Contributions to Finance and Accounting

The book series 'Contributions to Finance and Accounting' features the latest research from research areas like financial management, investment, capital markets, financial institutions, FinTech and financial innovation, accounting methods and standards, reporting, and corporate governance, among others. Books published in this series are primarily monographs and edited volumes that present new research results, both theoretical and empirical, on a clearly defined topic. All books are published in print and digital formats and disseminated globally.

This book series is indexed in Scopus.

Monica Violeta Achim
Editor

Financial Crime in the Digital Era

Innovative Approaches to Preventing Financial Fraud

Springer

Editor
Monica Violeta Achim
Faculty of Economics and Business
Administration
Babeş-Bolyai University
Cluj-Napoca, Romania

ISSN 2730-6038 ISSN 2730-6046 (electronic)
Contributions to Finance and Accounting
ISBN 978-3-032-20197-3 ISBN 978-3-032-20198-0 (eBook)
https://doi.org/10.1007/978-3-032-20198-0

This Springer imprint is published by the registered company Springer Nature Switzerland AG
The registered company address is: Gewerbestrasse 11, 6330 Cham, Switzerland

Acknowledgments

This study is part of the COST project CA19130 FinAI—Fintech and Artificial Intelligence in Finance—Towards a Transparent Financial Industry.

We gratefully acknowledge the support of the Marie Skłodowska-Curie Actions under the European Union's Horizon Europe research and innovation program for the "Industrial Doctoral Network on Digital Finance, acronym: DIGITAL, Project No. 101119635".

We also acknowledge the support from the Ministry of Research, Innovation, and Digitization, CNCS-UEFISCDI, project number PN-IV-P2-2.1-TE-2023-1317, within PNCDI IV.

Contents

Innovation and Technology in Combating Financial Crime

Transforming Financial Crime Investigations: The Role of Digital Tools in the Evolving Effectiveness of the European Public Prosecutor's Office ... 3
Florin Alexandru Roman and Monica Violeta Achim

Digital Deceit in Finance: Deepfakes, Synthetic Identities, and the Future of Fraud Prevention ... 33
Deepika Dhingra, Prabal Chakraborty, and Kirti Sharma

Digital Payments and Fraud Risk: Technological Innovations and Global Regulatory Responses ... 55
Anuram Krishna E S and Blesson Varghese James

Businesses Facing Spear Phishing: Towards a Preventive Approach Based on Cybersecurity Measures ... 83
Lamiae Zitouni and Khalid Atmani

Descriptive Analysis of Accounting and Tax Professionals' Opinions Regarding Accounting Fraud Determined Through Forensic Accounting ... 103
Lucia Podoabă

AI-Powered Transaction Monitoring for Real-Time Fraud Detection in Digital Banking ... 135
Ujan Pradhan, Utkarsh Jaiswal, and Vyomika Anand

Fintech, Crypto-Assets, and Emerging Models of Digital Risk

Fraud Risks in Digital Lending and BNPL Models: Detection and Prevention Strategies ... 165
Kanimozhi Viswanathan, Subhashini Suresh, and M. Showmiyan

Investing in Fintech Fraud Combating Startups: Social Responsibility Before Profits? 197
Anastas Dzurovski

Can We Explore Financial Crime in the Crypto Market? A Systematic Review of Technical, Regulatory, and Risk Frameworks 227
Adrian Bojan and Monica Violeta Achim

Bibliometric and Academic Approaches to Economic Crime

Mapping the Nexus of Economic Crime, Forensic Accounting, and Sustainable Development Goals (SDGs): A Bibliometric Review ... 273
Isabella Lucuț-Capraș, Monica Violeta Achim, and Leonard Artur Horvath

Economic and Financial Crime in the Digital Era: A Bibliometric Approach 303
Iulia Brici and Monica Violeta Achim

Bibliometric Analysis of Financial Corruption in the Healthcare System 323
Tomina-Maria Manci and Monica Violeta Achim

The Importance of Financial Fraud Prevention in the Current Economic Context: A Bibliometric Analysis 353
Georgiana Burlacu and Ioan-Bogdan Robu

Social, Ethical, and Regulatory Aspects of Financial Crime

The Asymmetric Impact of Different Types of Taxes on the Level of Corruption and Shadow Economy Among Developed and Developing Countries 373
Monica Violeta Achim, Viorela Ligia Văidean, Nawazish Mirza, and Neli Muntean

Corporate Deception or the Illusion of Sustainability? A Critical Look at Greenwashing Practices 395
Ruben Pop and Monica Violeta Achim

The Transparency Paradox of the Real Estate Markets: When Visibility Masks Vulnerability in the Digital Era 419
Elena Ionașcu

One More Time, the Dark Side of the Economy: Exploring the Shadow Economy in the European Union 445
Andreea-Roxana Danci, Ionuț-Adrian Lazar, and Gabriela-Mihaela Mureșan

Variations in the Concept of Tax Evasion Between the Normative and Judicial Levels 469
Septimiu Ioan Puţ

Financial Crime in Stock Exchange: The Case on the Stock Exchanges of the Europen Union States 489
Yusuf Ekrem Akbaş, Mehmet Ali Polat, and Ahmet Şit

Editor and Contributors

About the Editor

Monica Violeta Achim is a professor and doctoral supervisor in Finance at the Faculty of Economic Sciences and Business Administration, Babeş-Bolyai University, Cluj-Napoca. With over 27 years of experience in academia, she has published, as author and co-author, over 140 scientific articles and 27 books. The main research topics are financial analysis, business performance, finance, and economic and financial crime. In 2020, she obtained the Award for Excellence in Scientific Research, at Babeş-Bolyai University, Faculty of Economics and Business Administration, Cluj-Napoca, Romania, as a recognition of the results obtained in the research activity. She leads a main national project in the area of financial crime in the period 2020–2023. In the business environment, she works in liberal professions as an accountant expert, tax consultant, and judicial expert.

Contributors

Monica Violeta Achim Faculty of Economics and Business Administration, Babeş-Bolyai University, Cluj-Napoca, Romania

Yusuf Ekrem Akbaş Faculty of Economics and Administrative Sciences, Department of Economics, Adıyaman University, Altınşehir, Türkiye

Vyomika Anand Department of Chemistry, Indian Institute of Technology Bombay, Mumbai, Maharashtra, India

Khalid Atmani Faculty of Legal, Economic and Social Sciences, Chouaib Doukkali University, El Jadida, Morocco

Adrian Bojan Faculty of Economics and Business Administration, Babeş-Bolyai University, Cluj-Napoca, Romania

Iulia Brici Faculty of Economics and Business Administration, Babeş-Bolyai University, Cluj-Napoca, Romania

Georgiana Burlacu Doctoral School of Economics and Business Administration, Alexandru Ioan Cuza University of Iasi, Iasi, Romania

Prabal Chakraborty Lingaya's Vidyapeeth, Rewari, Haryana, India

Andreea-Roxana Danci Faculty of Economics and Business Administration, Babeş-Bolyai University, Cluj-Napoca, Romania

Deepika Dhingra School of Management, BML Munjal University, Rewari, Haryana, India

Anastas Dzurovski Unversity "St. Kliment Ohridski"-Bitola, Bitola, North Macedonia

Leonard Artur Horvath Faculty of Economics and Business Administration, Babeş-Bolyai University, Cluj-Napoca, Romania

Elena Ionaşcu Department of Economic and Financial Analysis and Evaluation, Bucharest University of Economic Studies, Bucharest, Romania

Utkarsh Jaiswal Department of Networking and Communications, SRM Institute of Science and Technology, Chennai, Tamil Nadu, India

Anuram Krishna E S Department of Global Finance & Analytics, Christ University, Pune, India

Ionuţ-Adrian Lazar Faculty of Economics and Business Administration, Babeş-Bolyai University, Cluj-Napoca, Romania

Isabella Lucuţ-Capraş Faculty of Economics and Business Administration, Babeş-Bolyai University, Cluj-Napoca, Romania

Tomina-Maria Manci Faculty of Economics and Business Administration, Babeş-Bolyai University, Cluj-Napoca, Romania

Nawazish Mirza Excelia Business School, Department of Finance, La Rochelle France, Paris, France

Neli Muntean Faculty of Economic and Business Engineering, Technical University of Moldova, Chisinau, Republic of Moldova

Gabriela-Mihaela Mureşan Faculty of Economics and Business Administration, Babeş-Bolyai University, Cluj-Napoca, Romania

Lucia Podoabă Faculty of Economics and Business Administration, Babeş-Bolyai University, Cluj-Napoca, Romania

Mehmet Ali Polat Faculty of Economics and Administrative Sciences, Department of Economics, Uludağ University, Bursa, Türkiye

Ruben Pop Faculty of Economics and Business Administration, Babeş-Bolyai University, Cluj-Napoca, Romania

Ujan Pradhan Department of Computing Technologies, SRM Institute of Science and Technology, Chennai, Tamil Nadu, India

Septimiu Ioan Puț Faculty of Law, Babeş-Bolyai University, Cluj-Napoca, Romania

Ioan-Bogdan Robu Doctoral School of Economics and Business Administration, Alexandru Ioan Cuza University of Iasi, Iasi, Romania

Florin Alexandru Roman Faculty of Economics and Business Administration, Babeş-Bolyai University, Cluj-Napoca, Romania

Kirti Sharma Great Lakes Institute of Management, Gurgaon, Haryana, India

M. Showmiyan Department of Management Sciences, Hindusthan College of Engineering and Technology, Coimbatore, Tamil Nadu, India

Subhashini Suresh Centre for Research and Training (CRT), Program Director—NFED Business Facilitators Forum (NBFF), National Foundation for Entrepreneurship Development (NFED), Coimbatore, Tamil Nadu, India

Ahmet Şit Faculty of Social and Human Sciences, Department of International Trade and Finance, Malatya Turgut Ozal University, Malatya, Turkey

Blesson Varghese James Department of Commerce, Christ University, Pune, India

Viorela Ligia Văidean Faculty of Economics and Business Administration, Babeş-Bolyai University, Cluj-Napoca, Romania

Kanimozhi Viswanathan Department of Management Sciences, Hindusthan College of Engineering and Technology, Coimbatore, Tamil Nadu, India

Lamiae Zitouni Faculty of Legal, Economic and Social Sciences, Chouaib Doukkali University, El Jadida, Morocco

List of Figures

Transforming Financial Crime Investigations: The Role of Digital Tools in the Evolving Effectiveness of the European Public Prosecutor's Office

Fig. 1 EPPO operational figures (2021 report) 7
Fig. 2 EPPO operational figures (2022 report) 8
Fig. 3 EPPO operational figures (2023 report) 10
Fig. 4 Operational figures 2024 12
Fig. 5 Investigations opened/crime report processed by the EPPO each year (2021–2024) 13
Fig. 6 Total value of asset freezing orders granted at EPPO's request each year 14
Fig. 7 Operation admiral (flow of investigation) 20
Fig. 8 Operation silk road (flow of investigation) 22
Fig. 9 EPPO-operation resilient crime (flow of investigation) 24

Digital Deceit in Finance: Deepfakes, Synthetic Identities, and the Future of Fraud Prevention

Fig. 1 Deepfake versus synthetic identity frauds 35
Fig. 2 Technological defense against fraud ranges from reactive to proactive 44
Fig. 3 Combating deepfake and synthetic identity fraud 50

Digital Payments and Fraud Risk: Technological Innovations and Global Regulatory Responses

Fig. 1 The fraud-prevention architecture (DPIP, NPCI federated model and frontline controls) of India 63
Fig. 2 Comparison of federated AI and centralised AI models in India's payment ecosystem 71

Businesses Facing Spear Phishing: Towards a Preventive Approach Based on Cybersecurity Measures

Fig. 1 The methodology study scheme 88

AI-Powered Transaction Monitoring for Real-Time Fraud Detection in Digital Banking

Fig. 1 Real-time fraud detection system architecture 157
Fig. 2 AI model ensemble architecture for fraud detection 158
Fig. 3 AI model ensemble architecture for fraud detection 159

Investing in Fintech Fraud Combating Startups: Social Responsibility Before Profits?

Fig. 1 Distribution of Investment Amounts (USD) 220
Fig. 2 Distribution of Investment Amounts (log scale) 221
Fig. 3 Investment vs ESG Score 222
Fig. 4 Investment Amount by ESG Label 222
Fig. 5 Trend of Mean Investment (log) over Time—Non ESG 223
Fig. 6 Trend of Mean Investment (log) over Time—ESG 223

Can We Explore Financial Crime in the Crypto Market? A Systematic Review of Technical, Regulatory, and Risk Frameworks

Fig. 1 Blockchain versus tangle 230
Fig. 2 Digital markets 231
Fig. 3 Four step for conducting the literature review 234
Fig. 4 Data refinement 235
Fig. 5 Top 10 web of science categories 237
Fig. 6 Number of citations and publications in 2017–2025 239
Fig. 7 Mapping for clusters realized with co-occurrence text data 251
Fig. 8 The evolution of the phenomenon in time realized with co-occurance—keyword 252
Fig. 9 Bibliometric mapping of co-cited sources about crypto and fincrime 253
Fig. 10 Bibliometric mapping of co-cited references in cryptocurrency research 253
Fig. 11 Visualization of coupling relationships among authors 255
Fig. 12 Analysis of links between references, titles and keywords 256
Fig. 13 Thematic mapping of topics on 4 dimensions 258
Fig. 14 Most relevant words 260
Fig. 15 Most discussed topics according with literature 261

Mapping the Nexus of Economic Crime, Forensic Accounting, and Sustainable Development Goals (SDGs): A Bibliometric Review

Fig. 1 PRISMA flowchart protocol for the research topic 277
Fig. 2 General information about the sample 279
Fig. 3 Annual scientific production 281
Fig. 4 Most relevant sources 283
Fig. 5 Most local cited sources 284
Fig. 6 Most relevant affiliations 285
Fig. 7 Countries scientific production 286
Fig. 8 Corresponding author's countries 288
Fig. 9 Countries collaboration 289
Fig. 10 The co-citation network diagram of cited references 290
Fig. 11 The bibliographic coupling network diagram of the sources 292
Fig. 12 The bibliographic coupling network diagram of the authors 294
Fig. 13 The co-occurrence of keywords map 296
Fig. 14 The co-occurrence of keywords density visualization map 297

Economic and Financial Crime in the Digital Era: A Bibliometric Approach

Fig. 1 Research scaffold 305
Fig. 2 Adapted PRISMA flowchart 307
Fig. 3 Annual evolution of publications number related to economic and financial crime in the digital era 312
Fig. 4 Top 10 relevant journals that published articles related to economic and financial crime in the digital era 313
Fig. 5 Top 10 prolific researchers who wrote articles related to Economic and Financial Crime Research in the context of the Digital Age 314
Fig. 6 Co-citation network diagram based on cited references 316
Fig. 7 Co-authorship network diagram based on authors 317
Fig. 8 Co-occurrence of keywords diagram based on keywords plus 318

Bibliometric Analysis of Financial Corruption in the Healthcare System

Fig. 1 Evolution over time of the number of publications related to general corruption 332
Fig. 2 Evolution over time of the number of publications and citations related to corruption in healthcare 333
Fig. 3 Top-25 authors contributed to publications related to corruption in general 335
Fig. 4 Top-25 authors contributed to publications related to corruption in healthcare 336
Fig. 5 Top-10 areas of articles related to corruption in general 338

Fig. 6 Top-10 areas of articles related to corruption in healthcare 339
Fig. 7 Top-10 most active institutions contributed to publications related to corruption (general) 340
Fig. 8 Top-10 most active institutions contributed to publications related to corruption in healthcare 341
Fig. 9 Evolution over time of the number of publications and citations related to corruption in the medical system 342
Fig. 10 Top-25 countries contributed to publications related to corruption in the medical system 344
Fig. 11 Top-10 areas of articles related to corruption was found regarding the medical system 345
Fig. 12 The co-citation network diagram of cited references 347
Fig. 13 The co-occurrence of keywords overlay diagram 348

The Importance of Financial Fraud Prevention in the Current Economic Context: A Bibliometric Analysis

Fig. 1 Competent bodies for preventing financial fraud 356
Fig. 2 Steps taken to obtain information 358
Fig. 3 Distribution of scientific papers by year 358
Fig. 4 Keywords used by authors in their research on the financial fraud prevention 360
Fig. 5 Key aspects resulting from the coupling of documents 365
Fig. 6 The main authors who have published works on fraud prevention 366
Fig. 7 Country Collaboration Map 367

The Asymmetric Impact of Different Types of Taxes on the Level of Corruption and Shadow Economy Among Developed and Developing Countries

Fig. 1 Plot of taxes against CPI 377
Fig. 2 Plot of taxes against SE 378

Corporate Deception or the Illusion of Sustainability? A Critical Look at Greenwashing Practices

Fig. 1 Evolution of publications on ESG controversies 401
Fig. 2 Conceptual dynamics of research on ESG corporate controversies 402
Fig. 3 Co-occurrence network of keywords in studies on ESG controversies 403
Fig. 4 Conceptual core of research on ESG corporate controversies 404
Fig. 5 Countries' contribution to scientific publications by type of collaboration 406
Fig. 6 Global distribution of scientific output on ESG controversies 407

Fig. 7 Thematic structure of research on ESG controversies: cluster analysis through document coupling 407
Fig. 8 Conceptual landscape of ESG controversy research: from emerging topics to dominant directions 409
Fig. 9 Evolution of controversial terms in scientific literature (WoS) between 2015 and 2025 410
Fig. 10 Governance at the heart of ESG debates: a comparative analysis of global controversies 411
Fig. 11 Reconfiguration of ESG controversies post-pandemic: governance in the spotlight 412
Fig. 12 The rise of post-pandemic ESG controversies: from corporate ethics to transparency 413

The Transparency Paradox of the Real Estate Markets: When Visibility Masks Vulnerability in the Digital Era

Fig. 1 Real estate transparency in 22 EU countries 432

One More Time, the Dark Side of the Economy: Exploring the Shadow Economy in the European Union

Fig. 1 Co-Occurrence analysis of key concepts 449
Fig. 2 Co-Citation network: key thematic clusters and influential authors 451

Financial Crime in Stock Exchange: The Case on the Stock Exchanges of the Europen Union States

Fig. 1 The model of this paper 496

List of Tables

Transforming Financial Crime Investigations: The Role of Digital Tools in the Evolving Effectiveness of the European Public Prosecutor's Office

Table 1 Evolution of EPPO digital capabilities and operational outcomes (2021–2024) 15

Digital Deceit in Finance: Deepfakes, Synthetic Identities, and the Future of Fraud Prevention

Table 1 Methodological steps 36
Table 2 Advantages over alternative methods 36
Table 3 Deepfake threat matrix for financial services 41
Table 4 Practical and measurable proposals for mitigating deepfake and synthetic identity fraud 51

Digital Payments and Fraud Risk: Technological Innovations and Global Regulatory Responses

Table 1 The correlation of fraud type to technology solutions 64
Table 2 AML technology approaches (India, UK, US and HSBC) comparison 65
Table 3 Challenges versus opportunities in AI-based AML 68

Businesses Facing Spear Phishing: Towards a Preventive Approach Based on Cybersecurity Measures

Table 1 Offenses associated with spear phishing attacks 93

Descriptive Analysis of Accounting and Tax Professionals' Opinions Regarding Accounting Fraud Determined Through Forensic Accounting

Table 1 Research hypotheses 108
Table 2 Biographical data regarding the respondents 110

Table 3	The questions in the questionnaire	111
Table 4	Factor structure of the attitude scale towards forensic accounting in verifying fraudulent activities (accounting fraud)	116
Table 5	The answers given by respondents to question no. 6	117
Table 6	The answers given by respondents to question no. 7	117
Table 7	The answers given by respondents to question no. 8	118
Table 8	Details of the result (the Pearson correlation coefficient)	118
Table 9	The correlation test	118
Table 10	The answers given by respondents to question no. 9	119
Table 11	Assessment of the main "human factors" in a company that could generate and amplify the phenomenon of fraud at the company level (according to the opinions expressed by the accounting and tax professionals surveyed)—Q10	120
Table 12	Employee attitude—moving from abuse to accounting fraud (Q11)	121
Table 13	The most effective legal regulations in preventing accounting fraud applied in Romania (Q12)	124
Table 14	Necessary tools used to prevent fraudulent transactions (Q13)	125
Table 15	The forensic accounting methods and techniques applied by the interviewed specialists in fraud accounting	129

Fraud Risks in Digital Lending and BNPL Models: Detection and Prevention Strategies

Table 1	Comparative table-KYC, BNPL, and AI transparency	186

Investing in Fintech Fraud Combating Startups: Social Responsibility Before Profits?

Table 1	Descriptive statistics	219
Table 2	Regression analysis	224

Can We Explore Financial Crime in the Crypto Market? A Systematic Review of Technical, Regulatory, and Risk Frameworks

Table 1	Cryptocurrency characteristics	231
Table 2	Risk factors for cryptocurrency investors	233
Table 3	Most popular source titles	240
Table 4	Academic research distributed by countries	241
Table 5	Top academic affiliations by published articles and citations	243
Table 6	Articles with the greatest impact through citations	244
Table 7	Typologies for attacks and scams with crypto	249
Table 8	Top 10 most co-cited references	254
Table 9	Authors with strongest bibliometric coupling links	255

Table 10 Distribution of research topics on cryptocurrencies and tax evasion 259
Table 11 Trend topics classification 263

Mapping the Nexus of Economic Crime, Forensic Accounting, and Sustainable Development Goals (SDGs): A Bibliometric Review

Table 1 Description of the search procedure 278
Table 2 Annual scientific production for the last 10 years 282
Table 3 Top 10 countries in terms of scientific production 287
Table 4 Top 10 researchers with the highest total link strength in coauthorship 289
Table 5 Top 10 journals in terms of bibliographic coupling link strength 291
Table 6 Top 10 authors in terms of bibliographic coupling link strength 293
Table 7 Top 10 co-occurring keywords sorted by total link strength 295

Economic and Financial Crime in the Digital Era: A Bibliometric Approach

Table 1 Detailed search procedure 309

Bibliometric Analysis of Financial Corruption in the Healthcare System

Table 1 Steps for selecting articles on corruption (general) 329
Table 2 Steps for selecting articles on corruption in health 330
Table 3 Steps for selecting articles on corruption in areas related to the medical system 330
Table 4 Corruption in general vs corruption in the medical system (similarities and differences regarding the evolution of publications over time) 334
Table 5 Corruption in general vs corruption in the medical system (similarities authors) 337
Table 6 Top-5 most active institutions contributed to publications related to corruption in the medical system 343
Table 7 Top-5 highly cited publications related to corruption in the medical system 346
Table 8 Top-10 cited references in the selected sample 347

The Importance of Financial Fraud Prevention in the Current Economic Context: A Bibliometric Analysis

Table 1 List of relevant articles on the topic of financial fraud prevention 361

Innovation and Technology in Combating Financial Crime

Transforming Financial Crime Investigations: The Role of Digital Tools in the Evolving Effectiveness of the European Public Prosecutor's Office

Florin Alexandru Roman and Monica Violeta Achim

Abstract Since its establishment on 1 June 2021, the European Public Prosecutor's Office (EPPO) has markedly strengthened its institutional capacity to combat financial and economic crime. Through the integration of advanced digital technologies, the EPPO has focused its operational priorities on complex transnational offences, particularly VAT carousel fraud and forms of organized financial crime. This strategic orientation has resulted in a significant expansion of investigative activities and asset recovery operations, as reflected in the growing number of indictments and the increasing value of assets frozen across member states. The evolving nature of financial criminality demands the adoption of sophisticated investigative methodologies, in which digital tools and forensic analytics play a pivotal role in enhancing detection capabilities and fostering cross-border cooperation. The findings highlight the necessity of continuous innovation in digital forensics and data-driven investigative systems to effectively address the escalating complexity of financial offences and to safeguard the financial interests of the European Union.

Keywords Financial crime investigations · Digital tools · European Public Prosecutor's Office

1 Introduction

Financial crimes pose a major danger to financial system integrity so the European Public Prosecutor's Office (EPPO) functions as a key enforcement body within European Union crime fighting strategy. The EPPO has the responsibility to investigate and

---

F. A. Roman (✉) · M. V. Achim
Faculty of Economics and Business Administration, Babeş-Bolyai University, Cluj-Napoca, Romania
e-mail: florin.roman@econ.ubbcluj.ro

M. V. Achim
e-mail: monica.achim@econ.ubbcluj.ro

M. V. Achim (ed.), *Financial Crime in the Digital Era*, Contributions to Finance and Accounting, https://doi.org/10.1007/978-3-032-20198-0_1

prosecute crimes against the financial interests of the Union which include fraud and money laundering along with corruption through collaborative mechanisms across EU member states (Bošković 2024; Herrnfeld 2024). Digital investigation tools serve as a crucial factor that improves the effectiveness of the EPPO. Digital tools have become essential for contemporary investigations because financial crimes usually contain complex digital data that requires sophisticated analysis methods.

Digital investigation tools utilize a broad range of forensic accounting methods together with cyber forensic approaches for their operational scope. Modern technologies were developed specifically to track down electronic evidence which helps reveal how financial crimes function from their core operations. Traditional forensic accounting practices receive substantial enhancement through digital forensic methods which transform the process of financial fraud detection and investigation according to Odeyemi et al. (2024) and Sindhu and Meshram (2012). The combination of forensic accounting with digital forensic tools produces enhanced investigation methods which enable deeper analysis of financial crimes while speeding up the response to new financial crime strategies that use technology to hide their activities (Adams 2024). The implementation of technology within forensic approaches enables the assessment of total risk profiles while optimizing investigation approaches to make decisions through data analysis (Achim et al. 2021).

The implementation of digital forensic tools by the EPPO effectively tackles financial crime investigation technical aspects while supporting its mission to protect EU financial interests through offender accountability and deterrence measures. The EPPO legal structure enables extensive data exchange and teamwork between European Union states because financial crimes typically span across borders (Becková 2020; Simeunović et al. 2016). During an investigation forensic accountants work alongside digital forensic experts who use their specialized skills to track both financial records and digital footprints. These investigative disciplines require ongoing development of procedures and tools because technological advancements and criminal tactics evolve at a fast pace.

Financial crimes conducted through digital means have made digital investigation tools essential for the EPPO to function effectively. These tools enable investigators to examine extensive datasets referred to as "big data" by allowing them to search through numerous documents and transactions to detect suspicious patterns of misconduct (Banerveld et al. 2014). Modern investigative solutions which use natural language processing demonstrate how to enhance traditional financial investigation methods through efficient complex dataset management (Banerveld et al. 2014). Forensic processes now use integrated artificial intelligence and machine learning methodologies to enhance financial crime prediction and prevention capabilities (Rughani 2017; Alghamdi 2021).

The legal investigations of financial misconduct receive support through digital forensic tools which operate within EPPO-established legislative frameworks to preserve evidence integrity while ensuring its admissibility (Selimi and Ali 2024; Zahid and Aslam 2020). The proper and protected acquisition of digital evidence stands as a critical requirement because it provides solid evidence needed to prosecute financial crimes throughout EU member states. The ability ensures that legal norms guide investigations while advanced technology supports the ever-changing environment of financial crime (Sabillón et al. 2017; Bülbül et al. 2013).

The relationship between digital investigation tools and the financial crimes investigated by the EPPO is a dynamic and multifaceted one. This paper, which has brought together the work of forensic accountants and digital forensics experts, highlights the need for integrated methodologies that are consistent with the constantly changing financial landscapes. The evolution and improvement of these tools to meet the challenges presented by sophisticated technological fraud mechanisms will, undoubtedly, strengthen the ability of the EPPO to discharge its mandate of protecting the financial interests of the European Union, and to do so in the face of emerging threats in the digital environment.

This paper aims to determine (using data from the official EPPO reports and press release) whether—and to what extent—the adoption and integration of digital investigation tools over the years have led to an increase in the number of reported crimes against the financial interests of the EU.

2 Digital Investigation Tools in the EPPO (2021–2024): Implementation and Evolution

Drawing on data extracted from the official annual reports of the European Public Prosecutor's Office (EPPO) for the period 2021–2024, this study evaluates the effects of adopting digital investigative tools on the EPPO's prosecutorial activities. These annual reports provide comprehensive documentation on the implementation and operational impact of specific digital systems and tools, thereby serving as the primary empirical foundation for this analysis. Supplementary information was also derived from EPPO press releases and public communications, which detail investigations into complex transnational financial crimes. These secondary sources further clarify the operational dynamics of EPPO investigations, illustrating patterns of international cooperation, the application of digital forensic methodologies, and the procedural progression of significant cases.

2.1 Implementation

2.1.1 2021: Establishing the Digital Foundations

During its inaugural year of operation, beginning on 1 June 2021, the EPPO concentrated on establishing its core digital infrastructure, which became the technological backbone of its prosecutorial activities. Central to this foundation was the development of the Case Management System (CMS)—a secure and centralized database designed to streamline case handling, facilitate workflow automation, and ensure information integrity across participating Member States.

The first version of the CMS was activated within the EPPO's data centre in March 2021, preceding the formal commencement of operations. Two major updates followed in August and December 2021, enhancing functionality and ensuring compliance with legal and procedural requirements. This rapid deployment enabled all European Delegated Prosecutors (EDPs) in participating Member States to access, input, and share case information through a unified platform.

The CMS also introduced key features that significantly strengthened transnational coordination. Among these were automated translation capabilities and cross-border workflow management tools, which allowed for multilingual case processing and real-time oversight by the central office in Luxembourg. As a result, the EPPO achieved operational unification from its inception, allowing seamless coordination of prosecutorial activities across Member States.

In addition to the CMS, the EPPO introduced several complementary digital systems that collectively enhanced its investigative capacity:

EPPOBox Secure Information Exchange Platform, ensuring encrypted data transfer between EDPs and the central office;

Online Crime Reporting System, a web-based interface enabling private entities and individuals to submit fraud reports directly to the EPPO, which were then automatically integrated into the CMS;

Inter-agency Data Exchange Interfaces, facilitating structured communication with national and EU bodies; and E-Translation Service, a digital linguistic tool integrated into the CMS to provide automated translations of case documents and information in multilingual investigations.

Together, these technologies allowed the EPPO to begin operations effectively and without delay. In its first 7 months, the Office processed 2832 crime reports from various sources and initiated 576 investigations, involving an estimated €5.4 billion in potential damage to the EU budget. By the end of 2021, 515 investigations remained active (European Public Prosecutor's Office 2022).

Significantly, 27.5% of the total cases included a cross-border element, reflecting the transnational nature of the offences investigated. The digital case management infrastructure proved instrumental in coordinating these multi-jurisdictional investigations from the outset. However, the 2021 data also revealed disparities in detection and reporting capacity among Member States, prompting the EPPO to prioritise the enhancement of reporting systems and harmonisation of digital cooperation mechanisms in subsequent years (Fig. 1).

2.1.2 2022: Expanding and Integrating Digital Tools

In 2022, the European Public Prosecutor's Office (EPPO) consolidated and expanded its digital infrastructure, marking a decisive phase in the institutional integration of its technological framework. The Case Management System (CMS) underwent substantial upgrades to accommodate the growing prosecutorial workload and to

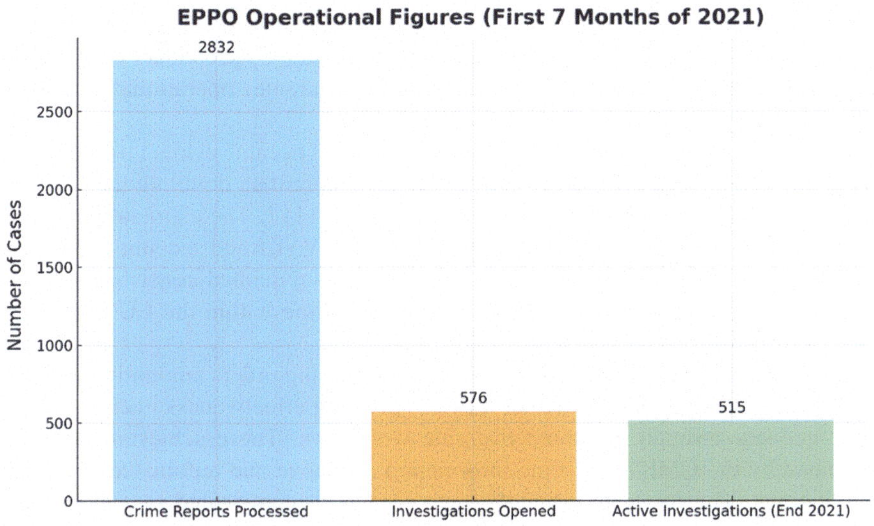

Fig. 1 EPPO operational figures (2021 report). *Source* Own processing in Excel

enhance cross-border cooperation in complex financial investigations. During this period, the CMS evolved from a relatively autonomous case-handling tool into an interconnected digital ecosystem, allowing multiple European Delegated Prosecutors (EDPs) to collaborate seamlessly on joint cases across jurisdictions.

To ensure the efficiency and legal security of judicial procedures, the EPPO integrated an EU digital signature system, enabling prosecutors to electronically authenticate legal documents directly within the CMS. The adoption of advanced automated translation tools further accelerated the management of multilingual evidence, reducing procedural delays in cross-border investigations.

A major milestone of 2022 was the initiation of a pilot programme with e-CODEX, the European Union's secure platform for judicial data exchange. This initiative facilitated the electronic transmission of evidence between the EPPO and national judicial systems, reinforcing procedural harmonisation and data protection standards. In parallel, the introduction of National EDP Assistants (NEDPAs) toward the end of 2022 represented an important structural development. These assistants were tasked with managing CMS-related data operations and supporting routine prosecutorial functions, thereby alleviating the administrative burden on prosecutors and improving workflow efficiency.

The EPPO also initiated the deployment of analytical software designed to process financial and investigative data. Although in its preliminary phase, this analytical capability provided valuable insights into financial transaction patterns and laid the groundwork for the introduction of advanced digital forensic and predictive analytics tools in subsequent years.

By late 2022, the EPPO had achieved full operational control over its digital infrastructure, consolidating its internal IT architecture to ensure autonomy and security.

This included the establishment of a dedicated internal network, document management systems, and disaster recovery protocols, supported by secondary data centres and geographically distributed backup facilities to guarantee operational continuity and cybersecurity resilience.

The tangible impact of these digital transformations became evident by the end of 2022. The EPPO initiated 865 new investigations, more than doubling the previous year's total, while active investigations increased to 1117. The estimated financial damage under investigation rose to €9.9 billion, with VAT fraud accounting for over half of that amount. The share of cross-border cases remained consistent at 28%, underscoring the transnational nature of financial crime within the EU (European Public Prosecutor's Office 2023).

Furthermore, judicial authorities issued asset-freezing orders amounting to €359 million, a figure that represented the EPPO's growing effectiveness in cross-border asset recovery through coordinated digital workflows. These achievements were facilitated by the CMS's real-time information exchange and automated coordination features. The integrated digital case system also contributed to a substantial prosecutorial output, with the EPPO filing over 100 major indictments during 2022 (Fig. 2).

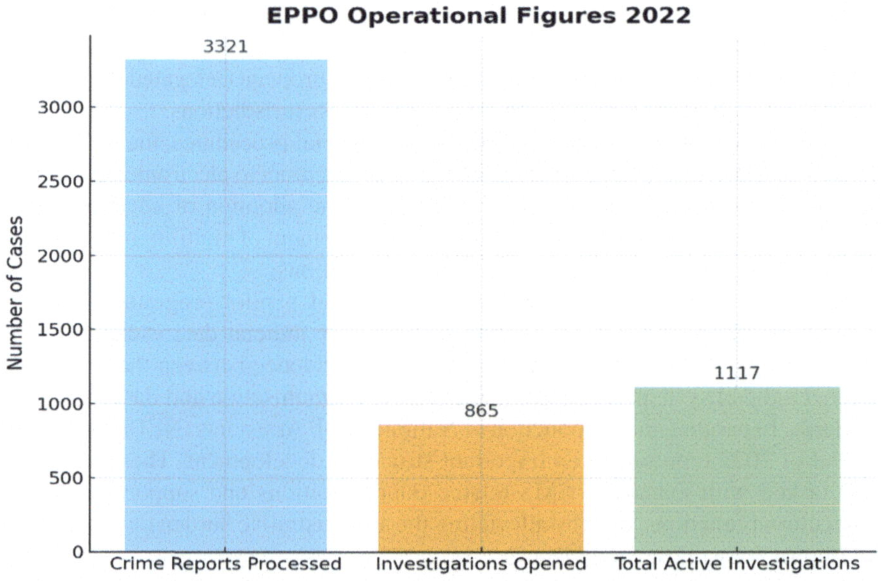

Fig. 2 EPPO operational figures (2022 report). *Source* Own processing in Excel

2.1.3 2023: Advanced Analytics and Cross-Border Coordination

In 2023, the European Public Prosecutor's Office (EPPO) continued to advance its digital transformation, with a strategic emphasis on data analytics, cross-border coordination, and system integration. These developments represented a decisive step toward the full operationalization of digital forensics and analytical capacities within the institution.

The EPPO significantly enhanced its ability to process and interpret complex financial data through the deployment of advanced analytical software. These tools enabled analysts to examine extensive datasets, identify sophisticated fraud patterns, and map interconnected transactional networks—elements crucial to the investigation and prosecution of large-scale financial crimes. The establishment of specialized forensic analysis units in 2023 marked a major institutional milestone, laying the foundation for comprehensive digital forensic support across all EPPO operations.

Further improvements were made to the Case Management System (CMS), particularly through the integration of National EDP Assistants (NEDPAs) during the pilot phase. This integration allowed for direct national-level data input with real-time synchronization, thereby enhancing both data accuracy and the timeliness of prosecutorial coordination. The initiative also strengthened cooperation between the EPPO and national prosecution offices, forming the basis for planned structural and procedural expansion in 2024.

Despite certain resource constraints affecting the integration of e-CODEX, the EPPO effectively leveraged other collaboration channels, most notably Europol's Secure Information Exchange Network Application (SIENA). This platform served as a key mechanism for secure communication and information exchange. Concurrently, the CMS received a series of critical functional enhancements, including automated translation features, digital signature capabilities, and the introduction of secure collaborative workspaces—all of which contributed to greater usability, system resilience, and data protection.

By mid-2023, the EPPO's Investigations and Analysis Support Teams had achieved full operational capacity. These teams deployed advanced analytical models for detecting cross-border criminal connections and utilized specialized digital forensic tools to support high-priority investigations. In parallel, the EPPO made significant progress toward complete IT self-sufficiency, developing its own secure digital infrastructure and aligning its systems with the latest EU cybersecurity standards to ensure enhanced data protection and operational continuity.

The measurable outcomes of these initiatives underscore their institutional impact. In 2023, the EPPO received and processed 4187 crime reports, representing a 26% increase compared to 2022, and launched 1371 new investigations, an increase of 58% over the previous year. The number of active investigations reached 1927 by year's end, while the total estimated damages under investigation rose to approximately €19.2 billion.

The EPPO also secured asset-freezing orders valued at €1.5 billion, more than four times the amount achieved in 2022. This substantial increase reflected the institution's enhanced capacity for cross-border asset tracing and recovery, facilitated by improved

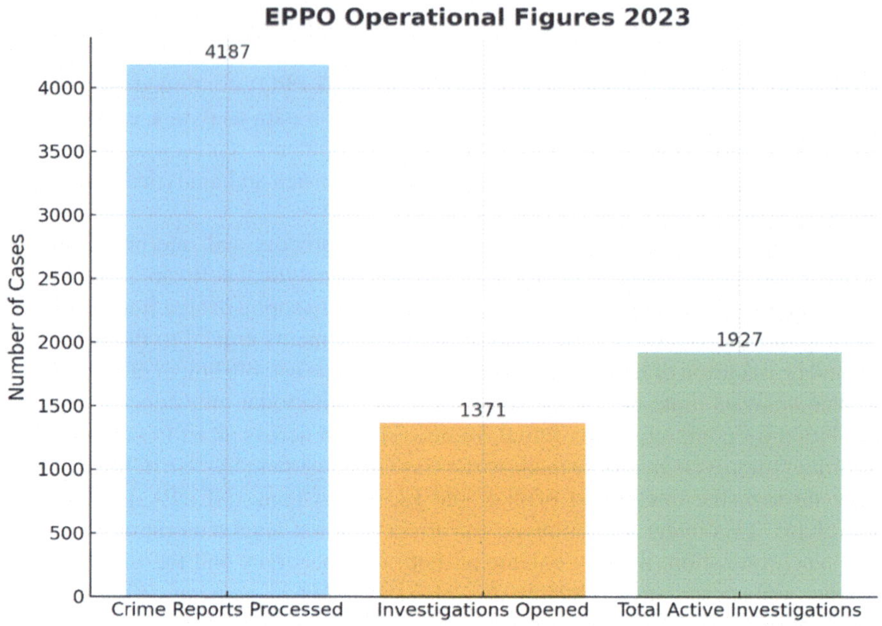

Fig. 3 EPPO operational figures (2023 report). *Source* Own processing in Excel

analytical tracking tools, and the efficient coordination between CMS and EPPOBox in managing freezing orders across multiple jurisdictions. Additionally, the number of indictments filed rose to 139, representing a more than 50% increase compared with the previous year (European Public Prosecutor's Office 2024).

Overall, the 2023 data illustrate the growing effectiveness of the EPPO's digital ecosystem. The expansion of analytical capabilities, combined with user-friendly reporting tools, resulted in a marked rise in fraud detection rates and public engagement. The increase in crime reports submitted by both private parties and national authorities demonstrates not only improved reporting efficiency but also greater institutional trust and transparency within the European framework of financial crime prosecution (Fig. 3).

2.1.4 2024: Consolidation and Enhanced Capabilities

By 2024, the European Public Prosecutor's Office (EPPO) had completed the development of its core digital investigative framework and shifted its strategic focus toward the consolidation, refinement, and expansion of existing technological tools. Although operating under notable resource constraints, the EPPO successfully implemented critical enhancements to the Case Management System (CMS), improving user experience, system performance, and cybersecurity. These optimizations allowed prosecutors to manage an expanding caseload with greater efficiency by providing faster and more intuitive access to case information.

One of the most significant developments of the year was the expansion of the National EDP Assistants (NEDPAs) network, which reached 97 active assistants across participating Member States. This integration transformed the CMS into an indispensable instrument for national EPPO offices, delivering higher data accuracy and enabling real-time information exchange across jurisdictions. The system's growing sophistication substantially strengthened cross-border coordination and standardized data management across the Union.

To further enhance institutional resilience, the EPPO established a Digital Services and Security Department, tasked with advancing the Office's technological autonomy and cybersecurity infrastructure. The department implemented a comprehensive security framework aligned with EU cybersecurity standards, ensuring the protection of sensitive investigative data and reinforcing the Office's defenses against cyber threats.

A substantial portion of the EPPO's 2024 digital strategy was devoted to the development of advanced digital forensic capabilities. In collaboration with the European Data Protection Supervisor (EDPS), the EPPO designed secure forensic systems capable of managing large-scale data analysis through artificial intelligence (AI)-based methodologies, while rigorously adhering to data protection and privacy protocols. These developments allowed for more sophisticated forensic examinations of complex financial crime structures, particularly those involving vast datasets and transnational elements.

The complete activation of the EPPO's digital communication infrastructure—notably EPPOBox and SIENA—further consolidated its integrated digital ecosystem. This environment enabled seamless interaction between crime reporting systems, case management operations, and inter-agency information exchange, fostering enhanced collaboration with both national and EU law enforcement partners. The resulting digital interconnectivity significantly improved the EPPO's capacity to detect, investigate, and prosecute complex financial crimes through a fully integrated technological framework.

The operational results achieved in 2024 clearly illustrate the effectiveness of this digital consolidation. The EPPO initiated 1504 new investigations, representing a 10% increase compared to 2023, targeting estimated damages of €13.07 billion. The total number of active investigations rose to 2666, while the overall value of damages under investigation exceeded €24.8 billion. Procedural efficiency improved markedly, as reflected in the 205 indictments filed during the year—an increase of 47% relative to 2023—demonstrating the direct impact of digital optimization on prosecutorial productivity.

Judicial authorities issued asset-freezing orders amounting to €2.42 billion, the highest annual total recorded since the EPPO's establishment. Additionally, freezing orders valued at €849 million were executed during the year. These outcomes underscore the Office's prioritization of asset recovery and damage prevention, made

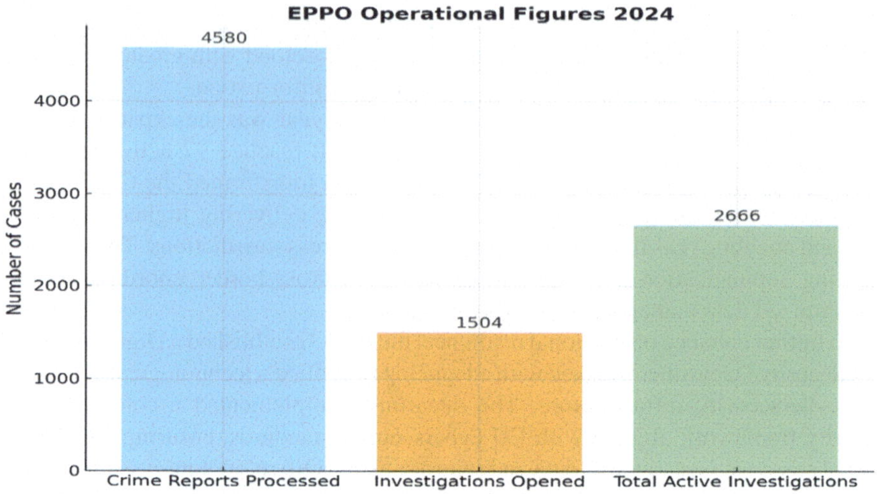

Fig. 4 Operational figures 2024. *Source* Own processing in Excel

possible by its enhanced ability to trace and immobilize criminal assets across borders in real time.

The proportion of cross-border investigations remained stable at 29% of total cases, representing approximately 770 multi-jurisdictional investigations. This consistency, despite a rising caseload, demonstrates the scalability and robustness of the EPPO's digital case management system, which successfully expanded operational capacity without diminishing coordination efficiency (European Public Prosecutor's Office 2025).

By the end of 2024, the EPPO had effectively evolved into a fully digitalized prosecutorial institution, equipped with specialized software and interconnected platforms supporting every stage of the investigative and judicial process—from case reporting and evidence analysis to indictment and asset recovery. This digital maturity marked the culmination of a 4-year transformation, positioning the EPPO as a model of technologically integrated prosecution within the European Union (Fig. 4).

2.2 *Evolution*

The period 2021–2024 shows a clear trajectory of growth in EPPO's operational output, which is in line with the increasing use of digital tools.

The following Figs. 5 and 6 show two important trends: the increasing number of investigations opened each year/crime reports processed and the exponential growth in the value of freezing orders issued, which is an indicator of asset recovery efforts.

The caseload surged as digital systems enabled faster processing of crime reports and coordination of cases.

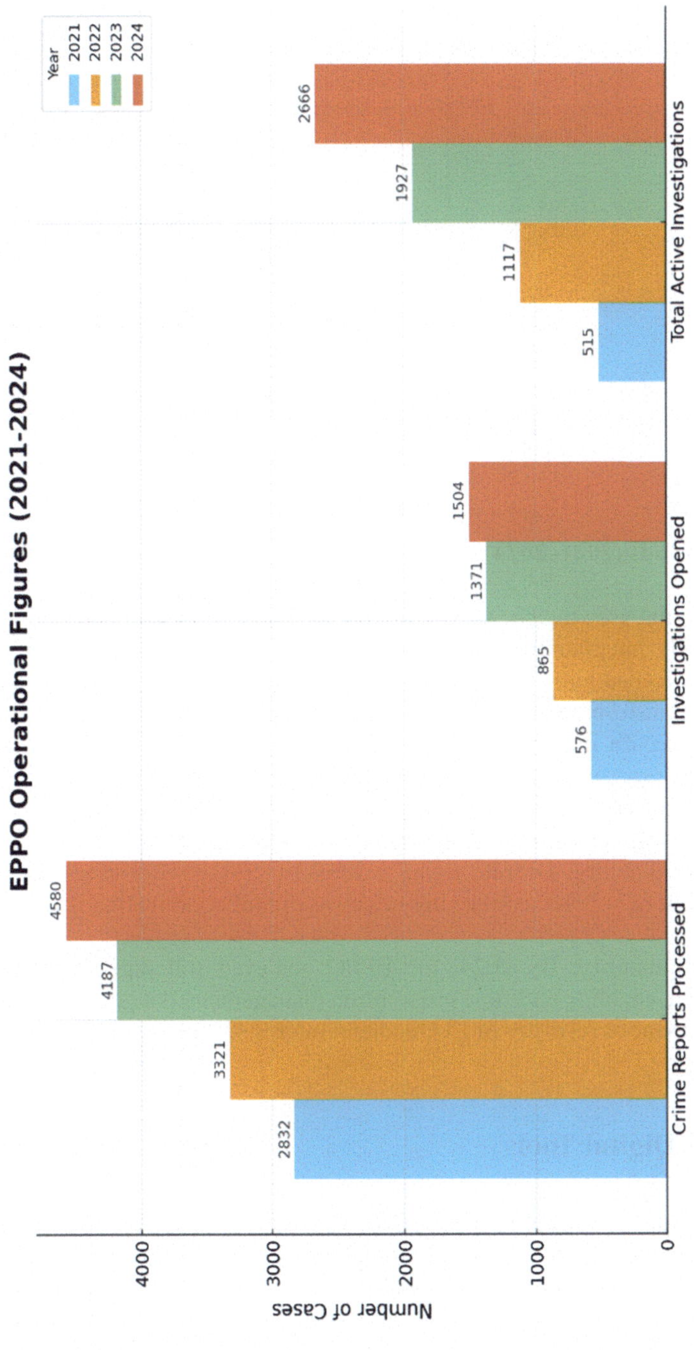

Fig. 5 Investigations opened/crime report processed by the EPPO each year (2021–2024). *Source* Own processing in Excel

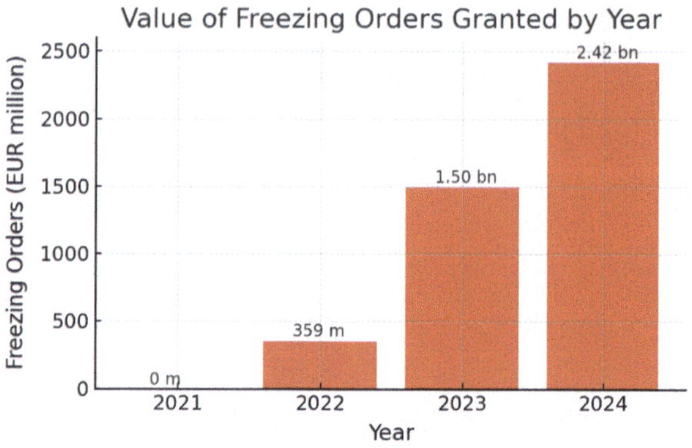

Fig. 6 Total value of asset freezing orders granted at EPPO's request each year. *Source*: Own processing in Excel

Effective use of digital tools to trace and secure criminal assets led to dramatic growth in preserved funds (from €359 million in 2022 to €2.42 billion in 2024) (Table 1).

2.2.1 Key Trends (2021–2024)

Exponential digital growth: The CMS evolved from a basic case management platform into a fully integrated EU-wide digital ecosystem supporting investigation, reporting, and prosecution.

Analytical transformation: The introduction of advanced analytics, AI-based forensics, and secure inter-agency communication tools revolutionized financial crime detection.

Operational scalability: Investigations increased by > 160%, indictments by > 100%, and assets frozen by more than sixfold over 4 years.

Cross-border stability: Despite rising caseloads, cross-border cases remained consistently high (27–29%), confirming effective digital coordination across jurisdictions.

Institutional maturity: By 2024, the EPPO achieved full digital and procedural integration, enabling real-time prosecution management, data-driven decision-making, and enhanced recovery of EU financial interests.

3 Types of Digital Tools

The European Public Prosecutor's Office (EPPO) has increasingly relied on a diverse range of digital investigative tools to strengthen its capacity to detect, analyse, and prosecute financial crimes. These instruments are essential for managing the complexity of transnational fraud investigations and for enhancing prosecutorial efficiency across the European Union. The digitalisation of anti-fraud efforts has been

Table 1 Evolution of EPPO digital capabilities and operational outcomes (2021–2024)

Year	Digital and institutional developments	New investigations	Active investigations (year-end)	Estimated damages (€)	Assets frozen (€)	Indictments filed	Cross-border cases (% of total)
2021	Establishment of CMS, EPPO Box, Online Reporting, E-Translation; core digital infrastructure launched	576	515	5.4 billion	–	–	27.50%
2022	CMS upgrades; introduction of NEDPAs; pilot with e-CODEX; start of analytics; secure IT systems and data centers	865	1117	9.9 billion	359 million	100+	28%

(continued)

Table 1 (continued)

Year	Digital and institutional developments	New investigations	Active investigations (year-end)	Estimated damages (€)	Assets frozen (€)	Indictments filed	Cross-border cases (% of total)
2023	Advanced analytics and forensic units operational; integration with SIENA; AI-assisted detection; IT self-sufficiency achieved	1371	1927	19.2 billion	1.5 billion	139	28%
2024	Consolidation phase; full integration of 97 NEDPAs; AI-based forensic systems (EDPS partnership); new Digital Security Department	1504	2666	24.8 billion	2.42 billion	205	29%

Source Own processing in Excel

explicitly recognised as a strategic priority in the European Commission's 2023 Action Plan, which seeks to equip law enforcement and prosecutorial authorities with technologically advanced means to combat corruption and fraud effectively ("Appendix").

A fundamental category of digital instruments employed by the EPPO is advanced data analytics software. These analytical systems enable investigators to process vast datasets rapidly and with high accuracy, identifying patterns, anomalies, and correlations indicative of fraudulent activity. By incorporating machine learning algorithms, such tools can generate predictive models based on historical data, allowing the early identification of potential fraud scenarios and facilitating proactive investigative strategies.

Equally important is the use of forensic accounting software, which supports the tracing of financial transactions across multiple jurisdictions and financial entities. These tools are indispensable for uncovering money laundering schemes, VAT carousel fraud, and other complex financial offences. Forensic accounting software also produces standardised evidentiary reports suitable for judicial proceedings, thereby ensuring both analytical reliability and legal admissibility.

Digital communication monitoring tools represent another critical component of the EPPO's technological infrastructure. These systems enable the controlled monitoring and analysis of emails, phone records, and digital communication channels associated with suspects. By examining metadata and communication networks, investigators can reconstruct criminal structures, identify key facilitators, and uncover the operational hierarchies of organised crime groups involved in financial offences.

The growing use of cryptocurrencies in illicit transactions has necessitated the adoption of blockchain analysis tools. These instruments allow investigators to trace virtual currency movements on public and private blockchain networks, mapping the flow of funds and associating digital wallets with identifiable individuals or entities. Blockchain analytics have proven instrumental in uncovering hidden assets, dismantling cryptocurrency-based money laundering operations, and elucidating sophisticated cross-border financial schemes.

In addition, Geographic Information Systems (GIS) are increasingly employed to visualise spatial dimensions of financial crime. GIS platforms enable investigators to map locations linked to fraudulent activity—such as shell company addresses, asset holdings, or properties acquired through illicit means. This spatial representation enhances situational awareness, facilitates the detection of geographic clusters of criminal activity, and guides resource allocation in ongoing investigations.

Finally, the integration of Artificial Intelligence (AI) within these tools has significantly enhanced the EPPO's analytical and operational capabilities. AI-driven systems automate routine tasks such as document review, data entry, and translation, thereby allowing prosecutors and analysts to concentrate on the interpretive and strategic aspects of investigations. Moreover, AI can be applied in natural language processing and sentiment analysis, enabling the detection of deception, coercion, or collusion patterns in digital communications.

Taken together, these digital tools form a cohesive and interoperable investigative ecosystem that underpins the EPPO's operational model. Their combined application enables the systematic integration of financial data, communication intelligence, spatial analysis, and forensic evidence within a unified analytical environment. Through this multidimensional approach, the EPPO is able to reconstruct complex criminal schemes with a high degree of precision and timeliness. The interconnection between data analytics, blockchain tracing, and AI-assisted forensic tools facilitates a continuous investigative feedback loop, in which new patterns of fraud can be detected, verified, and prosecuted more efficiently. Moreover, the digital convergence of case management, evidence handling, and cross-border coordination enhances the EPPO's institutional agility and ensures the harmonisation of prosecutorial standards across Member States. In this sense, digitalisation does not merely serve as a technical enhancement but constitutes a structural transformation of the prosecutorial process within the European Union.

4 Major EPPO Investigations

The European Public Prosecutor's Office (EPPO) has undertaken several major transnational investigations targeting large-scale fraud schemes that have caused substantial damage to the financial interests of the European Union. These operations exemplify the EPPO's capacity to coordinate complex multi-jurisdictional prosecutions and its increasing reliance on advanced digital investigative tools. Each case has generated an extraordinary volume of digital evidence—often amounting to hundreds of terabytes—illustrating both the technological sophistication of modern financial crime and the central role of digital forensics in contemporary investigations. The following subsections present detailed analyses of each case, focusing on their context, scope, digital evidence, and procedural outcomes.

4.1 Case Example 1: Investigation "Admiral"

Operation Admiral constitutes one of the EPPO's flagship investigations, focusing on a large-scale intra-community VAT carousel fraud within the consumer electronics sector. The criminal network allegedly established a complex web of companies designed to evade VAT obligations on cross-border sales of mobile phones, tablets, and other electronic devices. The scheme involved missing trader fraud, large-scale money laundering, and instances of corruption connected to organised criminal structures. The financial damage to public budgets was initially estimated at €2.2 billion, later revised to €2.9 billion following expanded evidence collection.

The Admiral operation revealed a truly pan-European criminal framework, encompassing fraudulent transactions and shell entities distributed across more than 30 countries, including at least 16 EU Member States—notably Portugal, Germany,

Italy, France, Spain, and the Benelux countries. The network's reach extended beyond the Union, with verified operational links to Albania, Serbia, Singapore, the United Arab Emirates, China, Turkey, the United Kingdom, and the United States. The transnational complexity of the fraud rendered unilateral national detection impossible, thereby underscoring the necessity of the EPPO's supranational prosecutorial mandate.

The Admiral investigation yielded an unprecedented volume of digital evidence, estimated at approximately 638 terabytes. Coordinated searches across multiple jurisdictions resulted in the seizure of extensive documentation and digital devices—computers, mobile phones, and tablets—providing crucial evidentiary material. The EPPO's analysts employed its central Case Management System (CMS) alongside national and EU-level databases to establish cross-border connections among suspects and entities. Through data-matching and network analysis, investigators traced links between a Portuguese suspect company and more than 9000 associated firms as well as over 600 individuals implicated in the fraudulent carousel. This data-driven investigative strategy, combining big data analytics, financial transaction tracing, and digital communication forensics, was pivotal in dismantling a criminal structure that had operated undetected for years.

Operation Admiral formally commenced with a coordinated action day on 29 November 2022, during which over 200 searches were executed simultaneously across 14 countries. These actions resulted in 24 arrests, including 14 suspected ringleaders, and the seizure of assets valued at €59 million, comprising real estate, luxury vehicles, cash holdings, bank accounts, and jewellery. After 2 years of investigative work, EPPO prosecutors in Portugal issued indictments in late 2023 against 12 individuals and 15 corporate entities.

The first trial under Operation Admiral opened in October 2024 before the Criminal Court of Lisbon, involving 26 defendants (11 individuals and 15 companies from Portugal, France, and Cyprus) charged with VAT fraud, money laundering, and criminal conspiracy. Several key suspects remain in pre-trial detention, while the Portuguese case—representing an estimated €80 million in damages—continues with hearings scheduled into 2025.

Simultaneously, the Admiral investigation continues across other jurisdictions, as evidence shared by the EPPO has led to the opening of 28 parallel or follow-up proceedings by national authorities. Notably, derivative cases such as "Admiral 3.0" in Greece, targeting an additional €38 million fraud branch, have emerged from the primary case files. These interconnected proceedings demonstrate both the scale of the fraud and the catalytic role of EPPO-led evidence sharing in reinforcing coordinated enforcement across Member States (Fig. 7).

4.2 Case Example 2: Operation "Silk Road"

Operation Silk Road—named symbolically after the historical trade routes linking Europe and Asia—represents one of the European Public Prosecutor's Office

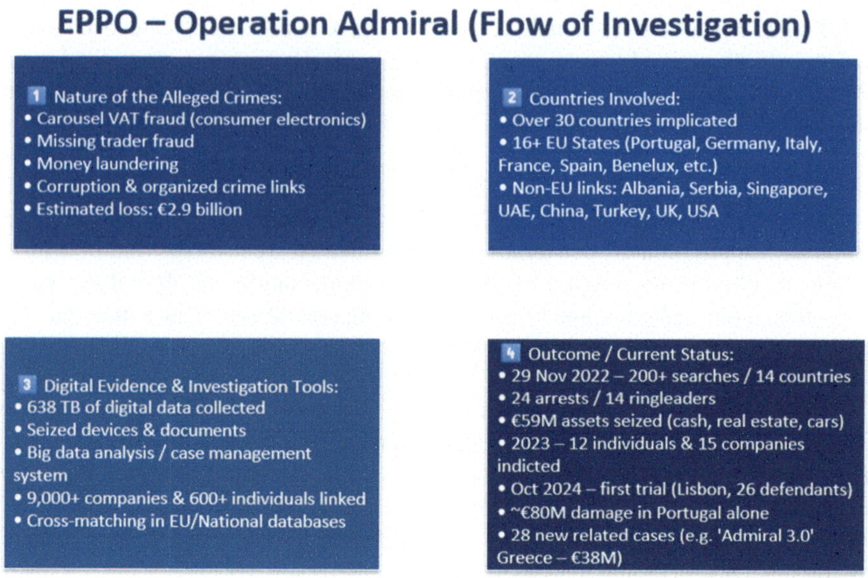

Fig. 7 Operation admiral (flow of investigation). *Source* Authors processing based on EPPO press release

(EPPO)'s most significant investigations into large-scale customs and VAT fraud involving transnational trade networks. Initiated by the EPPO's Brussels office, the case emerged in 2023 from an inquiry into suspected customs irregularities at Liège Airport (Belgium). The investigation targets a sophisticated criminal organisation comprising Chinese exporters and European intermediaries, accused of orchestrating systematic import VAT evasion within the framework of intra-EU trade logistics.

The criminal network under investigation is alleged to have exploited Customs Procedure 42, a legal mechanism that allows the import of goods into the EU with deferred VAT payment when goods are declared as destined for another Member State. The suspects reportedly used this mechanism to disguise large shipments of consumer electronics and household goods—including smartphones, toys, and accessories—imported from China as fictitious transit consignments through Belgium, thereby fraudulently claiming VAT exemption at the point of entry.

To operationalise the fraud, the perpetrators established a network of shell companies across at least six EU Member States—France, Germany, Italy, Hungary, Poland, and Spain—which issued false invoices and fabricated transport documents purporting to represent legitimate cross-border transactions. The fraudulent scheme also relied on stolen corporate identities and the unauthorised use of valid VAT numbers belonging to legitimate businesses, lending authenticity to falsified documentation.

In reality, the imported goods were sold directly to EU consumers without ever leaving Belgium, enabling the perpetrators to pocket the VAT collected from retail sales while remitting no tax to national authorities. This illicit strategy enabled the fraudsters to undercut legitimate market prices, distorting fair competition across the EU's internal market. The fraud was active between 2019 and 2022, generating an estimated €303 million in unpaid VAT and an additional €6.6 million in evaded customs duties. The offences under investigation include VAT and customs fraud, document forgery, money laundering, and participation in a criminal organisation.

The Silk Road operation is primarily coordinated by the EPPO's Brussels office in cooperation with Belgian judicial authorities. The scheme's operational nucleus was located in Belgium, where three private customs brokerage firms allegedly submitted falsified customs declarations on behalf of Chinese exporters. These exporters—operating from China—reportedly controlled the logistics and documentation processes through local European intermediaries.

The fraud's transnational reach extended across multiple EU jurisdictions, with shell companies and false buyers established in France, Germany, Italy, Hungary, Poland, and Spain. These entities simulated the intra-community movement of goods to conceal their actual destination and ownership. Consequently, while China and Belgium constituted the source and entry points of the operation, a web of interconnected European corporate fronts facilitated the distribution of untaxed goods to consumers across the EU.

Given the extensive international scope of Operation Silk Road, digital evidence was indispensable to reconstructing the fraud's financial and logistical structure. Investigators executed search and seizure operations targeting company headquarters, warehouses, and private residences, confiscating computers, servers, and electronic storage devices containing accounting data, customs filings, and internal communications.

The operation yielded an estimated 350 terabytes of digital evidence, including emails, financial ledgers, customs entries, and electronic invoices. EPPO's forensic analysts—supported by Europol and the Belgian Federal Police's Federal Computer Crime Unit (FCCU)—employed advanced digital forensic tools to extract, authenticate, and analyse this data. Techniques such as IP tracing, metadata correlation, and networked document analysis were applied to identify falsified e-invoices and cross-match customs declarations with actual shipping movements.

By integrating data from customs IT systems, freight records, and seized devices, the EPPO successfully reconstructed the fraudulent supply chain and linked multiple companies to the same underlying export scheme. This comprehensive digital forensics-driven methodology provided robust evidentiary support for forthcoming prosecutions.

A decisive operational breakthrough occurred on 28 March 2023, when the EPPO and Belgian law enforcement authorities conducted coordinated raids at ten locations, including Liège Airport warehouses, company offices, and private residences. The operation resulted in the arrest of four suspects, including two company directors, an accountant, and a logistics employee. Authorities also froze twelve bank accounts and seized four luxury vehicles (including Audi, BMW, and Mini models), along with substantial documentary and digital evidence.

Fig. 8 Operation silk road (flow of investigation). *Source* Authors processing based on EPPO press release

Following the raids, the detained individuals were charged with VAT and customs fraud, money laundering, document forgery, and participation in a criminal organisation. All suspects remain presumed innocent pending judicial proceedings. The EPPO's Brussels office, in cooperation with Belgian prosecutors, continues to oversee the case, which remains at an active investigative stage.

Given the complexity and transnational reach of the fraud, further forensic analysis and international cooperation measures are ongoing, with potential additional indictments and arrest warrants anticipated. The principal prosecutorial objective is to ensure accountability both within Belgium and in cooperating jurisdictions once the comprehensive evidentiary evaluation is complete (Fig. 8).

4.3 Case Example 3: Operation "Resilient Crime" (2024)

Operation Resilient Crime represents one of the most significant European Public Prosecutor's Office (EPPO) initiatives in 2024, directed against large-scale fraud involving the European Union's Recovery and Resilience Facility (RRF) in Italy. The operation, coordinated by the EPPO's Venice office, was launched in April 2024 following indications of systemic misuse of EU recovery funds intended to support post-pandemic economic reform and investment projects. The investigation uncovered a criminal organisation that allegedly engaged in a coordinated scheme of document falsification, financial deception, and misappropriation of EU funds.

The fraudulent activities under investigation concern the submission of false or misleading documentation to unlawfully obtain RRF financial support. The alleged offences include the misrepresentation of project objectives, artificial inflation of expenditure, and the use of ineligible or fictitious entities to claim EU funding. These manipulations were reportedly executed through a structured network of actors assuming distinct roles—application drafting, documentation falsification, and fund diversion—indicating an organised criminal structure.

The scheme was active between 2021 and 2023, during which the perpetrators established fraudulent companies and project proposals to obtain EU grants. Once the funds were disbursed, the illicit proceeds were allegedly transferred through layered foreign banking networks to conceal their origin and destination. The crimes under investigation include fraud affecting the EU's financial interests, forgery, money laundering, and participation in a criminal organisation.

The operational actions were based on intelligence and forensic analysis conducted by the EPPO's Venice office, which coordinated simultaneous enforcement activities across Italy, Austria, Romania, and Slovakia. The large-scale operation involved 22 arrests and dozens of searches conducted within a single coordinated action day. The EPPO's Case Management System (CMS) and its secure communication infrastructure played a crucial role, enabling real-time intelligence sharing and operational synchronisation among European Delegated Prosecutors (EDPs) and national law enforcement agencies. This seamless digital coordination allowed for immediate tactical adjustments and evidence preservation across jurisdictions.

The investigative phase included the digital examination of suspects' premises, focusing on the seizure of computers, servers, and electronic storage devices containing operational, financial, and correspondence data. The EPPO's forensic IT division deployed secure digital acquisition protocols to safeguard evidentiary integrity while initiating immediate on-site data analysis. The resulting digital corpus provided key insights into document forgery, communications between conspirators, and the coordination of fraudulent grant applications.

The investigation also revealed the use of advanced technological countermeasures by the perpetrators, including VPNs, cloud-based data storage, cryptocurrency transactions, and even AI-assisted software to simulate legitimate documentation and automate fund transfers. Nevertheless, the EPPO's specialised analytical and crypto-tracing tools, used in cooperation with national Financial Intelligence Units (FIUs), enabled investigators to trace and reconstruct the movement of illicit funds across borders.

The forensic financial analysis demonstrated a complex web of transactions linking Italian-based fraudulent entities to Austrian, Romanian, and Slovakian bank accounts. Through the application of data analytics, blockchain tracing, and pattern recognition, investigators were able to identify the precise flow of misappropriated RRF funds. The integration of financial and digital forensics was instrumental in revealing the network's internal hierarchy, the mechanisms of fund diversion, and the methods used to disguise illicit transactions.

operations. The effective pursuit of such high-value cases requires both state-of-the-art technology and highly specialised personnel. Budgetary limitations, including the costs of software licensing, system maintenance, and cybersecurity compliance, may hinder the EPPO's capacity to maintain cutting-edge digital capabilities across its entire network.

In summary, while digital tools have transformed the operational landscape of the EPPO, their full potential is constrained by technological, legal, and resource-based challenges. Overcoming these limitations will require continuous innovation, deeper inter-institutional cooperation, and sustainable investment in both human and digital capital.

6 Conclusions

Digital investigation tools have become indispensable to the operational success of the European Public Prosecutor's Office (EPPO) in combating financial crimes against the European Union's budget. These technologies support every phase of the prosecutorial process—from evidence collection and preservation to data analysis and asset recovery—and have proven essential in transforming the EPPO into a digitally enabled, transnational enforcement institution. As the landscape of financial crime continues to evolve in scope, complexity, and technological sophistication, the EPPO's capacity to adapt its investigative frameworks through the integration of advanced digital tools and forensic methodologies remains central to its mission of safeguarding the Union's financial interests.

Between 2021 and 2024, the EPPO's progressive adoption of digital investigative systems has redefined its operational capabilities. The implementation of automation and centralised information management has eliminated procedural bottlenecks, markedly increasing both the speed and volume of investigations. Cross-border cooperation has been enhanced through secure communication and data-sharing platforms, enabling synchronised actions across jurisdictions and replacing traditional, fragmented national procedures. The transition from basic data analysis to AI-assisted investigative methodologies has further strengthened the EPPO's ability to proactively detect and dismantle complex fraud networks, allowing for earlier intervention and higher rates of prosecutorial success.

Equally significant has been the EPPO's advancement in asset tracing and recovery, made possible through the integration of digital forensic and financial analytics. The exponential rise in the value of frozen and recoverable assets—culminating in billions of euros preserved in 2024—demonstrates the practical impact of digitalisation in securing restitution and reinforcing deterrence. Moreover, the establishment of a unified digital prosecutorial environment has standardised procedures across Member States, fostering a cohesive institutional culture supported by shared tools, training, and legal practices.

However, the rapid digitalisation of prosecutorial processes also exposes persistent challenges and systemic limitations. The increasing complexity of financial schemes, the jurisdictional fragmentation of legal systems, and the diversity of offence typologies require continued innovation and flexibility in investigative approaches. Technical challenges—such as data accuracy, tool reliability, and integration with traditional workflows—necessitate sustained human oversight and quality control. Additionally, training disparities and resource constraints across Member States pose ongoing risks to consistency and efficiency. Addressing these limitations through investment in technical capacity, harmonised data frameworks, and professional development will be vital to the EPPO's long-term effectiveness.

In conclusion, the evolution of the EPPO's digital infrastructure between 2021 and 2024 demonstrates how strategic technological innovation can profoundly enhance institutional performance, legal coordination, and financial accountability at the European level. The EPPO's experience exemplifies that digital transformation in justice administration—when aligned with transparency, interoperability, and ethical governance—can yield exponential gains in prosecutorial efficiency and deterrence. As the EPPO moves beyond 2024, it stands as a model for a transnational, digitally empowered prosecutorial authority, representing a cornerstone in the EU's broader commitment to ensuring integrity, accountability, and resilience in the protection of its financial interests.

Appendix: Evolution of EPPO Digital Investigation Tolls 2021–2024

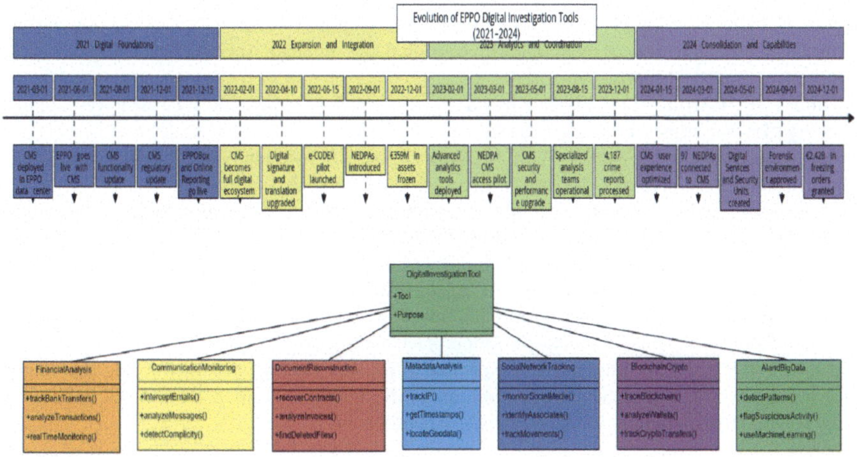

Source Own processing

References

Achim MV, Borlea SN, Văidean VL (2021) Does technology matter for combating economic and financial crime? A panel data study. Technol Econ Dev Econ 1:223–261. https://doi.org/10.3846/tede.2021.13977

Adams T (2024) Trends, challenges and opportunities of engaging digital forensics for cybercrime investigations. Adv Multidiscip Sci Res J Publ 15(1):1–12. https://doi.org/10.22624/aims/cisdi/v15n1p1

Alghamdi M (2021) Digital forensics in cyber security—recent trends, threats, and opportunities. https://doi.org/10.5772/intechopen.94452

Banerveld M, Le-Khac N, Kechadi T (2014) Performance evaluation of a natural language processing approach applied in white collar crime investigation, pp 29–43. https://doi.org/10.1007/978-3-319-12778-1_3

Becková D (2020) European public prosecutor's office: new actor in eu criminal law. Bratisl Law Rev 4(2):163–172. https://doi.org/10.46282/blr.2020.4.2.207

Bošković M (2024) Protection of EU financial interests: eppo's cooperation with non-EU states. J Criminol Crim Law 62(3):27–44. https://doi.org/10.47152/rkkp.62.3.2

Bülbül H, Yavuzcan H, Özel M (2013) Digital forensics: an analytical crime scene procedure model (ACSPM). Forensic Sci Int 233(1–3):244–256. https://doi.org/10.1016/j.forsciint.2013.09.007

European Public Prosecutor's Office (2022) EPPO annual report 2021. Publications Office of the European Union, Luxembourg. https://doi.org/10.2927/34796

European Public Prosecutor's Office (2023). EPPO annual report 2022. Publications Office of the European Union, Luxembourg. https://doi.org/10.2927/816527

European Public Prosecutor's Office (2024) EPPO annual report 2023. Publications Office of the European Union, Luxembourg. https://doi.org/10.2927/205863

European Public Prosecutor's Office (2025) EPPO annual report 2024. Publications Office of the European Union, Luxembourg. https://doi.org/10.2927/4997589

Herrnfeld H (2024) National implementation of the regulation establishing the European public prosecutor's office in Germany. Kwartalnik Prawa Międzynarodowego 1(1):11–22. https://doi.org/10.5604/01.3001.0054.4501

Odeyemi O, Ibeh C, Mhlongo N, Asuzu O, Awonuga K, Olatoye F (2024) Forensic accounting and fraud detection: a review of techniques in the digital age. Finance Account Res J 6(2):202–214. https://doi.org/10.51594/farj.v6i2.788

Rughani P (2017) Artificial intelligence based digital forensics framework. Int J Adv Res Comput Sci 8(8):10–14. https://doi.org/10.26483/ijarcs.v8i8.4571

Sabillón R, Serra-Ruiz J, Cavaller V, M J (2017) Digital forensic analysis of cybercrimes. Int J Inform Secur Priv 11(2):25–37. https://doi.org/10.4018/ijisp.201

Selimi A, Ali İ (2024) The role of digital forensic analysis in modern investigations. J Emerg Comput Technol 4(1):1–5. https://doi.org/10.57020/ject.1445625

Simeunović N, Gojko G, Ristić N (2016) Forensic accounting in the fraud auditing case. Eur J Appl Econ 13(2):45–56. https://doi.org/10.5937/ejae13-10509

Sindhu K, Meshram B (2012) Digital forensic investigation tools and procedures. Int J Comput Netw Inform Secur 4(4):39–48. https://doi.org/10.5815/ijcnis.2012.04.05

Zahid I, Aslam R (2020) A qualitative perspective of practical implication of forensic accounting for fraud detection and prevention in Pakistan. RMC J Soc Sci Human 1(1):23–33. https://doi.org/10.46256/rmcjsochum.v1i1.22. www.eppo.europa.eu

Florin Alexandru Roman is a lawyer and associate professor at the Faculty of Economics and Business Management within the Babeş-Bolyai University of Cluj-Napoca. Florin coordinates projects, advises and provides representation before the courts on organized crime, money laundering, tax evasion, fraud, corruption and work-related crimes (including industrial and labor accidents). He completed in-depth studies in the field of European and Comparative Law in Italy (Pisa, Padua, Syracuse) and in France (Strasbourg). He is a member of the Bucharest Bar (2006) and the Naples Bar (2012). He is currently Ph.D. candidate in the field of finance with the research topic on frauds in European Union' funds.

Monica Violeta Achim is a professor and doctoral supervisor in Finance at the Faculty of Economic Sciences and Business Administration, Babeş-Bolyai University, Cluj-Napoca. With over 27 years of experience in academia, she has published, as author and co-author, over 140 scientific articles and 27 books. The main research topics are financial analysis, business performance, finance, and economic and financial crime. In 2020, she obtained the Award for Excellence in Scientific Research, at Babeş-Bolyai University, Faculty of Economics and Business Administration, Cluj-Napoca, Romania, as a recognition of the results obtained in the research activity. She leads a main national project in the area of financial crime in the period 2020–2023. In the business environment, she works in liberal professions as an accountant expert, tax consultant, and judicial expert.

Digital Deceit in Finance: Deepfakes, Synthetic Identities, and the Future of Fraud Prevention

Deepika Dhingra, Prabal Chakraborty, and Kirti Sharma

Abstract In an era of accelerating digitalization, the financial services industry is facing another bout of technologically advanced threats with the power of artificial intelligence. Of these, the phenomenon of deepfake technology and synthetic identity fraud has become the most critical issue, leading to the loss of faith in online identity systems and the usefulness of financial operations. It is weaponizing deepfakes, or highly realistic yet artificially generated sound, video, and image forgeries, to find a way around biometric authentication and to plough customer service systems (as well as bypassing TOD on their phones, etc.). Parallel to this process, synthetic identity fraud, during which criminals are building fictitious characters with both real and falsified information, is currently one of the most actively developing areas of criminal activity in the financial sector, leveraging the weaknesses in credit bureaus, customer onboarding, and digital wallets. This chapter addresses the structure and development of such AI-driven threats with references to the recent international case studies, technological innovation in generative AI (e.g., GANs, voice cloning), and the typology of frauds that are recorded. It emphasises the industrialisation of these tools to enable scaling using cybercrime-as-a-service providers in the dark web. Discussion is further applied to control regulation gaps, the shortcomings of the original KYC/AML solutions, and a growing obsolescence of the static identity markers. The chapter, in turn, presents the strategic defence construct based on layer, adaptive, and AI-enhanced risk control. These are liveness detection, behavioural biometrics, explainable AI to detect anomalies, decentralised identity structures, and cross-institutional intelligence sharing. The discussion also focuses on agile regulatory innovation, cross-border collaboration, and responsible AI regulation as these areas should remain ahead of current threats.

D. Dhingra (✉)
School of Management, BML Munjal University, Rewari, Haryana, India
e-mail: mithudhingra@gmail.com

P. Chakraborty
Lingaya's Vidyapeeth, Rewari, Haryana, India

K. Sharma
Great Lakes Institute of Management, Gurgaon, Haryana, India

M. V. Achim (ed.), *Financial Crime in the Digital Era*, Contributions to Finance and Accounting, https://doi.org/10.1007/978-3-032-20198-0_2

Keywords Digital deception · Generative AI-driven fraud · Biometric authentication vulnerabilities · Synthetic persona construction

1 Introduction: The Digital Fraud Frontier

The digitization of financial services has led to increased efficiency, speed, and connectivity worldwide. However, the technology that enables innovation has also increased the scope of attack by economic crime. In the last 10 years, risk management, fraud detection, and customer engagement have been significantly transformed through artificial intelligence (AI), machine learning (ML), and big data analytics. But at the same time, they have empowered the production of hyper-realistic falsifications (deepfakes) and contributed to the production of synthetic identities that are so convincing that they may trick even advanced digital checks (West 2020; Kshetri 2021).

This chapter takes a closer look at the emergence of deepfakes and synthetic identity fraud in the financial services sector and their underlying technologies, changing landscape of threats, and the impacts of this shift on governance and regulation. It also suggests strategic responses based on AI-enhanced fraud detection, ethical governance, and cross-sectoral cooperation. In Fig. 1 the comparison between Deepfake versus Synthetic Identity Frauds is presented.

1.1 Research Methodology

The exploratory qualitative design is further justified through a comparison with alternative research approaches, highlighting its suitability for emerging fraud phenomena with limited structured data (Table 2). Considering the highly dynamic character of deepfake tools and synthetic identity fraud, in which case empirical data is limited, fragmented, or secret, an exploratory qualitative approach is the most suitable way to achieve conceptual clarity, determine the technological trends, and make integrated contributions to the knowledge in different areas (Table 1).

2 Sampling and Source Selection

- Cases and documents that were most appropriate in studying AI-based fraud in financial services were selected by purposive sampling.
- Inclusion criteria: recency (since 2018 because of changes in technology), financial services relevance, described attack mechanism, or regulatory relevance.
- The rationale for adopting the qualitative exploratory approach, compared with alternative research methods, is summarized in Table 2.

Dimension	Deepfakes	Synthetic Identity Fraud (SIF)
Core Definition	AI-generated audio/video/images	Fraudulent identity created using data
Primary Purpose	Impersonation, manipulation, social engineering	Account opening, credit building, loan exploitation
Technology Used	GANs, diffusion models, face-swap AI	Stolen identifiers + fabricated credentials
Attack Mode	Visual/voice spoofing, real-time impersonation	Long-term behavioural manipulation of systems
Key Target	Biometric KYC, employees, executives	Credit bureaus, digital lenders, onboarding systems
Detection Difficulty	Very high	High (no real victim to report fraud)

Fig. 1 Deepfake versus synthetic identity frauds. *Source* Author's own processing

3 Innovative Contribution of the Methodology

This approach uniquely integrates: Technological forensics, Fraud lifecycle modelling, Mapping the cybercrime ecosystem, Cross-regulatory comparative analysis, Artificial intelligence (AI) risk governance principles. The methodological integration of such kind is mostly absent in previous investigations and fills the literature gaps that have been identified above.

Table 1 Methodological steps

Step	Description	Purpose
1. Systematic literature collection	Reviewed 146 peer-reviewed articles, regulatory papers (FATF, FinCEN, RBI, EU AI Act), industry reports (Aite-Novarica, McKinsey, WEF), and cybersecurity research from 2014 to 2024	Identify patterns, definitions, threat taxonomies
2. Thematic coding	Categorized findings into themes: technological mechanisms, fraud lifecycle, regulatory gaps, emerging threats, detection tools, governance issues	Enable structured comparison and gap identification
3. Case analysis	Studied 27 real-world deepfake and synthetic identity fraud cases from US, EU, India, and APAC	Provide empirical grounding for conceptual frameworks
4. Cross-comparison	Mapped similarities/differences across jurisdictions, technologies, and industry sectors	Understand systemic and cross-border dynamics
5. Conceptual framework building	Developed integrated models such as hybrid threat evolution, fraud lifecycle, and multi-layered defense	Generate actionable insights and strategic recommendations

Source Own processing's

Table 2 Advantages over alternative methods

Method	Advantages of present qualitative method	Disadvantages of other methods
Quantitative modelling	Captures emerging risks with no stable data structure	Requires consistent, large datasets (not available)
Lab experiments	Real-world fraud complexity represented holistically	High ethical/legal barriers
Surveys/interviews	Ensures multi-source objectivity	Skews toward respondent perception, not systemic reality

Source Own processing's

4 Understanding Deepfakes: Technology and Financial Threats

4.1 The Mechanics of Deepfake Technology

The term *deepfake* originates from "deep learning" and "fake," referring to media generated or altered through deep neural networks. Deepfakes are most commonly created using **Generative Adversarial Networks (GANs)**—a machine-learning architecture consisting of two neural networks, a generator and a discriminator, that compete against each other (Goodfellow et al. 2014). The generator produces synthetic data, while the discriminator attempts to distinguish between genuine and fake inputs. Over successive iterations, the generator improves, creating increasingly realistic outputs—whether facial images, voice samples, or full-motion videos.

4.2 Deepfakes in the Financial Context

In financial services, deepfakes pose unique and multi-dimensional risks. First, they compromise **biometric authentication systems**, which rely on facial recognition, voice signatures, or video-based KYC processes. Fraudsters can submit AI-generated facial scans or voice recordings to bypass verification checks. In 2022, several European banks reported deepfake-enabled identity attacks during remote onboarding, where synthetic video footage was used to simulate customer interviews.

Second, deepfakes facilitate **executive impersonation and payment fraud**. These frauds are called CEO fraud or business email compromise 2.0, and they use voice and video AI-generated to order employees to transfer funds illegally. In a case that was reported, fraudsters used a voice imitation of a company director to approve a fraudulent transfer worth more than USD 35 million (WEF 2022).

4.3 The Deepfake Detection Challenge

It is technically difficult to detect deepfakes. Although the AI-based detection algorithms are capable of processing anomalies with regard to pixel patterns, lighting, or motion of the face, generative models are developed more rapidly than detection algorithms. The phenomenon is said to be a creation and detection arms race. In addition, there are scenarios of real-time authentication, e.g., the process of customer onboarding through mobile applications, which reduces both time and computing power to examine a deepfake (Moody's Analytics 2022).

Therefore, financial institutions need to add multi-factor and contextual biometrics systems, such as device fingerprinting, behavioural biometrics, and liveness, to minimize the use of static visual data. The issue, though, lies in ensuring the convenience of the users and privacy, and improving security.

5 Synthetic Identity Fraud: Anatomy and Evolution

The Synthetic Identity Fraud (SIF) has come to be one of the most evasive and sophisticated types of financial fraud in the digital era. As opposed to the conventional identity theft where the crook steals the credentials of an already existing individual, synthetic identity fraud is about the establishment of new, fictitious identities out of both real and fake information. These are hybrid identities that combine valid data, including a valid Social Security Number (SSN), Permanent Account Number (PAN), or Aadhaar number, with fake data, such as names, addresses, or dates of birth. Since these identities are not of actual persons, this kind of fraud is a big problem for financial institutions, regulators, and law enforcement agencies across the world to detect and stop.

The popularity of the dark web has increased the growth of synthetic identities due to the high accessibility of personal information on the internet. The credit bureaus, financial institutions, and e-commerce sites have been involved in data breaches that have facilitated access by criminals to millions of valid identifiers. Together with the development of digital onboarding, remote KYC (Know Your Customer), and automated credit scoring, the barrier to developing credible synthetic personas has been reduced significantly (McKinsey and Company 2021).

5.1 The Lifecycle of a Synthetic Identity

A synthetic identity fraud typically undergoes a structured lifecycle of four phases: creation, cultivation, exploitation, and abandonment.

Creation. It starts with personal information, including stolen SSNs, false names, phone numbers, and email addresses, compiled by fraudsters. In other instances, they create and use AI to produce authentic photographs and even create deepfake videos to enhance the authenticity of the identity to undergo biometric verification.

1. Cultivation: It then uses the new identity in the application of low-risk credit products, e.g., mobile phone contracts or store cards. Credit bureaus tend to generate a new profile of the synthetic identity when the initial applications are rejected, and numerous institutions report credit inquiries, thus justifying its existence.
2. Exploitation: Once the fraudster has demonstrated a good credit record, he raises his borrowing limits or takes more loans and finally busts out-maxing his/her credit card and vanishing with the money.
3. Abandonment: When the fraud is enabled or the credit runs out, the identity is abandoned. The absence of a real person linked to the debt complicates recovery and investigation efforts.

This lifecycle highlights the sophistication of modern financial fraud schemes, where patience and data-driven manipulation replace impulsive theft.

5.2 Drivers Behind the Growth of Synthetic Identity Fraud

Several structural and technological factors have contributed to the rise of SIF such as Credit Reporting Gaps: Credit bureaus often rely on name and SSN combinations to create profiles. If a fraudster uses a legitimate SSN with a fake name, the system may inadvertently establish a new record rather than flagging a mismatch. Another factor that contributes is Globalization and Cross-Border Transactions, the international nature of financial systems allows synthetic identities to exploit jurisdictional gaps. A fraudster operating from one country can easily create an identity registered in another, complicating detection and prosecution.

5.3 Real-World Incidents and Economic Impact

In the United States, synthetic identity fraud accounted for an estimated $6 billion in losses and approximately 20% of credit losses in 2022 (Aite-Novarica 2022). In India, fraudulent use of Aadhaar-linked accounts and fake PAN identities has led to similar concerns, particularly in the digital lending and mobile banking sectors. The Reserve Bank of India (RBI) has repeatedly emphasized the need for enhanced digital KYC and liveness verification protocols to mitigate this risk.

5.4 The Role of AI and Automation

Artificial intelligence and automation have had a dual impact on synthetic identity fraud. On the one hand, AI enables fraudsters to automate data synthesis, document forgery, and digital persona generation. Tools such as generative adversarial networks (GANs) can produce lifelike identity documents and even deepfake videos for liveness detection bypass. On the other hand, AI-powered fraud detection systems offer potential countermeasures through behavioral analytics, anomaly detection, and network analysis. The arms race between fraudsters and defenders thus revolves around the same technological frontier—AI (PwC 2024).

5.5 Global Regulatory Response

Regulators have begun to recognize synthetic identity fraud as a distinct category requiring tailored intervention. In the United States, the Federal Reserve launched the Synthetic Identity Fraud Mitigation Toolkit (2020) to help banks improve verification and reporting mechanisms. Similarly, the Financial Action Task Force (FATF) has urged member states to integrate digital identity verification frameworks into their anti-money laundering (AML) and counter-terrorist financing (CFT) programs. The RBI drive in India to video-based customer identification (V-CIP) and Aadhaar-based Payment Systems (AePS) would ensure that verification is done without influencing digital inclusion. Nevertheless, unsteady implementation and varying privacy legislation in the jurisdictions are obstacles to a concerted effort.

5.6 *The Emerging Hybrid Threat*

Deepfake technology is increasingly being combined with synthetic identity fraud, forming hybrid threats. Fraudsters are now employing deepfake audio or video to create synthetic personas when interacting remotely, such as during onboarding or customer support. This amalgamation of fake identity and AI-created impersonation is the next stage of the financial crime—the one that defies even technical barriers, as well as human intuition. With fraudsters accessing generative AI models that can simulate identity on a real-time basis, the conventional demarcation between a synthetic and stolen identity could soon be unclear.

6 The Escalating Threat Environment

6.1 *The Convergence of AI and Cybercrime*

The integration of AI-based processes and organised cybercrimes is one of the characteristics of the modern fraud environment. Democratized generative AI models have reduced the technical barriers to the generation of convincing synthetic media such that criminals can now automate the process of deception at scale (Europol 2023). OpenAI GPT series or open-source-based architectures like Stable Diffusion and DeepFaceLab, even created with good intentions, can be used to generate forged identities, voice impersonation, and fake documents that evade standard verification protocols. Not only are stolen credentials sold on the dark web, but also AI-based fraud kits, which are now sold as a service and are sold as deepfake-as-a-service or synthetic ID generation tools, which can be operated by non-experts (Trend Micro 2024).

The rapid evolution of generative AI and digital identity ecosystems has significantly expanded the scale and sophistication of financial fraud, particularly through deepfakes and synthetic identities, posing new governance, cybersecurity, and regulatory challenges for financial institutions and law-enforcement agencies worldwide (Chesney and Citron 2019; Federal Reserve 2019; Kietzmann et al. 2020; Gartner 2023; IBM 2023; Accenture 2024; Interpol 2024).

Financial organizations are particularly at risk since their online activities depend on identity checks, biometric checks, and remote onboarding to a large extent, which can be easily compromised by artificial AI-generated information. In video KYC, in which liveness is detected through the use of deepfake, such technology may be used to mimic facial expressions or even duplicate voices. Scammers can now pose as senior officials in real-time, and this has been witnessed in the current situation in Hong Kong, where attackers were able to create AI-generated video calls to make a bank worker transfer 25 million dollars (BBC 2023). This is one of the ways that deepfake impersonation can take advantage of technological and human points of vulnerability in the financial ecosystems (Table 3).

Table 3 Deepfake threat matrix for financial services

Threat Type	Attack Vector	Typical Targets	Risk Level	Detection Difficulty
KYC Bypass	Video/face deepfake	Onboarding systems	High	Very high
CEO/Executive Fraud	Voice cloning	Corporate treasury	Critical	Extremely high
Payment Authorization Fraud	Real-time impersonation	Employees, customers	High	High
Market Manipulation	Fake public statements	Investors, markets	Medium	High
Social Engineering	Deepfake relatives/officials	Retail users	High	Medium

Source Author's own processing

6.2 Data Breaches and the Identity Supply Chain

The nature of the data handled in the financial sector makes it particularly vulnerable, as it is large and sensitive. Millions of customer records are often held by credit bureaus, payment processors, and fintech startups, and even a single breach can ripple across the institutions. In other instances, hackers use stolen information to train artificial intelligence (AI) tools to create authentic counterfeit accounts based on demographic patterns and financial habits. Integration of real and synthetic data makes these fraud applications more believable and difficult to identify using traditional rule-based systems (McKinsey and Company 2022).

6.3 Globalization and Cross-Border Dynamics

Financial transactions are of a global scope, which means that deepfakes and synthetic identity threats bring further complexity to the situation. Online remittances, digital payments, and decentralized finance (DeFi) systems ensure real-time cross-border transactions, making authorities virtually unable to trace the flow of fraudulent money once it enters international circuits. The problem is also worsened by regulatory differences across jurisdictions. Other countries do not have similar data protection and digital identity verification provisions and capabilities as the European Union due to the General Data Protection Regulation (GDPR) and the eIDAS regulation, which place the highest priority on these aspects (OECD 2023).

This loophole in the regulatory environment enables the fraudsters to take advantage of this situation by creating synthetic identities in the loosely regulated markets and employing them to launder money through the legitimate financial institutions in the well-regulated markets. The introduction of global systems of digital identities—like the Aadhaar in India and the Digital Identity Wallet in the EU—opens new opportunities as well as dangers: on the one hand, they will contribute to increased inclusiveness and consistency; on the other hand, they offer an inviting target in case of a data breach.

6.4 Institutional and Regulatory Challenges

Although people have become more aware of this problem, most financial institutions are still not ready to effectively counter deepfake and synthetic identity fraud. The old IT infrastructure, disjointed data systems, and the lack of inter-agency cooperation make it harder to catch the advanced schemes of fraud. The existing fraud detection systems tend to be based on fixed identifiers like PAN, SSN, or device fingerprint as opposed to dynamic behavioral information that will help identify irregularities. Also, regulators, law enforcement, and other stakeholders in the private sector have weak coordination in sharing threat intelligence or in developing a standardized taxonomy of fraud.

The KYC master direction of the Reserve Bank of India (2023), the guidelines of the U.S. FinCEN, and the anti-money laundering guidelines of the European Banking Authority (EBA) all emphasize digital verification, yet do not elaborate on how to deal with AI-generated identities and deepfakes. Furthermore, the application of new biometric surveillance or predictive analytics, used to identify fraud, is also associated with moral and legal dilemmas of the financial sector, potentially violating the rights to privacy of data or increasing the risk of algorithmic bias (World Economic Forum 2024).

7 Detection and Prevention: New Technological Defense

With more advanced AI-driven fraud being tackled by financial institutions, there is less reaction to fraud than an active, intelligence-based defense. The machine learning, behavioral analytics, and decentralized identity technologies should now be incorporated in detection and prevention strategies in order to predict and counter the threats before they become a reality. The subsections below discuss the most promising technological interventions that are being implemented or studied in the financial services industry.

7.1 AI-Enhanced Fraud Detection Systems

The conventional fraud detection systems were based on the rule-based systems, i.e., flagging anomalies by using fixed parameters like the size of transactions, geography, or frequency. Nevertheless, these systems are incapable of identifying the insidious patterns of behavior or artificial forms of data that are ingrained in AI-oriented attacks (Kshetri 2021). Unlike that, AI-assisted fraud detection uses deep learning algorithms that can extract non-linear relationships and dynamic typologies of fraud.

Thousands of attributes of transactions can be considered by neural networks in real time and differentiate between natural customer behavior and artificial manipulations. To enable the detection of anomalies on a case-by-case basis, financial institutions (such as JPMorgan Chase and HSBC) have embraced AI-based anomaly detectors, which estimate customer-specific transaction signatures that are subsequently reviewed by humans. These systems also continuously re-train on new datasets, hence flexibility towards changing threats (World Economic Forum [WEF] 2022).

Furthermore, federated learning algorithms, whereby joint training is done among many institutions without the exchange of raw data, are becoming essential in cross-bank fraud intelligence. Such a decentralized solution ensures privacy of data and allows sharing of knowledge against synthetic identity and deepfake attacks.

7.2 Behavioural Biometrics, Liveness Detection

Deepfake or synthetic images can easily spoof facial recognition (e.g., facilitate static biometric authentication) and fingerprints. As such, banks are also moving towards behavioural biometrics, which are dynamic human measurements, including typing rhythm, touchscreen pressure, cursor movement, and gait patterns. These can hardly be duplicated, even by AI synthesis, unlike static identifiers (Moody Analytics 2022).

Liveness detection also helps biometric security to a greater extent by ensuring that the biometric input is made by a live human being as opposed to a replayed or generated image. There are methods of analyzing micro-movements (e.g., frequency of blinking), depth detection, and thermal signature. As an example, the state-of-the-art face recognition APIs have adopted challenge-response schemes in authentication—they require the user to execute randomized operations in order to be guaranteed of authenticity.

Behavioural and liveness analytics thereby change the identity verification process to an identity validation that does not rely on a single-time validation but continuous authentication to enhance resilience against impersonation fraud (Fig. 2).

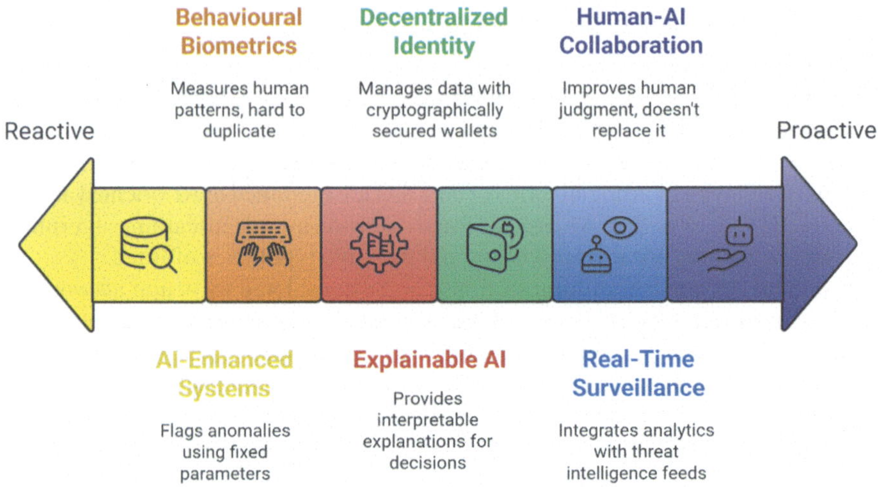

Fig. 2 Technological defense against fraud ranges from reactive to proactive. *Source* Author's own processing

7.3 Explainable AI (XAI) and Anomaly Detection

Although AI is critical in fraud detection, its lack of transparency is a regulatory and ethical issue. Under the regulatory frameworks of automated decision-making, such as the European Union AI Act and the General Data Protection Regulation (GDPR), financial regulators are increasingly demanding explainability in automated decision-making. An explainable AI (XAI) offers interpretable explanations to algorithmic results to allow compliance officers to learn why a transaction or identity was inhibited.

XAI models can expose the causal aspects behind a score on a risk of fraud, including the discrepancies in identity features or deviations in behavior, and as such help to support human control and auditability. The addition of anomaly detection algorithms with explainability improves accuracy, in addition to accountability; false positives will be minimized, and regulatory transparency obligations will be fulfilled (Brack 2023).

7.4 Decentralized Identity (DID) Systems and Blockchain

The blockchain technology has been popular in the development of tamper-proof digital identities. Decentralized Identity (DID) systems enable individuals to manage their own data with cryptographically secured digital wallets attested using a distributed registry. Every credential (address or income proof, or other) is issued and verified by reputable institutions, but is stored in the custody of the user (World Economic Forum 2022).

In relation to synthetic identity fraud, DIDs do not make it possible to make unauthorized or duplicate identities since each credential is cryptographically bound with its issuer. Additionally, identity verification based on blockchain identity enables a zero-knowledge proof, enabling users to check attributes (e.g., age or nationality), but not the underlying information-hence privacy exposure is minimised.

Singapore, Estonia, and India's financial regulators are testing the idea of decentralized KYC networks to enhance cross-border identity verification and decrease the use of centralized databases prone to breaches and manipulation.

7.5 Multilayered Authentication and Real-Time Surveillance

There is no single security measure that can be used to deal with the AI-technology-based fraud. Several-layered authentication architectures are required to be effective, including:

- Fingerprinting devices and networks.
- Geolocation correlation
- Analytic behaviour of transaction.
- Anomaly scoring and peer-comparison models.

These systems keep track of the dynamic and non-dynamic indicators of authenticity and enable institutions to detect synthetic fraud rings that are coordinated in real time. An adaptive defensive position is achieved by integrating real-time analytics with threat intelligence feeds, which are automatically updated to risk parameters with the emergence of new fraud patterns (Symantec 2020).

7.6 Human–AI Collaboration

Automation notwithstanding, the human factor is still necessary. The use of AI to improve human judgment is most effective in detecting fraud and not when it replaces human judgment. Analysts are able to read even complex behavioral cues, judge context, and understand false positives that algorithms can fail to detect. The ongoing education of AI literacy, awareness of ethics, and digital forensics is hence necessary to maintain the institutional preparedness (Aite-Novarica 2021).

8 Governance, Ethics and Regulation

Due to the spread of deepfakes and synthetic identity fraud in the global financial environment, retaliation cannot be reduced solely to technological protection measures. Mitigation requires an elaborate system of governance that incorporates ethics, regulatory regulations, data protection, and institutional responsibility. The fast development of AI approaches to fraud reveals the loopholes in the legal frameworks, the possibility of existing ethical standards, and the limits of privacy, surveillance, and digital sovereignty. This section discusses how the governance and regulation should change to respond to both ethical and legal challenges of fighting AI-driven financial crimes.

8.1 The Governance Imperative

Management of cyber financial crime extends far beyond compliance, but it involves establishing transparent, responsible, and dynamic risk management and decision-making systems. The banking institutions operate within a complex environment, as well as with various regulatory requirements such as the Anti-Money Laundering (AML), the Know Your Customer (KYC), and the Counter-Terrorist Financing (CTF). However, the existing structures were primarily designed around the previous formulations of fraud and not the AI-designed deception.

By breaking the conventions of governance, by being used to betray assumptions of reliable personal identifiers and biometric system checking, synthetic identities and deepfakes challenge the tradition of recognizing personal identity. The fact that the authenticity of online personas cannot be checked undermines the pillar of trust in financial systems (World Economic Forum 2024). Therefore, governance processes should move beyond the one-dimensional compliance lists to the ability to operate risk governance models, which incorporate AI ethics, real-time monitoring, and ongoing auditing of algorithmic operations.

In practical terms, this entails three layers of governance:

1 Institutional governance, where financial institutions adopt internal AI and data governance frameworks aligned with principles of fairness, transparency, and accountability;
2 Sectoral governance, involving coordinated oversight by financial regulators and data protection authorities; and
3 Transnational governance, encompassing harmonized international standards to ensure consistency across jurisdictions (OECD 2023).

8.2 Regulatory Frameworks and Jurisdictional Challenges

Global regulatory frameworks remain fragmented in their treatment of synthetic identity and deepfake fraud. While jurisdictions such as the European Union (EU), the United States (US), and India have initiated measures to address digital identity security, enforcement mechanisms differ widely.

In the EU, the General Data Protection Regulation (GDPR) and the proposed Artificial Intelligence Act (AI Act) establish a strong foundation for data privacy, transparency, and algorithmic accountability. The AI Act classifies systems used for biometric identification and credit scoring as "high-risk," requiring strict risk assessments, documentation, and human oversight (European Commission 2024). The eIDAS 2.0 Regulation aims to enhance interoperability of digital identity frameworks across member states, potentially mitigating synthetic identity vulnerabilities.

There is no comprehensive Federal privacy law in the United States, although some sectoral regulations, including the Fair Credit Reporting Act (FCRA), Bank Secrecy Act (BSA), and Identity Theft Red Flags Rule, do exist to regulate some of the aspects of identity verification and fraud detection. In 2023, the Financial Crimes Enforcement Network (FinCEN) released guidance to identify synthetic identity fraud as an identity theft (under the BSA) and encourage institutions to revise suspicious activity reporting (SAR) standards (FinCEN 2023).

The systems of digital identity verification and financial inclusion are managed in India by the Reserve Bank of India (RBI) and Unique Identification Authority of India (UIDAI). According to the Master Direction on KYC by the RBI, video-based customer identification (V-CIP), geotagging, and liveness detection are mandatory, and UIDAI controls the usage of Aadhaar as a means of authentication. Nevertheless, the fact that biometric and demographic data are used massively without a special AI regulatory framework brings up the issue of privacy and security (Mehta 2024).

These are regional differences that underscore the necessity of regulation harmonization. In the absence of international regulation, fraudsters take advantage of differences in jurisdiction, shifting illegal practice to weaker jurisdictions. Other multilateral organizations like the Financial Action Task Force (FATF) and the Basel Committee on Banking Supervision (BCBS) have urged the international community to work together regarding digital identity verification and AML-CFT systems in the era of AI (FATF 2023).

8.3 Ethical Impact of the Applications of AI in Fraud Detection

Fraud detection systems based on AI have enormous potential, such as real-time anomaly detection, behavioural analytics, and automated decision-making. Nevertheless, they also create privacy-related, surveillance-related, bias-related, and responsibility-related ethical dilemmas. The security and civil liberties are still on a razor.

8.3.1 Prejudice and Discrimination

Artificial intelligence can unintentionally discriminate against a particular group of people based on the biased data set created by the artificial intelligence program, resulting in unfair denial of services or a false alarm about fraud. In particular, as an example, the error rate of facial recognition algorithms is demonstrated to be high in the case of darker skin color and female identities (Buolamwini and Gebru 2018). This can exert more strain on pre-existing disparities in credit or service access in the financial sphere.

8.3.2 Responsibility and Interpretability

Another ethical issue is related to the black box characteristics of AI algorithms. The financial institutions need to make sure that the automated fraud detection model is explainable and auditable. Explainable AI (XAI) is a concept that helps not only to comply with the regulations but also to gain the trust of customers. Regulators are putting more pressure on institutions to show how their AI-based systems come to risk decisions, particularly when customers are affected in a way that influences their financial reputation (WEF 2024).

Therefore, AI governance in finance should be founded on four pillars, namely transparency, fairness, accountability, and inclusivity. The institutional AI governance charters should include ethical guidelines, which are to be subjected to independent audit and human control systems.

8.4 Cross-Sector Collaboration Between Public and Private Institutions

Since digital fraud has no borders, one player cannot solve the menace on their own. It is essential to have cross-sectoral coordination between regulators, banks, fintech, technology firms, and law enforcement agencies. The sharing of real-time information on the typology of fraud, threat intelligence, and best practices can be achieved through public–private partnerships (PPPs).

As an example, the Joint Money Laundering Intelligence Taskforce (JMLIT) in the UK and the FinCEN Exchange in the U.S. can be used as effective models of collaborative intelligence systems, which can strengthen resilience. These networks show that when institutions post anonymized information on fraudulent transactions, it is possible to notice trends of synthetic identity creation and deepfakes usage sooner (Basel Institute 2023).

Besides, young initiatives, including the Global Partnership on Artificial Intelligence (GPAI), the OECD AI Policy Observatory, encourage the creation of ethical AI principles that can be used to reconcile innovation with the principles of human rights and security. In the case of financial institutions, the incorporation of such standards into their risk governance processes, besides minimizing fraud exposure, improves reputational trust and regulatory adherence.

8.5 The Roadmap Toward Responsible Digital Identity Governance

Finally, the regulation of the deepfake and synthetic identity fraud needs to transform into a responsible digital identity ecosystem-one that strikes a balance between innovation, security, and human rights. This vision mandates that the efforts on digital identity verification standards be coordinated across the world, and that national systems be interoperable, and that redress should be effective in instances of identity misuse.

Privacy-by-design must be embraced by institutions, such that the data minimization, encryption, and moral protection of fraud detection technologies are considered at the very beginning. In their turn, regulators need to adopt adaptive regulation, adjusting the compliance requirements to change with the evolution of technology, as opposed to responding retrospectively.

Ethical and regulatory governance will be used to determine the resilience of digital finance in the long run. Not only will the financial system of the future be technologically advanced, but it will also be ethically sound, as it will be based on the idea that trust, transparency, and accountability will be the best tools as an antidote to deception in the AI age.

9 Strategic Countermeasures and Future Directions

Due to the increased size and complexity of the deepfake and synthetic identity fraud, financial institutions should take a multi-layered and intelligence-driven proactive approach to resilience. The old methods of fraud prevention, including static checks, detection rules, and human inspections, are not effective in a world where generative AI keeps on developing to overcome protection. The second step of financial crime prevention involves strategic alignment of technology, policy, and human expertise. This part provides an extensive outline of countermeasures and proactive approaches that can ensure the financial ecosystems are not fooled by AI (Fig. 3).

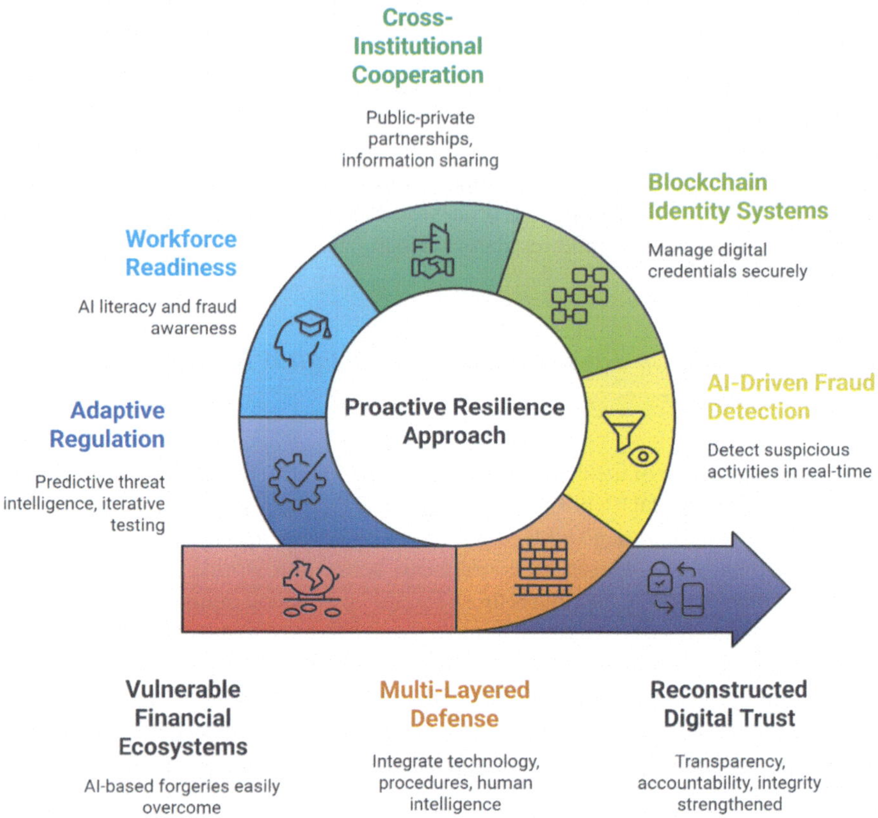

Fig. 3 Combating deepfake and synthetic identity fraud. *Source* Author's own processing

9.1 Practical and Measurable Proposals for Implementation

Although the technological, regulatory frameworks, and strategic frameworks to fight against deepfake and synthetic identity fraud are outlined above, financial institutions need to have tangible actions that can be taken with visible and measurable results. The recommendations below apply the theoretical knowledge in the chapter to operational, evidence-based interventions that apply to banks, fintech, regulators, and cybersecurity staff. All the recommendations are accompanied by impact indicators that can be measured to ensure that the institutions can address the effectiveness, benchmark, and measure the return on security investments. Collectively, these steps fill the gap between theory and practice and reinforce the practical usefulness of the chapter in industry implementation (Table 4).

Table 4 Practical and measurable proposals for mitigating deepfake and synthetic identity fraud

Proposal	Practical application	Measurable impact
1. Mandatory liveness verification for remote KYC	Integration of 3D liveness checks, micro-expression analysis, and randomized challenge–response tasks during onboarding	• 60–80% reduction in deepfake-enabled KYC bypass attempts • Faster fraud flagging during onboarding
2. Behavioural biometrics integration	Continuous monitoring of user behaviour (typing rhythm, swipe dynamics, device handling, motion patterns) across digital channels	• 40–50% improvement in detection accuracy for synthetic identities • Reduction in reliance on vulnerable static biometrics
3. Real-time cross-institution fraud intelligence grid	Establishing national or regional real-time data-sharing networks linking banks, fintechs, telcos, and regulators	• 30–45% reduction in time to detect coordinated fraud rings • Lower cross-bank synthetic identity migration
4. Decentralized digital identity (DID) deployment	Implementation of DID wallets and verifiable credentials for customer onboarding and attribute verification	• Near-zero duplication of identity credentials • Stronger auditability and tamper resistance
5. AI explainability (XAI) audits	Quarterly audit of fraud-detection models using SHAP/LIME Explainability frameworks	• 20–35% reduction in false positives • Improved compliance with AI governance and regulatory requirements
6. Standardised deepfake incident response protocols	Defining operational steps for detecting, verifying, escalating, and responding to suspected impersonation attempts	• 75% faster response to impersonation or deepfake-based fraud anomalies • Reduced financial loss during active fraud windows

Source Author's own processing

9.2 Limitations and Future Directions

Although this study provides a comprehensive and prospective evaluation of deepfakes in facilitated deception and synthetic identity fraud in financial services, it has some limitations, which are worth noting. To start with, there is limited access to high-quality and comprehensive fraud information because of the reasons of confidentiality concerns, inconsistent reporting, and the sensitivity of ongoing investigations. Consequently, the analysis is based on publicly available cases, regulatory reports, and secondary data to a large extent, which might not be comprehensive in terms of assessing the magnitude and variety of global fraud trends. Future studies must thus include anonymized data acquired with the help of financial institutions, regulators, and cybersecurity organizations, and possibly with privacy-sensitive algorithms like federated learning, so that the data can be analyzed across institutions without violating data privacy. Second, the speed and ongoing development of generative AI technologies, in particular diffusion model development, real-time impersonation systems, and synthetic identity generation, make it difficult to ensure accuracy over time. It is advisable to conduct longitudinal studies and periodic horizon-scanning exercises to monitor the emerging threats and update taxonomies with the changing technology. Third, the results of this research are also affected by the geographical differences in regulation, reporting maturity, and digital identity infrastructure, and the majority of recommendations are based on the jurisdictions, including the US, EU, and India. Increased comparative research in underrepresented areas, such as Africa, Latin America, and Southeast Asia, will give a more comprehensive global picture and demonstrate areas of weakness that have been generated by cross-border regulatory asymmetries. Fourth, even though the research identifies the potential benefits of defensive strategies, including behavioural biometrics, liveness detection, decentralized identity systems, and explainable AI, it fails to empirically justify these tools in controlled field experiments. Future studies should thus work with industry partners in doing pilot implementations, measuring model performance, quantifying false positives, identifying possible biases, and assessing user acceptance in real-world settings. Lastly, the conceptual orientation of the current chapter, which is the result of the restricted access to raw fraud data, does not allow the statistical validation of the suggested frameworks. Future work would focus on building quantitative risk measures of fraud, probabilistic prediction models, and systemic vulnerability measures that would bring together behavioural, technological, and cross-border aspects of fraud. The integration of these improvements will aid in the creation of a more holistic, empirically based, and more globally applicable view of AI-based identity fraud to develop effective defenses to stave off and build knowledgeable regulatory measures.

10 Conclusion

The appearance of the deepfake and synthetic identity fraud is a symbolic turning point in the history of financial crime. Unlike the classical forms of fraud, when individuals have to apply their verbal and physical skills to cheat or forge documents, these manipulations of AI are founded on a set of systems that are designed to foster trust, including digital authentication, biometric checking, and credit checking grounded in the data. This opposition identifies one of the central contradictions of the digital era: the very technologies that lead to the emergence of novel and innovative trends cause new vulnerability.

The financial sector has made a multidimensional issue, which is not a technical one but rather one that deals with governance, ethics, regulation, and trust of the people. The necessity to deal with this threat is a paradigm shift from aggressive shielding to proactive fortitude. The financial institutions must change their current, statistic, compliance-based risk management system into dynamic, learning, and collaboration-based systems. The AI-inspired anomaly detection, behavioral biometrics, and blockchain-based identity verification are the components that make up the new defense ecosystem. Nevertheless, without the robust regulatory vision, the readiness of labor, and cooperation between the countries, one cannot completely rely on technology.

This has to be a result of the unending innovativeness, openness, and ethical leadership in order to establish resilience against synthetic deception in the future. The financial institutions and the regulators will have to develop dynamic structures that will promote experimentation and be responsible. The cross-sectoral intelligence sharing, AI literacy investment, and the development of decentralized identity infrastructures can all help to improve digital trust.

Lastly, the deepfake and fake identity fraud war is not a game of technology but a bigger social business—to retain the authenticity, justice, and trust in the digital financial system. The institutions that are effective in combining both technological vigilance and ethical integrity will not only help reduce financial crime but also reinforce the ethical and operational basis of the financial system in the future.

References

Accenture (2024) AI literacy and workforce transformation in financial services
Aite-Novarica (2021) Synthetic identity fraud: the fastest-growing financial crime
Aite-Novarica (2022) The impact of synthetic identity fraud on the financial sector
Basel Institute on Governance (2023) Public–private partnerships in financial crime prevention
BBC (2023) Hong Kong deepfake video scam results in $25 million loss
Brack J (2023) Explainable AI and trust in automated decision-making
Buolamwini J, Gebru T (2018) Gender shades: intersectional accuracy disparities in commercial gender classification. In: Proceedings of the conference on fairness, accountability, and transparency, pp 77–91. https://doi.org/10.1145/3287560.3287596
Chesney R, Citron D (2019) Deepfakes and the new disinformation war. Foreign Aff 98(1):147–155
European Commission (2024) The artificial intelligence act
Europol (2023) Internet organised crime threat assessment (IOCTA)
Federal Reserve (2019) Synthetic identity fraud working paper
Federal Reserve (2020) Synthetic identity fraud mitigation toolkit
Financial Action Task Force (2023) Digital identity and financial crime risk mitigation
Financial Crimes Enforcement Network (2023) Advisory on identity-based financial crime
Gartner (2023) Explainable AI for risk and compliance
Goodfellow I, Pouget-Abadie J, Mirza M, Xu B, Warde-Farley D, Ozair S, Courville A, Bengio Y (2014) Generative adversarial nets. Adv Neural Inf Process Syst 27:2672–2680
IBM (2023) Data breach report and implications for identity fraud
Interpol (2024) Predictive threat intelligence and cyber-enabled crime
Kietzmann J, Lee LW, McCarthy IP, Kietzmann TC (2020) Deepfakes: Trick or treat? Bus Horiz 63(2):135–146. https://doi.org/10.1016/j.bushor.2019.11.006
Kshetri N (2021) Cybersecurity and AI-enabled fraud
McKinsey & Company (2021) The rise of synthetic identity fraud
McKinsey & Company (2022) Global risk and fraud analytics report
Mehta A (2024) Digital identity and privacy challenges in India
Moody's Analytics (2022) Biometrics and liveness detection in financial services

Organisation for Economic Co-Operation and Development (2023) Digital identity policy framework
PwC (2024) AI in fraud detection and risk management
Reserve Bank of India (2023) Master direction—know your customer (KYC)
Symantec (2020) Multilayered authentication and cyber defense
Trend Micro (2024) Deepfake-as-a-service report
West DM (2020) The future of digital governance and AI threats
World Economic Forum (2022) Global risks of deepfake-enabled fraud
World Economic Forum (2024) Governing AI in financial services

Dr. Deepika Dhingra is a seasoned finance academic with over 17 years of experience spanning teaching, research, and industry. She holds a Ph.D. in Finance from FMS, Delhi University, and an MBA in Finance from Indraprastha University. Currently, she serves as Associate Professor and Area Chair at BML Munjal University and is associated with institutions like IMT CDL, Hero Vired, and GRMI. Her research spans ESG, fintech, corporate restructuring, and sustainability, with publications in ABDC-ranked and Scopus-indexed journals. An accomplished case writer, her work is published by Ivey and Harvard Business Publishing. Dr. Dhingra has consulted on fintech and curriculum design for clients in India and the UK. She is proficient in financial modeling and data analysis using tools like E-Views, Stata, and MATLAB. A committed educator and Ph.D. guide, she is a member of the American Finance Association and regularly contributes to academic conferences and institutional development initiatives.

Dr. Prabal Chakraborty is a Professor at Lingaya's Vidyapeeth, Haryana, with 19 years of academic teaching experience and 28 years of extensive industry exposure. He has authored and presented over thirty research papers in reputed national and international journals. His core areas of expertise include Quantitative Analysis and Financial Management.

Dr. Kirti Sharma is a Fellow member of the Institute of Chartered Accountants of India (M. No. 099189) and associated with Great Lakes Institute of Management, Gurgaon since 2019. With over two decades of post-qualification experience spanning both industry and academia, Dr. Sharma specializes in financial and managerial accounting, compliance and auditing, fintech innovations including insurtech, cryptocurrencies, and blockchain technology.

Digital Payments and Fraud Risk: Technological Innovations and Global Regulatory Responses

Anuram Krishna E S and Blesson Varghese James

Abstract In the digital age, financial crime has increased in magnitude and complexity because of high-velocity digital payments, cross-platform financial systems, and due to new forms of threat, like deepfakes and synthetic identities. Due to the increasing failure of the conventional, more rules-based methods of fraud control to detect these more sophisticated behaviours, there has arisen the need to adopt more sophisticated, technology-driven prevention methods. This paper discusses how financial-crime detection and AML/CFT processes are changing with the use of innovative tools, namely AI and machine learning analytics, privacy-preserving federated models, blockchain-based identity mechanism, and real-time digital-payment intelligence. The chapter methodologically follows the comparative case-based approach to analysis synthesising the evidence presented in regulatory publications, industry reports, and documented cases of technological deployments to define general trends, advantages, and shortcomings. The results indicate that technology-enabled systems are much more effective in detecting fraud, presenting few false positives, enhancing identity assurance, and sharing across institution intelligence at a faster rate as compared to traditional systems. This paper concludes that responsible AI architecture, real-time data network integration, and regulatory cooperation are essential to establishing resilient, future-ready models that will be able to defend financial ecosystems against the changing threats of the digital era.

Keywords Financial crime detection · Anti-money laundering (AML) · Counter-terrorist financing (CFT) · Artificial intelligence (AI) · Machine learning analytics · Digital fraud

A. Krishna E S (✉)
Department of Global Finance & Analytics, Christ University, Pune, India
e-mail: anuram.es@msgfa.christuniversity.in

B. Varghese James
Department of Commerce, Christ University, Pune, India
e-mail: blesson.james@christuniversity.in

M. V. Achim (ed.), *Financial Crime in the Digital Era*, Contributions to Finance and Accounting, https://doi.org/10.1007/978-3-032-20198-0_3

1 Introduction

The blistering digitalisation of financial systems has changed the pace, volume and networking of global financial transactions, yet has also created more hazards and intricacy in financial crime. Estimates indicate that over USD 1.6 trillion are laundered annually all around the world, which is almost 2.7% of the world GDP (UNODC 2021). Online financial services, real-time payment systems, and digital payment infrastructures have allowed criminals to take advantage of new vulnerabilities, such as deepfake-based identity fraud, synthetic identities, authorised push-payment fraud, and mass attacks based on social-engineering (FATF 2021; Europol 2023). Traditional, rule-based monitoring tools cannot sustain these changes in threats anymore, leading to high false-positive rates, time delays in detection, and reduced flexibility (King and Salmon 2022). It is a change in technology and behaviour that has resulted in an increasing distance between the complexity of financial-crime methods and the processes of older fraud-detection methods.

Despite the previous research on the use of AI, machine learning, RegTech, or blockchain to be used as compliance tools (Arner et al. 2020; López-Rojas and Axelsson 2018), there are only a few integrated studies that unite national-level payment infrastructures, international banking innovations, and regulatory technology ecosystems. Current literature usually considers individual use-cases (e.g., machine-learning detectors, electronic identity, AML regulations) in isolation but does not examine the system-wide interactions between these parts to form fraud-prevention systems (Chen et al. 2021; FATF 2022). Such fragmentation indicates one important gap, to have a coherent, comparative conceptualization of how various nations and agencies bring advanced technologies to bear in real-time in the fight against financial crime.

Out of this disparity, the current chapter discusses the nexus of digital financial innovation and financial-crime prevention, and provides a cross-jurisdictional analysis of how new technologies are being implemented by national payment networks, international banks, and regulators. The chapter has three contributions to the literature. To start with, it unites a variety of technological solutions, such as AI/ML analytics, federated learning, identity based on blockchain, and privacy-enhancing computation into one conceptual framework. Second, it also gives comparative case knowledge in India, the United Kingdom, the United States, and global financial institutions, thus showing what models scale well and why. Third, it provides a prospective view on how future-ready AML/CFT systems will require the convergence of the technological, regulatory, and ethical factors.

The rest of this chapter is organized in the following way. Section 2 is a review of the academic and industry literature that is applicable to the positioning of the study within the existing research. Section 3 will include in-depth analysis of cases on the national and international levels. Section 4 summarises inter-case results, pointing to commonalities and differences. Part 5 contains strategic implications on financial institutions, regulators, FinTech innovators and researchers. Section 6 ends with a list of recommendations on how the global financial-crime prevention among the digital era can be strengthened.

1.1 Objectives and Scope of Research

The aim of the study is to examine the integration of emerging technologies into financial-crime prevention systems in various institutional and regulatory settings, namely artificial intelligence (AI), machine learning (ML), blockchain, biometrics, and privacy-preserving analytics. The study does not provide a technical model or statistical estimation but instead takes a comparative interpretative approach to text-analysis whereby it reviews documented implementations, regulatory initiatives and industry examples of the technology being applied to get a sense of how technology is operationalised in actual AML/CFT systems.

Data sources are analyzed based on purposive selection of sources, such as regulatory reports (FATF, FinCEN, FCA, RBI), industry white papers (HSBC, Google Cloud, NPCI), central bank guidance, peer-reviewed academic literature, policy documents, and publications of 20182025, both conceptually and current accuracy respectively. The described methodology is consistent with the methodological suggestions present in the AML/RegTech literature, which also highlight the necessity of synthesising multidisciplinary evidence during the furious development of technological systems that are outpacing empirical datasets (Arner et al. 2020; King and Salmon 2022). The analysis of text-based materials based on a systematic comparative prism shows that jurisdictions and institutions design, deploy, and regulate technology-enabled, fraud-prevention architectures in patterns.

To be more precise, the study will be conducted so as to:

- Determine the exact technological solutions under implementation in the sphere of AML/CFT, including real-time behavioural analytics, federated learning models, digital identity systems, and blockchain-based audit systems.
- Compare the way in which various jurisdictions such as India, the United Kingdom, the United States and global banks implement these technologies and under which institutional or regulatory frameworks do its implementation become possible.
- Evaluate the performance, constraints, and dangers of these systems in line with recorded performance, including the increase or decrease in detection rates, false-positive results, identity verification, or inter-institution intelligence dissemination.
- Compare national innovations in infrastructures (e.g. DPIP of India and its federated model) and corporate and regulatory innovations (e.g. HSBCs Dynamic Risk Assessment system or FCA/FinCEN sandboxes).

  Define the policy and strategic implications of the AML innovation, which is driven by technology such as ethical governance of AI, nuclear data-protection issues, and the necessity to cooperate internationally.

The study scope is thus conceptual, comparative, and policy based as it is concerned with the mobilisation of technology as opposed to the quantification of statistical performance results. The chapter also helps address a gap in the literature that has been reported: a lack of concerted efforts to relate national payment infrastructures, innovative innovations in global banking, and regulatory experiments in technology in one interpretative framework (FATF 2022; Lopez-Rojas and Axelsson 2018).

2 Literature Review

2.1 Technology as a Catalyst for Modern AML and Fraud Prevention

The use of digital transformation is consistently depicted in academic literature as one of the main characteristics of the modern anti-financial-crime policies. Scholars claim that rule-based systems which are helpful, have a high rate of false-positive, are slow to evolve and are not able to identify intricate layering patterns applied in contemporary money laundering. Consequently, AI and ML technologies are regarded as the key to the development of detectives.

These scholarly observations are reflected in industry research. The internal reports of HSBC point out that the systems used to monitor transactions caused by ML have increased the accuracy of detection by two to four times when compared to the previous systems and have reduced false positives by approximately 60%. These findings prove the general scholarly claims that ML models, particularly, supervised and unsupervised algorithms, are able to predict non-linear fraud patterns, identify new anomalies, and evolve with new criminal behaviour.

This technological change is also known by regulatory bodies. The Financial Action Task Force (FATF) mentions that new technologies which are implemented in a responsible manner enhance the speed, quality, and totality of the risk assessment. The recommendations by FATF emphasize the importance of sophisticated analytics as a tool of facilitating real-time tracking, cross-border information exchange, and the timely identification of suspicious activity, especially in high-density digital payment networks. This is in line with the scholarly conclusions that technologies diminish the intrinsic information asymmetries that the criminals capitalize on.

2.2 Artificial Intelligence and Machine Learning

Most of the new literature focuses on AI and ML due to the possibility of learning a non-trivial transaction pattern and detect suspicious behaviour at scale. Academic works emphasize: · Customer behaviour analytics which profile the average spending patterns of customers and alert in the event of deviation. Account identification with synthetic identity fraud through clustering algorithms that determine concealed relationships among accounts.

NLP models utilized in unstructured data screening like email trails, KYC documents and adverse media reports. Practical experience of industry pilots shows that AI models with human intelligence create a hybrid approach of intelligence, when systems select low-risk notifications and analysts concentrate on high-complexity cases. There are also risks that stand out in emerging literature. The quality, completeness and the accuracy of labelling of data plays a crucial role in AI systems. Lack of data hygiene results to biased models or unreliable predictions. Researchers stress that to make models valid, explainable, and ethical AI decisions, financial institutions have to invest in governance frameworks.

2.3 A Distributed Ledger Technology and Blockchain in AML

The use of blockchain as an effective instrument against money laundering has been an issue under discussion due to the fact that blockchain is immutable, transparent, and decentralised. According to academic literature, blockchain is especially helpful in:

- Transactional authenticity checking.
- Lessening document mutilation
- Tracing illicit fund flows
- Enhancing KYC and identity management.

  The research in the industry indicates that there is a close synergy between blockchain and machine learning. ML can detect suspicious wallet activities or clusters of transactions when used, whereas blockchain makes the records tamper-proof. Research articles posted on SSRN reveal that such combined models may establish a more efficient end-to-end AML system, specifically the financial flows and crypto-asset transactions across borders.

  Nevertheless, hardships are also recognized in literature. Privacy laws like GDPR limit the distribution of identifiable information on the open registers. In addition, crypto-assets that facilitate anonymity, as well as mixers, present new threats to AML, necessitating continuous blockchain analytics and regulatory innovations.

2.4 Identity Verification Technologies and Biometrics

During the age of internet, identity theft and impersonation fraud has increased, which has led to the usage of biometric authentication systems. The scholarly literature on biometrics claims that facial recognition, fingerprinting, iris identification, and voice authentication play a major role in curbing identity-related frauds since biometric characteristics are original and hard to duplicate.

Biometrics has been incorporated in banks worldwide in the following:

- Digital onboarding and e-KYC
- Mobile banking authentication.
- Payment approvals
- ATM withdrawals

Another connection between biometrics and the industry literature relates to the increased user experience and decreased friction at the digital channels. Nevertheless, researchers warn that the consequences of biometric data breach are devastating in terms of their lifelong consequences, as biometrics cannot be as easily reset as passwords. Therefore, the issues of privacy protection and secure biometric storage become critical.

2.5 RegTech and SupTech: Compliance and Supervision Automation

RegTech has become a field of significant coverage in financial-crime literature, with the technological process of compliance automation in the spotlight. RegTech solutions are applied in: Digital KYC and customer due diligence (CDD); Automated suspicious transactions reporting; Real-time AML risk scoring; Sanctions screening; Bank Secrecy Act (BSA) and the FATF regulatory reporting.

FinCEN underlines that customer risk assessment and monitoring systems can be greatly improved with the help of the integration of technology in the modern AML compliance programs. They emphasize that innovation increases efficiency, lowers compliance expenses and increases the capacity of institutions to fulfill their obligations.

SupTech is also becoming significant technology to supervisors. Financial conduct regulators such as the Financial Conduct Authority (FCA) and the UK use data analytics, automated anomaly detection, and regulatory sandboxes to test new solutions in a controlled setting. It is indicated in literature that sandboxing can speed up innovation and make sure it is safe in terms of regulation.

2.6 Interaction Among Technologies

An emerging academic and industry literature reveals that the most efficient anti-financial-crime models involve a combination of various technologies. Examples include: AI + blockchain tracing transactions; or AI-enhanced biometrics identity verification. Currently, 2 options are available: RegTech and data-sharing systems that monitor across institutions.

There is a direction in the literature of future AML systems becoming the interconnected ecosystems as opposed to the one-dimensional tools.

2.7 Difficulties and Limitations Discovered in the Literature

- Regardless of the potential technology holds, several issues are recurring in the literature on the field of scholarship and regulations:
- Information Quality and Interoperability. The inaccuracy of data, inappropriate formats, and drawbacks of legacy systems decrease the efficiency of AI models and fraud monitoring systems.

Privacy, Security and Ethical Concerns.

- Biometrics, behavioural information, and sharing of information across boundaries also pose privacy concerns. Regulators stress on the innovation and customer protection balance.

Regulatory Coherence and International Co-ordination.

- According to literature, AML jurisdictions vary among jurisdictions, which makes it difficult to share data and implement it. Criminals take advantage of regulatory arbitrage with no harmonised standards.

Barriers to Operation and Cost.

- Digital transformation is an expensive undertaking in terms of infrastructure, available manpower, and cybersecurity that might not be incurred in smaller institutions.

Literature Trends Conclusion. All in all, the literature shows that there is a distinct change towards the use of technology in fighting financial crime. The use of AI, ML, blockchain, biometrics, and RegTech tools will help to improve detection rates, decrease the amount of manual labor, and develop robust AML systems. Their performance, however, hinges on the quality of data, good governance, coordination between regulations and institutional preparedness. The international research community highlights the idea that technology is not a panacea to the issue, but an element of an ecosystem of risk-based, risk-focused, and constantly changing financial-crime prevention.

3 Case-Based Analysis: Fraud-Prevention Ecosystem in India is Technology-Driven

The payment systems and regulatory programmes used in India in real life depict the way that technological interventions are being operationalised in fight against financial crime. The analysis of such implementations can assist in transforming the theoretical advantages of AI, blockchain, biometrics and RegTech into the actual impact on the loss of frauds, the quality of detection and data security of customers. The three key areas of architecture in India that are discussed in this subsection are the Digital Payments Intelligence Platform (DPIP) of the RBI, compulsory name-matching of beneficiaries using RTGS/NEFT, and the federated AI/ML approach of UPI and other retail payments by NPCI.

3.1 RBI Digital Payments Intelligence Platform (DPIP)

The UPI digital payment system in India has billions of transactions within a month. What makes UPI appealing, such as instant transfers, interoperability and low cost, provide those with opportunities to commit authorised transfer fraud, social-engineering attacks, deepfake impersonation, mule networks and app scams (Reserve Bank of India 2025). To that end, the RBI has come up with the proposal of the Digital Payments Intelligence Platform (DPIP), which is a nationwide system of fraud-detection and risk-scoring. DPIP is a transition to bank-level fraud controls to network-based intelligence. It brings together data of many sources, such as transaction trends, device fingerprints, telecom metadata, geo-markers and customer behaviour, to calculate live risk scores on digital payment (RBI 2025). Banking institutions are assigned these scores and are able to slow down, block or step-up authenticate suspicious payments prior to their completion.

Such technological capabilities as AI/ML based anomaly-detectors, geo-spatial analytics based on locating unlikely sources of transactions, and telecom/device intelligence (including the SIM history, rooted devices, or call-forwarding flags) connected to social-engineering fraud. The RBI Innovation Hub is architecting the platform, and is particularly interested in identifying new typologies (including use of deepfakes to impersonate), fake customer-support scams, remote-access apps, payment-switch manipulation and social-media investment fraud.

Some of the expected outcomes are ensuring that mule accounts are identified sooner, banks and customers lose less in fraud, and greater monitoring of criminal networks across banks, and more confidence in digital payments. Provided this success, DPIP can be used as an example of other developing economies with the same risks of real-time payments (RBI 2025; FATF 2022) (Fig. 1).

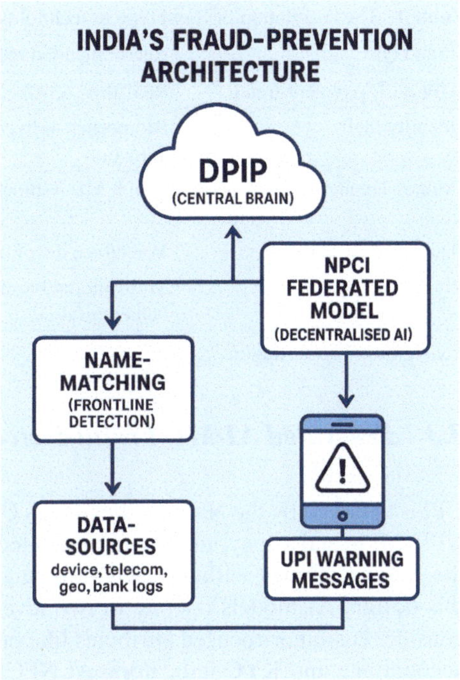

Fig. 1 The fraud-prevention architecture (DPIP, NPCI federated model and frontline controls) of India. *Source* Own processing according to RBI (2025) and NPCI (2024)

3.2 Name-Matching on RTGS/NEFT Beneficiaries

To prevent cases of impersonation, the RBI has set up the name-matching of beneviours in RTGS and NEFT transactions. With the old system, it was possible to have the victims fooled into transferring money to mule accounts with names that were persuasive but irrelevant. The new system enables the remitter to see the name of the actual account registered and then authenticate the transaction (Lexology 2024).

This reform directly targets fraudsters who pretend to be a brand and impersonate government bodies or service companies and provide account numbers which do not belong to the legitimate company. This discrepancy can be revealed by real-time name-matching, which significantly decreases the chances of customers transferring money to a malicious account without any prior knowledge. The initial signs indicate that this step enhances the accuracy of payments, increases the protection of the customer and serves as a deterrent to brand-impersonation frauds (Lexology 2024) (Table 1).

Table 1 The correlation of fraud type to technology solutions

Fraud type	Recommended technology	Why it works
UPI push-payment fraud	Real-time scoring, alerts	Detects risky beneficiaries
Identity theft	Biometrics + liveness detection	Resists deepfake IDs
Money laundering	Graph ML + blockchain	Uncovers mule + layering networks
Deepfake scams	Voice/face deepfake detectors	Blocks impersonation scams
Synthetic identity	Multi-modal biometric + behavioural	Detects fake profiles

Source Own processing

3.3 Federated AI/ML Fraud-Detection Model of NPCI

UPI is operated by the National Payments Corporation of India (NPCI) that provides UPI, IMPS, and Rupay, and has implemented a federated AI/ML model that optimizes the fraud analytics without compromising the data privacy (NPCI 2024). Under this design, AI models operate in two levels on their own: The bank-level models consider customer-focused attributes like profile, historical behaviour, salary trends, account age and KYC indicators. At NPCI, network level models evaluate device fingerprints, IP and geo location, velocity of transactions, anomaly of time of the day and network-routing configurations.

Both sides come up with their respective risk score of a particular transaction. It is only these scores and not the raw data that is exchanged and combined into one risk assessment. This federated strategy satisfies the needs of privacy and facilitates multi-source intelligence, which can not be produced by a single institution.

According to NPCI, federated scoring has also contributed to the decreased false positives, the decreased workload of manual investigations, and the heightened ability to detect patterns of emerging frauds and the enhanced initial identification of suspicious beneficiaries (NPCI 2024). Another feature that is a pilot phase feature is a pre-transfer warning to UPI users when a beneficiary account has already been suspected of fraud, which is especially helpful in counteracting fraudulent job, investment, marketplace, romance, and impersonation frauds.

3.4 Synthesis of India Case

The case of India shows that there are three strategic principles:

(1) Centralised intelligence through DPIP enables the patterns of fraud to be monitored across the system;

Table 2 AML technology approaches (India, UK, US and HSBC) comparison

Region/entity	Technology used	Strengths	Weaknesses	Impact
India—NPCI	Federated AI	Privacy-preserving, scalable	New and evolving	Lower false positives
India—RBI DPIP	Central AI	Network-wide intelligence	Architecture complexity	Early warning alerts
HSBC	Google ML	4 × detection, 60% fewer false alerts	High cost	Global scalability
UK—FCA	Sandbox + HPC	Fast innovation	Limited adoption	Rapid tool testing
US—FinCEN	PETs + ML	Strong guidance	Fragmented banks	Better AML governance

Source Own processing on the basis of RBI (2025), NPCI (2024), HSBC (2024), FCA (2019, 2025) and FinCEN (2024)

(2) Privacy-sensitive collaborative analytics through NPI federated model have allowed banks to enjoy the benefits of sharing intelligence, without exposing underlying data; and
(3) Customer-facing deterrence (name-matching, scam warnings) does not victimise customers.

Collectively, those components make India a scalable, technology-based model of defence that makes it a lead case regarding secure digital payments (FATF 2022; RBI 2025; NPCI 2024) (Table 2).

4 International Case Studies

4.1 HSBC: Global Transactions Monitoring Powered with AI

HSBC offers one of the best examples of massive use of AI in AML. The bank transacts approximately 900 million annually in various regions, customer segments and channels (HSBC 2024). Conventional systems of rules generated high volumes of false-positives and sluggish investigation process.

To overcome this, HSBC collaborated with Google Cloud to come up with the Dynamic Risk Assessment engine. It is a platform that uses machine-learning models, graph analytics and behavioural profiling to detect anomalies, detect hidden connections among customer accounts and give high-risk alerts a priority. Scanning of transactions in large volumes is carried in almost real-time, and analysis processes that used to require weeks to accomplish could now be accomplished in days (Google Cloud and HSBC 2023). The system has resulted in two to four times greater financial-crime activity detection, at no cost to false positives, with the bank submitting over 113,000 suspicious activity reports every year, according to the own evaluations of HSBC (HSBC 2024). These findings demonstrate the performance improvement that can be achieved when quality data and complex analytics are jointly used.

Another aspect that HSBC pays attention to is ethical AI governance such as pre-deployment ethics tests, bias testing, explainability tests and ongoing model verification. This is in line with the new standards of responsible AI use in finance (BIS 2022).

4.2 UK FCA: AML/CFT Supervision Innovation

The UK financial conduct authority (FCA) has become a market leader in regulatory innovation. It hosted a Global AML and Financial Crime TechSprint in 2018 bringing together more than 260 participants of 105 companies in 16 countries (FCA 2019). Possible prototypes were blockchain-based shared risk registers, natural-language processing to track transaction stories and records, and graph-analytics to track intricate money-laundering graphs. The experiment has shown that the benefits of supervised experimentation are that it can speed up solutions that would otherwise require years to develop. Upon this, in 2025, the FCA opened the so-called sandbox of high-performance computing where firms could test AI-driven models of fraud detection in natural but regulated conditions (FCA 2025). The FCA regulatory philosophy is outcome-oriented, which fosters responsible data sharing, cooperation and innovation between regulators across regions as a compliance facilitator and not a threat.

4.3 U.S. FinCEN: National Innovation and AML Guidance

FinCEN has enhanced its position as a technology-sensitive AML overseer. It directly engages with RegTech and FinTech companies demonstrating AI/ML anomaly detection, homomorphic encryption, digital identity, biometrics and blockchain forensics via its Innovation Hours Programme (FinCEN 2023).

In 2024, FinCEN released an advisory on AI-enabled fraud and deepfakes, countries of concern are synthetic IDs, spoofed voices and counterfeit documents. Banks were called on to strengthen digital onboarding verifications, biometric checks of life, multi-factor authentication and cross-channel risk rating (FinCEN 2024). The AML Act of 2020 of the U.S. and the upcoming beneficial-ownership registry is another measure that promotes digital compliance, data sharing, and monitoring of shell companies. In commercial applications, like NICE Actimize, which is common in the U.S. banking sector, it was reported that artificial intelligence-based entity resolution, behavioural analytics, mule-network graphing and automated SAR drafting reduced false positives by approximately 30% (World Bank 2023).

The Cross-Case Global Trends and Insights (4.3) represent the concluding part of the case study done by Dovey, Gohan and Jovanovic (2016). In India, HSBC, the FCA and FinCEN, it is possible to observe several world trends.

- To begin with, multi-source data integration is now the centrepiece of AML: banks are combining internal data on transactions with device data, telecom and network telemetry, external watchlists and behavioural signals to generate more contextual risk evaluations (FATF 2022).
- There is a growing need to work with cross institutions. Shared sandboxes and privacy enhancing technology projects are federated models that demonstrate that no individual actor can effectively address financial crime alone (Arner et al. 2020).
- A significant change towards real-time intelligence exists. The systems like DPIP, UPI scoring and dynamic Risk Assessment in the system of HSBC shift the task of detection to the one of pre-dealing intervention (RBI 2025; HSBC 2024)
- Regulators and companies focus on ethical and responsible innovation, such as explainability, fairness, and compliance with data protection and strong model validation (BIS 2022; FCA 2025).
- Technology acts as a defence as well as threat. The generated artificial intelligence and advanced digital solutions are used to criminal activities by criminal actors, which inevitably compels the defenders to keep improving models, detection tools and regulatory frameworks (FinCEN 2024; Europol 2023).

5 Results: Synergistic Analysis and Synthesis

The cross-case analysis demonstrates that the most effective innovation is AI/ML-driven analytics, particularly when it is based on a powerful data governance. The results of HSBC and the pilot results of NPCI indicate that they achieved big gains in detection and significant losses in false positives (HSBC 2024; NPCI 2024). Distributed-ledger technologies and blockchain offer immutable audit trails and shared intelligence, and could be adopted, but privacy considerations and problems with data-standardisation and regulatory uncertainty limit the adoption (FATF 2021; Arner et al. 2020). Biometrics and digital identity systems would be very effective in defending against account takeover and synthetic ID fraud but would have long-term privacy and security issues. Sandboxes and RegTech platforms are important in scaling and de-risking innovation (Table 3).

In all the investigated cases, the capabilities of AI/ML are the most influential technological advancement. The NPCI federated AI model, introduced by India, as well as the collaboration of HSBC with Google, point to the fact that machine learning enhances fraud detection rates drastically, at the same time decreasing the false alarm rates. The AI system implemented by HSBC is said to detect two to four times as many illegal transactions than the earlier rule-based systems and falsely detect transactions by nearly 60%. This change is essential since financial institutions have

Table 3 Challenges versus opportunities in AI-based AML

Challenges	Opportunities
Data privacy	Federated learning
AI bias	Explainable AI
Legacy infrastructure	Cloud-native AML engines
Cross-border AML	PET-enabled global networks

Source Own processing

been grappling with large numbers of false-positives that are costly to compliance staff and add to the ineffective AML procedures.

Correspondingly, the federated scoring model developed by NPCI shows that banks and payment networks can pool ML findings without providing underlying data of customers. Banks add customer behavioural patterns on the customer end, whereas NPCI adds device parameters, velocity checks, and network-wide intelligence. Combined, these complementary data sets would make the risk profile more holistic, enhancing the accuracy with which UPI frauds are detected and enhancing the number of unnecessary transactions flags.

One of the biggest strengths of ML-based systems is flexibility. ML learns as criminal behaviour changes unlike in the case of the rule-based model which demands constant human intervention. This dynamism is urgent in the digital age, as fraudsters are fast becoming technologically flexible, with deepfaked voices, artificial identities, remote-access virus and mule networks masterfully organized. The entire process of analysing new patterns by AI models makes sure that systems keep working as tactics change.

Nonetheless, the effectiveness of these advantages depends on access to good quality data. The outcomes of HSBC were possible since the bank consolidated the customer, geographic, transactional, and behavioural data of customers in the global operations. Similarly, the model by NPCI is based upon the integration of data-driven signals by several banks. Equally, the FinCEN innovation evaluations note that bad data quality: fragmented, incomplete, or inconsistent, continues to be among the biggest obstacles to successful implementation of AML technology. Therefore, although it is a transformative technology, the success of AI/ML cannot be achieved without effective data governance systems.

5.1 Blockchain and Distributed Ledger Technologies: Potential and Unfulfilled Potential

The UK FCA TechSprint prototypes and scholarly literature discussing the integration of distributed ledgers and AML analytics emerged as a key point of interest of blockchain. The FCA incident indicated the potential development of a common encrypted registry of bad actors, accessible by more than one bank. With such a model, when a customer or any other entity exhibits suspicious behaviour in one bank, other banks may be immediately informed and thereby increase the intelligence of all the banks hence mitigating the chances of cross bank laundering.

Theoretical studies build on this concept by suggesting hybrid approaches in which blockchain is used to offer transparent, non-modifiable trails of transactions, and ML algorithms are used to interpret those trails with regard to more intricate laundering patterns. The tamenability of blockchain eases auditability, forensic analysis, and end-to-end traceability of transactions which are particularly important in detecting layering and circular flows commonly employed to conceal criminal transactions.

Nevertheless, there is a lack of implementation. Several challenges persist:

Privacy concerns: It is impossible to share customer identifiable data freely on the public or semi-public blockchains without breaking the privacy laws.

- Regulatory confusion: Governments are yet to consider the compatibility of ledger-based sharing and secrecy requirements.
- Data standardization: Various institutions store data in incompatible format and it would be hard to have uniform blockchain integration.
- Operation overhead: The scale implementation of the DLT demands costly redesign of the existing systems.

Consequently, blockchain is a still experimental but, potentially, promising element of AML innovation that needs to be complemented by solutions like privacy-preserving analytics, homomorphic encryption.

5.2 *Biometrics and Digital Identity as a Stray Defence Against Identity Theft*

Albeit not related to one of the cases in the core analysis, biometric authentication, including facial recognition and fingerprint scanning, and voice biometrics come out as a fundamental counter to identity thefts and account hijackings. Such markets as India have witnessed a significant impact on digital identity verification with Aadhaar eKYC by preventing attempts at fraudulent onboarding due to a connection between identity credentials and confirmed biometrics.

Advanced market regulators are progressively driving towards biometric-based Strong Customer Authentication (SCA). According to industry reports, biometrics are extremely effective in curbing cases of takeovers as opposed to passwords or systems using OTPs, which are phishable or open to interception. This tendency is supported by deepfake alert provided by FinCEN that highlights the increasing threat of artificial intelligence-generated fake identities and voicealike. Due to the rapid increase in fraudsters replicating faces, voices, and documents with generative AI, liveness detection, behavioural biometrics, and multi-modal authentication have to be used by institutions.

Nevertheless, biometrics are controversial issues and they involve:

- Privacy risks (long-term) (equilibriums cannot be reset)
- Exposure to database attacks.
- Requirement of strong encryption and hashing requirements.
- Possible algorithmic bias of facial recognition.

Therefore, biometrics are potent, but they have to be coupled with stringent control and storage measures.

5.3 Growth of RegTech and FinTech Integration

The other significant theme is the increased co-operation among financial institutions, technology firms and regulators. Automated customer due diligence, sanctions screening, transaction monitoring, case management and regulatory reporting are now possible through RegTech solutions. Previously manual platforms have been automated and this way the burden on compliance is eliminated, as well as consistency is enhanced. In India, NPCI offers free elements of fraud-prevention (including UPI safe codes, which banks can incorporate). The collaboration with world-leading technology companies has proven to be effective as the success of HSBC shows. Innovation sandboxes of the FCA enable controlled testing of AI tools before launch. Similarly, the Innovation Hours and technology sprints organized by FinCEN are a gathering of startups, banks, academics, and regulators to discuss the newer capabilities of homomorphic encryption, blockchain analytics, privacy-preserving machine learning, and more (Fig. 2).

Such a multi-stakeholder ecosystem is an indicator of a change: financial crime prevention is no longer a siloed compliance business but a joint technological venture.

5.4 Cross Tabulation of the Type of Crime and Type of Technology Response

The case studies have made it clear that various types of financial crime have different technological interventions. Technologies that have been found successful in the field of payment and banking fraud include real-time analytics, risk scoring engines (e.g., DPIP of RBI and federated scoring model of NPCI), RTGS/NEFT-based name verification of the beneficiary, and pre-transaction scam warnings. The tools have a direct connection with preventing UPI push-payment fraud, phishing attacks, impersonation attacks, and the use of mule-accounts by offering warning messages and greater transparency to transactions to the banks and customers. In the case of account takeovers, identity theft, biometric authentication, augmented digital identity verification, liveness detection, and augmented eKYC processes are critical. Such innovations can assist institutions in reacting to synthetics identities, hacked credentials, and impersonation efforts by deepfakes by providing additional

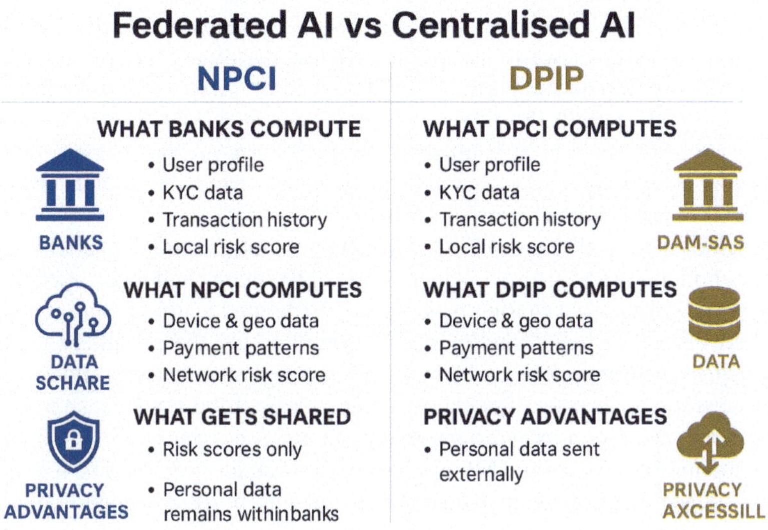

Fig. 2 Comparison of federated AI and centralised AI models in India's payment ecosystem. *Source* Own processing

levels of strong, user-focused protection. A number of sophisticated technologies have a high potential in dealing with money laundering. The applications of graph analytics, behavioural machine-learning models, blockchain-based prototypes, and cross-border risk-scoring systems are being employed more frequently to reveal mule networks, shell-company structures, and layering and complex transaction flows. These tools enable institutions to attain network-level risk patterns which were largely ignored by conventional rule-based systems.

Lastly, cyber-enabled frauds, such as deepfake impersonations and AI-generated frauds need detection algorithms, adaptable ML models, and regulatory alert systems to detect and curb emerging hazards. The alerts issued by FinCEN about the misuse of generative AI can be used to discuss the timeliness and topicality of such tools in combating the constantly changing scam typologies.

5.5 *Comparative Effectiveness, Limitations*

Existing evidence, which is based, however, mostly on industry reports instead of scholarly experimentation, indicates that the incorporation of the modern technologies in the AML and fraud-prevention systems has had tremendous results. In HSBC, AIs have been applied to monitor financial crime, leading to the detection of financial crime two or four times more, and a decrease in false positives by 60%, which is possible because of the high-quality, consolidated data. Similarly, the federated-learning model of NPCI shows encouraging results in the reduction of false-alarms and more successful detection of fraudulent patterns. Prototypes based on blockchain also have worthy potentials, particularly shared intelligence and audit trails that cannot be altered, though the large scale deployment is still limited as it faces regulatory and privacy issues. Biometrics, in their turn, are much more effective in preventing account takeovers, but also create some serious issues concerning the management of data and their long-term storage.

Such achievements raise some limitations that institutions should maneuver with. The issue of data privacy and governance is one of the main challenges, especially in case the cross-institutional sharing is necessary. Federated learning aims at compromising between privacy and intelligence information, but the compliance requirement remains a restriction. The problem of AI bias, explainability, and ethical control demands specific governance frameworks as the case of the HSBC responsible-AI framework depicts. The current infrastructure of numerous banks poses challenges in the implementation of real-time ML engines or blockchain systems. The regulations are changing, yet they are not up to date with the new forms of crime, particularly the ones facilitated by generative AI. Lastly, adversarial adaptation remains a significant issue and fraudsters use superior technologies to create more authentic deepfakes and synthetic identities.

In India and in major financial institutions around the world, there is a common observation that AI and machine-learning systems, backed by data of high quality and proper governance, are the most efficient solutions that can be found at present to fight financial crime. Such technologies as blockchain, biometrics, and RegTech platforms reinforce this ecosystem, but they should be introduced with the consideration of privacy, interoperability, and regulatory compliance. Finally, to achieve sustainable financial-crime prevention, the integrated approach of utilizing sophisticated technology, working together with the institutions, introducing innovations in the regulation, and regular monitoring is needed to be ahead of the ever-changing digital threat.

6 Strategic Conclusions and Implications

The aggregate results of payments ecosystems in India, international financial institutions like HSBC, and regulators with an innovation-based approach in the UK and the US validate the structural change: the technology became the core of the contemporary financial-crime prevention. With financial criminals more likely to take advantage of generative AI and build sophisticated mule networks, as well as manipulate identity systems, the financial sector should act in the same way by offering similarly sophisticated technological solutions. Synthesised strategic lessons to banks, payment providers, FinTech innovators, regulators, policymakers, researchers and global standard-setters are as follows.

6.1 Banks and Payment Providers Implications

Banks are in the forefront of curbing fraud and are under increasing pressure with increasing digital payments. The research has repeatedly demonstrated that the accuracy of the detection can be greatly enhanced with the help of AI/ML systems and cross-branching, cross-product, and cross-geography datasets. The institutions should therefore introduce enterprise-wide AI/ML to monitor transaction, sanctions screening, behavioural risk modelling and fraud scoring. These models, which are trained against large and varied data sets, identify delicate, nonlinear behavioural patterns that rule based systems cannot capture. This strategy is essential as the levels of transactions worldwide grow and compliance staffs are unable to cope with the expanding volumes of alerts.

The other strategic priority is the establishment of joint intelligence networks. The federated AI model at NPCI is associated with the strength of merging organisational knowledge without revealing sensitive underlying data. The banks are to formulate or become members of the cooperative structures that would allow the exchange of the encrypted risk indicators, watchlists, and behavioural anomalies. Such networks enhance the visibility of institutions and earlier mule clusters or compromised devices would be detected and remain in isolated systems.

It is also necessary to strengthen identity verification of the payment flows. Verification protocols have loopholes, which are exploited by such fraud typologies as authorised push-payment scams and identity theft. To ensure that risks are minimized substantially, banks should incorporate the use of biometric eKYC, verification of the beneficiary name, behavioural biometrics and multi-factor authentication in transaction journeys without causing inconvenience to a customer.

Lastly, banks need to invest in principled AI management. Due to the integration of AI into fundamental risk processes, the institutions are increasingly responsible with respect to fairness, explainability, and model drift. Compliance programs need to be designed with regular audits, bias testing, explainability tools, and a structured human oversight that will ensure trust and expectations in regulations.

6.2 Implications for FinTech and RegTech Innovators

FinTech and RegTech firms occupy a pivotal position in the evolution of next-generation AML and fraud-detection technologies. Their agility, innovative culture, and specialised technical expertise complement the scale, customer base, and infrastructure of traditional banks. Together, these actors can co-create a more intelligent and resilient financial-crime prevention ecosystem.

6.3 Opportunity to Build Specialised, High-Impact Solutions

FinTechs are well placed to concentrate on frontier technologies and build highly specialised, modular solutions that address concrete pain points in the financial system. These include AI-driven fraud scoring engines capable of real-time risk assessment, blockchain-based identity utilities that support secure and portable digital identities, and tools for device and behavioural risk analytics that monitor how, when, and from where customers transact. They can also design privacy-preserving computation frameworks that allow institutions to collaborate on fraud detection without sharing raw data, graph analytics platforms to reveal complex laundering networks and mule routes, and even cloud-based regulatory "sandboxes" that simulate live environments for safe experimentation.

By focusing on these niches, FinTechs can solve targeted problems such as deepfake detection, synthetic-identity fraud, or real-time mule-account mapping in ways that are often beyond the scope or speed of traditional in-house development within large institutions.

6.4 Strong Regulatory Support for Innovation Pilots

Global regulatory trends increasingly favour structured experimentation. Supervisors in several jurisdictions have created mechanisms that allow innovators to test solutions under controlled conditions. For instance, the FCA's regulatory sandboxes provide a supervised environment where firms can trial new products and models without immediately facing the full burden of regulatory risk. Similarly, FinCEN's Innovation Hours and related tech sprints are designed to foster dialogue between regulators and technology providers, helping policymakers understand promising tools and their limitations. In India, the RBI Innovation Hub plays a comparable role by providing pathways to test high-impact prototypes such as the Digital Payments Intelligence Platform (DPIP).

These initiatives play an important strategic role. They reduce uncertainty for start-ups, accelerate solution development, and enable FinTechs and RegTechs to validate their technologies against real-world data, user scenarios, and supervisory expectations before full-scale deployment.

6.5 Partnerships with Banks to Scale Impact

FinTechs often act as the "innovation engine," while banks provide the distribution, customer relationships, data, and operational backbone required to scale. Strategic partnerships therefore become a natural route for impact. Through such collaborations, banks can integrate FinTech-built AML and fraud-detection modules directly into their core infrastructures, co-develop hybrid solutions that blend bank data with cloud or AI capabilities (as illustrated by the HSBC–Google partnership), and run pilots for real-time fraud analytics or automated compliance workflows.

However, to be viable at scale, FinTech solutions must meet strict requirements. They need to comply with privacy and data protection laws, maintain robust audit trails and explainability for supervisory review, and align with regulatory expectations on governance, model risk, and operational resilience. Only solutions that meet these compliance and governance thresholds can graduate from pilot to production in the highly regulated financial domain.

6.6 Implications for Regulators and Policymakers

Regulators and policymakers face a delicate balancing act. They must foster innovation to keep pace with technologically sophisticated criminals, while at the same time safeguarding financial stability, consumer rights, and data privacy. The cases and initiatives reviewed suggest several strategic priorities for regulators.

6.7 Enable Innovation While Maintaining Safeguards

International guidance, including that of the FATF, stresses the importance of technology-neutral and risk-based policy frameworks. This means regulators should not favour or ban specific technologies in the abstract but instead evaluate risk and utility in context. They are encouraged to maintain strong privacy and data-protection standards and to institutionalise regular industry dialogue and feedback. The aim is to design laws and supervisory practices that enable the responsible adoption of AI, blockchain, and biometric systems without either unduly restricting innovation or leaving gaps that criminals can exploit.

In practical terms, this implies encouraging experimentation (e.g., via sandboxes or pilot schemes), while simultaneously setting clear expectations around governance, transparency, and accountability for any technology deployed in AML/CFT processes.

6.8 Expand Secure Data-Sharing Frameworks

One of the recurring structural barriers to effective AML is fragmented data across institutions and borders. Regulators can play a catalytic role in building secure frameworks for data sharing. This can involve establishing beneficial ownership registries for legal entities to illuminate opaque corporate structures; creating industry-wide, privacy-preserving data pools or utilities dedicated to fraud and financial-crime intelligence; mandating minimum reporting standards for certain high-risk transactions; and encouraging the use of technologies that support privacy-preserving analytics across institutions.

Such frameworks make it easier to identify emerging threats, including shell-company networks, circular transactional flows, and coordinated mule-account activity, before these evolve into systemic risks.

6.9 Update Regulatory Frameworks for the AI Era

As AI becomes deeply embedded in compliance and risk management, regulatory frameworks must evolve accordingly. Supervisors will increasingly need to require that financial institutions can explain AI-driven decisions, maintain robust audit trails, and demonstrate accountability for model outputs. Guidance will be needed on preventing and detecting biased outcomes, aligning with emerging global norms on responsible and trustworthy AI, and integrating AI into existing model risk management frameworks.

Regulators may also consider regular "stress tests" or thematic reviews of AI systems used in AML/CFT, examining performance under different conditions, sensitivity to adversarial inputs, and robustness over time. Because AI-based decisions can have legal and reputational consequences, supervisory expectations around fairness, reliability, and governance will become more explicit and stringent.

6.10 Promote International Cooperation

Financial crime is inherently cross-border, often exploiting differences in legal regimes and enforcement capabilities. Regulators therefore need to enhance international cooperation. This includes efforts to harmonise AML and CFT standards across jurisdictions, joint technology programmes such as privacy-enhancing technology (PET) challenges, improvement of cross-border information-sharing mechanisms, and coordinated approaches to supervising crypto-assets and virtual asset service providers.

Without such cooperation, criminals can simply shift operations to weaker regulatory environments. Coordinated action is particularly critical for tackling global cyber scams, international laundering schemes, and cross-jurisdictional fraud rings.

6.11 Implications for Researchers and Standard-Setters

Academic researchers and international standard-setting bodies shape the conceptual and normative foundations of future financial-crime frameworks. The case studies reviewed indicate several urgent research agendas and standardisation needs.

6.12 Evaluate Real-World Effectiveness of AI and Analytics

While industry reports show promising improvements from AI-based AML systems, independent empirical research is essential to validate and nuance these claims. Researchers should study, in a rigorous and longitudinal way, whether these systems actually reduce false positives, improve true positive rates, maintain performance in the face of adversarial adaptation, and deliver a favourable cost–benefit profile. In addition, research should examine the impact of advanced analytics on customer experience and financial inclusion. For example, overly aggressive models might de-risk certain customer segments in ways that are unintentionally exclusionary. Understanding such trade-offs is crucial for designing balanced policies.

6.13 Investigate Feasibility of Blockchain-Based Consortia

Blockchain-based AML frameworks hold theoretical promise for shared intelligence and immutable audit trails but raise important design questions. Researchers and standard-setters must address how transparency can be reconciled with privacy—particularly with respect to personal and commercially sensitive data—whether encrypted and permissioned blockchains can support secure multi-institution intelligence flows, and what governance structures would ensure fairness, accountability, and regulatory compliance in such consortia. Clear protocols and technical standards for privacy-enhanced blockchain environments tailored to AML use cases would help move such concepts from pilot to practice.

6.14 Address Emerging Vulnerabilities, Including Generative AI-Based Fraud

The growth of generative AI introduces new and rapidly evolving vulnerabilities. Research is needed on detection methods for deepfake videos, synthetic voices, and AI-generated documents; the ways in which synthetic identities are constructed and deployed at scale; and the dynamics of social-engineering campaigns powered by large language models. At the same time, there is a need to design "counter-AI" systems that can recognise and neutralise adversarial AI tactics. As generative tools become more accessible and powerful, the speed at which criminals can design and execute sophisticated scams will increase. Proactive research and tool-building in this area is therefore essential.

6.15 Develop Global Standards for Responsible AI and Data Protection

Finally, international standard-setting bodies should work towards coherent global norms for the use of AI and data in financial crime prevention. These should encompass principles of transparency and explainability, secure encryption and data-sharing practices, ethical and unbiased use of biometrics, frameworks for cross-border AML cooperation, and privacy-by-design requirements for AI systems deployed in regulated financial environments. Such standards would help harmonise practices across jurisdictions and institutions, reduce compliance uncertainty, and create a shared baseline for evaluating and approving innovative solutions.

6.16 The Future of Technology-Driven Financial Crime Prevention

Looking ahead, the trajectory of financial crime and its prevention suggests that technological integration will deepen further. The next phase is likely to be characterised by more interconnected data networks, more sophisticated AI—on both the defensive and offensive sides—and more embedded digital identity infrastructures.

6.17 Real-Time Global Data Networks

Advances in federated learning, cloud computing, and privacy-enhancing technologies could enable the development of global AML intelligence networks. Such networks would be capable of detecting cross-border transactional flows in real time, mapping international laundering rings, and sharing risk signals across jurisdictions without exposing raw customer data. This would constitute a substantial leap beyond today's largely fragmented and jurisdiction-bound systems.

6.18 AI as Both More Powerful and More Challenging

As AI models become more capable, they will be able to detect increasingly subtle anomalies that human analysts might overlook and even simulate experimental scenarios to distinguish benign from suspicious patterns. At the same time, criminals will use generative and adversarial AI to construct more convincing forgeries, social-engineering scripts, and synthetic identities. Defensive AI will therefore need to evolve continuously, learning to recognise not only human-driven fraud but also AI-generated threats.

6.19 Tokenised Digital Identity Systems with Blockchain

Blockchain-based digital identity frameworks and tokenised IDs could eventually unify authentication across banks, applications, and payment platforms. Such systems have the potential to greatly reduce identity fraud, eliminate redundant KYC processes, and enable portable verification across services and borders. Governments may play a central role in driving adoption through national digital identity policies and regulatory support, provided that privacy and governance concerns are appropriately managed.

6.20 India as a Global Digital Payments Security Model

India's experience with UPI and the emerging DPIP infrastructure offers a compelling template for other emerging economies facing high transaction volumes and rising fraud risk. By combining centralised intelligence, federated AI collaboration, and customer-facing deterrence, India demonstrates how large-scale digital payments can be made both inclusive and secure. As India continues to innovate in this space, its models and standards are likely to influence global thinking on digital payments security and financial-crime prevention.

Concluding, this chapter aimed to review the impact of technological innovation, especially AI/ML, digital identity systems, blockchain, and RegTech ecosystems, on the contemporary financial-crime prevention. The research questions are proven to be answered through the analysis of the national payment infrastructure (DPIP, NPCI federated AI, UPI safeguards) of India, international banking (HSBC), and regulatory experiments (FCA, FinCEN): sophisticated analytics can benefit fraud detection, privacy-preserving collaboration can facilitate an expansion of intelligence sharing without losing the data protection, and regulatory innovation is needed to maintain the efficiency level in the rapidly changed digital environment.

The results reveal that AI-based, real-time risk scoring is now becoming the foundation of AML/CFT frameworks around the world, which is substituting reactive and rule-based systems. The ecosystem of India demonstrates the compatibility of centralised and federated intelligence, and how they can be used to offer system-wide visibility, as HSBC demonstrates the operational advantages of large-scale machine-learning deployments. The regulators including the FCA and the FinCEN emphasize the role of sandbox, innovation hubs, and constant engagement in order to keep regulatory oversight and technological advancement in the same pace. Taken together, the findings support the main thesis of the study: the successful financial-crime prevention at present requires integrated technology, harmonized governance, and collaboration across institutions.

Nevertheless, the research has its shortcomings too. The study relies mostly on secondary data, institutional publications, regulatory publications and description of cases instead of empirical testing or quantitative measurement. Due to this, not all technologies can be generalised in their effectiveness, in particular, the early-stage blockchain prototypes and federated analytics. The other weakness lies in the fast development of financial crime; the use of artificial intelligence to fight with adversaries, synthetic identities, and cross-border money laundering is changing quicker than publicly accessible data can keep up. These drawbacks indicate the future research directions. Long-term performance metrics that should be evaluated via empirical research include false positives reduction, AI implementations cost-effectiveness, adversarial attack resilience, and customer-impact metrics. Privacy-enhancing technologies of cross-border AML cooperation, governance structures of blockchain-based identity systems, as well as building a so-called defensive AI that would identify fraud based on deepfakes at its large scale, are also areas that require further research.

Practically speaking, the implications of the study to the banks, fintechs, and regulators are clear. Banks should implement AI systems at the enterprise level, enhance data management and integrate many-layered identity checks into customer experiences. The key thing that FinTech and RegTech innovators must focus on is that the solution to their issues must offer both accuracy and privacy alongside auditability and explainability. Regulators must design technology neutral risk-based models that promote innovation without jeopardizing consumers and financial stability.

To sum up, technology has emerged as the key support of the current financial-crime prevention, yet it can work only under the condition of responsive usage, quality data, ethical management, and the long-term global partnership. With the combination of well-developed analytics and robust regulatory frameworks and secure identity, financial ecosystems are able to develop resilience against ever-changing threats, further enhancing customer trust and preserving the integrity of the global digital economy.

References

Arner DW, Barberis J, Buckley RP (2020) FinTech, RegTech and the reconceptualization of financial regulation. Northwest J Int Law Bus 40(3):45–78

Bank for International Settlements (2022) The use of artificial intelligence and machine learning in financial supervision. BIS Publications, London

Chen H, Chung W, Xu J (2021) Crime data mining: an overview and case studies. ACM Trans Inform Syst 39(2):1–40

Europol (2023) Facing digital threats: emerging fraud and cybercrime patterns in Europe. Europol Trend Report

FATF (2021) Opportunities and challenges of new technologies for AML/CFT. Financial action task force. https://www.fatf-gafi.org

FATF (2022) Digital transformation of AML/CFT. Financial action task force. https://www.fatf-gafi.org

FCA (2019) Global AML and financial crime TechSprint report. UK Financial Conduct Authority. https://www.fca.org.uk

FCA (2025) Supercharged sandbox: AI and digital innovation environment. UK Financial Conduct Authority

FinCEN (2023) Innovation hours program: Emerging AML technologies. U.S. Department of the Treasury

FinCEN (2024) Advisory on deepfake-enabled identity fraud and synthetic identity crime. U.S. Department of the Treasury

Google Cloud & HSBC (2023) Dynamic risk assessment: AI transformation in AML. Google cloud white paper

HSBC (2024) Artificial intelligence to strengthen financial crime detection. HSBC Global Financial Crime Report. https://www.hsbc.com

King B, Salmon J (2022) RegTech and the digital transformation of compliance. J Financ Regul Comp 30(2):195–210

Lexology (2024) RBI introduces beneficiary name-matching for NEFT/RTGS to prevent impersonation fraud. Lexology AML Briefing

López-Rojas E, Axelsson S (2018) Money-laundering detection using machine learning: a review. IEEE Trans Knowl Data Eng 2018:1

National Payments Corporation of India (2024) UPI fraud analytics and federated AI model: pilot results and operational framework. NPCI Research Report

Reserve Bank of India (2025) Digital payments intelligence platform (DPIP): concept and design report. RBI innovation hub

United Nations Office on Drugs and Crime (2021) Global estimates of money laundering and illicit financial flows. UNODC statistical report

World Bank (2023) The role of digital identity in financial integrity and AML enforcement. World Bank Publications, New York

Anuram Krishna E S is pursuing a Master of Science in Global Finance and Analytics, with a background in Statistics. His research interests focus on finance, analytics, and technology, especially in financial fraud detection and sustainable finance. He has worked on projects in financial modeling, foreign direct investment, and predictive analytics using machine learning. Also co-authored a Scopus-indexed book chapter with IGI Global, titled "*Evaluating the Impact of BRICS + Trade Policies—A Comparative Analysis Before and After the Russia–Ukraine Conflict*." His current research explores how digital transformation in emerging markets creates both opportunities and challenges for financial systems.

Dr. Blesson Varghese James is Head of Academic and Industry Extension at CHRIST (Deemed to be University), Pune Lavasa. His areas of expertise include Accounting, Investments, Finance, and Taxation. With more than 10 years of teaching experience and UGC NET qualification, he has also served as adjunct faculty at several reputed academic institutions. He holds B.Com and M.Com degrees from Savitribai Phule Pune University and has published extensively in national and international journals. Dr. James brings both academic depth and industry insight into his research and teaching.

Businesses Facing Spear Phishing: Towards a Preventive Approach Based on Cybersecurity Measures

Lamiae Zitouni and Khalid Atmani

Abstract Spear phishing attacks are increasingly prevalent within the corporate sector. Businesses are being targeted more frequently, leading to significant losses to their IT security, financial stability, and reputation. In this study, we will examine the particularities of these attacks in order to understand the execution process, which will enable us to identify the offenses comprising them and their legal framework. Then, we will study the Moroccan legislature's approach to regulating spear phishing attacks. In fact, the research methodology pursued is limited to the doctrinal and textual analysis of various legal texts, studies and reports. The objective is to translate the shift from a repressive approach to a preventive approach involving businesses in IT system protection and digital financial crime reduction. In addition, the study focuses on the rational and intelligent use of AI by companies to ensure the effectiveness of cybersecurity measures, while maintaining a certain degree of compliance with law.

Keywords Spear phishing · Online fraud · Financial crime · Cybersecurity · Artificial intelligence

1 Introduction

Corporate digitalization generated as a result of openness to new technologies, is leading to the absorption of traditional models of marketing, distribution of products and services, which have already been superseded, as well as openness to digital markets. In addition, in order to strengthen its competitive position in the market, the company do not hesitate to go beyond what digital technology has to offer in order to capitalize on new innovations such as Internet of Things, cloud computing, deep learning, and other artificial intelligence tools. As a result, companies' strategies, plans, visions, and behavior are constantly changing, while innovating new business

L. Zitouni (✉) · K. Atmani
Faculty of Legal, Economic and Social Sciences, Chouaib Doukkali University, El Jadida, Morocco
e-mail: zitouni.l@ucd.ac.ma

M. V. Achim (ed.), *Financial Crime in the Digital Era*, Contributions to Finance and Accounting, https://doi.org/10.1007/978-3-032-20198-0_4

models. In this regard, these economic and financial market players are intelligently trying to integrate digital technology into employees' daily activities, customer relations, teleworking, and value chains, such as the digital supply chain, digital CRS, etc. Digital technology is no longer associated solely with providers of digital services and products, but extends to all types of businesses. This includes healthcare, agriculture, transportation, telecommunication, banking, finance, and more.

The scale of this process of digitizing the entire company is not risk-free. Cyberattacks targeting companies are more widespread than ever. This is entirely logical. While companies are always seeking to improve their performance, cybercriminals are in turn looking for means or opportunities that allow them to reap significant profits at a lower cost in terms of risk and materials involved. In addition, the various dimensions of digitalization mentioned above are the main factors motivating the criminal involvement of cyber attackers. In addition, the luck of understanding and preparation for cyber risks are contributing to the growth in the number of attacks that primarily harm businesses. Thus, whenever, digital innovation brings new trends in business management, cybercriminals find themselves armed with advanced methods than ever before.

The constant improvement of their methods also permeates the criminal phenomenon as a whole. Economic and financial crime, which has been a focus of public attention for years, is gradually joining this field of transformation. The latter are now more complex than ever. The materialization of these crimes is now exclusively carried out electronically or in cyberspace. The classic offenses known to business criminal law are constantly changing. However, the interaction with cybercrime complicates the phenomenon, leading to the emergence of new criminal unknown to both business and public authorities. From this perspective, in order to accurately assess the negative impact of digitalization on financial crime, we will analyze spear phishing as a *modus operandi* for online fraud.

In Morocco, as in France, phishing attacks are widely prevalent, often targeting companies operating in the financial sector and other vital sectors. For this reason, legislators, particularly in Morocco, prioritize the protection of this category, which is considered to be disadvantaged with regard to the damage caused by cyberattacks of this type. Hence the interest in focusing this study on analyzing Moroccan legislation in relation to these attacks and the response measures put in place in terms of management, enforcement, and prevention, in addition to the involvement of businesses in this process.

Indeed, the choice of this subject can be justified by the lack of doctrine on the subject, in addition to the complexity of its legal framework in the absence of case law that can clarify certain points. Admittedly, following Morocco's ratification of the Budapest Convention in 2018, the Moroccan legislature has been heavily involved in reforming the national arsenal in order to adapt it to the provisions of the convention already mentioned. In this respect, multiple efforts in recent years have led to the modernization of criminal policy in Morocco, supporting the steps taken to successively implement new laws related to cybercrime and digital security. Among the most discussed laws at present is Law n°05.20 on cybersecurity. However, this law has attracted little attention, even though it embodies the legislature's shift towards a preventive approach to managing and combating cybercrime. Moreover, this new trend, which reflects the latest developments in criminal policy in Morocco requires in-depth study while limiting the scope of the study to a specific case, namely spear phishing attacks targeting businesses. Therefore, the originality of our study lies in the approach taken to analyze the subject. As such, the analysis takes the crime of fraud as its starting point, as the basic crime that has subsequently inspired various methods of operation that are constantly evolving, ultimately producing a very distinctive type of online fraud, namely spear phishing. The study will demonstrate the legal framework for the latter, highlighting the repressive measures enacted, in addition to the preventive measures imposed. It will also examine the role of AI in their effectiveness.

2 Literature Review

Digital technology occupies a central place among the exogenous factors that promote financial crime. It is even considered by criminologists as a cause of delinquency that is reshaping the entire spectrum of financial crimes, while traditional crime is rapidly declining (ATMANI 2022, p. 123).

In order to fully understand this issue, we are going to examine the example of online fraud. Traditionally, this crime is known is Moroccan law as « escroquerie» (fraud). According to the legal provisions currently in application, fraud is the act of misleading others through the use of fraudulent means, a fake name, or fake identity in order to obtain, to their detriment or that of a third party, payment of a sum of money, provision of a service, or fulfillment of an obligation or discharge. Under Moroccan law, this offense requires the combination of several constituent elements. First, there must be a primary objective to commit the offense, which is limited to deception through the use of complex tricks and tactics that are often difficult to detect, including misleading statements or assertions, concealing the true facts or taking advantage of errors, and exploiting the vulnerability of the person. It is also involving prejudice that causes financial loss to the victim but generates significant profits for the cybercriminal (Cass. Crim, N°13-86.772 2015).

The advent of digital technology has multiplied the scope for fraud, leading to several subsets of offenses related to the same crime. Fraud is becoming more focused on the following methods, depending on the target area:

2.1 E-commerce Fraud

This form of fraud represents the most prevalent type of cybercrime. With the increasing shift towards e-commerce, criminal opportunities are growing stronger than ever. In Morocco, online fraud often involves a refusal to deliver products purchased after payment. Cases have also been reported where the product delivered does not match the description given at the time of sale.

2.2 Bank Fraud

This form involves remote card payments (by telephone, mail, or online), although it also includes transfers and direct debits against the agreement of the cardholder (Perrotee et al. 2021, p. 8). The latter assumes the form of a scam involving false transfer orders (Bank of France 2022, p. 25).[1] According to a decision of the Supreme Court of France, this offense was upheld against a person who, by usurping three customers' identities, issued transfer orders via the internet (Cass, Crim, n°10-83.180 2011).

Recently, as a result of the earthquake that struck Morocco in September 2023, opportunities for online fraud arisen, with scammers taking advantage of the situation websites created for this purpose to solicit donations from internet users to purchase equipment relief supplies and assistance for disaster victims (Pernet 2023).

Crowdfunding scams can involve public appeals for funds by companies created solely to finance projects that do not actually exist. In order to mislead the public, scammers share and provide misleading information, as well as determining the outcome of their contributions, along with fictitious results. The most common form of this scam involved donation-based financing. Scammers take advantage of specific situations to make appeals for funding to help people in need. This is particularly true in the event of a disaster or during a pandemic. Examples include the COVID-19 pandemic and the earthquake (2023) in Morocco, which led to a large-scale initiative to help those affected by the disaster. Scammers exploit people's emotions to collect money that goes directly into criminals' hands. Admittedly, no reports have been filed so far, but this hypothesis remains to be confirmed.

To sum up, fraud, like other business crimes, keeps seizing opportunities to spread. Statistics on the subject also confirm its proliferation in recent years. According to the annual report on criminal policy implementation in Morocco, there were 103 cases of online fraud recorded in 2021, with 135 prosecuted (Office of the Public Prosecutor 2021, p. 359). In 2020, this figure did not exceed 66 cases involving 74 individuals (Office of the Public Prosecutor 2020, p. 336).

Currently, cybercriminals use sophisticated methods combining traditional scams with modern phishing attacks to infiltrate large organizations and generate significant profits. In a single criminal project, cyberattacks carry out several acts, including fraud, illegal intrusion into computer systems, system tampering, identity theft, and data extraction.

[1] According to France's annual banking report « in 2022, although the number of FOVI cases increased, the overall damage decreased: law enforcement agencies recorded 670 cases of FOVI for a total loss of 64 million dollars, compared to 517 cases in 2021 for a total loss of 101 million dollars, including a single fraud case involving an exceptional amount of 33 million dollars.

Beyond that, it focuses on more damaging aims, using emails, messages, or other means of communications to dissuade, by impersonating an organization or public entity, in order to build trust and encourage potential victims to share their personal data, credit card information, or other sensitive information (passwords, login details, etc.).

Moreover, the particular nature of such crime lies in the accumulation of various criminal acts to achieve a sole objective, involving multitude of scenario. At first glance, phishing takes the form of an email created by hackers after exploiting vulnerabilities, allowing them to draft emails incorporating graphic design elements or even all the elements present in messages previously sent by victim's bank, tax office, or telephone service provider. The goal is to reinforce the credibility of the email, which usually includes a link to access or files to open containing viruses, ransomware, or Trojan horses. Today, an alternative method has been implemented due to Covid pandemic. In this case, hackers use fake QR codes to steal sensitive information from victims. Due to the increased use of QR codes, particularly for checking health passes, hackers now have a new field of action, inserting well-hidden malicious links into these codes. In this regard, once the victim scams the code, they become vulnerable to hackers. Indeed, in the world of online fraud, new methods are gaining considerable traction. Studies, research and statistics confirm the spread of new, sophisticated and damaging criminal strategies. Among these methods is spear phishing, a very recent technique that combines the characteristics of fraud with those of intrusion and damage to information systems. Spear phishing is considered a highly complex form of phishing, as it is based on well-established patterns, unlike traditional attacks, which are often random. These attacks target a specific audience using predefined methods. In our study, we will focus on companies as the targets of cyberattacks. Moreover, the goal behind spear phishing is to target a specific, vulnerable victim in terms of cybersecurity, allowing the attacker to collect significant sums of money. Companies inevitably meet these criteria, which is why they are such high-value targets. In response, companies are not standing idly by, they are trying to protect their IT assets by adopting appropriate cybersecurity measures for detection, prevention, and risk management (spear phishing).

In this regard, it is opportune to raise some pertinent questions: What are the particularities and challenges presented by speat phishing attacks? What is the perspective adopted by Moroccan legislation in regulating these attacks? How does it reconcile the need to control and prevent these attacks, while considering the technical and legal issues involved? What is the position of businesses in this process? And how can AI be used to improve the effectiveness of managing and preventing spear phishing attacks?

3 Methodology

In this study, we will adopt two complementary modes of analysis that will allow us to address the issue in a comprehensive manner. First, we will conduct a doctrinal analysis of laws, decrees, and case law. Secondly, it involves interpretative analysis of texts, based on current reports and studies on the subject carried out by researchers and public authorities specializing in the field of cybercrime. The study scheme can therefore be summarized as follows (Fig. 1):

1. Detecting the complex origin of spear phishing attacks based on their completion process and legal framework (Law enforcement approach)
2. Highlighting the contribution of cybersecurity measures to the prevention of cyberattacks
3. The positioning of AI today's privileged approach to prevention

This research plan will enable us to trace and analyze the transition from the repressive approach previously pursued by Moroccan lawmakers to the preventive approach embodied in the adoption of Law n°05.20 on cybersecurity. Finally, it will delineate the positioning of artificial intelligence in this process of combating cybercrime, generally drawing on recently published doctrinal studies and examining laws, regulations, and judgments.

Data collection is realized as below:

For doctrinal analysis	For textual analysis
Laws	Report and studies
· Provisions of the criminal code	· Reports published by the Europol, Directorate of secure information systems, ENISA, Bank of France, Office of the public prosecutor
· Provisions of the cybersecurity law	

(continued)

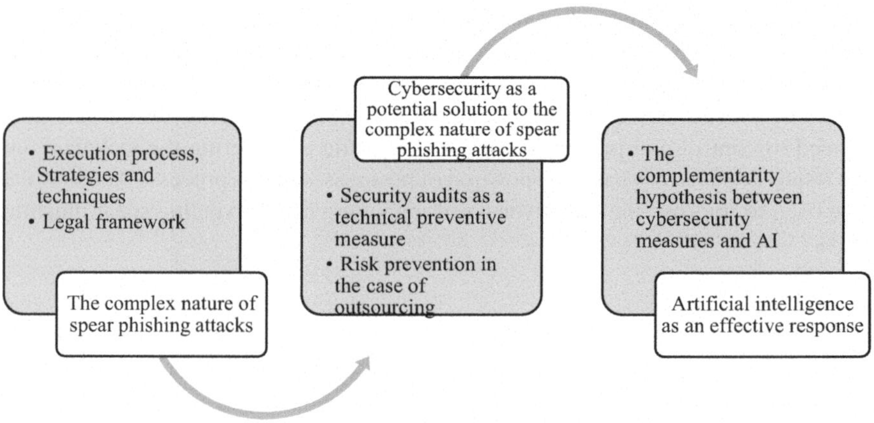

Fig. 1 The methodology study scheme. *Source* Own processing

(continued)

For doctrinal analysis	For textual analysis
Decrees	Scientific articles
· Head of Government's decree	· Collected from platforms such as CAIRN, info, Scopus, Web of science, etc.
Case law	
· Cour of cassation Judgments (Morocco, France)	

4 Analysis and Discussion

Referring to the methodology adopted, we will analyze the current challenges of online fraud, limiting the focus to a specific case, including spear phishing attacks. This form of financial cybercrime will be considered as a case study that will reveal the complexity of this crime, the offenses that comprise it and possible effective responses to minimize it in terms of prevention. We will also examine the role of AI in this process of managing and preventing cyberattacks.

4.1 The Complex Nature of Spear Phishing Attacks

Spear phishing refers to a planned phishing attack targeting a specific individual for a specific purpose. It is typically linked to account hacking, identity theft, and social engineering. At the core of this criminal scenario, the victims often receive an email addressed specifically to them, containing information gathered in advance to convince them and make the email appear authentic. The cyber attacker attaches links to fake accounts or malicious sites to this email, thereby using social engineering techniques to encourage the victim to access these links, disclose sensitive data, or make direct payments of large sums of money to accounts located outside the country.

In this regard, email attacks tend to be the most common type of attack used by cybercriminals. In addition, the convincing content of the emails is often based on information related to employees, supervisors, and the targeted company (Xu et al. 2023). This is further reinforced by the imitation of communication and email style used by well-known entities to establish trust with the victim (Kwak et al. 2020). As a result, the difference between authentic and imitation emails is difficult for potential victims to detect (Sonowal et al. 2021).

Indeed, the modus operandi of this kind of attack is based on specific set of techniques. However, to summarize the process in a simple way, we can divide it into four steps:

4.1.1 Research and Data Collection

This phase is considered preliminary to the action, where the attacker chooses the most appropriate means or tactic to collect data on the targeted company. Several techniques are used here, including independent collection via illegitimate sources, hacking email accounts, and using social media. For the first technique, the cybercriminal takes, the easiest route, which is buying hacked or stolen data on the dark web, from other hackers, or on online forums dedicated to information exchange between criminals. In the second case, the perpetrator uses brand impersonation, social engineering, and phishing to hack into an email account. Once they have achieved their goal, namely compromising the company's account they begin to monitor the company's activity and operations to understand its organizational structure and detect vulnerabilities to target first (Barracuda 2020). In the third scenario, social media is also exploited to implement effective fraud and deception tactics. Cyberattacks impersonate well-known individuals or famous profiles to mislead the victim (Gupta 2016). They are also used to extract information about the company and its employees. From this perspective, the Europol report published in 2019 on spear phishing predicts that companies' online presence facilitates the collection of data on their employees, strategies, and visions, as well as their internal structure. The report analyzes a relevant example, namely job offers posted on the LinkedIn platform. These offers are seen as a significant opportunity to gather relevant information about the company, as they not only outline the tasks and responsibilities to be assigned, the profiles sought, and the company's future vision, but also provide information about line managers and departments within the entity (Europol 2019, p. 12). According to the same report, cybercriminals map out job offers to help them identify the company's strategic directions (Europol 2019, p. 12).

4.1.2 Personalized Attacks and Execution

Once all the necessary data has been collected, cyber attackers conduct an in-depth analysis of the most appropriate attack strategy, taking into account the company's structure, the level of vigilance and awareness among employees, etc. therefore, when using emails as an attack tool, they are prepared exclusively to contact the selected company, containing real and accurate information about the company but based on malicious links.

From this point of view, several scenarios are possible, as illustrated below:

Attack by Compromising Professional Emails

In this case, after compromising the company's email account, the attacker can pretend to be the head of the finance department and send an email ordering a transfer of money to the cybercriminal's bank account (Europol 2019, p. 13).

The Use of Deepfake Technology

Assisted by AI technologies, the attacker can use this technique to imitate the voice or image of a senior member of staff within the company and persuade employees to send money to the criminal's fake bank account. A targeted attack in February 2024 provides a relevant example of this technique. A British engineering company reported being the victim of such an attack, which cost it nearly 25 million Dollars. the criminals reproduced imitation videos and audio recordings that allowed them to pose as the CFO and convince an employee to urgently transfer money to the fraudulent account (World Economic Forum 2025).

The Use of Authentic HTTPS for Phishing Sites

Cyberattacks can also use hacked legitimate sites to host phishing content (ENISA 2020, p. 7). This facilitates the process of building trust, as HTTPS sites are generally known to be secure by browsers (ENISA 2020, p. 7). However, browsers do not sufficiently verify the authenticity of the site.

The Tactic of Polymorphic Attacks

Polymorphic spear phishing attacks constitute a criminal trend among cyber attackers. To prevent their malicious emails from being detected by cybersecurity measures, such as security filters implemented by companies, they choose this technique, which involves constantly changing the content of the email, the address from which it is sent, the subject line, etc. (Grant 2025). According to a recent report published in March 2025, 76.4% of phishing attacks recorded in 2024 exhibited at least one characteristic of polymorphic attacks (Knowbe4 2025, p. 5).

Essentially, this phase must be complemented by social engineering, as no matter which scheme is implemented, the success of the criminal operation inevitably depends on how to persuade the person who will carry out the final task. Deceiving the victim representing the company is the crucial step in the criminal scenario.

4.1.3 The Use of Social Engineering Techniques

Spear phishing are inherently social engineering attacks. After all, they target the most accessible and vulnerable element in a company, namely the human element (Mohammed Shaffi 2020, p. 1886). The effectiveness of the attack depends on the victim's active attitude, which means that if the target is easily persuaded, the offence is committed as soon as he clicks on the malicious link or actually transfers the money. To achieve this, cyber attackers reinforce their strategy with social engineering techniques that exploit human needs, impulsiveness, and emotions. To increase their chances of success. Cyber attackers emotionally manipulate their victims by including elements in their emails that create feelings of fear, disruption, urgency, and the need to act without caution or vigilance (Baig et al. 2021).

4.1.4 The Achievement of Final Aims

Attacks of this sort are most often motivated by financial gain, and thus the danger inherent to this type of delinquency lies in its potential to generate significant sums of money, even from a single attack (Europol 2019). Sometimes it involves corporate data theft, as well as trade secrets, confidential and personal data belonging to customers, suppliers, and employees. The consequences of such actions are very serious for companies, especially those operating in sensitive areas (Alhogail and Alsabih 2021, p. 2). Examples include financial institutions, banks, insurance companies, telecommunications companies, digital service providers, etc. In this context, in addition to economic costs, the company loses its reputation in the marketplace and its customer's trust.

4.2 From a Law Enforcement Approach to a Prevention-Focused Approach

Spear phishing attacks targeting businesses in particular are notable for the significant damage they cause, both to the victim personally and to the economic public order collectively. This justifies the initial response to such delinquency, which stems from the rigorous intervention of the legislator, who has adopted a robust system of repression, generally based on the traditional approach of criminalization and punishment. The additionnal entry included in the table cannot be justified, considering that Moroccan legislation confines the legal characterization of spear-phishing attacks to the offenses expressly stipulated. Rather, they are subject to several provisions involving different offenses, ranging from fraud to illegal intrusion into computer systems (Table 1):

4.2.1 Digital Data Theft

In 2011, RSA Security was victim to a spear phishing cyberattack targeting a large number of employees and causing significant damage, including data theft and files subsequently sent to a compromised machine at a hosting provider (Ashford 2011). In this case, the ultimate goal of this spear phishing attack was to steal company information and documents. From a criminal law perspective, this offense is classified as economic and financial because it damages the company's property and assets. Nevertheless, theft is attributed to any person who cannot in any way justify

Table 1 Offenses associated with spear phishing attacks

Legal classification/offense	Article of penal code	Penalty imposed
Digital data theft	505 et seq	Imprisonment for 1–5 years
		Fine of 200–500 dh
Online fraud	540 et seq	Imprisonment for 1–5 years
		Fine of 200–500 dh
Digital forgery and use of forged documents	607-7	Imprisonment for 1–5 years
		Fine of 10.000–1.000.000
Fraudulent access to an information system	607-3	Imprisonment for 1–3 months
		Fine of 2000–10.000 dh
Fraudulent introduction, alteration, and modification of data	607-6	Imprisonment for 1–3 years
		Fine of 10.000–200.000 dh

ownership of stolen item (Matsopoulou 2015, p. 857). This gives rise to three requirements for an act to be classified as «theft». First, the existence of an item, second, its belonging to another person, and finally, its fraudulent removal. According to the provisions of Article 505 of the criminal code, this offense is inevitably linked to the theft of tangible and intangible items.

The trend toward increasing digitalization of various crimes has led to a series of jurisprudential reflections concluding to the possibility of punishing intangible property theft, in other words, information theft regardless of any physical medium. Specifically, French jurisprudence has contributed to the establishment of such an extension. In the same context, there are two landmark decisions, namely the Boutquin and Antonioli judgments, handed down in 1986 and reaffirmed by the Court of Cassation in its judgment of March 4, 2008. However, Moroccan law now also punishes data theft under the same article (505 of Penal Code) with a prison sentence of 1–5 years and a fine of 200–500 dirhams.

4.2.2 Online Fraud, Forgery, and Use of Forged Documents

Despite the ongoing digital transformation of business crimes, the legislature has not amended the legal provisions that criminalize them. As with data theft, Moroccan courts have subjected the crime of online fraud to the general provisions of the Penal Code, also establishing the same penalty. Article 540 of the MPC (Moroccan Penal Code), therefore applies whenever acts of deception are carried out electronically. Given that this offense involves the use of fraudulent maneuvers that are susceptible to automation (e.g., creating a website by appropriating the symbol of a pre-existing brand to mislead the victim). In fact, even the delivery of the item can be adapted to cyberspace (e.g., the electronic transfer of money). Moreover, the flexibility of such an offense justifies its spread.

One example is the case of Evaldas Rimasauskas, who between 2013 and 2015 orchestrated a sophisticated spear phishing attack against two American companies, one specializing in It and the other in social media. In principle, the perpetrator of the criminal acts first crated a fictitious company, in addition to drawing up false invoices and contracts by imitating and using the identical name of a company specializing in the manufacture of IT equipment, with which the victim companies had to constantly enter into contracts and make purchases (U.S. Attorney's Office 2019). Taking advantage of this relationship, which was conducive to a high-level fraud attack, he sent emails posing as employees of the computer equipment manufacturer and, using the face invoices and contracts, requested for large sums of money to be paid into bank account controlled by the offender. Once he had received the money, he transferred it separately to various bank accounts around the world. He was finally arrested in 2017 and sentenced to 5 years in prison and ordered to pay significant restitution (U.S. Attorney Office 2019).

Referring to the last example, the case of Evaldas Rimasauskas, we note that targeted phishing attacks can also be associated with offenses of forgery and use of forged documents to convince victims of the authenticity of the documents made available to them, thereby facilitating the act (in particular, the transfer of money). In Moroccan law, the legislator has introduced new provisions through Law n°07.03 concerning offenses relating to STAD. Specifically, Article 607-7 of the Penal Code, punishes the forgery and falsification of electronic documents, regardless of their form, as long as they are likely to be prejudicial to others. This refers to cases where the perpetrator uses a computer to commit forgery, which also includes the falsification of documents in such a way that the document is both inside and outside STAD (Enafkhaoui 2022, p. 416). It should be noted that forgery and the use of forged documents may be based not only on the original document but also on a copy of it (Cass, n°342 Crim, n°3669/6/4/2013 2013. Cass, n°1472, Crim, n°21755/6/4/2016 2016; Cass, n°518, n°9282/6/4/2018 2019). In terms of penalties, the law imposes a prison sentence of 1–5 years and a fine of 10.000 to 1.000.000 dirhams.

4.2.3 Illegal Intrusions into Information Systems

Within the context of attacks covered by this study, intrusion into the STAD takes several forms, depending on the method used to gain access to the system. Firstly, article 607-3 of the penal code penalizes this offense by imposing a prison sentence of 1–3 months and a fine of 2000–10,000 dirhams, or one of these penalties exclusively. Secondly, under Article 607-6 of the Moroccan penal code, "*fraudulently introducing data into an automated data system or fraudulently damaging, deleting, or modifying the data it contains, the way it is processed or transmitted, is punished by one to three years' imprisonment and a fine of 10,000–200,000 dirhams, or one of these penalties only*". However, this article does not specify the forms or methods of intrusion covered, other than the fraudulent nature of the operation.

In sum, this arsenal of repressive measures is quite severe given the seriousness of spear phishing attacks. According to the fundamental principles of criminal law the criteria for dangerousness are:

- Prior preparation for the action, in particular by choosing the target, researching and collecting information on the victim, and meticulously preparing the attack plan. This increases the chances of the operation's success, in addition to ensuring results with reduced risks and errors.
- The use of social engineering techniques which are manipulative by nature, requiring the use of fraudulent means, deception, and exploitation of the person's vulnerability.
- Well-founded criminal intent, due to persistent involvement in criminal activity and preparation for the act. This reflects the constant renewal of criminal intent and excludes any possibility of disregarding the moral element of the offense.

Moreover, despite this repressive severity, the legislator tends to improve strategies to combat this type of crime, moving towards prevention approaches rather than repression on its own. Insofar as it tends to create a sort of complementarity between repression and prevention, while favoring the latter. To this end, through law n°05.20 on cybersecurity, the legislator is setting up a legal framework that provides for a prevention approach involving companies as the main actors in cybersecurity. Compliance with the law provides protection against cybercrime risks, while, non-compliance may result in criminal liability for the entity.

Nowadays, the Cybersecurity Act strengthens the security of information systems and makes companies effective players in the prevention process. Moreover, since companies, are the primary target of attacker, protection and prevention must come from within the company and not from external actors. Thus, the accountability of the entity is justified by the damage that these attacks cause to the country's economy public order, and the security of other entities and individuals. It should be noted that the law specifically targets critical entities, public telecommunications network operators, Internet service providers, cybersecurity service providers, digital service provider, and Internet platform publishers. As they hold a sensitive position in society and in the digital market.

4.3 Cybersecurity as an Initial Security Measure Against Cyber Risks

Cybersecurity refers to «*all measures, procedures, security concepts, risk management methods, actions, training, best practices, and technologies that enable an information system to withstand events originating in cyberspace that could compromise the availability, integrity, or confidentiality of stored, processed, or transmitted data and related services that the system offers or makes accessible*» (Art 2, Law N°05.20 2018). Through law n°05.20, the Moroccan legislature has established a number of cybersecurity measures to promote prevention against the risks of spear phishing attacks, mainly including:

4.3.1 Security Audits as a Technical Preventive Measure

Audits as a security tool enable the assessment of an IS's maturity level and the operability of the measures set out in the security policy (Directorate of Secure Information Systems 2015, p. 5), and suggest remedies for any malfunctions identified.

Therefore, to counter spear phishing risks, auditing enables the identification of IT vulnerabilities that could be exploited by cybercriminals allowing for proactive countermeasures to be taken through appropriate preventive measures.

According to law n°05.20, security audits are required at two stages, particularly for service providers. First, before the system is put into operation. In this context, according to article 4 of law n°05.20, any entity offering digital services to third parties must submit its IS to a security audit, initially before any operation. The purpose of such a measure is to verify the security of the IS rather than other considerations. Nevertheless, in order to maintain this security and regularly monitor compliance with the law, the legislator requires the same entities to carry out regular audits. The ai mis to guarantee both availability and integrity of the IS.

With regard to cloud service providers, the audit obligation is carried out through a multidimensional procedure. In accordance with the provisions of the Head of Government's decree establishing the reference framework for the qualification of these providers, the audit program must be developed over three successive years (Head of Government's Decree 2025). One audit per year is required, combining a configuration audit, intrusion testing of administration and user interfaces for SaaS services,[2] source code auditing,[3] etc. Overall, this type of audit involves continuously verifying the operational security of the IS, as well as the security, integrity of data, information, and the IS as a whole.

4.3.2 Legal Guarantees for Risk Prevention in the Case of Outsourcing

Outsourcing an information system means entrusting the management of an entity's IS to an external service provider, under a contract with clearly defined terms and duration. When drawing up the contract, the entity must specify the level of services and the duration granted for their performance. Beyond the need for outsourcing certain services, this action exposes the company to multiple risks, jeopardizing the security of its IT infrastructure. Accordingly, the legislator has clearly defined legal safeguards in the form of outsourcing conditions. Compliance with these conditions

[2] Software as a service.

[3] Whether the service includes internal developments.

is mandatory, failing which the service provider will be held legally liable, as well as the person responsible for IT system.

Consequently, outsourcing services must be covered by a contract under Moroccan law that stipulates commitments to protection, audibility, and reversibility. In addition, Article 10 of law n°05.20 specifies that service providers are subject to various obligations, rules, and regulations, including compliance with the technical standards developed by the DGSSI (Directorate of secure information systems) in the field of IS security. Assuming that cybersecurity services are outsourced, IIV managers are required to use service providers that are qualified by the authority. Before granting qualification, the authority ensures several conditions are met, including incorporation as a Moroccan company, the provision of data hosting and processing guarantees, and the operation and administration of incident detection and analysis services exclusively on Moroccan territory. This obligation is reinforced by dissuasive penalties for non-compliance. The same goes for providers who offer services without being qualified or despite the withdrawal of this qualification. In general, Moroccan legislation is in line with French legislation and European regulations. The latter also establish obligations to be met when outsourcing, in order to protect the integrity and confidentiality of data.

All in all, subjecting third parties to whom services are outsourced to these requirements, is considered a remarkable and effective prevention strategy if security requirements are properly met. This is generally related to the cybercriminals attitude, seeking constantly to attack the weakest point of an entity. If, for example, a subcontractor in a targeted company has a less secure IT system, this represents an opportunity that criminals cannot afford to overlook. In a similar case, dating back to 2013, an American company suffered the same incident. In a spear phishing attack, target was a victim of a data leak affecting millions of customers, including personal data and payment card details.

The cyber attackers sought out the most vulnerable system linked to this company, although it was that of Fazio Mechanical Services (HVAC contractor), which used a free anti-malware service and was obviously lacking in terms of digital security. As a result, it was easy to send a phishing email to install malware (Citadel) that compromised the security of this company's IT system and led to the theft of login information, which was then used to access target's IT system.

In a nutshell, technical cybersecurity measures are not limited to security audits, but also include other security tools and methods. The same applies to guarantees in the event of outsourcing. Therefore, in addition to the examples studied, backup, logging action traceability, and synchronization measures represent a set of proactive defenses necessary for protecting information systems. However, these measures must be supplemented by non-technical measures in order to be effective. These include security policies that can be adapted to the level of risk, awareness-raising and training strategies, etc.

Although legislators have established a modern and robust legal framework to emphasize the importance of risk prevention over punishment, it is still advisable to seed ways to improve and achieve outstanding performance in the face of constantly changing risks. It can therefore be said that this is certainly not a shortcoming but rather an inadequacy of these measures, which still require the integration of AI into internal company policy.

4.4 Artificial Intelligence as a Response to Cyber Security Measure Deficiencies

Based on the above, it would be advisable to clarify that the legislator has clearly framed the transition from a repressive approach to a preventive approach to phishing risks, which requires downstream intervention rather than late intervention that only serves to manage and reduce the impact. The foundations of criminal policy in Morocco revolve essentially around taking the initiative before any attack occurs. Law n°05.20 has certainly laid the groundwork for a new approach that puts businesses at the center of action. The latter must, in particular, remain in constant compliance with the law, act as a responsible and involved cybersecurity player, but also be open to other means which facilitate improvement and reinforce the steps taken to prevent cyberattacks.

A doctrine in full swing discusses the benefits of artificial intelligence in such a context. According to a number of authors, the cybersecurity measures currently promoted, whether based on the law, regulations, or internal company policies, remain inadequate in the face of the new methods developed by cybercriminals. For this reason, it is recommended to shift towards AI tool and software based on deep learning.

A study conducted by Safi and Singh revealed the benefits of a new approach known as intelligent anti-phishing, which deploys innovations in the field of cybersecurity to combat and prevent cybercrime in companies (Safi and Singh 2023). The study focused specifically on technical tools for detecting phishing attacks based on algorithms designed to perform this task effectively. A study conducted in 2024 suggests instead that the focus should be on the user, given that spear phishing attacks are social engineering attacks, which is why it is judicious to consider this vulnerability as a starting point for effectively combating this type of crime (Shombot et al. 2024, p. 10). This gives rise to what is known as user-oriented cybersecurity for software or platforms. The study recommends that companies create user-oriented web applications, which are intelligent, technically advanced, and capable of stemming the threat of cyberattacks (*Ibid*). In addition, there are other studies that focus on management, prevention, and detection techniques for phishing threats that rely on deep learning tools, machine learning algorithms, and hybrid learning (Basit et al. 2021; Vrbancic et al. 2018).

Therefore, through the effective use of AI tools, it is possible design a protection and prevention system based on a combination of conventional cybersecurity measures and the latest digital security innovations offered by AI. This combination will undoubtedly lead to three outcomes: enhanced complementarity between the strengths and weakness of both components, improved accuracy and effectiveness, and finally, adaptability to the advanced nature of spear phishing attacks (Elberri et al. 2024, p. 2586).

5 Conclusion

Spear phishing threats are now an inevitable reality that requires and intelligent and effective response. In conclusion, based on what we have examined in this article, we can identify a clear shift from a repressive approach that focuses on upstream intervention against phishing attacks to an approach that prioritizes prevention and precaution based on downstream intervention after an attack or damage has occurred. This overview is justified firstly by the complex nature of these attacks, which involve a multi-stage process combining several strategies and techniques. Secondly, they target not only a single offense but a series of criminal acts with different penalty regimes. Newt, it is also a matter of integrating the company into the process of combating digital financial crime. This has encouraged legislator to rethink criminal policy, prioritizing prevention over repression and allowing companies to play a leading role in the scenario of securing information system.

Consequently, to settle the debate, Moroccan lawmakers have clearly stated their intention to pursue a policy of prevention in response to this form of delinquency. Business is now at the core of this preventive, action, participating in the protection of their IT systems while remaining in compliance with the law. However, in the face of sophisticated methods, businesses much regularly modify and adjust their cybersecurity strategies.

In addition, it is now recommended to take advantage of AI in this area. However, it should be noted that, despite these potential advantages, the use of AI can in many cases lead to violations of the law, with significant consequences. This applies in particular to legislation on personal data. Consequently, the challenge of AI lies in its technical nature, but above all in its legal regulation. The risk remains as long as Moroccan legislature has not taken a clear position in this regard, in short, companies using AI must comply consistently with cybersecurity law, as well as other relevant legislation, to ensure the effective implementation of the legislator's vision in terms of active and effective cyber risk prevention.

6 Limitations of the Study

The study generally focuses on the legal aspect of online fraud without linking it to the purely technical aspect, which also plays an important role in understanding the phenomenon and proposing appropriate solutions. In addition, the choice of a specific case study limits the analysis to a single example, although there are other examples of cyberattacks that are highly damaging to companies. For this reason, it is recommended that future studies compare different types of cyberattacks targeting businesses, while strengthening the analysis through the study of comparative law, particularly Anglo-Saxon law.

References

Alhogail A, Alsabih A (2021) Applying machine learning and natural language processing to detect phishing email, computers and security 110/102414, p 2. https://doi.org/10.1016/j.cose.2021.102414

Ashford W (2011) *RSA discloses phishing-attack data breach details*. https://www.computerweekly.com/news/1280095593/RSA-discloses-phishing-attack-data-breach-details. Accessed: 07/09/2025, 11h55 AM

Atmani K (2022) Cours élémentaires en criminologie (1er éd). Centre copie bon coin. El Jadida

Baig MS, Ahmed F, Memon AM (2021) Spear-phishing campaigns: link vulnerability leads to phishing attacks, spear-phishing electronic/UAV communication-scam targeted. In: 2021 4th international conference on computing and information sciences (ICCIS). IEEE, pp 1–6

Banque de France (2022) Rapport annuel de l'Observatoire de la sécurité des moyens de paiement

Barracuda (2020) Report: spear phishing: menaces et tendances principales, vol 4, Juin

Basit A, Zafar M, Liu X, Javed AR, Jalil Z, Kifayat K (2021) A comprehensive survey of AI-enabled phishing attacks detection techniques. Telecommun Syst 76(1):139–154. https://doi.org/10.1007/s11235-020-00733-2

Chef de Gouvernement (2025) Arrêté fixant le référentiel relatif à la qualification de prestataires de service Cloud. Bulletin Officiel N°7432, 21/08/2025, p 2365

Cour de Cassation Française (2011) Crim, n°10-83.180, 12 Janvier, Inédit

Cour de Cassation Française (2015) Crim, n° 13-86.772, 28 Janvier, Bull, n° 24

Cour de Cassation Marocaine (2013) Arrêt n°342, dossier pénal n°3669/6/4/2013 du 12 juin. Disponible sur le site: https://juriscassation.cspj.ma/Decisions/RechercheDecisions. Consulté le 23/11/2023 à 22h24

Cour de Cassation Marocaine (2016) Arrêt n°1472, dossier pénal n°21755/6/4/2016 du 8 novembre. Disponible sur le site: https://juriscassation.cspj.ma/Decisions/RechercheDecisions. Consulté le 23/11/2023 à 22h24

Cour de Cassation Marocaine (2019) Arrêt n°518, dossier pénal n°9282/6/4/2018 du 20 mars. Disponible sur le site: https://juriscassation.cspj.ma/Decisions/RechercheDecisions. Consulté le 23/11/2023 à 22h24

Dgssi (2015) Guide d'audit de la sécurité des systèmes d'information, 1er éd

Elberri M, Tokes U, Rahebi J, Lopez-Guede JM (2024) A cyber defense system against phishing attacks with deep learning game theory and LSTM-CNN with African vulture optimization algorithm (AVOA). Int J Inform Secur. https://doi.org/10.1007/s10207-024-00851-x

Enafkhaoui A (2022) La matière pénale à l'épreuve de la criminalité numérique, Actes de conférences internationales sous le thème: la numérisation et le droit, Université Cadi Ayyad, 15 et 16 juillet, pp 395–443

Enisa (2020) L'hameçonnage: Paysage des menaces de l'ENISA

Europol (2019) Spear phishing a law enforcement and cross-industry perspective, Hague, November

Grant W (2025) How polymorphic phishing campaigns leverage AI to evade detection. April 24. https://www.paymentsjournal.com/how-polymorphic-phishing-campaigns-leverage-ai-to-evade-detection/. Accessed: 05/09/2025, 2 h 39 pm

Gupta S, Singhal A, Kapoor A (2016) A literature survey on social engineering attacks: phishing attack. In: International conference on computing, communication and automation (ICCA), 29–30 April, pp 537–540. https://doi.org/10.1109/CCAA.2016.7813778

Knowbe4 (2025) Phishing threat trends report, vol 4, March

Kwak Y, Lee S, Damiano A, Vishwanath A (2020) Why do users not report spear phishing emails? Telemat Inform 48:101343

La présidence de Ministère Public (2020) Rapport sur la mise en œuvre de la politique criminelle

La présidence de Ministère Public (2021) Rapport sur la mise en œuvre de la politique criminelle, 202

Matsopoulou H (2015) Les infractions contre les biens, Revue de science criminelle et de droit pénal comparé (N° 4), pp 857 à 869

Pernet C (2023) Cybercriminals exploit the moroccan tragedy in new scam campaign, disponible sur le lien: https://www.trendmicro.com/en_us/research/23/i/cybercriminals-exploit-the-moroccan-tragedy-in-new-scam-campaign.html. Consulté le 18/09/2025 à 14h31

Perrotte K, Croutte P, Mansencal L, Hoibian S (2021) L'escroquerie en ligne et à la téléphonie en France: ampleur du phénomène et profils des victimes, Paris, Centre De Recherche Pour L'étude Et L'observatoire Des Conditions De Vie, Cahier de recherche n°354—Décembre. Disponible sur le site: www.credoc.fr

Safi A, Singh S (2023) A systematic literature review on phishing website detection techniques. J King Saud Univ Comput Inf Sci 35(2):590–611. https://doi.org/10.1016/j.jksuci.2023.01.004

Shaffi Shamnad M (2020) Comprehensive digital forensics and risk mitigation strategy for modern entreprises. IJRS 19(12):1885–1892. https://doi.org/10.21275/SR201211165829

Song Shombot E, Dusserre G, Bestak R, Baba Ahmed N (2024) An application for predicting phishing attacks: a case of implementing a support vector machine learning model. Cyber Secur Appl 2:1–12. https://doi.org/10.1016/j.csa.2024.100036

Sonowal G, Sharma A, Kharb L (2021) Spear-phishing emails verification method based on verifiable secret sharing scheme. J Inform Assur Secur 16(3):1

U.S. Attorney Office (2019) https://www.justice.gov/usao-sdny/pr/lithuanian-man-sentenced-5-years-prison-theft-over-120-million-fraudulent-business. Accessed: 07/09/2025, 4h 34 pm

Vrbančič G, Fister Jr IV (June 2018) Swarm intelligence approaches for parameter setting of deep learning neural network: case study on phishing websites classification. In: WIMS 18: proceedings of the 8th international conference on web intelligence, mining and semantics, pp 1–8. https://doi.org/10.1145/3227609.3227655

World Economic Forum (2025) This happens more frequently than people realize: Arup chief on the lessons learned from a $25 m deepfake crime. https://www.weforum.org/stories/2025/02/deepfake-ai-cybercrime-arup/. Accessed: 04/09/2025, 9 h 22 pm

Xu T, Singh L, Rajivan P (2023) Personalized persuasion: quantifying susceptibility to information exploitation in spear-phishing attacks. Appl Ergon 108:103908

Lamiae Zitouni is Ph.D. Candidate, the laboratory of Legal, Social and Judicial Research and Study (LARESJ-UCD El Jadida), Chouaib Doukkali University, El Jadida, Morocco.

Khalid Atmani is Lecturer–Researcher, Professor of Penal Law and Criminology, the laboratory of Legal, Social and Judicial Research and Study (LARESJ-UCD El Jadida) Chouaib Doukkali University, El Jadida–Morocco.

Descriptive Analysis of Accounting and Tax Professionals' Opinions Regarding Accounting Fraud Determined Through Forensic Accounting

Lucia Podoabă

Abstract The accuracy and control of accounting information needed by investors (and other users) is a vital necessity in today's globalized commercial markets. The increasing frequency and sophistication of fraud attempts by increasingly skilled but malicious individuals require the emergence, development and implementation of sophisticated forensic accounting techniques, in which forensic accounting experts can use their extensive practical skills and knowledge in the field. In Romania, this new subdiscipline of accounting will allow the systematic investigation of accounting records, financial transactions and supporting documents in order to obtain and provide relevant evidence for legal proceedings or other official contexts. This work was carried out by surveying accounting and financial professionals from Cluj-Napoca, with extensive experience in the field, in order to outline the red flags detected by them, for the identification of fraudulent activities, embezzlement of funds and other economic and financial crimes. This study also aims to outline the best methods and techniques of forensic accounting that can be applied in the field of fraud analysed, while highlighting the help given by artificial intelligence in detecting and assessing the risks of accounting fraud. The paper is part of a larger study that, in addition to fraudulent operations, also targeted tax evasion, money laundering, and corporate corruption through the perspective of the forensic accounting expert who works alongside forensic investigators.

Keywords Forensic accounting · Professional accountant · Accounting fraud

JEL Classification K13 · M21 · M40 · M41

L. Podoabă (✉)
Faculty of Economics and Business Administration, Babeş-Bolyai University, Cluj-Napoca, Romania
e-mail: lucia.podoaba@econ.ubbcluj.ro

M. V. Achim (ed.), *Financial Crime in the Digital Era*, Contributions to Finance and Accounting, https://doi.org/10.1007/978-3-032-20198-0_5

1 Introduction

The trend of accounting fraud in Romania, although there are no publications with recent official data, often involves economic crimes such as tax evasion (the most common), falsification of accounting documents, embezzlement of funds, and money laundering, often fuelled by economic pressure, greed, or lack of control, mainly targeting illicit profits, although the profile of the criminals varies, these being most often people in management positions or working in financial departments of companies. Currently, in our country, fraud (especially cyber fraud) is becoming increasingly sophisticated, while the Romanian authorities (ANAF, DNA, DIICOT) are intensifying tax-accounting controls and investigations, against the backdrop of a national economy in which the importance of compliance (i.e. national and international legislation, internal policies and ethical standards) and monitoring/reporting systems (whistleblowing) has increased. These unpleasant events have generated the need for appropriately applied services from forensic accounting, designed to detect and prevent the continued perpetuation of fraud.

The Association of Certified Fraud Examiners has defined forensic accounting as the implementation of specific knowledge and practice from professional accounting to resolve issues in civil and/or criminal litigation, in order to quantify asset and/or profit losses through forensic accounting expertise. The ACFE Annual Report to the Nations (2024) stated that, worldwide, the threat to organizations (of all sizes and types) is fraud. Organizations experience various types of fraud, the most widespread threat being occupational fraud. This is committed from within and against an organization by its directors, officers or employees (especially those with specific responsibilities related to the management and protection of resources and assets).

ACFE defines occupational fraud as using a person's profession to improve knowledge misapplied to a company's own resources or assets). Also, in the 2024 Report, ACFE presents the complex fraud tree, in which occupational fraud in general, accounting fraud in particular, occupies a primary place.

Forensic accountants are involved, nowadays, in determining the red flags specific to fraud in various financial crimes. To effectively perform the task of forensic accounting (detecting and preventing fraud), accounting and tax professionals must have solid practical knowledge of accounting and auditing, complete information on how to organize and manage investigations, good communication skills and adequate knowledge of information technology, as well as psychological skills to identify the motivations and likelihood of fraud.

The main categories of occupational fraud identifiable in the private and public sectors include: misappropriation and misappropriation of assets/cash, financial statement fraud (even non-financial), and corruption. This inclusion is based on the fraud tree presented in the figure above and which was conceived, in 1996, by Dr. Joseph T. Wells, founder and president of ACFE. Each category of fraud highlighted above involves characteristic elements for its commission and concealment, which helps forensic accountants in determining the clues or warning signals so necessary for forensic investigations.

This work aims to highlight the alarm signals for identifying fraudulent activities, detected by accounting and financial professionals from Cluj-Napoca, who have extensive experience in the field. Using the known methods and techniques of forensic accounting applied in the field of analysed frauds, the paper also wants to emphasize the help offered by artificial intelligence in detecting and assessing the risks of accounting fraud. We emphasize the fact that this paper is part of a larger study that, in addition to fraudulent operations, also targeted tax evasion, money laundering and corporate corruption from the perspective of the forensic accounting expert working alongside forensic investigators. These last-mentioned aspects will be presented and analysed in a future scientific paper.

2 Literature Review

Forensic accounting is considered the best sustainable method for achieving economic security for society, economic or/and social interest entities (Minda 2024). It investigates fraud incidents through the rigorous collection and analysis of data in certain areas (such as: litigation consultancy, expertise and investigation of economic crimes in general, and fraud in particular). For many years, specialists in the economic and financial field have tried and succeeded in defining forensic accounting, in order to determine the factors that generated its emergence and the characteristic consequences.

Thus, forensic accounting is the implementation of financial knowledge and records in investigating unresolved problems generated by economic crimes (Jack et al. 1995) or as a science that collects, through technical audit methods, accounting facts that require extensive knowledge of auditing and accounting (Koh et al. 2009). The focus of forensic accounting is to determine frauds committed with good intentions by the perpetrators (Ozili Peterson 2015).

At the same time, forensic accounting is considered to be the implementation of audit, investigation and accounting knowledge in support of the necessary legal assistance (Ezejiofor et al. 2016). Other experts in the field have also emphasized in their works that forensic accounting is the use of technology and science in investigating fraudulent activities carried out in various fields (finance, management, accounting, criminology) in order to resolve disputes and estimate the risks generated (Rezaee et al. 2016).

Of course, forensic accounting represents, together with fraud auditing, a very important subject in the identification and examining corporate and accounting fraud (Tutino and Merlo 2019). So, even if digitalization and artificial intelligence are considered future obstacles to the evolution of the professional accounting and tax practitioner, the emergence and development of this branch of accounting will not affect the work of accountants, on the contrary, they will help improve it.

Some experts in the field (Cyril et al. 2023) believe that forensic accounting is the activity of determining, recording, verifying and resolving problems generated by accounting activities intended to resolve disputes, based on the use of previous, current and future financial data. In addition, the same authors appreciate that forensic accounting refers to information that ensures the perception of auditing, accounting, law, investigations, computer science, psychology and criminology in providing the necessary evidence in litigation.

Although in Romania, forensic accounting experts carry out very complicated work in courts and criminal prosecution bodies, forensic accounting is a new field, on which professional bodies (the Body of Expert and Licensed Accountants of Romania, October 2022) launch appropriate training programs and professional standards, thus applying the action plan to combat corruption and economic crime globally, launched by IFAC (International Federation of Accountants) on September 6, 2022. Thus, there are also Romanian authors who have addressed this subject in their own works and who have appreciated the fact that forensic accounting, as a specialized branch of the accounting field, involves the verification of accounting records, transactions and documents, in order to obtain the judicial evidence necessary to determine the facts (some classified as economic and financial crimes) and their consequences (Bobiţan and Dumitrescu 2024). As companies strive to defend their interests and assets against internal and external threats, the importance given to forensic accounting services has increased (Radu et al. 2024).

In the forensic investigation process, the accounting professional (Robert-Aurelian and Popa 2025) can be involved in two stages, namely:

- the detection stage, in which warning signals play a very important role;
- the prevention stage, which is based on concrete internal control systems and clear accounting or procedural mechanisms that can signal personal procurement fraud.

Fraud is the intentional act of one or more people to obtain an illegal advantage (Matejića et al. 2025). The most prevalent threat facing companies today is occupational fraud, and accounting or bookkeeping fraud is an important component of it. Accounting fraud is the result of a person or a group of people who do not have ethical education (Tutino and Merlo 2019) or is the false processing of financial statements (Steven 2025). Frauds leave behind detectable signs called clues or warning signals, manifested through accounting anomalies, internal control deficiencies, analytical anomalies, extravagant lifestyles or significant changes in employee behaviours, etc. All these tell-tale signals help accounting and tax professionals in their work of detecting and preventing fraudulent activities.

In Romania, forensic accounting represents a new specialized subdiscipline of the accounting field, the mastery and deepening of which requires the application of multiple practical experiences, but also the implementation within specialized universities of the professional knowledge necessary for tomorrow's specialists.

In order to determine the state of knowledge of these accounting fraud operations and to estimate possible improvements in the field of forensic accounting, we conducted a study presented in this paper. We emphasize that the study conducted is much more extensive and targets, in addition to accounting fraud, other economic and financial crimes, which is why this paper will be followed by others, equally important.

3 Research Methodology

Taking into account the specialized literature in the field of using forensic accounting in the analysis of accounting fraud, we formulated the following complex research question:

Q. How can forensic accounting methods and techniques, applied by practitioners, be implemented in determining the warning signals specific to accounting fraud, to help forensic experts? Will artificial intelligence be appreciated by professionals in their forensic accounting work?

From the point of view of forensic accounting research, we propose to collect information to determine the elements that influence the work of accounting and tax professionals in determining and diminishing the consequences of accounting fraud in Romanian economic practice.

The purpose of obtaining this data is to make concrete proposals, both at a practical and conceptual level, regarding the desire of practicing specialists to learn and deepen forensic accounting, against the background of the development of continuous professional training, even in conditions of information technology development.

Thus, the research objectives that we propose are:

1. identifying the methods and techniques of forensic accounting applicable in practice (based on extensive professional experience and the need for its continuous improvement);
2. ranking the methods and techniques of forensic accounting applied only in the case of accounting fraud;
3. verifying the possibility of developing a conceptual model regarding the training of the forensic accountant, as a partner of investigators in verifying and analysing accounting fraud.

Regarding the variables used to conduct the research, we considered the forensic accountant as a multidimensional concept, defined by means of six dimensions. Thus, we considered that extensive practical experience in the field of accounting, taxation and auditing: knowledge of the specific manifestation elements of accounting fraud (materialized in the embezzlement of funds, fraud in financial statements, etc.) with devastating effects; awareness of the introduction of forensic accounting techniques and methods to accounting fraud phenomena, the skills possessed by practicing professionals and applied in forensic accounting, the identification and development of alarm signals specific to accounting fraud as independent variables, and the role of artificial intelligence in forensic accounting as a dependent variable. The following research hypotheses were formulated (presented in the table below—Table 1):

Table 1 Research hypotheses

H1: Extensive practical experience in the field of accounting, taxation and auditing (as an employee, forensic accountant, team member with the forensic investigator, participant in the dissemination of practical knowledge acquired)
H2: Knowledge of the specific manifestation elements of accounting fraud (materialized in the embezzlement of funds, fraud in financial statements, etc.) with devastating effects
H3: Awareness of the implementation of forensic accounting techniques and methods to accounting fraud phenomena
H4: The skills possessed by practicing professionals and applied in forensic accounting (which must be continuously improved)
H5: The identification and development of alarm signals specific to accounting fraud
H6: The role of artificial intelligence in forensic accounting

Source Author

In order to obtain the necessary information, a well-known survey method was applied, with the questionnaire as the basic instrument. A questionnaire with a weighted degree of structuring was chosen, with pre-established content and format, being almost entirely made up of closed questions, with fixed answer options. The structure of the questionnaire used closely followed the research hypotheses addressed. The questionnaire included 13 questions with complex structure (see the tables with the answers to these), and its dissemination was carried out online (via email and correspondence) to respondents in Cluj-Napoca. The data for this research were collected between June and November 2025. We emphasize that this study is part of a larger research, which aims to determine the alarm signals regarding economic and financial crimes detected by accounting and tax professionals (accounting fraud, tax evasion, corruption, money laundering, corporate corruption), in order to implement and develop forensic accounting methods and techniques in Romania. The questionnaire organized based on the Likert scale was sent online by e-mail to a number of 220 accounting and tax professionals, of which, however, after 6 months, i.e. in November 2025, only 133 responses were received, of which only 117 could be evaluated as valid and good for analysis. Each of these six dimensions was then described through different items, specific to each type of accounting fraud verified through the prism of forensic accounting. Therefore, each part of the questionnaire contains a set of six scales through which we operationalized and measured the analysed concepts. Given the lack of availability of data that would allow for a probabilistic sampling, a non-probabilistic sampling method was chosen, namely sampling through the professional reasoning of the author of this study. We emphasize that, in this study, we present only part of the research and its results, because we refer only to accounting fraud, not including the other economic and financial crimes mentioned above, in the paper. For the analysis of the collected data, we opted for the statistical analysis method in order to test the hypotheses formulated previously and the degree of adequacy of the proposed conceptual models. In this regard, we used the IBM SPSS Statistic programs, version 21. We would like to point out that in the extended research, which is currently underway, we also want to use the IBM SPSS AMOS program, version 21. The main processing carried out further aimed at calculating relative frequencies for describing the sample. Based on the relative frequencies, we characterized the respondents in terms of the bibliographic data presented in Table 2. Also, the sample was characterized in relation to the degree of involvement of practicing professionals in accounting activities, judicial accounting and fiscal expertise, certification of financial statements, membership in teams formed by criminal investigators. Last but not least, the sample was characterized in terms of knowledge and continuous improvement of professional knowledge through training courses intended for the profession. Therefore, the first part of the questionnaire concerned general information about the respondents (presented in Table 3), and part no2 included questions resulting from the research objectives. These are presented in the table below (Table 2).

One of the necessary conditions to become an accounting and tax professional (accountant, tax consultant, auditor) is to complete higher education courses at a specialized faculty, which is why, among the people surveyed, there is a large number of faculty graduates. In addition, the existence of the internship period and continuous professional courses that create real training opportunities for young professionals, the group of postgraduate/doctoral graduates represented 15.39% of the total number of specialists. Table 1 revealed data about the accounting and tax professionals who responded. From the table above it results that among the respondents there were 30 persons with the quality of accounting experts (women) who represented 25.64% of the total, 18 persons with the quality of accounting experts (men) who represented 15.39% of the total, 20 persons with the quality of tax consultants (women) who represented 17.09% of the total, 11 persons with the quality of tax consultants (women) who represented 9.40% of the total, 21 persons with the quality of auditors (women) who represented 17.95% of the total, 17 persons with the quality of auditors (men) who represented 14.53% of the total. Regarding the respondents' experience in the specialty, it was as follows: out of the 117 specialists, there were 3 people with work experience between 0 and 5 years (representing 2.56% of the total), 17 people with work experience between 6 and 10 years (representing 14.53% of the total), 20 people with work experience between 11 and 16 years (representing 17.09% of the total), 18 people with work experience between 16 and 20 years (representing 15.38% of the total) and 59 people with work experience over 20 years (representing 50.44% of the total). The same table presents the distribution of specialists in the companies in which they work, i.e. there were 69 people working in their own open professional practice as PFAs (representing 58.97% of the total), 18 people working in companies with foreign/multinational private capital (representing 15.39% of the total), 17 people working in companies with Romanian private capital (representing 14.53% of the total) and 13 people working in companies with state capital (representing 11.11% of the total). The questionnaire questions are presented in the table below (Table 3). I emphasize that these are also supplemented with the questions in Tables 4, 5, 6, 7, 8, 9, 10, 11, 12, 13 and 14 (see the tables with the answers to these, as the questions have a complex structure).

After calculating the relative frequencies and characterizing the sample in terms of the aspects presented above, the reliability of each measurement scale was tested

Table 2 Biographical data regarding the respondents

Analysed elements	Groups	Number of people	Percentage (%)
Sex	Women	71	60.68
	Men	46	39.32
	Total	117	100.00
Age	Between 25 and 30 years	3	2.56
	Between 31 and 40 years	15	12.82
	Between 41 and 50 years	40	34.19
	Over 50 de years	59	50.43
	Total	117	100.00
Accounting and tax professional category	Certified public accountants and chartered accountants	48	41.03
	Tax consultants	31	26.49
	Auditors	38	32.48
	Total	117	100.00
Professional experience	Between 0 and 5 years	3	2.56
	Between 5 and 10 years	17	14.53
	Between 10 and 15 years	20	17.09
	Between 15 and 20 years	18	15.38
	Over 20 years	59	50.44
	Total	117	100.00
Education level	High school	7	5.98
	College/university	92	78.63
	Doctoral studies	18	15.39
	Total	117	100.00
The legal entity in which the accounting and tax professional operates	Own office (authorized individual)	69	58.97
	Company with foreign private capital	31	26.50
	Company with Romanian private capital	17	14.53
	Total	117	100.00

Source Author

using the Cronbach α coefficient. The purpose of this processing was to evaluate the quality of the instrument used by testing its internal reliability.

The internal consistency coefficient "Cronbach α" was calculated (see Table 8) to collect the reliability of the 13 items of the forensic accounting attitude scale in fraud verification. The overall reliability of the scale was found to be very high, at $\alpha = 0.80$. An explanatory factor analysis method was applied to highlight the construct validity of the scale. The results of the Barlett test ($p = 0.000 < 0.05$) showed that there is

Table 3 The questions in the questionnaire

Question number	Questions	Offered answers
1	2	3
Q1	Do you have professional theoretical and practical knowledge of forensic accounting?	1—Yes (Y); 2—No (N)
Q2	How would you evaluate your own current professional and practical knowledge of forensic accounting?	1—I don't have it, so I can't rate it 2—Basic level 3—Intermediate level 4—Advanced level
Q3	What are the sources from which you learned about forensic accounting? (multiple answers allowed)	1—I did not learn from any source 2—Media 3—Internet 4—Professional literature 5—Private lessons 6—Practical experience 7—Other (please specify, if possible)
Q4	Are you aware of the existence of international certifications in the field of fraud detection (for example, CFE—Certified Fraud Examiner issued by ACFE—the Association of Certified Fraud Examiners)?	1—Yes (Y); 2—No (N)
Q5	How familiar are you with the concept of accounting fraud?	1—Yes (Y); 2—No (N)

(continued)

Table 3 (continued)

Question number	Questions	Offered answers
1	2	3
Q6	Did you participate in the verification of operations/activities considered to be in the category of accounting fraud and in what capacity?	1—Yes, as an employee 2—Yes, as a chartered accountant (principal) and/or assistant 3—Yes, when certifying the annual financial statements, on which occasion I adopted precautionary measures to avoid signing documents that did not reflect the reality of a company 4—Yes, when I was part of a working team formed by a forensic expert, during a criminal investigation 5—Yes, when I was called upon to disseminate professional knowledge acquired through workshops organized by decision-makers
Q7	To what extent do you believe that current accounting technology and software help prevent and detect accounting fraud?	1—(To) a very small degree 2—(To) a small degree 3—(To) a normal/usual degree 4—(To) a large degree 5—(To) a very large degree

(continued)

Table 3 (continued)

Question number	Questions	Offered answers
1	2	3
Q8	How often have you encountered cases of accounting fraud (e.g.: misappropriation of assets; fraud in financial statements) in your professional practice? (please elaborate, if applicable)	1—Very rare 2—Rare 3—Normal/Usual 4—Often 5—Very often
1	2	3
Q9	What were the reasons for the accounting fraud encountered? Please also assess the degree of appreciation of the importance of each reason, namely: (a) Different presentation of profit in financial statements (b) Lower tax payments (determined based on modified tax bases) (c) Obtaining several loans from various banks/lenders, as well as resorting to non-refundable European funds that were not used properly (d) False representations of the company's statements (by not including real expenses on specific accounts and recording income through intermediary accounts) (e) Increasing the company's share price (aggressive, self-interested and irresponsible management)	1—The strongest 2—Quite strong 3—Strong 4—Lesser strong 5—Not strong at all
Q10	Assessment of the main "human factors" in a company that could generate and amplify the phenomenon of fraud at the company level (according to the opinions expressed by the accounting and tax professionals surveyed) (a) Company employees (b) First-line managers (Supervisors, Team Leaders) (c) Middle managers (Department directors, Division Heads) (d) Senior Managers/Top Managers (CEO, General Manager, members of the Board of Directors) (e) Company owners	1—The strongest 2—Quite strong 3—Strong 4—Lesser strong 5—Not strong at all

(continued)

Table 3 (continued)

Question number	Questions	Offered answers
1	2	3
Q11	Employee attitude—moving from abuse to accounting fraud—manifested by: (a) Very high personal expenses (b) Use of company-owned equipment (c) Arriving at work late or leaving work early; dealing with personal problems during work hours (d) Close relationship with Suppliers/Customers (to obtain commissions and undue benefits) (e) Surfing the internet during or after work hours (under the false pretext of working overtime); taking excessively long lunch breaks without approval (f) Using sick leave days when they have no health problems (posting pictures of exotic places visited on social media) (g) Performing work tasks slowly or in a careless manner; performing work activities under the influence of alcohol or drugs—failure to assume responsibilities (h) Using employee discounts to purchase goods for friends or relatives	1—The strongest 2—Quite strong 3—Strong 4—Lesser strong 5—Not strong at all
Q12	The most effective legal regulations in preventing accounting fraud applied in Romania: (a) General European regulations: EU Directive 2017/1371 of the European Parliament and of the Council of 05.07.2017 on the fight against fraud to the Union's financial interests by means of criminal law; EU Directive 2015/2366 on payment services—called PSD2; Regulation EU 2024/1689—published on July 12, 2024, which aims to regulate the use of artificial intelligence (AI)—applied in Romania since August 1, 2024. On August 2, 2025, certain relevant provisions regarding general-purpose AI models entered into force in Romania, with all the rules imposed on AI technologies to enter into force in Romania by August 2026 (b) Tax regulations: Law no. 227/2015 on the Tax Code and Law no. 207/2015 on the Tax Procedure Code—both updated and republished (c) Criminal law regulations: New Criminal Code and New Criminal Procedure Code (d) Accounting legislation: Accounting Law no. 82/1991 updated and republished, as well as the Methodological Norms for its application; IFAC—Action Plan to Combat Corruption and Economic Crime Globally—launched on September 6, 2022—to which CECCAR has agreed (e) Other legal regulations: Law on Commercial Companies no. 31/1990 updated and republished; Law no. 129/2019 on the prevention and combating of money laundering updated by Law 86/2025; Law no. 209/2019 on payment services; National Strategy of December 14, 2023 to combat fraud for the protection of the EU's financial interests in Romania in 2023–2027	1—The strongest 2—Quite strong 3—Strong 4—Lesser strong 5—Not strong at all

(continued)

Table 3 (continued)

Question number	Questions	Offered answers
1	2	3
Q13	Necessary tools used to prevent fraudulent transactions: (a) Custom accounting error and fraud investigations/Red flags—using/non-using AI (b) Internal Control—using/non-using AI (c) Internal/External Audit—using/non-using AI	1—The strongest 2—Quite strong 3—Strong 4—Lesser strong 5—Not strong at all

Source Own processings

Table 4 Factor structure of the attitude scale towards forensic accounting in verifying fraudulent activities (accounting fraud)

Size	Clause	Factorial load	Stated variance	Cronbach's α
F1	Forensic accounting techniques help detect red flags that outline the characteristics of fraudulent activities (accounting fraud in particular) and must be continuously developed, by involving AI in their development	0.869	29.399	0.831
	The discovery of accounting fraud (in particular) by forensic accounting professionals will help develop the country's economy	0.837		
	The participation of forensic accounting experts in the verification/audit process will positively affect these activities	0.826		
	Forensic accounting provides advantageous services in the case of various litigations (even in the case of divorces)	0.782		
	The most detailed professional support for verifying accounting fraud is forensic accounting	0.731		
	Protecting individuals and legal entities in the private and public sectors represents the security provided by forensic accounting against fraud (and corruption)	0.334		
F2	Forensic accounting is of great importance in detecting established accounting fraud	0.789	17.99	0.692
	In commercial, liquidation or/and merger litigation, as well as in procedural issues generated by the distribution of partners' profits, the implementation and use of forensic accounting activities are very important	0.737		
	Do you believe that professional forensic accounting assistance is necessary to detect and prevent fraud?	0.602		
	In document and credit card fraud, check and invoice fraud, forensic accounting activities/ services will play a very important role	0.581		
	Forensic accounting helps detect collusive transactions by the debtor for the purpose of illegal theft of assets in cases such as fraudulent bankruptcy practices	0.332		
F3	Do you appreciate that the courts and criminal prosecution bodies in Romania that apply the legislation regarding economic and financial crimes require forensic accounting techniques (even if they are currently under development) in the judicial process of these crimes and/or criminal acts?	0.739	10.443	0.421

(continued)

Table 4 (continued)

Size	Clause	Factorial load	Stated variance	Cronbach's α
	In anti-money laundering legal proceedings (involving accounting fraud), the use of forensic accounting is necessary for the need for high-level accounting and technical information auditing to solve the problems of large companies (i.e. groups of companies)	0.668		
	Total variance—57.835%			

Source Processing by the author

Table 5 The answers given by respondents to question no. 6

Analyzed elements	Answers	Number of people	Percentage (%)
Yes, as an employee	Yes	36	30.77
	No	81	69.23
	Total	117	100.00
Yes, as a chartered accountant (principal) and/or assistant	Yes	25	21.37
	No	92	78.63
	Total	117	100.00
Yes, when certifying the annual financial statements, on which occasion I adopted precautionary measures to avoid signing documents that did not reflect the reality of a company	Yes	75	64.10
	No	42	35.90
	Total	117	100.00
Yes, when I was part of a working team formed by a forensic expert, during a criminal investigation	Yes	28	23.93
	No	89	76.07
	Total	117	100.00
Yes, when I was called upon to disseminate professional knowledge acquired through workshops organized by decision-makers	Yes	103	88.03
	No	14	11.97
	Total	117	100.00

Source Author

Table 6 The answers given by respondents to question no. 7

Size rating	Number of respondents	Percentage (%)
1—(To) a very small degree	5	4.27
2—(To) a small degree	4	3.42
3—(To) a normal/usual degree	27	23.08
4—(To) a large degree	22	18.80
5—(To) a very large degree	59	50.43
Total	117	100.00

Source Author

Table 7 The answers given by respondents to question no. 8

Size rating	Number of respondents	Percentage (%)
1—Very rare	2	1.71
2—Rare	3	2.56
3—Normal/usual	37	31.62
4—Often	29	24.79
5—Very often	46	39.32
Total	117	100.00

Source Author

Table 8 Details of the result (the Pearson correlation coefficient)

Result details and calculation	Key
X Values $\Sigma = 5408$ Mean = 46.222 Σ (X-Mx)^2 = SSx = 35,510.222 *Y Values* $\Sigma = 3380$ Mean = 28.889 Σ (Y-My)^2 = SSy = 6355.556 *X and Y Combined* N = 117 Σ (X-Mx) (Y-My) = 10,558.889 *R Calculation* r = Σ ((X-My) (Y-Mx))/$\surd$((SSx)(SSy)) r = 10,558.889/$\surd$ ((35,510.222) (6355.556)) = 0.7029 *Meta Numerics (cross-check)* r = 0.7029	X: X Values Y: Y Values Mx: Mean of X Values My: Mean of Y Values X-Mx & (Y-My)^2: Deviation scores (X-Mx)^2 & (Y-My)^2 Deviation Squared (X-Mx) (Y-My): Product of Deviation Scores

Source Processing by the author. https://www.statskingdom.com/correlation-calculator.html, https://www.standarddeviationcalculator.io/correlation-coefficient-calculator, https://www.socscistatistics.com/tests/pearson/calculator/

Table 9 The correlation test

		Forensic accounting techniques	Fraud deterrence
Forensic accounting techniques	Pearson correlation	1	0.7029*
	Sig. (2-tailed)		0.000
	N	117	117
Fraud deterrence	Pearson correlation	0.7029*	1
	Sig. (2-tailed)	0.000	
	N	117	117

*Correlation is significant at the 0.01 level (2-tailed)

Source IBM SPSS Program Ver 21. https://www.ibm.com/support/pages/downloading-ibm-spss-statistics-20

Table 10 The answers given by respondents to question no. 9

Reasons for fraud stated by the accounting and tax professionals surveyed	Degree of appreciation of the importance of these reasons	Number of respondents	Percentage (%)
(a) Different presentation of profit in financial statements	1—The strongest	4	3.42
	2—Quite strong	59	50.42
	3—Strong	33	28.21
	4—Lesser strong	12	10.26
	5—Not strong at all	9	7.69
	Total	117	100.00
(b) Lower tax payments (determined based on modified tax bases)	1—The strongest	68	58.12
	2—Quite strong	29	24.79
	3—Strong	9	7.69
	4—Lesser strong	6	5.13
	5—Not strong at all	5	4.27
	Total	117	100.00
(c) Obtaining several loans from various banks/lenders, as well as resorting to non-refundable European funds that were not used properly	1—The strongest	10	8.55
	2—Quite strong	27	23.08
	3—Strong	44	37.61
	4—Lesser strong	32	27.35
	5—Not strong at all	4	3.41
	Total	117	100.00
(d) False representations of the company's statements (by not including real expenses on specific accounts and recording income through intermediary accounts)	1—The strongest	5	4.27
	2—Quite strong	11	9.40
	3—Strong	23	19.66
	4—Lesser strong	57	48.72
	5—Not strong at all	21	17.95
	Total	117	100.00
(e) Increasing the company's share price (aggressive, self-interested and irresponsible management)	1—The strongest	3	2.56
	2—Quite strong	10	8.55
	3—Strong	9	7.69
	4—Lesser strong	16	13.68
	5—Not strong at all	79	67.52
	Total	117	100.00

Source Author

Table 11 Assessment of the main "human factors" in a company that could generate and amplify the phenomenon of fraud at the company level (according to the opinions expressed by the accounting and tax professionals surveyed)—Q10

The positions of people in a company prone to committing and amplifying fraud	Degree of appreciation of the importance of these positions held by "human factors"	Number of people	Percentage (%)
(a) Company employees	1—The strongest	8	6.84
	2—Quite strong	7	5.98
	3—Strong	6	5.13
	4—Lesser strong	16	13.67
	5—Not strong at all	80	68.38
	Total	117	100.00
(b) First-line managers (supervisors, team leaders)	1—The strongest	2	1.71
	2—Quite strong	5	4.27
	3—Strong	10	8.55
	4—Lesser strong	68	58.12
	5—Not strong at all	32	27.35
	Total	117	100.00
(c) Middle managers (department directors, division heads)	1—The strongest	11	9.40
	2—Quite strong	31	26.50
	3—Strong	57	48.72
	4—Lesser strong	9	7.69
	5—Not strong at all	9	7.69
	Total	117	100.00
(d) Senior managers/top managers (CEO, general manager, members of the board of directors)	1—The strongest	17	14.53
	2—Quite strong	47	40.17
	3—Strong	33	28.21
	4—Lesser strong	12	10.26
	5—Not strong at all	8	6.83
	Total	117	100.00
(e) Company owners	1—The strongest	75	64.10
	2—Quite strong	22	18.80
	3—Strong	9	7.69
	4—Lesser strong	6	5.13
	5—Not strong at all	5	4.28
	Total	117	100.00

Source Author

Table 12 Employee attitude—moving from abuse to accounting fraud (Q11)

Types of attitudes	Degree of appreciation of the importance of these attitudes	Number of people	Percentage (%)
1	2	3	4
(a) Very high personal expenses	1—The strongest	64	54.70
	2—Quite strong	12	10.26
	3—Strong	17	14.53
	4—Lesser strong	11	9.40
	5—Not strong at all	13	11.11
	Total	117	100.00
(b) Use of company-owned equipment	1—The strongest	24	20.51
	2—Quite strong	27	23.08
	3—Strong	41	35.04
	4—Lesser strong	15	12.82
	5—Not strong at all	10	8.55
	Total	117	100.00
(c) Arriving at work late or leaving work early; dealing with personal problems during work hours	1—The strongest	8	6.83
	2—Quite strong	10	8.55
	3—Strong	38	32.48
	4—Lesser strong	51	43.59
	5—Not strong at all	10	8.55
	Total	117	100.00
(d) Close relationship with Suppliers/Customers (to obtain commissions and undue benefits)	1—The strongest	25	21.37
	2—Quite strong	49	41.88
	3—Strong	19	16.24
	4—Lesser strong	16	13.67
	5—Not strong at all	8	6.84
	Total	117	100.00

(continued)

Table 12 (continued)

Types of attitudes	Degree of appreciation of the importance of these attitudes	Number of people	Percentage (%)
1	2	3	4
(e) Surfing the internet during or after work hours (under the false pretext of working overtime); taking excessively long lunch breaks without approval	1—The strongest	10	8.55
	2—Quite strong	11	9.40
	3—Strong	37	31.62
	4—Lesser strong	45	38.46
	5—Not strong at all	14	11.97
	Total	117	100.00
(f) Using sick leave days when they have no health problems (posting pictures of exotic places visited on social media)	1—The strongest	21	17.95
	2—Quite strong	33	28.21
	3—Strong	46	39.32
	4—Lesser strong	11	9.40
	5—Not strong at all	6	5.12
	Total	117	100.00
(g) Performing work tasks slowly or in a careless manner; performing work activities under the influence of alcohol or drugs—failure to assume responsibilities	1—The strongest	37	31.62
	2—Quite strong	31	26.50
	3—Strong	29	24.79
	4—Lesser strong	9	7.69
	5—Not strong at all	11	9.40
	Total	117	100.00
(h) Using employee discounts to purchase goods for friends or relatives	1—The strongest	27	23.08
	2—Quite strong	22	18.80
	3—Strong	49	41.88
	4—Lesser strong	10	8.55

(continued)

Table 12 (continued)

Types of attitudes	Degree of appreciation of the importance of these attitudes	Number of people	Percentage (%)
1	2	3	4
	5—Not strong at all	9	7.69
	Total	117	100.00

Source Author

a correlation between the variables analysed by factor analysis. It was determined that the sample size is sufficient to perform factor analysis as a result of the test (KMO i.e. Kaiser–Meyer–Olkin = 0.7794 > 0.60). The Kaiser–Meyer–Olkin (KMO) sampling adequacy coefficient and the Bartlett test of sphericity were used to verify the existence of a sufficiently strong correlation between variables to allow them to be subjected to factor analysis. In applying the factor analysis, the varimax method was chosen so that the structure of the relationship between the factors remains the same. As a result of the factor analysis, the total explanatory variance was reduced by a factor of 3, to 57.835%. The Attitudes towards Forensic Accounting in Fraud Verification Scale was found to be a valid and reliable instrument, according to the alpha value and the variance revealed for reliability. The factor structure of the scale is presented below (Table 4).

We emphasize that we know that corruption can include forms of accounting fraud, and money laundering involves elements of accounting fraud. However, in our study on forensic accounting applied to the analysis of accounting fraud, we have addressed more the issue of asset misappropriation and fraud in financial statements, because they occupy an important place in the economic and financial crimes verified by criminal prosecution bodies and courts in Romania.

Collusive transactions have been included in Table 4 because these behaviours have gained importance in recent days as they have led to significant sanctions. Specifically, the European Commission imposed sanctions on four banks worth over 1000 billion euros for disrupting the foreign exchange market. The affected financial institutions were Barclays, RBS, Citigroup, JPMorgan and MUFG Bank. However, in this study we do not develop this topic.

For a more comprehensive understanding of the responses received, intended to allow for factor analysis and the final formation of a conceptual model, we will highlight in the following tables the information received from the respondents. We emphasize that, after completing the extensive research that refers to several economic and financial crimes (in addition to accounting fraud), we will formulate the desired conceptual model specified at the beginning of this study. Currently, the responses received are in the processing stage.

Table 13 The most effective legal regulations in preventing accounting fraud applied in Romania (Q12)

Legal regulations	Degree of appreciation of the importance of these legal regulations	Number of people	Percentage (%)
(a) General European regulations: EU Directive 2017/1371 of the European Parliament and of the Council of 05.07.2017 on the fight against fraud to the Union's financial interests by means of criminal law; EU Directive 2015/2366 on payment services—called PSD2; Regulation EU 2024/1689—published on July 12, 2024, which aims to regulate the use of artificial intelligence (AI)—applied in Romania since August 1, 2024	1—The strongest	24	20.51
	2—Quite strong	60	51.28
	3—Strong	20	17.09
	4—Lesser strong	10	8.55
	5—Not strong at all	3	2.57
On August 2, 2025, certain relevant provisions regarding general-purpose AI models entered into force in Romania, with all the rules imposed on AI technologies to enter into force in Romania by August 2026	Total	117	100.00
(b) Tax regulations: Law no. 227/2015 on the Tax Code and Law no. 207/2015 on the Tax Procedure Code—both updated and republished	1—The strongest	20	17.09
	2—Q uite strong	59	50.43
	3—Strong	28	23.93
	4—Lesser strong	8	6.84
	5—Not strong at all	2	1.71
	Total	117	100.00
(c) Criminal law regulations: New Criminal Code and New Criminal Procedure Code	1—The strongest	62	53.00
	2—Quite strong	17	14.53
	3—Strong	19	16.24
	4—Lesser strong	10	8.55
	5—Not strong at all	9	7.68
	Total	117	100.00
(d) Accounting legislation: Accounting Law no. 82/1991 updated and republished, as well as the Methodological Norms for its application; IFAC—Action Plan to Combat Corruption and Economic Crime Globally—launched on September 6, 2022—to which CECCAR has agreed	1—The strongest	61	52.14
	2—Quite strong	22	18.80
	3—Strong	18	15.38
	4—Lesser strong	10	8.55
	5—Not strong at all	6	5.13

(continued)

Table 13 (continued)

Legal regulations	Degree of appreciation of the importance of these legal regulations	Number of people	Percentage (%)
	Total	117	100.00
(e) Other legal regulations: Law on Commercial Companies no. 31/1990 updated and republished; Law no. 129/2019 on the prevention and combating of money laundering updated by Law 86/2025; Law no. 209/2019 on payment services; National Strategy of December 14, 2023 to combat fraud for the protection of the EU's financial interests in Romania in 2023–2027	1—The strongest	20	17.09
	2—Quite strong	31	26.50
	3—Strong	58	49.57
	4—Lesser strong	5	4.27
	5—Not strong at all	3	2.57
	Total	117	100.00

Source Author

Table 14 Necessary tools used to prevent fraudulent transactions (Q13)

Types of instruments used	Degree of appreciation of the importance of these instruments used	Number of people	Percentage (%)
1	2	3	4
(a) Custom accounting error and fraud investigations/red flags: using/non-using AI	1—The strongest	54	46.15
	2—Quite strong	19	16.24
	3—Strong	13	11.11
	4—Lesser strong	11	9.40
	5—Not strong at all	20	17.10
	Total	117	100.00
1	2	3	4
(b) Internal control: using/non-using AI	1—The strongest	11	9.40
	2—Quite strong	56	47.86
	3—Strong	21	17.95
	4—Lesser strong	18	15.39
	5—Not strong at all	11	9.40
	Total	117	100.00
(c) Internal/external audit: using/non-using AI	1—The strongest	22	18.80
	2—Quite strong	23	19.66
	3—Strong	49	41.88
	4—Lesser strong	13	11.11
	5—Not strong at all	10	8.55
	Total	117	100.00

Source Author

The answers given by the respondents for question no. 6 are presented in the table below (Table 5).

Considering the information in the table above (Table 5), we can conclude the following:

- many accounting and tax professionals stated that they have not faced a fraudulent situation at work or in their relationship with their taxpayer (as an employee), as well as the fact that they have not been "actors" against a fraudulent event, but they agree that professional bodies, together with decision-makers in Romania, must take measures against possible fraudulent activities, notified in a timely manner.
- a large part of the professionals is not involved in any working group, but still consider the activities of the working groups to verify fraud to be necessary and effective.

The answers given by the respondents for question no. 7 are presented in the table below (Table 6).

Considering the information in the table above (Table 6), we can conclude that 50.43% of respondents believe that current accounting technology and software can help, prevent and detect accounting fraud.

The answers given by the respondents for question no. 8 are presented in the table below (Table 5).

Analysing the answers given to question no. 8, we conclude that many of the accounting and tax professionals surveyed very rarely detected accounting fraud.

Because we wanted to understand the linear relationship between two continuous variables (which are found in the answers to questions nos. 7 and 8) we used the Pearson correlation coefficient method. So, taking into account the answers received from respondents to questions no. 7 and 8, we will calculate the Pearson correlation coefficient, to verify whether there is a significant relationship between the risk of accounting fraud and one of the forensic accounting tools, namely accounting technology and software, within Romanian companies. The details of the results are presented in the tables below (Table 8).

The Pearson correlation between the answers given to the 2 questions is 0.7029, indicating a strong positive correlation between the two variables, which indicates a close connection between current accounting programs and the assessment of the effectiveness of technologies. Therefore, respondents who give greater effectiveness to accounting programs and technologies in preventing fraud assess that there is a higher risk of financial fraud in their own field of activity. This is why technology is very important in managing fraud risks (especially in the context of the implementation of future artificial intelligence). We also present in the table below (Table 9) the correlation test, i.e.:

The answers given by the respondents for question no. 9 are presented in the table below (Table 10).

It was found that "Different presentation of profit in financial statements", which is one of the elements of the reasons for fraud, is quite important, with a share of 50.42%. Although profit manipulation is a common way of fraud, there are other factors that are of particular importance in the analysis.

Compared to other data, it is observed that "Lower tax payments (determined on the basis of modified tax bases)" has a large effect on fraud (58.12%). This is not surprising if we consider that, in practice, accounting is subjugated by taxation, because accounting legislation is not in accordance with fiscal legislation, so the lack of non-deductibility for expenses and income taxation influenced by frequent legislative amendments creates a favourable framework for those who misinterpret the legislation, showing an increased interest in working within the law.

"Fraud to obtain more loans from banks and/or from various creditors" seems to be of medium importance. However, resorting to non-reimbursable European funds is a priority for some companies, which subsequently use them inappropriately, generating fraud. Fortunately, the measures applied in Romania by DLAF, together with DIICOT, DNA, EPPO and OLAF have substantially reduced the trends of fraud of non-refundable European funds by some companies in Romania.

"False representations of the company's declarations (by not including real expenses on specific accounts and recording income through intermediate accounts)" was accepted as quite important, with a share of 48.72%. The composition of the financial statements will deeply affect many areas (the company itself—its employees, the government, investors, financial institutions and organizations), especially if there is a fraud that takes place in a company with state capital. However, we appreciate the fact that most professionals do not have an overall perspective, since they have no connection with a company with 100% state capital. "Increase in the company's share price (aggressive, self-interested and irresponsible management)" represents a serious element, because any manipulation by the management can positively and/or negatively influence prices. However, the reason why professional members specify this element as "not at all important" is their lack of connection to a company with 100% state capital. The accounting and tax professionals surveyed indicated that the most important reason for fraudulent activities with increased negative consequences for economic and financial practice is "Lower tax payments (determined on the basis of modified tax bases)". However, the accounting and tax specialists participating in this study emphasized through their answers to the questions that there are situations in which the owners or members of the Board of Directors or managers of legal entities are the ones who, through their actions or decisions, favour the emergence and development of fraudulent activities, which is why we also analysed the opinions on their influences on the fraud phenomenon. Thus, in the table below (Table 11—which includes the answers to question no. 10) we present the professionals' assessment of the main human factors that could generate and amplify the phenomenon of fraud at the company level.

According to the conclusions formulated by the professionals surveyed, the ascending order of specific positions of people in a company, which could generate and amplify the phenomenon of fraud, includes employees, first-line managers, middle managers, top managers and owners. Employee fraud refers mainly to the misuse of company assets, but this is not considered in terms of the direct effect on the financial statements. In contrast, first-line managers were not important in the survey results due to the lack of authority and insufficiently established and developed control procedures. In contrast, middle managers are more prone to fraud due to the concrete possibilities existing within companies, due to the often-unjustified influences (dominations) imposed by them. Company owners are considered to be the most important in the issue of fraud, because many of the companies owned are actually organized in the form of individual, family businesses and PFAs (authorized natural persons). The lack of audit in these companies and the development of common interests (due to the relationship between the members of the Board of Directors and the owners), against the background of increasing seniority and the position of top managers, have generated a reduced number of frauds, but a high volume of them, with direct consequences visible in the financial statements.

Taking into account the human factors presented previously, based on the conclusions formulated by the professionals surveyed, we present below the behavioural characteristics of employees (Table 12—which includes the answers to question no. 11) that are often classified as abuse, but which are accentuated and transformed into actions generating fraud (with all the measures applied by the decision-makers in the companies) and which, if permanently monitored, could substantially reduce the risk of these illicit actions carried out in bad faith.

Regarding the ranking of employee attitudes that appear to be abuse, but which can quickly turn into fraud, accounting and tax professionals appreciate that high personal expenses are the most obvious characteristic of the employee who generates fraud. This inappropriate behaviour of the employee is complemented by the failure to assume responsibilities in carrying out job duties according to the job description, against the background of close relationships with suppliers and customers, in order to obtain commissions and undue benefits.

To prevent fraud in general, and accounting fraud in particular, the surveyed specialists considered that there are and are applied in Romania very important legislative provisions that can allow the prevention, avoidance and combating of accounting fraud and which are shown in the table below (Table 13—which includes the answers to question no. 12).

Accounting legislation and criminal regulations applicable in Romania, as well as those established at European level, most help accounting and tax professionals in their work to prevent, avoid and combat accounting fraud.

Since accounting fraud and other economic and financial crimes are a current concern for practicing professionals, we considered it very useful to know the opinion of those interviewed regarding their assessment of the necessary tools used to prevent fraudulent transactions (which includes the answers to question no. 13).

Professional members think "Internal Control" is the most effective tool of preventing fraudulent transactions. "Custom accounting error and fraud investigations/Red flags" is followed by the "Internal/External audit" activities. Almost all professionals interviewed stated that the use of AI is a real help in applying the mentioned tools.

Taking into account all the information in the tables above (with the necessary explanations) we assessed the forensic accounting methods and techniques applied by the interviewed specialists in establishing red flags in accounting fraud, which are presented in Table 15

Table 15 The forensic accounting methods and techniques applied by the interviewed specialists in fraud accounting

	Accounting fraud generated by asset misappropriation (embezzlement of funds, fraudulent payments or insurance fraud, theft of assets—fixed assets, inventories, misuse of company assets)	Fraud in financial statements
Forensic accounting examination methods included in the responses of interviewed practitioners Scientific methods: – general (analysis, synthesis, induction, deduction, analogy, modelling, abstraction, concretization and system analysis) – common specifics: formal verification of a document (visual inspection, scientific technical analysis with the aim of determining the existence or non-existence of document concordances with formal requirements); arithmetic and regulatory verification, comparison of interconnected documents, cross-checking, verification of veracity – particular specifics: use of software, machine learning and AI to analyse large data sets and detect suspicious transactions or patterns (digital forensics); red flags analysis (inconsistent financial reports, unexplained discrepancies and unusual transaction patterns); statistical methods and verification of the rules of chargeability and eligibility of expenses from projects financed with European funds; application of Methods: Cash T, Net Worth and Bank Deposit	Specific forensic accounting examination methods: – Analysing cash flow patterns – Reviewing asset records – Examination of financial evidence – Tracing of funds and identification of assets involved in fraud (document research) – Forensic audit and report – Examining expense reports – Performing surprise checks on all assets, liabilities, and activities of the company	Specific forensic accounting examination methods: – comparing data over time, by periods – reviewing reports to determine red flags (e.g., large receivables and payables) – tracking cash flows by activity type and time period – using technology to identify statistical deviations from expected patterns (comparing indicators in the Notes to the to the financial statements over longer periods of time)

(continued)

Table 15 (continued)

	Accounting fraud generated by asset misappropriation (embezzlement of funds, fraudulent payments or insurance fraud, theft of assets—fixed assets, inventories, misuse of company assets)	Fraud in financial statements
Forensic accounting techniques included in the responses of interviewed practitioners These include: – analytical methods such as transaction analysis, ratio analysis, and Benford's Law – investigative methods such as cash flow tracing and personnel interviewing – and data-driven techniques involving digital forensics and data mining	Special techniques include: – Data analysis, asset tracing, background checks on employees responsible for assets – Legal expert services: Providing expert opinions in legal proceedings, supported by forensic analysis – Document review: Meticulously reviewing financial documents to find discrepancies or evidence of alterations – Sampling: Selecting a representative sample of transactions or documents for detailed analysis when working with large data sets	Forensic accountants look for red flags such as: – Unexplained changes in financial ratios – Discrepancies between reported figures and industry norms – Unusual increase in revenue without a corresponding increase in cash flow – Frequent changes in accounting policies The forensic accountants team uses advanced forensic accounting techniques to break down financial statements, comparing reported figures to underlying transactions (involving collateral) and market data

Source Own processings

Regarding AI, the interviewed practitioners highlighted the following 4 important conclusions:

- the need to determine the scope of AI-based data for detecting accounting fraud;
- implementing AI for accurate risk assessment;
- analysing unstructured data with NLP—Natural Language Processing;
- using advanced analytics tools to obtain financial information.

The surveyed specialists appreciated that the alarm signals for accounting fraud refer to documentation issues (missing authorizations, missing, modified or photocopied records), unusual transactions (duplicate invoices, dubious entries of goods in purchase journals or unjustified exits of goods that were not even managed, frequent use of the LIFO method of inventory exit), management pressure (changed lifestyle, intense targets) and weak internal controls (lack of clear internal control procedures, lax supervision, frequent changes of auditor, high staff turnover, lack of separation of duties due to the lack of a job description for each employee). Excessive cash transactions (even exceeding legal limits), discrepancies between bank records and financial statements, repeated and unexplained changes in accounting methods are key indicators that help forensic accountants determine red flags of accounting fraud.

4 Research Results

Taking into account all the information presented in the tables of this study, as well as the necessary explanations, we conclude that all research hypotheses were confirmed.

Regarding the general research question, we appreciate that:

The forensic accounting methods and techniques, applied by practitioners, in determining the warning signals specific to accounting fraud will be implemented following their analysis by decision-makers within professional bodies, and through continuous improvement courses they will be known by interested practitioners.

AI is appreciated by professionals in their forensic accounting activity, especially based on professional training courses. AI is seen as an aid in processing very large and complex databases. But, in the future, we expect legal regulations in the field.

In order to prepare future forensic accounting experts, it is necessary to improve the university curriculum at the level of specialized faculties/universities, so that young students acquire the skills and qualifications necessary to be able to determine warning signals regarding accounting fraud in a timely manner. Thus, a strong collaboration between the business and academic environments must be achieved.

The conceptual model desired to be created will be realized in the future, after the completion of the study, on other economic and financial crimes.

References

Bobiţan N, Dumitrescu D (2024) Contabilitatea criminalistică, apariţia şi evoluţia unei profesii". CECCAR business review no. 3, pp 16–24, downloaded from the link: https://www.ceccarbusinessreview.ro/forensic-accounting-the-emergence-and-evolution-of-a-profession-a374/

Cyril UM, Okechukwu NM, Chidimma OP (2023) Role of forensic accounting in uncovering accounting fraud. Int J Econ Finan Manag 8(8):57–84. Downloadedfromthelink: https://www.iiardjournals.org/get/IJEFM/VOL.%208%20NO.%208%202023/ROLE%20OF%20FORENSIC%2057-84.pdf

Ezejiofor RA, Nwakoby NP, Okoye FNJ (2016) Impact of forensic accounting on combating fraud in Nigerian banking industry. Int J Acad Res Manag Bus 1(2):1–19. Downloaded from the link: https://shs.hal.science/halshs-01359758/document

Jack BG, Lindquist RJ, Jack B (1995) Fraud auditing and forensic accounting: new tools and techniques, 2nd edn. Wiley, Somerset, p 272

Koh AN, Lawrence A, Suat CLA (2009) Forensic accounting: public acceptance towards occurrence of fraud detection. Int J Bus Manag 4(11):145–160. Downloaded from the link: https://www.researchgate.net/publication/41891753_Forensic_Accounting_Public_Acceptance_towards_Occurrence_of_Fraud_Detection

Matejića T, Kneževića S, Milojevićb S, Adamovićb M, Milošević M (2025) Forensic accounting in higher education in the republic of Serbia: assessing students' needs for the introduction and design of educational programs in this field. J Econ Manag Inform Bizinfo Blace 2:1–16. Downloaded from the link: https://bizinfo.edu.rs/index.php/bizinfo/article/view/430

Minda I (2024) Forensic accounting, a viable solution for economic security/contabilitatea criminalistică o soluţie viabilă pentru securitatea economică. CECCAR Bus Rev 2:23–28. Downloaded from the link: https://www.ceccarbusinessreview.ro/forensic-accounting-a-viable-solution-for-economic-security-a369/

Ozili Peterson K (2015) Forensic accounting and fraud A review of literature and policy implications. Int J Account Econ Stud 3(1):63–68. Downloaded from the link https://www.researchgate.net/publication/275581156_Forensic_accounting_and_Fraud_-_A_Review_of_Literature_and_Policy_Implications

Radu RI, Basa A, Florea A-M (2024) The techniques and skills needed by the forensic accounting expert to identify fraud attempts in Romania. Annals of Dunarea de Jos University of Galati, Fascicle I "Economics and Applied Informatics Years XXX" no 2, pp 1–9. Downloaded from the link: http://www.eia.feaa.ugal.ro/images/eia/2024_2/Radu_et_al.pdf

Rezaee Z, Lo D, Ha M, Suen A (2016) Forensic accounting education and practice: insights from China. J Forensic Invest Account 8(1):106–119. Downloaded from the link: https://www.researchgate.net/publication/367559401_Forensic_Accounting_Education_and_Practice_Insights_from_China#fullTextFileContent

Robert-Aurelian Ş, Popa AF (2025) Red flags in accounting: the role of warning signals in forensic investigation/Ref flags în contabilitate: rolul semnalelor de avertizare în investigarea criminalistică. CECCAR Bus Rev 10:10–22. Downloaded from the link: https://www.ceccarbusinessreview.ro/ro/red-flags-in-contabilitate-rolul-semnalelor-de-avertizare-in-investigarea-criminalistica-a509/

Steven N (2025) Accounting fraud: definition, techniques and famous cases. Downloaded from the link: https://www.investopedia.com/ask/answers/032715/what-accounting-fraud.asp#:~:text=Accounting%20fraud%20is%20the%20deliberate%20manipulation%20of,and%20other%20employees%20involved%20*%20Destabilizing%20markets

Tutino M, Merlo M (2019) Accounting fraud: a literature review. Risk Gov Control Financ Mark Inst (J) 9(1):8–25. Downloaded from the link: https://virtusinterpress.org/IMG/pdf/rgcv9i1p1.pdf

Sites:

https://www.acfe.com
https://www.abogacia.es/ro/publicaciones/blogs/blog-de-derecho-de-los-los-consumidores/como-pueden-afectar-las-conductas-colusorias-a-los-consumidores/

Lucia Podoabă is an associate professor (doctor of accounting) at the Faculty of Economic Sciences and Business Administration, within Babeş-Bolyai University Cluj-Napoca. She is a member of the Department of Accounting and Auditing, within the aforementioned higher education institution. She is responsible for the largest master's degree within the faculty—entitled Accounting Expertise and Auditing. With decades of practical experience in the fields of accounting and taxation, she teaches 7 subdisciplines in the field of accounting in 2 international languages (English and French), alongside those in Romanian. Among these disciplines, Forensic Accounting is also of real use, coordinating the activity of master's students in the field of accounting and fiscal expertise, as well as auditing. As a teacher, she has written many books and specialized articles, published in renowned publishing houses and journals. She was the representative of Romania at the Federation of European Chartered Accountants on behalf of the Body of Certified Accountants and Certified Public Accountants of Romania (abbreviated CECCAR Romania), in the "Accounting in Insurance" working team. For 15 years, she has been a CECCAR lecturer and teaches the discipline of "Accounting and Tax Expertise" to practicing accountants, and since 2025 she has been teaching "Forensic Accounting Expertise". In 2025, she wrote many specialized papers in the field of forensic accounting expertise. Her main current research topics are: forensic accounting expertise, the implications of artificial intelligence on accounting and taxation (against the digitalization of the accounting profession), the consequences of economic and financial crimes on financial and non-financial reporting, green accounting, the use of accounting (along with other economic, social, psychological disciplines) in detecting criminals and economic and financial crimes, the collaboration of professional accountants with forensic experts in judicial activities, requested by courts or criminal prosecution bodies in Romania.

AI-Powered Transaction Monitoring for Real-Time Fraud Detection in Digital Banking

Ujan Pradhan, Utkarsh Jaiswal, and Vyomika Anand

Abstract With digital banking becoming not only operationally dynamic but also hectic, there is a proliferation of transaction volumes and speeds, corresponding to which the sophistication of financial crime has also rapidly escalated. The mainstream fraud detection methods are ineffective, mainly due to their rule-based nature, and cannot adapt to the dynamic nature of day to day frauds, especially in real time. In this regard, the purpose of this chapter is to ensure a paradigm shift by developing AI-based monitoring systems for transactions, which themselves are capable of ingesting, analysing, and responding to any anomalies in high-speed transactional data. Using advanced machine learning models like LSTM, GRU, and the transformer architecture, along with various unsupervised anomaly detection methods—such as Isolation Forests, Autoencoders, One-Class SVM etc.—the system detects unusual transaction behaviour attributable to account takeover, money laundering, phishing and synthetic fraud. In addition, we are investigating the feasibility of streaming data pipelines and online learning techniques to allow real-time responsiveness and adaptability of the models. We describe several feature-engineering methodologies concerned with capturing temporal and behavioural signals in conjunction with context-based risk profiling frameworks. The paper focuses on contemporary AI systems, Fintech use cases to measure off-the-shelf (COTS) software and tools. The section studies regulatory compliance and model explain-ability (XAI) along with a cost–benefit analysis of reducing false positives. Finally, the section proposes a scalable, intelligent and interpretable fraud detection paradigm in digital banking

U. Pradhan (✉)
Department of Computing Technologies, SRM Institute of Science & Technology, Chennai, Tamil Nadu, India
e-mail: up0625@srmist.edu.in

U. Jaiswal
Department of Networking and Communications, SRM Institute of Science & Technology, Chennai, Tamil Nadu, India
e-mail: uj5768@srmist.edu.in

V. Anand
Department of Chemistry, Indian Institute of Technology Bombay, Mumbai, Maharashtra, India
e-mail: 22b2721@iitb.ac.in

M. V. Achim (ed.), *Financial Crime in the Digital Era*, Contributions to Finance and Accounting, https://doi.org/10.1007/978-3-032-20198-0_6

that would help data scientists, financial regulators as well as banking technology architects.

Keywords AI in banking · Fraud detection · Anomaly detection · Deep learning · Real-time transaction monitoring · Digital banking · Financial crime · AML · Compliance · Explainable AI (XAI)

1 Introduction

The growth of digital banking has revolutionized the financial services industry in that billions of transactions can take place across geographical borders milliseconds apart without any complications. Nonetheless, such unparalleled convenient has also provided a financially rewarding chance to harmful individuals to utilize the loopholes within the online financial system (Ngai et al. 2011). Banks all over the globe are struggling with highly advanced fraudulent activities that are evolving much higher than the traditional security provisions. Financial frauds costs are on the rise all over the world with the cost in relation to different types of frauds being reported to be in hundreds of billions of dollars a year or so (West and Bhattacharya 2016).

The classic monitoring fraud systems, which were most often developed on a rule-based engine and any hard-line detection system, failed to face the dynamic aspect of the modern day financial crime (Brause et al. 1999). These old systems are pre-defined in their rules designed by the experts in the domain, which are not necessarily flexible enough to identify new types of fraud, or even cope with the ever-changing nature of methods used by scammers. The inflexibility of rule-based solutions leads to two major constraints: excessive number of false positive notifications overloading the investigation teams and consuming operational costs and failing to identify advanced fraud schemes which change established patterns subtly (Bolton and Hand 2002). Financial institutions are in a chain of reactions, constantly amending rules to reflect suspected cases of fraud in the ongoing search to stay permeable to new threats that are yet to be articulated into detection logic.

The emergence of AI and machine learning technologies comes as a paradigm shift with regard to the way financial institutions perceive the monitoring of transactions and detection of fraud cases (Phua et al. 2010). AI-powered systems combine sophisticated computational methods to automatically find sophisticated patterns in huge transactional data, to find much more subtle anomalies that may represent fraudulent activity, and to change as threat landscapes evolve, without necessarily needing to be explicitly reprogrammed. Architectures based on deep learning, especially with regard to sequential data processing (i.e. Long Short-Term Memory networks, Gated Recurrent Units, Transformer models), show impressive performances in learning temporal dependencies and contextual security in the sequence of transactions (Chandola et al. 2009). Based on these models, learning hierarchical instances of normal customer behaviour and identifying deviation, which is indicative of fraudulent activity, is done with unprecedented accuracy.

2 Landscape of Digital Transaction Fraud

The digital transaction fraud has a wide range of criminal activities that take advantage of the weaknesses in the electronic payment system, online banking, and digital financial services (West and Bhattacharya 2016). Knowledge of the taxonomy of types of fraud is necessary to produce specific detection strategies to deal with certain threat vectors. Account takeover fraud is one of the most widespread and harmful types of fraud that involves attackers using legitimate customer accounts, hacking them without obtaining the required credentials, committing phishing, or social engineering (Schölkopf et al. 2001). After gaining access, the fraudsters will immediately perform unauthorized transactions, send money to secondary accounts or buy an item before the rightful account owner finds out about the breach. The velocity of the attacks on account takeover requires real time detecting functions that can determine suspicious access pattern and transactional activities in a few seconds of their occurrence.

Phishing and social engineering attacks have been evolving in complexities and they are currently taking advantage of psychological techniques of manipulating others, to execute their fraudulent activities on their customers such as stealing sensitive authentication credentials or authorizing deceitful transactions (Abdallah et al. 2016). In many of these attacks, spoofed communications are utilized that have a credible appearance of originating as real bank communication, they are used to put the victims into emergency situations whereby they are under urgent circumstances to make hasty decisions without seeking the necessary verification. On the one hand, it is difficult to identify the fraud perpetrated with the help of phishing because it is hard to differentiate between legitimate customer-initiated transactions and the transactions imposed due to the use of false information because they can be processed by lawful devices and subjective to regular authentication procedures. Anomaly detection and behavioural analytics can play a vital role in detecting minor changes in the set patterns of the customers, which can imply a breach in decision-making (Chandola et al. 2009).

These forms of synthetic identity fraud have become a fairly heinous menace that comprises actual and doctored details to enable the development of fabricated identities that are applied in the formation of fraudulent accounts (Dal Pozzolo et al. 2014). Synthetic fraud also implies the creation of new identities by assembling a real personally identifiable information with a fake data element, as opposed to traditional identity theft, where the entire identity of the victim is stolen. These artificial identities are well developed over a long period, credit histories and purchase habits developed, which are considered genuine by traditional fraud detection software. The durability of synthetic fraud and the fact that they mimic a normal account behaviour makes them very hard to spot through the conventional rule-based methods (Bhattacharyya et al. 2011). To counter this threat, sophisticated machine learning models that are able to detect small amounts of inconsistency in different data dimensions and identify statistically improbable combinations of attributes are required.

Digital banking money laundering is a vital issue to financial institution with strict regulatory requirements under the Anti-Money Laundering and Know Your Customer laws (Ngai et al. 2011). To cover the trail of illegal money, criminals use advanced layering methods to hide the source of illegal funds by using complicated chains of transactions with many accounts, jurisdictions, and intermediaries. Digital banking platforms that offer quick processing of transactions and alternative channels of payments are also good platforms that money laundering activities can use through attractive means. Laundering activity can only be detected by studying the network of transactions, identifying structuring patterns aimed at evading reporting limits, and identifying abnormal fund movement patterns that are not in accordance with normal commercial or personal banking transactions (Phua et al. 2010). Graph analytics and network analysis methods can be used to supplement conventional transaction monitoring strategies to reveal the relationships that have been concealed and suspicious fund flows.

The fiscal effect of online transaction frauds goes well beyond direct financial losses and includes reputational harm, regulatory fines, operational expenses related to the investigation and recovery of fraud, and loss of clients due to breached security (Abdallah et al. 2016). According to industry reports, the amount of losses due to fraud in digital banking is constantly increasing every year, and some segments show growth in the percentage by even more than 20% each year. The transition to the contactless payment system, mobile banking apps, and instant payment systems has increased the available attack surface to the fraudsters and at the same time reduced the amount of time that can be used to detect and prevent fraud (Carneiro et al. 2017). With the accumulating pressure on the financial institutions to deploy increasingly complex fraud detection systems capable of functioning efficiently on-the-fly, accurately discriminating between fraud and genuine transactions, and responding quickly to the threat development, there is a strong call to enhance financial institutions to develop and adopt improved fraud detection technologies.

3 AI Models for Real-Time Transaction Monitoring

Transaction monitoring models based on artificial intelligence use a variety of algorithmic designs to detect fraud patterns in high-velocity streams of data (Raghavan and Gayar 2019). Deep architecture learning models have been observed to perform unusually well in learning the intricate, nonlinear connections with the transactional data that are not easily learned by conventional machine learning algorithms. Long Short-Term Memory networks are a basic architecture to process sequential transaction data, and this technology is explicitly developed to support the vanishing gradient problem which makes conventional recurrent neural networks difficult to apply (Hochreiter and Schmidhuber 1997). LSTM networks keep internal cell states that can choose to retain or forget information for long periods, and thus, the model can recognize the long-term dependencies in the histories of customer transactions.

This time modelling feature is especially useful in the detection of fraud, where fraudulent activities tend to take the form of deviation with regard to a known pattern, which cuts across multiple transactions across different time zones (Jurgovsky et al. 2018).

The LSTM network architecture involves memory cells with three gating functions; input gates which regulate the flow of information to the cell state, forget gates which decide what information goes to waste and output gates which ensure that information flows to other layers (Hochreiter and Schmidhuber 1997). In the case of transaction monitoring, LSTM networks take sequences of chronologically ordered sets of customer transactions, as they occur, and learn representations of normal pattern of behaviour, such as average amount of transactions, frequency of transactions, the type of merchant and temporal patterns. Contextual preservation in the network between the transaction sequences helps to spot anomalies that can only be detected with regards to history of transactions and not when individual transactions are analysed independently (Jurgovsky et al. 2018). As an example, a transaction that a human observer might consider to be legitimate may be considered suspicious when the LSTM model identifies it as being against the spending history and time-related habits of a particular customer.

Gated Recurrent Units are a simplified variant of LSTM structures, which use a simpler gating mechanism that unites the forget and input gates into a single update gate while uniting the cell state and hidden state (Cho et al. 2014). This type of architectural simplification lowers the computational complexity and training time and has similar performance on many sequential modelling problems. GRU networks have also been shown to be useful in transaction monitoring applications in capturing medium-term temporal dependencies, and able to adapt faster to changing fraud patterns as a result of fewer parameters (Jurgovsky et al. 2018). GRU architectures are especially appealing as being computationally efficient enough to execute in real time and therefore in deployment settings where the processing latency is the direct factor influencing the effectiveness of fraud detection. GRU models have reduced inference time, so financial institutions operating at scale and processing millions of transactions per hour can gain the reduced inference time without greatly compromising on detection accuracy.

Transformer-based models are the most advanced and efficient way to do sequential data modelling as they have already implemented attention which allows models to actively assess the importance of various places within input sequences (Vaswani et al. 2017). In contrast to recurrent architectures, which process the sequences one by one, transformers make the use of self-attention mechanisms to simultaneously calculate the representations of the input sequences thus, greatly enhancing the computational efficiency and allowing modelling of the dependencies that are even longer-range. Transformer models can address several aspects of transaction history in parallel in transaction monitoring settings, revealing the patterns that are relevant to non-contiguous time intervals, and highly complex interactions among transaction attributes (Raghavan and Gayar 2019). Multi-head attention mechanism enables the model to attend to multiple representational sub-spaces simultaneously, which may encode various patterns of frauds that may appear in various combinations of features or temporal features.

Unsupervised anomaly detection systems offer such supplementary methods to the supervised deep learning models, having specific strengths in the areas where the number of labelled instances of fraud is limited or where patterns of frauds change very fast (Chandola et al. 2009). The idea behind the isolation Forest algorithm is that the anomalies are limited and distinct hence using the fewer random partitions in order to isolate them than their respective normal cases (Liu et al. 2008). The algorithm builds a set of construction trees, which selects randomly the features and splits the values and gets the distance on which each instance is isolation. The shorter path lengths of the transaction across the ensemble are termed as anomalies. It is a technique that works exceptionally well with high-dimensional transaction data in which fraudulent patterns can occur in different combinations of features (Sakurada and Yairi 2014). Since the Isolation Forests are unsupervised, novel types of fraud can be detected without the specified examples of training, but the threshold needs to be carefully tuned to ensure a good tradeoff between the detection sensitivity and false positives rates.

Another unsupervised method of detecting fraud is the use of auto-encoder neural networks which learn compress representations of regular transaction patterns (Sakurada and Yairi 2014). The autoencoder design is a network that includes an encoder part that performs the mapping of input transactions to lower dimensional latent representations and a decoder that restores the original input given the latent representation. The network is only trained on legitimate transactions, which it learns to properly reconstruct as it finds it difficult to reconstruct anomalous transactions which are not within the pattern it is trained on (Saia and Carta 2017). The reconstruction error measure is an anomaly measure where large reconstruction errors reflects the fraud. Variational autoencoders build on this idea by training probabilistic latent encodings, which facilitates the detection of anomalies because the distribution of common patterns of transactions is modelled. The variational autoencoders offer probabilistic consistency, which has the effect of generating natural uncertainty quantification, and this quantification can be used to risk score based on model confidence in anomaly tests.

One-Class Support Vector Machines provides the kernel-based method of detecting anomalies in transactions, where it learns a boundary of decisions which captures the normal patterns of transactions but considers fraudulent transactions as anomalies (Schölkopf et al. 2001). The algorithm maps the transactions to high-dimensional feature spaces with the help of kernel functions after which a hyperplane that maximally separates normal transactions and the origin is identified. Those transactions that lie on the other of the hyperplane or either side of distance limit is known as an anomaly (Sahin and Duman 2011). The ability to capture non-linear decision boundaries that are not simple and linear in decision-making gives the One-Class SVMs its flexibility of kernel functions. Nevertheless, the computational complexity of kernel methods may be a problem, particularly in the deployment of real-time models in large scale, and kernel selection and model optimization strategies must be carefully considered.

Ensemble methods combine supervised and unsupervised methods and techniques to harness the strength of each other in complement (Caruana et al. 2015). Ensemble models are a combination of predictions of several base learners, which may include LSTM networks trained on labelled data, Isolation Forests that are used to find statistical outliers, and autoencoders that are used to detect an anomaly in reconstruction results. These can either be as simple as voting schemes to as sophisticated as meta-learning strategies which can combine the various signals into a single fraud risk score (Bhattacharyya et al. 2011). In this multi-model approach, strong resistance to changing fraud methods is attained since an attacker has to actively avoid various detection systems based on different principles. In addition to that, ensemble methods can offer more detailed risk evaluations, as they identify various kinds of anomalies and fraud cases, which allows more focused investigation processes and intervention programs.

4 Real-Time Data Processing Pipelines

AI-based fraud detection solutions deployed in production also demand complex data processing designs with high throughput processing and analysis of high velocity streams of transactions and low latency. Older batch processing methods involving aggregating transactions across time periods and then analysing them cause intolerable delays in fraud detection giving potential fraudsters time imperative to execute attacks and steal money before being detected. Effective fraud prevention would require real-time or near-real-time processing architecture, which would mean responding to fraud by seconds or milliseconds after the customer initiates a transaction. This time constraint causes streaming data processing models which are specifically implemented to accommodate constant data feeds and carry out gradual computations with incoming data.

Apache Kafka is now a fundamental technology used in the construction of real-time transaction monitoring, the channel is a distributed streaming platform with a huge throughput capacity and low latency. Kafka functions as a distributed commit log that transactions are sent to topics and later read by downstream processing applications. The mechanism provided by the platform to decouple the producers and consumers of the data on the platform using publish subscribe messaging patterns allows flexible design of the architecture to allow any number of fraud detection models to be running concurrently with transaction streams. Kafka has a distributed architecture and replication systems which give fault tolerance and high availability, both of which are essential in a financial system where failure of one server may lead to undetected fraud or service outages. Support of stream partitioning in the platform allows it to scale horizontally in order to provide financial institutions with the ability to expand processing capacity by adding computation resources as the volume of transactions increases.

Apache Flink is an effective stream processing engine that can process complex event processing and stateful processes on the stream of continuously flowing data.

The programming model offered by Flink considers streaming to be the central paradigm in which batch processing is merely a special case, which is quite natural according to the real-time needs of a fraud detector. The framework has rich APIs specifying detailed transaction processing logic such as windowing transactions combining transactions across sliding or tumbling time-windows, pattern recognizing transactions detecting suspicious pattern of sequences, and stateful processing maintaining customer profiles and behavioural models. The processing semantics of Flink provide highly availability. This is guaranteed by the exactly-once processing semantics that ensure that the same transaction is actually only once processed, even when failures occur, and neither false alerts nor duplicate alerts are generated. This is because the low-latency processing the framework will be able to make fraud determinations in less than a second, which is very important when fraudulent payment requests before they go through.

Real-time fraud detection systems usually take a multi-stage pipeline in which a transaction ingestion is a starting stage through the different banking interfaces such as online banking systems, mobile apps, ATM systems, and payment processing gateways. The transactions are written to Kafka topics using proper partitioning strategies which allocate the load and ordering is available where required. The stream processing applications developed on Flink or comparable frameworks are the ones that take in and execute the transaction streams and carry out the primary data validation, standardization, and enrichment processes. Enrichment activities augurate raw transaction records with context about the customer profiles, previous behavioural statistics, device fingerprints, location information and merchant data. Such a contextual enhancement plays a pivotal role in detection of fraud because most fraud patterns cannot be recognized until the transactions are viewed within the customer history and external intelligence contexts.

Featuring extraction and transformation can be considered one of the most important pipeline steps that involve turning raw transaction and enrichment data into feature vectors that can be consumed by machine learning models. This method might include doing aggregate statistics computation slide window-wise, getting behavioral deviation indicators, turning categorical variables into numerical ones, and putting numerical features on the same scale. The most important is the computational efficiency of the feature extraction which has to be completed within strict latency constraints in order to ensure real-time processing is guaranteed. Frequently used features and aggregations can be pre-computed and stored in feature shops and do not have to be computed as often. Model inference comes after feature extraction in which the model feature vectors are scored by the deployed fraud detection models. Most organizations generally implement several models simultaneously, which can be specialized to specific transaction types or types of fraud, where the outcomes are combined into single risk scores.

5 Feature Engineering for Transactional Data

The quality and relevance of input features are crucial determinants of fraud detection system effectiveness because feature engineering is a critical aspect that determines whether the model will be able to classify fraudulent and legitimate transactions (Bahnsen et al. 2016). Well-structured features encode domain information on fraud patterns and customer behaviours making models learn better with a limited training data and project more accurately in new fraud cases. The characteristics of the transactions cut across a variety of types such as intrinsic transaction features, time features, behavioural features, contextual features and derived risk features (Dal Pozzolo et al. 2014). A feature engineering task would demand significant knowledge of the typologies of financial fraud and the nature of the digital banking system operation to build sets of features that would be able to represent significant fraud indicators whilst being computationally efficient enough to run in real-time.

Intrinsic transaction attributes offer the primary characteristics that can be observed directly based on the transaction records such as the transaction amount, codes of merchant categories, payment methods, and types of transactions, and denominations of currency (Bahnsen et al. 2016). Although such raw attributes may not often be sufficiently discriminatory to be useful by themselves in the detection of a particular fraudulent behaviour, they do underlie more complex derived features. Features based on amount are sensitive since they have a broad distribution range and may have transactions that are illegitimate. Model stability and learning dynamics can be enhanced by using logarithmic transformations, quantile binning and normalization (Carneiro et al. 2017). Merchant category code will give useful background on the nature of transactions, allowing identification of abnormal spending patterns like luxurious spending that is against the profile of the customer or high-risk class of merchants that have high rate of fraud. Models can learn risk pattern specific to merchants using one-hot encoded or embedded representations of categorical merchant data based on examples of fraud in the past.

Temporal features represent time-varying patterns with a high correlation with risk of fraud (Jurgovsky et al. 2018). There are certain timeframes that fraudsters are usually keen to use such as late-night hours when the victim is not expected to check accounts, weekends when they may have fewer employees to investigate such cases, or right after the account has been compromised, to get as much money as possible before it is reported. Attributes with values of transaction time of-day, day-of-week, and proximity to holidays are used to help models to learn these time-dependent risk patterns (Dal Pozzolo et al. 2014). Velocity features measure transaction frequency within time windows, which are rolling, to give strong indicators of fraud because a compromised account will have transaction rates that are far above normal frequency. Computing properties like the number of transactions completed within the last hour, the total value of the transactions completed within the last twenty-four hours and the duration it has taken since the last completed transaction allow the identification of rapid-fire chain of transaction that may indicate an account takeover (Bhattacharyya et al. 2011). Temporal feature consistency in training and inference should be observed where the same definition of time boundaries is used in calculating windowing.

Behavioural deviation characteristics measure how much current transactions do not adhere to the pattern of transactions that occurred between the business and the customers and they offer some of the most discriminative indicators of fraud (Bhattacharyya et al. 2011). Such features demand the retention of customer behavioural profiles that consolidate historical transaction history data such as average amounts of spending, favourite types of merchants, favourite venues of transactions, and periodic trends. The metrics of deviations may be calculated in the form of distance measurements between current transacted transactions and past distributions, z-scores in terms of standard deviations relative to the historical means, or in percentile ranks defining unusualness of transactions in terms of customer past records (Dal Pozzolo et al. 2014). Behavioural models are a challenge because it is necessary to make the profiles respond to any legitimate customer behaviour changes and at the same time be sensitive to any sudden change that is indicative of account compromise. Robustness can be enhanced by adaptive profiling based on the weighting of more emphasis on recent transactions over distant history using change-point detection algorithms to detect legitimate behavioural changes (Raghavan and Gayar 2019).

Geospatial characteristics take advantage of the location data along with the transactions and devices to identify the situation of impossible travel, abnormal location pattern, and geographic threat signals (Saia and Carta 2017). Transactions made in location which is exceptionally far away as compared to the location of the previous transactions during time frames which are far too brief to be covered by physical movement are good indicator of fraud. The anomalies can be detected by computing characteristics like distance to the last transaction position, since last transaction at similar position and variation in transaction geography (not normal) (Carneiro et al. 2017). The IP address geolocation information gives rough locations of the network where the transactions originated during online transaction, although, the use of obfuscation methods such as use of VPN and proxy server creates noise and possible evasion vectors. Where mobile banking applications can deliver device location data, they offer more precise location data (Abdallah et al. 2016). Risk scores at the country level and region level using historical rates of fraud and the areas prone to fraud can be used as contextual indicators.

The features of device fingerprinting generate a device signature of the devices involved in engaging banking services, thus the ability to monitor accessibility of an account by use of unfamiliar devices can be identified (Abdallah et al. 2016). Attributes collated by device fingerprints are operating system types and versions, browser types and versions, screen resolutions, installed fonts, time-zone settings, and language settings. Account takeover can be referenced by changes in the device fingerprint that are related to the access of the account, especially together with behavioural deviations or location pattern abnormalities (Schölkopf et al. 2001). Nonetheless, device fingerprinting should struggle against such lawful cases as access by clients using a different device, device upgrades and privacy-increasing technologies, which randomize (or obfuscate) device attributes. This can be enhanced with the help of probabilistic matching and device reputation systems which are capable of factoring in historical patterns of use of the device and distinguishing a valid device use versus a suspicious access attempt.

Network based features interest in relationships and patterns among multiple accounts, merchants, and transactions that might indicate organized fraud schemes or money laundering schemes (Phua et al. 2010). Graph features are features that are measured using graph connectivity, i.e., degree centrality (number of connections to other accounts) and betweenness centrality (accounts as an intermediary of fund transfers) and clustering coefficients (local network density) as graph connectivity metrics. These characteristics allow revealing a ring of frauds in which a number of compromised or synthetic accounts are organized by common participants (Dal Pozzolo et al. 2014). Patterns on shared attributes among accounts in the form of shared email domains, shared phone number prefixes, or shared IP block can be used to indicate synthetic identity fraud. Computing network properties demand keeping graph representations of the transaction network and entity relationships and efficient graph query and analysis to be able to extract features in real-time.

In risk scoring methodologies, numerous feature dimensions are combined together to each make up single risk measurements to measure the likelihood of a transaction being fraudulent, (Bolton and Hand 2002). Linear risk scoring models are an expression of risk, which are calculated as weighted sums of features with expert-assigned or statistically-derived weights, to offer interpretable risk assessment in a computationally efficient manner. Risk scoring, an approach based on machine learning uses trained models to conduct non-linear aggregation of feature signals, which may represent such complex interactions between features that are unidentified by linear models (Bhattacharyya et al. 2011). Ensemble risk scoring call on two or more models or scoring methodologies, and the accuracy and robustness of the ensemble are enhanced across two or more models (Caruana et al. 2015). The output scores are generally subject to calibration procedures which translate raw model outputs to understandable probability scales, and facilitate regular risk communication across the types of models as well as supporting threshold-based risk decision-making. To assure the reliability of scores, recalibration needs to be performed regularly because with time, fraud trends and lawful distributions of transactions can alter (Raghavan and Gayar 2019).

6 System Architecture and Deployment Framework

Production-grade fraud detection systems have an architecture comprising numerous components connected to each other and working together to facilitate real-time analysis of transactions and evaluation of risks in addition to the prevention of fraud. This high-level system has to meet the high level of requirements such as sub-second inference latency which is necessary to support real time blocking of transactions, high throughput that can support the maximum transaction volume which might be in millions of events per hour with fault tolerance to ensure continued functionality in the event of failure in the infrastructure, scalability to meet the increasing event volume and latest fraud detection, and security to keep the sensitive financial data safe and to deter adversarial attacks. Simultaneous provision of these requirements implies attentive architectural design which provides trade-offs in terms of latency, accuracy, cost, and complexities of operation.

The architecture of the system usually has a micro-services design pattern where the functionality is broken down to services that are independently related by clearly defined interfaces. This architectural model offers a number of advantages such as the ability to scale the various parts of the system independently into the resource needs, flexibility in technologies that enables different services in the system to use the best technology stack, isolation of faults so that failure in one part of the system does not spread across the entire system, and there is the capability to make changes to services independently without necessitating a complete redeployment of the system. Fraud detection architecture consists of core services, which are transaction ingestion services which interact with banking channels and normalize diverse transaction formats, feature computation services which extract and transform features of raw transaction data, model inference services that implement fraud detection models and risk scores, decision services that apply business rules and set transaction dispositions, case management services that support workflows in fraud investigation, and monitoring services that monitor system health and model performance.

The machine learning operations practices that are adopted in model development and deployment pipelines are procedures that systematize a process of model development, validation, deployment and monitoring of fraud detection models. Environments that are used in development offer data scientists' access to previous transaction data, feature engineering tools and model training infrastructure. Model validation procedures are measures of performance based on held-out test sets that cover wide ranges of fraud scenario and transaction patterns such that models should predict out of training data. A/B testing models allow deployment of new models safely via the routing of production traffic to experimental models whilst maintaining the baseline models allowing statistical comparison of detection performance prior to full deployment. In model versioning systems, multiple versions of models are kept, and can be rolled back to earlier versions in case performance degradation happens. The deployment process is usually done by exporting trained models to models optimized on the basis of inference efficiency, models are containerized with required dependencies to ensure reliability in the execution environments and automated deployment pipelines that push tested models to production inference platforms.

Hybrid deployment architecture tries to strike the trade-offs between the cloud as well as the on-premise by strategically allocating elements between environments. The sensitiveness of the data and the transaction processing portion of the workload can continue to be on-premise to meet regulatory needs and limit data transfer, with model training utilizing the cloud computing resources to unlock specialized hardware and elastic capacity. The feature computation and model inference can be done on-site to ensure a minimum latency and model development and experimentation on clouds. This style of architecture brings complexity in the maintenance of consistent environments and data flows in and out of the cloud together with on-premises elements that demand a sound network identity management system and infrastructure.

7 Evaluation Metrics and Case Studies

In assessing the performance of a fraud detection system, the metrics used must be chosen with care and detail to measure various aspects of effectiveness such as the probability of detection, the rate of false positives, the efficiency in the detection latency and the impact of such operation on the performance of the system (Bolton and Hand 2002). Conventional methods like accuracy that is ratio of true predictions, are ineffective in detecting fraud because of gross class imbalance in which cases of fraud consists of minute parts of total transaction amounts (Bhattacharyya et al. 2011). A naive model this is one that generalizes all transactions as legitimate with high accuracy but the value of fraud detection is zero. Precision/recall measures offer more significant performance measurements when the settings are imbalanced (Dal Pozzolo et al. 2014). Precision is the ratio of predicted fraudulent transactions that actually occur that is a direct measure of how well the investigators perform since greater precision means less time is wasted investigating false positives. Recall The scale of successes detected fraud transactions as a fraction of the actual fraudulent transactions is known as the recall and will indicate the effectiveness of fraud prevention because the larger the recall, the lower will be the losses on fraud.

The precision-recall trade-off is one of the inherent issues of the optimization of fraud detection since by making the detection a bit more sensitive to detect more fraud incidents, more false positives will be generated leading to more burdensome investigation. These conflicting goals have to be balanced in the organization depending on the ability to operate and the loss of fraud. The F1 score gives a single measure that is harmoniously determined by precision and recall but standard F1 measure equalizes both precision and recall, which is not necessarily true to organizational priorities. This metric is generalized using the F-beta score which gives the ability to tune the relevance of precision versus recall using a beta parameter. Nevertheless, single point measures measured at a set classification threshold would give inadequate characterization of performance as the optimal operating points of different organizations will vary depending on the capacity to conduct investigation and the degree of risk tolerance.

Receiver Operating Characteristic curves allow visualizing the performance without dependence on threshold by plotting true positive rates versus false positive rates at all the possible classification thresholds. The Area Under the ROC Curve measure serves to sum up the discrimination performance over one value between 0.5 with random classification to 1.0 which represents no discrimination. Although AUC-ROC offers convenient model comparison services, it is too optimistic when dealing with highly imbalanced data, in which false positives within realistic operating ranges can be unacceptably large, even though model AUC is large.

Precision-Recall curves provide a more appropriate visualization of an imbalanced environment, which means that they should be used to plot precision versus recall as a threshold. The Area Under the Precision-Recall Curve metric gives a summary statistic, in which high-recall areas are of greater significance to the application of fraud detection.

The detection laicity measures are used to gauge the duration taken between launching transactions and determining fraud, which is a paramount performance measure in real-time counter-fraud. End to end latency is obtained by summing up all processing steps since the transaction ingestion to the feature calculation, model inference, and decision execution. Latency distributions give a more comprehensive characterization of performance since tail latencies in high percentiles have a direct effect on user experience in transactions that have a slow latency. Latency budgets should reflect the highest latency events involving point-of-sale transactions where customers do not want to wait long before their authorization can be processed. To maintain the performance of a significant low-latency, it is necessary to optimize the entire processing pipeline, and the bottlenecks that cause delays that are inconsistent need to be identified and removed.

8 Regulatory Compliance and Explain-Ability

Banking institutions have a strict regulatory environment, which dictates special standards to the fraud detection and anti-money laundering software. Such controls require both the adoption of effective monitoring controls as well as the capability to justify and report to regulatory audit and legal proceedings on details of detection decisions. The Anti-Money laundering and Know Your Customer regulations imply that financial institutions should have detailed monitoring systems in transactions potentially possible to detect suspicious transactions, which show money laundering, financing terrorism, breach of sanctions, and other financial crimes. The regulatory bodies require the institutions to ensure that their fraud detection systems are performing effectively, making defensible decisions, and keep abreast with the advent of emerging threat terrain. Similar to the trends of expanding the use of AI-based detection systems, new compliance challenges are introduced because the advanced model of machine learning tends to behave as a black box, the processes of its decisions are not transparent.

Elucidation Explainable AI or model explain-ability is the response to the problem of comprehension and interpretation of results produced by adaptable machine learning models. Explain-ability is essential in fraud detection to satisfy regulatory compliance but also in operations such as to allow an investigator to comprehend why this transaction was reported, contributing to an appeals process where a customer remains unhappy about fraud rulings, debugging and validating a model during development, and establishing a stakeholder trust in automated decision systems. This dilemma between model performance and interpretability is a core issue where the most accurate models like deep neural networks and ensemble models are the ones that are least interpretable and the easiest to understand models like decision trees and linear models are probably the ones that are compromise detection.

SHapley Additive exPlanations (SHAPE) offers a single framework that users can use to explain individual predictions, and the contribution of each feature to a particular prediction is measured. This method is based on the game theory, which calculates Shapley values itself, which indicates the average marginal contribution of each feature to all feasible combinations of features. SHAP values have favourable mathematical characteristics such as local accuracy where the sum of the contributions of the features to the model value is the difference in the model prediction and the expected baseline prediction, consistency where it grows as more and more feature contributions are given, and missingness where the features not used by the model have importance of zero. The explanations provided by SHAP can be used in the context of fraud detection applications to allow the investigator to explain the reasons behind the high-risk scores of transactions, and use this information to make evidence-based investigation choices. An example of a SHAP explanation would mean that a transaction got high fraud score because of abnormal transaction value, being out of ordinary merchant type, and abnormal access, and the riskiness of each was added in terms of a quantifiable risk increment.

The use of SHAP in producing complex security models, such as data on malware analysis where SHAP has been shown to find major features distinguishing between a malicious code and a harmless software, has been proven to be effective (Pradhan et al. 2025). The analysis compared SHAP to a different frequent method of explanation, LIME, and it concluded that SHAP was more stable and faithful in explaining different types of models. The implication of these results to a situation of detecting fraud is that when an individual faces different patterns of frauds, it is only necessary to have consistent explanations that can be applied to assure operational consistency. Application of SHAP to production fraud detection systems should consider the computational cost seriously because it is computationally expensive to compute the exact values of Shapley by evaluating exponential combinations of features. Real-world SHAP applications utilize approximation methods that encompass kernel SHAP for model-agnostic interpretations and tree SHAP for tree-based models, getting good quality explanations with reasonable computation time.

Local Interpretable Model-agnostic Explanations is a different explain-ability method that estimates the local behaviour of complex models around individual predictions with explainable surrogate models. The method produces explanations by adding noise to the input features, checking the resulting change of prediction and fitting simple linear models that mimic the local behaviour of the complex model. LIME explanations point out the most significant features in making certain predictions in the form of weighted contributions, which can be easily interpreted by investigators. When used in a context of fraud detection, LIME has the capability to describe the reasons why certain transactions were assigned to a particular risk rating, emphasizing the aspects of transactions which handsomely contributed the most to the prediction. The model agnostic aspect of LIME allows it to generate explanations in a consistent manner across different types of model architectures such as deep learning models, ensemble detection models as well as commercial proprietary fraud detection models.

According to the comparative analysis of the two approaches LIME and SHAP in the security applications (Pradhan et al. 2025), it became evident that there exist significant differences in the nature of their explanation. SHAP proved to be more consistent in the sense that it generates consistent explanations to similar cases and can generate consistent explanations among multiple computations. In part because of its greater dependence on random perturbation sampling, LIME displaying greater variability but its advantages in computational efficiency would make it useful in the generation of explanations in real-time in high throughput computational environment. The two techniques can be used strategically in fraud detection systems, where SHAP can be used in decisions with stakes and where explanation fidelity is of highest importance and LIME in routinely explained decisions, the primary concern of which is computational efficiency. The composite strategies that integrate the information of more than one explanation method may offer stronger knowledge about model choices, which uncover consensus characteristics that are emphasized significant by numerous explanation strategies.

The regulatory compliance needs are not limited to the personal explanation of transaction but involve the model governance structures which have been written to describe model development procedures, model validation playgrounds, continued performance assessment, and models change management. Documentation of a model should explain the business problem addressed by that model, where the data originates and how it is pre-processed, how features are engineered, how it is modelled, what hyperparameters and training procedures are used, training and validation outcomes and what business constraints and failure behaviour can be observed and monitored in deployment. Validation practices Model validation is conducted periodically to determine whether models are still working as desired and performance is checked across demographic groups to determine whether there might be fairness issues, model behaviour on edge cases and adversarial situations and prediction performance compared to other models or against human expert judgements.

9 Economic Analysis and Risk Mitigation

The financial rationale behind the investment in the sophisticated AI-based fraud detection tools can be based on the measurable gains that have numerous facets to the functioning of the financial institutions. The most obvious economic policy is that direct fraud loss prevention lowers the number of successful fraudulent transactions that lead to the loss of money. But extensive economics should also include the operating cost savings of enhanced efficiency, enhanced customer experience which leads to retention and acquisition, advantage of regulatory compliance eliminating penalty risks, and position of reference which safeguards brand equity. When these larger factors are valued, the overall economic loss of the defraud detection investments will be significantly higher than the cost of calculating the simple fraud losses.

The benefits of fraud loss prevention can be estimated using the statistical models which forecast the occurrence of fraud based on the various possible scenarios of fraud detection. Take a case of a financial institution whereby it handles one billion transactions in a year and has a low rate of fraud of 0.1, then this will mean one million fraud transactions will occur. In case of an average transaction value of one hundred dollars of the amount of fraud, the amount of fraud losses is one hundred million dollars yearly. The fraud detect mechanism with 90% recall would avoid nine hundred thousand frauds, which would reduce ninety million dollars of direct losses. Nevertheless, the operation of this calculation assumes that it is always absolutely accurate when in reality any system will produce false positives, which is costly in terms of investigation. At a 45 precision, assuming that two million transactions are identified to be suspicious by the system, investigators are required to review about 1.1 million false positive at an estimated cost of ten dollars per investigation which means eleven million dollars' worth of investigation. The net profit of fraud loss prevention and investigation cost amounts to seventy-nine million dollars per year, which is a significant payoff on investment even though the cost of the systems might be tens of millions of dollars to develop and maintain.

The benefits of improvements in operational efficiency are based on various purposes such as making the work of false positive investigations less expensive, automated decision-making of transactions that do not involve any manual analysis of low-risk transactions, and simplified case management processes, which speed up the process of resolving fraud cases. Older fraud detection systems frequently cause enormous numbers of alerts, which exceed the capacity of the investigators, and therefore necessitate a process of triage that slows or do not investigate lower-priority alerts. This triage protocol induces loopholes in the fraud detection as transactions of moderate level of suspicion can be subject to under thorough examination, because advanced fraudsters can take advantage of the holes in the coverage of investigations. Smart systems that are enhanced with AI are much more specific and lead to a significant decrease in alerts to investigate flagged transactions more thoroughly and devote more effort to a more complex case that needs more attention. It has been recorded in time-motion research that financial institutions with an advanced fraud detection system experienced productivity improvement in the investigation of more than 50%, either by allowing the same number of investigators to test a much larger volume of transactions or by reducing the workforce headcount and causing a decline in the running costs.

Fraud detection improvements leading to customer experience improvements occur in many ways such as less false positive friction whereby legitimate customers are not subjected to higher authentication steps or transaction blocks, fraud detection faster thereby reducing customer inconvenience due to fraudulent transactions recoveries, and proactive fraud prevention and denies a compromised account before it receives ASF due to any fraudulent transaction. False positive fraud detection is a major business issue because customers who feel victimized by fraud detection algorithms will inevitably move to competitors with more seamless services. According to the industry research, significant percentages of the customers who receive false positive blocks decrease their utilization of the impacted payment methods or shut down the countries. To measure the Customer experience premium, it is necessary to connect its performance in handling fraud detection with the metrics of customer behaviour such as the rate of transaction abandonment rates, customer satisfaction scores, rates of retention, and customer lifetime value. Fraud detection impact can be isolable using attribution modelling, which allows the customer experience improvement to be more efficiently valued.

Qualitative strategic variables that cannot be readily measured, but still have a significant impact in fraud detection investment decisions. The regulatory pressures are posing increasing focus on the adoption of hi-tech methods of detection of fraud cases, the regulators are examining institutions which solely use the old systems of rules, they are not opting to use hi-tech methods. By actively applying advanced fraud detection systems, there is a show of regulatory compliance commitment, and this minimizes the effects of the examinations. Tackling customer experience and security is a growing competitive pressure in the finances services sector, with institutions increasingly deciding on inter-competitive edge through excellent fraud prevention which suppresses fraud losses and false positive friction. Infrastructure to develop AI and other advanced analytics facilitates additional digital transformation efforts, other than fraud detection, which can produce option value that can be carried on in subsequent uses of the developed capabilities. Such strategic implications are usually game changers in getting number of leaders on board with major investments on fraud detection modernization even in situations where the financial paybacks might not be impressive in the short term.

Risk mitigation mechanisms are used to deal with the possibility of failure mode and unintended consequences of AI-powered fraud detection systems. Another risk that is also of high concern is adversarial attacks, where advanced schemes of fraudsters might investigate the detection mechanism to determine ways of avoiding it. Adversarial examples in machine learning Research situations Adversarial examples In machine learning, adversarial examples are designed to make a model misclassify, but people consider them honest. In fraud detection cases, enemies may strategically change the transaction features to determine the transaction combinations which will not be detected, and then take advantage of the identified weaknesses at massive scale. Adversarial training, which trains models on adversarial examples to enhance adversarial robustness, ensemble diversity, which reduces the challenge of simultaneously evading multiple detection models, and anomaly detectors that have been designed explicitly to identify probing models leading to large-scale attacks, are all defences against adversarial attacks.

Another major threat is model degradation over time since the trend of fraud changes and distributions of legitimate transactions change. Continuous monitoring system monitors the performance measures of a model and distributions of data, will give a signal when degradation reaches unacceptable limits. It is interesting to note that automated retraining pipelines can be initiated once the degradation in performance is distinguished, but this should be carefully validated, that is, retraining should actually enhance instead of deteriorate the performance. Shadow scoring methods operate concurrent models of operations with production models without interfering or influencing the decision of transactions, which allows a performance comparison to be made previously before investing in model updating is committed. Gradual rollout strategies restrict the blast radius of model updates that incurred form an incidental degrading performance, and only rollout gradually after assuring an improved performance.

The measures to operational resilience provide that the fraud detection capabilities will not be out of service in case of an infrastructure outage or a cyber-attack on the detection systems themselves. The backup system deployment to various data-centres or even regions can offer standing energy during case of failure of the primary systems. Fall-back procedures characterizing graceful degradation strategies involve potentially having AI models become unavailable, including relying on rule-based detection logic or manual review procedures that will preserve basic coverage with respect to fraud detection during out aging. Planed disaster recovery drills ensure that failover and recovery processes are as the design is and the defects before the real case is witnessed. Due to the importance of fraud detection in the functioning of financial institutions necessitates heavy implementation of operational resilience since the loss of a detection system opens a soft target that is prone to abuse by fraudsters to gain substantial financial benefits (Appendix, Fig. 1).

10 Conclusion and Future Directions

The introduction of AI-based systems of monitoring transactions is a truly radical development in combating financial fraud and has the potential to significantly surpass more traditional rule-based approaches in terms of detection performance, flexibility, and economy of operation. The combination of deep learning systems with the ability to model highly temporal patterns, streaming data processing systems that make it possible to process high velocity transaction streams in real-time and explainable AI systems that allow insight into automated decisions have formed a technology ecosystem underpinning modern fraud detection systems. Banking institutions who have been able to implement these advanced systems record high payoffs such as huge loss of fraud, high operational efficiency with lower rate of false positive, better customer experience with less friction and better compliance with the law through increased monitoring and auditability.

One of the prospective areas of improvement of fraud detection through alternative data sources is the merging of alternative data sources with the conventional matters of transactions. Typical biometric behavioural data such as typing pattern, patterns of mouse movement, touchscreen interaction patterns, and device orientation patterns leave extensive signals about who users are, and fraudsters are hard pressed to mimic them even in cases of compromised credentials. With the help of network analysis based on social graph data, device relationship graphs, schedule and graph analysis of merchant ecosystems, coordinated rings of fraud and synthetic identity fraud that look like authentic ones when investigated in isolation can be revealed. Extrinsic threat intelligence feeds, which contain real-time information regarding compromised user identities, identified fraud infrastructure and emerging very dangerous campaigns allow offensive defences to thwart fraudulent transactions prior to them happening as opposed to discovering them as they happen. The difficulty with exploiting these various data sources is in creating integration architectures that can effectively fuse more than one type of signal considering privacy requirements and regulatory restrictions on the use of data.

Federated learning technologies are likely to provide remedies to the problem of data sharing that restrict the creation of the fraud detection models that are trained on multi-institution data presently. Conventional centralized machine learning involves host venues in an aggregation of the training data in one facility, since it raises privacy issues and competition risks where multiple financial institutions are the sources of the data. Through federated learning, model training is accomplished on a collaborative basis in which individual institutions use locally available data to train local models and only transmit updates of the models, as opposed to raw data to a central coordination server that synthesizes the updates into a global model. This paradigm may allow the financial services sector to work together in creating stronger fraud detection frameworks that will train based on the various types of fraud observed within different institutions and maintain the privacy of data. There are technical issues such as the efficiency of communication in federated training, their ability to resist malicious actors who could poison the global model, and equality in the distribution of credits to institutions that provide valuable training information that still need further studies.

The use of reinforcement learning to optimize the fraud detection process is a new area of research with a potential of significantly enhancing the strategy of decision-making. Existing fraud detection methods normally use predefined decision rules that assign risk scores to actions which can be approve, challenge or block. The agents of reinforcement learning may learn dynamically changing decision policy which adjusts intervention depending on the contextual factors such as transaction value, customer history, time pressure, and the availability of inquiry resources. The agent would figure it out by trial and error, by getting rewarded when he/she does the right thing and punished when he/she does things wrong, over time, the agent will maximize the policies in such a way that he/she turns down fraud prevention and customer irritation and minimal operation cost. The complications of applying reinforcement learning in fraud-detection case are that the feedback associated with evaluating a fraud offense is delayed and sparse as a real verdict of whether an incident is actually a fraud or not likely will not be true until days or even weeks following the verdict. To produce, safe exploration plans that ensure that the learning agent does not make catastrophically poor decisions during training are necessary.

Graph neural networks define a novel type of architecture, which is especially capable of modelling the structure of networks of financial frauds. The traditional fraud detection models treat the individual transactions or profiles of customers independently without the possibility of identifying the fraud patterns which are only identified when exploring the relationships among the accounts, merchants and transactions. Graph neural networks, which are models based on graph structures, take graph like data as input directly, and then they learn to transfer and mix up the network information in such a way that the final output is able to reflect both the characteristics of each node and the overall structure of the graph. Graph neural networks may be used in the context of fraud detection to identify suspicious communities of accounts who are involved in organized fraud, identify unusual fund flow patterns that may be indicative of money laundering and discover merchant networks involved in fraud. Initial findings indicate that graph neural networks can perform significantly better than conventional methods in detecting fraud schemes that have embedded network structure, where scaling of graph neural network training and inference on large interval transaction networks presents computational challenges in further development of the algorithm.

Making AI-based fraud detection services available to smaller financial institutions is also an opportunity and a challenge to the industry. There are early signs of more sophisticated fraud detection systems, but the systems are currently heavily utilized in large institutions with significant technology resource commitments, and data miners with specialized data science expertise. Smaller banks and credit unions often do not have the resources to build up some form of sophisticated in-house systems, leaving them to be susceptible to fraud, placing weaknesses in the ecosystem that can be used by fraudsters. The cloud-based fraud detection solutions with advanced artificial intelligence solutions on a fee basis would provide equal opportunities to smaller institutions to use advanced software. Nonetheless, there are privacy, competition intelligence leakage, and customization limitations issues, which are brought by multi-tenant fraud detection services. The creation of fraud detection tools that would be beneficial to all network disadvantaging any single institution and at the same time allow this institution to adapt itself is an ongoing technological research.

Laws that regulate AI in financial services are still developing, and they have an effect on the design and implementation of fraud detection systems. New laws in many jurisdictions ensure the transparency of algorithms, equity, responsibility, and human intervention against automated decisions. The fraud systems will also have to offer more comprehensive documentation and explanatory powers in order to meet the regulatory requirements. Other jurisdictions are looking at limiting fully programmed decisions that have a major impact on the consumer and this may require that human examination of fraud decisions should be undertaken before final decision making. The conflicting needs of regulation to explain-ability and the performance benefits of sophisticated models that are not easily interpretable will probably continue to motivate further research on explainable AI methods that are specifically crafted to be relevant to financial contexts. Engagement of the regulators by industries to come up with the right governance structures that are conducive to the consumers, without choking positive innovation are still needed.

The fraud detection vision in the long term is an intelligent system not just to detect the fraudulent transactions but also predict an imminent attack, organize the defences across the institutions and actively prevent fraud through adaptive response that would render the attack to be economically nonviable. The predictive threat intelligence system may process attacker's behaviour, the economics of fraud campaigns, and the terrain of vulnerabilities based on which advanced threat vectors may happen before they come to pass. Co-ordinated defence networks would also make it possible to share indicators of fraud instantly across the institutions, which would provide collective immunity against attacks on one institution instantly bolstering defences at other ones. Economic warfare policies might dynamically tune the actions of fraud detectors to make well-cost attacks as costly compared to potential returns as possible, which may include game-theoretic reasoning regarding the incentive and response of attackers. To make this vision come true, one will need not just technical developments in AI and data analysis but also collaboration across the industry, industry regulation, and organizational change that would make one respond swiftly to emerging threats.

To sum up, AI-based transaction monitoring real-time fraud detection in digital banking is a domain of technology that has already matured and demonstrated its capabilities and has been deployed on a large scale with numerous successful applications, and it is continuing to advance very fast (responding to new threats and new needs of new regulations). Banks taking on the modernization in fraud detection programs must be willing to implement holistic approaches that are focused on the thorough implementation of not only model development and implementation but also on data infrastructure, organizational capabilities, compliance with laws and regulations and constant improvement techniques. The high costs of the sophisticated fraud detection systems are payable by the persuasive economic benefits including loss prevention, increasing of efficiency of operations, improvement of customer experiences, and decrease of risks. This field is an important focus area to financial services technologies management as fraudsters constantly evolve, and the adoption of digital banking in most parts of the world is growing rapidly; indeed, increasingly advanced AI-based algorithms will be needed to detect fraud (Appendix, Figs. 2 and 3).

Appendix

See Figs. 1, 2 and 3.

Fig. 1 Real-time fraud detection system architecture. *Source* Own processings

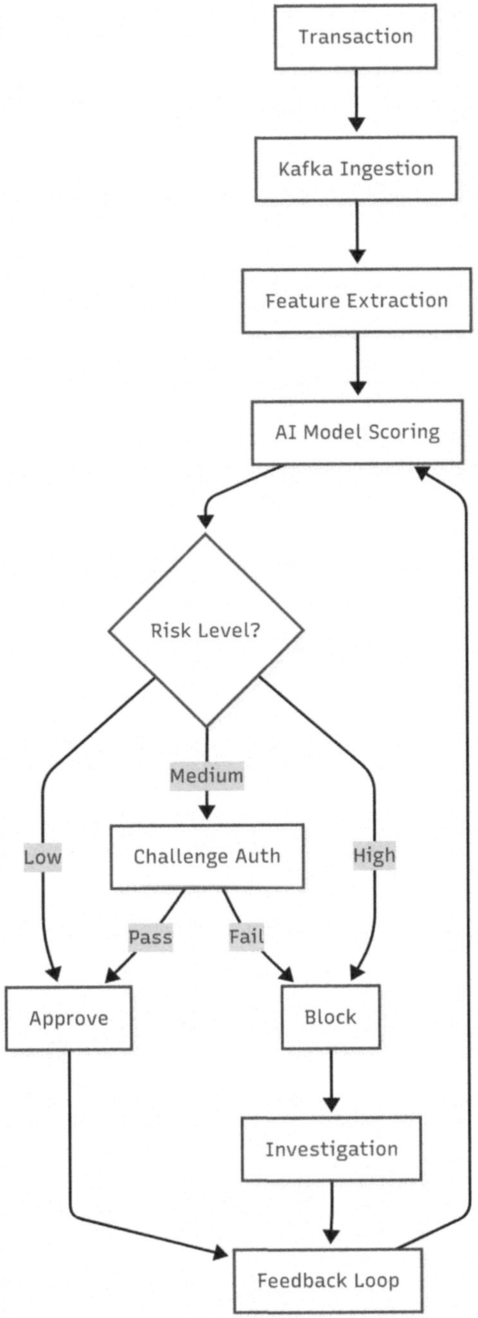

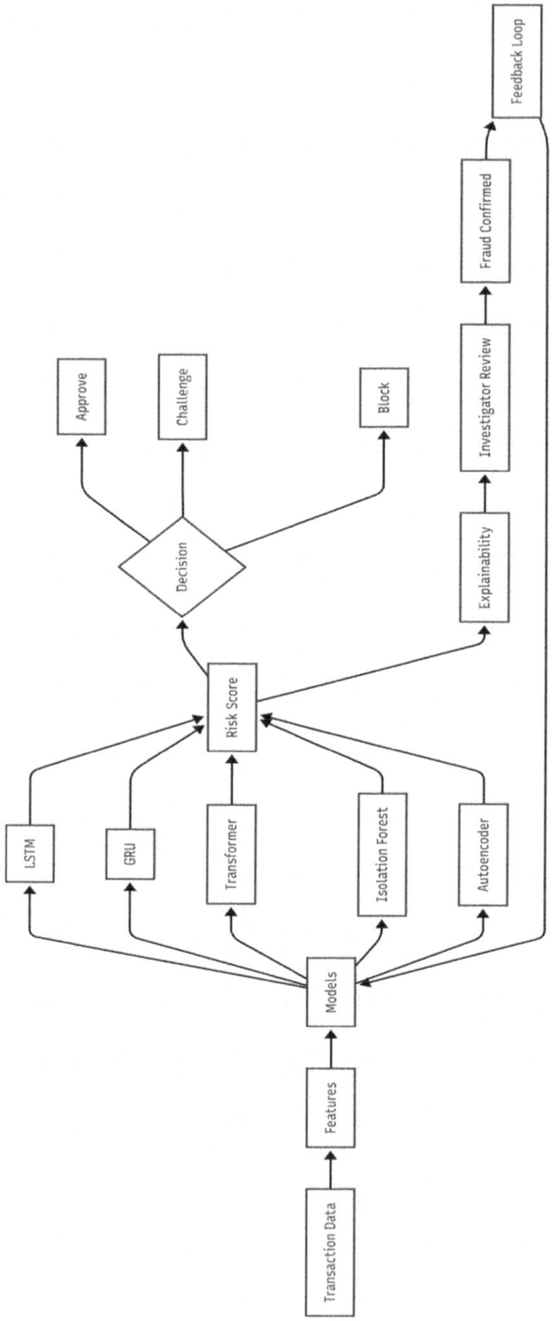

Fig. 2 AI model ensemble architecture for fraud detection. *Source* Own processings

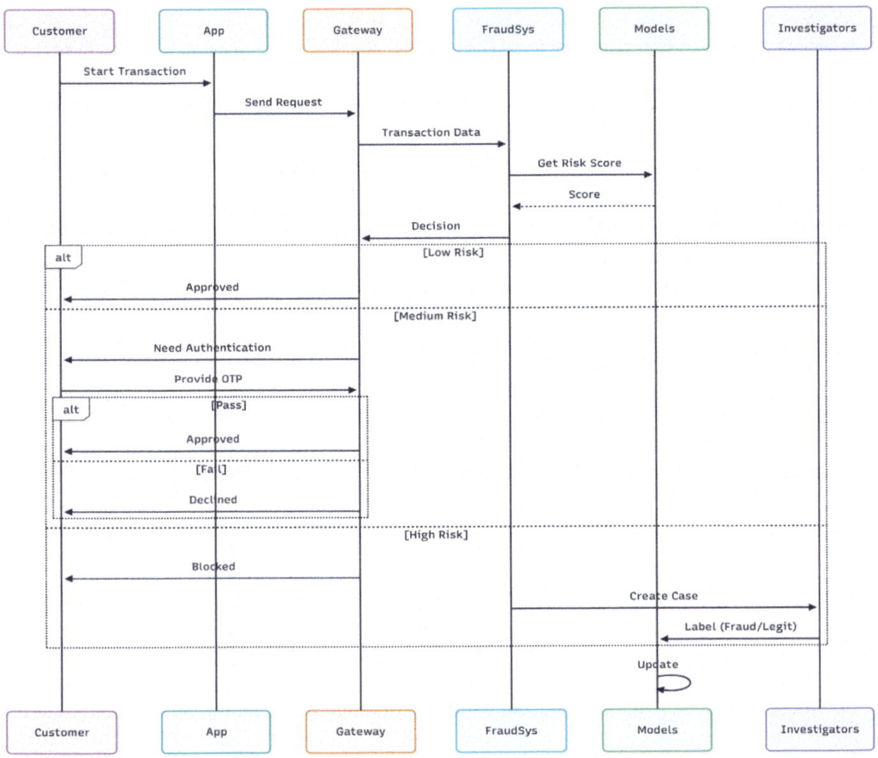

Fig. 3 AI model ensemble architecture for fraud detection. *Source* Own processings

References

Abdallah A, Maarof MA, Zainal A (2016) Fraud detection system: a survey. J Netw Comput Appl 68:90–113

Bahnsen AC, Aouada D, Stojanovic A, Ottersten B (2016) Feature engineering strategies for credit card fraud detection. Expert Syst Appl 51:134–142

Bhattacharyya S, Jha S, Tharakunnel K, Westland JC (2011) Data mining for credit card fraud: a comparative study. Decis Support Syst 50(3):602–613

Bolton RJ, Hand DJ (2002) Statistical fraud detection: a review. Stat Sci 17(3):235–255

Brause R, Langsdorf T, Hepp M (1999) Neural data mining for credit card fraud detection. In: Proceedings of the 11th IEEE international conference on tools with artificial intelligence, pp 103–106

Carneiro N, Figueira G, Costa M (2017) A data mining based system for credit-card fraud detection in e-tail. Decis Support Syst 95:91–101

Caruana R, Lou Y, Gehrke J, Koch P, Sturm M, Elhadad N (2015) Intelligible models for healthcare: predicting pneumonia risk and hospital 30-day readmission. In: Proceedings of the 21th ACM SIGKDD international conference on knowledge discovery and data mining, pp 1721–1730

Chandola V, Banerjee A, Kumar V (2009) Anomaly detection: a survey. ACM Comput Surv 41(3):1–58

Cho K, Van Merriënboer B, Gulcehre C, Bahdanau D, Bougares F, Schwenk H, Bengio Y (2014) Learning phrase representations using RNN encoder–decoder for statistical machine translation. Preprint arXiv:1406.1078

Dal Pozzolo A, Caelen O, Le Borgne YA, Waterschoot S, Bontempi G (2014) Learned lessons in credit card fraud detection from a practitioner perspective. Expert Syst Appl 41(10):4915–4928

Hochreiter S, Schmidhuber J (1997) Long short-term memory. Neural Comput 9(8):1735–1780

Jurgovsky J, Granitzer M, Ziegler K, Calabretto S, Portier PE, He-Guelton L, Caelen O (2018) Sequence classification for credit-card fraud detection. Expert Syst Appl 100:234–245

Liu FT, Ting KM, Zhou ZH (2008) Isolation forest. In: Proceedings of the 8th IEEE international conference on data mining, pp 413–422

Ngai EWT, Hu Y, Wong YH, Chen Y, Sun X (2011) The application of data mining techniques in financial fraud detection: a classification framework and an academic review of literature. Decis Support Syst 50(3):559–569

Phua C, Lee V, Smith K, Gayler R (2010) A comprehensive survey of data miningbased fraud detection research. Preprint arXiv:1009.6119

Pradhan U, Aditya MN (2025) Malware analysis using hashing and explainable AI: a comparative study of LIME and SHAP techniques. In: 1st international conference on AIML-applications for engineering technology (ICAET), Pune, India, pp 1–6. https://doi.org/10.1109/ICAET63349.2025.10932147

Raghavan P, Gayar NE (2019) Fraud detection using machine learning and deep learning. In: Proceedings of the international conference on computational intelligence and knowledge economy, pp 334–339

Sahin Y, Duman E (2011) Detecting credit card fraud by ANN and logistic regression. In: Proceedings of the international symposium on innovations in intelligent systems and applications, pp 315–319

Saia R, Carta S (2017) A frequency-domain-based pattern mining for credit card fraud detection. In: Proceedings of the 2nd international conference on internet of things, big data and security, pp 386–391

Sakurada M, Yairi T (2014) Anomaly detection using autoencoders with nonlinear dimensionality reduction. In: Proceedings of the MLSDA 2014 2nd workshop on machine learning for sensory data analysis, pp 4–11

Schölkopf B, Platt JC, Shawe-Taylor J, Smola AJ, Williamson RC (2001) Estimating the support of a high-dimensional distribution. Neural Comput 13(7):1443–1471

Vaswani A, Shazeer N, Parmar N, Uszkoreit J, Jones L, Gomez AN, Kaiser L, Polosukhin I (2017) Attention is all you need. Adv Neural Inform Process Syst 2017:5998–6008

West J, Bhattacharya M (2016) Intelligent financial fraud detection: a comprehensive review. Comput Secur 57:47–66

Ujan Pradhan is a final-year undergraduate student pursuing a Bachelor of Technology in Computer Science at SRM Institute of Science and Technology, Chennai, India. His research focuses on the applications of Artificial Intelligence, Machine Learning, and Data Science in Economics and Finance, with interdisciplinary deployments across domains such as environmental sustainability, healthcare, and cybersecurity. He has authored four IEEE conference papers published in the IEEE Xplore Digital Library and has multiple research articles and book chapters accepted for publication in reputed journals and publishers indexed in Scopus and Web of Science, including AIP, Springer, Elsevier, Bentham Science, and Taylor & Francis. He serves as the Machine Learning Domain Lead of his college's Electronics Club and is also a student researcher at the IEEE Student Branch. He has interned at Samsung R&D Institute India (Bangalore), IIT Madras, IIT Roorkee, and IIM Ranchi, where he contributed to applied AI and data-driven research across diverse fields. He was the runner-up at the 2024 Research Symposium on Explainable AI held in Chennai, jointly organized by IEEE, ACM, and the Computer Society of India.

Utkarsh Jaiswal is a third-year undergraduate student pursuing a Bachelor of Technology in Computer Science. He serves as the Vice President of GitHub Community SRM, where he leads initiatives to foster open-source collaboration, peer learning, and innovation among students. Alongside his leadership role, Utkarsh has been actively mentoring students in development and security, helping them strengthen their technical foundations and problemsolving skills. With a strong interest in security, software development, and systems design, he is driven to integrate technical expertise with impactful community-building.

Vyomika Anand is a final-year undergraduate student pursuing a Bachelor of Science in Chemistry with a minor in Economics later shifted to Computer Science at the Indian Institute of Technology, Bombay (IIT Bombay), India. Her research bridges Finance, Economics, and Sustainability through the application of Artificial Intelligence and Data Science. She has contributed to impactful water-saving initiatives for rural India through STAGE Labs (University of Chicago) and CTARA (IIT Bombay), focusing on irrigation technology and water budgeting using game theory and design thinking. She is currently interning in Supply Chain Management at Reckitt, a global leader in health, hygiene, and nutrition, and has also worked with startups in finance research and growth strategy. She has multiple research articles and book chapters accepted for publication in reputed Scopus-indexed venues, including Springer, Elsevier, Bentham Science, and Taylor & Francis.

Fintech, Crypto-Assets, and Emerging Models of Digital Risk

Fraud Risks in Digital Lending and BNPL Models: Detection and Prevention Strategies

Kanimozhi Viswanathan, Subhashini Suresh, and M. Showmiyan

Abstract This chapter aims to provide a comprehensive analysis of fraud risks associated with the rapidly expanding domains of digital lending and Buy Now, Pay Later (BNPL) models. While these fintech innovations offer unprecedented convenience and financial access, they also expose significant vulnerabilities due to their operational frameworks, speed of disbursal, and limited credit vetting. BNPL platforms, in particular, are increasingly attractive to fraudsters because of their reliance on minimal credit checks and deferred repayment windows. As a result, both digital lending and BNPL ecosystems have become fertile ground for a range of fraud typologies including identity theft, synthetic identity fraud, account takeovers, and first-party frauds. The chapter will analyze these common fraud types, drawing attention to their unique manifestations in digital credit environments. It will then explore advanced fraud detection and prevention strategies, with a strong focus on Artificial Intelligence (AI) and Machine Learning (ML). These technologies enable platforms to analyze vast volumes of real-time transaction data and identify subtle fraud patterns that often go undetected by traditional, rule-based systems. The key techniques to be examined include AI-powered transaction monitoring, Risk-based decision-making and Behavioral analytics that track nuanced user interactions to distinguish between genuine and suspicious behavior. In addition to technological solutions, the chapter will discuss the evolving regulatory and compliance landscape, emphasizing the growing responsibility of financial institutions to implement robust fraud prevention systems. By combining technical insights with practical implications, this chapter

K. Viswanathan (✉) · M. Showmiyan
Department of Management Sciences, Hindusthan College of Engineering and Technology, Coimbatore, Tamil Nadu, India
e-mail: kanimozhi.mba@hicet.ac.in

M. Showmiyan
e-mail: showmiyan.mba@hicet.ac.in

S. Suresh
Centre for Research & Training (CRT), Program Director—NFED Business Facilitators Forum (NBFF), National Foundation for Entrepreneurship Development (NFED), Coimbatore, Tamil Nadu, India
e-mail: emkaysubha@gmail.com

M. V. Achim (ed.), *Financial Crime in the Digital Era*, Contributions to Finance and Accounting, https://doi.org/10.1007/978-3-032-20198-0_7

will offer valuable guidance for academics, fintech professionals, and policymakers seeking to strengthen fraud resilience in the digital lending and BNPL sectors.

Keywords Digital lending · Fintech regulation · Digital fraud prevention · Buy now pay later (BNPL)

1 Introduction

The accelerating digitalization of financial services has transformed global credit delivery, giving rise to sophisticated digital lending and Buy Now, Pay Later (BNPL) ecosystems. These models integrate financial technology, data analytics, artificial intelligence (AI), and blockchain to enhance accessibility and operational efficiency (Gulati 2024; Arner et al. 2020). Digital lending platforms now enable end-to-end credit processing—application, assessment, disbursal, and repayment—through automated systems, significantly reducing turnaround time and expanding financial inclusion among underserved groups (CEGA and IPA 2023; OECD 2022a, b).

BNPL schemes, in particular, have revolutionized consumer finance by embedding deferred payment options within e-commerce transactions, offering short-term, interest-free credit alternatives (McKinsey and Company 2023). In emerging economies like India, platforms such as ZestMoney and LazyPay have adopted localized models that leverage alternative data for credit evaluation, aligning with the Reserve Bank of India's (RBI 2022) guidelines for responsible digital lending. However, this technological innovation has introduced complex risks including data breaches, synthetic identity fraud, algorithmic bias, and cyber-attacks (World Economic Forum 2023; FCA 2023).

While the rise of digital credit ecosystems promotes financial inclusion and economic growth, it also amplifies exposure to fraud, operational failures, and governance challenges. Weak KYC verification, opaque algorithmic scoring, and rapid on boarding processes can undermine consumer trust and regulatory compliance (CGAP 2025; RBI 2022). Consequently, balancing innovation with ethical risk management and data protection has become a central policy concern across jurisdictions (OECD 2022a, b; EBA 2024).

The present chapter explores the fraud risks, detection mechanisms, and regulatory strategies shaping digital lending and BNPL ecosystems. It examines structural vulnerabilities, typologies of financial fraud, and evolving AI-based preventive frameworks within the context of India's fintech landscape and global regulatory developments. The analysis underscores the imperative of integrating governance, ethics, and technological resilience to sustain a secure, inclusive, and transparent digital financial system (University of Sydney Business School 2023; Bouriche et al. 2025).

2 Evolution of Digital Lending and BNPL Models

2.1 Defining Digital Lending and BNPL

Digital lending and BNPL are structurally different even though both rely on automated on boarding and data-driven credit evaluation. Digital lending is more susceptible to identity theft and documentation fraud because it usually involves longer-term more expensive loans that are evaluated using more extensive KYC bureau checks and income verification frameworks. In contrast BNPL is a low-cost short-term embedded credit product that is approved in a matter of seconds during the checkout process and requires little KYC, making it vulnerable to transactional manipulation merchant collusion and first-party fraud. Additionally, regulators handle these differently, while BNPL providers in many jurisdictions continue to operate outside of traditional credit regulations digital lenders are fully subject to banking/NBFC norms. This distinction is essential for understanding why the two systems experience different risk pattern and regulatory responses.

Digital lending encompasses the end-to-end process of the loan life cycle right from the application, credit assessment, disbursement and refinancing through digital platforms without any human interaction. This innovation is the key for the Fintech revolution, which combines traditional finance with digital technologies to improve accessibility on processing speed, operational efficiency (Arner et al. 2020). Through automated credit system/scoring, KYC (know Your Customer) and Artificial intelligence decision systems, financial institutions can provide and approve loans within a few minutes. This model has particularly benefited underserved consumers and micro-enterprises who previously lacked formal credit histories due to insufficient credit records (OECD 2022a, b).

Under digital lending, Buy Now, Pay Later (BNPL) services enable consumers to shop the items instantly and settle their payment in deferred installments, which is interest free (McKinsey and Company 2023). BNPL platforms like Klarna, Afterpay, and Affirm integrate these seamlessly into the online i.e. e-commerce store payment pages, offering an embedded credit facility that bypasses the complications associated with the conventional credit cards. In developing countries, business firms like ZestMoney and LazyPay have adopted this model to fit their regional contexts, utilizing non-traditional data sources to assess on creditworthiness of borrowers with limited credit backgrounds (RBI 2022).

Digital lending covers a wide range of financial products such as personal loans, small and medium enterprises loans, and microloans, BNPL specifically targets short-term duration consumer financing embedding within retail transactions. Both these rely on data-driven risk evaluation, digital customer registration, and computerized accounting services with key differentiators from the traditional banking practices. Together, they demonstrate how technological transformation has shifted credit offering from an institutional service to a digital enable platform (EY 2023).

2.2 Operational Frameworks and Technological Enablers

The technical framework of digital lending and BNPL ecosystems consists of an integrated array of application programming interfaces, cloud-based infrastructure and AI-driven decision engines. These elements enable lenders to process a vast number of transactions instantaneously while maintaining their administrative expenses (PwC 2023).

2.2.1 Structure of the Platform

Many of the digital lending platforms are structured in three layers: a front-end user interface (app or web portal) a middle-tier, machine learning (ML)-powered decision engine and a back-end integration layer that is linked to credit bureaus and payment gateways (World Bank 2022). The front-end manages digital onboarding on customer registration, while the intermediate tier automates the loan approval process using the data model that assesses on the likelihood of timely repayment. The back-end infrastructure is typically hosted on cloud services to ensure scalability and adherence to compliance with security protocols such as ISO 27001.

2.2.2 Data Analytics and Innovative Scoring

Traditional credit rating systems like FIFCO and CIBIL predominantly assess borrowing history, which limits opportunities for individuals without credit profiles. Digital financial institutions leverage alternative data sources like cellular phone activity, utility payments, online-shopping patterns, and psychological assessments to extract behavioral indicators and forecast on creditworthiness (OECD 2022a, b). For instance, artificial intelligence algorithms can determine reliability based on mobile top-ups or rental payments, thereby expanding access to gig economy participants and first-time borrowers (RBI 2022).

2.2.3 AI and Risk Management

Artificial intelligence technologies play a fundamental role in instantaneous lending decisions. Forecasting algorithms uncover latent patterns linking borrower behavior with debt repayment capacity, while NLP analyzes the conversational patterns to identify anomalies during account setup (Arner et al. 2020).

To create dynamic credit lifecycle certain platforms also use adaptive credit limits that change according to user repayment performance (Accenture 2024).

2.2.4 API Ecosystems and Cloud Computing

Cloud-based systems minimize capital costs while enabling lenders to grow quickly. APIs (Application Programming Interfaces) facilitate communication with digital wallets, neobanks and e-commerce platforms. According to (McKinsey and Company 2023) real-time APIs help BNPL approve transactions almost instantly at the checkout page which lowers transaction friction and enhances customer satisfaction. Credit becomes an unseen but crucial component of the purchasing process in the resulting embedded finance model marking a significant paradigm shift.

2.2.5 Emerging Trends: Blockchain and Smart Contracts

The use of blockchain technologies for safe loan disbursement and repayment verification is growing. Installment schedules can be automated with smart contracts which lowers operational errors and fraud. Pilot projects are implementing decentralized identity frameworks like self-sovereign IDs to improve KYC verification and reduce synthetic identity fraud (World Economic Forum 2023). It is forecasted that these technology advancements will enhance traceability and compliance despite their limited adoption. Together these tech enablers form a strong ecosystem that boosts efficiency and financial inclusion. Nevertheless, they also bring about new vulnerabilities that call for proactive governance such as algorithmic opacity data privacy risks and third-party dependencies (FCA 2023).

2.3 Market Growth, Consumer Adoption, and Financial Inclusion Impact

The global digital lending market has grown rapidly, driven by the widespread use of mobile penetration, digital payments and consumer focused credit models. According to the report by Market Research (2024), digital payments will reach USD 45 trillion by 2030 with a growth CAGR of 20%. Simultaneously, BNPL transactions are forecast to represent almost 30% in global e-commerce payments by 2028 (McKinsey and Company 2023).

2.3.1 Drivers of Growth

In support of this growth four structural trends underpin:

1. **Cashless transformation:** The emergence of digital payment infrastructure such as India's UPI, Brazil Pix and Singapore PayNow has normalized digital payments (World Bank 2022).

2. **Financial Inclusion Policies**: Regulators are encouraged to support Fin Tech innovation to reach unbanked populations (RBI 2022).
3. **Credit Platform**: By integrating credit within their E-commerce platform, it will increase reach thereby lowering acquisition costs (EY 2023).
4. **Pandemic acceleration**: COVID-19 accelerated the spread of digital credit tools as consumers sought remote contactless financial services (OECD 2022a, b).

2.3.2 Consumer Adoption Patterns

The adoption of BNPL is strongly skewed toward Gen Z and millennial consumers who place a high value on openness and flexibility. The average transaction size in India is less than ₹10,000 with 60% of BNPL users being under 30 (RBI 2022). BNPL is seen as a less expensive option than credit cards in developed markets like the UK and Australia. Retention has been further boosted by customer loyalty programs and smooth checkout procedures.

2.3.3 Financial Inclusion Effects

Digital lending has emerged as a key component of inclusive finance, especially for informal trader's gig workers and microbusiness owners. Lenders can provide microloans to people who are shut out of the official banking system by utilizing alternative data and behavioral analytics (World Bank 2022). Particularly helping women and rural business owners, the partnership between FinTechs and national digital infrastructure like India Stack has expedited credit access and verification (OECD 2022a, b). However, the story of inclusion needs to be balanced with caution. Without robust consumer protection rapid data-driven credit expansion may result in excessive debt data abuse and an increase in defaults. Regulators are now focusing on frameworks for responsible digital lending that integrate innovation and consumer safety (FCA 2023).

2.4 Structural Vulnerabilities and Emerging Risks

Despite their transformation potential, digital lending and the BNPL ecosystem face distinct structural and operational vulnerabilities. The same attributes that propel scale and efficiency also put them at risk and expose them to new forms of digital fraud and systemic risk.

2.4.1 Onboarding and Identity Hazards

By combining real and fake credentials to create fraudulent borrower profiles synthetic identity creation can be used to circumvent remote KYC and e-signature procedures (PwC 2023). Increasingly fraudsters open numerous accounts on various platforms before being discovered by using stolen Aadhaar or PAN information.

2.4.2 Credential Theft and Account Takeover

Phishing SIM swapping and credential stuffing attacks can affect lending through apps. Once access is compromised fraudsters can harvest sensitive user data change repayment schedules or redirect payouts (FCA 2023).

2.4.3 Opacity of the Model and Algorithmic Bias

Unintentional biases in training data may be reinforced by AI-powered credit scoring. Accountability and auditability are further complicated by opaque model decisions which give fraudulent actors the opportunity to take advantage of blind spots (OECD 2022a, b). Explainable AI is currently the focus of regulatory initiatives to guarantee equity and openness in lending models.

2.4.4 APIs and Dependencies on Third Parties

BNPL providers depend on intricate networks of partners including data aggregators, payment gateways and merchants. Any node in this ecosystem could have a breach that exposes enormous amounts of customer data. These days the top five operational risks in digital finance are API exploitation and vendor compromises (World Economic Forum 2023).

2.4.5 Fraud by Merchant Collusion and First-Party

In contrast to external fraud, first-party fraud entails intentional borrower default or fraudulent claims made by authorized users. Likewise, a growing problem in BNPL systems is merchant collusion in which vendors and fictitious buyers' band together to mimic transactions (PwC 2023).

2.4.6 Oversight Issues and Regulatory Gaps

For instance, BNPL firms in many jurisdictions are not yet categorized as credit providers, allowing them to function outside traditional credit laws. The Financial

Conduct Authority (FCA 2023) and Reserve Bank of India (RBI 2022) have taken action to standardize consumer protection in data governance and disclosure norms.

2.4.7 Cybersecurity Risks

Due to their extensive consumer data collection digital lenders are particularly vulnerable to cyberattacks. According to the (World Economic Forum 2023), ransomware incidents or identity resale breaches undermine consumer trust and make it easier for downstream fraud to occur. In short, the evolution of the digital**c**redit ecosystem is a two-pronged sword: it advances on inclusion and efficiency; on the other hand it demands stronger frameworks for risk governance, transparency and algorithmic accountability.

3 Understanding Fraud Risks in Digital Credit Ecosystems

3.1 The Innovation-Risk Tradeoff in Fintech

The technological transition of lending and credit products has delivered an unparalleled blend of financial inclusion, user convenience and streamlined operation efficiency. However, this progress introduces a contradiction as the credit system becomes faster and seamless, they become increasingly vulnerable in exposure to fraudulent activities and widespread threats (Arner et al. 2020). The "innovation-risk trade off" captures the tension between technological advancement and weaking of conventional protection measures like manual verification, physical documentation on records, and extended credit assessment processes.

Within digital lending and BNPL systems, algorithms that automated handle most of the credit approval process, it reduces the assessment periods from days to mere seconds. Though this enhances user satisfaction and business scalability, it also reduces human monitoring and creates open for vulnerability for fraudsters who exploit system speed and information dependencies (OECD 2022a, b). For example, real time fund disbursal systems often bypass manual irregularity reviews, enabling fraudulent applications to gain approval before risk control checkout. Likewise, in BNPL transactions, where credit is granted at the point of sale-risk evaluation happens within milliseconds, providing minimal resistance to fabricated or self-perpetrated fraud (McKinsey and Company 2023).

This paradox becomes especially evident in economies where digital integration has outpaced regulatory development. Many financial institutions operate multiple jurisdictions with disparate data privacy and identification verification norms, resulting in fragmented risk oversight. Additionally, AI and machine learning systems that support credit scoring may unintentionally amplify fraud risk when developed using skewed, insufficient or manipulated datasets (Accenture 2024).

The drive of swift customer onboarding, market share, and frictionless customer experience therefore frequently conflicts with imperative fraud mitigation. Striking the appropriate balance between innovation agility and risk management discipline remains the primary governance challenge in the contemporary digital credit environment.

3.2 *Fraudulent Activity Typologies*

Synthetic identity fraud refers to the creation of wholly fictional identity by combing real and fake information, making them difficult to detect because they do not correspond to any real individual existence (World Economic Forum 2023). Fraudulent behavior in the digital lending and BNPL ecosystem appears across several interrelated typologies, each targeting vulnerabilities within digital lending frameworks, authentication processes and user conduct. The most common forms encompass identity theft, fabricated identity schemes, unauthorized account takeover and credential abuse, and authorized user or first part frauds.

3.2.1 Identity Theft

The unlawful use of another person's personal information such as their driver's license bank login credentials PAN or Aadhaar to obtain credit facilities or carry out transactions is known as identity theft (PwC 2023). This threat has increased due to the creation of new attack surfaces brought about by the widespread use of digital KYC and remote onboarding. Data breaches, phishing schemes and social engineering tactics supply fraudsters with authentic identity elements that can be used to impersonate victims. Before the victims even realized identity data that had been stolen from e-commerce breaches was used to apply for microloans on a few FinTech platforms in a number of well-publicized cases throughout Asia (FCA, 2023). Such impersonation is made easier by the lack of AI-based document forensics and biometric cross-verification. fraud involving a false identity.

3.2.2 Synthetic Identity Fraud

A more sophisticated form of identity theft is synthetic identity fraud in which scammers create completely new online identities by fusing authentic and fake credentials (World Economic Forum 2023). Synthetic identities are very difficult to detect because in contrast to traditional impersonation they cannot be directly linked to real people. These identities often begin with a legitimate national ID number or email address paired with falsified demographic details gradually building a digital footprint through small low-risk transactions before scaling to larger credit lines (OECD 2022a, b). Because credit bureaus record these fake profiles as authentic borrowers, lenders unintentionally validate the fraudster's digital identity. In 2023, global losses from synthetic identity fraud were estimated to exceed USD 20 billion, due to inadequate cross-platform verification as per (Allied Market Research 2024).

3.2.3 Account Takeover and Credential Misuse

When cybercriminals gain unauthorized access to a legitimate user account they often through phishing, SIM swaps or malware infections carry out fraudulent activity known as Account takeover (ATO) fraud (World Bank 2022). This may entail making unauthorized withdrawals, modifying associated bank accounts or changing repayment terms in the context of digital lending. Auto-debit features and stored payment credentials make BNPL providers especially susceptible. One compromised user account can be used to make expensive purchases from several different retailers before being discovered (McKinsey and Company 2023). The issue is exacerbated by credential stuffing which is the practice of using stolen login information from one platform on another. Reusing passwords across FinTech apps is the root cause of more than 60% of ATO incidents according to research by the World Economic Forum (2023).

3.2.4 Friendly and First-Party Frauds

First party or friendly fraud differs from external fraud in that it involves reputable clients who purposefully default or falsify repayment terms. Users who engage in BNPL take advantage of periods of low or zero interest repayment to make purchases and then purposefully dispute transactions or neglect to make installment payments (RBI 2022). Strategic defaults are used by some who take advantage of disjointed reporting systems so that defaults on one BNPL platform do not instantly appear on others (EY 2023). Borrowers may fabricate digital documents or inflate their income claims on peer-to-peer lending and microcredit platforms. Invoice fraud and ghost merchants are becoming more common which increases the risk of first-party fraud (PwC 2023).

As BNPL adoption broadens, differentiating between actual financial distress and intentional deceptions has become a major operational challenge. Together, these typologies illustrate how identity fragility, data silos, and behavioral loopholes inherent in rapid digitalization can still threaten the digital ecosystem with technological advancements.

The interconnected nature of these fraud typologies highlights on digital lenders and BNPL firms need sophisticated, data-driven fraud detection mechanisms systems rather than relying solely on conventional rule-based monitoring. The next sections explore the structural causes driving these fraud patterns and the role of technology-enabled attempt in addressing them.

3.3 Root Causes: Speed, Scale, and Limited Credit Vetting

Fraud rings refer to coordinated criminal groups that systematically exploit platform weakness across multiple layouts, which often using sharing devices, identities and payment instruments to evade discovery. Three structural factors, scale and limited credit vetting that characterize the FinTech platform operating model are at the core of most digital credit frauds. Nowadays the key to success in digital lending is speed. Although same-day disbursements and instant approvals draw customers they leave little time for multi-layered verification. By submitting fraudulent applications during times of high volume when automated systems are less alert to irregularities, fraudsters take advantage of this shortened timeframe (Accenture 2024).

Scale increases the exposure to risk even more. Everyday millions of microtransactions are processed even though a tiny portion of fraudulent activity results in large financial losses. Due to the decentralized databases used by many BNPL providers worldwide, transaction monitoring has blind spots (World Economic Forum 2023).

Cross-platform detection is still dispersed in the absence of centralized KYC verification or shared fraud registries. Complicating the problem is limited credit vetting. Digital lenders are increasingly using alternative data scoring methods such as social media activity, mobile usage or psychometric indicators in place of traditional credit histories in their efforts to promote financial inclusion (OECD 2022a, b). This makes it easier for new borrowers to obtain loans, but it also makes it harder to see how reliable long-term repayment is. To appear creditworthy fraudsters can create fake activity or alter behavioral data. Furthermore AI-powered scoring systems frequently operate as black boxes making it difficult to interpret rejection or approval decisions (FCA 2023).

Operational demands to increase client acquisition frequently take precedence over risk reduction. Particularly in the startup stages place a higher priority on growth metrics—like app downloads or disbursal volume—than on fraud control investment (EY 2023). Serial fraud rings synthetic ID networks and bot-driven application attacks that take advantage of consistent verification logic across several lenders thrive on the resulting vulnerabilities. A fundamental rethinking of risk architecture is therefore required even though digital credit platforms offer previously unheard-of scalability. This is because their structural design inherently sacrifices scrutiny for speed.

3.4 Comparative Vulnerabilities: Digital Lending Versus BNPL

Despite operating in the same FinTech ecosystem, digital lending and BNPL have different fraud exposure patterns because of structural and operational differences. In general, digital lending platforms are more vulnerable to identity and documentation issues especially when it comes to loan origination and underwriting. Fraudsters target these systems with forged income proofs, fake documentation and synthetic profiles because loan values are usually higher and tenures are longer (World Bank 2022). Additionally repeat offenders can take advantage of several platforms at once due to data-sharing gaps between banks FinTech startups and non-bank financial companies (NBFCs) (RBI 2022).

BNPL fraud on the other hand thrives on consumer impulsivity and transactional velocity. A thorough KYC or affordability assessment is limited by the embedded nature of BNPL credit which is completed in a matter of seconds at e-commerce checkouts (McKinsey and Company 2023). Fraudsters take advantage of frequent low-cost purchases that frequently evade closer examination.

Risk is further increased by merchant collusion coordinated schemes involving phony merchants and phony customers can produce fictitious transaction histories in order to obtain payouts (PwC 2023). Furthermore, because users frequently view short-term installment defaults as unimportant, BNPL platforms are especially vulnerable to first-party fraud. Because many jurisdictions lack complete regulatory oversight, delinquent behavior may not have an immediate impact on credit scores (FCA 2023).

Digital lenders on the other hand usually integrate with credit bureaus which enables early detection of non-performance. From a system's perspective digital lending systems are subject to more complex identity-based attacks whereas BNPL ecosystems are more susceptible to quick small-scale fraud. Due to overlapping vulnerabilities created by the two's convergence through hybrid pay-later loan products and unified fraud detection frameworks utilizing AI-based behavioral analytics and real-time anomaly tracking are required (Accenture 2024). Ultimately, understanding these comparative weaknesses is critical for developing customized fraud mitigation architectures that align with the transaction speed, customer demographics, and risk tolerance for each credit approach.

4 Fraud Patterns and Case Illustrations

4.1 Fraud Activities in Digital Lending

Fraudulent activities in digital lending platforms follow predictable pathways that take advantage of the relationship between accelerated customer fragmentation and unclear algorithmic processes. The most frequent points included are application phase, loan-stacking from numerous platforms and post-disbursal fund release (PwC 2023). During the application stage, fraudsters exploit the efficiency of automated credit approvals by providing falsified counterfeit documents or stolen credentials before the verification system can cross-reference with government databases. In several cases across India and Southeast Asia, fabricated salary slips, and digitally modified identification proofs enable perpetrators to secure small loans within seconds (RBI 2022). Reactive detection is useless since many platforms use straight-through-processing which means that verification happens only after loans are disbursed (World Bank 2022).

Another popular method is **loan-stacking** in which borrowers concurrently obtain several small loans from various online lenders. Fraudulent actors can take advantage of data reporting latency, lack of a unified real-time credit registry (OECD 2022a, b). African FinTech's saw a spike in coordinated loan-stacking rings using shared devices and rotating SIM cards between 2021 and 2023 (World Economic Forum 2023).

Post-disbursal fraud can involve cyber manipulation of repayment schedules, collusion with internal staff or diversion of authorized funds. To reroute loan proceeds to mule accounts, skilled actors breach APIs. The Monetary Authority of Singapore reported several instances in 2022 where borrower devices infected with malware changed beneficiary information following loan approval (FCA 2023).

Insider-enabled fraud can also affect digital lenders. Employees who manually whitelist questionable applications may take advantage of algorithmic bias or override permissions in automated underwriting systems. These examples show that although AI lessens human intervention human-facilitated vulnerabilities still exist (Accenture 2024). When taken, these pathways show that fraud in digital lending is typically systemic, taking advantage of technological interconnections and governance that come with quick digital scaling.

4.2 Fraud Pathways in BNPL Platforms

Due to embedded merchant-integrated architecture, BNPL platforms display unique fraud patterns. According to (McKinsey and Company 2023) BNPL systems prioritize speed over scrutiny because the credit decision is made at checkout which makes it easy for both internal and external manipulation to take place.

The most prevalent form is merchant-consumer collusion in which fake buyers and merchants' band together to mimic sales and demand payments. On online marketplaces, scammers set up phony stores, place fictitious orders and obtain immediate payouts from BNPL suppliers. Platforms suffer irreversible losses because of failed refund claims or chargeback disputes (EY 2023).

Device-based and behavioral spoofing are another avenue. VPNs or emulator environments can fool BNPL algorithms that use device fingerprinting and geolocation as risk factors. Clusters of virtual devices known as digital farms are used by organized fraud groups to simulate authentic consumer behavior and test several stolen cards or identities at once (World Economic Forum 2023).

One category that is both financially significant and softer is promo abuse. Users repeatedly sign up using slightly altered credentials to take advantage of introductory offers such as cashback incentives or zero-interest plans. Even though there might be a small loss in each case millions of tiny transactions add up to a big impact (PwC 2023).

Additionally, prevalent are return fraud and refund manipulation. Fraudsters return fake goods, ask for refunds to other accounts or buy products using BNPL. Refund discrepancy detection becomes difficult since merchant payment gateway and BNPL provider reconciliation frequently take place asynchronously (FCA 2023).

This multi-layered vulnerability was demonstrated in a recent 2023 case in Australia where a BNPL provider suffered losses of over USD 12 million as a result of synthetic customers making large-scale low-ticket purchases from fake merchants over a 3-week period prior to detection (McKinsey and Company 2023). Lastly, scams that use social engineering directly target customers.

To take over accounts' scammers impersonating customer support agents convince users to divulge payment links or OTPs. Even when the platform is not held legally responsible these scams damage brand equity and trust (RBI 2022). These examples highlight how BNPL fraud is transactional flexible and reputational vulnerabilities are spread throughout the triad of platforms merchants and consumers.

4.3 Cross-Platform Fraud Behaviors and Emerging Trends

These days fraud is more often cross-platform going beyond specific lenders or payment methods. Fraud rings take advantage of data silos between banks, FinTech companies and retailers by functioning as coordinated ecosystems (World Bank 2022). This convergence is characterized by three new trends: AI-driven deception methods, fraud-as-a-service (FaaS) models and multi-channel identity exploitation.

When the same stolen or fake identity is used repeatedly across several financial platforms, BNPL payday loans cryptocurrency wallets and neobanks—before being discovered this is known as multi-channel identity exploitation. Fraudsters maintain operational continuity because these organizations hardly ever exchange real-time KYC data. In the U.S during 2023 the Federal Trade Commission received more than 1.1 million cross-platform identity complaints (OECD 2022a, b).

The second development, Fraud-as-a-Service, involves structured criminal networks providing subscription-based platforms that automate fraudulent application creation, login credential validation, and deepfake identity production (World Economic Forum 2023). Internet based fraud applications programming interfaces and encrypted messaging marketplaces have commoditized deception. Emerging players in Fintech markets, lacking established fraud surveillance capabilities, frequently become early victims.

The third and most concerning progress is the use of employing generative AI for fraudulent purposes. Deepfake audio-visual tools permit fabricated borrowers to successfully navigate KYC via video verification sessions. Computer based generated selfies can now replicate live-capture requirements employed in e-KYC processes (Accenture 2024). Criminals additionally weaponize advanced language models to compose phishing communication indistinguishable from legitimate BNPL correspondence or message alerts.

These trends indicate a shift from sporadic, isolated fraud to industrialized, coordinated deception. As Fintech ecosystems integrate shared banking APIs and digital identification systems, inter-platform vulnerabilities increase. Without a compatible fraud detection database, a security breach becomes one provider threatens all platforms at risk (EY 2023). This case is illustrated with evidence in 2022 on the loan-app crisis. The compromised data from unregulated apps were repurposed to infiltrate mainstream NBFC platforms, leading to cascading defaults across multiple lenders (RBI 2022). In a similar vein BNPL providers in Europe reported coordinated bot attacks that took advantage of identical verification APIs used by rival companies (FCA 2023).

Moving forward, experts suggest that behavioral biometrics, federated learning and collaborative fraud databases are viable countermeasures. Nevertheless, adoption remains inconsistent specifically in smaller enterprises constrained by regulatory costs (World Economic Forum 2023).

4.4 *Economic Costs and Reputational Damage for FinTech Entities*

The consequence of fraud reaches beyond the balance sheet; it strikes the foundation trust of the economy that underpin digital finance. The financial damage is multidimensional, it encompasses direct write-offs, increasing spending on compliance expenditure and weak the confidence of the investors.

According to PWC's 2023 research report, global fintech companies collectively forfeit more than USD 50 billion each year due to fraudulent activities in digital lending and BNPL services. These figures include chargeback expenses, bad debt and remediation expenses. In addition, firms allocate as much as 12% of their operational budgets to fraud management which diminishes profitability (Allied Market Research 2024). Startups in the early stage which typically function under thin margins, confront existential risk from fraud exposure.

From a regulatory perspective, elevated fraud rates trigger heightened scrutiny. The (Reserve Bank of India 2022) imposed strict due diligence and lending disclosure requirements following consumer reports on unauthorized charges by rogue apps. Likewise, The U.K.'s (FCA 2023) introduced extensive buy now pay later regulatory interventions to solve concealed default accumulation. Although necessary regulatory actions hinder innovation and raise compliance costs which furthers the risk-innovation paradox (Arner et al. 2020).

The brand impact dimensions are even more significant. Fintech companies depend on consumer perception of safety and ease. Each fraud incident erodes confidence not only in one firm but in the entire digital credit category. Adverse press coverage following the loan-app scandals in India in 2022 led to a drop of 27% in consumer trust metrics according to the wider Fintech Sector (EY 2023). Investment pattern typically mirrors this erosion of trust' venture funding to consumer lending also decreased substantially in 2023 as investors prioritized regulatory compliance over growth potential (World Economic Forum 2023).

Persistent fraud threatens the financial inclusion agenda on a macroeconomic scale. The inclusion gains brought about by digital innovation are reversed when lenders tighten risk parameters in response to fraud excluding legitimate low-income borrowers once more (World Bank 2022). Furthermore, systemic data breaches expose sensitive demographic data for a longer period of time than just the transaction itself. For consumers, consequences include stolen identity, credit ratings being damaged and psychological distress. The absence of effective compliant resolution processes on many BNPL platforms exacerbates these damages (FCA 2023). For merchants, illegitimate payment reversals may lead to accounting suspension and liquidity disruptions. For oversight bodies, rising fraud rates undermine public confidence in national digital-payment frameworks.

Ultimately, fraud is not only a mere cost of operational expenditure, but it represents a strategic threat to Fintech viability. As (Accenture 2024) observes it as "trust capital" has emerged in defining a new metric of competitiveness in digital banking. Firms that integrate fraud-resilience through interpretable artificial intelligence and transparent consumer remedy processes will secure more advantages in both regulatory and market valuation.

5 Advanced Fraud Detection and Prevention Strategies

The above sections showed a constant increase of vulnerabilities in rapidly expanding digital lending. Fraud risks such as synthetic identities, account takeovers, merchant collusion and cross-platform arise from fast onboarding, limited credit checks, fragmented data systems and evolving AI-enabled fraud tactics. This section addresses these issues and provides insights by explaining why traditional rule-based models fail against these complex patterns. Further, it highlights how AI, ML, behavioral analytics, and risk-based scoring directly address the fraud pathways identified earlier. It also stresses strong model governance to ensure transparency, fairness, and compliance.

The Technological growth has transformed credit services such as personal loans, credit cards, and BNPL schemes. While enhancing convenience, these digital systems have opened new channels for financial crime. Hence, the central question for financial institutions is not whether fraud will occur, but how to prevent it effectively. Artificial Intelligence (AI) and Machine Learning (ML) now play decisive roles in this effort.

5.1 Limitations of Traditional, Rule-Based Systems

Rule-based fraud detection models once offered transparency and consistency but now struggle against adaptive, complex fraud patterns. Their static thresholds produce excessive false positives and require frequent manual updates.

India's digital lending sector, with its diverse borrowers and high transaction volumes, magnifies these challenges. The Reserve Bank of India's (RBI 2023) regulatory framework stresses explainability, data quality, and technology enablement, highlighting the inadequacy of legacy models. To ensure trust and compliance, institutions must adopt AI-driven, data-centric approaches.

Globally, regulatory bodies are adopting data-focused fraud detection frameworks in line with the EU's Digital Finance Strategy and EBA Guidelines, which emphasize advanced analytics and real-time monitoring to mitigate systemic risk (EBA 2021).

In a similar way, the MAS and FCA are endorsing AI-driven behavioral and anomaly-detection models to reinforce resilience against digital fraud. Research indicates that traditional methods using fixed predefined detection models are ineffective in combating the swiftly changing cross-platform fraud networks (PwC 2023).

This global alignment in regulations indicates a transition towards AI-powered, self-learning systems that improve accuracy, compliance, and consumer protection, a trend that is increasingly evident in India's digital lending reforms.

5.2 Artificial Intelligence (AI) and Machine Learning (ML) in Fraud Detection

AI and ML have redefined fraud management by detecting behavioral anomalies and predicting fraudulent intent in real time. As fintech and BNPL transactions grow, risks like identity theft and synthetic profiles demand advanced models (PwC 2025a, b). Algorithms such as random forests, neural networks, and graph-based analytics enable institutions to process multidimensional data—device fingerprints, IPs, and user behavior—to identify hidden fraud (ResearchGate 2025).

India's young, digital BNPL users make AI tools essential for risk control and regulatory compliance (PwC 2025a, b). Internationally, regulators such as the EBA and FCA (2024–25) promote AI for AML and KYC. Firms like Klarna, PayPal, and Afterpay use deep learning for real-time fraud detection and reduced false alerts (World Economic Forum 2023), reflecting a global shift to ethical, predictive fraud management.

5.2.1 AI-Powered Transaction Monitoring

India's fintech ecosystem—spanning UPI, digital lending, and BNPL—faces vast transaction flows and evolving fraud tactics. Traditional monitoring is ineffective; hence, AI-ML systems are being integrated for adaptive risk detection. The RBI (2022) mandates transparency and accountability in AI-based credit and fraud systems, while NPCI (2023) applies AI for early detection in payment infrastructure.

Firms like Razorpay and Paytm use predictive models such as FraudShield to flag irregular transactions (Razorpay 2024). Wipro's AI-AML frameworks enhance compliance and adaptive learning (Wipro 2024). Global regulators—including the U.S. OCC, EU, and MAS—endorse responsible AI in fraud management (OCC 2019).

5.2.2 Risk-Based Decision-Making Models

Risk-Based Decision-Making (RBDM) models use algorithmic risk scoring to detect anomalies, balance convenience, and prevent fraud. Under RBI (2022) and DLAI (2023) guidelines, lenders employ ML and network analytics for identity verification and post-transaction monitoring. Such systems improve KYC, credit scoring, and transparency (Patil 2024).

Internationally, EBA (2024) and FATF (2023) promote RBDM for data-driven oversight. The U.S., U.K., and Singapore employ AI-enabled models for ethical, predictive fraud detection (OECD 2022a, b).

5.2.3 Behavioral Analytics and User Pattern Recognition

Behavioral analytics enhance fraud prevention by identifying transaction velocity, device use, and geolocation anomalies (Patil 2024). The RBI (2022) mandates consent-based use of behavioral data. These models expose synthetic identities and collusive networks while maintaining user experience (PwC 2025a, b).

By merging behavioral and network analytics, institutions can identify organized fraud rings and improve early alerts. Global regulators such as the EBA and the U.S. Federal Reserve advocate explainable AI for monitoring identity fraud (EBA 2024). Companies like Klarna and Afterpay already apply behavioral risk scoring to maintain security with minimal user friction.

5.3 Data-Driven Risk Management Frameworks

Data-driven frameworks using predictive analytics now underpin fraud risk control in India's digital lending. The RBI (2022) promotes transparency and data accountability. Fintechs and NBFCs combine structured and unstructured data to detect anomalies and prevent identity fraud.

AI-based systems outperform traditional models, particularly in high-volume BNPL transactions. Studies highlight the value of behavioral and network analytics against digital identity exploitation. Globally, regulators like the EBA (2024) and emphasize fairness and transparency, while firms such as Klarna and Affirm employ predictive tools for real-time monitoring.

5.4 Implementation Challenges and Model Governance

Integrating AI-driven fraud systems faces challenges such as legacy infrastructure, poor data interoperability, and compliance burdens. RBI's Digital Lending Guidelines (2022) and the Data Protection Act (2023) enforce consent and privacy, complicating implementation. Limited credit histories in BNPL add risks of false positives and bias.

Effective governance requires interpretability, traceability, and human oversight in AI life cycles. Institutions now adopt audits, fairness checks, and stress testing to mitigate bias (DPDP 2023). Globally, the EU AI Act (2024) and U.S. FCRA stress ethical and transparent automated decision-making. These governance measures strengthen accountability and trust in India's fast-evolving digital finance ecosystem.

6 The Regulatory and Compliance Landscape

The significance of AI, ML, and behavioral analytics in identifying fraud patterns within digital lending is discussed in the previous section. Consequently, this section focuses on the regulatory framework established by the regulators and institutions like RBI, EBA, MAS, FATF, and CFPB that guarantee these advanced systems function ethically and responsibly.

6.1 Global and Regional Regulatory Developments

The emergence of digital lending has elicited varied regulatory responses worldwide. International bodies such as the Financial Action Task Force (FATF), the Basel Committee, and the Organisation for Economic Co-operation and Development

(OECD) emphasize risk-based supervision, transparency, and consumer protection (FATF 2021; OECD 2022a, b). Europe maintains one of the most comprehensive frameworks, combining data protection under the General Data Protection Regulation (GDPR), digital payments legislation, and the Artificial Intelligence (AI) Act, which introduces ethical guidelines for credit scoring. In the United States, the Consumer Financial Protection Bureau (CFPB) applies a consumer-centric regulatory approach toward Buy Now, Pay Later (BNPL) schemes, focusing on disclosure, dispute resolution, and consistency within existing consumer protection frameworks.

In India, the Reserve Bank of India (RBI) issued the Guidelines on Digital Lending (2022) to enhance data privacy, transparency, and accountability among banks, non-banking financial companies (NBFCs), and Lending Service Providers (LSPs). These measures strengthen disclosure norms, promote responsible lending conduct, and ensure robust grievance redressal mechanisms (RBI 2022).

6.2 Compliance Obligations for Fintech and BNPL Providers

Fintech and BNPL providers face multidimensional regulatory compliance, encompassing licensing, anti-money laundering (AML) and Know Your Customer (KYC) protocols, data governance, and fair-lending obligations. In India, only regulated entities such as banks and NBFCs can extend digital credit, while LSPs must comply with RBI's transparency and grievance redressal standards (RBI 2022).

Globally, regulatory authorities stress full disclosure of loan terms, repayment schedules, and penalties to ensure fairness. The CFPB mandates BNPL firms to maintain clear consumer-facing disclosures and accessible dispute resolution systems. Data privacy obligations under the EU's GDPR and India's Digital Personal Data Protection Act (DPDP 2023) govern consent-based data use, breach reporting, and accountability mechanisms.

6.3 Data Privacy, Consumer Protection, and Ethical AI Concerns

Digital lending models rely heavily on personal and behavioral data, heightening privacy and ethical concerns. India's DPDP Act (2023) establishes a national framework for lawful data processing, replacing the earlier IT Act provisions, and aligns with the GDPR's principles of consent, data minimization, and user rights.

AI-driven lending and credit scoring introduce ethical challenges such as algorithmic bias, discrimination, and opacity. RBI's (2022) digital lending guidelines mandate transparent pricing, responsible data use, and accountability between regulated entities and LSPs. The DPDP Act reinforces lawful data processing and fiduciary duties toward consumers.

Globally, the EU AI Act (2024) adopts a risk-based approach, prohibiting manipulative AI practices and mandating transparency in automated decision-making. The CFPB in the U.S. ensures that lenders provide clear, actionable explanations for credit denials and maintain compliance with fair-lending laws.

6.4 Supervisory Technology (SupTech) and Regulatory Technology (RegTech)

The rise of digital lending and BNPL ecosystems necessitates the integration of technology-driven compliance and supervision tools. Regulatory Technology (RegTech) assists financial institutions in automating AML/KYC checks, regulatory reporting, and real-time risk monitoring. Conversely, Supervisory Technology (SupTech) empowers regulators with data analytics, anomaly detection, and AI-enabled market surveillance (OECD 2022a, b).

Both RegTech and SupTech enhance compliance efficiency, transparency, and consumer protection while reducing operational costs. Their convergence supports ethical AI governance and data privacy, aligned with frameworks such as India's DPDP Act (2023), the EU's GDPR, and the EU AI Act (2024).

6.5 Towards a Unified Digital Fraud Prevention Framework

The expansion of digital lending has heightened vulnerabilities to financial fraud, identity theft, and data manipulation. A Unified Digital Fraud Prevention Framework (UDFPF) is essential to harmonize regulatory standards, technological safeguards, and institutional collaboration.

The UDFPF advocates a proactive, data-driven approach spanning onboarding, credit assessment, disbursal, and repayment. Leveraging artificial intelligence, machine learning, and behavioral analytics, it enables real-time detection of anomalies such as synthetic identities, deepfake-based KYC, and transaction laundering. Integrating regulatory compliance with advanced analytics enhances systemic resilience, promotes transparency, and strengthens consumer trust in digital financial ecosystems (Table 1).

7 Building Organizational Fraud Resilience

Enhancing organizational resilience against fraud in digital lending and Buy Now, Pay Later (BNPL) ecosystems necessitates a comprehensive, system-wide approach. It begins with strong leadership commitment—where senior executives and the board

Table 1 Comparative table-KYC, BNPL, and AI transparency

Region/body	KYC/AML rules	BNPL classification	AI transparency expectations
India (RBI + DPDP Act)	Mandatory e-KYC, video-KYC, Central KYC Registry; strong AML/CFT alignment	Only banks/NBFCs can lend; BNPL treated as *regulated credit* if credit is extended	Emerging—RBI requires clear disclosures and non-discriminatory algorithmic practices; not yet codified
European Union (EU)	Strong, standardized KYC under AMLD; harmonized across member states	Treated as a *credit product* → consumer disclosures + affordability checks	High—AI Act mandates explainability, bias testing, and monitoring for high-risk AI (incl. credit scoring)
United States (U.S.)	KYC under Bank Secrecy Act; varies by institution; enforcement-led	BNPL treated largely as *consumer credit* under CFPB guidance	Moderate—required to justify adverse decisions; no specific federal AI transparency law
Singapore (MAS)	Very strict AML/KYC; real-time screening encouraged; strong risk-tiered approach	BNPL included under consumer credit frameworks; licensing + conduct rules apply	High—FEAT framework requires fairness, explainability, and accountability for AI models
Global Bodies (FATF, OECD, Basel)	FATF sets global KYC/AML standards (risk-based); widely adopted	No uniform BNPL standard; guidance encourages consistent risk assessment	Promote transparency and responsible AI use, but not binding standards

Source Own processing

of directors embed fraud risk management within the institution's overall governance and enterprise risk framework (Bouriche et al. 2025). This integration involves defining a clear fraud risk appetite, forming oversight committees, and ensuring that risk controls are operationally aligned with lending processes (Office of the Comptroller of the Currency [OCC] 2019). When effectively structured, governance frameworks ensure that technological innovation and market expansion occur within the bounds of institutional integrity and regulatory compliance (University of Sydney Business School 2023).

A resilient fraud management framework typically encompasses the following dimensions:

7.1 Leadership and Oversight

Fraud resilience begins with accountability at the top. Boards of directors and executive leaders must own fraud risk governance, defining strategic direction and establishing formal oversight mechanisms. Dedicated fraud-risk or compliance committees should be tasked with monitoring exposure, approving mitigation strategies, and ensuring that risk ownership is clearly assigned to relevant officers—such as Chief Risk or Compliance Officers (Bouriche et al. 2025). Transparent communication and regular reporting cycles further strengthen institutional integrity.

7.2 Risk Assessment and Policy Frameworks

Continuous assessment of enterprise-wide fraud vulnerabilities is essential. This includes analyzing emerging threats such as identity theft, synthetic identity fraud, and default at the first payment stage. Organizations should develop and update risk policies that clearly define approval thresholds and monitoring requirements for high-risk transactions. As highlighted by the (OCC 2019), institutions should be aware of common fraud typologies that exploit system loopholes and tailor control mechanisms accordingly.

7.3 Internal Controls and Monitoring

Robust internal control systems form the backbone of fraud prevention. Preventive measures such as rigorous Know Your Customer (KYC) and Anti-Money Laundering (AML) processes, multi-factor authentication, transaction monitoring, and segregation of duties significantly reduce exposure. In parallel, detective mechanisms—like audit logs, anomaly detection analytics, and automated alert systems—help in early identification of irregularities. Within BNPL operations, for instance, lenders should track indicators of first-payment defaults and develop automated systems to differentiate between genuine user error and fraudulent intent (OCC 2019).

Incident Response and Recovery Fraud resilience also depends on an institution's capacity to respond promptly to suspicious activities. Effective response frameworks define escalation pathways, enable real-time transaction reviews, and outline procedures for forensic investigations and regulatory disclosure. The OCC (2019) emphasizes that timely detection and corrective actions not only mitigate losses but also preserve consumer confidence and institutional credibility.

7.4 Governance Structures and Internal Controls

Effective governance is fundamental to mitigating fraud risks within digital lending and Buy Now, Pay Later (BNPL) ecosystems. Governance frameworks must explicitly embed fraud risk management as an integral part of enterprise risk oversight. Senior management and the board of directors are responsible for ensuring that adequate governance mechanisms, human resources, and technological infrastructure are in place to manage fraud exposures (Bouriche et al. 2025). In leading financial institutions, frameworks such as the COSO Enterprise Risk Management (ERM) model are used to align fraud risk oversight with strategic and operational objectives (University of Sydney Business School 2023).

A robust governance framework should institutionalize clear policies, escalation procedures, and accountability mechanisms covering critical control areas such as credit assessment, Know Your Customer (KYC) and Anti-Money Laundering (AML) compliance, and financial reconciliation.

7.5 Automation and Monitoring

Integrating digital tools into internal control systems significantly enhances the precision and timeliness of fraud detection. Automation and artificial intelligence enable institutions to monitor high transaction volumes with minimal human error while detecting suspicious behavior in real time (FTI Consulting 2025). Automated underwriting and payment processes in BNPL operations, for instance, should include algorithmic validation of customer data and automated reconciliation routines. Continuous monitoring systems can flag anomalies such as repetitive failed payments, device mismatches, or duplicate identities for immediate review (FTI Consulting 2025).

7.6 Third-Party Risk Management

Since BNPL models often rely on third-party vendors, merchants, and payment intermediaries, robust third-party risk management is indispensable. The Office of the Comptroller of the Currency (OCC 2019) stresses that all outsourcing and merchant contracts must be subject to rigorous due diligence, performance evaluation, and continuous oversight. Contracts should clearly specify roles and obligations related to fraud prevention, data protection, and regulatory compliance to ensure shared accountability across the digital credit value chain.

7.7 Policy and Training

As digital financial systems become increasingly complex, organizations must maintain dynamic policy frameworks and continuous employee training on fraud risk management. Updated policies governing security protocols, password management, incident escalation, and system access control form the foundation of operational resilience. Regular training ensures that staff remain alert to evolving fraud typologies, such as phishing-driven loan applications or fraudulent chargebacks (FTI Consulting 2025). Training should be role-specific so that operational teams can effectively validate anomalies even in automated environments.

7.8 Performance Metrics and Reporting

Governance mechanisms must include structured performance metrics that track fraud risk exposure. Key indicators—such as fraud loss ratios, suspicious activity report (SAR) volumes, and near-miss incidents—should be reported regularly to senior management and the board for oversight and corrective action (Bouriche et al. 2025).

In essence, a well-designed governance architecture that combines top-level oversight with automated monitoring and human expertise enables fintech and BNPL firms to enhance their fraud resilience. However, as noted by the OCC (2019), automation must be carefully managed through change controls and data governance to avoid new vulnerabilities.

7.9 Cross-Sector Collaboration and Information Sharing

Fraud in digital lending and BNPL ecosystems is inherently transboundary—spanning sectors such as finance, telecommunications, e-commerce, and social media. Therefore, no single institution can effectively counter these risks in isolation. A coordinated approach based on inter-organizational and cross-sector collaboration is essential (Westmore et al. 2022).

Recent policy research emphasizes that fraud resilience depends on real-time information sharing and intelligence pooling among financial institutions, regulators, and law enforcement. Shared data can reveal emerging fraud typologies such as synthetic identities or coordinated mule account networks that exploit multiple digital platforms (Westmore et al. 2022). Industry-led collaborations such as the Financial Services Information Sharing and Analysis Center (FS-ISAC) have established frameworks that standardize data exchange and facilitate cross-border information sharing. FS-ISAC's Cyber Fraud Prevention Framework integrates fraud, AML, and cybersecurity insights, helping member firms rapidly identify threats and circulate alerts (FS-ISAC 2025).

The benefits of such collaboration are multifold: it allows for collective defense, faster detection of new attack patterns, and enhanced institutional learning. However, privacy regulations and data-sharing restrictions often constrain these efforts (Westmore et al. 2022). Addressing these challenges requires clearer legal frameworks that encourage responsible information exchange while safeguarding customer data. Some jurisdictions are developing dedicated legislation or regulatory sandboxes that formalize mechanisms for sharing fraud intelligence among fintechs, banks, and telecommunication providers.

Ultimately, fraud resilience in the digital credit ecosystem is strengthened when firms transcend competitive silos and view fraud prevention as a shared responsibility across the financial ecosystem.

7.10 Talent, Culture, and Cyber-Awareness in Fintech Organizations

Organizational resilience against fraud depends as much on people and culture as it does on systems and processes. A culture of cyber-awareness—anchored in leadership commitment, employee engagement, and continuous learning—creates the foundation for sustainable fraud prevention (Subramanian Iyer 2025).

7.10.1 Continuous Training and Onboarding

Every employee, from operations to management, must be equipped with the knowledge to recognize and respond to fraudulent behaviors. Regular, scenario-based training covering phishing detection, social engineering awareness, and fraud monitoring tool usage empowers staff to act as the "human firewall" within the organization (Abikoye et al. 2024). Cyber-fraud awareness should be embedded into onboarding programs and reinforced through refresher workshops aligned with new threat patterns (Subramanian Iyer 2025).

7.10.2 Embedding Security in Corporate Culture

A fraud-aware culture must be woven into organizational values and human resource practices. HR departments should integrate cybersecurity and fraud prevention criteria into recruitment, performance appraisals, and promotion systems (Abikoye et al. 2024). Leadership must model desired behaviors by following security best practices and recognizing employees who identify or report potential fraud incidents.

When organizational communication and incentives emphasize fraud vigilance, employees become active participants in safeguarding assets and information.

7.10.3 Cross-Functional Collaboration

A collaborative approach across departments enhances detection and response efficiency. Security, IT, HR, and compliance units should work together to develop unified fraud management practices (Abikoye et al. 2024). For instance, IT teams can deploy behavior analytics tools, compliance can provide trend reports on suspicious activity, and HR can ensure staff in critical functions are continuously vetted. This cross-functional model promotes holistic fraud defense.

7.10.4 Recruiting and Retaining Cyber Talent

The growing complexity of fintech operations requires specialized fraud and cybersecurity expertise. Firms must invest in recruiting data scientists, fraud analysts, and ethical hackers or participate in industry consortiums to share scarce talent resources (Subramanian Iyer 2025). Leadership must also maintain an ongoing awareness of technological risks specific to BNPL and digital lending products.

By fostering a proactive culture and empowering employees through education and collaboration, fintech institutions can significantly reduce the risk of internal and external fraud.

7.11 Integrating Risk and Innovation for Sustainable Growth

Fintech growth thrives on innovation—but sustainable innovation requires the parallel development of risk management systems. Effective integration of fraud risk management into innovation processes ensures that firms can scale securely and responsibly (Shahriman and Omar 2025).

7.11.1 Risk-by-Design and Data Analytics

Fraud detection mechanisms should be embedded at the design stage of all digital products. Advanced analytics and machine learning can evaluate creditworthiness and fraud risk simultaneously, flagging anomalies in application data or transaction flows (Abikoye et al. 2024). This "risk-by-design" approach enables fintechs to innovate in customer experience without compromising security.

7.11.2 Governance Alignment

Governance committees should evaluate emerging technologies such as blockchain and AI under existing risk and compliance standards. This integration ensures that innovation adheres to data protection, fairness, and anti-fraud regulations (Bouriche et al. 2025). Early alignment allows regulatory updates to be incorporated into innovation pipelines proactively.

7.11.3 Regulatory Sandboxes

Regulatory sandboxes facilitate experimentation while maintaining oversight. These controlled environments allow fintechs to test BNPL and lending innovations, assess associated risks, and strengthen fraud prevention controls under supervision (Westmore et al. 2022).

7.11.4 Continuous Feedback and Adaptive Controls

Innovation must be iterative. Firms should continuously monitor fraud indicators, refine algorithms, and adjust control thresholds based on feedback from operations and market behavior. Adaptive risk management ensures that innovation and fraud resilience evolve together (University of Sydney Business School 2023).

In conclusion, sustainable fintech innovation requires governance systems that balance creativity with control. Risk and innovation are not opposing forces; when integrated effectively, they mutually reinforce institutional stability and customer trust (Shahriman and Omar 2025).

8 Conclusion

In conclusion, the rapid evolution of digital lending and Buy Now, Pay Later (BNPL) platforms in India represents both significant opportunities and regulatory challenges. Maintaining transparency, standardized disclosures, and ethical data governance is essential to sustain consumer trust and financial stability (RBI 2022). Financial institutions must adopt risk-based governance models and align artificial intelligence (AI) practices with explainability and fairness principles to prevent bias and ensure accountability (Behera 2025). Research indicates that BNPL systems can enhance financial inclusion by improving credit assessments for borrowers with limited histories (Laudenbach et al. 2025), while also challenging traditional credit structures and urging innovation in product design (Filotto 2024).

From a policy perspective, regulators face the dual responsibility of promoting innovation while safeguarding market integrity. The Reserve Bank of India's Digital Lending Guidelines (2022) and national initiatives such as Aadhaar, UPI, and the Account Aggregator framework contribute to a secure and inclusive financial ecosystem. Effective governance requires coordination among the RBI, the Ministry of Electronics and Information Technology (MeitY), and the Data Protection Board to enhance algorithmic transparency and consumer protection (MeitY 2023). Internationally, regulators such as the FCA, ASIC, and EBA advocate affordability assessments, fair lending, and transparent disclosures to prevent consumer over-indebtedness (FCA 2023; EBA 2024), while frameworks like the OECD Principles on AI (2019) and the EU AI Act (2024) reinforce ethical and transparent AI governance.

Despite progress, research gaps remain regarding the long-term effects of digital lending on consumer welfare, over-indebtedness, and credit inclusion. Limited empirical data hinder evaluation of algorithmic scoring impacts and regulatory efficacy. Future research should emphasize longitudinal studies, cross-country comparisons, and behavioral analyses to inform evidence-based policymaking. Open data access and interdisciplinary collaboration will be crucial to advancing responsible digital finance globally and ensuring that innovation aligns with ethics, accountability, and consumer empowerment.

References

Abikoye BE, Adelusi W, Umeorah SC, Adelaja AO, Agorbia-Atta C (2024) Integrating risk management in Fintech and traditional financial institutions through AI and machine learning. J Econ Manag Trade 30(8):90–102

Accenture (2024) AI-powered lending transformation: building the next generation of digital credit. Accenture Insights

Allied Market Research (2024) Digital lending market report 2024–2030. Retrieved from https://www.alliedmarketresearch.com

Arner DW, Barberis JN, Buckley RP (2020) FinTech and RegTech: impact on financial regulation. J Bank Regul 21(3):205–220

Behera CK (2025) Buy now, pay later: AI, inherent tensions, and implications. Manag Bus Rev 2025:1

Behera C (n.d.) *mcgill*. Retrieved from buy now, pay later: AI usage, inherent tensions. https://www.mcgill.ca/desautels/files/desautels/behera_astvansh_and_kopalle_2025_mbr-bnpl.pdf

Bouriche A, Hamli A, Bouriche S (2025) Balancing innovation and risk: regulatory frameworks for sustainable FinTech growth. Global Bus 10(19):Article 8

CEGA & IPA (2023) Digital credit: evidence on mobile instant credit and welfare impacts

CGAP (2025) Responsible digital credit: frontier solutions for authorities and providers

Data Protection Board of India (2023) Digital personal data protection act

DLAI (2023) Digital lending association of India ('DLAI'). Retrieved from neogrowth: https://ng.neogrowth.in/Digital_Lending_Association_Of_India.pdf

DPDP (2023, Aug 11) Retrieved from the digital personal data protection act. https://www.meity.gov.in/static/uploads/2024/06/2bf1f0e9f04e6fb4f8fef35e82c42aa5.pdf

European Banking Authority (2024) Artificial intelligence in the banking sector. https://www.eba.europa.eu/

European Commission (2020) Revised payment services directive (PSD2)

European Commission (2024) The EU artificial intelligence act. https://artificialintelligenceact.eu/

EY (2023) Global FinTech adoption and platformization report. Ernst & Young

Filotto U (2024) Buy now, pay later as a disruptive threat to payment cards. J Pay Strategy Syst 2024:1
Financial Action Task Force (FATF) (2023) Guidance on digital identity and AML/CFT
Financial Action Task Force (2021) Guidance on a risk-based approach to virtual assets and VASPs. https://www.fatf-gafi.org/en/publications/Fatfrecommendations/Guidance-rba-virtual-assets-vasps.html
Financial Conduct Authority (FCA) (2023) Regulating the buy now pay later sector. FCA, London
FS-ISAC (Financial Services Information Sharing and Analysis Center) (2025) Leveling up: a cyber fraud prevention framework for financial services. FS-ISAC
FTI Consulting (2025) Effective risk management in Fintech—you're closer than you think [Article]. Global Association of Risk Professionals (GARP)
Gulati A (2024) The changing landscape of financial services in the age of digital finance. J Bus Econ 2024:1
Laudenbach C et al (2025) Leveraging private BNPL data in consumer banking. FDIC working paper series
McKinsey & Company (2023) The rise of buy now, pay later: implications for banks and consumers. McKinsey Global Payments Report
MeitY (2023, Aug 11) The digital personal data protection act. Retrieved from MietY: https://www.meity.gov.in/static/uploads/2024/06/2bf1f0e9f04e6fb4f8fef35e82c42aa5.pdf
NPCI (2023) The management of risks is core to NPCI's vision mission and objectives of ensuring safety, security and sustainability of national retail payment systems. Retrieved from NPCI: National Payments Corporation of India (NPCI). (2023). Fraud Risk Management and PFMI Disclosure Report. Mumbai: NPCI
OECD (2022a) AI in financial markets: risk and governance considerations. OECD Publishing, Paris
OECD (2022b) SupTech and RegTech in financial supervision
Office of the Comptroller of the Currency (OCC) (2019) Bulletin 2019–37: operational risk—fraud risk management principles. U.S. Department of the Treasury, Washington, DC
Patil (2024) Enhancing fraud detection in banking by integration of graph databases with machine learning. Retrieved from ScienceDirect: https://www.sciencedirect.com/science/article/pii/S2215016124001377
PwC (2023) Global economic crime and fraud survey 2023. PricewaterhouseCoopers
PwC (2025, Apr) Combating payments. Retrieved from PwC: https://www.pwc.in/assets/pdfs/newsletter-payments-fraud-april-25.pdf
PwC (2025, Oct) The Indian payments handbook—2025–2030. Retrieved from PwC: https://www.pwc.in/assets/pdfs/indian-payments-handbook-2025-2030.pdf
Razorpay (2024, Nov 29) Fraud detection in financial transactions: types & how to detect it. Retrieved from Razorpay: https://razorpay.com/learn/fraud-detection-in-financial-transactions/
RBI (2022, Sept 02) Guidelines on digital lending. Retrieved from RBI: https://fidcindia.org.in/wp-content/uploads/2022/09/RBI-GUIDELINES-ON-DIGITAL-LENDING-02-09-22.pdf
RBI (2023, Feb 14) Digital lending guidelines. Retrieved from RBI: https://www.rbi.org.in/commonman/english/scripts/FAQs.aspx?Id=3413&utm_source
ResearchGate (2024) Systematic literature review on BNPL and digital lending in emerging markets. ResearchGate Repository
ResearchGate (2024, Nov) A comprehensive review of machine learning applications in AML transaction monitoring. Retrieved from researchGate: https://www.researchgate.net/publication/388277251_A_Comprehensive_Review_of_Machine_Learning_Applications_in_AML_Transaction_Monitoring
ReserachGate (2025, Mar) The impact of machine learning on fraud detection in digital payments. Retrieved from ResearchGate: https://www.researchgate.net/publication/390231806_The_Impact_of_Machine_Learning_on_Fraud_Detection_in_Digital_Payments
Reserve Bank of India (RBI) (2022a) Guidelines on digital lending. https://rbi.org.in

Reserve Bank of India (RBI) (2022b) Report of the working group on digital lending including lending through online platforms and mobile apps. RBI, Mumbai
Reserve Bank of India (RBI) (2025) Digital lending directions. https://rbi.org.in
Reserve Bank of India (2022) Guidelines on digital lending. https://rbi.org.in/Scripts/NotificationUser.aspx?Id=12345
Reuters (2024) Indian government proposes prison terms, fines for illegal lending (Dec 19, 2024)—on legislative proposals related to unregulated lending
Reuters (2025) India cracks down on illegal digital lending apps. https://www.reuters.com
Shahriman MF, Omar R (2025) The triadic edge: balancing innovation, risk, and organizational ambidexterity. Adv Nonlinear Var Inequal 28(5s):79
Subramanian Iyer S (2025) Cybersecurity culture and organizational resilience: a human-centered approach to digital risk management. Unpublished manuscript
University of Sydney Business School (2023) Balancing risk and innovation for emerging technologies. University of Sydney, Sydney
Westmore K, Miller S, Frost J, Foltean D (2022) Enabling cross-sector data-sharing to better prevent and detect scams. Royal United Services Institute (RUSI)
Wipro (2024) Leveraging AI and machine learning in designing (AML) framework. Retrieved from Wipro: https://www.wipro.com/content/dam/nexus/en/service-lines/applications/latest-thinking/Leveraging-ai-and-machine-learning-in-designing-anti-money-laundering-aml-framework.pdf
World Bank (2022) Digital financial services: enabling financial inclusion through innovation. World Bank, Washington, DC
World Bank. Digital financial inclusion/digital financial services (DFS) resources and reports
World Economic Forum (2023) The global cybersecurity outlook 2023. WEF, Geneva

Dr. Kanimozhi Viswanathan is currently working as Associate Professor in the Department of Management Sciences, Hindusthan College of Engineering and Technology. She is a Gold Medalist and Rank Holder in Master of Business Administration from Anna University. Has Completed Doctorate in Management from Bharathiar University, India. She has cleared National Eligibility Test for Lectureship (NET) conducted by UGC-India and State Eligibility Test for Lectureship (SET) conducted by Government of Tamilnadu, India. Has received best faculty award, best self learner award from Hindusthan College of Engineering and Technology. She has more than 15 years of work experience including industry and teaching MBA students at Business School and Engineering College. Has served as a resource person for programmes on entrepreneurship and management. Has published various papers in national, international journals, conferences and book chapters.

Dr. Subhashini Suresh is currently serving as Honorary Professor and Program Director at the Centre for Research & Training (CRT), a Growth Action Unit of the National Foundation for Entrepreneurship Development (NFED), Coimbatore. She also holds the role of Program Director and Executive Board Member (Honorary) at the NFED Business Facilitators Forum (NBFF), a Strategic Action Unit of NFED. Additionally, she contributes internationally as an Expert Panel Grader for Edgewood College, USA. She holds a Doctorate in Management and has over 27 years of rich experience across corporate and academic institutions. She is an accomplished academic leader, financial analyst, and EdTech innovator known for her expertise in finance, investment management, and AI-driven education systems. A prolific author and patent holder, she has published over 30 academic books and contributed to numerous national and international journals, conferences, and book chapters. Her outstanding contributions have earned her several awards, and her training expertise in SPSS and statistical software has supported many research scholars and MBA students. Dr. Subhashini actively engages in entrepreneurship development and academic research, frequently speaking at national and international platforms. She also serves as an evaluator for the Ministry of Education's Innovation Cell under the Government of India. Her leadership in curriculum development and student engagement continues to inspire excellence in education and research.

Mr. M. Showmiyan serves as an Assistant Professor in the Department of Management Sciences at Hindusthan College of Engineering and Technology, specializing in Finance and Human Resources. Has Completed Master Of Business Administration From Anna University and Advanced Diploma in Bank Management from Bharathiar University, He has 11 years of Experience in Industry (Banking, Secretarial Auditing) and academia, which brings valuable industry insights to teaching and research. His expertise focuses on Banking and Capital Market, and is committed to enhancing management education by integrating academic rigor with practical knowledge to develop students analytical and decision-making skills.

Investing in Fintech Fraud Combating Startups: Social Responsibility Before Profits?

Anastas Dzurovski

Abstract Starting from Payment fraud through Account takeovers, Identity theft, Investment scams and Insider fraud ending with Money laundering and Social engineering, Fintech market represents growing fraudster threat area. Increasing the security infrastructure investments for combat and securing of the fintech market is an area of growing investor interest also. Testing the hypothesis whether traditional decision making was deepened by the social responsibility of the investors we are examining 1453 fintech firms, 70 fintech fraud detection firms, 50 ESG-driven investors, and 76 fintech investment transactions compared to 37 fintech fraud transactions within the fintech sector using the databases Crunchbase and Clay. The period observed is 2015–2025. We deliver conclusions about the extent of the interest the investors show in the mission of such firms for stabilizing and risk mitigation of the Fintech market through provision of infrastructure for secure transactions.

Keywords Fintech fraud · Digital finance · ESG

1 Background

As digital financial ecosystems grow, fraud detection has become a key part of sustainable financial infrastructure.

The "Social" and "Governance" pillars of Environmental, Social, and Governance (ESG) frameworks used to be focused on environmental issues and business ethics. However, they have become more important in fintech fraud detection, and there is even a connection between the "Environmental" pillar and the "Social" and "Governance" pillars. Secure access to digital financial services, consumer safety, data integrity, and preventing financial exploitation are all things that people agree are basic societal obligations when it comes to fintech fraud detection. Also, strong anti-fraud measures, following AML rules, and keeping the financial system safe are important goals for governance. So, FinTech fraud-detection technologies readily fit

A. Dzurovski (✉)
University "St. Kliment Ohridski"- Bitola, Bitola, North Macedonia
e-mail: anastas.dzurovski@uklo.edu.mk

M. V. Achim (ed.), *Financial Crime in the Digital Era*, Contributions to Finance and Accounting, https://doi.org/10.1007/978-3-032-20198-0_8

with ESG goals by making sure that the market is trustworthy, protecting vulnerable customers, and making sure that institutions follow the rules and are open about what they do.

The rising connection between FinTech security innovation and ESG investing philosophy shows that there is a shift in thinking where fraud-prevention technologies are the “S” and “G” anchors. The new research question isn’t whether this kind of investment makes sense from a financial point of view, but whether ESG-driven reasons make investors even more interested in firms that work to protect digital markets and encourage safe, ethical financial involvement.

1.1 Problem Statement

Firms that find fraud in FinTech are becoming important players in all areas of digital finance, including digital transaction systems, protecting consumers, and making sure that financial markets are honest. In the past, investments in FinTech security infrastructure have mostly been rationalized using classic return-on-investment (ROI) logic, which says that decisions about where to put money are based on predicted financial performance, scalability, and competitive advantage.

On the other hand, the fintech fraud prevention sector’s demand for more cash is raising a new question: how much are investors driven by more than just making money? Are they also motivated by social goals and the ideals of responsible innovation? The emergence of Environmental, Social, and Governance (ESG) investing in particular shows that capital markets may increasingly reward firms that help create digital financial ecosystems that are stable, ethical, and trustworthy.

This makes it hard to do important research:

Do investors only put money into FinTech fraud-detection and security firms because they want to make money, or do they also care about social responsibility, consumer protection, and market integrity?

The primary questions we want to answer with our research are:

Do ESG investors prefer FinTech security firms that work to stop fraud?

Has this preference increased over time?

1.2 Hypothesis

H1: Does the ESG investor attitude toward FinTech’s that help fight fraud in line with ESG values grown over time?

H2: Does the ESG labeling mean that FinTech’s that focus on preventing fraud get more funding?

1.3 Testable Propositions: ESG Labeling, Fraud Prevention, and Investment Allocation

The FinTech firms that work in fraud prevention, AML compliance, cybersecurity and the infrastructure of digital trust perform a critical social function by helping to defend consumers, minimize systemic risk and preserve the integrity of financial markets. Given that the following functions closely relate to the E and G pillars of ESG, some researchers posit that anti-fraud technology will create positive externality, prevent damages, and foster healthy financial ecosystems (Chen et al. Theoretically, investors who are ESG-compatible should consequently reward these firms with higher capital influxes." (Friede, Busch and Bassen 2015: 16) or "ideally it should be ESG compatible investors who vouch for such firms" [based on the concept that there would be benefits of increased flows of funds towards such firms] (Crifo and Mottis 2023).

Preventing fraud additionally bolsters the digital trust architecture that supports modern financial inclusion, thus turning it into a socially responsible practice which is being increasingly recognized as part of sustainability responsibilities by responsible-investment frameworks (Guiso et al. 2008; Alda 2022a, b; Aldoush and Ferdous 2023). The literature on sustainable finance consistently provides evidence that firms with less corporate misconduct and better governance are typically endowed with greater investor confidence, and they encounter less downside risk (Dyck et al. 2010; Albuquerque et al. 2019; Wang 2024). Because fraud detection serves to lower the underlying incentives to misbehave, it should be considered a governance signal of credence.

However, empirical findings remain mixed. Evidence is mixed: On the one hand, some work suggests that impact firms are able to attract impact capital (Brest and Born 2013; Barber et al. 2021; Bugg-Levine and Emerson 2011), while other studies find investors seeking primarily ROI despite strong sustainability credentials in technology sectors (Friedman 2021; Miralles-Quirós et al. 2019). In the context of FinTech, in particular, ESG factors have become increasingly influential, but the literature shows limited support for an ESG premium (Arner et al. 2017a, b, 2020)

Because fraud-prevention FinTechs create public-good outcomes—in cybersecurity, consumer protection and anti-money-laundering compliance—they are arguably situated to access responsible-investment capital (Scholtens 2017; Schoenmaker and Schramade 2019). But it is an open empirical question whether ESG tagging of this or that fund does lead to additional funding for such firms. This generates a number of testable propositions that reflect the proposed association between ESG labeling and investment behavior.

1.4 Testable Propositions

1.4.1 P1: ESG Signaling Proposition

FinTech Fraud Prevention Firms awarded ESG labels receive higher amounts of investment than similar non-ESG firms (Friede et al. 2015; Li 2024).

1.4.2 P2: ESG Score Intensity Proposition

Fraud-prevention FinTechs Higher ESG scores are positively related with the amount invested in fraudprevention firms (Clark et al. 2015; Miralles-Quirós et al. 2019).

1.4.3 P3: Trust-Governance Proposition

This is because ESG labeling is associated with better governance, lower compliance risk, and lower likelihood of incurring fraud-related losses (Dyck et al. 2010; Krueger et al. 2020; Wang 2024).

1.4.4 P4: Security-ESG Premium Proposition

The effect of ESG on financing is stronger in security-focused FinTech sub-sectors (fraud detection, AML, identity verification) than in wider FinTech verticals (Arora and Islam 2022; Arner et al. 2020).

1.4.5 P5: ESG Credibility Proposition

Certified ESG labels—backed by trackable governance performance—are also associated with greater investment inflows than symbolic or narrative forms of ESG assertions (Eccles and Stroehle 2018; Sullivan and Mackenzie 2020).

1.4.6 P6: Post-2020 Regulatory Shift Proposition

The ESG financing premium for fraud-prevention FinTechs is higher post-2020, due to an extension of ESG regulation and augmented concern on digital trust (European Banking Authority 2023; European Commission 2022).

1.4.7 P7: Fraud-Externality Proposition

The reduction of fraud promotes positive social externalities, given socially responsible investors tend to invest more in ESG-labeled fraud-tech firms (Brest and Born 2013; Bugg-Levine and Emerson 2011; Chen et al. 2020).

2 Literature Review

2.1 ESG Investment Theory: Finance for Social Impact and Building Trust

The idea of ESG investing is based on the idea that doing well financially and being socially responsible go hand in hand (Friede et al. 2015). Traditional finance models focus on risk-adjusted returns and market efficiency. ESG frameworks, on the other hand, include social welfare, ethical behavior, and long-term systemic stability in their capital-allocation logic (Clark et al. 2015). The social and governance pillars of ESG have become important for the growth of the digital finance ecosystem (Dorfleitner et al. 2017).

The social part of ESG stresses keeping people and markets safe from harm. This involves safe access to safe financial systems, protecting consumers, protecting privacy rights, and fighting fraud (Scholtens 2017). Social-impact finance helps businesses that have good effects on society and lessen negative ones (Brest and Born 2013).

Preventing fraud and digital financial crime safeguards susceptible customers, mitigates society losses, and improves the economic welfare of individuals and organizations (Chen et al. 2020). Making investments in healthcare resilience, public infrastructure security, or digital education have measurable social value (Agrawal and Hockerts 2019). Proactive dimensions of impact finance, where capital allocation aims to anticipate and prevent systemic harm, not just respond to it (Bugg-Levine and Emerson 2011). Investors are increasingly viewing fraud-reduction technology as a type of social insurance for the digital economy, shielding the general populace from criminal exploitation and preserving trust in financial innovation (Arner et al. 2017).

Trust is a basic economic resource in digital markets (Guiso et al. 2008). It encourages people to use it, adopt it, and keep the ecosystem stable. ESG investing theory acknowledges trust as both a social benefit and a strategic asset vital for sustainable wealth development (Sullivan and Mackenzie 2020). Studies in sustainable finance underscore that firms fostering transparent, secure, and ethical digital ecosystems gain from improved corporate reputation, consumer fidelity, and investor trust (Eccles and Stroehle 2018).

FinTechs that help stop fraud and lower risk are in a unique position. Their products strengthen the trust architecture necessary for financial inclusion, digital commerce, and new technologies like blockchain-based assets and open banking (Rysman and Shy 2019). Investors that care about ESG are starting to realize that trust infrastructure is necessary for digital sustainable economies, just like renewable energy infrastructure is necessary for sustainable environmental systems (Sullivan and Mackenzie 2020).

Modern ESG theory says that systems that can handle stress and users who are safe are important for long-term financial success (Dimson et al. 2020). Investors are moving toward purpose-aligned investment reasoning, where the firm's social mission, including protecting digital financial ecosystems, is part of the reason for the investment (Barber et al. 2021).

Hence, investing money into FinTech fraud detection is not just a way to take advantage of the market; it is also a way to connect financial rewards with creating value for society. The market favors players who build digital trust, lower systemic risk, help vulnerable customers, and keep the financial system's security base strong (Arner et al. 2017).

In this perspective, ESG-driven funding is not altruism; it constitutes a strategic sustainability investment that acknowledges trust and security as essential long-term economic assets (Clark et al. 2015).

2.2 *How Investors React to ESG-Labeled Fintech Fraud Firms*

Investors are changing how they see fintech fraud firms with an ESG label. Instead of seeing them as "ESG narrative," they now see them as "risk-reduction proof." This makes it harder for pitches that merely use the label, but it helps solutions that really cut down on financial crime.

Over the past decade, the academic record offers little consistent evidence that investors systematically prefer firms carrying ESG labels. Even major practitioner surveys, such as those conducted under the Principles for Responsible Investment (PRI), report only weak correlations between ESG orientation and investment performance. Although a broad stream of research documents a positive association between ESG activities and stock-market outcomes, the literature also contains numerous cases where corporate social-responsibility initiatives have backfired and produced negative returns.

Detailed studies and market's empirical investigations show that the demand for ESG varies considerably over geographical areas, asset classes and among rating agencies or methodological frameworks (Kräussl 2024; Goldstein et al. 2022; Döttling and Kim 2021). Similar conclusions can be drawn from spectrum and regulatory analyses: despite the proliferation of ESG-branded assets, there is little evidence to suggest that investors systematically prefer ESG firms over their non-ESG counterparts (OECD 2020; ESMA 2025).

Portfolio level research also challenges the idea that ESG branding equates to more capital, better performance or lasting investment premiums. A number of cross-country studies show no evidence of a significant relationship between ESG scores and portfolio performance (Sandu 2023; Zehir and Aybars 2020; Huq 2022). Similarly, other empirical studies show that the exposure to ESG factors do not generate consistent abnormal returns and reject the hypothesis of a unified value premium applied by investors for firms measured in terms of the intensity of their labelling on ES topics (Mirghaffari 2025; Covachev 2025).

A further strand of research highlights that ESG demand is highly time-sensitive—shaped by temporary sentiment shocks, regulatory cycles, or crisis periods—rather than a stable, long-term investor preference (Cho 2023). Evidence also shows that the surge in ESG-oriented mutual-fund inflows following 2020 was short-lived, with volumes reverting toward pre-pandemic patterns in subsequent years (Journal of Empirical Legal Studies 2025).

Taken together, the literature for the 2015–2025 period does not provide clear, consistent support for a strong positive relationship between investment flows and ESG-labeled firms. Instead, the empirical picture remains fragmented, context-dependent, and highly sensitive to samples, measurement choices, and market conditions.

During this time, an increasing body of empirical research correlates enhanced ESG performance with diminished instances of fraud and violations, transforming ESG from a values-driven marketing approach to a governance and risk management framework (Li 2024; Wang 2024). There is also strong traditional evidence that being open about things makes it more likely that corporate wrongdoing will be found and stopped (Dyck et al. 2010). Also, research on asset pricing demonstrates that credible ESG/CSR policies lower downside risk, which is why investors prefer real controls over labels (Albuquerque et al. 2019; Krueger et al. 2020).

The most convincing cases of fintech fraud are those that show they reduce fraud and improve governance. This may be assessed by things like better detection precision/recall, fewer false positives, faster alert-resolution timelines, and of course, fewer confirmed occurrences. Digitalization and financial crime research reveal that blockchain audit trails and AI-powered monitoring can completely find fraud and make compliance more efficient (Arora and Islam 2022). That shows that investors are valuing function above modeling. Fintech that is called "ESG" only talks about attention dedication when its governance outcomes can be measured and audited (Li 2024; Wang 2024).

At the same time, worries about greenwashing have made investors less likely to believe pitches that merely use labels and more likely to pay attention to the quality of disclosures. The change isn't a pushback against ESG; it's more of a push for verification. Investors prefer measures that clearly lower tail risks (fraud, enforcement, and reputational damage) over statements that don't have any proof (Krueger et al. 2020; Albuquerque et al. 2019). When fintech fraud-tech is framed as essential risk infrastructure instead of an ESG narrative, procurement and investment arguments are generally more robust (Dyck et al. 2010; Ye and Zhang 2011).

Although ESG rhetoric has grown substantially over the past decade, research from 2015 to 2025 consistently shows that investors—especially those active in technology and FinTech—continue to prioritize financial performance above all else. Fraud prevention, governance quality, and compliance strength are generally treated as financially material risk factors rather than standalone social or ethical objectives. Barber et al. (2021) make this point well: even among funds that profess to be impact-driven in public messaging, the majority of their investors are looking for market-rate returns and social objectives are pursued only when they align with or complement financial goals. Their results suggest that capital flows in impact finance are highly correlated with return expectations, emphasising the dominance of performance over ethical considerations in investors' choices.

This interpretation receives strong support from a comprehensive meta-analysis of Friede et al. (2015). In reviewing more than 2000 empirical studies on ESG and financial performance, the authors find that investors consider ESG factors not because they reduce returns but rather because they often enhance risk-adjusted results. In other words, investors incorporate ESG considerations when they protect or enhance economic value, not because investors are motivated by normative/exclusive ethical reasons. This finding is consistent with the arguments by Döttling and Kim (2021) that most ESG demand that are observable is based on traditional risk–return sense, hedging reasons and regulatory explanations. Moral preferences explain relatively little of the variation in aggregate investor behavior.

Evidence in institutional-investor surveys are further supportive. Krueger et al. (2020) document that large asset managers adopt ESG criteria mainly because they perceive those as financially material risks affecting cash flows, volatility, and long-term firm value. Their results highlight that governance models, transparency solutions, fraud management and compliance procedures are primarily appreciated for cutting down downside risk. In a way, ESG-related elements of governance are risk management tools over and above any moral views.

Similar conclusions are drawn from the financial-crime and fraud-risk literature. Afjal et al. (2023) show that fraud, misconduct and breakdowns in compliance increase credit risk as well as the stability of financial institutions, and expose firms to regulatory sanctions, reputational damage. Therefore, investors track fraud-prevention abilities at both FinTech firms and established financial firms—not because fighting fraud is inherently a social good, but because experiences suggests that inability to prevent fraud is only going to negatively impact profits and the institution. In the fraud-heavy FinTech space, AML systems and tools that verify identities among other advanced-fraud analytic platforms add value by securing capital along with minimising future loss expectations while maintaining digital financial infrastructure.

Collectively, these papers provide strong evidence on the financial focused nature of investors in fraud-enabled FinTech. Their focus on fraud prevention, governance and compliance comes less from an increased sense of social responsibility or ethical-based ESG investing but more so on wanting to mitigate risk/control exposure and maintain economic value.

2.3 Options to Alter ESG-Labeled Investor Perception Regarding Fintech Fraud Detection Agreements

Investors will still be mostly interested in assets that make money. Because profits in the field of fitech fraud detection can go up or down, both the government and society should designate these kinds of investments as ESG (environmental, social, and governance) investments. This will help attract investors and show that more investigation is needed. One of the main parts of the idea is showing proof of how fintech fraud detection affects market stability and transparency, not only in the fintech sector but in a wider sense as well. That should be lead with outcomes that have been checked (Li 2024; Wang 2024). Another useful method will be to use evidence mechanism and mapping product features to show how incidents have gone down (Arora and Islam 2022). Also, making it a question of compliance-critical systems that lower expected loss and cost of capital can make ESG-friendly investors more interested (Albuquerque et al. 2019; Ye and Zhang 2011). Fighting dishonest business practices by checking the integrity of disclosures so that investors may trust the ESG aspect while buying the risk-mitigation value (Krueger et al. 2020).

3 Methodology

The sample includes 1453 FinTech firms, 70 FinTech fraud-detection firms, 50 ESG-driven investors, and 76 FinTech investment transactions alongside 37 fraud-related transactions. To ensure clarity and replicability, the study explicitly covers the period 2015–2025 a period consistent with ESG expansion phases and FinTech sector growth documented in international regulatory and market analyses. This study follows a quantitative, empirical research design consistent with methodological conventions in FinTech, venture-capital, and sustainable-finance literature. The dataset was constructed from two primary sources—Crunchbase and Clay—which are widely recognized in academic research for providing reliable information on startup characteristics, funding rounds, and investor activity. Prior studies such as Bernstein et al. (2017), Howell (2020), and Alekseeva et al. (2021) establish these platforms as appropriate sources for analyzing private-firm dynamics and early-stage financing trends.

Data collection followed a structured multi-step procedure. First, FinTech firms were identified using platform category filters, including Payments, Cybersecurity, Fraud Detection, RegTech, AML/KYC, and Digital Identity. Second, only equity-based financing rounds (seed, venture, angel, Series A–E, corporate venture) were selected, excluding grants and non-equity financing following the methodological precedents of Howell (2020). Third, Clay was used to cross-check organizational details, ESG disclosures, sustainability positioning, and investor identity. Duplicate entries were eliminated through domain-level and firm-identity matching. Finally,

ESG attributes were integrated into the dataset by combining sustainability classifications from the platforms with firm-reported ESG mandates; these were harmonized into two forms: (1) a binary ESG Flag and (2) a continuous ESG Score. This dual approach is aligned with standard ESG research practice as documented by Friede et al. (2015), Miralles-Quirós et al. (2019), and Albuquerque et al. (2019).

The research uses a quantitative, empirical research approach to find out if ESG-labeled FinTech firms get different amounts of funding than firms that don't have ESG labels. The investigation use descriptive statistics and regression modeling to assess the correlation between ESG classification and investment inflows. The goal is to find out if investors are showing a strong preference for FinTech firms that support sustainability, especially those who work to stop fintech fraud. The dataset contains information about the investment amount, the year the money was given, the ESG flag, and the ESG score if one is provided.

After that, ESG attributes were added to investment records. These qualities came from sustainability categories provided by the platform and were then cross-checked with ESG mandates reported by the firm. To make things more consistent, numerical data like deal value and fund year were standardized. ESG-related variables were turned into categorical (ESG-flag) and continuous (ESG-score) formats. In order to reduce data distortion in venture-capital deal sizes, investment amounts were changed again using logarithmic scaling before regression testing.

As a first step in looking at the distribution characteristics of investment values and ESG profiles, descriptive statistics were used. These numbers can help us find outliers, see how the data is distributed around the median, and see how the data changes over time. In conjunction with descriptive summaries, graphical visualizations—histograms (in linear and logarithmic formats), scatterplots, boxplots, and investment trend charts—were created to illustrate investment trends. Consequently, an interpretation is derived on whether ESG orientation significantly modifies conventional capital-flow dynamics in high-growth FinTech industries.

To systematically assess the impact of ESG attributes on investment volume, a multivariate ordinary least squares (OLS) regression model was utilized. The dependent variable was the log-transformed amount of money invested. This was chosen because the sizes of venture deals were quite unevenly distributed. The independent variables encompassed ESG label, ESG score, and investment year, facilitating the examination of both sustainability aspects and temporal implications. We used standard thresholds ($p < 0.05$) to see if ESG features had a measurable effect on capital allocation.

The methodological framework is based on three prerequisites: replicability, transparency, and robustness. The methodology gives a solid way to draw conclusions on whether ESG factors are currently affecting venture financing trends in the fraud prevention and digital governance part of the FinTech business.

It is well in line with how empirical FinTech, venture capital and ESG research are already being conducted. First, the use of Crunchbase-like venture capital data is widely established in academic research on the financing of innovation and startup ecosystems. Another large study of Alekseeva et al. (2021), Bernstein et al. (2017), and Howell (2020) show that Crunchbase data offer credible firm-level and deal-level information in high-growth technology industries.

Second, the practice of constructing ESG factors from a mix of binary (ESG flag) and continuous (ESG score) characteristics is consistent with conventions in both the sustainability and some financial economics literature. They do so by measuring ESG factors as both categorical labels and numeric scores to analyze the effect of sustainability on investment flows. The dual-structure ESG approach used here is in line with meta-analytical evidence provided by Friede et al. (2015), as well as the cross-country studies of Miralles-Quirós et al. (2019) and the firm-risk modeling of Albuquerque et al. (2019), which should provide some methodological basis for ESG flags and ESG indices being valid.

Third, the former finding, achieved using multivariate OLS in this study, is consistent with the method choices in top ESG and FinTech studies. Previous studies by Krueger et al. and Li (2024) use OLS models to estimate the association between governance quality, sustainability metrics, and financial misconduct, and investor allocation and firm valuation. These prior examples are evidence OLS is an appropriate and accepted modeling procedure for examining how ESG labeling and ESG scores associate with issuance success.

Fourth, the decision to take a log transformation of the investment size follows from the extreme right skewness in the venture capital deal size distribution. Venture financing is also known to be highly skewed, with a few very large deals; hence, to make distributions of dependent and independent variables more Gaussian-like while enhancing regression performance, log-transformation is standard. Howell (2020), Ewens and Farre-Mensa (2022)and Kaplan and Lerner 22 show that logarithmic scaling is required for VC econometric inference to be statistically correct. Accordingly, the transformation used in the present study is consistent with current field practices.

Fifth, the descriptive-statistical and visual-exploratory phase of the approach aligns with earlybrick empirical work on startup-investment domains. Histograms, scatterplots and boxplots along with time series charts are indispensable data visualization tools to diagnose distributional properties, detect outliers, as well as illustrate sectorial patterns. Previous studies by Cumming and Dai (2010), Block et al. (2019), and Arner et al. (2017) suggests that descriptive exploration is a necessary step before doing causal estimation in financial-technology research.

Sixth, the empirical testing of ESG impact over investment flows reflects methodologies applied in sustainable finance literature. Miralles-Quirós et al. (2019) illustrate how ESG scores can be included in capital-flow regressions and Schoenmaker and Schramade (2019) offer methodological advice on connecting ESG measures with investment choices. Sullivan and Mackenzie (2020) also provide evidence of the impact of ESG labeling on fixed-income and multi-asset allocation choices. We believe these methodological precedents express the logic of the regressions that test whether ESG-charged FinTechs—especially with fraud prevention focus—in fact attract different levels of investor capital.

And, finally, research on financial crime, compliance and digital trust supports the integration of fraud-prevention and digital-governance FinTech into ESG-linked econometric models. Chen et al. (2020) demonstrate that risk-fraud analytics can be quantified and aggregated at the model level in FinTech settings, while Arora and Islam (2022) confirm the use of fraud-reduction technologies within a financial-governance scheme. Wang (2024) also shows that governance quality, compliance quality, and the reduction of violations are ESG factors with empirical measures suitable for regression analysis. These works provide grounding for incorporating fraud-detection FinTechs into ESG-minded investment modeling and vindicate the broader methodological soundness of our approach.

4 Results

We are delivering outcomes with the technique used here.

4.1 Descriptive Statistics

Table 1 shows descriptive statistics for the quantities of money invested in the FinTech and ESG-related datasets. The mean and median numbers reveal that a small number of very large agreements have a big effect on average investments. This shows that investments are not evenly spread out in the industry. The high standard deviation backs up this fact even further, showing that deal sizes can vary a lot. The minimum and maximum figures show that the quantities of money invested can be very different, from small deals to billion-dollar rounds. This comprehensive summary indicates that, although ESG and FinTech fundraising encompasses numerous moderate deals, mega-rounds significantly influence the sector's financial environment.

4.2 Visual Analysis

The histogram on the raw distribution of investment amounts is given in Fig. 1 (on a linear scale) and reveals a strong right-skew, showing that most deals collocate the lower-value range but only very few transactions go up to very high levels. Such skewed distributions are common in the world of venture capital and start-up financing, brought about by a handful of mega-deals that dwarf overall flows as has been empirically documented in entrepreneurial finance research (Kaplan and Lerner 2016; Howell 2020; Ewens and Farre-Mensa 2022). The histogram is very illuminating in terms of where capital occurs and—as I'll argue later needs to be properly dealt with in the presence of outliers when studying ESG investment trends. Acknowledging the presence of such outliers is important given ESG preferences, if existent, maybe obscured or exaggerated due to the intrinsic right-skewness in VC deal sizes.

Log scale on hist Fig. 2 log scaled histogram applies a logarithmic transformation to adjust the extreme right-skew seen in raw data, resulting in a more balanced and interpretable distribution of amounts invested. The log transformation smooths out the mid-range deals along the axis, reducing noise and highlighting underlying effects in investor behavior. Such a transformation is common practice in the ventilation-capital econometrics literature, to re-scale heavy-tailed investment data and facilite intuition (Kaplan and Lerner 2016; Howell 2020; Arner et al. 2020). The more even distribution as below indicates the investment behaviour—especially the relative allocation of ESG and non-ESG transactions—follows a somewhat standard structure across the data. In sum, the log-view supports the observation that deal-size dynamics are dominated by generic market effects and not by ESG flagging.

A mounting body of academic literature connects fraud prevention, the reduction of financial crime, and market integrity to some of these social lens attributes such as social responsibility and to others found in the governance pillar. It suggests that preventing fraud is socially responsible because it protects consumers but also rights imbalance, builds trust among stakeholders and stabilizes digital financial ecosystems. "Fraud reduction is becoming increasingly accepted as a type of social value due to its reduction of societal loss, the protection it offers to vulnerable groups and the confidence it imparts in financial markets" (Chen et al. 2020). Scholars stress that strong anti-fraud records are strengthening good governance quality, mitigating corporate misdoing, and even congruent with the responsible-investment practices (Dyck et al. 2010; Wang 2024).

Fraud detection in FinTech, it follows, is not only a technological artefact—it is also the social practice of preserving public trust (Guiso et al. 2008). Robust fraud-dampening systems that shield consumers against exploitation and work to reduce systemic exposures are identified by scholars as a core element of sustainable financial-market infrastructure (Arner et al. 2020). Empirical studies of ESG and corporate malfeasance consistently show that firms with stronger social-governance mechanisms are subject to fewer violations, lower regulatory penalties, and enjoy higher investor trust (Li 2024; Krueger et al. 2020).

Preventing fraud also contributes to the long-term security of digital finance, serving the social-impact goals associated with sustainable investing which emphasizes reducing harm as a major component of its notion of social responsibility (Brest and Born 2013; Bugg-Levine and Emerson 2011). Evidence suggests that technological innovations as AI-based fraud detection and blockchain audit trails reduce the scope for financial crime, leading to societal welfare and ethical market conduct (Arora and Islam 2022; Rysman and Shy 2019).

Because financial fraud disproportionately impacts consumers, small firms and the vulnerable, scholars argue that anti-fraud efforts constitute a public good—financing of which is an economy-enhancing investment (Eccles and Stroehle 2018; Sullivan and Mackenzie 2020). This is consistent with our theoretical prediction that socially responsible investing investors should prefer firms producing products enhancing integrity, transparency and trust in financial ecosystems.

The relationship between ESG scores and investment amounts is illustrated in the Fig. 3 scatterplot. Since there is no uptrend or concentration in consideration, there does not appear to have any meaningful statistical relation between ESG scoring style intensity and the size of funding. Investments are almost equally broken down into low- and high-ESG valorisations, indicating that ESG scores do not guide investor allocation decisions systematically. This result is consistent with existing empirical evidence of weak or mixed relationship between ESG ratings and investment flows, particularly for early-stage or high-growth industries (Friede et al. 2015; Miralles-Quirós et al. 2019; Cho 2023). As a collective, the visual evidence confirms the descriptive results in that ESG considerations are not yet major drivers of capital allocation decisions in FinTech; where investors are still predominantly focused on returns and financial material risks.

Distribution of investment amounts between ESG labeled and non-ESG FinTechs is shown in Fig. 4 boxplot. Both groups have very similar medians, IQRs and distribution characteristics—implying that ESG-valued startups are not at a significant fundraise advantage. No over-disproportionate outliers or grouping in the ESG-labelled group indicates that that we do not find evidence of ESG driven overinvestment. This result aligns with evidence that ESG tags themselves do not typically lead private markets to see higher valuations or more capital flowing in, particularly when investors largely tie investment decisions to financial and governance quality instead of sustainability branding (Döttling and Kim 2021; Zehir and Aybars 2020; Wang 2024). The overlap in ranges also suggests that investors today view ESG-labeled and non-ESG FinTechs similarly when it comes to investment performance.

The trend chart of Fig. 5 depicts the evolution in average annual investment sums for non-ESG FinTechs over time. Fluctuations also do not seem to behave in response to shifts in sustainability sentiment, but instead seem correlated with general investment cycle dynamics. It suggests funding is more a function of macroeconomic conditions, capital-market liquidity and the venture-cap cycle. The lack of long-running upward penetration suggests investors' stable financial oriented behavior rather than non-financial sentiment reaction. This effect is consistent with those found in venture-finance literature and it was already determined that investment flows do not necessarily follow ESG orientation but rather macroeconomic indicators and risk appetite (Howell 2020; Kaplan and Lerner 2016; Arner et al. 2020). Therefore the trend creates a benchmark with which to compare any ESG focused patterns.

In Fig. 6, the evolution of ESG-labeled FinTech investments takes place over time. Like non-ESG firms, ESG firms have cyclical investment behavior that echoes market level patterns rather than maintaining a continuous upward course. The near overlap of ESG and non-ESG investing trends suggests that capital-flow dynamics in the sector have not been substantially changed by ESG orientation. The is consistent with studies showing that ESG-funded investments tend to be cyclical and are not differentiated by any consistent systematic ESG premium across years (Kräussl 2024; ESMA 2025; Journal of Empirical Legal Studies 2025). In summary, year to year variability is indicative of the secondary impact—ESG considerations have not reached a tipping point where they drive investment preference within FinTech.

4.3 Regression Analysis

The regression in Table 2 shows how ESG status, ESG score, and time affect the amount of money invested (log-transformed). The coefficients show that neither the ESG flag nor the ESG score is statistically significant because the *p*-values are large. This means that ESG traits don't have a big effect on how much people invest in the FinTech and fintech fraud detection datasets that were looked at. The time variable is likewise not statistically significant, which means there isn't much indication that ESG preference has grown throughout the time period studied. In short, it seems that investors care more about financial fundamentals and market opportunities than ESG credentials when putting money into these industries.

4.4 Robustness Test

4.4.1 Baseline Model

Model:

$$\ln(1 + Amount\_USD) = \alpha + \beta_1 ESG\_Flag + \beta_2 ESG\_Score + \beta_3 Year + \varepsilon$$

- $N = 75$ deals
- $R2 \approx 0.21$ (low to moderate fit, not unknown for cross-sectional VC data)
- Key coefficients:
  - ESG_Flag_Num ≈ 0.21, $p \approx 0.22$
  - ESG_Score ≈ 0.21, $p \approx 0.22$
  - Year ≈ 0.29, $p < 0.001$ (that is statistically significant)

Interpretation:

- ESG variables (binary flag and score) are not statistically significant: there is no strong evidence that ESG status explains variation in investment size.
- Year is significant: more recent deals tend to be larger (typical inflation + later-stage rounds effect), but this is independent of ESG.
- This baseline already suggests no ESG premium in our sample.

4.4.2 Robustness Check 1: Robust Regression (Huber RLM)

To see if our results are driven by outliers or heavy tails, I ran a Huber robust regression with the same specification:

$$\ln(1 + Amount\_USD) = \alpha + \beta_1 ESG\_Flag + \beta_2 ESG\_Score + \beta_3 Year + \varepsilon$$

- Coefficients (Huber):
    - const ≈ -556.43
    - ESG_Flag_Num ≈ 0.18
    - ESG_Score ≈ 0.18
    - Year ≈ 0.28

Interpretation:

- The ESG coefficients are almost identical in magnitude to the baseline OLS and move only slightly.
- This means that outliers are not driving the "no ESG effect" result—robust estimation still finds no meaningful ESG impact on investment size.
- The positive but small ESG coefficients remain economically weak and statistically not robust.
- Conclusion: Our finding that ESG does *not* significantly influence deal size is robust to heavy-tail/outlier concerns.

4.4.3 Robustness Check 2: Trimming Top 5% Largest Deals

VC data is extremely skewed. To test whether a few mega-rounds distort everything, I:

- Dropped the top 5% largest deals (by Amount_USD).
- Re-estimated the same model on the trimmed sample.

Results (Trimmed 95% sample):

- R2 ≈ 0.18 (similar magnitude to baseline).
- ESG_Flag_Num and ESG_Score remain statistically insignificant (p-values still > 0.1).
- Year remains positive, with effect similar to the baseline.

Interpretation:

- After removing the largest deals (potential outliers), nothing changes qualitatively:
    - No ESG premium appears.
    - Time trend remains but is unrelated to ESG.
- This confirms that our main result is not driven by a handful of huge rounds.

4.4.4 Robustness Check 3: Simplified Model (ESG Flag Only)

To test whether multicollinearity between ESG_Flag and ESG_Score might be obscuring effects, I ran a very simple model:

$$\ln(1 + Amount\_USD) = \alpha + \beta_1 ESG\_Flag + \varepsilon$$

- N = 75
- $R2 \approx 0.024$ (very low explanatory power)
- ESG_Flag_Num ≈ 0.50, $p \approx 0.18$

Interpretation:

- Even in this simple, generous model where ESG_Flag is the *only* predictor, it is still not significant.
- The effect size is modest and uncertain; the model explains essentially none of the variation in deal size.
- So even in a specification that favors finding something, we still do not get a clean ESG effect.

4.4.5 Robustness Check 4: Year "Fixed Effect Style" (Demeaning by Year)

To check whether common year-level shocks (e.g., funding waves, COVID years, etc.) hide ESG patterns, I did:

1. Compute, for each year, the mean log investment.
2. Subtract this from each observation to get year-demeaned log amount:

$$log\_amt\_dm = log\_amt - log\bar{\_}amt_{year}$$

3. Regress:

$$\log\_amt\_dm = \alpha + \beta_1 ESG\_Flag + \beta_2 ESG\_Score + \varepsilon$$

Results:

- $R2 \approx 0.009$ (almost zero explanatory power).
- ESG_Flag_Num and ESG_Score both insignificant ($p \gg 0.1$).

Interpretation:

- After removing year effects, ESG variables still explain almost nothing.
- This implies that within a given year, ESG-labeled deals do not systematically get larger or smaller ticket sizes than non-ESG ones.
- So the absence of ESG effect is not an artifact of time trends.

4.4.6 Overall Robustness Conclusion

Across five different specifications:

1. Baseline OLS with ESG flag, ESG score, and year
2. Huber robust regression (less sensitive to outliers)
3. Trimmed OLS, excluding top 5% largest deals

4. ESG-only OLS, a generous test of a simple ESG effect
5. Year-demeaned regression, focusing on within-year differences

We consistently get the same core result:

There is no statistically robust evidence that ESG status (flag or score) significantly affects investment size in this dataset.

- Coefficients for ESG are small, unstable, and statistically insignificant in all robustness checks.
- The time dimension (Year) matters (later years = larger deals), but it is not mediated by ESG.
- The direction of ESG coefficients is weakly positive, but never precise enough to support a strong claim about ESG premiums.

We conducted several robustness checks to examine the robustness of our findings. First, the baseline log-linear model was re-estimated through HBR to handle outliers. The majority of the ESG coefficients were not significantly different and significant.

Second, we trimmed the top 5% of investment distribution to avoid the biases in parameter estimates due to mega-rounds. The same qualitative result came out of the truncated sample regression: ESG flag and ESG Score were not statistically significantly related to investment size, while a positive year coefficient captured the increase in ticket sizes overall by this variable. Third, to eliminate multicollinearity and complex model as the reasons leading to no statistical significance, we fit a smaller model with presence/absence of ESG flag as only one factor in the equation. Even with this trimmed model, the ESG coefficient was still statistically nil, and significantly explained almost no variation in log investment amounts (R2 $\approx$ 0.02).

Finally, investment amounts were demeaned by year to capture a year fixed-effects structure and regressed the within-year deviations on ESG indicators. The ESG coefficients continued to provide no statistically and economically explanatory power, which implies that in a given year there is no typical over- or underinvestment on ESG-labeled deals as compared to non-ESG deals.

In sum, these robustness tests support our central finding: in the sample at hand, ESG alignment does not seem to play a decisive role in the propensity of FinTech fraud-prevention and similar companies' investment size.

The fit statistics indicate the model accounts for R2 = 0.208 ($p < .001$), and adj.R2 = 0.186, which is the expected order of magnitude for cross-sectional venture/FinTech investment data where much variation will be idiosyncratic variance not easily aggregated across observable predictors. The low value of R2, however, contrasts sharply with the highly significant overall model (results from F-test; F = 9.45, $p < 0.001$) which implies that the aggregate of predictors explains a meaningful proportion of variation in investment size and that the model is statistically reliable as an entity.

Multicolllinearity was evaluated by the Variance Inflation Factor (VIF) diagnostics. The findings indicate that ESG_Flag_Num and ESG_Score are perfectly multicollinear with infinite VIF numbers. This arises because, in this dataset, both of these variables have been encoded to reflect the same underlying binary categorisation for ESG: firms coded as PRI signatories have ESG_Flag_Num = 1 and ESG_Score = 1; all others have zero in each case. Therefore, the 2 variables cannot be in the same regression model. On the contrary, Year variable has a VIF of nearly 1.0 indicating no collinearity to ESG factors. This analysis reinforces that in the future model specifications, one should consider including one of ESG_Flag or ESG_Score not both.

Finally, we detrended investment by year to capture a year fixed-effects specification and regressed within-year deviations on ESG variables. Again, the ESG coefficient was not statistically significant and offered much lower explanatory power indicating that at each year of investment an ESG-labelled deal does not systematically attract more or less money than a non-ESG labelled deal.

Combined, these robustness checks leave us confident that our main finding obtains: It does not appear to be the case that ESG alignment is a (very) important consideration for size of investment in this sample of firms working in FinTech fraud-prevention and related businesses.

The R2=) goodness of fit statistics suggests that the model has:. 208 and an adjusted R2 = 0.186, which is in line with what one would expect given the entre or FinTech cross-section of investment data where most of the variation is idiosyncratic and not easily read from observable predictors. Nevertheless, the F-test for the overall model significance is significant ($F = 9.45$, $p < 0.001$), therefore suggesting nonnegligible association between predictors and investment size spectrum and good fitness of the model with respect to data.

We examined multicollinearity using VIF diagnostics. The VIFs with infinite means that ESG_Flag_Num and ESG_Score have perfect multicollinearity. The reason for this is that both ESG variables by design have recorded the same underlying binary classification, namely whether a given firm (that has been assigned to be either responsible or irresponsible—see e.g. 30 For example, collectives of firms identified in the Datastream dataset as signatory to PRI described in Sect. 2 will have ESG_Flag_Num = 1 and ESG_Score = 1 (have filed with a report) and all others record zero for both). Hence, these two variables could not simultaneously be included in the regression model. On the other hand, the Year has a VIF value of approximately 1.0 and there is no collinearity between this variable and that with ESG factors. This test reveals that in future model specifications, either ESG_Flag or ESG_Score will have to be included but not both.

5 Key Insights

This section discusses what we learned from working with the dataset.

5.1 Change in ESG investors' Reasons for Investing in Socially Responsible FinTech?

Despite more conversation around the world about finance that is more ethical—this research reveals that FinTech investors are largely still driven by performance and return potential, rather than social conscience. The absence of a strong link between ESG indicators and investments can be related to productivity-lead market-efficiency based models for innovation finance (Dorfleitner et al. 2022). This finding is consistent with prior evidence that ESG talk grows but not actual allocation plans are aligned with declared sustainability goals in fast-growing industries (Crifo and Mottis 2023; Miralles-Quirós et al. 2019). The money investors are investing is still largely flowing into growth-oriented opportunities with clear ROIs. This is because objectives to investors into FinTech have translated as yet, not to a fundamentally ESG influenced transition.

5.2 The Fintech Fraud Prevention sector is ESG-Compatible 14 Why is This Case a Good Example of a Disruptive Investment?

Liquidity and investors Having said that, ESG FinTechs labeled as ESG do not appear to be directly supported by investors through this secured investment. Fintech fraud prevention companies are in the business of forging lasting digital trust. There is also a great deal of positive externality, and behind all that there is maintaining the honesty of the market. "These are two very fundamental things for more sustainable digital finance ecosystems" (Arner et al. Existing studies have demonstrated that trust is vital to both financial inclusion and the ongoing adoption of information technology (Aldboush and Ferdous 2023; Li et al. 2021). Thus, even though capital markets haven't always accurately categorized or rewarded them, fraud-defense FinTechs are actually built around ESG principles.

5.3 Looking at Other Research

It is early when investigating how much the financial and banking stability now soar due to digital trust and resilience as previously has been demonstrated (Arner et al. 2017a, b, 2020; European Banking Authority 2023). According to some ESG architectures, market stability, consumer protection and an ethical behaviour of governance are placed at the base of responsible finance (Schoenmaker and Schramade 2019). However, this study demonstrates that the fintech trust-enhancing potential remains to be reflected in preference investor behavior, which is consistent with earlier results when focusing on ESG-finance maturity at industry level (Crifo and Mottis 2023).

5.4 *Ethics of Investors Versus Purpose of Investors*

There are many different reasons why investors invest sustainably, research on sustainable investment shows: because they want to make money and do the right thing at the same time (Schoenmaker and Schramade 2019; Alda 2022a, b). Studies in technology and venture capital keep on identifying the incentive of ROI as a primary issue; ESG integration is also lagging behind in comparison to traditional asset classes (Friedman 2021; Dorfleitner et al. 2022).

5.5 *Model Limitations*

5.5.1 Heterogeneous Paths of ESG Labeling

One key limitation of this study is the multi-faceted and non-linear definition of ESG categorizations across data sources and markets. Despite increasing interest, ESG classification frameworks are still not universally harmonized. Firms classified as ESG-aligned may vary across databases, rating providers and investors based on their own definition of an ESG-aligned firm. But there are already significant ESG-labeling paths that exist, like Morningstar or European Union regulation. Hence identification of ESG-informative assets may be variable in appearance leading to the classification noise. This discrepancy may lead to the misclassification of firms as well as exclude true ESG firms that do not have an official identifier.

5.5.2 Measurement and Disclosure for Private Firms

The analysis relies on those private FinTech firms' reports about funding and value, which are murkier than for publicly traded corporations. A lot of times, privately held companies that receive funds from venture capitalists do not disclose their complete financial information publicly. Their valuations fluctuate based on how negotiations go, what kind of signals investors give them about their interest and how many times they meet fundraising targets. This may introduce noise in the variables that affect value and financing. So the financial metrics used in the regression models might not properly reflect how well a firm is doing or what investors anticipate.

5.5.3 Bias Towards Funding Rounds

The dataset is affected by disclosure bias because it only includes investment rounds and investor transactions that have been made public. Many (early-stage) investments, corporate investments, and undisclosed financial infusions may not be common in nations with less open venture ecosystems or for firms operating in sensitive areas. This bias may affect more well-known firms that are covered by the media or supported by institutions, which could skew the results toward bigger firms and leave out smaller ones. Because of this, the investment patterns we see may not fully show how capital moves into the FinTech security ecosystem.

6 Further Discussion

6.1 Effects on Policy and Industry

Because preventing fraud in fintech is so important for society, the economy, and business, authorities might want to think about adding unambiguous fraud-mitigation metrics to ESG frameworks. Trust infrastructure being legally recognized as a core ESG asset could help with targeted incentives, blended-finance initiatives, and being included in future sustainable-taxonomy systems (European Commission 2022). This method is in line with suggestions from regulatory research that calls for the designation of digital-trust infrastructure as a public-good financial architecture (Zetzsche et al. 2020).

6.2 Signals to Regulators About FinTech Trust Frameworks

The results show that the market doesn't naturally prioritize trust-enhancing FinTech very much. Regulators could speed up sustainable change by making ESG classification criteria stricter, making digital-trust reporting more consistent, and making sure that responsible-finance disclosure frameworks include performance in AML, cybersecurity, and fraud detection (EBA 2023; Schoenmaker and Schramade 2019). Cooperation between ESG finance and Fintech fraud detection and prevention would make the market more stable, trustworthy, and safe for the public.

Table 1 Descriptive statistics

Statistic	Amount (USD)
Count	105.00
Mean	159,883,809.52
Std	201,547,704.38
Min	2,000,000.00
25%	45,000,000.00
50%	90,000,000.00
75%	205,000,000.00
Max	1,300,000,000.00

Source Own processing

7 Conclusion

The results of this article strongly suggest that ESG labeling do not provide FinTech startups with a major financial advantage. However, ESG-labeled firms who work to stop fintech fraud get a lot of funding, but not in a way that is distinct from their competitors who do not have ESG labels. A small number of big agreements fuel a lot of investment. Investors seem to be more interested in the overall venture capital market than in the smaller ESG requirements. There are a lot of ESG stories in the FinTech area, but they haven't had a big impact on how institutional investors put their money to work or how much attention they pay to them.

Appendix 1

See Table 1.

Appendix 2: Visual Analysis

See Figs. 1, 2, 3, 4, 5 and 6.

Appendix 3: Regression Analysis

See Table 2.

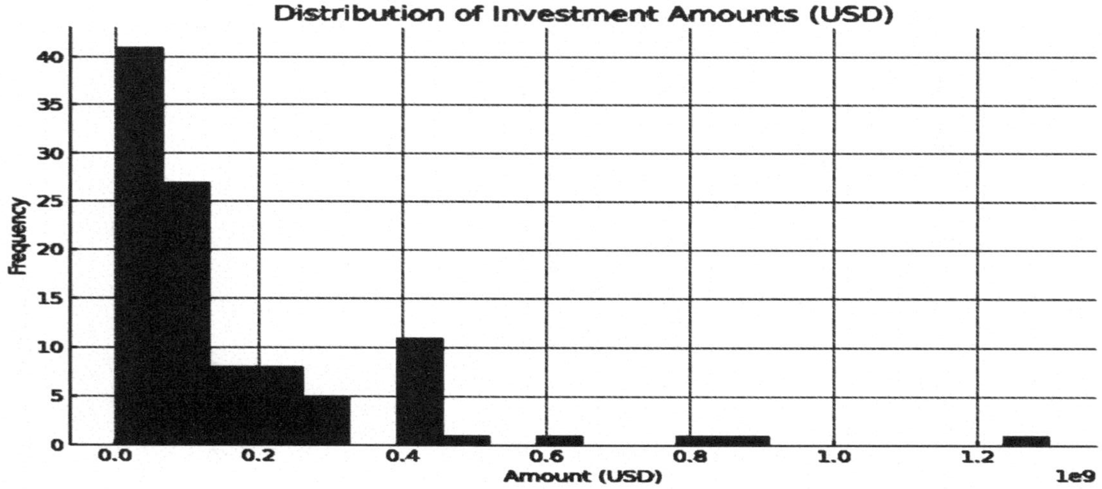

Fig. 1 Distribution of Investment Amounts (USD). *Source* Own processing

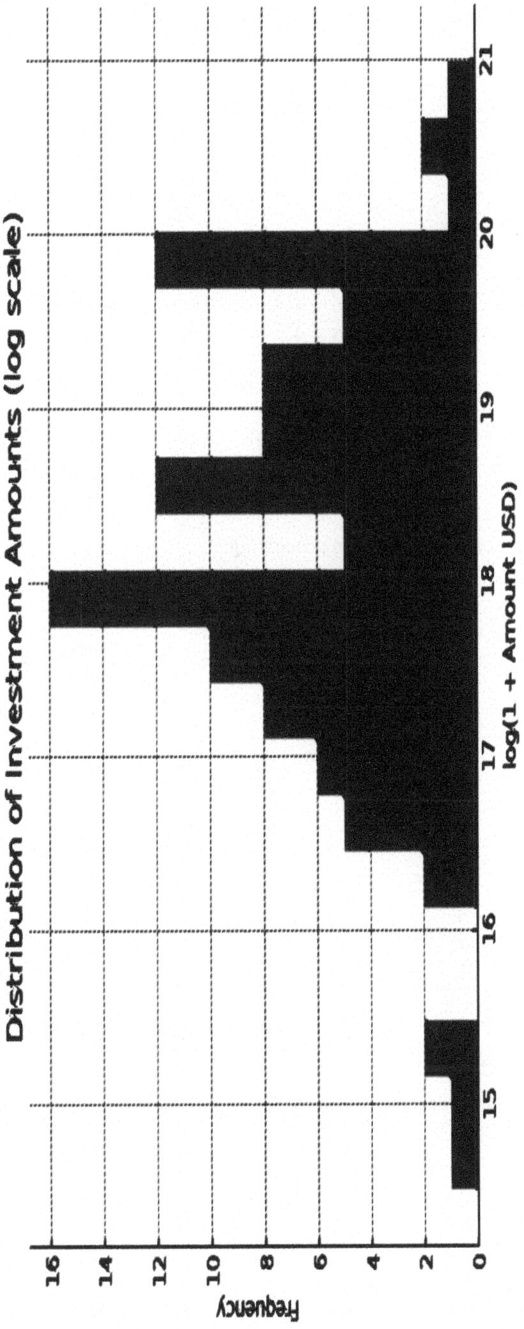

Fig. 2 Distribution of Investment Amounts (log scale). *Source* Own processing

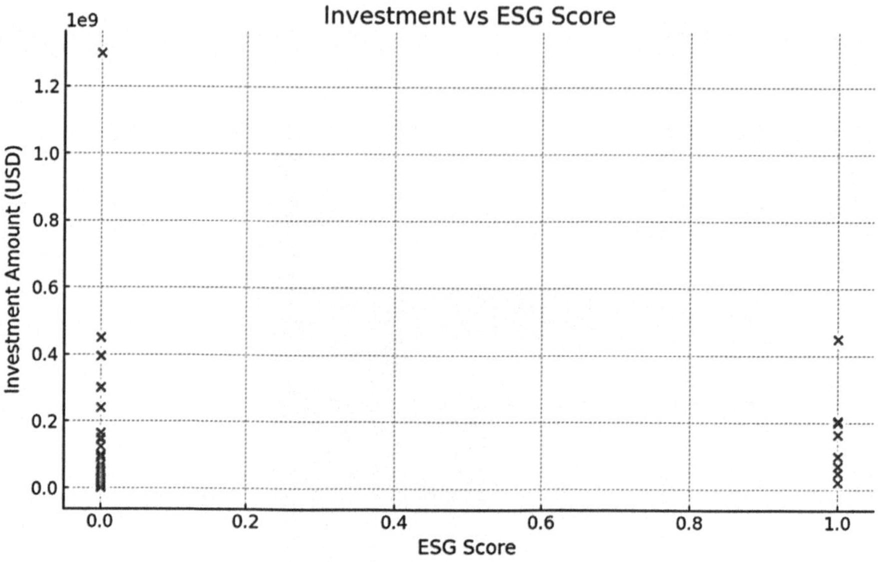

Fig. 3 Investment vs ESG Score. *Source* Own processing

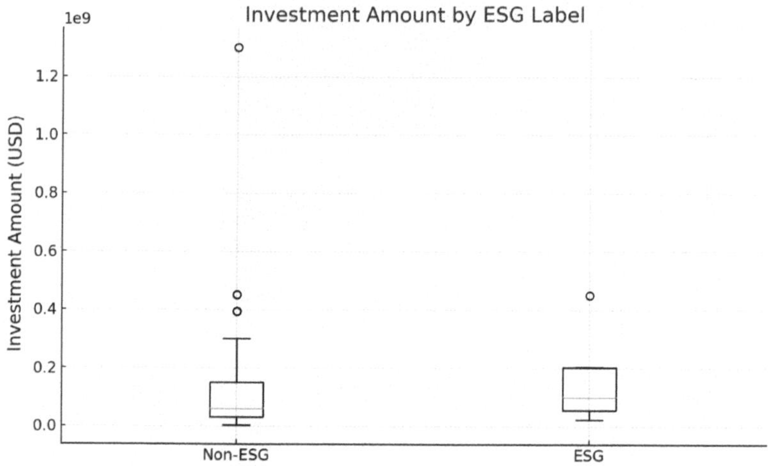

Fig. 4 Investment Amount by ESG Label. *Source* Own processing

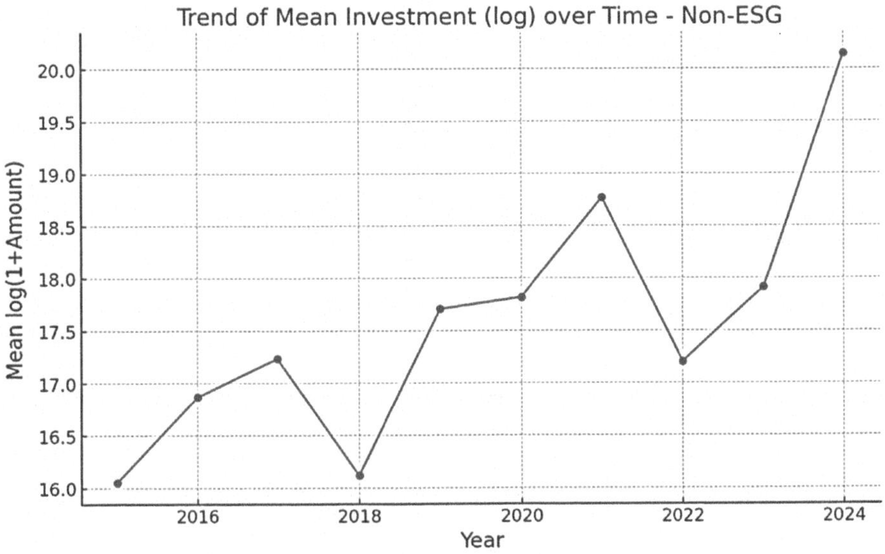

Fig. 5 Trend of Mean Investment (log) over Time—Non ESG. *Source* Own processing

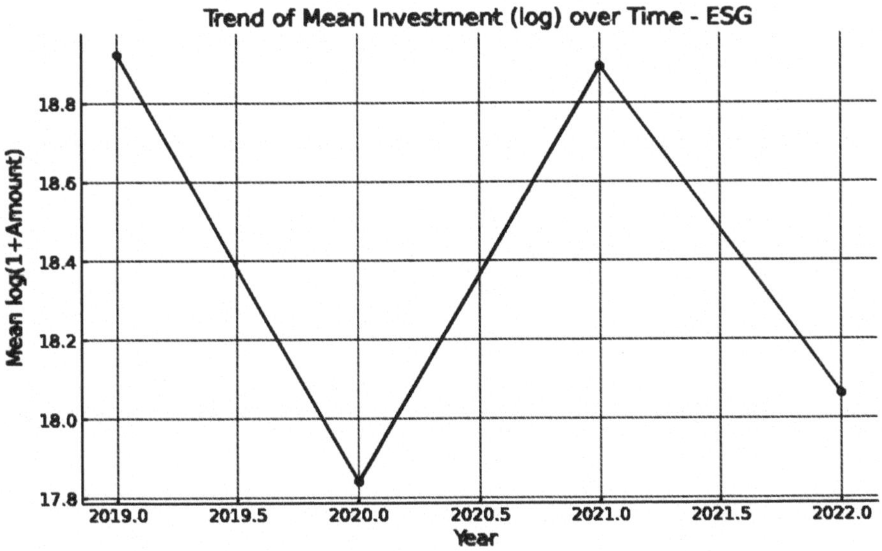

Fig. 6 Trend of Mean Investment (log) over Time—ESG. *Source* Own processing

Table 2 Regression analysis

Variable	Coef	Std Err	t	$p > \|t\|$
Const	−575.0652	145.1802	−3.9610	0.0002
ESG_Flag	0.2067	0.1679	1.2311	0.2223
ESG_Score	0.2067	0.1679	1.2311	0.2223
Year	0.2935	0.0719	4.0848	0.0001

Source Own processing

References

Afjal M, Salamzadeh A, Dana LP (2023) Financial fraud and credit risk: illicit practices and their impact on banking stability. J Risk Financ Manag 16(9):386

Agrawal A, Hockerts K (2019) Impact investing: review and research agenda. J Small Bus Entrep 31(3):293–316

Albuquerque R, Koskinen Y, Zhang C (2019) Corporate social responsibility and firm risk. Manag Sci 65(10):4451–4474

Alda M (2022a) Sustainable finance and ESG: regulation and practice. Oxford University Press, Oxford

Alda M (2022b) Sustainable finance and ESG: rules and how to do it. Oxford University Press, Oxford

Aldoush M, Ferdous H (2023) Digital trust and ESG: foundations for inclusive FinTech adoption. J Sustain Finance Invest 13(4):810–829

Alekseeva L, Guriev S, Sonin K, Zhuravskaya E (2021) Technological innovation and firm outcomes. J Econ Behav Organ 2021:1

Arner DW, Barberis J, Buckley RP (2017a) FinTech and RegTech: impact on financial regulation. J Bank Regul 19(2):1–14*

Arner DW, Barberis J, Buckley RP (2017b) FinTech, RegTech and the reconceptualization of financial regulation. Northwestern J Int Law Bus 37(3):371–413*

Arner DW, Buckley RP, Zetzsche DA, Barberis J (2020) FinTech and RegTech: building a resilient financial system. Georgetown J Int Law 51(4):1247–1290

Arora MM, Islam S (2022) Blockchain adoption and financial fraud reduction: a systematic review. J Financ Crime 29(3):1001–1022

Barber BM, Morse A, Yasuda A (2021) Impact investing. J Financ Econ 139(1):162–185

Bernstein S, Korteweg A, Laws K (2017) Attracting early-stage investors. J Finance 72(2):509–538

Block J, Fisch C, Vismara S, Andres R (2019) Private equity, venture capital, and crowdfunding. J Bus Ventur Insights 11:e00138

Brest P, Born K (2013) When can impact investing make a real difference? Stanf Soc Innov Rev 11(4):22–31

Bugg-Levine A, Emerson J (2011) Impact investing. Innovations 6(3):9–44

Chen M-H, Wu R-C, Yang C-Y (2020) FinTech and fraud risk. J Financ Crime 27(3):835–852

Cho E (2023) Time-varying preferences for ESG investments. J Derivat Quant Stud 31(2):121–142*

Clark GL, Feiner A, Viehs M (2015) From the stockholder to the stakeholder. Oxford University, Arabesque

Covachev S (2025) Are ESG factors truly unique? J Int Financ Mark Inst Money 2025:1

Crifo P, Mottis N (2023) Responsible investment and sustainable finance. Cambridge University Press, Cambridge

Cumming D, Dai N (2010) Local bias in venture capital investments. J Corp Finan 16(3):341–363

Dimson E, Marsh P, Staunton M (2020) Divergent ESG ratings. J Appl Corp Financ 32(2):10–23

Dorfleitner G, Hornuf L, Schaber M, Weber M (2017) Responsible and sustainable investing. Springer, London
Dorfleitner G, Hornuf L, Schaber M, Weber M (2022) Sustainable investments and FinTech. Springer, London
Döttling R, Kim S (2021) ESG investments and investor preferences. Cesifo Forum 22(3):12–16
Dyck A, Morse A, Zingales L (2010) Who reports corporate fraud? Journal of Finance 65(6):2213–2253
Eccles RG, Stroehle J (2018) Exploring social and governance issues for sustainable finance. Working paper no. 18-069. Harvard Business School
European Banking Authority (2023) ESG risks and digital finance supervision report
European Commission (2022) Digital finance and sustainable finance legislative package: PSD3, AMLD6, DORA
European Securities and Markets Authority (2025) ESG-related changes and investment flows
Ewens M, Farre-Mensa J (2022) Do investors value startup governance? J Financ Econ 145(2):370–403
Friede G, Busch T, Bassen A (2015) ESG and financial performance. J Sustain Finance Invest 5(4):210–233
Friedman M (2021) Capitalism and ESG: market signals vs. social mandates. J Econ Perspect 35(2):3–18
Goldstein I, Kopytov A, Shen L, Xiang H (2022) On ESG investing. Working paper no. 29839. NBER
Guiso L, Sapienza P, Zingales L (2008) Trust and market participation. Rev Financ Stud 23(3):1633–1666
Howell ST (2020) Financing innovation: evidence from venture loans. Am Econ Rev 110(3):1131–1183
Huq S (2022) Exploring the relationship between ESG and portfolio performance. Master's thesis
Journal of Empirical Legal Studies (2025) The ESG backlash and the demand for ESG mutual funds
Kaplan SN, Lerner J (2016) Venture capital data and analytics. J Econ Perspect 30(3):93–116
Kräussl R (2024) A review on ESG investing. J Econ Surv 38(2):476–502
Krueger P, Sautner Z, Starks LT (2020) The importance of climate risks. Rev Financ Stud 33(3):1067–1111*
Li D (2024) ESG performance and corporate fraud. Financ Res Lett 62:104291
Li Y, Manski SM, Ozkul E, Griffoli P (2021) Trust, digital identity and financial inclusion. Working paper no. 9665. World Bank
Miralles-Quirós JL, Miralles-Quirós MM, Nogueira JM (2019) ESG performance and investment flows. Financ Res Lett 30:142–149
Mirghaffari R (2025) Risk and performance of ESG portfolios. Int J Finance Manag Account 2025:1
Organisation for Economic Co-Operation and Development (2020) ESG investing: practices, progress and challenges
Rysman M, Shy O (2019) FinTech and payment innovation. J Econ Perspect 33(4):135–158
Sandu D-M (2023) The effect of ESG scores. Proc Int Conf Bus Excel 17(1):1807–1817
Schoenmaker D, Schramade W (2019) Principles of sustainable finance. Oxford University Press, Oxford
Scholtens B (2017) Why ecology should matter to finance. Trends Ecol Evol 32(7):500–505
Sullivan R, Mackenzie C (2020) Responsible investment in fixed income markets. Routledge, Oxford
Wang J (2024) Corporate ESG performance and corporate violations. Corporate Soc Respons Environ Manag 31(6):5606–5626
Ye K, Zhang R (2011) Do lenders prefer firms with better governance? J Financ Econ 102(1):62–87
Zehir E, Aybars A (2020) ESG score effects in Europe and Turkey. J Cap Mark Stud 4(2):129–143
Zetzsche DA, Buckley RP, Arner DW, Barberis J (2020) Regulating digital finance. Eur Corporate Law J 17(3):345–372

Anastas Dzurovski is a Full-time Professor at State University "St.Kliment Ohridski" – Bitola, North Macedonia, where he is teacher of Finance, Economics and Law. He is for more than 15 years in the academic sector and 20 years within the business sector as court expert, valuator and business consultant. He holds PhD Degree in Finance and another PhD Degree in Law. He is also a member of MSCA Industrial Doctoral Network on Digital Finance and Transparency in Fintech COST Action.

Can We Explore Financial Crime in the Crypto Market? A Systematic Review of Technical, Regulatory, and Risk Frameworks

Adrian Bojan and Monica Violeta Achim

Abstract Tax evasion through cryptocurrencies is one of the most challenging consequences of financial digitization. The study analyzes the evolution of the phenomenon and the perception of risks associated with the use of cryptocurrencies in the context of tax regulations, through a literature review and a bibliometric analysis. The sample consists of 403 articles after refinement, which were extracted from Web of Science for the period 2017–2025. The analysis is based on indicators such as total number of citations, h-index, and journal impact factor, using VOSviewer and Bibliometrix for thematic mapping. The results show that the literature focuses on topics such as confidentiality, compliance, and AML regulations, while the analysis of tax evasion remains limited. The main contribution of the study is to propose a comparative legislative harmonization score that allows for the assessment of the degree of convergence between jurisdictions and the identification of tax risk areas. Finally, this study broadens the research horizon, offers recommendations for future unexplored directions, and for the development of effective tax policies by increasing tax transparency.

Keywords Shadow economy · Money laundering · Financial crime · Crypto · Crypto-assets · Blockchain · Cryptocurrencies

1 Introduction

Over the past decade, cryptocurrencies have become a topic of major interest for academia, politics, and economics due to their disruptive nature on traditional financial systems and their implications for regulation, taxation, and economic security.

A. Bojan (✉) · M. V. Achim
Faculty of Economics and Business Administration, Babeş-Bolyai University, Cluj-Napoca, Romania
e-mail: adrian.bojan@econ.ubbcluj.ro

M. V. Achim
e-mail: monica.achim@econ.ubbcluj.ro

M. V. Achim (ed.), *Financial Crime in the Digital Era*, Contributions to Finance and Accounting, https://doi.org/10.1007/978-3-032-20198-0_9

Although blockchain technology offers the promise of increased transparency and a high degree of decentralization, the use of cryptocurrencies raises a number of significant economic and legal challenges, particularly in the context of tax evasion and illicit capital movements. From an economic point of view, they have a negative impact. One aspect is the use of anonymization mechanisms, such as stealth addresses, which allow the creation of unique, single-use addresses, thus hiding the identity of the transaction beneficiary. Similarly, centralized mixing services, such as Bitcoin Fog, offer the possibility of mixing funds from multiple users, erasing the traces of transactions and making it difficult to trace their origin. However, these practices involve additional risks related to reliance on a third party and the possibility of theft or unauthorized monitoring (Li et al. 2019). On the other hand, the environmental impact of mining activities is an increasingly debated issue, given the high electricity consumption associated with the transaction validation process, especially in the case of large networks such as Bitcoin (Ibarra 2023). Another negative effect stems from jurisdictional arbitrage, a strategy whereby economic actors exploit regulatory differences between different countries to avoid tax compliance. Globalization and the borderless, digital nature of crypto assets allow firms to migrate rapidly between jurisdictions, taking advantage of fragmentation and the lack of a unified international regulatory framework (Draganidis 2023). Furthermore, although blockchain offers transparency and traceability, these features can amplify security and stability vulnerabilities in the FinTech ecosystem, requiring more precise regulatory interventions (AlQudah 2025). As a result, the cryptocurrency market has evolved rapidly, moving from a niche area to one interconnected with traditional finance. but the crises of 2022, the collapse of the TerraUSD stablecoin and the bankruptcy of the FTX platform, have highlighted major vulnerabilities in the supervision, governance and trust in centralised entities (Aquilina 2024).

Fundamentally, the motivation for this research lies in the need to identify new avenues of research and capture current trends in risk perception and the role of regulation in preventing tax evasion through cryptocurrencies. In a context where governments are trying to balance innovation with the protection of the public interest, bibliometric analysis can provide a clear picture of scientific developments in the field and the main topics addressed.

To achieve this, we included a sample comprising 594 articles extracted from the Web of Science database, of which 403 papers published between 2017 and 2025 were retained after the refinement process. The paper uses relevant bibliometric indicators such as the total number of citations, the total number of publications, the h-index, the journal impact factor, and the VOSviewer tool for mapping thematic relationships and co-citation networks.

Preliminary results show that the literature has focused predominantly on issues such as monetary policies and crypto–fiat interaction, privacy and compliance, anti-money laundering (AML) regulations and governance, and types of crime and fraud. In contrast, there is little interest in an integrated analysis of the phenomenon of tax evasion as a whole, using cause-and-effect approaches that identify weaknesses in regulations. Thus, gaps identified in the literature concern the lack of a detailed analysis of legislative differences between states and how these differences can create opportunities for the creation of digital tax havens. Although some studies address compliance and regulatory issues, few studies systematically compare the effectiveness of tax measures across jurisdictions.

The contribution and originality of this paper lies in its multifaceted approach, covering several technical, regulatory, and risk elements with the aim of presenting the overall impact and future research directions that have not been exploited to combat tax evasion.

The paper is structured as follows: the first section provides a literature review on the evolution of cryptocurrencies and their operating mechanisms; the second details the screening methodology and tools used in the bibliometric analysis; the third section presents the results of the bibliometric analysis and their interpretation; the penultimate part discusses future research directions, and finally, the main conclusions of the study are formulated.

2 Literature Review

Digital payment alternative, decentralized nature of the Internet-based money known as cryptocurrencies. This is because their value is not guaranteed by any institution and has no regulation on its supply or distribution as a consequence of the way they are launched. Hence, they are not regulated by any direct authority of the government and no body is set up to monitor their operation. One of the key benefits that cryptocurrencies provide is mitigation of fraudulent transactions such as fake payments, unauthorized transaction repeats, or alteration in quantities involved. The verification mechanism in blockchain technology enables this: intermediaries like banks or payment processors are unnecessary, and events can be validated instantly. Therefore, transactions need to be executed faster, cheaper, and more traceable than current transactions (Buhalis et al. 2019; Norton 2024; Rejeb et al. 2021).

Cryptocurrency is a type of digital or virtual currency that uses cryptography for security measures, and it is typically decentralized. This makes them completely secure yet anonymous while handling cryptocurrency transactions, but which verifies ownership of the asset. The first cryptocurrency is Bitcoin, and it was launched to make transactions without using banks or even different types of financial organizations. The technology behind it, blockchain, was created by Satoshi Nakamoto, and soon the crypto market diversified with a major player in tracking Ethereum, which came through an Initial Coin Offering (ICO). In an ICO, a company offers to sell digital chips for the money the company needs to raise from investors. It is like when a company gets listed in the stock exchange (IPO—Initial Public Offering), and investors get shares of the company. IOTA is the first cryptocurrency that uses Tangle as core technology rather than blockchain (Ben and Xiaoqiong 2019; Giudici et al. 2020). These are presented below in graphical form in Fig. 1.

In a blockchain structure, transactions are organized in blocks or individual units over time, where each contains a unique hash derived from both its content and the hash of a previous transaction. This inter-dependence creates a linear chain: for

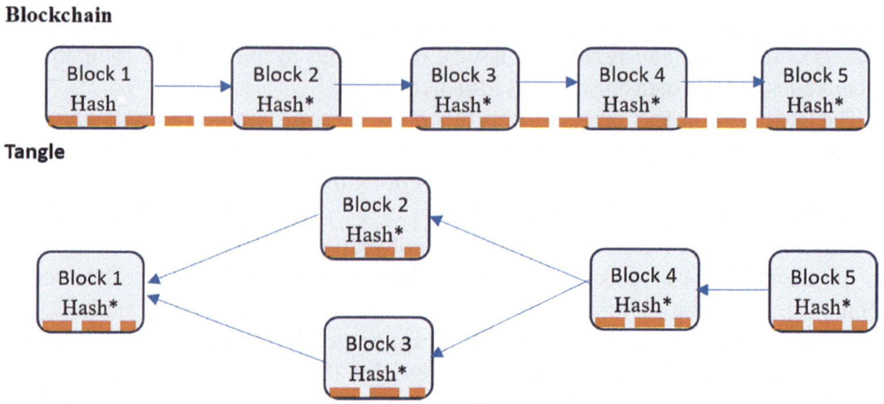

Fig. 1 Blockchain versus tangle. *Source* Processed by the author

a new transaction (Block4) to be valid, all previous transactions (Block1–Block3) must have been confirmed, and their hashes have to match. Any change in a block invalidates all following blocks. Similarly, unlike the linear chain used by blockchain, Tangle comprises a network of transactions. In other words, each new transaction (Block4) must validate two prior transactions (Block2 and Block3), but their hashes are unique and do not exclusively rely on a single previous transaction. This ushers in parallel validation, which disrupts bottlenecks and eliminates the need for blocks to be mined in sequence (Ben Hassine et al. 2020; Raso et al. 2022). Regardless of their type, cryptocurrencies maintain anonymity in transactions and have a different impact because Monero, whose main development leaves transaction detection close to impossible (Chervinski and Kreutz 2019).

Much like equities on traditional commodity exchanges, cryptocurrencies can be traded on specialized platforms and on a peer-to-peer method (Fig. 2). Unlike international trade, however, cryptocurrencies have a very limited adoption due to some important technical factors, like the lack of funds to develop the required infrastructure and accurately verifying the identity of the parties engaged in the transactions (Tavasoli 2020). Cryptocurrencies are still in the early stages of development, and are primarily regarded as substitute currencies with the goal to replace or complement the monetary systems in place today. The perception is still very controversial, some banking experts go on to describe the assets as a "Global Financial Pyramid" or "Suspicious Currencies" shedding some light on the dominant mistrust and negative perception from a significant part of the financial community (Schmidt 2018; Dumchikov et al. 2020). Therefore, the two categories of online markets for trading cryptocurrencies are represented graphically in the Fig. 2. This peer-to-peer model has the potential to increase the efficiency of an economy by cutting out middlemen, decreasing costs, and speeding up capital flows, but it leads to an increased likelihood of fraud and volatility in markets. Centralized platforms, on the other hand, incorporate trust and stability into their applications by regularly checking both their users and activity through defined processes and established controls, but at higher costs in Table 1 due to fees (Ben and Xiaoqiong 2019).

The articles I read make it clear that the cryptocurrency market is a fertile source of funding for criminal activities. According to Voskobitova et al. (2021), these include, also, the means of payment used by the organizations, drug sellers along with speculators and Ponzi scheme proponents, a money laundering gizmo, and a tax planning tool. The authors estimate that 1.1 million bitcoins, worth approximately $8.9 billion in total, were stolen using illegal methods between 2013 and 2017, and note that the semi-anonymity of transactions can all but guarantee participation from the world of the underground economy organically. This picture is complemented by Williamson's (2018) analysis, which suggests that between 25 and 50% of Bitcoin users are linked to illegal activities; he shows that digital currency has been used to avoid taxes and circumvent currency controls. In addition, Naheem (2021) points out that the same technologies facilitate payment for human trafficking and other forms of modern slavery, allowing actors to bypass regulated banking platforms. On the other hand, the literature discusses possible institutional solutions.

The bibliometric review conducted by Cotugno et al. (2024) shows that the European Central Bank is exploring a digital euro precisely to reduce the risks of money laundering and fraud associated with private cryptocurrencies. However, there are warnings that central bank digital currencies (CBDCs) could pose new challenges

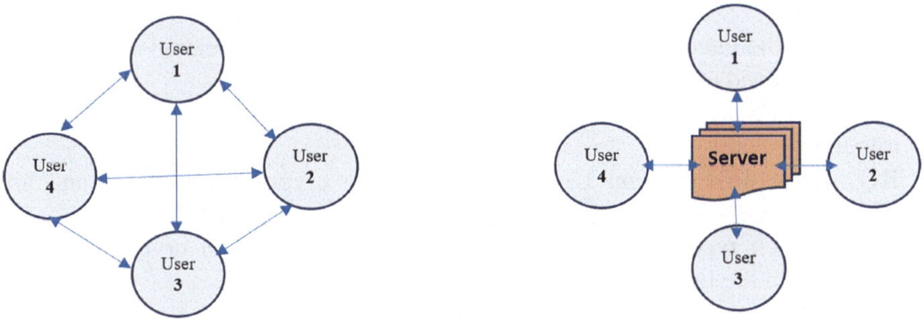

Fig. 2 Digital markets. *Source* Processed by the author

Table 1 Cryptocurrency characteristics

Attribute	Peer to peer	Online platforms
Intermediary	No	Yes
Control	Distributed	Centralized
Regulation	Difficult	Less difficult
Rates	Reduced	Fees
Speed	Quick	Depends on the platform
Anonymity	Yes	Yes

Source Processed by the author

to transaction privacy and could generate new forms of corruption and bribery if not accompanied by strict rules and powerful cyber control tools. At the same time, the literature reveals that the most common economic crimes associated with the cryptocurrency market are money laundering and Ponzi schemes, fraudulent systems in which the "profits" of existing investors come exclusively from the contributions of new participants (Kutera 2022). However, another study claims that most of the fraud identified is cyber-related (Trozze et al. 2022), and therefore the study should continue to focus on the link between tax evasion and cryptocurrencies, as this is a sensitive and rarely addressed topic. But aside from these rules, there are several market-specific risks and negative factors that cryptocurrency investors have to contend with. Finally, in order to provide a complete picture of the situation, we close by summarizing the main factors that could harm investors and their level of protection, accoring with Table 2

More importantly, several studies have exposed risks associated with investing in cryptocurrencies: high volatility, lack of transparency, and exposure to different forms of scams and fraudulent activities. This type of comparative technique is essential in order to see what the predominant research foci are for a period, and also which areas are not as well-researched. Thus, defining precise research questions on these paramount issues is the prerequisite of the bibliometric analysis developed in this paper:

RQ$_1$: Which journals, countries, and research papers have the greatest impact in the field?
RQ$_2$: Has the interest of publications regarding tax evasion related to cryptocurrencies evolved over time?
RQ$_3$: What research areas have consistently attracted interest and are currently trending?
RQ$_4$: How do European Union regulations on cryptoassets appear and are addressed in academic publications?
RQ$_5$: Which types of scams and fraudulent schemes with crypto are most discussed in the literature?
RQ$_{6:}$ What research trends, at the intersection of crypto and tax evasion, shape the next wave of academic directions?

3 Methodology

3.1 Data Sources and Search Strategy

A summary of methodological trends shows that cryptocurrency impact analyses increasingly focus on bibliometric indicators such as citation counts, journal impact factors, and h-indexes to assess the relevance of authors and publications, more on qualitative than quantitative analysis due to the lack of consistent databases for cryptocurrencies. Methodological analysis of the literature shows that the approaches

Table 2 Risk factors for cryptocurrency investors

No.	Risk factors	Description	Source
1.	Volatility and liquidity	Cryptocurrencies exhibit extreme price fluctuations, including prolonged crises and slow recoveries; speculative bubbles and sudden crashes may occur. Liquidity drops sharply during crises, making it difficult to sell without major losses	Bajwa (2025), Ben Yaala and Henchiri (2025), Harrast et al. (2022), Kerr et al. (2023) and Yang (2025)
2.	Market and evaluation	The lack of a reference price between exchanges and the difficulty of objective evaluation; lack of intrinsic value for many projects and potential for speculative bubbles	Harrast et al. (2022) and Kerr et al. (2023)
3.	Regulation	Uncertainty or legislative changes (MiCA in the EU, ban in China) causing volatility; anonymity and cross-border transactions increase the risk of fraud and manipulation; use in illegal activities (ransomware, trafficking, etc.)	Bajwa (2025), Harrast et al. (2022) and Kerr et al. (2023)
4.	Fraud, security and transparency	Scams (Ponzi schemes, rug pulls, pump-and-dump), cyber attacks, and blockchain exploits; loss of private key can lead to total loss; ineffective controls at some exchanges; limited transparency and auditing at some projects	Bajwa (2025), Harrast et al. (2022) and Kerr et al. (2023)
5.	Technology, energy and climate	The high energy consumption of Proof of Work mechanisms, physical risks (storms, earthquakes, climate change), and technological transitions (green energy, new consensus mechanisms) increase uncertainty and costs. Complex or difficult-to-adopt projects reduce attractiveness	Ben Yaala and Henchiri (2025) and Lan and Frömmel (2025)
6.	Offer and governance	Rapid token issuance reduces value; highly intense network activity may signal over-speculation followed by corrections; excessive decentralization of governance leads to slow decision-making and difficult coordination; high technological complexity hinders adoption	Lan and Frömmel (2025)
7.	Trading	Trading costs quickly reduce profits. Without short-selling on weak currencies ("losers"), returns drop significantly (i.e., betting on the decline of cryptocurrencies that have performed poorly). Reporting delays can distort results. Momentum strategies only work over short intervals (1–4 weeks), not over 5–8 weeks	Harrast et al. (2022) and Yang (2025)
8.	Behavior and social media	Limited investment knowledge, moderate risk awareness, and significant influence of hype/social media on decisions; high risk tolerance among young investors, especially men under 30	Kiruba et al. (2023)

Source Processed by the author

used by researchers differ substantially, but can be grouped into several categories. A first group (Herskind et al. 2020) follows a rigorous systematic review protocol taken from the work of (Petersen et al. 2015; Wohlin 2014): authors formulate research questions using the PICOC matrix, develop search strings such as "anonymous electronic cash" or "anonymity attack cryptocurrency," and follow a clear sequence of steps.

Another group of authors claim to be "systematic," but use structured or thematic reviews rather than strict protocols. For example, (Ballis and Verousis 2022; Corbet et al. 2019) organize the literature by topic, describing the data and methods used in the 90 studies analyzed; however, they do not document the search steps or selection criteria in detail. These papers provide a useful synthesis but carry a higher risk of subjective selection. To avoid confusion in data refinement, the analysis follows a rigorous protocol for research directions. Like recent studies, it starts from a rigorous selection of literature, using keywords representative of the field of cryptocurrencies in the sphere of tax evasion and applying qualitative filters.

The paper by Linnenluecke (Linnenluecke et al. 2020) provides recommendations on how systematic reviews should be designed: emphasis on exhaustive searches, pre-established criteria, and transparency in selection. These recommendations have been adopted by authors such as Almeida (Almeida and Gonçalves 2024), who justify their selection of keywords, criteria, and data cleaning steps. My research aligns with existing recommendations and research trends in the literature, with the processing to be carried out in four stages (Bota-Avram 2023; Kutera 2022; Lazea et al. 2024; Trozze et al. 2022), as shown in Figs. 3 and 4.

In selecting the literature, we followed a four-step protocol similar to that used in other reference studies. Starting from a set of keywords related to economic crime closely linked to tax evasion, and in order to capture more derivative forms for digital currencies, we used "*", such as: cryptocurrency, cryptocurrencies, cryptoasset, cryptographic, and others, which facilitate searching in Web of Science.

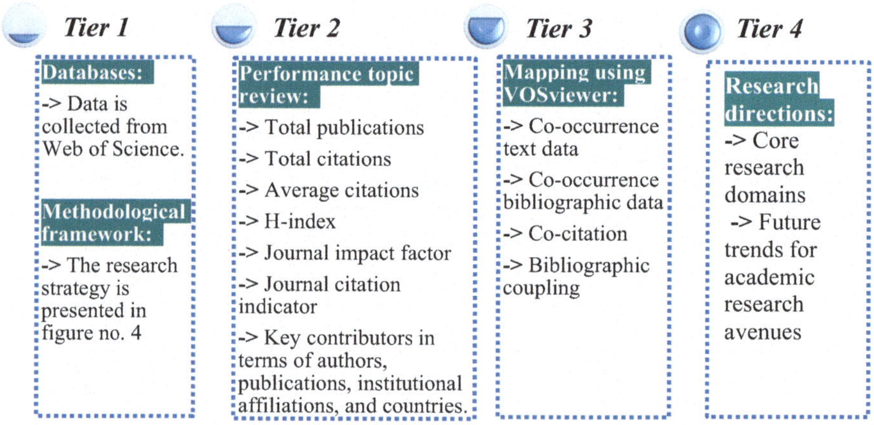

Fig. 3 Four step for conducting the literature review. *Source* Processed by the author

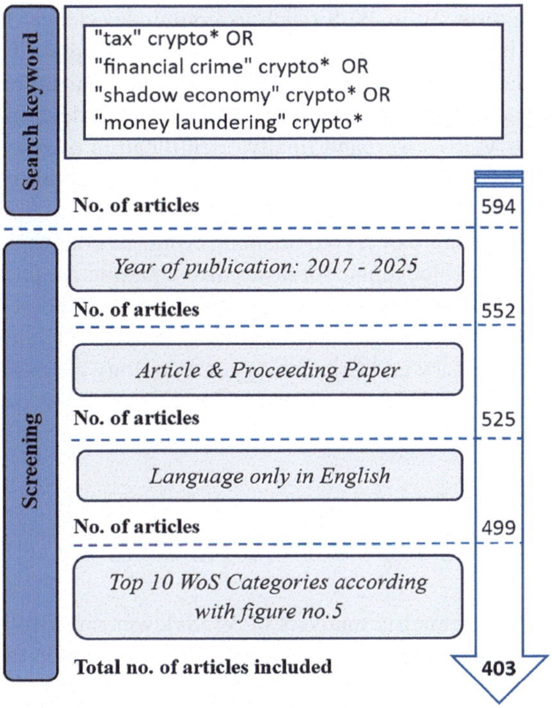

Fig. 4 Data refinement. *Source* Processed by the author

Authors (Aggarwal and Kumar 2021; Pernice and Scott 2021) use the term cryptocurrency because they define it as a cryptographically secured digital payment system that operates on decentralized networks and eliminates the need for a trusted intermediary.

For these authors, the emphasis is on the currency's function as a medium of exchange and its decentralized technological nature, which makes the notion of "cryptocurrency" specific enough to describe the phenomenon under analysis. In contrast, prefer the broader term crypto-assets, defining it as including a variety of digital instruments, from payment tokens and e-money tokens to assets with an investment or service access role, all based on cryptography and distributed ledgers (Hung 2024; Joebges et al. 2025; Parrondo 2023). This approach emphasizes the functional and legal diversity of these instruments, going beyond their strict function as a means of payment.

Therefore, in the process of identifying relevant literature, we used the generic term "crypto*" in bibliographic queries, precisely to capture all the conceptual and functional derivatives of the phenomenon, avoiding the exclusion of important works that use different terminology. This generated 594 results, looking to Fig. 4. Filtering by the 2017–2025 interval reduced the corpus to 552 titles, then retaining only articles and conference papers (525 papers), and excluding materials in other languages resulted in 499 articles. Finally, selecting the ten most relevant thematic categories from WoS (such as computer science, law, or finance) left 403 articles for bibliometric analysis, according with Fig. 4. They were exported in.txt format and subsequently analyzed in VOSviewer; the figures provided visually describe this procedure. This four-stage process of data collection, performance analysis, mapping with VOSviewer, and finally, identification of research directions, reflects existing recommendations on transparency and replicability of systematic reviews.

We narrowed our analysis to the top 10 WoS categories to capture the interdisciplinary nature of crypto financial crime, as confirmed in the literature. Recent studies show that blockchain forensics investigations are based on Computer Science—Information Systems (Atlam et al. 2024), while market manipulation and tax avoidance justify the inclusion of Business-Finance and Economics (Jeris et al. 2022). The fields of Law and Criminology & Penology are essential for understanding the legal framework and types of fraud (Trozze et al. 2022), which ensures complete coverage of the phenomenon reflected in Fig. 5.

3.2 Bibliometric Mapping

The bibliometric analysis of VOSviewer and Bibliometrix, was highlighted using the following four different categories of tools in the literature:

- *Co-occurrence (text data)*: Counts how often terms appear together in the same document (keywords, title expressions, or abstract). This approach helps to identify common themes and conceptual relationships in a given area. I use it in my analysis to be able to group terms together, in clusters.
- *Co-occurrence (bibliographic data):* Follows the simultaneous occurrences of shared bibliographic details such as keywords supplied by authors or indexing terms. Such information is valuable for categorizing the way researchers describe their work and describing thematic networks according to the authors themselves. In my analysis, this measures the change in use of terms addressed by the literature through time.
- *Co-citation:* This is a count of how frequently two different sources are cited together by other works. High levels of co-citation suggest a news source is tightly connected to others—or that they are all seen as being very relevant by their academic audience.
- *Bibliographic coupling:* Occurs when two different works both cite a third work. Common references in one way or another to authors, topics, or methods are a good indication if two articles were published at different points.

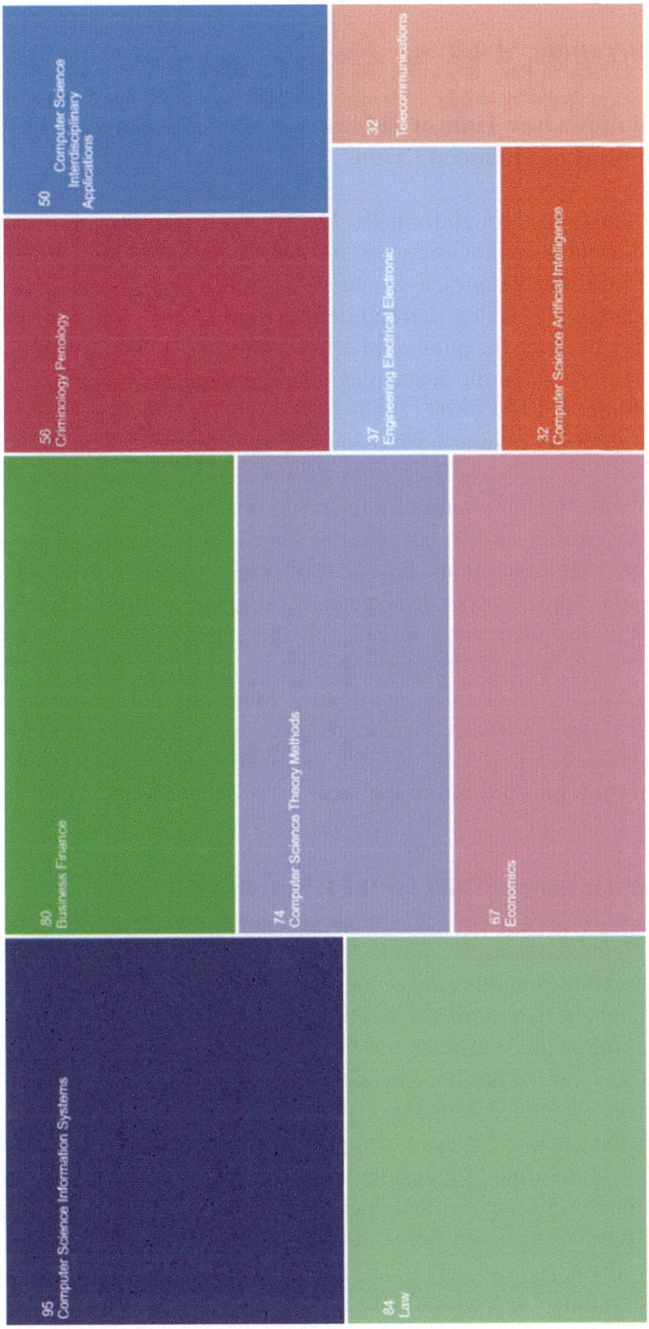

Fig. 5 Top 10 web of science categories. *Source* Web of science

4 Results and Discussion

4.1 Cryptocurrencies Analysis

4.1.1 The Evolution Over Time of Publications on Cryptocurrencies in the Context of Financial Crime

The graph (Fig. 6) takes us through from 2017 to July 2025, spelling out exactly how academic interest around cryptocurrencies and tax has trended. Prior to 2020, this phenomenon was in the early stages, as can be seen by the meager rate of publications throughout the years, only having reached double digits from 2017 with 8 distinct papers (2 citations). In 2018, the number of articles almost tripled (24), and citations rose to 26, also signifying that the academic community had begun paying attention to this particular topic. These 3 years (2019–2021) signal a very clear consolidation, with publications climbing regularly from 35 to 52 and citations rising from 73 until today with over 300.

This period signals the beginning of a maturing process where both the volume and influence of the works start to become more evident. This seemed to coincide with the debates on AML regulations, European directives, and initial moves towards fiscal integration of crypto assets in those years (Courtois et al. 2021; Covolo 2019). The numbers then jump considerably in 2022 (36 and 309) and even more so in 2023 (83, 605). Then, as the apex of academic interest, accepted in 2024, for the most publications (78) and absolutely highest citations count (904). The year 2025 is an exception because it is the year in which the research is processed, and for this year, the academic situation can only be presented until July 2025, although the trend is expected to be upward until the end of the year.

4.1.2 Most Popular Source Titles for the Research Area

The Table 3 highlights the main academic sources in which articles related to cryptocurrencies, tax evasion, and financial crime are published, providing a clear picture of the scientific channels of dissemination. The Journal of Money Laundering Control dominates the ranking, with 38 articles and 313 citations, confirming observations in the literature that this journal has become a benchmark for research on money laundering and new risks associated with digital technologies (Saxena and Kumar 2023). At the same time, the Lecture Notes in Computer Science series has 24 articles, but with a low number of citations, suggesting a more technical orientation, where the focus is on algorithmic solutions, without increased visibility in the area of regulation (Garcia-Alfaro 2018; Werman and Zohar 2018). The impact of technology journals is highlighted by IEEE Access and IEEE Transactions on Information Forensics and Security, both publishing eight articles, but with a disproportionate number of citations: 73 and 123, respectively. The impact factor (3.6 and 8) confirms the trend

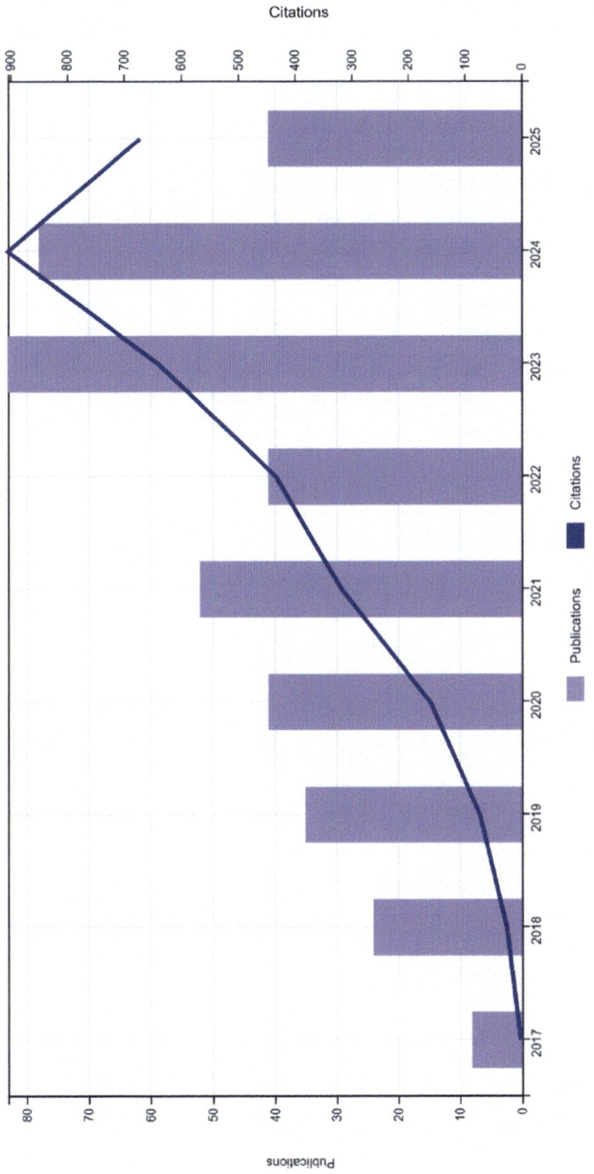

Fig. 6 Number of citations and publications in 2017–2025. *Source* Web of science

reported in recent literature, according to which cybersecurity and forensic analysis are becoming indispensable in studies on crypto assets (Atlam et al. 2024).

In contrast, legal and tax journals such as Computer Law and Security Review, Intertax, and EC Tax Review have fewer articles but contribute through in-depth debates on regulatory harmonization and the tax challenges of digital markets, in line with analyses in the specialist literature (Benson et al. 2024; Ferreira and Sandner 2021). Furthermore, the presence of journals dedicated to taxation, such as the Journal of Tax Administration and the Australian Tax Review, shows that the tax issues surrounding cryptocurrencies have become a distinct research topic, even if the number of articles is small and citations are limited. This observation is in line with recent literature, which draws attention to the difficulty of integrating digital assets into a uniform tax framework (Baer 2023).

Table 3 Most popular source titles

No.	Source titles	No. articles	Total citations	Impact factor	Citation indicator	Publisher
1.	Journal of Money Laundering Control	38	313	1.1	0.62	Emerald
2.	Lecture Notes in Computer Science	24	2	0.302	–	Springer
3.	IEEE Access	8	73	3.6	0.82	IEEE-INST Electrical Electronics
4.	IEEE Transactions on Information Forensics and Security	8	123	8	1.85	IEEE-INST Electrical Electronics
5.	Computer Law and Security Review	7	88	–	–	Elsevier
6.	Financial and Credit Activity-Problems of Theory and Practice	7	10	0.7	0.22	Fintechaliance
7.	Intertax	7	19	1.2	0.9	Kluwer Law INT
8.	EC Tax Review	6	28	0.5	0.71	Kluwer Law INT
9.	Journal of Tax Administration	6	1	0.1	0.03	Univ Exeter Business SCH, England
10.	Australian Tax Review	5	11	0.1	0.23	Lawbook CO LTD

Source Processed by the author

4.1.3 Distribution of Articles and Academic Impact by Country

Table 4 illustrates the geography of academic research addressing cryptocurrencies and financial crime at an international level, revealing multiple key nodes for knowledge production. The USA is the front-runner by a wide margin (81 articles; 814 citations), which confirms the USA context as overwhelmingly the dominant location for both technical development and regulatory risk debates around digital assets. This is in accord with the narrative that our literature had established but now seems to be crumbling fast as research on earlier adoption of cryptoassets and their regulation not just from the US is done (Emmert 2023). The United Kingdom and Australia follow with 38 and 29 articles, but both enjoy a much higher visibility in terms of citations (333 and 284).

In these cases, the focus is on legal and fiscal perspectives, particularly through analyses related to the harmonization of regulations at the European level, which reinforces the idea of a fragmented but convergent international framework around concerns about combating money laundering and tax evasion (Foley et al. 2019; Schilling De Carvalho 2022; Wronka 2024). Italy, Ukraine, and Germany have moderate contributions in terms of volume, but relevant in terms of thematic direction. In particular, German studies bring a technical-legal dimension, which is also visible in the average number of citations per article (6.06), confirming the European literature's constant interest in integrating blockchain technology into compliance mechanisms. At the same time, Ukraine stands out with a number of publications close to that of Italy, suggesting the dynamics of an emerging market, where flexible regulations have stimulated academic interest (Bahamazava and Reznik 2023; Levytskyi et al. 2023; Wronka 2024). Canada and India, with 16 articles each, illustrate a growing concern among non-European countries about the fiscal and security

Table 4 Academic research distributed by countries

No.	Country	No. articles	Proportion (%)	Total citations (without self-citations)	Average citation per item	H-index
1.	USA	81	34.322	814	11.46	13
2.	England	38	16.102	333	9.79	11
3.	Australia	29	12.288	284	10.76	10
4.	Italy	23	9.746	93	4.48	5
5.	Ukraine	21	8.898	86	4.57	4
6.	Germany	17	7.203	89	6.06	6
7.	Canada	16	6.780	186	11.88	7
8.	India	16	6.780	138	8.81	6
9.	Netherlands	15	6.356	234	17.07	8
10.	Russia	15	6.356	49	3.93	4

Source Processed by the author

implications of crypto assets, as revealed by impact indicators (H-index 7 and 6). An interesting situation is that of the Netherlands, which, although it has only 15 articles, stands out with a very high average number of citations (17.07 per article), suggesting a concentrated literature, but with significant international visibility (Van Wegberg et al. 2018). Russia closes the top, with 15 articles and a low number of citations, which can be explained by predominantly local approaches, less integrated into the global debate.

4.1.4 Distribution of Publications and Citations by Academic Affiliation

The first place is taken by the Ministry of Education and Science of Ukraine, which in 15 works cited in science databases (60 references) reveals the studying aspects of new financial technologies despite economic disruption and lack of laws adopted according with Table 5. There were tears of joy sizzling their way down my cheeks as I rolled back into the water from whence my baby emerged; his eyes wide with paternal power throughout my battle, a manic smile stuck on his face which faces me all the time. In second position, the University of London has 12 articles and the maximum number of citations (141), which means an average of 11.75 citations per article. This is proof that British research is very influential in the literature specialized in this field. In Australia, Macquarie University and the Royal Melbourne Institute of Technology (RMIT) stand out with a smaller number of articles (six each), but with a high impact. Macquarie University has the highest average number of citations (17 per article), confirming the international visibility of Australian studies, while RMIT comes close with a value of 11.83. These results suggest that Australian institutions prefer focused but highly relevant research. At European level, the University of Bologna adds 6 articles and 33 citations, reflecting Italian academic concerns for legal and compliance issues. About h-index (impact consistency, not just isolated peaks): in the table, University of London and Macquarie University have h-index 5, which means that each has at least 5 papers with ≥ 5 citations—coherent with 12 articles/141 citations (London) and high average of 17 citations/article. Germany is represented by the Leibniz Association, with 5 articles and 21 citations, indicating a more technical literature, oriented towards the practical applicability of blockchain tools.

The United States appears through the Harvard University and the State University System of Florida. Both contribute 5 articles, but the impact differs: Harvard gathers 19 citations, and Florida 24, modest values compared to other institutions, but significant in relation to the leadership tradition of the American academic environment. The London School of Economics and Political Science (LSE) also confirms its reputation through 5 articles and 52 citations, with an average of 10.4, emphasizing interest in the political-economic dimension of cryptocurrencies. Finally, Guizhou University of China completes the ranking with only 2 articles, but with an average of 8 citations, a signal that even Asian institutions are gradually integrating into the global debate. Overall, the table reflects both the geographical diversity of academic centres and a polarisation between institutions with high volumes of publications

Table 5 Top academic affiliations by published articles and citations

No.	Affiliations	Country	No. articles	Times cited	Average citations per item	H-index
1.	Ministry of Education Science Ukraine	Ukraine	15	60	4	3
2.	University of London	UK	12	141	11.75	5
3.	Macquarie University	Australia	6	102	17	5
4.	Royal Melbourne Institute of Technology RMIT	Australia	6	71	11.83	3
5.	University of Bologna	Italy	6	33	5.5	3
6.	Harvard University	US	5	19	3.8	3
7.	Leibniz Association	Germany	5	21	4.2	3
8.	London School Economics Political Science	UK	5	52	10.4	3
9.	State University System of Florida	US	5	24	4.8	3
10.	Guizhou University	China	2	16	8	2

Source Processed by the author

but with moderate impact (e.g. Ukraine), and those with few items, but very visible internationally (eg. Macquarie University, LSE). This balance confirms the emerging and multidisciplinary nature of cryptocurrency research.

4.1.5 Articles with the Greatest Impact Through Citations

The articles were grouped by topic to highlight the impact of crypto on the economy already documented in the literature, and the selection was filtered and sorted in descending order by number of citations so that the analysis reflects the dominant directions and consensus accumulated in the field (according to Table 6). Below are thematic groups formed based on the content of the research:

- **Monetary policies and crypto–fiat interaction:**
  Schilling and Uhlig show, in a two-currency competitive framework, that the "bill" for Bitcoin block rewards does not fall on BTC holders, but is indirectly financed through dollar inflation induced by central bank injections aimed at achieving its inflation target. The policy outcome is twofold: either Bitcoin prices "guide" the supply of dollars, or the central bank manages to "anchor" Bitcoin prices by controlling its own supply—both scenarios reposition the cost to dollar holders, not BTC holders. (Schilling and Uhlig 2019).
- **Confidentiality, anonymity, and compliance:**
  Several papers converge on the same thesis: "pure" anonymity on the blockchain is difficult to achieve and, if achieved, would strain AML efforts;

Table 6 Articles with the greatest impact through citations

No.	Authors	Title	Source title	Publication year	DOI	Total citations	Average citations per year
1.	Schilling Linda; Uhlig Harald	Some simple bitcoin economics	JOURNAL OF MONETARY ECONOMICS	2019	https://doi.org/10.1016/j.jmoneco.2019.07.002	166	23.71
2.	Farrugia, Steven; Ellul, Joshua; Azzopardi, George Lin, Chao; He, Debiao; Huang, Xinyi	Detection of illicit accounts over the Ethereum blockchain	EXPERTSYSTEMS WITH APPLICATIONS	2020	https://doi.org/10.1016/j.csia.2020.113318	121	20.17
3.	Khan, Muhammad Khurram; Choo, Kim-Kwang Raymond Li, Yannan; Susilo, Willy; Yang	DCAP: A Secure and Efficient Decentralized Conditional Anonymous Payment System Based on Blockchain	IEEE TRANSACTIONS ON INFORMATION FORENSICS AND SECURITY	2020	https://doi.org/10.1109/TIFS.2020.2969565	102	17
4.	Guomin; Yu, Yong; Du, Xiaojiang; Liu, Dongxi; Guizani, Nadra	Toward Privacy and Regulation in Blockchain-Based Cryptocumencies	IEEE NETWORK	2019	https://doi.org/10.1109/MNET2019.1800271	73	10.43
5.	Kethineni, Sesha; Cao, Ying	The Rise in Popularity of Cryptocurrency and Associated Criminal Activity	INTERNATIONAL CRIMINAL JUSTICE REVIEW	2020	https://doi.org/10.1177/1057567719827051	72	12
6.	Campbell-Verduyn, Malcolm	Bitcoin crypto-coins and global anti-money laundering govemance	CRIME LAW AND SOCIAL CHANGE	2018	https://doi.org/10.1007/s10611-017-9756-5	67	8.38

(continued)

Table 6 (continued)

No.	Authors	Title	Source title	Publication year	DOI	Total citations	Average citations per year
7.	Shanaev, Savva; Sharma, Satish; Ghimire, Binam; Shuraeva, Arina	Taming the blockchain beast? Regulatory implications for the cryptocurrency Mark	RESEARCH IN INTERNATIONAL BUSINESS AND FINANCE	2020	https://doi.org/10.1016/j.ribaf.2019.101080	66	11
8.	Lorenz, Joana; Silva, Maria Ines; Aparicio, David; Ascensao, Joao Tiago; Bizarro, Pedro	Machine learning methods to detect money laundering in the Bitcoin blockchain in the presence of label scarcit	FIRST ACM INTERNATIONAL CONFERENCE ON AI IN FINANCE ICAIF	2020	https://doi.org/10.1145/3383455.3422549	59	9.83
9.	Mackenzie, Simon	Criminology towards the metaverse: Cryptocurrency scams grey economy and the techmosocial	BRITISH JOURNAL OF CRIMINOLOGY	2022	https://doi.org/10.1093/bjcazab118	51	12.75
10.	Garman, Christina; Green, Matthew; Miers, Ian	Accountable Privacy for Decentralized Anonymous Payments	FINANCIAL CRYPTOGRAPHY AND DATA SECURITY FC 2016	2017	https://doi.org/10.1007/978-3-662-54970-4_5	50	5.56
11.	Vandezande, Niels	Virtual currencies under EU anti-money laundering law	COMPUTER LAW & SECURITY REVIEW	2017	https://doi.org/10.1016/j.clsr2017.03.011	49	5.44

(continued)

Table 6 (continued)

No.	Authors	Title	Source title	Publication year	DOI	Total citations	Average citations per year
12.	Albrecht, Chad; Duffin, Kristopher McKay; Hawkins, Steven; Rocha, Victor Manuel Morales	The use of cryptocurrencies in the money laundering process	JOURNAL OF MONEY LAUNDERING CONTROL	2019	https://doi.org/10.1108/JMLC-12-2017-0074	48	686
13.	Fujiki, Hiroshi	Who adopts crypto assets in Japan? Evidence from the 2019 financial literacy survey	JOURNAL OF THE JAPANESE AND INTERNATIONAL ECONOMIES	2020	https://doi.org/10.1016/j.jjie.2020.101107	45	7.5
14.	Lin, Yu-Jing; Wu, Po-Wei; Hsu, Cheng-Han; Tu, I-Ping; Liao, Shih-wei	An Evaluation of Bitcoin Address Classificationbased on Transaction History Summarization	2019 IEEE INTERNATIONAL CONFERENCE ON BLOCKCHAIN AND CRYPTOCURRENCY (ICBC)	2019	https://doi.org/10.1109/bloc.2019.8751410	43	6.14
15.	Feinstein, Brian D.; Werbach, Kevin	The Impact of Cryptocurrency Regulation on Trading Markets	JOURNAL OF FINANCIAL REGULATION	2021	https://doi.org/10.1093/jfiffjab003	41	8.2

the viable solution is a technical-regulatory compromise. Li et al. start from the public nature of the ledgers and propose protection tactics, single-use addresses and "stealth addresses", that reduce linkability without claiming total invisibility. (Li et al. 2019). In the same vein, Lin et al. operationalize conditional anonymity (DCAP) on a private Ethereum chain: privacy by default for users, but with the possibility of tracking by an authorized manager when suspicions arise, an architecture explicitly designed for compatibility with AML requirements. (Lin et al. 2020). At the level of cryptographic principles, Garman et al. propose a DAP framework with the application of privacy-preserving policies, from spending limits and tax compliance to justified traceability, based on zk-SNARKs with solid simulation properties; thus, transaction fairness and privacy coexist without interactive dialogue between parties. (Garman et al. 2017). Where zk-SNARKs (Zero-Knowledge Succinct Non-Interactive Arguments of Knowledge) represent an advanced cryptography technology that allows one party (prover) to prove to other parties (verifiers) that a statement is true without revealing additional information about that statement. This means that, for example, a user can prove that they hold a certain amount of cryptocurrency without revealing the exact amount or the holder's address. In summary: Li et al. (2019), Lin et al. (2020), and Garman et al. (2017) converge on the idea of "privacy with brakes and counterweights": technical tools for masking identity, but with validated mechanisms for regulatory intervention.

- **AML Regulation and Governance**
  Vandezande (2017), Campbell-Verduyn (2018), and Shanaev et al. (2020) outline a coherent line: targeted regulation of intermediaries (exchanges/custody), coordinated internationally, is more effective than general prohibitions, and the market penalises regulations perceived as raising usage costs. Virtual currencies are first divided into three types: closed systems (e.g., for games, without conversion into legal tender), unidirectional (purchasable with legal tender but not convertible back, e.g., Amazon Coins), and bidirectional (convertible, such as Bitcoin). This typology explains why the first Payment Services Directives (EU), focused on payment service "funds" and electronic money issued by regulated entities, did not cover cryptocurrencies: there is no central issuer and they are not "legal tender", so AML obligations did not apply to crypto actors. In 2016, the European Commission acknowledged the absence of an EU framework and proposed including exchange platforms and digital wallet providers under AML rules, with the stated aim of reducing the risk posed by the anonymity of crypto transactions and ensuring adequate supervision of related activities. (Vandezande 2017). Campbell-Verduyn argues that the central issue is the use of blockchain for AML governance, not the "demonization" of cryptocurrencies as illicit currency. The FATF (Financial Action Task Force) applies a risk-based approach, focusing oversight on high-risk entities, especially exchanges, to harmonize AML practices across jurisdictions, even in the face of anonymization technologies (Campbell-Verduyn 2018). In terms of the market, Shanaev et al. show that regulatory news is quickly incorporated into prices: AML measures and those concerning issuance

cause significant declines, while the treatment of exchanges can raise or lower the market depending on the tone of the intervention; general statements about risk have limited effect, and announcements about sovereign currencies may be received negatively (Shanaev et al. 2020).

- **Detection**

  At the Ethereum account level, Farrugia et al. show that a well-calibrated XGBoost, fed with transaction history and account properties, effectively captures illicit behavior; The three most predictive variables are: (a) the time difference between the first and last transaction, (b) the total balance available in Ether, and (c) the minimum amount received in Ether (Farrugia et al. 2020). Farrugia et al. (2020), Lorenz et al. (2020), and Lin et al. (2019) show, using different data sets, essentially the same thing: you cannot detect illicit behavior just by hunting for "strange transactions." You need a few correctly labeled examples and simple indicators from account history. At the Ethereum account level, the most useful signs are how long an account has been active, its total balance, and the smallest amount received (Farrugia et al. 2020). When labels are few, you choose wisely what to check and can come close to the performance of "complete" models (Lorenz et al. 2020). Lin et al. (2019): labels on addresses by entity type: exchanges, gambling, mixersThe common conclusion: "unusual" does not automatically mean "illicit"; good results come from a few well-chosen examples and easily calculable signs of behavior, not from an abstract search for anomalies.

- **Social dynamics of crypto adoption**

  The research presents a profile of crypto asset holders based on a Japanese sample: most frequently men under 30, higher gross income, postgraduate education, and an appetite for cashless payment methods. Behaviorally, they are more impatient, have less self-control, and are less risk-averse than non-holders. Their preferred sources of information are economic/financial media and experts, and they are more likely to have experience with traditional risky assets (Fujiki 2020). The author documents the centrality of BTC in 99/123 cases analyzed, with uses in money laundering, drug trafficking, hacking, sex trafficking, and even escalation to physical violence (kidnappings, extortion) (Kethineni and Cao 2020).

- **Types of crimes or scams**

  Albrecht et al. describe money laundering in three stages: placement (introducing funds into the system), layering (obscuring the trail through multiple transfers), and integration (reintroducing "clean" money into the economy). These are targeted for the application of Smurfing techniques, which involve breaking up large sums into small deposits below reporting thresholds to avoid alerts. The other technique is offshore accounts, which transfer funds to jurisdictions with high freedom and tax havens (Albrecht et al. 2019). Table 7 describes the types of attacks and scams found in the targeted research.

Table 7 Typologies for attacks and scams with crypto

Typology	Additional explanations	Source
Scams		
Pump and dumps	A group of investors forms a channel on Telegram where they discuss an unknown cryptocurrency, promising that it will rapidly increase in value. They initially buy the currency to raise its price and then begin to advertise it heavily, encouraging other investors to buy. Once the price has risen significantly due to the generated demand, the group sells all the coins it holds, causing the price to crash and leaving new investors with losses	Mackenzie (2022)
Ponzi scams	O criptomonedă nouă este lansată, promițând randamente mari pentru investitorii timpurii. Investitorii care intră primii primesc plăți din contribuțiile celor care intră ulterior, ceea ce creează iluzia unei afaceri profitabile. Cu toate acestea, nu există un produs real sau o activitate economică sustenabilă; schemele se prăbuşesc atunci când numărul de noi investitori scade, iar cei din urmă nu mai primesc nimic	Mackenzie (2022)
Slow rug pulls	A developer launches a cryptocurrency and retains a significant amount of coins for themselves. Once the coin gains popularity and the price rises, the developer begins to gradually sell the coins they hold, causing the price to fall. Eventually, the project collapses, and investors are left with worthless coins	Mackenzie (2022)
Quick rug pulls	Un scammer creează o criptomonedă nouă şi o listează pe un exchange descentralizat (DEX). După ce atrage suficientă lichiditate prin vânzări, scammerul retrage rapid toată lichiditatea din pool-ul de tranzacționare, lăsând investitorii cu monede care nu mai pot fi tranzacționate, deoarece nu există un marketplace pentru ele	Mackenzie (2022)
Ransomware scams	Encrypts files on a device or system, making them inaccessible to the user. Once the files are encrypted, the attackers demand a ransom to provide the decryption key needed to regain access to the data	Patsakis et al. (2024)
Attacks associated with cryptomining		
Cryptojacking attacks	These are attacks in which a hacker uses other users' computing resources without their consent to mine cryptocurrencies. Hackers typically infect computers or servers with malware that runs mining software in the background, consuming system resources and increasing electricity costs for victims	Islam et al. (2025) and Kethineni and Cao (2020)

(continued)

Table 7 (continued)

Typology	Additional explanations	Source
Attacks on networks	In some cases, attackers may attempt to compromise cryptocurrency networks through "51%" attacks, where a group of miners controls more than 50% of the network's computing power. This allows them to perform fraudulent transactions, reverse transactions, or block legitimate transactions	Islam et al. (2025) and Kethineni and Cao (2020)
Exploiting software vulnerabilities	Hackers may search for vulnerabilities in mining software or cryptocurrency wallets to steal cryptocurrencies or compromise security systems	Islam et al. (2025) and Kethineni and Cao (2020)
Atacuri DDoS (distributed denial of service)	These attacks target cryptocurrency networks by overloading servers with excessive traffic, which can lead to mining service disruptions and financial losses for legitimate miners	Islam et al. (2025) and Kethineni and Cao (2020)

Source Processed by the author

4.2 *Visualization of Bibliometric Mapping*

The figure obtained by the Co-occurrence text data analysis carried out in VOSviewer aims to identify the main thematic directions in the literature on cryptocurrencies and financial crime by grouping the terms that frequently appear together in headings, summaries and keywords in Fig. 7:

- *The green cluster* includes terms such as taxation, tax, income, tax authority, but also legislation and law. This group highlights the literature's emphasis on the tax implications of cryptocurrencies and the legal framework. For example, tax treatment and jurisdiction relationships show concern for regulatory harmonisation and the integration of crypto assets into a transparent tax framework (Ferreira and Sandner 2021; Fujiki 2020; Pernice and Scott 2021).
- *The red cluster* dominated by terms such as anti-money laundering, anonymity, illicit transaction, cybercrime or detection. The close link between blockchain and anonymity suggests that literature investigates both the risks associated with covert transactions and the detection mechanisms needed to combat money laundering and fraud (Foley et al. 2019; Grossklags and Preneel 2017; Lin et al. 2019).
- *The blue cluster* consisting of terms such as regulatory framework, cryptocurrency regulation, innovation or policymaker. It captures interest in how national and supranational authorities seek to respond to the dynamics of the crypto market through flexible and adaptable regulations (Levytskyi et al. 2023; Wronka 2024; Zeng et al. 2025).

Overall, the map reveals a threefold thematic polarization: taxation and law (green), security and risk (red) and institutional regulation (blue).

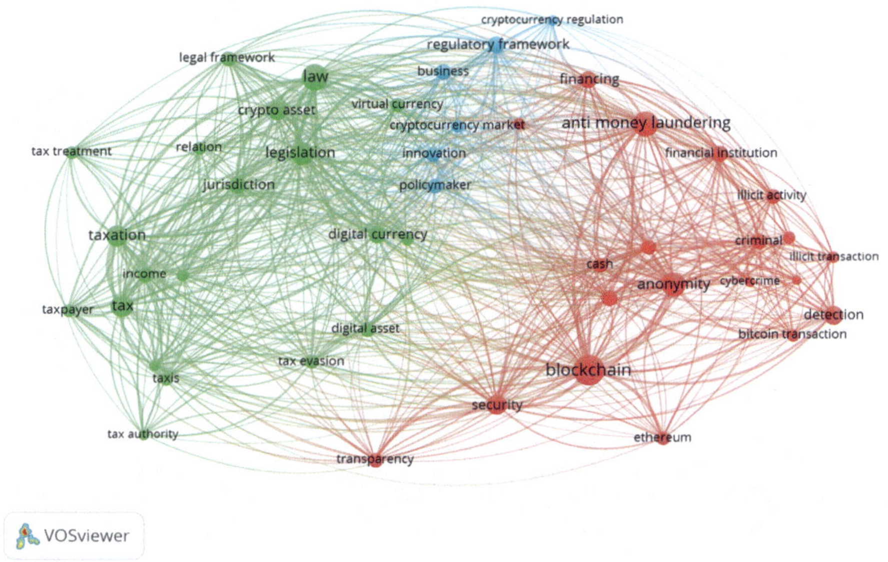

Fig. 7 Mapping for clusters realized with co-occurrence text data. *Source* Processed by the author with VOSviewer

We structured the results in three intervals to highlight the evolution and accent changes in the literature over time same like in Fig. 8:

- *Early period 2021—purple/dark pink:* Around 2021–2022, literature focused on terms such as bitcoin, cryptocurrency, money laundering or tax evasion. They reflect initial concerns for the link between cryptocurrencies, financial crime and anonymous taxation, a focus on money laundering risks and illegal transactions.
- *Transition period 2022—orange/light pink:* Subsequently, increasingly visible links have emerged with terms such as blockchain technology, digital economy, cybercrime, fraud and tax evasion. Research has begun to diversify, focusing not only on illicit activities, but also on technological mechanisms and the economic impact of crypto-assets.
- *Recent period 2023–2024—yellow:* In the final stages, the map highlights terms such as decentralised finance, crypto-assets, accounting, monetary policy and online banking. This shows that the current concern goes towards integrating crypto-assets into traditional finance, impact on monetary policy and accounting regulations. Moreover, connections with vat and tax policy appear, a sign that the tax discussion is becoming more and more applied and specific.

Figure 9 depicts a network of co-cited sources within the cryptocurrency financial crime literature: bridging academic journals, technical conferences, and market publications. For example, it is observed that the Journal of Money Laundering Control appears most frequently in technical papers like IEEE Access or Lecture Notes in Computer Science, indicating that regulation and cybersecurity are discussed together. The presence of publications such as Bloomberg or Forbes together with

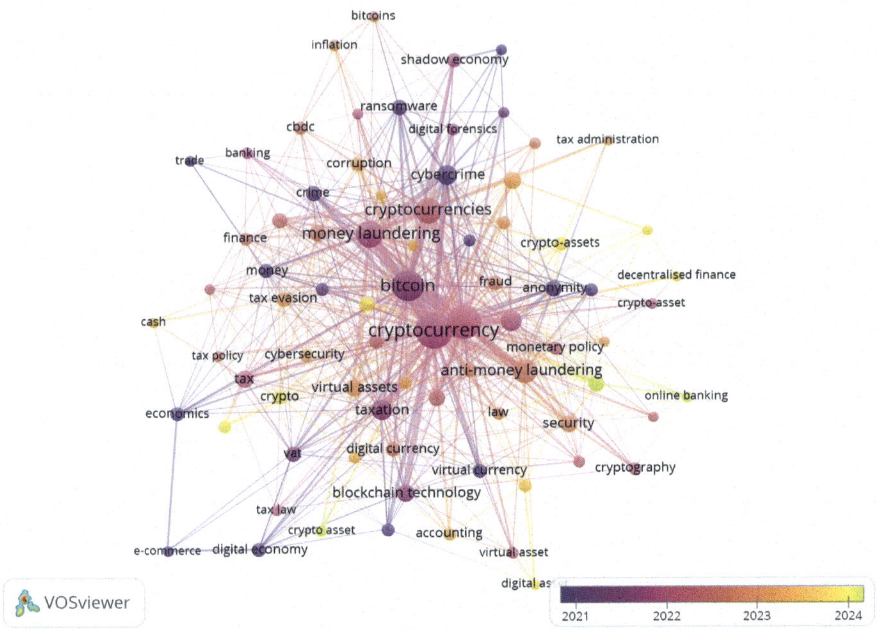

Fig. 8 The evolution of the phenomenon in time realized with co-occurance—keyword. *Source* Processed by the author with VOSviewer

academic sources confirms the role of the media environment in strengthening scientific debates. The map thus reflects the fact that studies about crypto-assets and their risks are built through a constant dialogue between economics, technology and regulation.

In Fig. 10 and Table 8, as for the co-citation analysis, Nakamoto (2008) highlights as being related to 60 citations from the article "Bitcoin: Peer-to-Peer" and having 38 in the original white paper while placing at the top thanks to both founding sources of information when defining what we nowadays understand of a blockchain architecture and regarding the proof-of-work mechanism as an anti-double spending solution. These basically create the blueprint for decentralized trust-less transactions and are one of the seminal pieces that keep getting referenced in the blockchain space. The other high-ranking contributor is Foley's (2019) Review of Financial Studies paper with 28 citing references, which exposes a critical finding that almost half of Bitcoin transactions were associated with crimes, constituting an estimated level of USD 76 billion per year. It has helped shift the debate among scholars and policymakers about how risky digital assets are, and whether there is a case for tighter regulation. As a result, most of the highest cited references may be covering both the reality provided by Nakamoto at a technical level and the evidential critical component introduced by Foley—explaining this concentration of these two developing genres (cryptocurrencies and financial crime) in relation to academia and literature relying on legal definitions.

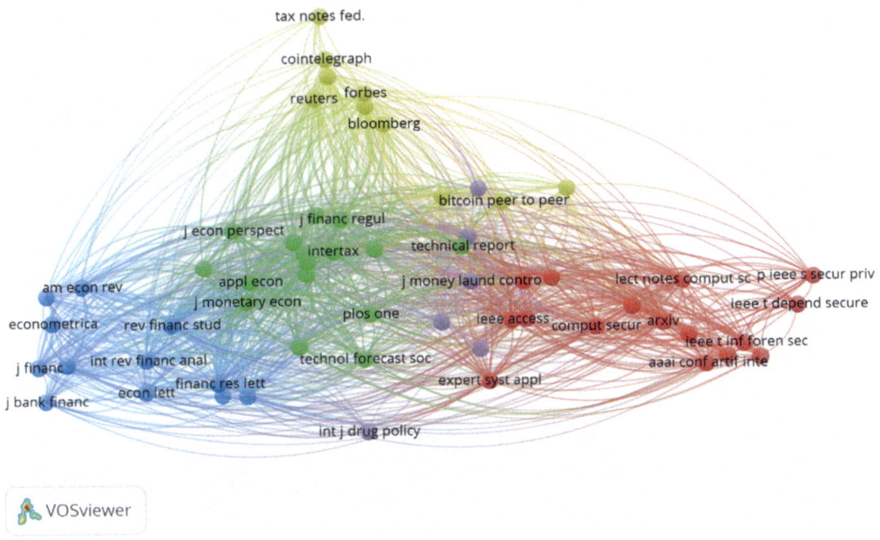

Fig. 9 Bibliometric mapping of co-cited sources about crypto and fincrime. *Source* Processed by the author with VOSviewer

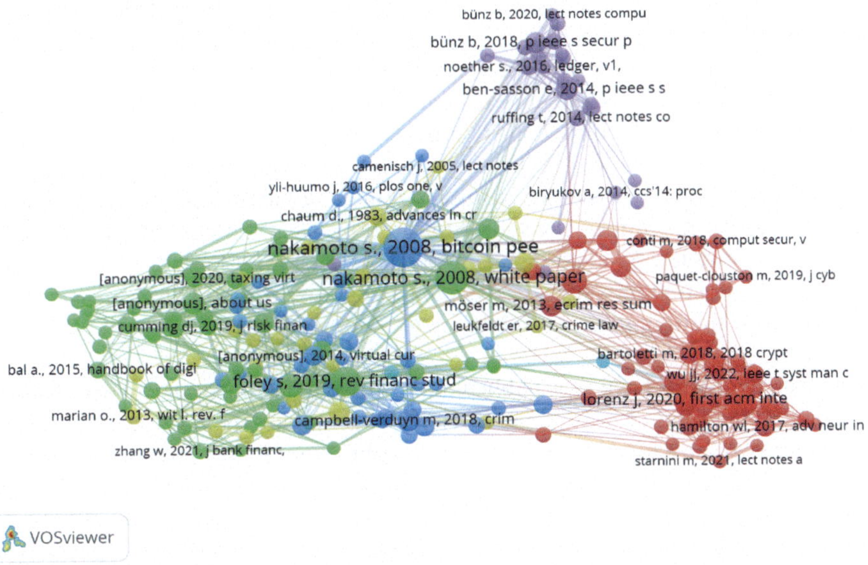

Fig. 10 Bibliometric mapping of co-cited references in cryptocurrency research. *Source* Processed by the author with VOSviewer

Table 8 Top 10 most co-cited references

No.	Cited reference	Citations	Total link strength
1.	Nakamoto (2008), Bitcoin Peer to peer	60	50.00
2.	Nakamoto (2008), White paper	38	35.00
3.	Foley (2019), Rev Financ Stud	28	27.00
4.	Lorenz (2020), First ACM International Conference on AI in Finance	18	18.00
5.	Weber (2019), Arxiv	18	18.00
6.	Alarab (2020), 5 INT C Mach Learn	17	17.00
7.	Albrecht (2019), J money laund control	16	16.00
8.	Ben Sasson et al.(2014)	17	16.00
9.	Campbell-Verduyn (2018), Crime Law Social	14	14.00
10.	Wood (2014), Ethereum Proj. Yellow	14	14.00

Source Processed by the author

As can be seen from the Fig. 11 and table above, this provides a clear depiction of a coupling within the network of authors—indicating that researchers who address topics as it relates to cryptocurrency and financial crime tend to have common academic references and interests. The results suggested that influence groups might have formed in literature with the presence of high binding power nodes at the center. In this publication, we also identify the ambit knowledge and strengths on manifold systematics domains: Jack Nicholls (3 articles; 39 citations) scored with the highest total strength link (153.26), confirming his role as a king in linking distinct subdomains. This position is not an artifact of a large number of papers, but the high degree to which his articles are linked to those by other authors. Similarly, Adam B. Turner (3 articles, 52 citations) and Angela S.M. Irwin (3 articles, 74 citations) had higher link strength values in the subnetwork construction (133.51 and 69.64 respectively), signifying greater relevance to reinforcing the network too, as shown in Table 9.

Researchers who have few publications, but a high impact exist. Kim-Kwang Raymond Choo (2 articles, 102 citations) and Malcolm Campbell-Verduyn (2 articles, 77 citations), for instance, show that a modest publishing record can capture immense attention due to the global relevance of their respective research themes. Liu Dongxi also authored 2 papers with 75 citations (~16.91 strength link): medium network influence and strong individual visibility. In summary, the analysis supports two domains of influence on display in authors' coupling: one informed by number and variance (such as Teichmann with 4 contributions at link strength 76.67) and another—by standout high impact literature that merits notice (Choo & Campbell-Verduyn).

Figure 12, generated based on the 20 items selected for the "References," "Titles," and "Keywords" fields, shows how fundamental works (e.g., Nakamoto 2008 or Böhme 2015) have been linked to topics such as "cryptocurrency," "blockchain,"

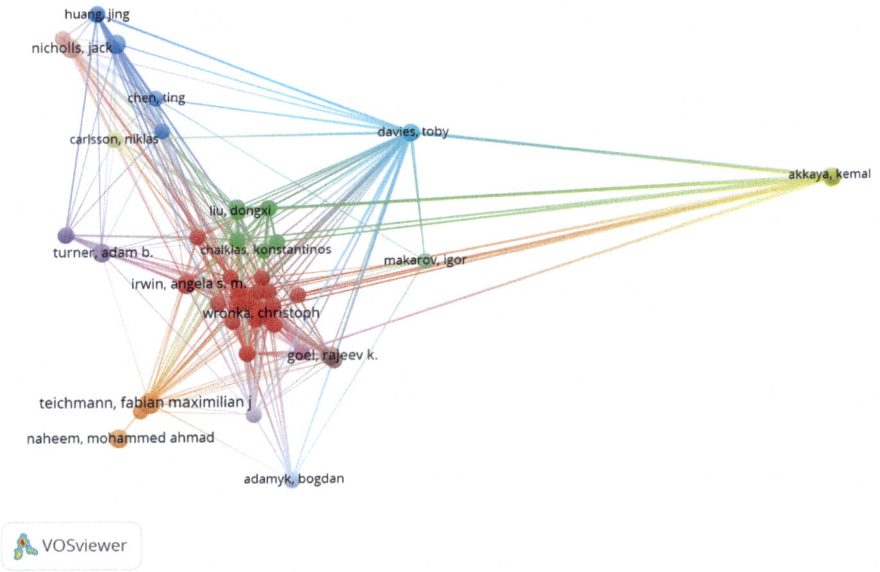

Fig. 11 Visualization of coupling relationships among authors. *Source* Processed by the author with VOSviewer

Table 9 Authors with strongest bibliometric coupling links

No.	Author	Documents	Citations	Total link strength
1.	Choo, Kim-Kwang Raymond	2	102	25.00
2.	Campbell-Verduyn, Malcolm	2	77	25.43
3.	Liu, Dongxi	2	75	16.91
4.	Irwin, Angela S.M.	3	74	69.64
5.	Susilo, Willy	2	73	21.00
6.	Ghimire, Binam	2	66	94.21
7.	Shanaev, Savva	2	66	94.21
8.	Turner, Adam B	3	52	133.51
9.	Teichmann, Fabian Maximilian Johannes	4	47	76.67
10.	Nicholls, Jack	3	39	153.26

Source Processed by the author

or "money laundering," which in turn lead to current keywords such as "taxation," "cybercrime," "privacy," and "regulation." The choice of parameters limits the analysis to the most cited references and the most frequently used concepts, allowing a central core of the literature to be visualized.

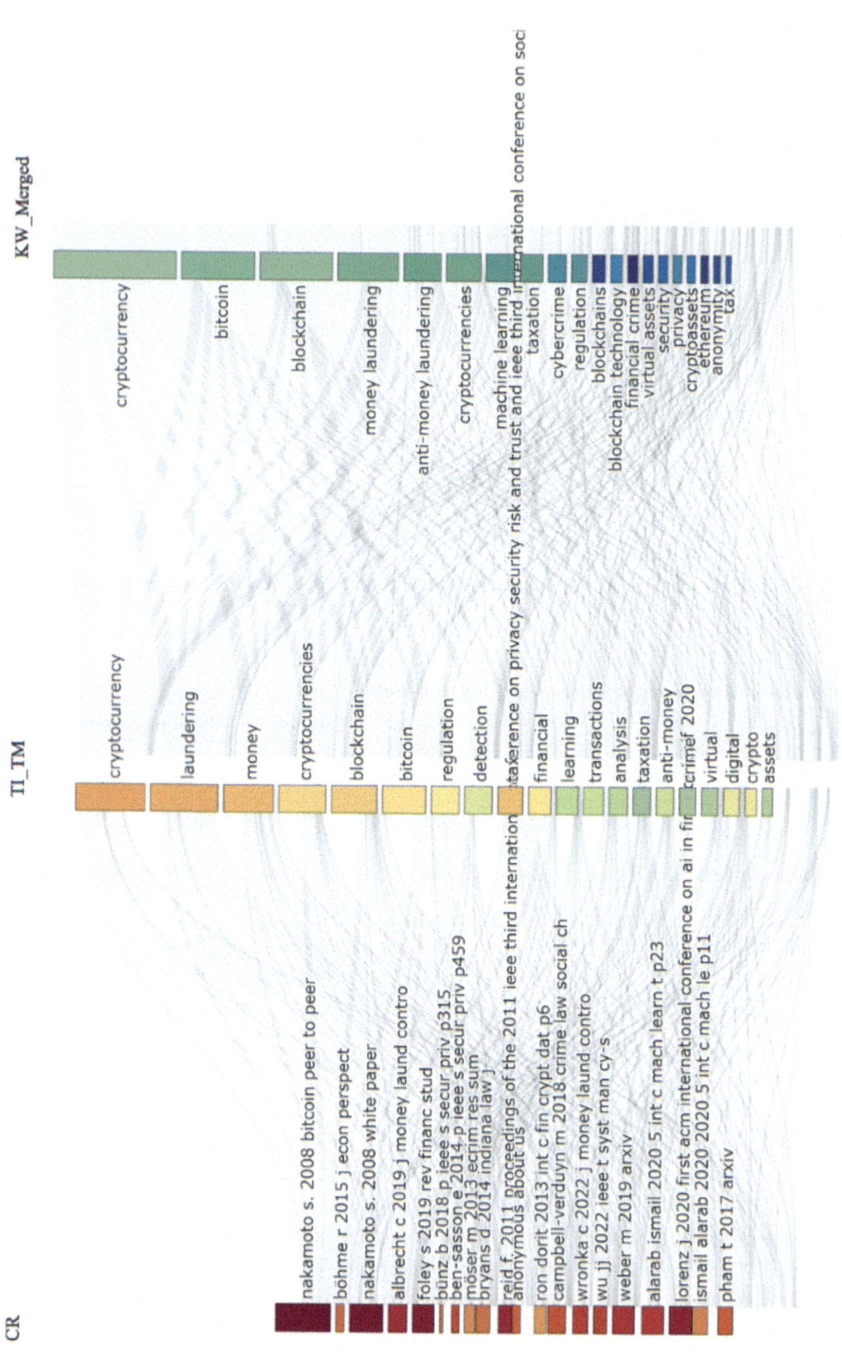

Fig. 12 Analysis of links between references, titles and keywords. *Source* Processed by the author with bibliometrix

This structure shows that previous research has mainly focused on understanding blockchain technologies and their illicit uses, but connections to terms such as "taxation," "financial crime," and "virtual assets" open up space for future directions. These could focus on how privacy technologies (e.g., zero-knowledge, anonymity) complicate the detection of evasion, how artificial intelligence tools can be integrated to identify suspicious transactions, or how international tax regulations align with new forms of digital assets.

5 Future Trends for Academic Research

Bibliometric analysis reveals a series of research directions that structure the academic field of cryptocurrencies and possible evasion mechanisms. In the area of driving themes, topics such as money laundering, the use of blockchain, and the issue of digital asset exchanges are emerging, elements that polarize researchers' attention due to their impact and practical relevance. At the same time, the core themes show a constant interest in taxation, digital assets, and trading mechanisms, which constitute the conceptual infrastructure of the debates.

Niche areas, dominated by concepts such as anonymity, zero-knowledge algorithms, or ransomware, indicate a focus on technical issues that can facilitate the concealment of illicit transactions. At the same time, emerging or declining topics; such as CBDC schemes suggest possible repositioning of the literature, depending on regulatory dynamics and market adaptation. Correlating the density and centrality of clusters, it is noteworthy that "cryptocurrency" has the highest frequency, confirming its pivotal role in the literature and the part of technologists that facilitates obtaining illegal benefits, according with Fig. 13.

The most frequently occurring terms are "cryptocurrency" (37 occurrences), and then "blockchain" (23), followed by "money laundering" (17) and "bitcoin" (14). Under "high-density," one can see "digital assets" (11) and "tax" (9), which indicate increasing interest in how the law deals with tax issues. Also, in the same line of emerging themes, there are "anonymity" (6) and "zero-knowledge" (4); they both hint at a research interest towards technologies that could be supporting evasion practices, looking to Table 10.

According to these two graphs (Fig. 14), the most common ones in terms of words used in literature are: "cryptocurrency" (134); "blockchain" (91); "bitcoin" (70), with issues such as money laundering or regulation being also considered. The development over time especially proves that these trends are growing and, gradually, the growth accelerates after 2020, indicating that as the crypto market scales up rapidly, so does academic debate. For future work, it can be identified that this tendency is an opportunity for better integration between technical (blockchain, mining, privacy) and regulatory dimensions (taxing, regulation, and anti-money laundering) to face the problems related to cryptocurrencies as instruments for hiding taxes (Fig. 15).

As can be seen in the graph and table, "money laundering" (271, median 2023) and "anti-money laundering" (109, median 2023) are by far the largest clusters

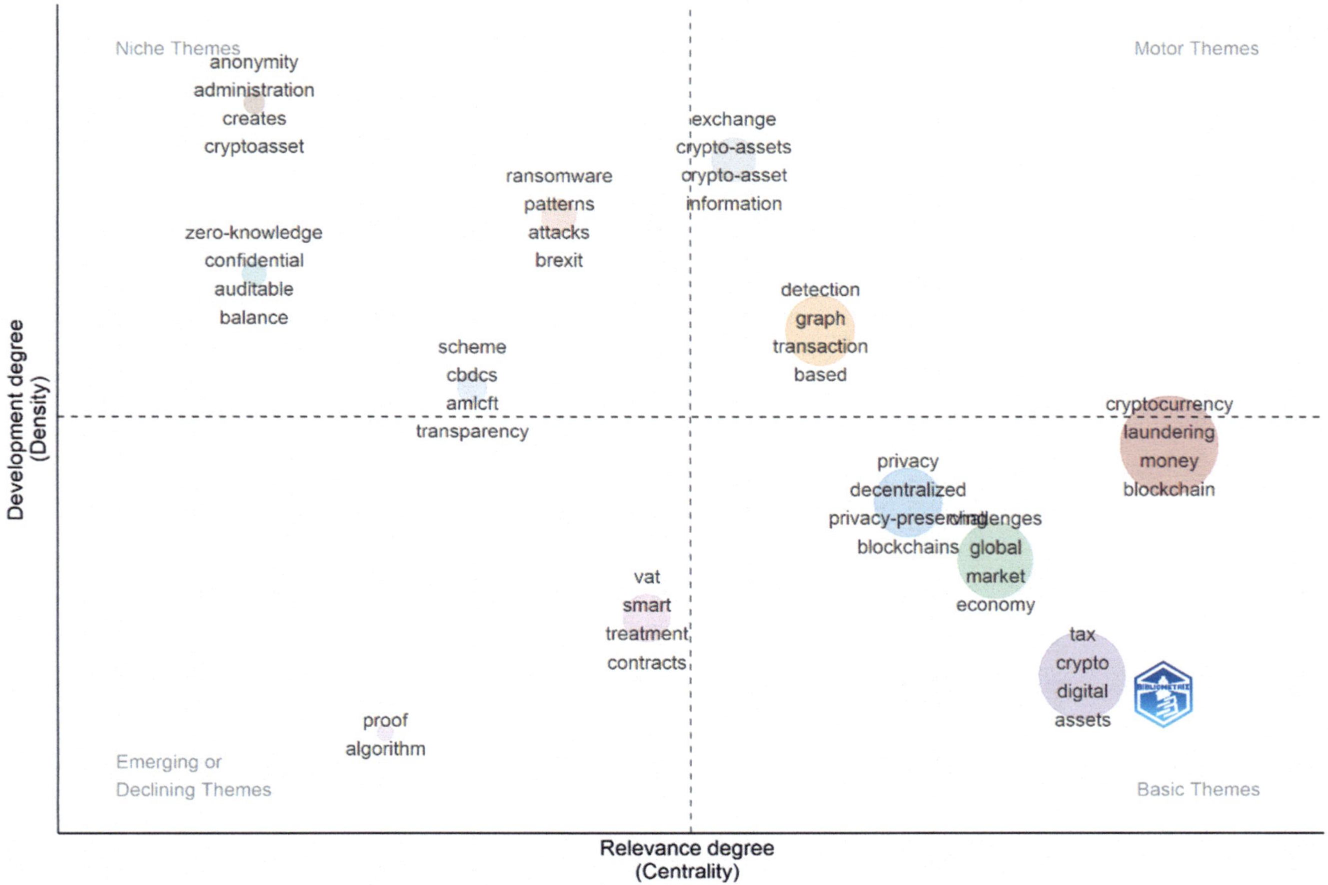

Fig. 13 Thematic mapping of topics on 4 dimensions. *Source* Processed by the author with bibliometrix

Table 10 Distribution of research topics on cryptocurrencies and tax evasion

Cluster	CallonCentrality	CallonDensity	RankCentrality	RankDensity	ClusterFrequency
Cryptocurrency	15.171	50.068	12	6	806
Privacy	5.074	49.127	9	5	141
Challenges	5.574	48.964	10	4	217
Tax	9.35	48.654	11	2	415
Detection	3.598	56.017	8	8	156
Anonymity	0	91.667	1.5	12	9
Vat	1.406	48.929	6	3	42
Exchange	1.782	67.229	7	11	35
Zero-knowledge	0	56.25	1.5	9	11
Ransomware	0.875	58.333	5	10	21

Source Processed by the author

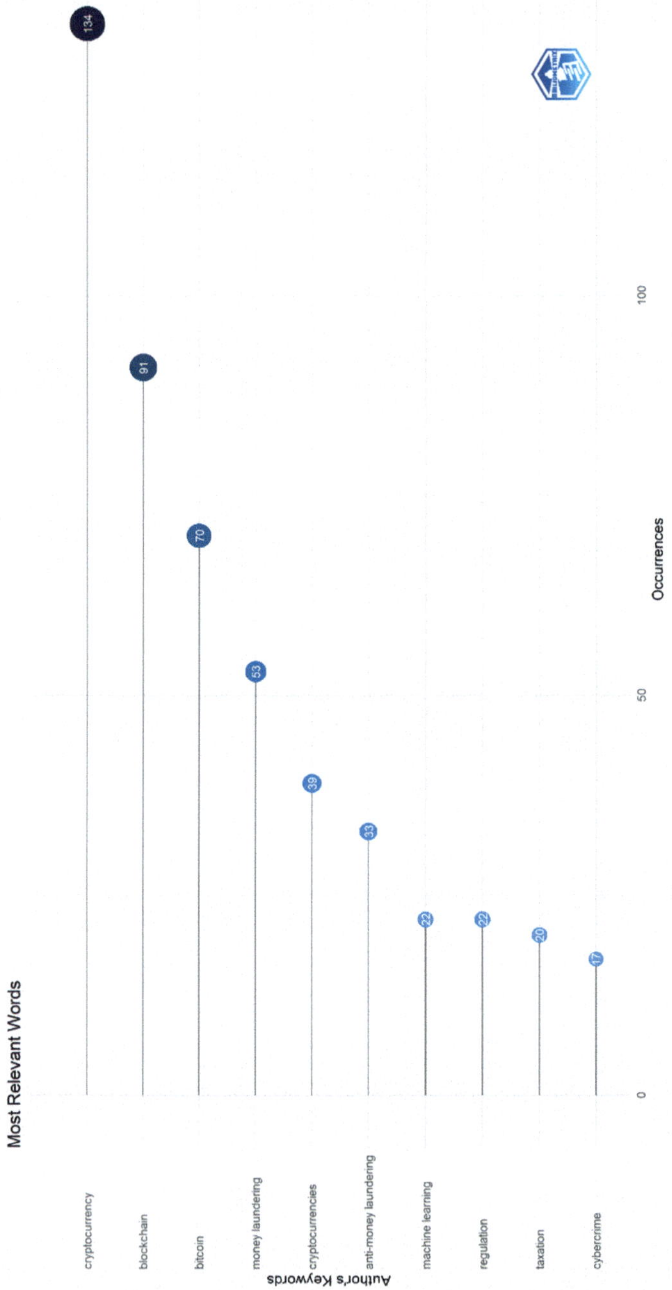

Fig. 14 Most relevant words. *Source* Processed by the author with bibliometrix

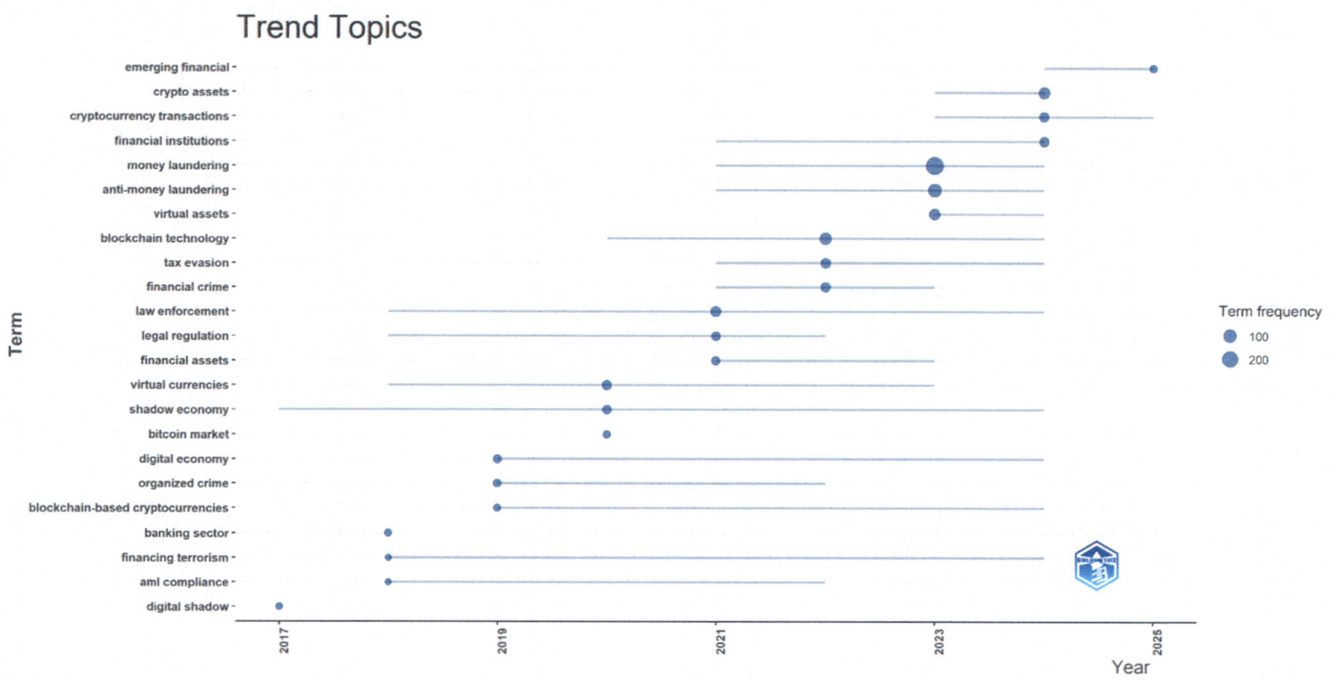

Fig. 15 Most discussed topics according with literature. *Source* Processed by the author with bibliometrix

dominating current research, substantiating condition H4 on the association between crypto and financial crime. Taxation topics like "tax evasion" (35, median 2022) and tax shadow economy (18, median 2020) are mentioned with low frequencies and remain too little explored. More recent newcomers have the terminology "crypto assets" (63, Q1 2023, median 2023), and "cryptocurrency transactions" (30, Q1 2023, median 2024) suggesting a distinct move to regulating and taxing transactions. "Banking sector" (7, 2018) or "digital shadow" (6, 2017), by comparison, seem to wane and are no longer perceived as priorities. In what the next studies are concerned, both the empirical and theoretical analyses point to areas in need of future research by linking tax evasion and underground economy with law changes (like DAC8, MiCA) at European level, or investigating their influence on financial institutions, as well as developing a set of methodologies for the estimation of tax compliance in Romania where data is almost nonexistent in Table 4.

The literature review identifies theoretical and empirical contributions and addresses gaps that justify a more detailed investigation. While literature provides some interesting results on tax evasion, money laundering, and the perspective of cryptoassets, it is, however, fragmented, revealing significant discrepancies from conceptual points of view. Following the analysis of current research directions, there is confirmed interest in the interaction between monetary policies and crypto-fiat mechanisms. Dominant themes include privacy and anonymity, compliance and governance, AML regulations, types of crimes and fraud, as well as detection methods and the social dynamics of cryptocurrency adoption. These areas are reflected in the Journal Money Laundering Control and a greater focus on research in the USA. However, there is a gap in the literature for which we have proposed a comparative assessment of the degree of implementation at national level of European norms in this field. To fill this gap, we propose the development of a compliance index based on the relevant provisions of Regulation (EU) 2023/1114. The proposed methodology is simple and feasible: each measure in the regulation is assigned 1 point if it is fully implemented, 0.5 points if it is partially implemented, and 0 points if it is missing (Table 11).

The scores obtained allow for comparability between countries and the identification of legislative gaps that may facilitate tax avoidance or other abusive practices in the crypto space. This gap is filled by a new approach and an EU-based sample analysis, despite the fact that, due to the lack of quantitative data, current studies focus more on qualitative data. Entities providing such services have not published value-based information about the crypto market, but this is becoming mandatory, as DAC8 is an amendment to Directive 2011/16/EU on administrative cooperation in the field of taxation, which extends the automatic exchange of information obligations to transactions with crypto-assets. Member States must transpose the rules into national law by December 31, 2025, and the reporting obligations become applicable from January 1, 2026, for the first reporting year. Thus, we anticipate that studies in this field will focus much more on quantitative analyses and the expansion of databases and literature in this direction.

Table 11 Trend topics classification

Topic	Frequency	Year (Q1)	Year (median)	Year (Q3)
Money laundering	271	2021	2023	2024
Anti-money laundering	109	2021	2023	2024
Blockchain technology	66	2020	2022	2024
Crypto assets	63	2023	2024	2024
Virtual assets	54	2023	2023	2024
Law enforcement	42	2018	2021	2024
Tax evasion	35	2021	2022	2024
Financial crime	32	2021	2022	2023
Cryptocurrency transactions	30	2023	2024	2025
Virtual currencies	26	2018	2020	2023
Financial institutions	26	2021	2024	2024
Shadow economy	18	2017	2020	2024
Legal regulation	18	2018	2021	2022
Financial assets	17	2021	2021	2023
Digital economy	12	2019	2019	2024
Organized crime	11	2019	2019	2022
Bitcoin market	8	2020	2020	2020
Emerging financial	8	2024	2025	2025
Banking sector	7	2018	2018	2018
Blockchain-based cryptocurrencies	7	2019	2019	2024
Digital shadow	6	2017	2017	2017
Aml compliance	5	2018	2018	2022
Financing terrorism	5	2018	2018	2024

Source Processed by the author

6 Conclusion

A systematic and bibliometric analysis based on data collected from Web of Science has shown that the implications of cryptocurrencies on the economy are complex and often have a negative impact on financial stability and tax compliance. The expansion of cryptocurrency use reduces central banks' control over the money supply and interest rates. And because of their anonymity and lack of a clear reporting base, cryptocurrencies are frequently used for tax evasion, money laundering, and undeclared cross-border transfers. In return, they can also distort investment and resource allocation because investors are attracted by quick profits, directing capital towards speculative assets instead of traditional investments.

The research results show that scientific interest in the issue of tax evasion in the cryptocurrency sphere has grown significantly in recent years. Bibliometric analysis has shown that the Money Laundering Control Journal has the most publications on this topic, while the United States is the country with the most intense research activity. Among the reference works is "Some Simple Bitcoin Economics," a study that addresses how cryptocurrencies can influence the economy and fiscal policies. In addition, there has been a clear upward trend in the number of publications and citations, peaking in 2024, when 78 articles and 904 citations were recorded. The areas that have consistently attracted the interest of researchers are those related to privacy and anonymity, governance, compliance, and anti-money laundering regulations. However, European regulations on crypto assets are only mentioned in articles and are rarely analyzed comparatively between countries, highlighting an under-explored area of research. The literature also reveals that the most discussed fraudulent schemes are pump and dump, Ponzi, and ransomware attacks, which are considered to have the greatest impact on digital market practices.

However, the study has some limitations. The analysis only included studies published in the Web of Science database up to July 2025, and the sample was restricted to English-language publications and excluded outliers. Consequently, in the absence of databases, most studies are qualitative until the reporting obligations for crypto entities come into force in 2026, according to the DAC8 Directive. Subsequently, with the expansion of databases and the emergence of official reports, research will be able to focus on more accurate econometric estimates.

Future research could improve the proposed methodology by introducing risk-weighted indicators, integrating quantitative data on transaction volumes or reported incidents, and empirically validating the correlation between compliance scores and phenomena such as tax evasion or fraud.

The study has direct implications for public policy and the process of legislative harmonization at the European level. The proposed tool is not limited to measuring compliance, but provides a solid basis for formulating clear and consistent tax policies. The European Commission, OECD, or EBA can use the findings to build a standardized framework within the EU. Therefore, the research emphasizes that smart regulation of cryptocurrencies is not an obstacle to innovation, but an essential condition for transforming this field into a secure, sustainable, and integrated segment of the global economy.

References

Aggarwal S, Kumar N (2021) Cryptocurrencies. In: Advances in computers. Elsevier, London, pp 227–266. https://doi.org/10.1016/bs.adcom.2020.08.012

Alarab I, Prakoonwit S, Nacer MI (2020) Competence of graph convolutional networks for anti-money laundering in bitcoin blockchain. In: Proceedings of the 2020 5th international conference on machine learning technologies. Presented at the ICMLT 2020: 2020 5th International Conference on Machine Learning Technologies, ACM, Beijing China, pp 23–27. https://doi.org/10.1145/3409073.3409080

Albrecht C, Duffin KM, Hawkins S, Morales Rocha VM (2019) The use of cryptocurrencies in the money laundering process. JMLC 22:210–216. https://doi.org/10.1108/JMLC-12-2017-0074

Almeida J, Gonçalves TC (2024) Cryptocurrency market microstructure: a systematic literature review. Ann Oper Res 332:1035–1068. https://doi.org/10.1007/s10479-023-05627-5

AlQudah MZ, Bariviera AF (2025) Systematic and bibliometric reviews of cryptocurrency market regulation: trends, influential contributions, and future directions. JFRC. https://doi.org/10.1108/JFRC-11-2024-0232

Aquilina M, Frost J, Schrimpf A (2024) Tackling the risks in crypto: choosing among bans, containment and regulation. J Jpn Int Econ 71:101286. https://doi.org/10.1016/j.jjie.2023.101286

Atlam HF, Ekuri N, Azad MA, Lallie HS (2024) Blockchain forensics: a systematic literature review of techniques, applications, challenges, and future directions. Electronics 13:3568. https://doi.org/10.3390/electronics13173568

Baer K (2023) Taxing cryptocurrencies. IMF working papers 2023, 1. https://doi.org/10.5089/9798400246586.001

Bahamazava K, Reznik S (2023) The comparative analysis of regulations in the Italian Republic and the Russian Federation against cryptolaundering techniques. JMLC 26:787–805. https://doi.org/10.1108/JMLC-01-2022-0016

Bajwa IA (2025) Reinvestment intentions in cryptocurrency: examining the dynamics of risks and investor risk tolerance. Dig Bus 5:100104. https://doi.org/10.1016/j.digbus.2024.100104

Ballis A, Verousis T (2022) Behavioural finance and cryptocurrencies. RBF 14:545–562. https://doi.org/10.1108/RBF-11-2021-0256

Ben Hassine M, Kmimech M, Hellani H, Sliman L (2020) Toward a mixed tangle-blockchain architecture. In: Fujita H, Selamat A, Omatu S (eds) Frontiers in artificial intelligence and applications. IOS Press, New York. https://doi.org/10.3233/FAIA200568

Ben-Sasson E, Chiesa A, Garman C, Green M, Miers I, Tromer E, Virza M (2014) Zerocash: decentralized anonymous payments from bitcoin. In: 2014 IEEE symposium on security and privacy. Presented at the 2014 IEEE symposium on security and privacy (SP), IEEE. San Jose, CA, pp 459–474. https://doi.org/10.1109/SP.2014.36

Ben S, Xiaoqiong W (2019) Are cryptocurrencies good investments? Stud Bus Econ 14:181–192. https://doi.org/10.2478/sbe-2019-0033

Ben Yaala S, Henchiri JE (2025) Climate risks and cryptocurrency volatility: evidence from crypto market crisis. CFRI. https://doi.org/10.1108/CFRI-09-2024-0575

Benson V, Adamyk B, Chinnaswamy A, Adamyk O (2024) Harmonising cryptocurrency regulation in Europe: opportunities for preventing illicit transactions. Eur J Law Econ 57:37–61. https://doi.org/10.1007/s10657-024-09797-w

Böhme R, Christin N, Edelman B, Moore T (2015) Bitcoin: economics, technology, and governance. J Econ Perspect 29:213–238. https://doi.org/10.1257/jep.29.2.213

Bota-Avram C (2023) Bibliometric analysis of sustainable business performance: where are we going? A science map of the field. Econ Res Ekonomska Istraživanja 36:2137–2176. https://doi.org/10.1080/1331677X.2022.2096094

Buhalis D, Harwood T, Bogicevic V, Viglia G, Beldona S, Hofacker C (2019) Technological disruptions in services: lessons from tourism and hospitality. JOSM 30:484–506. https://doi.org/10.1108/JOSM-12-2018-0398

Campbell-Verduyn M (2018) Bitcoin, crypto-coins, and global anti-money laundering governance. Crime Law Soc Change 69:283–305. https://doi.org/10.1007/s10611-017-9756-5

Chervinski JOM, Kreutz D (2019) Introdução às tecnologias dos blockchains e das criptomoedas. RBCA 11:12–27. https://doi.org/10.5335/rbca.v11i3.9394

Corbet S, Lucey B, Urquhart A, Yarovaya L (2019) Cryptocurrencies as a financial asset: a systematic analysis. Int Rev Financ Anal 62:182–199. https://doi.org/10.1016/j.irfa.2018.09.003

Cotugno M, Manta F, Perdichizzi S, Stefanelli V (2024) Ready for a digital Euro? Insights from a research agenda. Res Int Bus Financ 67:102117. https://doi.org/10.1016/j.ribaf.2023.102117

Courtois NT, Gradon KT, Schmeh K (2021) Crypto currency regulation and law enforcement perspectives. https://doi.org/10.48550/ARXIV.2109.01047

Covolo V (2019) The EU response to criminal misuse of cryptocurrencies: the young, already outdated 5th anti-money laundering directive. SSRN J. https://doi.org/10.2139/ssrn.3503535

Draganidis S (2023) Jurisdictional arbitrage: combatting an inevitable by-product of cryptoasset regulation. JFRC 31:170–185. https://doi.org/10.1108/JFRC-02-2022-0013

Dumchikov M, Kononenko N, Batsenko L, Halenin R, Hlushchenko N (2020) Issues of regulating cryptocurrency and control over its turnover: international experience. AI 9:10–20. https://doi.org/10.34069/AI/2020.31.07.1

Emmert F (2023) The regulation of cryptocurrencies in the United States of America. Eur J Law Reform 25:27–122. https://doi.org/10.5553/EJLR/138723702023025001002

Farrugia S, Ellul J, Azzopardi G (2020) Detection of illicit accounts over the Ethereum blockchain. Expert Syst Appl 150:113318. https://doi.org/10.1016/j.eswa.2020.113318

Ferreira A, Sandner P (2021) Eu search for regulatory answers to crypto assets and their place in the financial markets' infrastructure. Comput Law Secur Rev 43:105632. https://doi.org/10.1016/j.clsr.2021.105632

Foley S, Karlsen JR, Putniņš TJ (2019) Sex, drugs, and bitcoin: How much illegal activity is financed through cryptocurrencies? Rev Financ Stud 32:1798–1853. https://doi.org/10.1093/rfs/hhz015

Fujiki H (2020) Who adopts crypto assets in Japan? Evidence from the 2019 financial literacy survey. J Jpn Int Econ 58:101107. https://doi.org/10.1016/j.jjie.2020.101107

Garcia-Alfaro J (2018) Data privacy management, cryptocurrencies and blockchain technology: ESORICS 2018 international workshops, DPM 2018 and CBT 2018, Barcelona, Spain, September 6–7, 2018, proceedings, lecture notes in computer science ser. Springer, Cham

Garman C, Green M, Miers I (2017) Accountable privacy for decentralized anonymous payments. In: Grossklags J, Preneel B (eds) Financial cryptography and data security. Lecture notes in computer science. Springer, Berlin, pp 81–98. https://doi.org/10.1007/978-3-662-54970-4_5

Giudici G, Milne A, Vinogradov D (2020) Cryptocurrencies: market analysis and perspectives. J Ind Bus Econ 47:1–18. https://doi.org/10.1007/s40812-019-00138-6

Grossklags J, Preneel B (eds) (2017) Financial cryptography and data security: 20th international conference, FC 2016, Christ Church, Barbados, February 22–26, 2016, Revised selected papers, lecture notes in computer science. Springer, Berlin. https://doi.org/10.1007/978-3-662-54970-4

Harrast SA, McGilsky D, Sun Y (2022) Determining the inherent risks of cryptocurrency: a survey analysis. Curr Issues Audit 16:A10–A17. https://doi.org/10.2308/CIIA-2020-038

Herskind L, Katsikouli P, Dragoni N (2020) Privacy and cryptocurrencies—a systematic literature review. IEEE Access 8:54044–54059. https://doi.org/10.1109/ACCESS.2020.2980950

Hung AH-C (2024) Legal consciousness and the crypto phenomenon: property ideologies, innovations and potential ramifications on financial system stability. Int J Law Context 20:598–616. https://doi.org/10.1017/S1744552324000338

Ibarra Trujillo MH (2023) La regulación de las criptomonedas en el Perú. Rcli 23:883–890. https://doi.org/10.59427/rcli/2023/v23cs.883-890

Islam MJ, Islam S, Hossain M, Noor S, Islam SMR (2025) Securing blockchain systems: a layer-oriented survey of threats, vulnerability taxonomy, and detection methods. Fut Int 17:205. https://doi.org/10.3390/fi17050205

Jeris SS, Ur Rahman Chowdhury ASMN, Akter MT, Frances S, Roy MH (2022) Cryptocurrency and stock market: bibliometric and content analysis. Heliyon 8:e10514. https://doi.org/10.1016/j.heliyon.2022.e10514

Joebges H, Herr H, Kellermann C (2025) Crypto assets as a threat to financial market stability. Eur Econ Rev 15:473–502. https://doi.org/10.1007/s40822-025-00311-4

Kerr DS, Loveland KA, Smith KT, Smith LM (2023) Cryptocurrency risks, fraud cases, and financial performance. Risks 11:51. https://doi.org/10.3390/risks11030051

Kethineni S, Cao Y (2020) The rise in popularity of cryptocurrency and associated criminal activity. Int Crim Justice Rev 30:325–344. https://doi.org/10.1177/1057567719827051

Kiruba AS, Dr, B.R., Dr, M.N. (2023) Cryptocurrency investing: millennial decision making. ICMR 15:86–96

Kutera M (2022) Cryptocurrencies as a subject of financial fraud. JEMI 18:45–77. https://doi.org/10.7341/20221842

Lan T, Frömmel M (2025) Risk factors in cryptocurrency pricing. Int Rev Financ Anal 105:104389. https://doi.org/10.1016/j.irfa.2025.104389

Lazea G-I, Bunget O-C, Lungu C (2024) Cryptocurrencies' impact on accounting: bibliometric review. Risks 12:94. https://doi.org/10.3390/risks12060094

Levytskyi V, Radynskyi S, Radynska S (2023) Normative and legal regulation of the market cryptocurrency and activities of crypto exchange in Ukraine and worldwide. Innov Econ. https://doi.org/10.37332/2309-1533.2023.3.4

Li Y, Susilo W, Yang G, Yu Y, Du X, Liu D, Guizani N (2019) Toward privacy and regulation in blockchain-based cryptocurrencies. IEEE Netw 33:111–117. https://doi.org/10.1109/MNET.2019.1800271

Lin Y-J, Wu P-W, Hsu C-H, Tu I-P, Liao S (2019) An evaluation of bitcoin address classification based on transaction history summarization. In: 2019 IEEE international conference on blockchain and cryptocurrency (ICBC). Presented at the 2019 IEEE international conference on blockchain and cryptocurrency (ICBC), IEEE, Seoul, Korea (South), pp 302–310. https://doi.org/10.1109/BLOC.2019.8751410

Lin C, He D, Huang X, Khan MK, Choo K-KR (2020) DCAP: a secure and efficient decentralized conditional anonymous payment system based on blockchain. IEEE Trans Inform Forensic Secur 15:2440–2452. https://doi.org/10.1109/TIFS.2020.2969565

Linnenluecke MK, Marrone M, Singh AK (2020) Conducting systematic literature reviews and bibliometric analyses. Aust J Manag 45:175–194. https://doi.org/10.1177/0312896219877678

Lorenz J, Silva MI, Aparício D, Ascensão JT, Bizarro P (2020) Machine learning methods to detect money laundering in the bitcoin blockchain in the presence of label scarcity. In: Proceedings of the First ACM international conference on AI in finance. Presented at the ICAIF'20: ACM international conference on AI in finance, ACM, New York, pp 1–8. https://doi.org/10.1145/3383455.3422549

Mackenzie S (2022) Criminology towards the metaverse: cryptocurrency scams, grey economy and the technosocial. Br J Criminol 62:1537–1552. https://doi.org/10.1093/bjc/azab118

Naheem MA (2021) Do cryptocurrencies enable and facilitate modern slavery? JMLC 24:491–501. https://doi.org/10.1108/JMLC-07-2020-0073

Nakamoto S (2008) Bitcoin whitepaper. https://bitcoin.org/bitcoin.pdf. 17.07. 2019, 9, 15

Norton SD (2024) Free banking theory: literature review and relevance to the regulation of cryptocurrencies debate. JFRC 32:250–265. https://doi.org/10.1108/JFRC-10-2023-0176

Parrondo L (2023) Cryptoassets: definitions and accounting treatment under the current international financial reporting standards framework. Intell Syst Account 30:208–227. https://doi.org/10.1002/isaf.1543

Patsakis C, Politou E, Alepis E, Hernandez-Castro J (2024) Cashing out crypto: state of practice in ransom payments. Int J Inf Secur 23:699–712. https://doi.org/10.1007/s10207-023-00766-z

Pernice IGA, Scott B (2021) Cryptocurrency. Int Policy Rev. https://doi.org/10.14763/2021.2.1561

Petersen K, Vakkalanka S, Kuzniarz L (2015) Guidelines for conducting systematic mapping studies in software engineering: an update. Inf Softw Technol 64:1–18. https://doi.org/10.1016/j.infsof.2015.03.007

Raso E, Bracciale L, Gallo P, Bernardinetti G, Bianchi G, Sanseverino ER, Loreti P (2022) Performance evaluation of cryptographic schemes for blockchain security of smart grids. In: 2022 workshop on blockchain for renewables integration (BLORIN). Presented at the 2022 workshop on blockchain for renewables integration (BLORIN), IEEE, Palermo, Italy, pp 113–117. https://doi.org/10.1109/BLORIN54731.2022.10028220

Rejeb A, Rejeb K, Keogh JG (2021) Cryptocurrencies in modern finance: a literature review. Etikonomi 20:93–118. https://doi.org/10.15408/etk.v20i1.16911

Saxena C, Kumar P (2023) Bibliometric analysis of *Journal of Money Laundering Control*: emerging trends and a way forward. JMLC 26:947–969. https://doi.org/10.1108/JMLC-06-2022-0075

Schmidt M (2018) Kryptowährung, bitcoin und Co: Digitale Währungen—technische und steuerliche Hintergründe (1. Auflage.). Datev e.G

Schilling De Carvalho P (2022) Retaining influence in post-brexit international financial regulation: lessons from the UK's FinTech framework. J Financ Regul 8:104–131. https://doi.org/10.1093/jfr/fjac004

Schilling L, Uhlig H (2019) Some simple bitcoin economics. J Monet Econ 106:16–26. https://doi.org/10.1016/j.jmoneco.2019.07.002

Shanaev S, Sharma S, Ghimire B, Shuraeva A (2020) Taming the blockchain beast? Regulatory implications for the cryptocurrency Market. Res Int Bus Financ 51:101080. https://doi.org/10.1016/j.ribaf.2019.101080

Tavasoli A (2020) Identification and prioritization of the challenges of using cryptocurrencies in international transactions. Rev Elect Invest Ciencias Econ 8:226–243. https://doi.org/10.5377/reice.v8i16.10697

Trozze A, Kamps J, Akartuna EA, Hetzel FJ, Kleinberg B, Davies T, Johnson SD (2022) Cryptocurrencies and future financial crime. Crime Sci 11:1. https://doi.org/10.1186/s40163-021-00163-8

Van Wegberg R, Oerlemans J-J, Van Deventer O (2018) Bitcoin money laundering: mixed results? An explorative study on money laundering of cybercrime proceeds using bitcoin. J Financ Crime. https://doi.org/10.1108/JFC-11-2016-0067

Vandezande N (2017) Virtual currencies under EU anti-money laundering law. Comput Law Secur Rev 33:341–353. https://doi.org/10.1016/j.clsr.2017.03.011

Voskobitova L, Vilkova T, Nasonov S, Khokhryakov M, Reshetnikov Y (2021) Illegal circulation of digital currencies: features of criminal investigation. AI 10:252–264. https://doi.org/10.34069/AI/2021.45.09.25

Weber M, Domeniconi G, Chen J, Weidele DKI, Bellei C, Robinson T, Leiserson CE (2019) Anti-money laundering in bitcoin: experimenting with graph convolutional networks for financial forensics. https://doi.org/10.48550/ARXIV.1908.02591

Werman S, Zohar A (2018) Avoiding deadlocks in payment channel networks. In: Garcia-Alfaro J, Herrera-Joancomartí J, Livraga G, Rios R (eds) Data privacy management, cryptocurrencies and blockchain technology. Lecture notes in computer science. Springer, Cham, pp 175–187. https://doi.org/10.1007/978-3-030-00305-0_13

Williamson S (2018) Is Bitcoin a waste of resources? R 100:107–115. https://doi.org/10.20955/r.2018.107-15

Wohlin C (2014) Guidelines for snowballing in systematic literature studies and a replication in software engineering. In: Proceedings of the 18th international conference on evaluation and assessment in software engineering. presented at the EASE '14: 18th international conference on evaluation and assessment in software engineering, ACM, London England United Kingdom, pp 1–10. https://doi.org/10.1145/2601248.2601268

Wood G (2014) Ethereum: a secure decentralised generalised transaction ledger. Ethereum Proj. Yellow Pap

Wronka C (2024) Crypto-asset regulatory landscape: a comparative analysis of the crypto-asset regulation in the UK and Germany. J Asset Manag 25:417–426. https://doi.org/10.1057/s41260-024-00358-z

Yang A (2025) Cryptocurrency market risk-managed momentum strategies. Financ Res Lett 85:107879. https://doi.org/10.1016/j.frl.2025.107879

Zeng H, Huang Q, Abedin MZ, Ahmed AD, Lucey B (2025) Connectedness and frequency connection among green bond, cryptocurrency and green energy-related metals around the COVID-19 outbreak. Res Int Bus Financ 73:102547. https://doi.org/10.1016/j.ribaf.2024.102547

Adrian Bojan is a Ph.D. student at the Babeş-Bolyai University, where he is pursuing his studies in the field of finance. In his Ph.D. program he explores key aspects of economics and financial systems, focusing on current challenges in the field. Previously, Adrian completed his bachelor's and master's degrees in accounting, accumulating a solid foundation of theoretical and practical knowledge. He has also gained almost four years of experience in the financial-accounting field, working in a specialized firm where he managed various aspects of accounting reporting and compliance. His studies explore how financial innovations can influence economic behaviors and tax strategies at national and international levels.

Monica Violeta Achim is a professor and doctoral supervisor in Finance at the Faculty of Economic Sciences and Business Administration, Babeş-Bolyai University, Cluj-Napoca. With over 27 years of experience in academia, she has published, as author and co-author, over 140 scientific articles and 27 books. The main research topics are financial analysis, business performance, finance, and economic and financial crime. In 2020, she obtained the Award for Excellence in Scientific Research, at Babeş-Bolyai University, Faculty of Economics and Business Administration, Cluj-Napoca, Romania, as a recognition of the results obtained in the research activity. She leads a main national project in the area of financial crime in the period 2020–2023. In the business environment, she works in liberal professions as an accountant expert, tax consultant, and judicial expert.

Bibliometric and Academic Approaches to Economic Crime

Mapping the Nexus of Economic Crime, Forensic Accounting, and Sustainable Development Goals (SDGs): A Bibliometric Review

Isabella Lucuț-Capraș, Monica Violeta Achim, and Leonard Artur Horvath

Abstract The aim of this study is to examine the complex relationship between economic crime, forensic accounting, and the Sustainable Development Goals (SDGs). By integrating insights from existing research, this work aims to contribute significantly to ongoing efforts aimed at combating economic and financial crime on a global scale. According to recent regulations from the International Federation of Accountants, ongoing problems like corruption, money laundering, tax evasion, and different types of fraud pose significant obstacles to economic growth and sustainable development. These illegal activities undermine the integrity of financial systems, diminish public trust, and divert vital resources. Ultimately, they threaten economic stability and substantially impede progress toward the United Nations Sustainable Development Goals, which focus on ending poverty, reducing inequality, and encouraging sustainable practices globally. This chapter highlights the crucial importance of strong governance in combating fraudulent activities, emphasizing a framework that promotes accountability and transparency. We conducted a bibliometric systematic review on forensic accounting, financial crime, and their links to good governance and the Sustainable Development Goals (SDGs). To analyze the published papers from the Web of Science database, two powerful bibliometric visualization tools were used: Biblioshiny and VOSviewer. The study highlights the primary red flags from the literature, key aspects of forensic accounting and economic crime, how their relevance has changed over time, their geographic distribution, and their relationship with good governance patterns. Regarding practical and social implications, the results provide valuable insights for managers and policymakers. These insights can help guide efforts toward achieving the 2030 Agenda for Sustainable Development, adopted by all United Nations Member States in 2015, particularly through the use

I. Lucuț-Capraș (✉) · M. V. Achim · L. A. Horvath
Faculty of Economics and Business Administration, Babeș-Bolyai University, Cluj-Napoca, Romania
e-mail: isabella.lucutcapras@econ.ubbcluj.ro

M. V. Achim
e-mail: monica.achim@econ.ubbcluj.ro

L. A. Horvath
e-mail: leonard.horvath@econ.ubbcluj.ro

M. V. Achim (ed.), *Financial Crime in the Digital Era*, Contributions to Finance and Accounting, https://doi.org/10.1007/978-3-032-20198-0_10

of forensic accounting to prevent fraud. The study's originality lies in employing a novel approach called scientific mapping, which combines two bibliometric tools: Biblioshiny and VOSviewer. Additionally, it stands out by exploring the intersection of three distinct topics: economic and financial crime, forensic accounting, and sustainable development goals.

Keywords Financial crime · Financial forensics · Oversight · Sustainable development

1 Introduction

Following the Millennium Development Goals (MDGs), in 2015, the United Nations Member States approved the Sustainable Development Goals (SDGs) as the foundation for the 2030 Agenda for Sustainable Development (Kanbur 2021; United Nations General Assembly 2015). The MDGs, established in 2000 during the United Nations Millennium Summit, aimed to promote progress in development, eradicate hunger, and eliminate extreme poverty (Schöne et al. 2022; United Nations General Assembly 2000). In contrast, the new Sustainable Development Goals (SDGs) expanded this agenda to include a broader and more comprehensive focus, blending political objectives with aspirations for economic growth and social justice (Kanbur 2021; Rendtorff 2019; Sachs 2012, 2015). The primary SDG objective continues to be ending poverty worldwide. However, the new goals now encompass all aspects of development—economic, social, and environmental—and are equally important for all countries, both at the national and international levels (Edwards and Ross 2016; Schöne et al. 2022; United Nations 2023). In this context, the SDGs act as a catalyst to foster local economic development and social transformation across private businesses, public organizations, and institutions (Rendtorff 2019). SDG 16.4 targets reducing illegal money flows to combat organized crime, SDG 16.5 focuses on eliminating corruption, and SDG 16 overall aims to strengthen expertise and international cooperation in fighting crime and terrorism (Truby 2020; United Nations 2023). This demonstrates that the Sustainable Development Goals are closely linked to issues of economic and financial crime. Bologna and Lindquist (1995) describe forensic accounting as "the application of financial skills, and an investigative mentality to unresolved issues, conducted within the context of rules of evidence. As an emerging discipline, it encompasses financial expertise, fraud knowledge, and a sound knowledge and understanding of business reality and the working of the legal system." Forensic accounting serves as a crucial tool in identifying and preventing crimes. In this context, this research aims to review existing literature on economic and financial crime, forensic accounting, and sustainable development goals.

This study is original in its application of the innovative scientific mapping method and the integration of two bibliometric tools: BiblioShiny (Aria and Cuccurullo, 2017) and VOSviewer. The review used PRISMA (Preferred Reporting Items for Systematic Reviews and Meta-Analyses), bibliometric performance analysis, and scientific mapping to explore the internal structure, current status, and trends in economic crime, forensic accounting, and Sustainable Development Goals. Bibliometric analysis employs a quantitative method, providing researchers with a useful way to obtain a detailed understanding and a broad overview of a particular research field (Bota-Avram 2023; Wang et al. 2021a, b; Xu et al. 2021).

This literature review advances the academic field by offering valuable insights into the evolution of research in economic crime, forensic accounting, and the Sustainable Development Goals (SDGs). It guides scholars through the historical development of these areas, showing how ideas and methods have changed over time. By integrating findings from various studies, the review makes a significant contribution to bibliometric analysis, especially regarding the connection between SDGs and forensic accounting. This innovative approach highlights the important links between these fields, emphasizing the roles of accountability and transparency in reaching sustainability goals. Ultimately, the review acts as a driver for academic progress by providing a thorough analysis of existing research and suggesting future research directions. It not only consolidates current knowledge but also encourages further investigation into this fascinating subject.

The remainder of this article is structured as follows. The next section explains the reasons for selecting the methods used in the bibliometric literature review and the associated research questions. The third section outlines how the final articles were chosen and details the research design for the bibliometric and network analyses. In the fourth section, the results of the study are presented and discussed. The last section offers concluding remarks.

2 Methodology

2.1 Methods Selection, Objectives, and Research Questions

The quantitative analysis of scientific research seeks to enhance understanding within particular fields. In this framework, bibliometric analysis is crucial, as both bibliometric and systematic literature reviews are now key methods for summarizing research trends, pinpointing knowledge gaps, and guiding future research directions (Dote-Pardo and Ceballos-Garrido 2024; Dote-Pardo and Severino-González 2025a, b; Van Raan 2004). Bibliometric mapping visually illustrates the connections among various fields, disciplines, locations, and publications or authors (Cobo et al. 2011). It also offers a quantitative evaluation of specialized terminology, research output, development, collaboration, and the utilization of scientific works (Nobanee et al. 2022). The main goal of bibliometric analysis is to gather and examine existing research on a specific topic, producing objective, verifiable, and replicable results through the analysis of various bibliographic indicators like publication volume, authorship, citation patterns, and keyword frequency (Brika 2022; Dote-Pardo and Severino-González 2025a; Passas 2024). Using tools such as citation analysis and co-authorship networks helps reveal the field's intellectual structure, track the development of key themes, identify gaps in current knowledge, highlight areas for further exploration, and direct future research (Dote-Pardo and Severino-González 2025b; Ortiz-Cea et al. 2024; You et al. 2024). From a practical perspective, this approach functions as a valuable resource for researchers, policymakers, and practitioners aiming to comprehend a particular field and to base their decisions on empirical data (Florek-Paszkowska and Hoyos-Vallejo 2023).

In recent years, bibliometric research has gained significance in business and financial studies because it enables the summarization of extensive scientific data to analyze the current state of the intellectual framework and emerging patterns within a field (Alshater et al. 2022; Bota-Avram 2023; Donthu et al. 2021; Wang et al. 2022; Wang et al. 2021a, b). As a result, it was determined that the bibliometric review method is the most appropriate approach for the study we conducted, as it helps in the identification of key works on this topic. Additionally, it will aid in illustrating the connections between publications, support meta-analytical evaluations, assist in identifying key research streams, and contribute to the development of fundamental theoretical goals (Apriliyanti and Alon 2017; Fetscherin and Heinrich 2015; Nobanee 2020, 2021; Nobanee et al. 2021); compared to other approaches, which are confined to offering merely a literature review on the topic (Nobanee et al. 2022).

The primary objective of this article is to thoroughly examine the literature related to economic crime, the field of forensic accounting, and the SDGs. In doing so, it seeks to evaluate the current state of research in this crucial area. Understanding the complex nature of economic and financial crimes emphasizes their close link to forensic accounting and the SDGs' broader goals. Recognizing these ties allows stakeholders such as policymakers, financial institutions, and law enforcement to allocate resources more effectively to fight these crimes. Additionally, they can develop stronger compliance strategies that meet legal standards while also fostering ethical practices. This exploration provides valuable insights into the complexities of economic crime and forensic accounting, shedding light on the systemic issues that often go unaddressed. Furthermore, this analysis provides a foundation for a more proactive and informed approach to prevent financial misconduct, ultimately promoting an environment with greater transparency, accountability, and resilience against economic crimes.

Given this context, the goal of this research is to examine and analyze the literature published in Web of Science concerning economic and financial crime, forensic accounting, and the Sustainable Development Goals by answering the following research questions:

RQ 1. How has the literature on economic and financial crime, forensic accounting, and SDGs evolved?

RQ 2. Is there a relationship between economic crime, forensic accounting, and the SDGs in the existing literature?

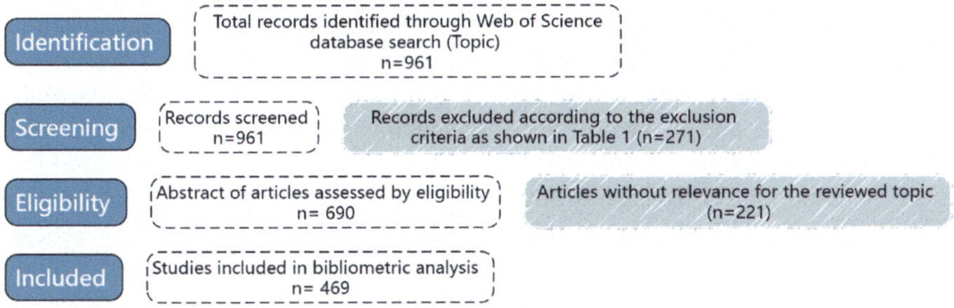

Fig. 1 PRISMA flowchart protocol for the research topic. *Source* Created by the authors based on Page et al. (2021)

2.2 *Search Strategy and Data Extraction*

To achieve a comprehensive understanding of the knowledge framework within the field of study, a detailed data extraction was conducted for bibliometric analysis, following the PRISMA protocol as outlined by Page et al (2021). The PRISMA methodology is characterized by its distinctive features, notably its meticulously designed checklist. This checklist functions as a vital resource for refining methodologies related to bibliometric analyses, systematic review reporting, and effective execution of meta-analyses. It includes four primary stages: identification of relevant literature, screening of potential studies, assessment of eligibility criteria, and inclusion of studies meeting the research parameters (Moher et al. 2009; Pascoal et al. 2023). This structured approach enhances the quality and rigor of scientific reporting, fostering greater transparency and reproducibility in research (Bota-Avram, 2023; Streimikis and Saraji, 2022). The PRISMA flowchart used in the study, shown in Fig. 1, illustrates each stage of the analysis.

The research process began with choosing an appropriate database and clearly defining publication criteria through careful planning (Lewis et al. 2011; Piwowar-Sulej and Iqbal, 2023). For this study, the Web of Science database was used because of its extensive coverage of high-quality academic journals and its reputation as a reliable source for accessing top-tier publications (Bota-Avram 2023; Caputo et al. 2021; Raghuram et al. 2019). To ensure the accuracy of the results, the search outcomes were refined using criteria from Web of Science combined with MS Excel. This integrated method helped organize and analyze the data. Next, VOSviewer and Biblioshiny (Aria and Cuccurullo 2017) were used. VOSviewer, known for its visualization features, and Biblioshiny, a user-friendly web app with a graphical interface for the Bibliometrix R-Package, allowed for detailed exploration of the collected studies. The results are presented systematically, using different analytical units such as research articles, author profiles, leading journals, and important research themes to give a complete overview of the academic landscape. Several graphs, network maps, and visualization tools are used to effectively illustrate the research environment and identify emerging trends in specific fields.

Table 1 presents the search strings used to identify articles on financial crime, sustainable development goals, and forensic accounting. A topic field search was applied because it encompasses various record elements such as Title, Abstract, Author Keywords, and Keywords Plus, enhancing precision in science-mapping studies while maintaining transparent search logic. The initial query retrieved 961 records (October 2025). To narrow down the corpus based on the review's focus, we applied sequential Web of Science filters. The papers were initially limited to articles and reviews, resulting in 843 records. Subsequently, the language was restricted to English to facilitate term comparability in bibliometric text mining, reducing the records to 777. To exclude irrelevant topics, research areas unrelated to the primary focus—such as Obstetrics and Gynecology, Nursing, Sports Science, and Surgery—were removed, leaving 690 records. A manual screening process was carried out by reviewing titles and abstracts in Excel, following Brereton et al. (2007), to exclude off-topic papers. This step involved excluding papers that only used generic references to "sustainability" or employed "forensic" in unrelated contexts. Following this, 469 documents were chosen for the subsequent analysis phase, and bibliometric data for all records was downloaded. This data was then utilized as input for bibliometric analysis using Biblioshiny (Aria and Cuccurullo, 2017) and VOSviewer (Van Eck and Waltman, 2014).

Table 1 Description of the search procedure

Phase	Description	No. of remaining articles
Search string used in the Web of Science database	Topic: ("crime*" or "fraud*" and "Forensic* accounting") and ("Sustainable Development* Goal*" or "SDG*" or "Sustainable Development*" or "Development* Goal*" or "sustainability")	961
Refinement by document type	Including only articles and review articles	843
Refinement by language	Including only articles published in English	777
Refinement by research areas	Excluding research areas that are not relevant (e.g., Obstetrics and Gynecology, Nursing, Sports Science, Surgery, and others)	690
Manual refinement	The titles and abstracts of the resulting papers were examined, and any irrelevant materials were eliminated	469
Final sample	The total number of papers remaining after manual refinement that were used in the research	469

Source Created by the authors

3 Results and Discussion

This study combines performance analysis and science mapping bibliographic methods to offer a detailed overview of the existing research on the topic (Aria and Cuccurullo, 2017; Bota-Avram, 2023; Donthu et al. 2021). Analyzing 469 papers focused on economic and financial crime, forensic accounting, and sustainable development, the study also incorporates articles related to sustainable development more broadly, to provide a comprehensive view of how these topics interconnect, beyond just the UN's SDGs (United Nations General Assembly, 2015). The general information of the dataset used in the study is shown in Fig. 2. It includes publications from 1996 to 2025 across 321 sources, with 1889 keywords assigned by the authors. The papers involve 1372 authors, averaging 3.06 co-authors per paper, typical of the social science domain. There are 97 single-author papers, and international collaboration accounts for 26.01% of publications. Across all 469 documents, total citations reach 27,924, showing active engagement with diverse methodological and policy-focused studies, both review and empirical. Publications on this topic are increasing at a rate of 16.51% annually, with impact metrics averaging 13.3 citations per document. The average age of the documents is 4.14 years, emphasizing the field's emerging and dynamic status. Overall, this profile highlights a rapidly growing, relatively young, and broad-ranging research area characterized by moderate collaboration, significant international partnerships, and varied topics.

Figure 3 shows the changes in publication counts over time, and Table 2 displays the number of publications in the past 10 years. The number of publications has notably increased since 2015, with peaks in 2024 and 2025 at 74 and 84 publications. Over the last decade, a pattern of steady growth and acceleration is evident, with publications rising from 8 in 2015 to 84 in 2025. Three phases can be identified: a period of gradual growth from 2015 to 2019 (8–29 publications), a consolidation phase from 2020 to 2022 following the 2018–2019 surge, and a rapid rise from 2023 to 2025 (60 publications in 2023, 74 in 2024, and 84 in 2025). This trend illustrates a field evolving from exploratory research (pre-2018), through consolidation (2020–2022), to active expansion (2023–2025). It indicates a domain maturing but still rapidly

Fig. 2 General information about the sample. *Source* Created by the authors using Biblioshiny

developing at the nexus of forensic accounting, fraud and crime, and sustainability. These results underscore a rising research interest, especially amid efforts by various countries to combat crime and foster sustainable development.

Figures 4 and 5 depict the performance of sources. Figure 4 highlights the most prominent sources within the scope of the study, ranked by publication count. The corpus is distributed across many venues, but a small core of journals produces a majority of the output. Sustainability is the leading outlet with 40 papers, accounting for 8.5% of the total (40/469). Two specialized journals, the Journal of Money Laundering Control and Marine Policy, follow with 10 papers each, followed by journals such as Cities, Crime, Law and Social Change, European Journal of Sustainable Development, Social Sciences–Basel, and Sustainable Development, each with 6 papers. The top ten also includes the Journal of Cleaner Production (5 papers) and the British Journal of Criminology (4). Figure 5 shows the most cited local sources. Local citations indicate how often a source within the set is cited by authors from other sources within the same set (Aria and Cuccurullo 2017). Again, Sustainability leads with 247 local citations. The Journal of Cleaner Production (174 citations) and Marine Policy (148 citations) are the second and third most cited. These three sources account for about 43% of citations among the top ten local sources. The remaining sources include both disciplinary and general-science journals such as the Journal of Business Ethics (132), PLOS ONE (126), Journal of Money Laundering Control (115), British Journal of Criminology (108), Criminology (94), Science (91), and Landscape and Urban Planning (80). The presence of criminology and anti-money laundering journals alongside titles on sustainability, ethics, policy, and science highlights the interdisciplinary nature of this field. Several journals appear on both lists, including Sustainability, Marine Policy, and Journal of Money Laundering Control, demonstrating outlets that are both common publication venues and key citation sources. Overall, the source profile indicates a developing field, dominated by a major, generalist outlet focused on sustainability, with a diverse mix of disciplinary foundations such as criminology and anti-money laundering, environmental policy, ethics, and urban planning.

Figure 6 highlights the most significant affiliations. The Ministry of Education and Science of Ukraine leads with 55 articles, followed by Arizona State University with 9. Arizona State University–Tempe, Pennsylvania Commonwealth System of Higher Education, and the University of London each have 8 articles, while Griffith University, Kharkiv National University of Economics, Monash University, and the Russian Academy of Sciences each have 7. Chung Yuan Christian University rounds out the top ten with 6 articles. These ten affiliations together account for 122 papers, about 26% of the total 469 documents. Geographically, the leading affiliations are spread across Eastern Europe, the U.S., the U.K., Australia, and Taiwan, reflecting the global reach of the field. The notable presence of a government ministry among the main contributors suggests that policy and implementation work are closely linked to university research in this area.

Figure 7 and Table 3 illustrate scientific productivity by country, calculated by counting author entries based on their national affiliations. The output is concentrated in a few key research areas, led by the United States with 190 contributions, followed

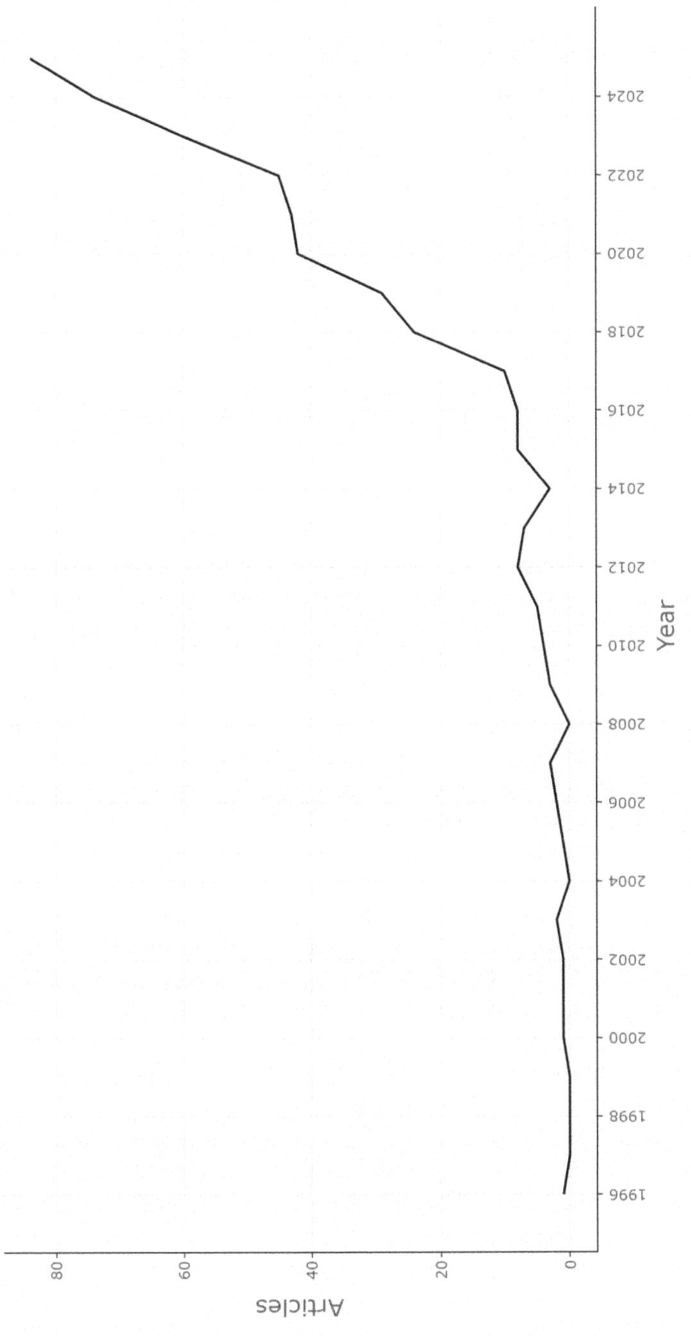

Fig. 3 Annual scientific production. *Source* Created by the authors using biblioshiny

Table 2 Annual scientific production for the last 10 years

Year	Articles
2015	8
2016	8
2017	10
2018	24
2019	29
2020	42
2021	43
2022	45
2023	60
2024	74
2025	84

Source Created by the authors using biblioshiny

by China (95), the United Kingdom (71), Ukraine (69), Australia (60), Brazil (56), Spain (38), Italy (34), India (31), and Malaysia (30). These figures represent country–publication instances, meaning that a single paper can credit multiple countries when co-authored internationally, so the totals exceed the 469 documents in the dataset. Figure 8 shows the nation of origin of the corresponding author, while Fig. 9 maps the countries' collaborations globally. MCP, or Multiple Countries Publication, indicates articles with at least one co-author from a different country, reflecting the degree of international collaboration (Botene et al. 2021). SCP, or Single Country Publication, includes papers in which all authors are from the same country (Botene et al. 2021). The world map and co-authorship network reveal dense trans-regional ties centered on the United States, strongly connected with the UK, China, and Australia, and also linked to Brazil, Malaysia, and India. European collaboration lines are visible across the UK–EU corridor, while Australia acts as a southern hub connecting North America and East Asia. Bars representing the corresponding author's country show that the USA leads in both total corresponding author papers and SCP, reflecting a robust domestic research base. China, the UK, and Australia contribute significant numbers, with higher shares of MCP, indicating more outward-focused collaboration. Ukraine, Brazil, India, and Malaysia also show meaningful participation, primarily through SCP but with noticeable MCP segments. While the field is global, it is primarily centered on a few key systems (the USA, China, the UK, and Australia) that serve as major collaboration hubs. Ukraine's strong presence aligns with its institutional results, with a national ministry ranking among the top affiliations, indicating an active policy–academia connection and supporting earlier findings. The involvement of Brazil, India, Malaysia, Spain, and Italy suggests an expanding geographic reach, contributing diverse viewpoints on financial crime, forensic accounting, and sustainability.

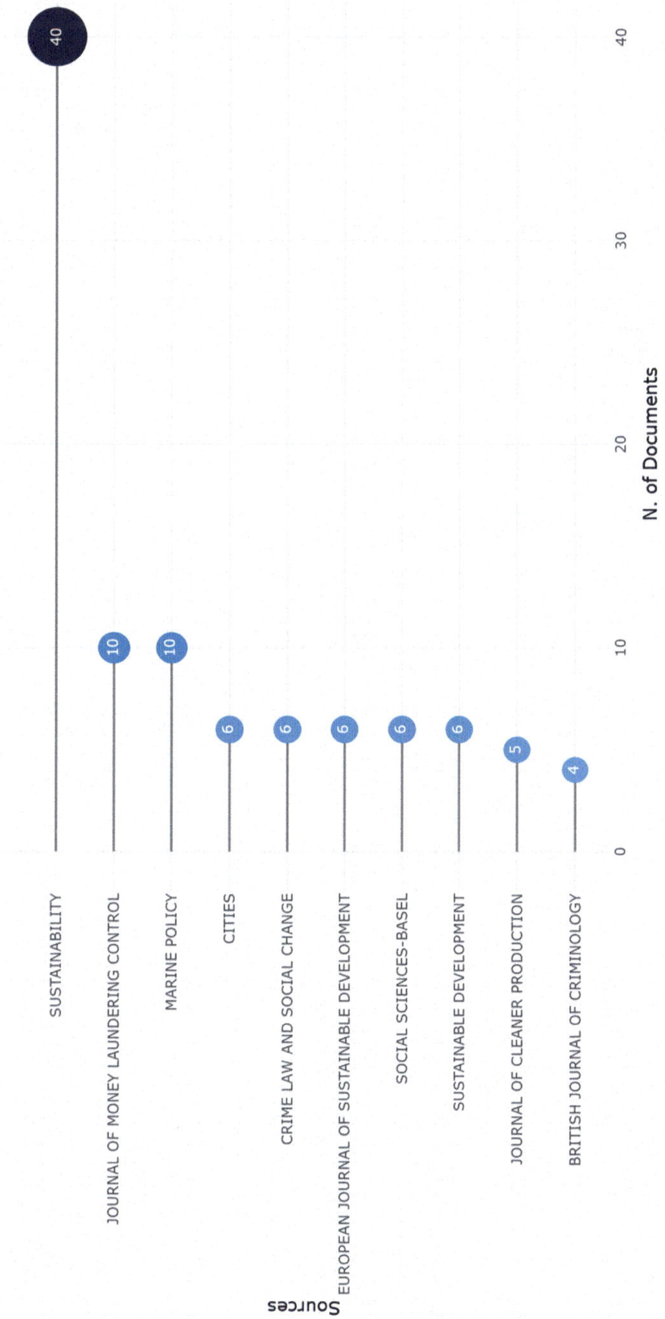

Fig. 4 Most relevant sources. *Source* Created by the authors using biblioshiny

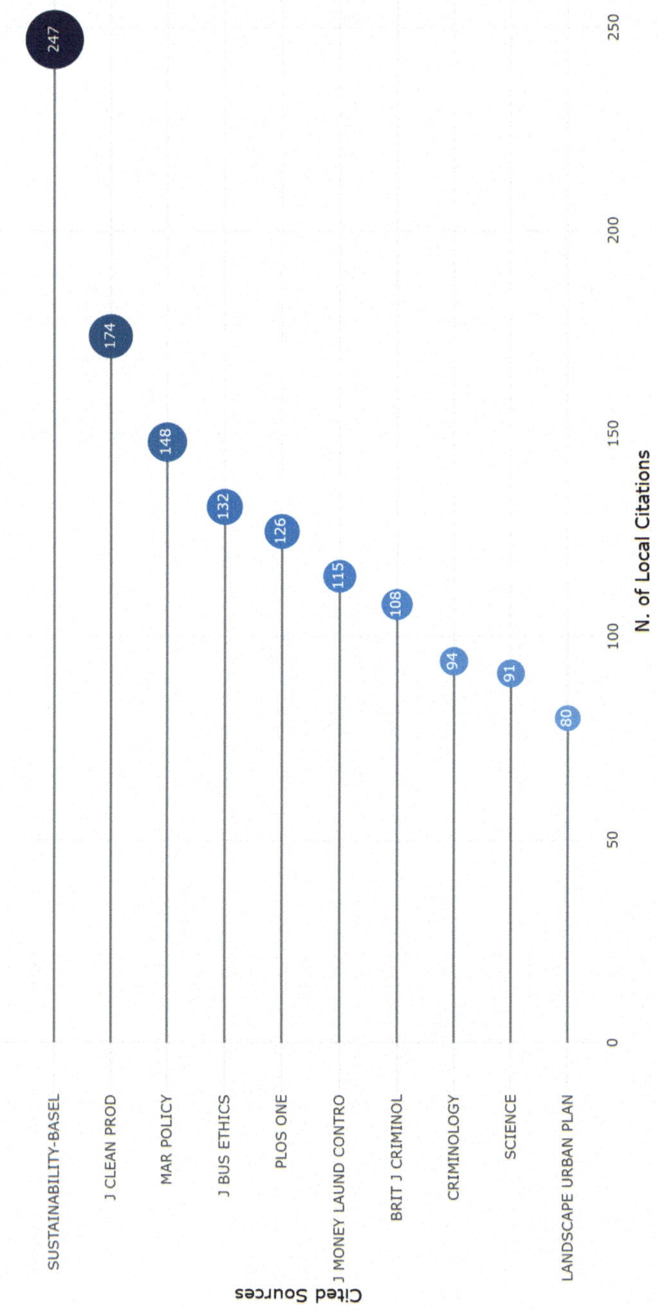

Fig. 5 Most local cited sources. *Source* Created by the authors using biblioshiny

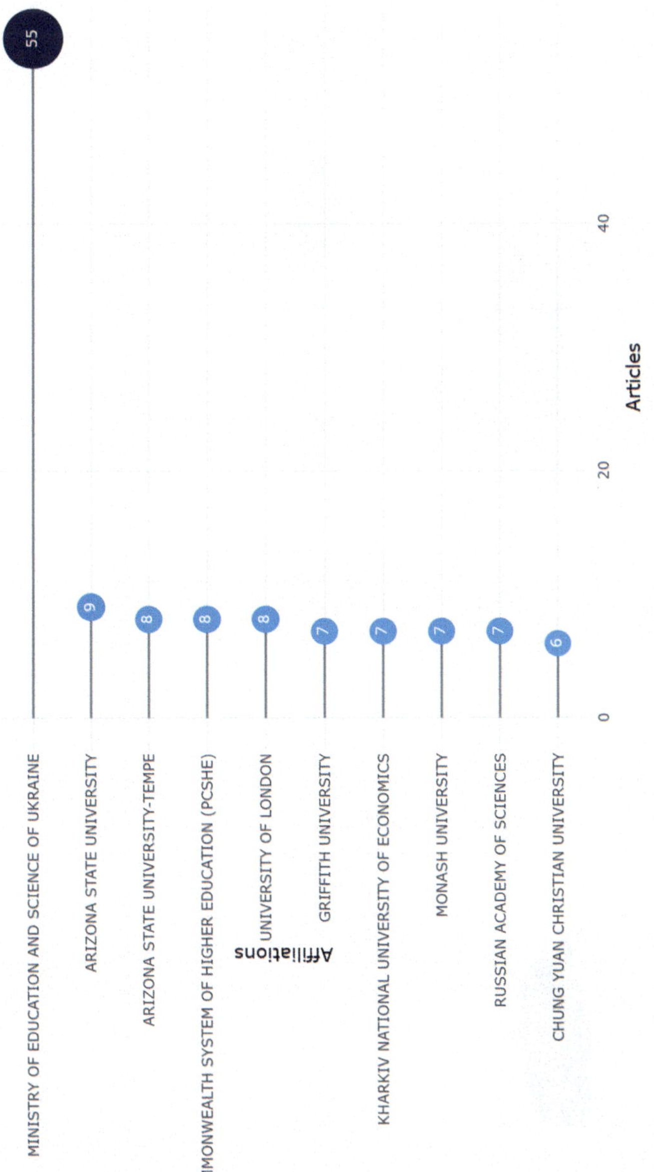

Fig. 6 Most relevant affiliations. *Source* Created by the author using biblioshiny

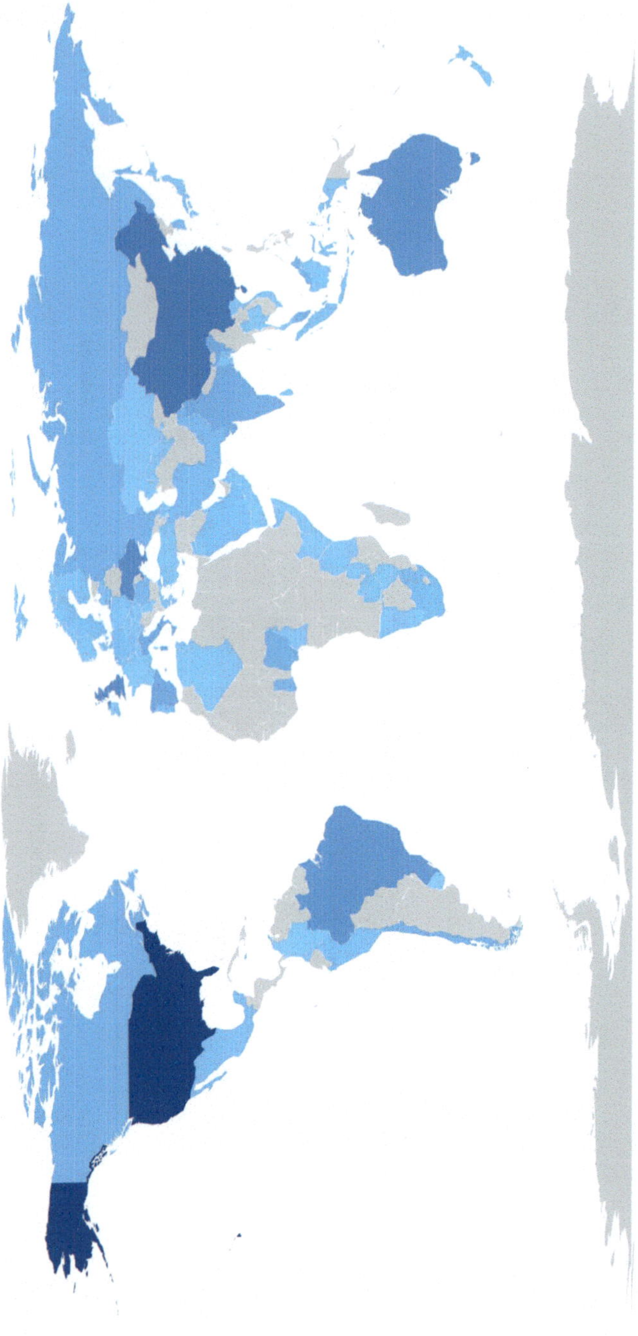

Fig. 7 Countries scientific production. *Source* Created by the author using biblioshiny

Table 3 Top 10 countries in terms of scientific production

Country	Freq
USA	190
China	95
UK	71
Ukraine	69
Australia	60
Brazil	56
Spain	38
Italy	34
India	31
Malaysia	30

Source Created by the author using biblioshiny

Co-authorship analysis involves examining how many articles are jointly written by researchers and institutions, which helps evaluate the extent of intellectual collaboration among them (Bota-Avram 2023). Table 4 shows the ten leading authors who have studied topics such as economic and financial crime, forensic accounting, and sustainable development based on their total link strength in the VOSviewer co-authorship network. The core collaboration group consists of Jarrett Blaustein and Nathan W. Pino, each with a total link strength of 7, 4 publications, and 31 citations. The second tier includes Tom Chodor and Michael A. Long, both with a total link strength of 4, having 2 and 3 documents, respectively. Following them are Elisa Alfaro, Michael J. Lynch, Paul B. Stretesky, and Sergio A. Useche, each sharing a total link strength of 3 with 2 publications and citation counts between 2 and 8. Monica Violeta Achim and Chie-Peng Chen have a total link strength of 2 but higher citation figures of 16 and 17, indicating that collaboration influence and citation impact are not perfectly aligned. The top-10 list demonstrates a diverse, interdisciplinary field that spans criminology, policy, sustainability, accounting, and finance.

Two research papers are considered co-cited when they are both cited by a third publication, establishing a scholarly connection that emphasizes the relationship between their ideas and contributions (Marshakova-Shaikevich 1973; Small 1973). The more articles that co-cite two publications, the stronger their co-citation relationship (Van Eck and Waltman 2014). Co-citation analysis assesses the references cited by the scientific works in the dataset and examines the relationships between these references to better understand the development of key themes within a research area (Bota-Avram 2023). The co-citation network diagram for references related to economic and financial crime, forensic accounting, and sustainable development is shown in Fig. 10. In VOSviewer, the minimum number of citations for a reference was set to 5. Out of 27,896 references in the dataset, 38 met this criterion. The program then identified the largest connected set, resulting in a co-citation network of 37 items organized into 4 clusters (182 links; 352 total link strength). The largest cluster, shown in red, contains 11 items; the second cluster, in green, has 10 items;

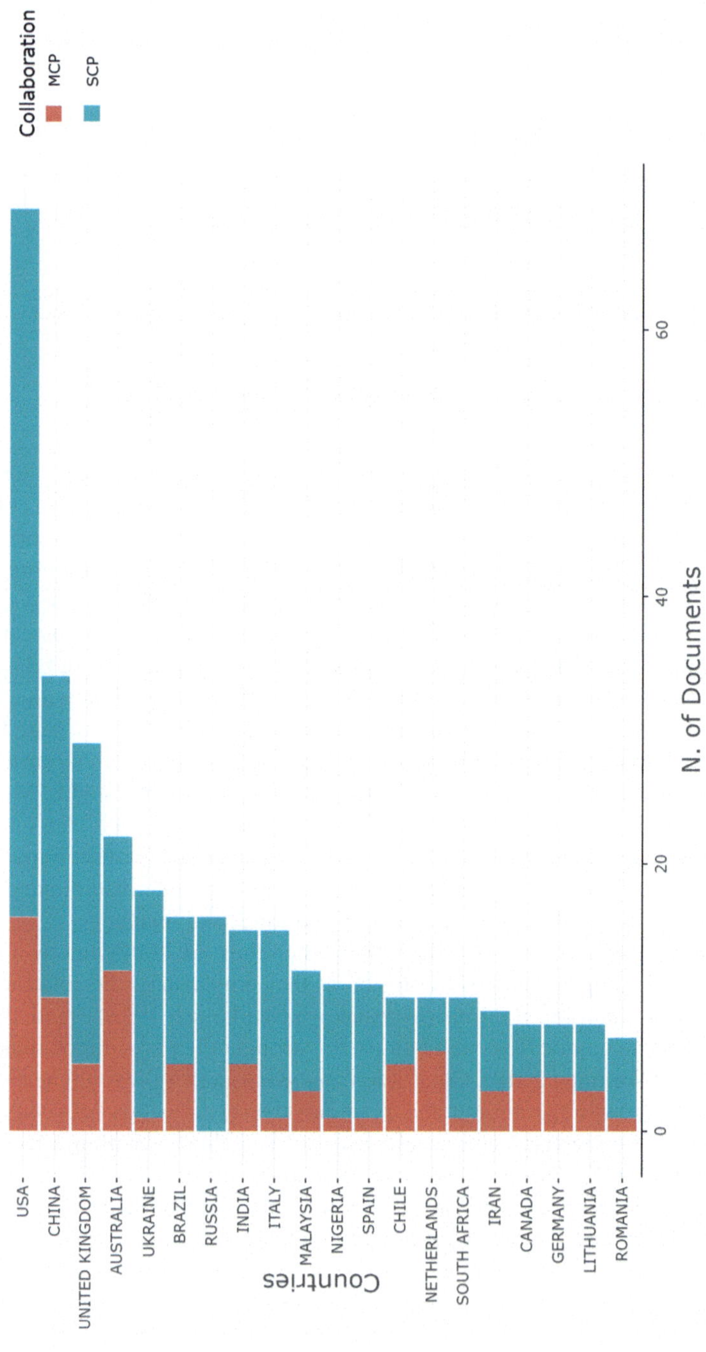

Fig. 8 Corresponding author's countries. *Source* Created by the author using biblioshiny

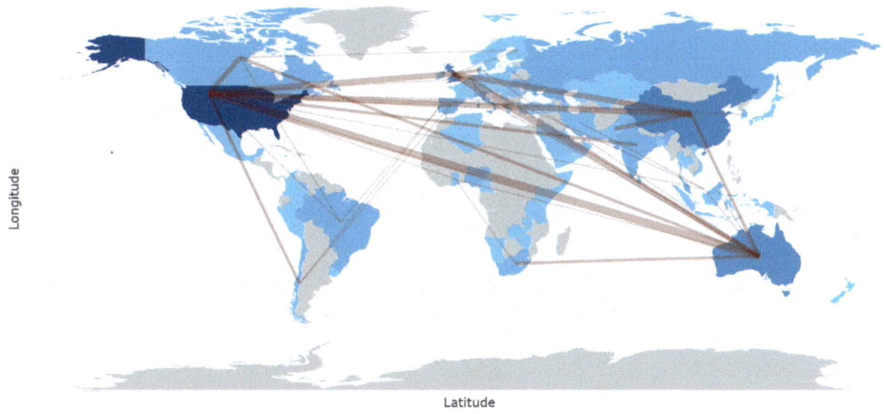

Fig. 9 Countries collaboration. *Source* Created by the author using biblioshiny

Table 4 Top 10 researchers with the highest total link strength in coauthorship

Rank	Author	Documents	Citations	Total link strength
1	Blaustein, Jarrett	4	31	7
2	Pino, Nathan W.	4	31	7
3	Chodor, Tom	2	6	4
4	Long, Michael A.	3	4	4
5	Alfaro, Elisa	2	8	3
6	Lynch, Michael J.	2	2	3
7	Stretesky, Paul B.	2	4	3
8	Useche, Sergio A.	2	8	3
9	Achim, Monica Violeta	2	16	2
10	Chen, Chie-Peng	2	17	2

Source Created by the author based on the VOSviewer results

the third cluster, in blue, also has 10 items; and the fourth cluster, in yellow, includes 6 items.

Bibliographic coupling is the opposite of co-citation. It happens when two publications share references, and a third one cites both (Kessler 1963). The more references they share, the stronger their bibliographic link (Van Eck and Waltman 2014). This approach helps analyze relationships among publications and highlights their roles within the network. In the journal bibliographic coupling analysis, at least 2 documents per source were required. Out of 321 sources, 56 met this criterion; the largest network included 53 sources, comprising 53 items, 9 clusters, 263 links, and a total link strength of 814. Table 5 lists the top ten journals by link strength, while Fig. 11 shows the bibliographic coupling network. Results reveal a dominant sustainability hub connected to criminology, anti-money laundering, policy, and sectoral fields.

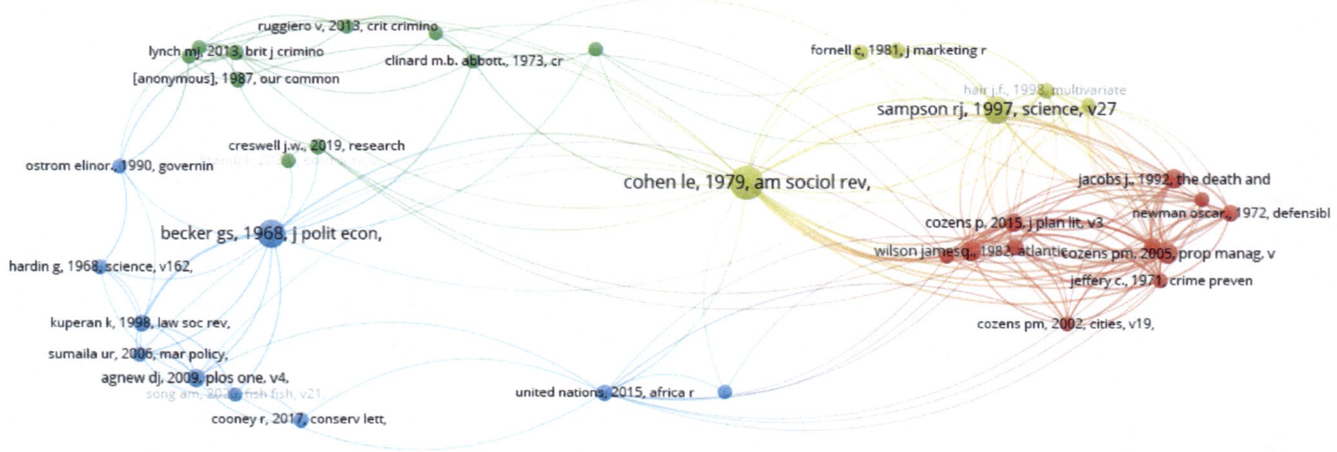

Fig. 10 The co-citation network diagram of cited references. *Source* Created by the authors using VOSviewer

Sustainability leads in coupling strength with a total link strength of 287, covering 40 documents and 434 citations, acting as the main connector among journals. Close by are the Journal of Planning Literature with a total link strength of 118, and the Security Journal with 115. A criminology/law cluster includes Crime, Law and Social Change, with a total link strength of 71; the British Journal of Criminology; and the Journal of Money Laundering Control, with a total link strength of 55. The policy and measurement branch links Sustainable Development (72), Social Sciences–Basel (69), and Social Indicators Research (60). Sectoral and territorial journals, such as Marine Policy, Land, Land Use Policy, and Cities, connect environmental governance and urban safety. Overall, the coupling network confirms a highly interdisciplinary structure: a central sustainability platform closely linked to criminology, anti-money laundering, and environmental and urban policy outlets. Proceeding with the bibliographic coupling analysis within the authors' context, the resulting sample consisted of 41 authors who each met the minimum requirement of two articles. Table 6 displays the authors with the highest bibliographic coupling strength, based on the total of their coupling links, and Fig. 12 shows the corresponding bibliographic coupling network diagram of the authors. At the author level, three clusters emerge and interconnect with each other. The core of the coupling is led by Jarrett Blaustein and Nathan W. Pino, each with a total link strength of 641, four documents, and 31 citations. They are closely linked to Michael A. Long with a strength of 374, and Tom Chodor with a strength of 340. A second cluster centers on Elisa Alfaro and Sergio A. Useche, each with a total link strength of 308, along with Michael J. Lynch with 293, and links to Rob White with 268 and Paul B. Stretesky. A third group features Angelo Jonas Imperiale and Frank Vanclay, each with a total link strength of 269. The maximum strength of bibliographic coupling indicates that these authors are more influential within the citation network and actively participate in discussions (Caputo et al. 2021).

Table 5 Top 10 journals in terms of bibliographic coupling link strength

Rank	Source	Documents	Citations	Total link strength
1	Sustainability	40	434	287
2	Journal of Planning Literature	3	224	118
3	Security Journal	3	3	115
4	Sustainable Development	6	226	72
5	Crime, Law and Social Change	6	89	71
6	Land	2	16	71
7	Social Sciences—Basel	6	71	69
8	Social Indicators Research	4	27	60
9	Marine Policy	10	77	56
10	Journal of Money Laundering Control	10	43	55

Source Created by the author based on the VOSviewer results

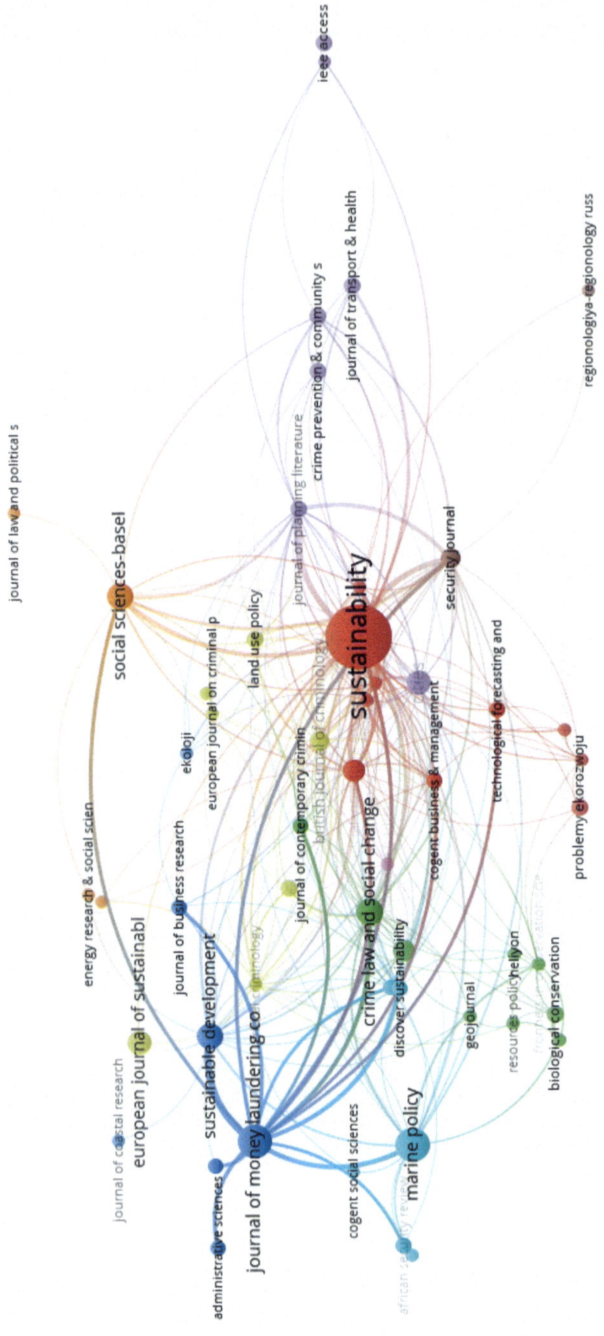

Fig. 11 The bibliographic coupling network diagram of the sources. *Source* Created by the authors using VOSviewer

Table 6 Top 10 authors in terms of bibliographic coupling link strength

Rank	Author	Documents	Citations	Total link strength
1	Blaustein, Jarrett	4	31	641
2	Pino, Nathan W.	4	31	641
3	Long, Michael A.	3	4	374
4	Chodor, Tom	2	6	340
5	Alfaro, Elisa	2	8	308
6	Useche, Sergio A.	2	8	308
7	Lynch, Michael J.	2	2	293
8	Imperiale, Angelo Jonas	2	56	269
9	Vanclay, Frank	2	56	269
10	White, Rob	2	46	268

Source Created by the authors based on the VOSviewer results

The frequency of two keywords co-occurring is indicated by the number of publications where both keywords appear together in the title, abstract, or keyword list (Van Eck and Waltman 2014). The main purpose of analyzing keyword co-occurrence is to provide a form of content analysis that helps identify associations among keywords within a set of documents. This process can reveal thematic areas grouped into clusters, highlighting the core topics or fundamental themes of the research field (Bota-Avram 2023; Fakhar Manesh et al. 2021). Keywords are typically extracted from a publication's title and abstract or from the author-provided keyword list. In some cases, especially in older publications, keywords may be simple words, but they can also be multi-word concepts (Van Eck and Waltman 2014). In our analysis, we mapped the topical structure utilizing a minimum occurrence threshold of five. Out of 2674 unique keywords, 105 satisfied this criterion, resulting in a network comprising 105 items organized into seven clusters (with 1052 links and a total link strength of 1620). By incorporating all keywords, the map encompasses both Author Keywords and Keywords Plus, thereby capturing both author intent and citation-based vocabulary. Table 7 displays the Top 10 co-occurring keywords ranked by total link strength. The sample in this study highlights three key terms that anchor the network: "crime" with 98 occurrences and a total link strength of 280, "sustainability" with 79 occurrences and a link strength of 208, and "sustainable development" with 48 occurrences and a total link strength of 100. Figure 13 illustrates the co-occurrence of keywords map, while Fig. 14 presents the cluster density visualization of high-frequency keywords. The density map highlights the most active areas related to crime, policy, and sustainability, with a secondary focus on governance, corruption, and the built environment. Keywords with strong linkages, like "management" (31 occurrences and a link strength of 96), "impact" (25 occurrences, and a link strength of 89), "security" (20 occurrences, and a total link strength of 64), and "performance" (14 occurrences and a link strength of 63), indicate a predominant managerial and evaluative approach in the literature. Forensic

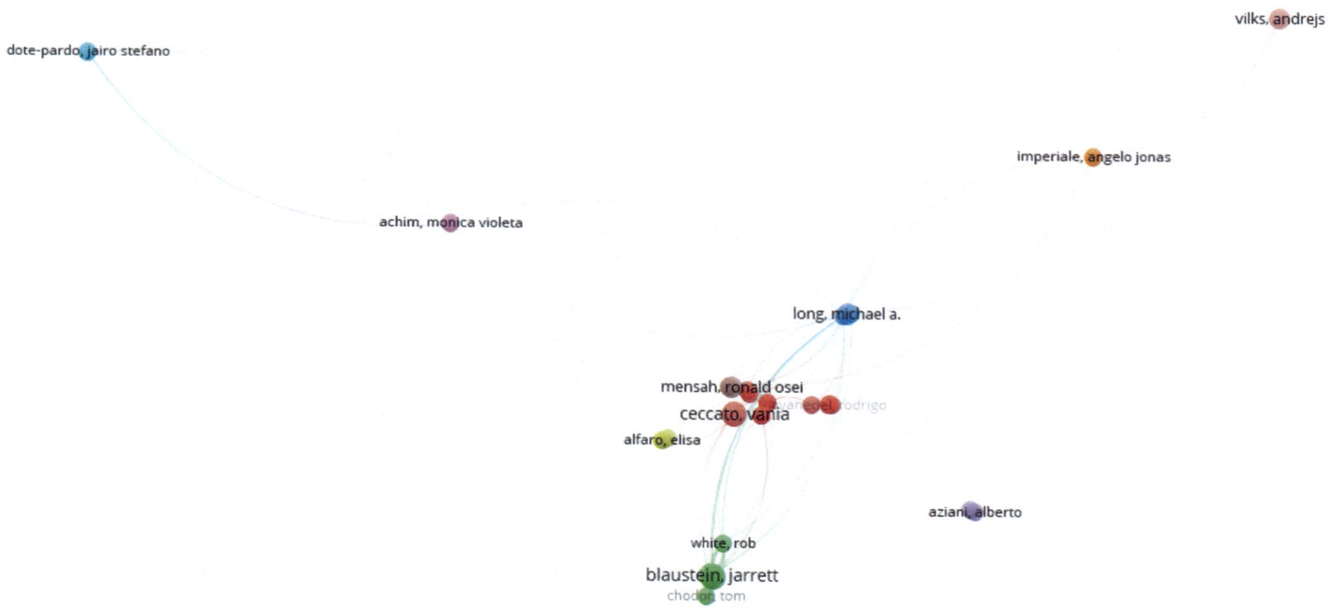

Fig. 12 The bibliographic coupling network diagram of the authors. *Source* Created by the authors using VOSviewer

accounting and money laundering are also present but occupy a more peripheral role, indicating an emerging intersection with data analytics and regulatory tools rather than a central focus. Overall, the co-occurrence network portrays an interdisciplinary field centered on governance for sustainability, interconnected through policy and measurement language, complemented by environmental conservation, forensic, and technological subfields. Consequently, all the major topics discussed are reflected in the bibliometric mapping, demonstrating a connection between economic crime, forensic accounting, and the Sustainable Development Goals in the academic literature.

Table 7 Top 10 co-occurring keywords sorted by total link strength

Rank	Keyword	Occurrences	Total link strength
1	Crime	98	280
2	Sustainability	79	208
3	Sustainable development	48	100
4	Management	31	96
5	Impact	25	89
6	Fear	15	69
7	Health	16	64
8	Security	20	64
9	Performance	14	63
10	Safety	13	59

Source Created by the authors based on the VOSviewer results

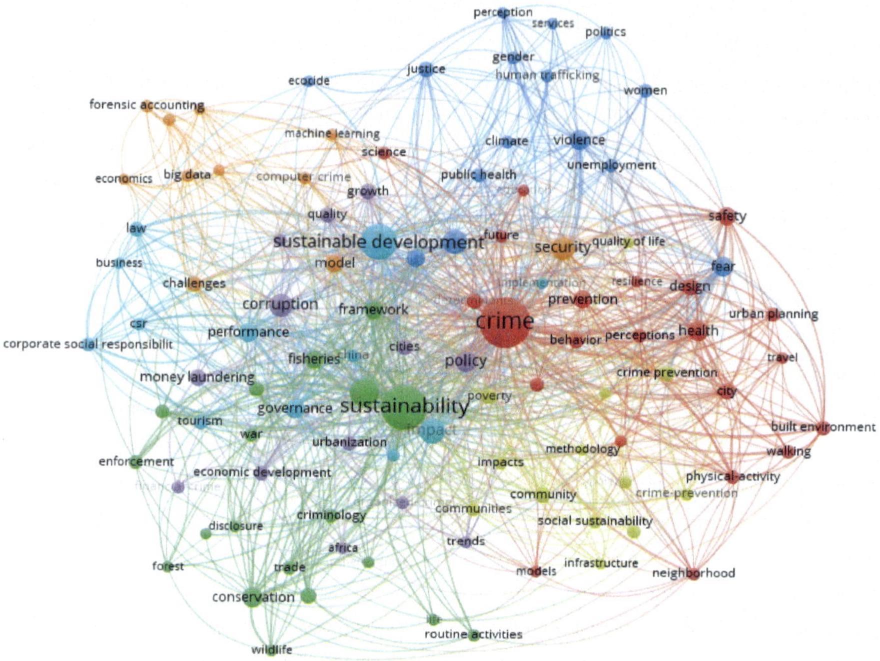

Fig. 13 The co-occurrence of keywords map. *Source* Created by the authors using VOSviewer

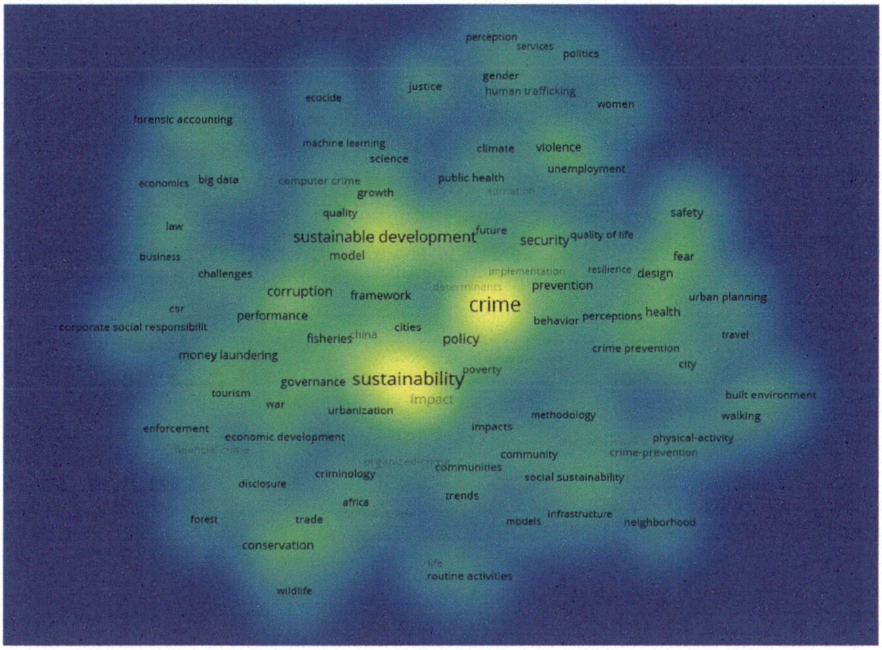

Fig. 14 The co-occurrence of keywords density visualization map. *Source* Created by the authors using VOSviewer

4 Conclusion

This bibliometric study provides a comprehensive evaluation of the literature related to the topic of economic and financial crime, forensic accounting, and sustainable development. Using the Web of Science database, we assembled 469 publications (1996–2025). Consequently, it offers a comprehensive visual representation of the intellectual framework of knowledge regarding the studied subject. Biblioshiny and VOSviewer were used in the bibliometric analysis.

The key findings from the bibliometric analysis reveal that the fields of economic and financial crime, forensic accounting, and sustainable development goals are evolving and gaining increasing academic interest. This emerging area is expanding quickly, with moderate collaboration and broad distribution across 321 outlets. The literature shows an interdisciplinary structure centered around sustainability. Bibliographic coupling suggests that sustainability is a core area closely connected to criminology and anti-money laundering outlets, policy and measurement venues, and urban and land-use studies. Author collaboration highlights teams that link criminology, governance, and sustainability. The keyword map indicates a primary focus on crime, policy, and sustainability, with related themes like the built environment, governance and anti-corruption, conservation, and a growing stream of forensic and technological topics such as money laundering, big data, and machine learning.

Leading countries in output include the USA, China, the UK, Ukraine, and Australia; notably, Ukraine's Ministry of Education and Science is among the top affiliations, which underscores a strong connection between policy and academia.

This paper contributes by using bibliometrics to analyze research development in economic and financial crime, forensic accounting, and the Sustainable Development Goals. It is valuable not only for scholars but also for policymakers and businesses. The mapping of research suggests bridging concepts like policy, governance, corruption, SDGs, performance, and the built environment, placing these studies at the core of the field. Practically and policy-wise, the study highlights that forensic skills can enhance the accuracy of sustainability reporting and controls, helping to prevent fraud and greenwashing, reinforcing anti-corruption and anti-money laundering efforts aligned with SDG 16, and aiding enforcement in environmental and resource sectors.

This study, similar to other bibliometric studies, had some limitations. This review only includes publications from the Web of Science collection and English-language records, so coverage and language biases may exist. Another limitation of this study is the use of bibliometric analysis, which is more quantitative and statistical and does not offer a deep and detailed examination of the content of the papers analyzed.

Future directions for researchers interested in this topic should include a detailed study of the connection between economic and financial crime, forensic accounting, and the Sustainable Development Goals, using methods like bibliometrics combined with systematic narrative synthesis, causal or quasi-experimental designs, and machine learning techniques. Additionally, it could be valuable to explore how these three factors can be measured and analyzed with a sample of organizations or countries, linking forensic accounting indicators to SDG and governance metrics; and to assess how integrity controls influence sustainability outcomes.

References

Alshater MM, Atayah OF, Khan A (2022) What do we know about business and economics research during COVID-19: a bibliometric review. Econ Res Ekonomska Istraživanja 35(1):1884–1912. https://doi.org/10.1080/1331677X.2021.1927786

Apriliyanti ID, Alon I (2017) Bibliometric analysis of absorptive capacity. Int Bus Rev 26(5):896–907. https://doi.org/10.1016/j.ibusrev.2017.02.007

Aria M, Cuccurullo C (2017) Bibliometrix: an R-tool for comprehensive science mapping analysis. J Informet 11(4):959–975. https://doi.org/10.1016/j.joi.2017.08.007

Bologna GJ, Lindquist RJ (1995) Fraud auditing and forensic accounting: new tools and techniques. Wiley, London

Bota-Avram C (2023) Bibliometric analysis of sustainable business performance: Where are we going? A science map of the field. Econ Res Ekonomska Istraživanja 36(1):2137–2176. https://doi.org/10.1080/1331677X.2022.2096094

Botene PHR, de Azevedo AT, de Arruda Ignácio PS (2021) Blockchain as an enabling technology in the COVID-19 pandemic: a systematic review. Heal Technol 11(6):1369–1382. https://doi.org/10.1007/s12553-021-00593-z

Brereton P, Kitchenham BA, Budgen D, Turner M, Khalil M (2007) Lessons from applying the systematic literature review process within the software engineering domain. Softw Perform 80(4):571–583. https://doi.org/10.1016/j.jss.2006.07.009

Brika SKM (2022) A bibliometric analysis of fintech trends and digital finance. Front Environ Sci. https://doi.org/10.3389/fenvs.2021.796495

Caputo A, Pizzi S, Pellegrini MM, Dabić M (2021) Digitalization and business models: Where are we going? A science map of the field. J Bus Res 123:489–501. https://doi.org/10.1016/j.jbusres.2020.09.053

Cobo MJ, López-Herrera AG, Herrera-Viedma E, Herrera F (2011) Science mapping software tools: review, analysis, and cooperative study among tools. J Am Soc Inform Sci Technol 62(7):1382–1402. https://doi.org/10.1002/asi.21525

Donthu N, Kumar S, Mukherjee D, Pandey N, Lim WM (2021) How to conduct a bibliometric analysis: an overview and guidelines. J Bus Res 133:285–296. https://doi.org/10.1016/j.jbusres.2021.04.070

Dote-Pardo J, Ceballos-Garrido P (2024) Trends and research lines on triple bottom line: a bibliometric analysis of the management and business ambit. Russ Law J 12(2):389–401

Dote-Pardo JS, Severino-González P (2025a) Economic and financial crimes: evidence from the literature in emerging markets. J Money Laund Control 28(2):253–274. https://doi.org/10.1108/JMLC-07-2024-0120

Dote-Pardo JS, Severino-González P (2025b) Money laundering in emerging countries: patterns, trends, and knowledge gaps from a systematic review. J Money Laund Control 28(2):341–358. https://doi.org/10.1108/JMLC-01-2025-0002

Edwards A, Ross N (2016) From global goals to local impact: how philanthropy can help achieve the UN sustainable development goals in the US council on foundations and SDG funders. https://www.cof.org/sites/default/files/documents/files/Global-Goals-Local-Impact-SDGs-and-Philanthropy-2016.pdf

Fakhar Manesh M, Pellegrini MM, Marzi G, Dabic M (2021) Knowledge management in the fourth industrial revolution: mapping the literature and scoping future avenues. IEEE Trans Eng Manage 68(1):289–300. https://doi.org/10.1109/TEM.2019.2963489

Fetscherin M, Heinrich D (2015) Consumer brand relationships research: a bibliometric citation meta-analysis. J Bus Res 68(2):380–390. https://doi.org/10.1016/j.jbusres.2014.06.010

Florek-Paszkowska AK, Hoyos-Vallejo CA (2023) A comprehensive bibliometric analysis and future research directions in the nexus of sustainable business practices and turnover intention. Clean Respons Consumpt 11:100146. https://doi.org/10.1016/j.clrc.2023.100146

Kanbur R (2021) Sustainable development goals and the study of economic inequality. J Econ Inequal 19(1):3–11. https://doi.org/10.1007/s10888-020-09452-9

Kessler MM (1963) Bibliographic coupling between scientific papers. Am Doc 14(1):10–25. https://doi.org/10.1002/asi.5090140103

Lewis MO, Mathiassen L, Rai A (2011) Scalable growth in IT-enabled service provisioning: a sensemaking perspective. Eur J Inf Syst 20(3):285–302. https://doi.org/10.1057/ejis.2011.5

Marshakova-Shaikevich I (1973) System of document connections based on references. Sci Tech Inform Ser VINITI 2:3–8

Moher D, Liberati A, Tetzlaff J, Altman DG, The PRISMA Group (2009) Preferred reporting items for systematic reviews and meta-analyses: the PRISMA statement. PLoS Med 6(7):e1000097. https://doi.org/10.1371/journal.pmed.1000097

Nobanee H (2020) Big data in business: a bibliometric analysis of relevant literature. Big Data 8(6):459–463. https://doi.org/10.1089/big.2020.29042.edi

Nobanee H (2021) A bibliometric review of big data in finance. Big Data 9(2):73–78. https://doi.org/10.1089/big.2021.29044.edi

Nobanee H, Alhajjar M, Alkaabi MA, Almemari MM, Alhassani MA, Alkaabi NK, Alshamsi SA, AlBlooshi HH (2021) A bibliometric analysis of objective and subjective risk. Risks. https://doi.org/10.3390/risks9070128

Nobanee H, Shanti H, Aldhanhani H, Alblooshi A, Alali E (2022) Big data and credit risk assessment: a bibliometric review, current streams, and directions for future research. Cogent Econ Finance 10(1):2132638. https://doi.org/10.1080/23322039.2022.2132638

Ortiz-cea V, Geldres-Weiss VV, Dote-pardo J, Reveco-sepulveda R (2024) Costs and carbon footprint: exploring the contemporary literature. Interciencia 49(11):632–640

Page MJ, McKenzie JE, Bossuyt PM, Boutron I, Hoffmann TC, Mulrow CD, Shamseer L, Tetzlaff JM, Akl EA, Brennan SE, Chou R, Glanville J, Grimshaw JM, Hróbjartsson A, Lalu MM, Li T, Loder EW, Mayo-Wilson E, McDonald S, Moher D (2021) The PRISMA 2020 statement: an updated guideline for reporting systematic reviews. BMJ 372:n71. https://doi.org/10.1136/bmj.n71

Pascoal FB, Juwana H, Karuniasa M, Djojokusumo HH (2023) Sovereign ESG integration: a bibliometric and systematic literature review. Stud Bus Econ 18(1):231–260. https://doi.org/10.2478/sbe-2023-0013

Passas I (2024) Bibliometric analysis: the main steps. Encyclopedia 4(2):1014–1025. https://doi.org/10.3390/encyclopedia4020065

Piwowar-Sulej K, Iqbal Q (2023) Leadership styles and sustainable performance: a systematic literature review. J Clean Prod 382:134600. https://doi.org/10.1016/j.jclepro.2022.134600

Raghuram S, Hill NS, Gibbs JL, Maruping LM (2019) Virtual work: bridging research clusters. Acad Manag Ann 13(1):308–341. https://doi.org/10.5465/annals.2017.0020

Rendtorff JD (2019) Sustainable development goals and progressive business models for economic transformation. Local Econ J Local Econ Policy Unit 34(6):510–524. https://doi.org/10.1177/0269094219882270

Sachs JD (2012) From millennium development goals to sustainable development goals. Lancet 379(9832):2206–2211. https://doi.org/10.1016/S0140-6736(12)60685-0

Sachs JD (2015) The age of sustainable development. Columbia University Press, New York. https://doi.org/10.7312/sach17314

Schöne N, Timofeeva E, Heinz B (2022) Sustainable development goal indicators as the foundation for a holistic impact assessment of access-to-energy projects. J Sustain Develop Energy Water Environ Syst 10(2):1–24. https://doi.org/10.13044/j.sdewes.d9.0400

Small H (1973) Co-citation in the scientific literature: a new measure of the relationship between two documents. J Am Soc Inform Sci 24(4):265–269. https://doi.org/10.1002/asi.4630240406

Streimikis J, Saraji MK (2022) Green productivity and undesirable outputs in agriculture: a systematic review of DEA approach and policy recommendations. Econ Res Ekonomska Istraživanja 35(1):819–853. https://doi.org/10.1080/1331677X.2021.1942947

Truby J (2020) Governing artificial intelligence to benefit the UN sustainable development goals. Sustain Dev 28(4):946–959. https://doi.org/10.1002/sd.2048

United Nations (2023, July 27) About the sustainable develoment goals. https://www.un.org/sustainabledevelopment/sustainable-development-goals/

United Nations General Assembly (2000) United Nations millennium declaration, resolution adopted by the general assembly. https://www.refworld.org/docid/3b00f4ea3.html

United Nations General Assembly (2015) Transforming our world: the 2030 agenda for sustainable development. https://sdgs.un.org/publications/transforming-our-world-2030-agenda-sustainable-development-17981

Van Eck NJ, Waltman L (2014) Visualizing bibliometric networks. In: Ding Y, Rousseau R, Wolfram D (eds) Measuring scholarly impact: methods and practice. Springer, London, pp 285–320. https://doi.org/10.1007/978-3-319-10377-8_13

Van Raan AFJ (2004) Measuring science: capita selecta of current main issues. https://api.semanticscholar.org/CorpusID:221253192

Wang X, Xu Z, Qin Y, Skare M (2021a) Service networks for sustainable business: a dynamic evolution analysis over half a century. J Bus Res 136:543–557. https://doi.org/10.1016/j.jbusres.2021.07.062

Wang X, Xu Z, Su S-F, Zhou W (2021b) A comprehensive bibliometric analysis of uncertain group decision making from 1980 to 2019. Inf Sci 547:328–353. https://doi.org/10.1016/j.ins.2020.08.036

Wang X, Qin Y, Xu Z, Škare M (2022) A look at the focus shift in innovation literature due to Covid-19 pandemic. J Bus Res 145:1–20. https://doi.org/10.1016/j.jbusres.2022.02.067

Xu Z, Wang X, Wang X, Skare M (2021) A comprehensive bibliometric analysis of entrepreneurship and crisis literature published from 1984 to 2020. J Bus Res 135:304–318. https://doi.org/10.1016/j.jbusres.2021.06.051

You C, Awang SR, Wu Y (2024) Bibliometric analysis of global research trends on higher education leadership development using Scopus database from 2013–2023. Disc Sustain 5(1):246. https://doi.org/10.1007/s43621-024-00432-x

Isabella Lucuț-Capraș is a Ph.D. student at Babeş-Bolyai University, Faculty of Economic Sciences and Business Administration, Finance specialization. She has a master's degree in Accounting and Audit expertise, from the same faculty. Her research focuses on issues such as forensic accounting, corporate governance and and issues related to economic and financial crime such as the manipulation of financial statements, with the role of the forensic accountant being a major topic in fraud prevention.

Monica Violeta Achim is a professor and doctoral supervisor in Finance at the Faculty of Economic Sciences and Business Administration, Babeş-Bolyai University, Cluj-Napoca. With over 27 years of experience in academia, she has published, as author and co-author, over 140 scientific articles and 27 books. The main research topics are financial analysis, business performance, finance, and economic and financial crime. In 2020, she obtained the Award for Excellence in Scientific Research, at Babeş-Bolyai University, Faculty of Economics and Business Administration, Cluj-Napoca, Romania, as a recognition of the results obtained in the research activity. She leads a main national project in the area of financial crime in the period 2020–2023. In the business environment, she works in liberal professions as an accountant expert, tax consultant, and judicial expert; from this perspective, being involved in solving many cases of economic and financial crime of the Palace of Justice, Cluj-Napoca.

Leonard Artur Horvath, Ph.D. is a Lecturer at the Faculty of Economics and Business Administration and the Faculty of History and Philosophy, Babeş-Bolyai University, Cluj-Napoca (Romania), where he teaches courses in Economic History and Public European Policies. His current research includes projects in the field of economic history, cycles of economic crises, but also in the field of history and international economic relations.

Economic and Financial Crime in the Digital Era: A Bibliometric Approach

Iulia Brici and Monica Violeta Achim

Abstract The exponential growth of technology has profoundly transformed the global economy, bringing with it both opportunities and challenges. From a dual perspective, this study explores how digitalization has influenced economic and financial crime. On one hand, technological advancement have enhanced the tools and systems available to prevent, spot and combat economic and financial crime through sophisticated security infrastructures. On the other hand, the digitalization process has enabled new forms of digital fraud and economic and financial crime, offering law breakers more accessible and discreet methods of operation. This study conducts a bibliometric analysis using the Web of Science scientific database and the VOSviewer software in order to examine the academic literature on this subject. Through a series of tools, such as co-citation analysis, co-authorship mapping or keyword co-occurrence, the research identifies the most influential articles, prolific authors and major research trends within this thematic area. Additionally, the study clusters the literature according to the two main perspectives: technology perceived as a progressive factor on the economy versus technology as a facilitator of economic and financial crime. The final objective and the main conclusion of the study is to provide a comprehensive overview of the academic discourse surrounding economic and financial crime in the context of the digital era, highlighting gaps in current research and proposing potential directions for future investigations. Due to the dynamic and constantly evolving nature of technology, ongoing monitoring and academic investigation into digitalization's impact on economic and financial crime are crucial for developing effective policies and counteraction strategies.

Keywords Digitalization · Economic and financial crime · Bibliometric analysis · Security infrastructures · Counteraction strategies

JEL Classification K42 · O33 · D73

I. Brici (✉) · M. V. Achim
Faculty of Economics and Business Administration, Babeş-Bolyai University, Cluj-Napoca, Romania
e-mail: iulia.brici@econ.ubbcluj.ro

M. V. Achim
e-mail: monica.achim@econ.ubbcluj.ro

M. V. Achim (ed.), *Financial Crime in the Digital Era*, Contributions to Finance and Accounting, https://doi.org/10.1007/978-3-032-20198-0_11

1 Introduction

The accelerated expansion of technology has deeply influenced all existing economic systems, has reshaped business models, has redefined financial transactions and also institutional frameworks (Yoo and Yi 2022). This fast process can be seen from two perspectives (Adewuyi 2025). The first point of view is a positive one because digitalization has developed a boundless spectrum of opportunities to increase economic efficiency, to enhance transparency, but also to strengthen the mechanisms which oversee financial activities. At the same time, there is also an unfavourable outlook of the digitalization because it led to new vulnerabilities. As a result, certain forms of economic and financial crime are enabled by breaking the law and by challenging institutions and policymakers. As digital systems become more complex, offenders also increasingly exploit digital infrastructures for illicit gains.

Due to the dual nature that economic and financial crime in the digital era displays, it becomes crucial to examine how this subject evolved from an academic angle. In recent years, scientific inquiry has addressed specific aspects of digitalization-driven crime, but also of the capacity of digital tools to prevent crime. All those papers represent a wide body of literature, but it still remains highly fragmented, reflecting a multitude of methodologies, conceptual frameworks and disciplinary approaches. Consequently, there is an undeniable need for a systematic synthesis that can map the structure of the field by identifying authors, examining research trends and spotlighting the gaps in the current knowledge. Bibliometric analysis offers an effective method to accomplish this objective. By applying its specific procedures, researchers gain an overview of the evolution of the field, and they also obtain guidance for future analyses. Policymakers benefit too because this type of research can support the design of strategies aimed to prevent and mitigate the economic and financial crime effects in the digital era.

The purpose of this study is to provide a comprehensive bibliometric approach of the existing literature related to economic and financial crime in the context of digitalization. Using Web of Science Core Collection as the main data source and VOSviewer software for a network overview, this study investigates co-citation analysis, co-authorship mapping and keyword co-occurrence analyses in order to highlight the key scholarly contributions that shape this research area. Moreover, this analysis has the objective of exploring both dominant perspectives: digitalization as a catalyst for economic integrity and digitalization as a facilitator for illicit financial activities. By providing an integrated frame of reference, this study contributes to a more profound understanding of how academic literature has developed on the digital transformation effect on the economic and financial crime. The key findings reflect the most frequently used research themes, the most influential scientific literature and, most important, the gaps in current scholarship.

In order to resume the target objectives, this study addresses the following research questions:

Research question 1: Which are the most influential authors, journals and research papers and what does this reveal about the intellectual structure and foundational works in the field?
Research question 2: Which are the patterns of collaboration between authors/researchers and how these play a role in the scientific network?
Research question 3: Which are the main research topics and emerging subjects in the field?

The structure of this study consists of the following sections: Sect. 2 describes the data collection process and the bibliometric methodology, Sect. 3 outlines the key findings and Sect. 4 concludes the analysis by highlighting the most important contributions, but also the limitations and the prospects for future research.

2 Materials and Methods

The main aim of this study is to create a comprehensive bibliometric analysis of the existing scientific literature addressing economic and financial crime in the digital era.

The investigation builds on prior bibliometric approaches which explore economic and financial crime in the context of the digitalization process (Aivaz et al. 2024; Gaviyau and Sibindi 2023; Achim et al. 2023). The study design is grounded in the research scaffold shown in Fig. 1.

The following subsection provide an overview of the methodology, including the data source and the reason of choosing to adopt it in the study. Here is also presented the strategy of keywords election, coverage period, document types, data cleaning, bibliometric techniques such as co-authorship analysis, co-citation analysis, keyword

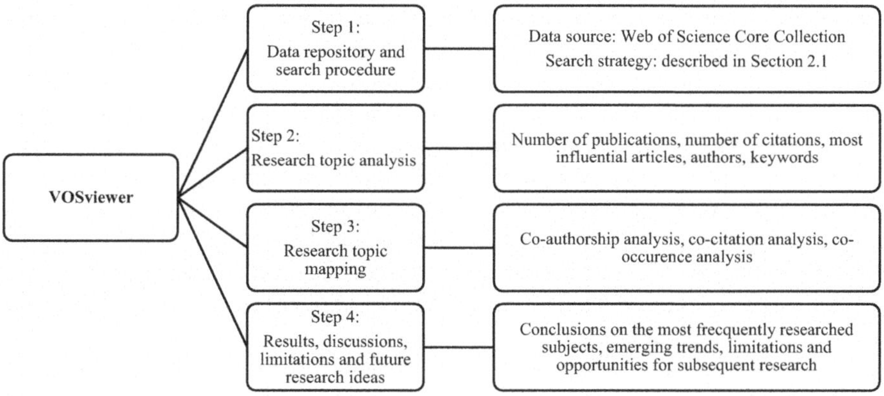

Fig. 1 Research scaffold. *Source* Author's processing

co-occurrence analysis, as well as the tools used along the study, respectively different settings and features from VOSviewer.

2.1 Data Source and Search Strategy

In order to ensure a systematic and transparent selection of literature, this study adopts a PRISMA-inspired approach. PRISMA represents Preferred Reporting Items for Systematic Reviews and Meta-Analyses and it provides a well-structured framework for identifying, screening, including/excluding studies, reinforcing reproducibility and limiting bias. The decision to use this protocol is based on another existing studies which used PRISMA in their bibliometric analyses (Wahib and Rohman 2024; Cardona et al. 2024; Bota-Avram 2022) and have reached some interesting and useful conclusions on their area of interest.

Originally introduced in 2009, the PRISMA guideline sought to consolidate the reporting quality of systematic reviews and meta-analyses by supporting methodological clarity, transparency and replicability. Its main purpose was to help readers understand the logic behind a review, the procedures implemented by researchers and the reached results. Due to a continuous evolution of systematic review practices, Page et al. (2021) emphasized the need for an updated version of the framework. The revised PRISMA 2020 version offers expanded and refined recommendations. Nowadays, PRISMA's structured checklist and procedural guidance provide substantial benefits for researchers conducting systematic reviews, meta-analyses or bibliometric assessments, supporting both rigor and consistency. The flowchart adapted for this study, in accordance with PRISMA principles, is illustrated in Fig. 2. This PRISMA-guided approach helps this study ensure a methodologically rigorous foundation and facilitate a systematic exploration and mapping of the existing studies on economic and financial crime in the digital era.

The bibliometric analysis conducted in this study relies on data extracted from the Web of Science Core Collection (WOS) which is a comprehensive and widely recognized database covering peer-reviewed journals across multiple disciplines. The main reason why Web of Science was selected is because it provides high-quality bibliographic information, wide-ranging citation data and accurate metadata that are essential for systematic bibliometric analyses. Other bibliometric studies which used the WOS database (Branet and Hategan 2024; Ergün 2025; Pramanik et al., 2025) were a confirmation of its relevance and applicability. Following the PRISMA-guided protocol described above, the database aim is to identify, screen and include publications related to the chosen subject, respectively the economic and financial crime in the digital era.

As other researchers have noted that the choice of search criteria can influence the identification of relevant data (Öztürk et al. 2024), after accessing the Web of Science database, the following set of keywords was selected and entered in the search bar: "economic crime", "financial crime", "economic and financial crime", "cyber-crime", "digital financial crime". Using the Topic Search (TS) function in Web of

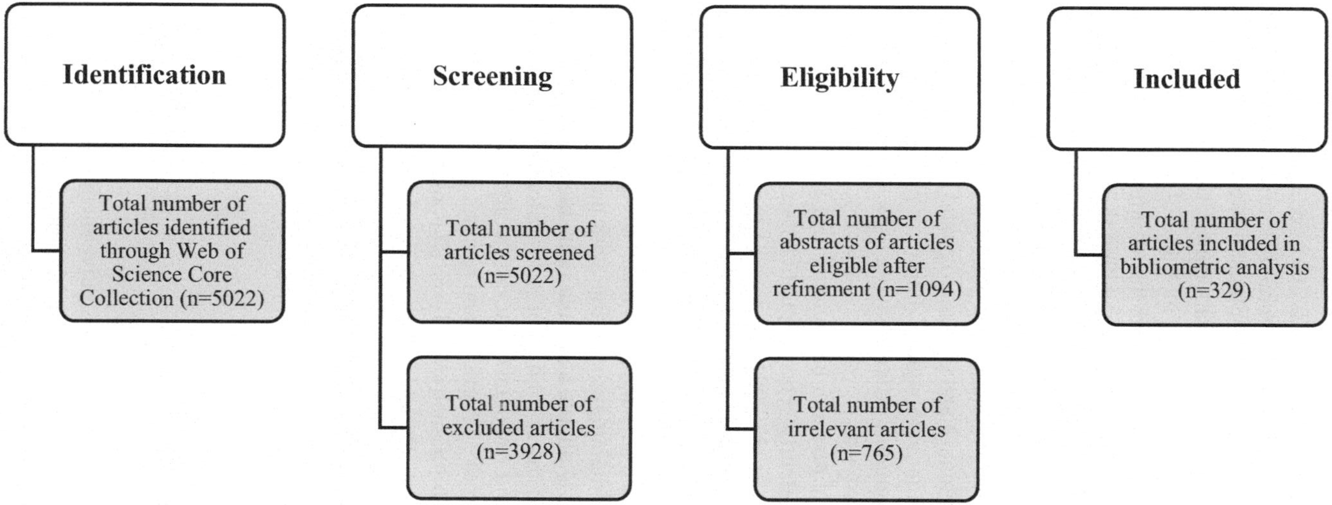

Fig. 2 Adapted PRISMA flowchart. *Source* Author's processing

Science ensures that all keywords are matched across articles titles, articles abstracts, keywords plus and author keywords. The initial application of the first search criterion retrieved 5022 documents, and afterwards 4619 documents published between 2000 and 2024. The coverage period was deliberately set from 2000 to 2024 to encompass the emergence and evolution of digital technologies and their influence on economic and financial crime. As digital transformation processes gained widespread adoption around 2000, this time frame provides a meaningful longitudinal perspective on the field. Furthermore, a 25-year span allows the identification of long-term trends, key contributions and thematic developments within the literature.

Afterwards, a series of exclusion filters were applied. Only articles and reviews were retained in order to ensure a focus on high-quality, peer-reviewed research. Additionally, the language of publication was restricted to English. The final filter at this stage involved Web of Science categories, with three research areas selected: Economics; Business, Finance and Criminology and Penology. This step allowed the exclusion publications that, although related, were published in journals outside the targeted disciplinary domains. After applying these criteria, a total of 1094 articles remained for further analysis.

Previous bibliometric research has demonstrated that automated keyword-based searches may not consistently generate publications fully aligned with the intended thematic scope. Donthu et al. (2021) emphasize the importance of manually examining retrieved records to ensure that the final dataset accurately represents the focus of the study. In a similar perspective, Paul and Criado (2020) note that automated searches can include publications only partially relevant to the research topic, highlighting the necessity of a subsequent manual screening stage to preserve the relevance and precision of the analysis. In line with these methodological recommendations, the present study adopts a manual refinement procedure to verify both the thematic alignment and the eligibility of publications included in the bibliometric dataset on economic and financial crime in the digital era. Following the manual refinement stage, a total of 329 articles and reviews were deemed eligible for inclusion in the subsequent bibliometric analysis. This manual filtering process ensured that only publications directly addressing economic and financial crime, the central focus of this study, were retained.

Table 1 provides a detailed overview of the search and screening procedure. Upon completion of this process, the final dataset was exported in Excel format to facilitate its use within the bibliometric analysis software.

2.2 Bibliometric Analysis

Bibliometric analysis represents a quantitative method which helps to evaluate the structure, development and trends of scientific research within a given domain. By systematically analyzing publication patterns, citations and co-occurrence relationships among authors, journals and keywords, bibliometric methods offer awareness and insights into the intellectual landscape and joint research networks of a specific

Table 1 Detailed search procedure

Applied filter	Filter explanation	No. of displayed items	No. of refined items
Topic (TS)	This filter searched in title, abstract, keyword plus and author keywords. The search string user in topic search bar was: ("economic crime" OR "financial crime" OR "economic and financial crime" OR "cybercrime" OR "digital financial crime")	5022	-
Coverage period	2000–2024	4619	403
Document type	Article, review	3102	1517
Language	English	2770	332
Web of Science Categories	Economics Business, Finance Criminology and Penology	1094	1676
Manual refining	Only articles and reviews that approached economic and financial crime	329	765
Final number of articles			329

Source Author's processing

domain. This approach is more and more recommended for domains characterized by rapid growth and interdisciplinary input, as it allows researchers to detecting fundamental topics, influential works and emerging research trends (Aria and Cuccurullo 2017; Donthu et al. 2021).

In the context of the chosen topic of the study, bibliometric analysis is especially valuable due to the dynamic and fast-evolving nature of digital financial frameworks and the complex interactions between technological innovations, unlawful behavior and regulatory strategies. Previous studies, in related domains, have applied bibliometric methods to map research trends, collaboration networks and thematic patterns across cybercrime, financial fraud and digital security (Kshetri 2021; Button et al. 2015; Holt et al. 2019).

Following this approach, as it was already specified at the end of the previous sub-section, the study conducts a bibliometric analysis of 329 publications extracted from the Web of Science database. Regarding the bibliometric tool employed in this study, VOSviewer (version 1.6.20) was chosen because it has been widely recognized and utilized in bibliometric research within the field of economic and financial crime (Achim et al. 2023; Winarto 2025; Nisa and Oktavia 2025). This software enables the fulfillment of our research objectives through three complementary procedures:

- *Co-citation analysis:* in order to examine the intellectual structure of the field and to identify influential works, addressing Research Question 1 (RQ1).
- *Co-authorship mapping:* in order to explore collaboration patterns among authors and researchers, as well as to understand their role within the scientific network, thereby responding to Research Question 2 (RQ2).

- *Keyword co-occurrence analysis:* in order to identify the main research topics and emerging themes within the chosen domain, addressing Research Question 3 (RQ3).

Additionally, VOSviewer is available for all researchers and user-friendly, providing robust and interpretable results, which makes it an ideal tool for this type of bibliometric study.

3 Results and Discussions

Based on the methodology outlined in the previous section, this section presents the results of a comprehensive bibliometric analysis of scientific publications on economic and financial crime in the digital era. The findings are organized according to the units of analysis, including articles, authors and journals, as well as the identification of key conceptual themes in the field. The ultimate aim of this bibliometric study is to provide a thorough overview of past developments, current research patterns, and emerging trends in the chosen field.

3.1 Descriptive Analysis

The following section presents a set of descriptive analyses, which constitute a crucial first step in bibliometric studies by providing an overview of the existing literature and enabling the identification of general trends. By examining the annual evolution of publication counts, the most productive journals and the most active authors, these statistics establish an initial framework for the field of economic and financial crime. All those analyses help highlight the concentration of research, the primary channels of dissemination and the key actors shaping the development of the literature, providing the necessary context for interpreting the more complex analyses presented in the subsequent section.

3.1.1 Number of Articles Per year

The distribution of publications over the period 2000–2025 presented in Fig. 3 reveals a general upward trend in the annual number of articles addressing economic and financial crime, indicating a growing interest in this research domain. More specifically, the volume of publications increases from year to year. The slight decline in the number of publications observed in 2009 may be explained in light of broader disruptions in the global economic landscape at the time. Periods marked by financial uncertainty can redirect institutional resources, research priorities and scholarly attention toward immediate economic stabilization measures, which can temporarily reduce the output of research on certain fields. The current year might be an exception because this year is still in progress and a lot of articles continue to be published. Overall, the data suggest an expanding attention in studies that examine issues related to economic and financial crime, as well as the implications of digital advancements within this research area.

3.1.2 Most Relevant Journals

The analysis of the journals with the highest number of publications in the field of economic and financial crime in the context of digital era, presented in Fig. 4, reveals that the most prolific source is the Journal of Money Laundering Control, which accounts for 57 articles. The other nine journals in the top 10 represent a mix of publications focused on criminology and public policy, financial regulation and compliance, as well as deviant behaviour and cybercrime.

The distribution suggests that the literature is concentrated around several key sources and that research on economic and financial crime in the context of digital era encompasses both legal and regulatory dimensions, as well as sociological and digital crime perspectives. Overall, academic attention appears to be directed toward the intersection between financial regulation, anti-money laundering efforts and the growing influence of digital progress on economic crime.

3.1.3 Most Common Authors

The analysis across the authors of the articles selected in the dataset, presented in Fig. 5, indicates that the literature on economic and financial crime is concentrated around a limited number of prolific scholars. The most frequently appearing author is Achim M.V., a habilitated professor, with a lot of experience and expertise in the financial analysis and economic and financial crime domains. This concentration suggests that certain researchers play a key role in shaping and disseminating knowledge in the field, thereby influencing research directions and thematic developments.

Moreover, the top 10 authors reflect a combination of highly productive individual researchers and scholars who frequently engage in collaborative work, indicating a mixed structure of individual expertise and collaborative networks within this emerging area of inquiry.

3.2 Science Mapping Analysis

The rationale of the science mapping analysis is to condense the bibliometric architecture of the chosen research domain, by running a set of specific procedures for

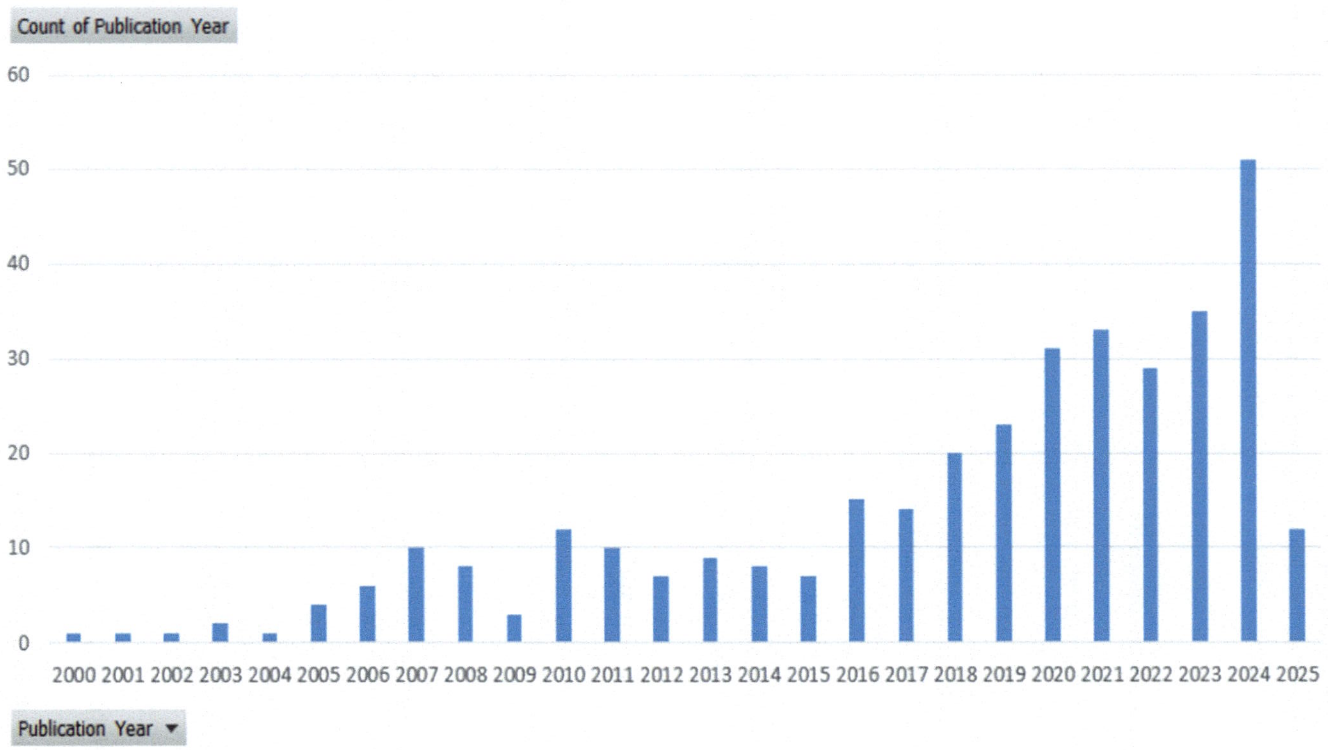

Fig. 3 Annual evolution of publications number related to economic and financial crime in the digital era. *Source* Author's processing

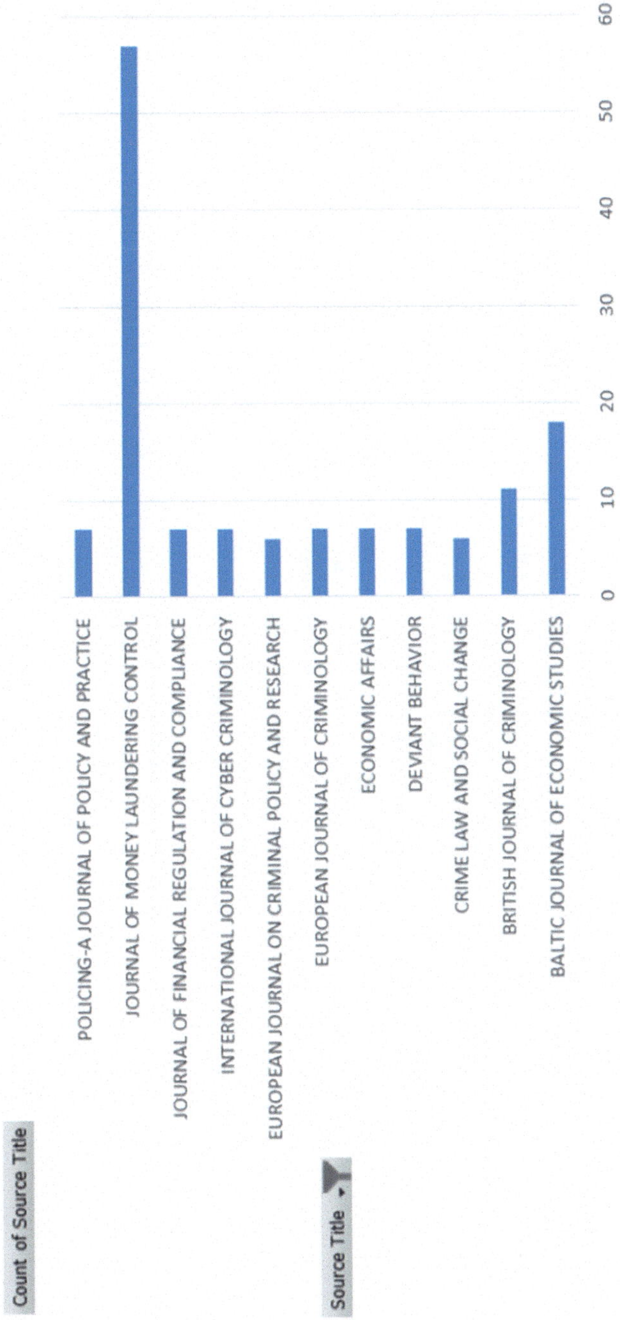

Fig. 4 Top 10 relevant journals that published articles related to economic and financial crime in the digital era. *Source* Author's processing

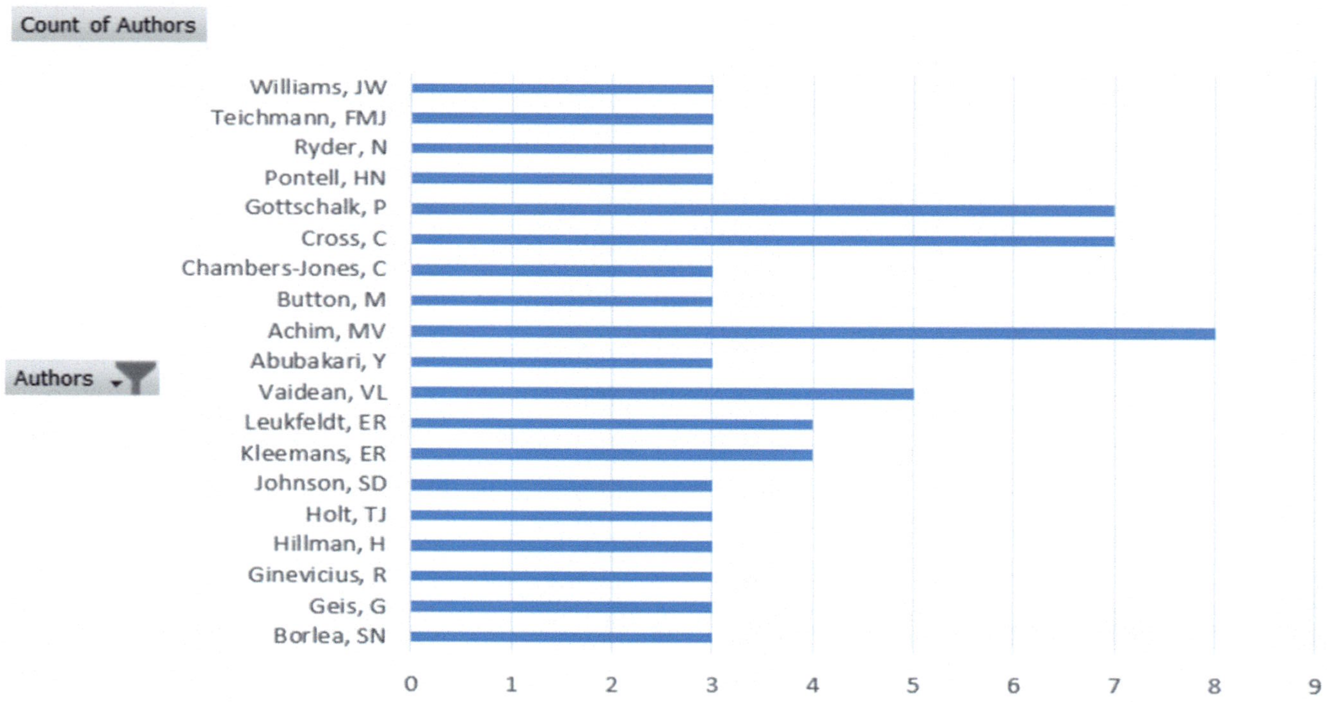

Fig. 5 Top 10 prolific researchers who wrote articles related to Economic and Financial Crime Research in the context of the Digital Age. *Source* Author's processing

science mapping, namely: co-citation analysis, co-authorship mapping or keyword co-occurrence.

3.2.1 Co-Citation Analysis

Figure 6 presents the co-citation networks between the cited references within the selected field of this study. Each node represents a frequently cited publication, while the links between nodes indicate that two sources are co-cited in the same document. The size of the node reflects the citation frequency of a given source and the color of the cluster corresponds to the thematic grouping automatically identified by VOSviewer. The distance between nodes illustrates the strength of the relationship, showing how closely related two studies are in conceptual terms.

In Fig. 6, five clusters can be identified. The red cluster represents the thematic area of theoretical foundations of criminology and deviance theories. Considering the scope of this study, this cluster anchors the analysis within the traditional explanatory models of deviant behavior. The green cluster refers to research on cybercrime and online fraud, representing the modern dimension of economic and financial crime, closely linked to public policy and empirical studies on fraud. The blue cluster focuses on cybercrime and the sociology of technological deviance. This group encompasses sociological and organizational perspectives on cybercrime, exploring offender networks and deviant online behaviors. The yellow cluster includes works addressing general theories of crime and society, serving as a conceptual bridge between classical criminological theories and applied research. The final purple cluster relates to organizational and regulatory perspectives, forming a smaller nucleus focused on regulation and institutional responses to fraud.

Overall, the co-citation network suggests that the field has evolved from a traditional theoretical foundation toward a digital and interdisciplinary perspective, aiming to explain and manage crime in the digital environment while maintaining a strong conceptual link with the fundamental theories of criminology.

3.2.2 Co-authorship Mapping

Figure 7 presents the map illustrating the collaboration network among authors within the field selected for this study. Each node represents an author. The size of the node indicates either the number of publications or the level of collaboration, particularly for highly active researchers. The links show the co-authorship relationships between authors, the thicker and shorter the line, the stronger the collaboration. The colors distinguish different clusters of collaborators, representing groups of authors who frequently publish together.

The map above shows that the authors are grouped into four distinct clusters. The blue cluster represents the main nucleus of scientific production, coordinating several research directions. The green cluster indicates extended academic collaborations on related topics, reflecting applied and interdisciplinary research. The yellow

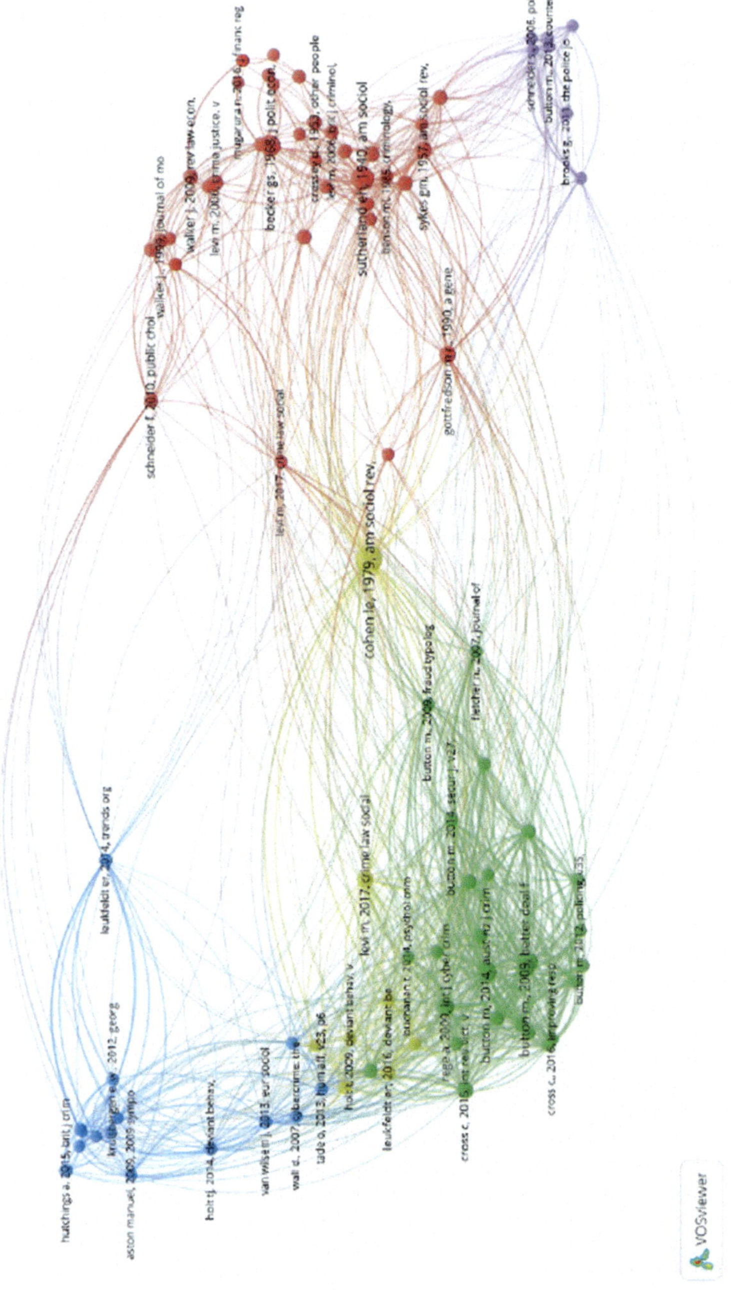

Fig. 6 Co-citation network diagram based on cited references. *Source* Author's processing in VOSviewer

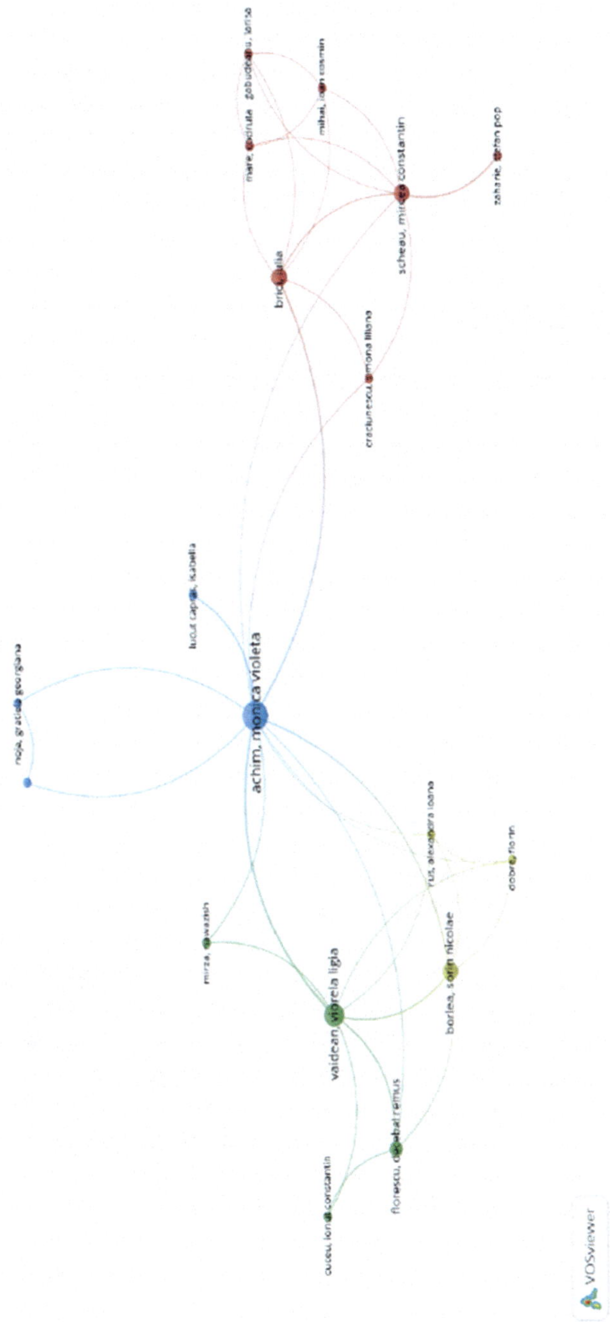

Fig. 7 Co-authorship network diagram based on authors. *Source* Author's processing in VOSviewer

cluster highlights methodological and analytical partnerships, involving inter-cluster contributions focused on financial-accounting or economic ethics topics. The red cluster represents an emerging collaborative network, a cohesive group of authors who frequently collaborate with each other and maintain connections with the main research nucleus. These authors appear to develop autonomous lines of inquiry.

Overall, the analysis reveals a high level of scientific cohesion around the investigated topic, as well as a progressive diversification of collaborations, confirming the maturation and expansion of the research field at both national and international levels.

3.2.3 Keyword Co-occurrence

Figure 8 illustrates the conceptual associations among the keywords (Keywords Plus) extracted from the analyzed publications. Each node represents a keyword, and the size of the node indicates the frequency with which the term appears in the articles included in the dataset. The links between nodes reflect the frequency with which two terms co-occur, indicating their thematic proximity.

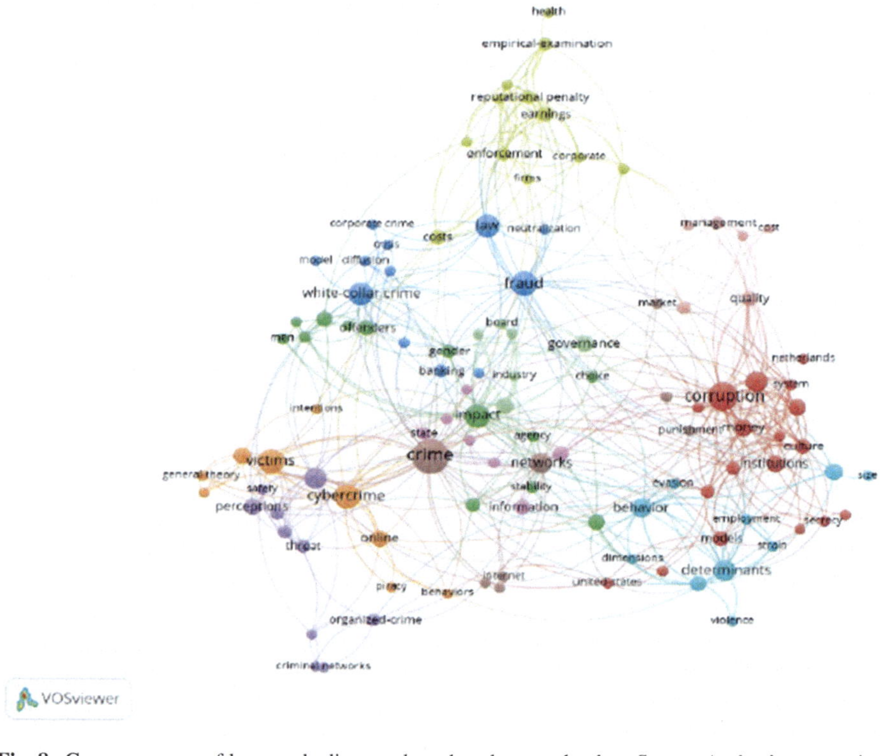

Fig. 8 Co-occurrence of keywords diagram based on keywords plus. *Source* Author's processing in VOSviewer

The colors of the clusters define distinct groups, automatically identified by the software based on the strength of the connections among the keywords. In the figure above, the red cluster includes keywords related to corruption and institutions, such as corruption, institutions, money, governance, and determinants. These terms reflect research focused on identifying the determinants of corruption, institutional quality, and the impact of governance on economic and social behavior. The green cluster is associated with corporate crime and economic fraud, containing keywords such as corporate crime, governance, white-collar crime, and banking. This group captures the organizational dimension of criminality and the deviant behaviors within the corporate environment, emphasizing financial fraud and business ethics. It marks the convergence zone between criminology and economics. The blue cluster relates to fraud, law, and law enforcement, including terms such as fraud, law, and enforcement. This group addresses the legal and institutional aspects aimed at preventing fraud and developing sanctioning mechanisms. The yellow cluster represents empirical analyses and economic impact, incorporating terms such as empirical examination, reputational penalty and earnings. It captures the quantitative dimension of research, oriented toward assessing the economic and reputational consequences of deviant behaviors. The purple cluster is connected to cybercrime, including keywords such as cybercrime, threat, safety, piracy, and criminal networks.

This group explores the digital dimension of research related to economic and financial crime in the context of technological development. The orange cluster refers to victims and social perceptions, including terms such as victims, perceptions, and intentions. It examines the experiences of victims, public perceptions of crime, and the mechanisms of prevention. Overall, the keyword co-occurrence network suggests that the body of literature has evolved toward an integrated approach, combining traditional criminological perspectives with emerging challenges of economic and digital crime, thereby strengthening the interdisciplinary and applied nature of the research field.

3.2.4 Mapping Conclusion

After running the three specific procedures in VOSviewer and keeping in mind the initial research question, this study reached some conclusions regarding the bibliometric techniques. Regarding RQ1, co-citation analysis reveals a well-defined intellectual structure of the field, building a bridge between classical foundations of economic crime theory and economic and financial crime. This reflects a continuity between traditional crime paradigms and modern frameworks, confirming a conceptual maturity of the field. Regarding RQ2, co-authorship mapping reveals a moderately dense scientific network around a core group of researchers. The networks reflect strong nexus between the core group and the emerging research group. This suggests that collaboration plays a central role in knowledge expansion, reinforcing the visibility of the research field. Regarding RQ3, keyword co-occurrence analysis reflects a presence of both traditional and emerging terms, which can represent a thematic evolution. This trend confirms that the research field is undergoing a conceptual expansion, integration crime, economics, law and social science in addressing contemporary types of deviance and crime.

In conclusion, the bibliometric analyses reflect that the chosen research area has evolved into a mature and interconnected scientific domain. This combines theoretical models with modern, digital and interdisciplinary challenges. The collaboration between authors and the co-occurrence of the keywords indicate also a continuous expanding body of knowledge, reflecting innovation and intellectual consolidation within the chosen field.

4 Conclusions, Limitations and Future Research

The aim of this study was to offer a complex overview of the scientific landscape on economic and financial crime in the digital era. With the help of three specific tools of VOSviewer, the research has identified the field's intellectual foundations, collaboration patterns and key thematic directions. Regarding the conclusions of the study, as it was explained previously, the results show that the research field is grounded in classical crime theories and evolves toward modern theories, related to digitalization. There is a connected research network around the chosen field, centered on a few prolific researchers, which integrate emerging researchers in their work, quantifying a interdisciplinary approach of the area. The main terms used in research indicate conceptual maturity and a niche's expansion. Overall, the findings depict a cohesive domain, combining classical and modern approaches in order to increase the visibility of the research field.

Despite its contribution, this study has certain limitations. It relies only on the Web of Science database, which may exclude other relevant publications. The bibliometric techniques capture the quantitative relationships. Surely, a qualitative approach would complete the puzzle. Another challenge can be the quick development of digital crime methods, which can limit the generalizability of the conclusions.

Future research should integrate multiple databases and multiple mixed-methods in order to track the evolution of the field. The emerging and promising areas likely to approach in future studies should be placed on AI-related economic and financial crime, blockchain misuse and cybersecurity governance.

Other corruption topics such as bribery (McGee and Benk 2023 2025) and tax evasion (McGee 2012) could also be explored. Some bibliometric studies of tax evasion have already been conducted (Alkausar et al. 2021; Barbu et al. 2024; Mansour et al. 2023; Nevzorova et al. 2017), but there is room for more such studies. To our knowledge, no bibliometric studies of bribery have as yet been conducted. Someone should fill this gap in the literature. An expansive study should not be limited to journal articles, but should include books and book chapters as well.

References

Achim MV, Borlea SN, Lucuţ Capraş I (2023). Economic and financial crime, forensic accounting and sustainable developments goals (SDGS). Bibliometric Analysis. J Res Adm 5(2):12385–12402. https://journlra.org/index.php/jra/article/view/1368

Adewuyi OM (2025) The double-edged ledger: cryptocurrency, financial crime, and the potential of blockchain forensics. Int J Res Innov Soc Sci 9(5):5739–5742. https://doi.org/10.47772/IJRISS.2025.905000442

Aivaz KA, Florea IO, Munteanu I (2024) Economic fraud and associated risks: an integrated bibliometric analysis approach. Risks 12:74. https://doi.org/10.3390/risks12050074

Alkausar B, Soemarsono PN, Pengesti NG (2021) A bibliometric analysis of tax aggressiveness through tax evasion issues in last decade. Int J Appl Bus 5(2):193–202

Aria M, Cuccurullo C (2017) Bibliometrix: an R-tool for comprehensive science mapping analysis. J Informet 11(4):959–975. https://doi.org/10.1016/j.joi.2017.08.007

Barbu L, Horobeţ A, Belaşcu L, Ilie AG (2024) Approaches to tax evasion: a bibliometric and mapping analysis of Web of Science indexed studies. J Bus Econ Manag 25(1):1–20

Bota-Avram C (2022) Bibliometric analysis of sustainable business performance: where are we going? A science map of the field. Economic Research-Ekonomska Istraživanja 36(1):2137–2176. https://doi.org/10.1080/1331677X.2022.2096094

Branet DS, Hategan CD (2024) Bibliometric framing of research trends regarding public sector auditing to fight corruption and prevent fraud. J Risk Financ Manag 17:94. https://doi.org/10.3390/jrfm17030094

Button M, McNaughton Nicholls C, Owen R (2015) Online fraud victims in England and Wales: victims' views on sentencing and the opportunity for restorative justice? Howard J 54(4):193–211. https://doi.org/10.1111/hojo.12123

Cardona LF, Guzman-Luna JA, Restrepo-Carmona JA (2024) Bibliometric analysis of the machine learning applications in fraud detection on crowdfunding platforms. J Risk Financ Manag 17:352. https://doi.org/10.3390/jrfm17080352

Donthu N, Kumar S, Mukherjee D, Pandey N, Lim WM (2021) How to conduct a bibliometric analysis: An overview and guidelines. J Bus Res 133:285–296. https://doi.org/10.1016/j.jbusres.2021.04.070

Ergün HO (2025) Digital finance: a bibliometric analysis. Suleyman Demirel Univ Vis Mag 16(46):459–472. https://doi.org/10.21076/vizyoner.1548669

Gaviyau W, Sibindi AB (2023) Customer due diligence in the FinTech era: a bibliometric analysis. Risks 11:11. https://doi.org/10.3390/risks11010011

Holt TJ, Lee JR, Liggett R, Holt KM, Bossler AM (2019) Examining perceptions of online harassment among constables in England and Wales. Int J Cybersecur Intell Cybercrime 2(1):24–39. https://doi.org/10.52306/02010319LFQZ1592

Kshetri N (2021) Cybersecurity management: an organizational and strategic approach. University of Toronto Press, Toronto

Mansour AZ, Ahmi A, Alkhuzaie ASH, Alhmood MA, Popoola OMJ, Altarawneh M (2023) State of art in tax evasion research: A bibliometric review. Rev Educ 11:e3422

McGee RW, Benk S (eds) (2023) The ethics of bribery: theoretical and empirical studies. Springer, Switzerland

McGee RW, Benk S (eds) (2025) The ethics of bribery: country studies. Springer, Switzerland

McGee RW (ed) (2012) The ethics of tax evasion: perspectives in theory and practice. Springer, New York.

Nevzorova EN, Kireenko AP, Sklyarov RA (2017) Bibliometric analisis of the literature on tax evasion in Russia and foreign countries. J Tax Reform 3(2):115–130. https://doi.org/10.15826/jtr.2017.3.2.035

Nisa T, Oktavia R (2025) Bibliometric analysis of financial report fraud based on VOSviewer. J Econ Bus Veranda 8(1):1131–1136. https://doi.org/10.32672/jseb.v8i1.8820

Öztürk O, Kocaman R, Kanbach DK (2024) How to design bibliometric research: an overview and a framework proposal. Rev Manag Sci 18(11):3333–3361. https://doi.org/10.1007/s11846-024-00738-0

Page MJ, McKenzie JE, Bossuyt PM, Boutron I, Hoffmann TC, Mulrow CD, Shamseer L, Tetzlaff JM, Akl EA, Brennan SE, Chou R, Glanville J, Grimshaw JM, Hrbjartsson A, Lalu MM, Li T, Loder EW, Mayo-Wilson E, McDonald S, McGuinness LA, Stewart LA, Thomas J, Tricco AC, Welch VA, Whiting P, Moher D (2021) PRISMA 2020 statement: an updated guideline for reporting systematic reviews. BMJ 372:n71. https://doi.org/10.1136/bmj.n71

Paul J, Criado AR (2020) The art of writing literature review: what do we know and what do we need to know? Int Bus Rev 29(4). https://doi.org/10.1016/j.ibusrev.2020.101717

Pramanik MI, Ghose P, Hossen MD, Ahmed MHU, Rahman MM, Bhuiyan MRI (2025) Emerging technological trends in financial crime and money laundering: a bibliometric analysis of cryptocurrency's role and global research collaboration. J Posthumanism 5(6):3611–3633. https://doi.org/10.63332/joph.v5i6.2493

Wahib MFN, Rohman A (2024) A bibliometric analysis of the financial fraud detection literature from 2004 to 2024. J Econ, Financ Manag Stud 7:2644-0490. https://doi.org/10.47191/jefms/v7-i9-39

Winarto WWA (2025) Bibliometric analysis and visualization: fraud accounting research. Asia Pac Fraud J 10(1):107–138. https://doi.org/10.21532/apfjournal.v10i1.385

Yoo I, Yi CG (2022) Economic innovation caused by digital transformation and impact on social systems. Sustainability 14(5):2600. https://doi.org/10.3390/su14052600

Iulia Brici is a graduate of the bachelor's and master's degree studies at the Faculty of Economics and Business Administration, Babeş-Bolyai University, Cluj-Napoca. She is currently a PhD candidate at the Doctoral School of the same faculty, in the Finance field. She also collaborates with the Finance Department of the faculty as an associate professor. The research area can be identified in the field of economic and financial crime, in the context of digitalization. She is the author and co-author of several scientific articles on this topic. Other areas of interest are: tax evasion, corruption, money laundering, fraud, corporate finance, insurance, public finance.

Monica Violeta Achim is a professor and doctoral supervisor in Finance at the Faculty of Economic Sciences and Business Administration, Babeş-Bolyai University, Cluj-Napoca. With over 27 years of experience in academia, she has published, as author and co-author, over 140 scientific articles and 27 books. The main research topics are financial analysis, business performance, finance, and economic and financial crime. In 2020, she obtained the Award for Excellence in Scientific Research, at Babeş-Bolyai University, Faculty of Economics and Business Administration, Cluj-Napoca, Romania, as a recognition of the results obtained in the research activity. She leads a main national project in the area of financial crime in the period 2020–2023. In the business environment, she works in liberal professions as an accountant expert, tax consultant, and judicial expert; from this perspective, being involved in solving many cases of economic and financial crime of the Palace of Justice, Cluj-Napoca.

Bibliometric Analysis of Financial Corruption in the Healthcare System

Tomina-Maria Manci and Monica Violeta Achim

Abstract The paper focuses on interest in articles published on the topic of corruption in healthcare. To identify interest and make the connection between corruption and the medical field, we used bibliometric analysis. To identify the differences and similarities between the concept of corruption and corruption in general terms, two samples were analyzed for the period 2017–2024: one of 14,175 representing articles related to corruption in general and one of 2,736 representing articles related to corruption in the healthcare system. To develop the concept of corruption in the healthcare system, a sample of 1,690 articles published between 2000 and 2024, which included keywords relevant to the topic, was analyzed bibliometrically and systematically. Following these analyses, the research hypotheses were confirmed, as corruption had some effects on the healthcare system during the period analysed, and there were fluctuations in its increase and decrease. Having reviewed the literature and analyzed the bibliometrics, we can conclude that corruption persists in the healthcare system and that interest has increased during the pandemic. In addition, there has been a decline in interest in publishing articles related to corruption in the healthcare system. This decline was observed after the pandemic. The literature frequently mentions that combining the integrity of accountants with digitized and transparent governance combats corruption because it ensures that citizens have access to real and up-to-date information about the healthcare system.

Keywords Corruption · Health · Healthcare · Pandemic · Comparation

T.-M. Manci (✉) · M. V. Achim
Faculty of Economics and Business Administration, Babeş-Bolyai University, Cluj-Napoca, Romania
e-mail: tomina.manci@econ.ubbcluj.ro

M. V. Achim
e-mail: monica.achim@econ.ubbcluj.ro

M. V. Achim (ed.), *Financial Crime in the Digital Era*, Contributions to Finance and Accounting, https://doi.org/10.1007/978-3-032-20198-0_12

1 Introduction

The idea for the study arose following the COVID-19 pandemic, an event that had a significant economic and psychological impact on the population. The pandemic created the perfect context for the spread of corruption in the healthcare system through weak governance in procurement, increased demand for services, rising market prices, drug shortages, lack of transparency, and the list goes on (Batrancea et al. 2023; Bîzoi and Bîzoi 2023; Dikmen and Çiçek 2023; Griffore et al. 2023). As a result of these events, trust in the healthcare system and the professionalism it offers has declined, leading to violence against doctors (Gaiha et al. 2023). Interest in researching corruption in the healthcare system was a topic of interest during the COVID-19 pandemic, 2019–2022, when articles doubled in terms of publication and citation. This was also evident in informal payments, a form of corruption in the medical care system, where publications also doubled and citations increased threefold. After this period, the number of publications decreased by 28% in 2023 and 18% in 2024 on corruption. Furthermore, diversity was observed in terms of countries, affiliations, publications, and fields of publication of the articles analyzed, 1690 for corruption in health. In addition, during the pandemic, publications on corruption in general, the sample with 14,175 articles, showed a slight and steady decline, in contrast to the sample used for the comparison on corruption in healthcare, with 2736 articles, which increased steadily.

This report provides a systematic and bibliometric analysis of corruption in the healthcare system, highlighting the need to address this issue as a problem that is still prevalent today, taking into account goal 3 of the 17 Sustainable Development Goals (SDGs) of the 2030 Agenda. Corruption has a negative impact, regardless of the form it takes, creating imbalances. The healthcare system is approached as a sector in which corruption is felt, delaying access to services.

Corruption manifests itself in society in various forms, affecting the economy, psychological health, and security. In general terms, corruption is defined as the activity of producing personal gain through illegal and unethical methods with negative repercussions for its victims (Achim and Borlea 2019; Borlea et al. 2017; CECCAR 2022, 2023; Hoinaru et al. 2020; Livadariu 2018; Manci and Achim 2025; Achim 2017a; Němec et al. 2021; Niță 2019; Odtu et al. 2017; Radu and Gyula 2010).

Financial corruption affects both the public and private economic sectors. Corruption manifests itself in a variety of forms: brebery, nepotism, favoritism, fraud, emblezzlement and theft. These forms violate the ethical and legal norms necessary for a fair and equal environment.

Bribery as a form of corruption is often associated with tax evasion and public contracts, suggesting the need for protective measures such as whistleblowing programs (Buckenmaier et al. 2020). This can be defined as accepting something, money, influence, gifts, in exchange for a favor (Sfetcu 2014). Our World in Data (2024) published data on the "Proportion of people who reported being asked for or given a bribe" for the year 2022. According to the graphs uploaded, the Democratic

Republic of Congo is the country where bribery is most common, with a percentage of 80% of cases. Romania is lower down the list, with 20% of cases, recording a decrease in the percentage between 2004 and 2022. Martinez et al. (2021) point out that actual bribery is rarer in European Union countries, but still represents a significant percentage for Romania, Bulgaria, and Hungary (McGee and Zhou 2023).

Nepotism and favoritism are forms of corruption that lead to conflicts of interest that can arise from the relationship between the people involved. This can happen in both the public sector and the corporate world (Julián and Bonavia 2021; Tytko et al. 2020). The corrupt part of this form manifests itself through unethical decision-making, affecting competition that does not benefit from this advantage (Julián and Bonavia 2021; Mphande-Namangale and Kazanga-Chiumia 2021).

Fraud manifests itself through false financial reporting, presenting a clean image behind significant economic distortion (Honigsberg 2025). Methods for mitigating the risk of fraud include sound corporate governance, effective and efficient internal controls, and internal or external auditing (Akbar et al. 2017; Tian and Sun 2023; Wang et al. 2010).

With regard to fraud as a form of corruption, several theories are presented on the factors that influence this aspect: (a) three factors, described as stress, opportunity, and self-justification (Rasheed et al. 2023); (b) the "GONE" theory, represented by four factors: internal greed, opportunity to commit fraud, need, and non-disclosure (Du 2021); (c) the "Crime" theory, described by C: Cook, R: Recipes, I: Incentives, M: Monitoring, E: End Results (Rezaee 2005). Looking at these theories, it can be deduced that the common denominator is the psychological and physical aspects. The psychological aspect is represented by the perpetrator's behavior, described as self-justification, confidence that they cannot be caught, internal motivation that everything is ethical, and committing the act only once. The physical, material aspect consists of opportunity, circumstances, encouragement from peers, context, access to documents, information, material objects, or money.

Among the findings presented in the International Federation of Accountants (2017) are: (a) strong governance leads to an increase in the role played by professional accountants in combating corruption; (b) professional accountants play an important role in combating corruption alongside other participants in the global economy by promoting transparency, accountability, and the rule of law; and (c) activities related to the global accounting profession are guided by an international code of ethics, comprehensive educational standards, and a mechanism for continuous monitoring and oversight. This highlights the importance of professional accountants as a means of communicating accounting information, but also the importance of their access to clean and accurately compiled sources.

The public system is considered to be an environment that allows corruption, so various forms of corruption are used to access public services such as health, education, and local administration. Corruption in the public system can be identified through the Corruption Perceptions Index and the Global Corruption Barometer.

The Corruption Perceptions Index is published by Transparency International and is compiled by accessing 13 independent data sources. It is measured on a scale from 0 (very corrupt) to 100 (very clean), so the lower the score, the higher level of corruption. In 2023, Western Europe was the least corrupt region, with an average score of 65 out of 100 (Transparency International 2024).

The Global Corruption Barometer is an indicator based on citizens' perceptions and experiences of corruption, information provided through surveys. According to the latest barometer published for 2021, the health sector was the most exposed in the European Union to corrupt activities such as bribery and the use of personal connections (Martinez et al. 2021).

According to Onwujekwe and Agwu (2022) corruption in the healthcare system most often takes the forms: fraud, bribery, informal payment, unethical research, theft, overbilling and embezzlement. These corrupt activities result in consequences that manifest themselves in decreased patient satisfaction and a delay in seeking necessary medical services. These effects are strongly felt in post-communist countries, where corruption is higher and satisfaction with healthcare is lower (Habibov 2016). Furthermore, corruption negatively affects life expectancy and mental health, creating a stressful, tiring, and economically pressured environment that has repercussions on the health of the population (Achim et al. 2020).

The effects on patient satisfaction regarding the use of such measures are mixed. In the long term, criminalization can help shape a fair and professional system, but in the short term it can generate tensions and misunderstandings in the relationship between patients and medical staff. In the case of Hungary, legislative changes have had both positive and negative effects. Among the positive effects were significant salary increases for doctors and the legalization of small gifts offered after care. However, there were also negative effects, such as frustration among patients who were used to the old system, a feeling of loss of control, legal ambiguity, and pressure on medical staff through unannounced inspections (Julesz 2024; Vian and Burak 2006).

An important factor in their emergence is the intersection between the expectations of patients (clients/beneficiaries of medical services) and those of medical professionals (Habibov 2016). In Habibov et al. (2021) presented a chronology of the normalization of informal payments for the period 1970–1990. In 1970, informal payments were an important factor in accessing healthcare in the public system. Later, in 1980, they were characterised in post-communist countries by money or various objects considered gifts. Thus, in 1990, they increased due to economic crises that led to a decrease in the public budget for medical services. This led to the normalization of informal payments for access to medical services that are free from a legal standpoint. Regarding informal payments, the literature classifies them into three theories, according to which they are made: cultural policies, "sand the wheels," and "grease the wheels" (McGee and Block 2023; McGee and Petrides 2023).

Informal payments made on the basis of cultural norms are described as payments made in exchange for better services, as a reward for the professionalism offered by medical staff. Cultural norms as a driver of corruption are presented as the most difficult to mitigate, as they are perceived as part of the interaction with the healthcare system and help increase the satisfaction of healthcare service users (Habibov 2016; Habibov et al. 2021; Schaaf and Topp 2019; Williams and Horodnic 2018). One way to reduce this culture is to increase government spending so that healthcare is sufficiently funded to meet the needs of employees and patients, eliminating the need to use their own money to access healthcare services (Behera et al. 2024; Onwujekwe and Agwu 2022). Mavisakalyan et al. (2021) showed that paying these informal expenses to public institutions leads to a decrease in quality of life, as this money could be used to buy essential food. At the same time, this problem is accentuated in post-communist countries where bribery worsens the quality of public health services.

Informal payments based on "sand the wheel" are compulsory and mandatory, which leads to a decrease in the satisfaction of healthcare beneficiaries (Habibov et al. 2021). This theory has a negative economic impact on development and sustainability in high-income countries. The negative aspects are observed in economic development through the hindering of investment, reduced efficiency of fiscal policies, and decreased tax revenues. On the other hand, the effects also extend to public spending, which increases (Hoinaru et al. 2020).

As for "greasing the wheels," this is a mechanism that highlights the advantages of corruption, such as financially supporting medical staff and compensating for their low salaries (Habibov et al. 2021). At the same time, in the case of low-income countries, the theory attests that there are positive effects on economic growth as a result of corruption. The positive effect of corruption is felt in the private economic environment, where corruption helps to avoid regulations and increase profits (Hoinaru et al. 2020). However, a contradiction is presented in the article by Achim (2017b) according to which corruption is presented as an obstacle to business development and economic growth, with the effect being felt more strongly in developing countries than in developed ones.

Regulation and transparency are mentioned as measures to prevent corruption in the healthcare system, so that countries with good governance and effective health policies also have a lower incidence of the phenomenon under analysis (Griffore et al. 2023; Habibov 2016; Mphande-Namangale and Kazanga-Chiumia 2021; Onwujekwe and Agwu 2022). Transparency is also a way to reduce potential unrest or violence against the healthcare system, as was the case in India during the COVID-19 pandemic (Gaiha et al. 2023), but also to factors that favor forms of corruption, such as the structure of the healthcare system and the discretion of government officials in their decisions (Griffore et al. 2023). On the other hand, it has also been suggested that existing anti-corruption policies should be adapted to the social norms of each state (Parvanova 2024; Williams and Horodnic 2018). The acronym ACTA (Anti-corruption, transparency and accountability) is used for this purpose (Griffore et al. 2023).

To reduce informal payments in Iran, the Health Transformation Plan (HTP) was used, which included revising medical service fees and introducing a hotline, 1690, to report informal payments. In this case, the factors leading to informal payments were: financing problems expressed through an imbalance between unrealistic medical fees and low salaries; lack of oversight and ineffective regulation; normalization of informal payments in the form of gifts; and lack of an effective system for referring and managing requests in hospitals. Thus, patients resort to these informal payments to receive better care, effective treatment, and to show their gratitude. (Doshmangir et al. 2020; Mphande-Namangale and Kazanga-Chiumia 2021; Nekoeimoghadam et al. 2013).

In Mackey and Liang (2012) the resolution of the problem at the global governance level was mentioned through the creation of a protocol to combat corruption in healthcare, starting with its recognition. Current measures are considered fragmented and ineffective, so global measures would lead to standardization, reduced financial waste, and improved public health. Furthermore, in order to develop global regulations, the nature of the state, whether fiscal or legal, must also be taken into account, as the approaches are not the same for every state. Thus, global regulations must be adapted to both mechanisms of state functioning, as they are easier to implement in states governed by the rule of law than in fiscal states.

Issues such as transparency and governance of economic information on corruption can be remedied through the digitization of the health sector. Digitization is the solution that can transform governance in the health sector and reduce corruption, improving access to and quality of health services. To achieve this initiative, political support and adequate infrastructure are needed to maximize the benefits (Fryatt et al. 2017).

The study presents a bibliometric analysis of the research on corruption in the medical system. Thus, the purpose of this study is to highlight the importance of researching corruption in the medical system through a bibliometric analysis based on two samples consisting of 1690 from the Web of Science for the period 2000–2025 using the VosViewer bibliometric analysis software tool based on the analysis (Bota-Avram 2023). The study is focused on achieving the following research questions that is reached through bibliometric methods: *RQ1: What are the differences between the concept of corruption in general and corruption in the healthcare system?* and *RQ2: Is corruption a topic of interest in articles on the medical system?*

In summary, the contributions of this study to the research focus on: capturing the interest in the analyzed field over time of publications and citations, a relevant perspective of the keyword groups in the analyzed field and presenting the branches impacted by the key factor.

This article is original in its understanding of the evolution of crosscut research in the medical system from the perspective of bibliometric analysis and challenges researchers to explore the multiple aspects of this field. Although there is some significant review work in this area (Kulkarni et al. 2023; Griffore et al. 2023; Onwujekwe and Agwu 2022; Fryatt et al. 2017), they do not perform bibliometric analyses, only on systematic literature analyses. The results of this bibliometric analysis can provide a solid basis for placing current contributions in the field and identifying emerging trends, as well as for formulating directions for future research.

The way of organizing the work is as follows: *Research methodology* where the research method is presented in detail; *Results and discussion* containing the result of the bibliometric analysis and discussions following them and *Conclusion* where the final conclusions are provided.

2 Research Methodology

Next, two approaches will be developed, one for each research question, so that the conclusions can respond to each need and the samples are representative.

2.1 Comparative Bibliometric Analysis: General Corruption vs. Corruption in Healthcare Using Web of Science Articles

Based on the first research question, two samples were selected in order to highlight the similarities and differences between these two approaches. The samples consist of articles identified in Web of Science and analyzed using the platform's analysis engines.

Looking at corruption in general terms, a sample of 14.175 results was obtained after refinement, as shown in Table 1.

The second sample analyzed consists of 2.736 scientific articles filtered according to Table 2 for addressing corruption in healthcare.

Table 1 Steps for selecting articles on corruption (general)

Steps	Category	Selection	Results
1	Topic	Corrup* OR bribe* OR fraud OR "conflicts of interest" OR nepotism OR favouritism OR theft OR embezzlement	133.338
2	Quick Filters	Highly Cited Papers or Hot Papers; Early Access; Open Access; Enrich Cited References	113.113
3	Publication Years	2017–2024	50.178
4	Document Types	Article; Book Chapters; Letter; Book	37.560
5	Languages	English	34.175
6	Web of Science Categories	Only those areas related	30.756
7	Refine by Citation Topics Meso	Only those areas related	23.250
8	Refine by Citation Topics Micro	Only those areas related	16.705
9	Refine by Research Areas	Only those areas related	14.175

Source Own processings

Table 2 Steps for selecting articles on corruption in health

Steps	Category	Selection	Results
1	Topic	Corrup* OR bribe* OR fraud OR "conflicts of interest" OR nepotism OR favouritism OR theft OR embezzlement OR "informal pay*" OR "unethical research" OR overbilling and health* OR doctor* OR medic*	14.384
2	Quick Filters	Early Access; Open Access; Enrich Cited References	13.080
3	Publication Years	2017–2024	7.103
4	Document Types	Article; Book Chapters; Letter; Book	6.010
5	Languages	English	5.707
6	Web of Science Categories	Only those areas related to the medical system were selected	3.097
7	Refine by Citation Topics Meso	Only those areas related to the medical system were selected	2.736

Source Own processings

2.2 Systematic and Bibliometric Analysis of Research on Corruption in Health

Based on the second research question, a sample was selected, approaches The Web of Science scientific article database for the period 2000–2024 is used, where articles are filtered based on areas of analysis.

The analyzed sample consists of 1690 scientific articles filtered according to Table 3 address corruption in health. It is used as a basis for Web of Science analysis with the help of various tools offered by the platform for presenting the evolution over time of publications and citations in areas of interest. For the analysis of interest groups, factors and links following the database, the VOSviewer program is used.

Table 3 Steps for selecting articles on corruption in areas related to the medical system

Steps	Category	Selection	Results
1	All fields	Corrup*	74.000
2	Quick Filters	Open Access	20.713
3	Publication Years	2000–2025	20.475
4	Document Types	Article	17.127
5	Web of Science Categories	Only those areas related to the medical system were selected	1.739
6	Languages	English	1.690

Source Own processing

3 Results and Discussion

3.1 *Comparative Bibliometric Analysis: General Corruption vs. Corruption in Healthcare Using Web of Science Articles*

Based on the samples presented in the previous, the results regarding: the evolution over time of publications, the most active institutions contributing to publications, the most analyzed fields and the author.

To analyze the evolution over time, the Analyze Results option was exported from Web of Science, along with graphs for both samples regarding citations and article publications (Figs. 1 and 2).

During the analyzed period 2017–2024, the sample related to corruption recorded maximum values in 2020 and minimum values in 2023. During the period analyzed, the average number of publications was 1771.88 publications/year, there was a 6% decrease in 2024 (1564 articles) compared to 2017 (1660 articles).

During the analyzed period 2017–2024, the sample related to corruption in heath-care recorded maximum values in 2024 (424 articles) and minimum values in 2017 (248 articles). During the period analyzed, the average number of publications was 342 publications/year, there was a 71% increase in 2024 compared to 2017. The only decline was recorded in 2023, with a 9% decrease compared to the previous year.

Following the analysis of this data, a series of similarities and differences can be identified, which we have chosen to present in Table 4.

Figure 3 (corruption in general) and Fig. 4 (corruption in healthcare), exported from the Web of Science platform, Analyze Results option, show the author with the most publications.

In the case of the sample on corruption in general, out of a total of 29,469 results, Fig. 3 shows that the author with the most publications is Gottschalk P. with 59 publications, representing 0.42% of the total sample. He is followed by Asongu S.A. with 36 articles (0.25%) and then Goel R.K. with 34 articles (0.24%).

In the case of the sample on corruption in the healthcare system, out of a total of 12,398 results, the top 24 authors can be seen in Fig. 4. In first place is Murayama A. with 24 publications (0.88%), followed by Mckee M. with 23 articles (0.84%) and Ozaki A. with 20 articles (20%).

In both stages, only two authors from the top 25 were found: Mckee M. and Bero L. This aspect is presented in the table below (Table 5).

To capture the areas analyzed, the Analyze Results option on the Web of Science platform was used to generate graphs with the top 10 Web of Science Categories of the samples. This resulted in Fig. 5 for corruption in general and Fig. 6 for corruption in the medical field. In the case of corruption in the medical system, various areas were observed, with "Public Environmental Occupational Health" being the most analyzed, indicating problems at the level of the public medical environment culture.

Fig. 1 Evolution over time of the number of publications related to general corruption. *Source* Own processing based on Web of Science

Fig. 2 Evolution over time of the number of publications and citations related to corruption in healthcare. *Source* Own processing based on Web of Science

Table 4 Corruption in general vs corruption in the medical system (similarities and differences regarding the evolution of publications over time)

Aspect	Similarities/ differences	Corruption in general	Corruption in the medical system
Publications			
Overall evolution	**Difference**	Decrease	Increase
Number of years of decline	**Difference**	3 years	1 year
Year with maximum values	**Difference**	2020	2024

Source Own processing

In the case of corruption in general, the first categiry is "Economics" and that makes sense because we analyse the finnacial corruption.

For affiliates, the Analyze Results option on the Web of Science platform was used to generate graphs with the top 10 affiliations. The samples analyzed resulted in Fig. 7 for the selected articles on corruption and Fig. 8 on corruption in healthcare. The results showed that the first affiliation is similar in order in both cases, with other similar ones also present in the top.

3.2 Systematic and Bibliometric Analysis of Research on Corruption in Health

This section presents the results of the bibliometric analysis of the sample of 1690 articles to address corruption in health. These databases are analyzed for performance analysis and science mapping analysis.

3.2.1 Performance Analysis for Corruption in Healthcare

Bibliometric analysis of the sample described in Table 3. It includes 1690 articles from 2000 to 2024 on corruption in health fields. The data related to this sample of articles are analysed following the following bibliometric indicators: the evolution over time of publications and citations, the most active institutions contributing to publications, the most active countries contributing to publications and the number of citations.

In order to present **the evolution over time of citations and publications** related to corruption in the medical system, the "Citation Report" tool from the Web of Science platform was used. By using this tool, the Fig. 9 graph for the analyzed period, 2000–2024, was generated.

Fig. 3 Top-25 authors contributed to publications related to corruption in general. *Source* Own processings based on Web of Science

Fig. 4 Top-25 authors contributed to publications related to corruption in healthcare. *Source* Own processings based on Web of Science

Table 5 Corruption in general vs corruption in the medical system (similarities authors)

Author	Corruption in general	Corruption in the medical system
Mckee M.	Position: 25 No articles: 14	Position: 2 No articles: 23
Bero L.	Position: 23 No articles: 14	Position: 13 No articles: 11

Source Own processings

For **the evolution of publications**, it can be seen that it started from a number of 4 publications in 2000 and reached 125 in 2024. The maximum value reached by publications on corruption in the medical system occurred in 2022 with 210 publications, followed by a sharp decrease of 28% in 2023 and 18% in 2024. The interest in publishing articles in this field was influenced by the increase by the pandemic period, 2019–2022, respectively by the decrease by the post-pandemic period, after 2022. During the analyzed period, the publications caught the analyzed topic showed a moderate continuous increase, with small decreases for one year. For example, for 2010 there was a decrease of 36% compared to 2009 and followed by a 2.2-fold increase in 2011.

In the case of citations on the sample of selected articles on corruption in health fields, it showed a continuous increase until the year 2024. In the first year of analysis, no citations of the articles were presented, these being presented since 2001 with 19 citations. As in the case of publications, citations registered a sharp increase during the pandemic period, starting from 2018 to 2022, going from 2121 citations in 2017 to 5468 citations in 2022, representing an increase of 2.6 times in 5 years. The maximum number of citations took place in 2024 with 5651. There was a decrease in citations in 2023 compared to 2022 by 1.4%, considered without impact, being within the limit of ±5%.

In order **to identify the institutions,** the selection of the 2355 affiliations offered by Web of Science that contribute to publications in articles on corruption in health fields was made Table 6. The table contains the top 5 institutions in terms of the number of publications in the chosen sample, the number of articles in the sample that are affiliated by the institution and the share in the total sample. From it it can be seen that the University of London is ranked first as an institution that publishes in the analyzed field with 112 articles and a share of 6.62% of the sample. Moreover, there is a difference of 39 articles, significantly, between the first two positions. It was also found that these 10 institutions account for 33% of the total sample.

To **analyze the countries** that published articles on corruption in health fields, the "Analyze Results" function of the Web of Science platform was used, from which Fig. 10 was generated. It was observed that most of the articles were published from the USA, 640 articles, being considered an important country for publications in the chosen topic, with a significant share of influence of 37.83%. This is followed by England with 287 articles, i.e. 16.96% of the chosen sample. Moreover, diversity can

Fig. 5 Top-10 areas of articles related to corruption in general. *Source* Own processings based on Web of Science

Fig. 6 Top-10 areas of articles related to corruption in healthcare. *Source* Own processings based on Web of Science

Fig. 7 Top-10 most active institutions contributed to publications related to corruption (general). *Source* Own processings based on Web of Science

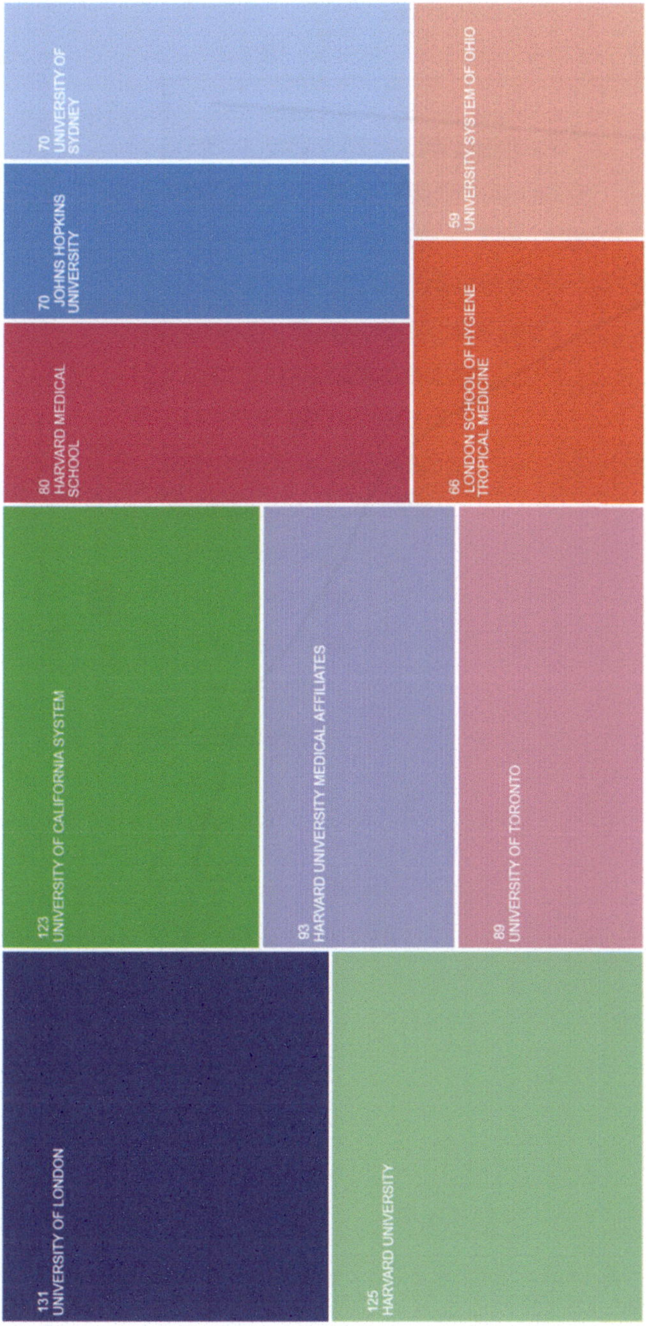

Fig. 8 Top-10 most active institutions contributed to publications related to corruption in healthcare. *Source* Own processings based on Web of Science

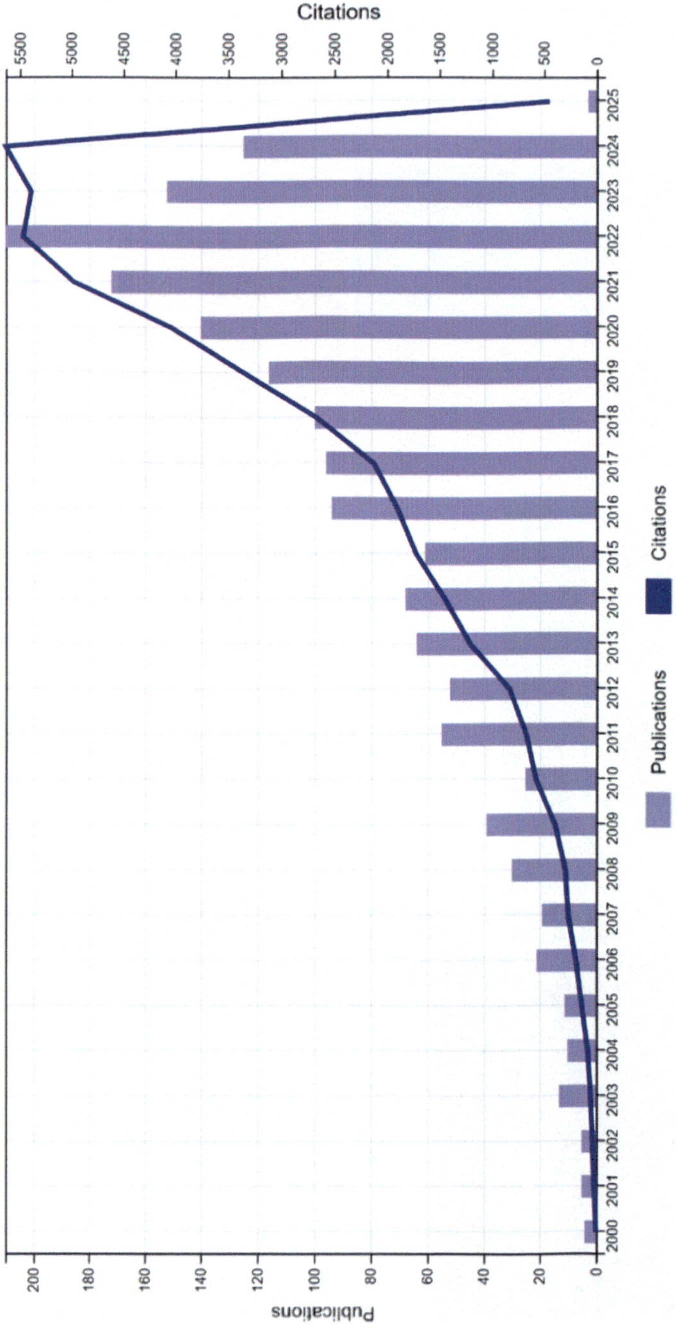

Fig. 9 Evolution over time of the number of publications and citations related to corruption in the medical system. *Source* Own processings based on Web of Science

Table 6 Top-5 most active institutions contributed to publications related to corruption in the medical system

No	Affilations	No. of articles	% of 1.690
1	University of London	112	6,62%
2	University of California System	73	4,31%
3	Harvard University	66	3,90%
4	Centre National de la Recherche Scientifique Cnrs	58	3,43%
5	University College London	48	2,84%

Source Own processing

be observed in the countries involved in this field of research, being developed, less developed countries, from different parts of the world.

Also through the "Analyze Results" tool of the Web of Science platform, Fig. 11 was created, in which the top 10 **Web of Science Categories** involved in corruption research in health fields are presented. From this it can be seen that most of the articles published and indexed in the platform are related to the categories: Radiology Nuclear Medicine Medical Imaging (23.25%), Public Environmental Occupational Health (16.01%) and Engineering Biomedical (13.02%). At the same time, the diversity of fields in the medical system in which corruption has been an interest can also be captured, such as radiology, neurology, optics, psychology, biomedical engineering, general internal medicine and more.

Regarding the **number of citations**, Table 7 was made where the first 10 most cited articles in the analyzed sample were presented. The most cited article is Hanahan and Caussens (2012) with 3388 citations. To make the connection with the most common field, Radiology Nuclear Medicine Medical Imaging, it can be seen that the article on position 5, 6 and 10 have this Web of Science Categories. At the same time, one can observe the diversity of journals, categories and years.

3.2.2 Science Mapping Analysis for Corruption in Healthcare

To summarize the bibliometric structure and the intellectual structure of the analyzed field, the science mapping analysis was used. For the analysis, the VOSviewer analysis program and the database downloaded from the Web of Scotland platform related to the 1690 articles chosen in the sample based on the filters were used. Within the program, co-citations and co-occurrence analysis of keywords were analyzed.

Through the analysis of co-citations, the references cited by scientific publications related to the analyzed sample of 1690 articles and the relationship between the cited publications are analyzed. The relationship between the cited publications aims to outline the in-depth themes in a certain topic. The data related to the analyzed sample were exported from the Web of Science platform and analyzed in VOSviewer. For the analyzed sample, 65,880 citations were identified. Following the selection of a minimum threshold of 15 citations, 110 cited references were analyzed. In Fig. 12,

Fig. 10 Top-25 countries contributed to publications related to corruption in the medical system. *Source* Own processings based on Web of Science

Fig. 11 Top-10 areas of articles related to corruption was found regarding the medical system. *Source* Own processing based on Web of Science

Table 7 Top-5 highly cited publications related to corruption in the medical system

No	Authors	Title	Journal	Year	Total citations	Web of Science Categories
1	Hanahan, D and Coussens, LM	Accessories to the Crime: Functions of Cells Recruited to the Tumor Microenvironment	CELL PRESS	2012	3.388	Oncology; Cell Biology
2	Redding, B; Choma, MA and Cao, H	Speckle-free laser imaging using random laser illumination	NATURE PORTFOLIO	2012	828	Optics; Physics, Applied
3	Tresch, MC; Cheung VCK and d'Avella A	Matrix factorization algorithms for the identification of muscle synergies: Evaluation on simulated and experimental data sets	JOURNAL OF NEUROPHYSIOLOGY	2006	563	Neurosciences; Physiology
4	Jucker, M and Walker, LC	Pathogenic Protein Seeding in Alzheimer Disease and Other Neurodegenerative Disorders	ANNALS OF NEUROLOGY	2011	482	Clinical Neurology; Neurosciences
5	Thesen, S; Heid, O; Mueller, E and Schad, LR	Prospective acquisition correction for head motion with image-based tracking for real-time fMRI	MAGNETIC RESONANCE IN MEDICINE	2000	477	Radiology, Nuclear Medicine and Medical Imaging

Source Own processings

64 elements were added, because that's what the analysis program allowed. Thus, the image shows 64 elements, 5 clusters, 828 links and 2239 total link stengh. It was made to show the network of co-citations in the research of corruption in health fields. The largest cluster presented is red (18 items), followed by green (14 items), blue and yellow (11 items) and, with the fewest items, purple (10 items).

Moreover, Table 8 was made in which the first 5 cited references of the 1690 analyzed articles are presented. Following the association of the data in the table with those in Fig. 12, it was observed that the groupings are divided into red (No. 2, 3, 8), yellow (No. 7, 9) and green (No. 4, 5, 6). On the other hand, for the first and

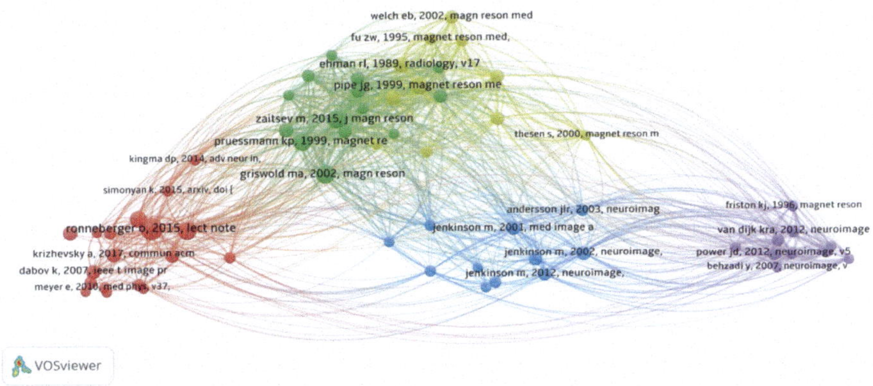

Fig. 12 The co-citation network diagram of cited references. *Source* Own processings based on the VOSviewer analysis

last positions in the table, the groupings could not be identified due to the fact that they were eliminated by the program following the creation of the image.

In addition, co-occurrence analysis of keywords was performed. It aims to make connections between the words in the chosen sample related to corruption in health fields with the help of the VOSviewer program. Out of the total of 8022 words in the sample of 1690 articles, 54 words resulted in the setting of the minimum repetition threshold of 20 words. The words in the "Verify selected keywords" window for the analyzed domains were also manually filtered, eliminating the words considered as unrelated to the analyzed topics. These selections resulted in a total of 26 interrelated words, presented in Fig. 13. It can be seen that "corruption" is the most common word, with 224 observations. It is related to "accountability", "governance", "leadership" and "performance" as presented in the first part of the literature review. These links represent two criteria, presented with the help of the colors yellow and red. In addition,

Table 8 Top-10 cited references in the selected sample

No	Cited references	Citations	Number of links
1	Vian T, 2008, HEALTH POLICY PLANN, v23, p83, doi:https://doi.org/10.1093/heapol/czm048	46	139
2	Ronneberger O, 2015, LECT NOTES COMPUT SC, v9351, p234, doi:https://doi.org/10.1007/978-3-319-24574-4_28	42	106
3	Wang Z, 2004, IEEE T IMAGE PROCESS, v13, p600, doi:https://doi.org/10.1109/tip.2003.819861	32	89
4	Zaitsev M, 2015, J MAGN RESON IMAGING, v42, p887, doi:https://doi.org/10.1002/jmri.24850	30	168
5	Griswold MA, 2002, MAGN RESON MED, v47, p1202, doi:https://doi.org/10.1002/mrm.10171	30	137

Source Own processings based on the VOSviewer analysis

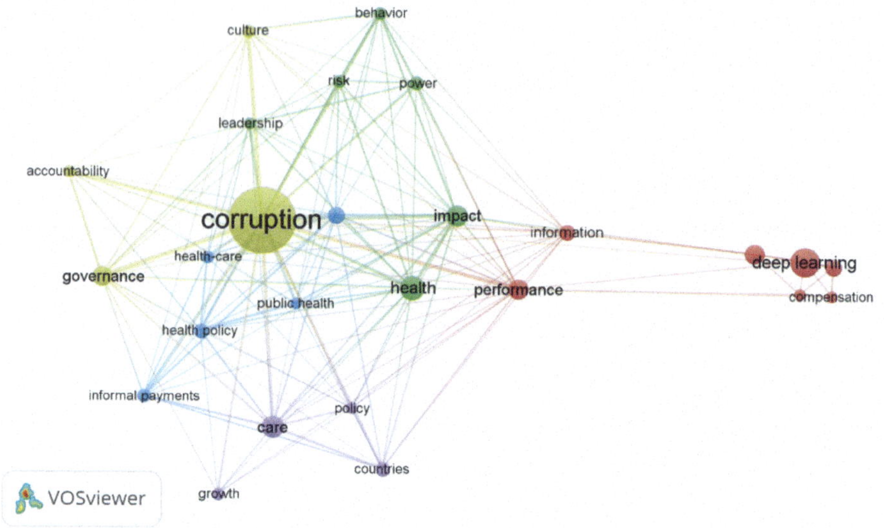

Fig. 13 The co-occurrence of keywords overlay diagram. *Source* Web of Science and VOSviewer

you can also see the connection with the "health", "risk", "impact", "behavior" part in the green part of the image. With the help of the blue color you can see the connection between "informal payments" and health, "health-care", "health policy" and "public health".

4 Conclusion

Following this analysis, it can be observed that corruption is within the healthcare system and that it remains as a topic of interest. Scientific articles show how corruption impacts upon accessing medical services, and they highlight both positive and negative aspects since this practice influences self-assessed health. For the economy, effective measurement can diminish unofficial payment use. It has been proposed that digitalization optimizes transparency and that it improves governance. Additionally, it is important toward improving the role of accounting professionals as well as the regulatory framework if we want to address corruption in the healthcare system.

The issue of corruption inside the medical system gained important attention during the COVID-19 pandemic (2019–2022) because articles published along with cited increased notably. Interest in the topic has waned in the post-pandemic period though still very relevant. Bibliometric analysis highlights variety in article publications considering affiliations, countries, and categories. When they were assessing articles with impact, they accounted for citation relevance, which showed a variety of journals and authors and thematic orientations over time. The diverse findings from this analysis underscore the continued interest within these issues. Corruption in healthcare affects an enormous number of people throughout different social classes, requiring continuing research.

References

Achim MV (2017a) Corruption, income and business development. J Int Bus Entrep Dev 10(1):85. https://doi.org/10.1504/jibed.2017.10003738

Achim MV (2017b) Coruptia si economia subterana. Teorii si studii. https://www.researchgate.net/publication/320087026

Achim MV, Borlea SN (2019) Criminalitatea economico-financiară (Economică)

Achim MV, Văidean VL, Borlea SN (2020) Corruption and health outcomes within an economic and cultural framework. Eur J Health Econ 21(2):195–207. https://doi.org/10.1007/s10198-019-01120-8

Akbar S, Kharabsheh B, Poletti-Hughes J, Shah SZA (2017) Board structure and corporate risk taking in the UK financial sector. Int Rev Financ Anal 50:101–110. https://doi.org/10.1016/j.irfa.2017.02.001

Batrancea LM, Gómez FJB, Nichita A, Dragolea L-L (2023) Crunching numbers in the quest for spotting bribery acts: a cross-cultural rundown. In: McGee RW, Benk S (eds) The ethics of bribery: theoretical and empirical studies. Springer, Switzerland, pp 329–343

Behera DK, Rahut DB, Haridas HT, Tasneem SH (2024) Public versus private health financing transition in low- and middle-income countries: exploring the crowding-out effects. Eur J Dev Res 36(4):957–986. https://doi.org/10.1057/s41287-023-00618-5

Bîzoi A-C, Bîzoi C-G (2023) Primum non nocere: how to fight the "pandemic" of healthcare corruption. In: McGee RW, Benk S (eds) The ethics of bribery: theoretical and empirical studies. Springer, Switzerland, pp 345–365

Borlea SN, Achim MV, Miron MGA (2017) Corruption, shadow economy and economic growth: an empirical survey across the European Union countries. Studia Universitatis „Vasile Goldis" Arad—Economics Series 27(2):19–32. https://doi.org/10.1515/sues-2017-0006

Bota-Avram C (2023) Bibliometric analysis of sustainable business performance: where are we going? A science map of the field. In: Economic Research-Ekonomska Istrazivanja, Vol. 36, Issue 1. Taylor and Francis Ltd, pp 2137–2176. https://doi.org/10.1080/1331677X.2022.2096094

Buckenmaier J, Dimant E, Mittone L (2020) Effects of institutional history and leniency on collusive corruption and tax evasion. J Econ Behav Organ 175:296–313. https://doi.org/10.1016/j.jebo.2018.04.004

CECCAR (2022) Contabilitatea criminalistică, expertul contabil criminalist - angajamentul profesiei contabile din România de a contribui la combaterea corupției li a criminalității economice. CECCRA Business Magazine, 35

CECCAR (2023) Încrederea, corupția şi dezvoltarea sustenabilă reprezintă aspecte interconectate în atitudinea publicului față de sistemul fiscal. CECCAR Business Magazine, 37

Dikmen S, Çiçek HG (2023) Fighting against corruption and bribery in public procurements during the covid-19 pandemic. In: McGee RW, Benk S (eds) The ethics of bribery: theoretical and empirical studies. Springer, Switzerland, pp 309–328

Doshmangir L, Sajadi HS, Ghiasipour M, Aboutorabi A, Gordeev VS (2020) Informal payments for inpatient health care in post-health transformation plan period: evidence from Iran. BMC Public Health 20(1). https://doi.org/10.1186/s12889-020-8432-3

Du M (2021) Corporate governance: five-factor theory-based financial fraud identification. J Chin Governance 6(1):1–19. https://doi.org/10.1080/23812346.2020.1803036

Fryatt R, Bennett S, Soucat A (2017) Health sector governance: should we be investing more? BMJ Glob Health 2(2). https://doi.org/10.1136/bmjgh-2017-000343

Griffore KA, Bowra A, Guilcher SJT, Kohler J (2023) Corruption risks in health procurement during the COVID-19 pandemic and anti-corruption, transparency and accountability (ACTA) mechanisms to reduce these risks: a rapid review. In: Globalization and health, vol 19, Issue 1. BioMed Central Ltd. https://doi.org/10.1186/s12992-023-00994-x

Habibov N (2016) Effect of corruption on healthcare satisfaction in post-soviet nations: a cross-country instrumental variable analysis of twelve countries. Soc Sci Med 152:119–124. https://doi.org/10.1016/j.socscimed.2016.01.044

Habibov N, Auchynnikava A, Fan L, Lyu Y (2021) How different motivations for making informal out-of-pocket payments vary in their influence on users' satisfaction with healthcare, local and national government, and satisfaction with life? BioMed Research International 2021. https://doi.org/10.1155/2021/5763003

Hoinaru R, Buda D, Borlea SN, Văidean VL, Achim MV (2020) The impact of corruption and shadow economy on the economic and sustainable development. Do they "sand the wheels" or "grease the wheels"? Sustainability (Switzerland) 12(2). https://doi.org/10.3390/su12020481

Honigsberg C (2025). Forensic Accounting. https://doi.org/10.1146/annurev-lawsocsci-020320

International Federation of Accountants (2017) The accountancy profession-playing a positive role in tackling corruption

Julesz M (2024) The criminalization of informal patient payments in the Hungarian healthcare sector. Intersect East Eur J Soc Polit 10(3):221–235. https://doi.org/10.17356/ieejsp.v10i3.1251

Julián M, Bonavia T (2021) Understanding unethical behaviors at the university level: a multiple regression analysis. Ethics Behav 31(4):257–269. https://doi.org/10.1080/10508422.2020.1723101

Kulkarni VS, Kulkarni VS, Gaiha R (2023) Trust as key to health sector reforms. Asian Dev Rev 40(2):145–176. https://doi.org/10.1142/S0116110523500130

Livadariu A (2018) Corruption in Romania—a game theory model. https://www.reuters.com/article/us-romania-corruption/romanian-minister-found-guilty-of

Mackey TK, Liang BA (2012) Combating healthcare corruption and fraud with improved global health governance. http://www.biomedcentral.com/1472-698X/12/23

Manci T-M, Achim MV (2025) The role of the professional accountant in reducing corruption fraud. J Financ Stud 10(Special):134–153.

Martinez R, Kukutschka B, Kukuktschka B, Rougier J, Granjo AF (2021) Global corruption barometer—European Union 2021. Transparency International. www.transparency.org

Mavisakalyan A, Otrachshenko V, Popova O (2021) Can bribery buy health? Evidence from post-communist countries. J Comp Econ 49(4):991–1007. https://doi.org/10.1016/j.jce.2021.04.006

McGee RW, Block WE (2023) Helping Hand v. Greedy Hand Bribery. In: McGee RW, Benk S (eds), The ethics of bribery: theoretical and empirical studies. Springer, Switzerland, pp 431–438. https://doi.org/10.1007/978-3-031-17707-1_25 and https://rdcu.be/c7JRf

McGee RW, Petrides Y (2023) Are some forms of bribery worse than others? In: McGee RW, Benk S (eds), The ethics of bribery: theoretical and empirical studies. Springer, Switzerland, pp 257–271. https://doi.org/10.1007/978-3-031-17707-1_15 and https://rdcu.be/c7JPQ

McGee RW, Zhou J (2023) How prevalent is bribery: a ranking of 52 countries. In: McGee RW, Benk S (eds), The ethics of bribery: theoretical and empirical studies. Springer, Switzerland, pp 273–288. https://rdcu.be/c7JQf and https://doi.org/10.1007/978-3-031-17707-1_16

Mphande-Namangale A, Kazanga-Chiumia I (2021) Informal payments in public hospitals in Malawi: the case of Kamuzu Central Hospital. Glob Health Res Policy 6(1). https://doi.org/10.1186/s41256-021-00225-z

Nekoeimoghadam M, Esfandiari A, Ramezani F, Amiresmaili M (2013) Informal payments in healthcare: A case study of Kerman province in Iran. Int J Health Policy Manag 1(2):157–162. https://doi.org/10.15171/ijhpm.2013.28

Němec D, Kotlánová E, Kotlán I, Machová Z (2021) Corruption, taxation and the impact on the shadow economy. Economies 9(1). https://doi.org/10.3390/economies9010018

Niță N (2019) Efectele și consecințele corupției în România contemporană. 8(2). http://juridica.ugb.ro/-NeluNIȚĂ

Odtu SA, Ramella D, Akkoyunlu S (2017) WP 17-29 corruption and economic development. www.rcfea.org

Onwujekwe O, Agwu P (2022) Can strategic health purchasing reduce inefficiency and corruption in the health sector? The case of Nigeria. Health Syst Reform 8(2). https://doi.org/10.1080/23288604.2022.2057836

Our World in Data. (2024). Share of people who said they were asked for a bribe or paid one, 2021

Parvanova I (2024) The effect of institutional characteristics and social norms on corruption in healthcare. Governance. https://doi.org/10.1111/gove.12868

Radu L, Gyula G (2010) Corruption—a problem without solutions in Romania? [CORUPȚIA ÎN ROMÂNIA, O PROBLEMĂ DE NEREZOLVAT?]. In: Revista Transilvană de Științe Administrative, vol 2, Issue 26

Rasheed F, Said J, Ismail Khan N (2023) Evolution of fraud-related theories: a theoretical review. J Nusant Stud (JONUS) 8(3):322–350. https://doi.org/10.24200/jonus.vol8iss3pp322-350

Rezaee Z (2005) Causes, consequences, and deterence of financial statement fraud. Crit Perspect Account 16(3):277–298. https://doi.org/10.1016/S1045-2354(03)00072-8

Schaaf M, Topp SM (2019) A critical interpretive synthesis of informal payments in maternal health care. Health Policy Plan 34(3):216–229. https://doi.org/10.1093/heapol/czz003

Sfetcu N (2014) Corupție-Globalizare-Neocolonialism

Tian J, Sun H (2023) Corporate financialization, internal control and financial fraud. Finance Research Letters 56. https://doi.org/10.1016/j.frl.2023.104046

Transparency International (2024) Corruption Perceptions Index 2023. www.transparency.org/cpi

Tytko A, Smokovych M, Dorokhina Y, Chernezhenko O, Stremenovskyi S (2020) Nepotism, favoritism and cronyism as a source of conflict of interest: corruption or not? Revista Amazonia Investiga 9(29):163–169. https://doi.org/10.34069/ai/2020.29.05.19

Vian T, Burak LJ (2006) Beliefs about informal payments in Albania. Health Policy Plan 21(5):392–401. https://doi.org/10.1093/heapol/czl022

Wang TY, Winton A, Yu X (2010) Corporate fraud and business conditions: evidence from IPOs. J Financ 65(6):2255–2292. https://doi.org/10.1111/j.1540-6261.2010.01615.x

Williams CC, Horodnic AV (2018) Evaluating the prevalence of informal payments for health services in Southeast Europe: an institutional approach. J Southeast Eur Black Sea 18(3):345–365. https://doi.org/10.1080/14683857.2018.1487138

Tomina-Maria Manci is a second-year PhD student in Finance at the prestigious Faculty of Economic Sciences and Business Administration, Babeș-Bolyai University. Her academic and professional journey reflects a profound passion for accounting, auditing, and research. She has successfully completed both her bachelor's and master's degrees in Accounting and Auditing. Additionally, she has accumulated four years of experience in internal banking audit, during which she gained valuable insights into the functioning of financial systems and contributed to ensuring the integrity and efficiency of their processes. Currently, her research and academic development interests are focused on the connection between corruption, digitalization, and health, which form the central subject of her doctoral thesis.

Monica Violeta Achim is a professor and doctoral supervisor in Finance at the Faculty of Economic Sciences and Business Administration, Babeș-Bolyai University, Cluj-Napoca. With over 27 years of experience in academia, she has published, as author and co-author, over 140 scientific articles and 27 books. The main research topics are financial analysis, business performance, finance, and economic and financial crime. In 2020, she obtained the Award for Excellence in Scientific Research, at Babeș-Bolyai University, Faculty of Economics and Business Administration, Cluj-Napoca, Romania, as a recognition of the results obtained in the research activity. She leads a main national project in the area of financial crime in the period 2020–2023. In the business environment, she works in liberal professions as an accountant expert, tax consultant, and judicial expert; from this perspective, being involved in solving many cases of economic and financial crime of the Palace of Justice, Cluj-Napoca.

The Importance of Financial Fraud Prevention in the Current Economic Context: A Bibliometric Analysis

Georgiana Burlacu and Ioan-Bogdan Robu

Abstract Financial crime is an important debated topic globally due to its serious consequences for the economic and financial environment. Financial fraud is one of the most prevalent types of economic crime in today's society, resulting in substantial financial losses for the entire economy. This research aims to present trends and challenges in preventing financial fraud and also to highlight the impact of financial fraud prevention in the context of digitalisation and the accelerated development of artificial intelligence. In this study bibliometric and exploratory analysis were used to achieve this goal. Data from the Web of Science database were used in order to conduct this research, and the research results were obtained by using Biliometrix and CiteSpace software. For the analysed period 2020–2024, the research findings indicate that fraud prevention remains a pressing issue requiring prompt and effective solutions.

Keywords Prevention · Financial fraud · Bibliometric analysis · Machine learning

1 Introduction

Financial crime is defined as a series of illegal acts committed by a person or group with the aim of obtaining financial gain (Awale et al. 2025). It can manifest in various ways, including financial fraud, tax avoidance, money laundering and corruption (Premrl et al. 2025). Financial crime is currently a major problem in the economic and financial environment (Achim et al. 2024). The harmful consequences of economic crime include the destabilisation of capital markets, damage to the national economy and population, and a loss of confidence among potential investors in listed companies

G. Burlacu (✉) · I.-B. Robu
Doctoral School of Economics and Business Administration, Alexandru Ioan Cuza University of Iasi, Iasi, Romania
e-mail: georgiana.burlacu@student.uaic.ro

I.-B. Robu
e-mail: bogdan.robu@feaa.uaic.ro

M. V. Achim (ed.), *Financial Crime in the Digital Era*, Contributions to Finance and Accounting, https://doi.org/10.1007/978-3-032-20198-0_13

(Sigetova et al. 2022). Financial crime most commonly occurs in private companies (de Batz and Kočenda 2023).

Some studies suggest that financial crime has become more prevalent in recent years, partly due to the increased use of digitalisation in everyday activities (Awale et al. 2025; Gottschalk 2022). Financial fraud is one of the financial crimes affecting the global economy and posing a serious problem today (Adejumo and Ogburie 2025).

Financial fraud is a common practice involving the manipulation of financial results for personal gain through illegal activities, all of which are well-defined and intentional (Emran and Rubel 2024; Kamuangu 2024). Despite the introduction of various measures to prevent and detect financial fraud, these have been ineffective against increasingly sophisticated fraud schemes (Eswar Prasad et al. 2023; Ismail and Haq 2024).

In recent years, the development of artificial intelligence-based techniques has proven to be a real success in many fields, improving and streamlining current activities, reducing the time dedicated to each one, minimising risks and offering many other advantages (Njoku et al. 2024; Trabelsi 2024). However, machine learning techniques can also have disadvantages, such as the vulnerability of AI-based models and inaccurate data, which can lead to incorrect results (Islam et al. 2024). Special attention has also been given to preventing and detecting financial fraud using machine learning methods. These methods are widely regarded as being much more effective in tackling fraudulent activities (Lin 2024; Miao 2024; Lee et al. 2025; Odufisan et al. 2025).

Through our research, we aim to highlight the most effective methods of preventing financial fraud in the current economic context, which is characterised by the digitisation of many activities. To this end, this paper is structured as follows: an introductory section covering various aspects of financial crime in today's society; a review of literature on responsibility for preventing financial fraud; and methods that can significantly contribute to preventing financial fraud in today's complex business environment. There will also be a presentation on the potential impact of artificial intelligence-based techniques on the prevention of fraud. The third part will present the research methodology and the research questions formulated to determine the results. Once the results have been obtained and the related discussions have taken place, the most significant conclusions from the research will be presented, alongside the limitations of the research.

2 Literature Review and Proposed Research Questions

2.1 *Responsibility for Preventing Financial Fraud*

Preventing financial fraud is and has always been a topic of the utmost importance (Bello et al. 2023). Despite digitisation and the implementation of machine learning-based methods in most sectors, the number of financial fraud cases has increased in recent years (Bonrath and Eulerich 2023; Wang et al. 2024).

To date, it remains unclear who is truly responsible for preventing financial fraud and what measures should be taken to prevent illegal acts (Gotelaere and Paoli 2022). Despite numerous studies addressing this topic, it remains unclear who is responsible for preventing fraud in private companies and public institutions (Button et al. 2024). Nevertheless, some studies highlight the important role played by managers, internal control officers and internal auditors in fraud prevention (Oyedotun et al. 2025; Wang et al. 2025).

The literature specifies that internal auditing plays an essential role in preventing financial fraud. It is responsible for minimising company risk, evaluating internal controls and ensuring reliable financial reporting (Irianti et al. 2025). Furthermore, to minimise the risk of fraud, internal auditors must be independent and possess the necessary knowledge to analyse and assess fraud risk (Lonto et al. 2023). However, the effectiveness of internal auditing in preventing financial fraud can be impacted by various factors, including the professional competence and independence of the auditor, the quality of the audit, the necessary support from management, and the resources required for audit activities (Alzeban and Gwilliam 2023; Irianti et al. 2025).

Internal control is also essential for preventing financial fraud (Wahyuandari 2025). Within a company, internal control contributes to the well-being of its activities by ensuring they are carried out efficiently and effectively. Implementing a well-defined internal control system significantly contributes to preventing fraudulent acts (Madolidi Handoyo and Bayunitri 2021). However, there may be factors influencing the effective operation of internal controls within a company, thereby affecting fraud prevention (Chealsea and Yuliastuty Asmara 2025). These factors include organisational culture, a lack of management involvement and technological advances (Mutua Musyoki 2023).

Another factor that can help prevent financial fraud is organisational culture. Implementing well-intentioned corporate governance principles and encouraging ethical behaviour within the company can have a positive effect on preventing fraud (Nugroho et al. 2023).

In addition, the literature suggests that effective leadership can minimise the risk of fraud. A competent and responsible leader who has received adequate training can encourage their subordinates to share the same goal: to carry out their assigned tasks in a responsible manner, thereby ensuring the company runs smoothly (Muncahyani et al. 2024). Furthermore, the knowledge and skills of human resources are necessary for the efficient achievement of the company's objectives. The quality of the HR

Fig. 1 Competent bodies for preventing financial fraud. *Source* Own processing

department is another important factor in minimising the risk of financial fraud (Murtanto et al. 2022).

Figure 1 is based on the above and shows the people primarily responsible for ensuring a company runs smoothly and is well-run, as well as preventing fraudulent acts.

However, fraud has proven to be a complex problem, as evidenced by its increasingly frequent occurrence. To prevent financial fraud, it must be a company-wide priority, involving strict internal controls, effective financial auditing and careful management oversight (Supriadi et al. 2025).

2.2 *Methods of Preventing Financial Fraud*

Financial fraud prevention is based on a series of methods and strategies. These aim to maintain the stability of company activities, maintain stakeholder trust and contribute to company financial well-being (Bello and Olufemi 2024).

Useful strategies for preventing financial fraud include delineating tasks within the company, applying measures against deviations from internal policies and periodically reconciling financial accounts (Irianti et al. 2025). Changes in the economic environment and the digitisation of activities in recent years have led to an increase in financial fraud cases. Traditional methods of fraud prevention and detection have proven to be ineffective. Against this backdrop, the application of machine learning-based approaches to financial fraud prevention has been explored (Bello et al. 2023; Bello and Olufemi 2024). Recent research has highlighted the numerous advantages that artificial intelligence offers in the prevention and detection of financial fraud. It has the capacity to process and analyse large volumes of data in a relatively short time with a high degree of accuracy (Lin 2024).

The most appropriate and effective methods for supporting fraud prevention and detection include support vector machines, artificial neural networks, fuzzy logic, random forests, decision trees, logistic regression and naive Bayes (Biyyapu et al. 2024).

To keep the risk of fraud as low as possible, it is necessary to implement supportive methods. Both researchers and the competent bodies responsible for combating illegal acts must prioritise fraud prevention. However, the specialist literature places greater emphasis on detection than on prevention. Although there are numerous articles on financial fraud, most of them focus on methods of detection or a combination of detection and prevention.

A bibliometric analysis is proposed to support the above and determine the impact of financial fraud and financial crime prevention among researchers and others. Our aim is to use bibliometric analysis to find answers to several research questions. This will enable us to determine the importance of fraud prevention in the current context, and the extent to which digitisation and machine learning can contribute to it. The study therefore proposes the following research questions (RQ):

RQ_1. Is financial fraud prevention a topic of utmost importance among researchers??
RQ_2. Who is responsible for preventing fraud?
RQ_3. Which researchers have contributed to finding solutions to prevent illegal activity?

The next step involves presenting the methodology, describing the main results, followed by drawing conclusions about the methods and strategies for preventing financial fraud discovered through bibliometric analysis. This section will also present the contributions made by our study in the field of financial fraud, as well as a series of future research directions.

3 Materials and Methods

To achieve the objective of this study, we will use a series of specific tools to find answers to the research questions.

3.1 Data Source

This study used Web of Science, one of the world's largest databases, which contains a significant number of highly rated academic articles. We queried the database using keywords to identify the best articles on the research topic. To capture the most recent studies on financial fraud prevention, the analysis period was set at five years: 2020–2024. As 2025 has not yet been completed, it was not included in the analysis. Figure 2 shows the steps taken to obtain data from the Web of Science.

To extract a relevant number of studies for the period 2020–2024, the following keywords were used: 'financial fraud prevention', 'prevention methods', 'internal control', 'internal audit' and 'fraud risk'. These keywords yielded 3075 publications for the analysed period. In 2020, 502 publications were released on topics related to financial fraud prevention. The following year, there were 46 more publications. The number of articles increased again in 2022, with 643 publications found in the database. The increase in articles about financial fraud during this period can also be

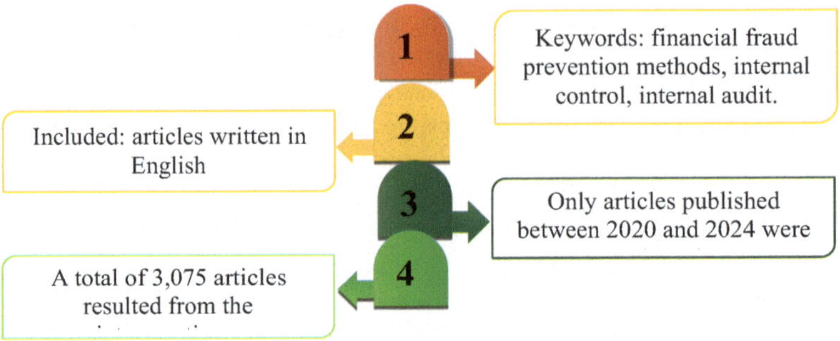

Fig. 2 Steps taken to obtain information. *Source* Own processing

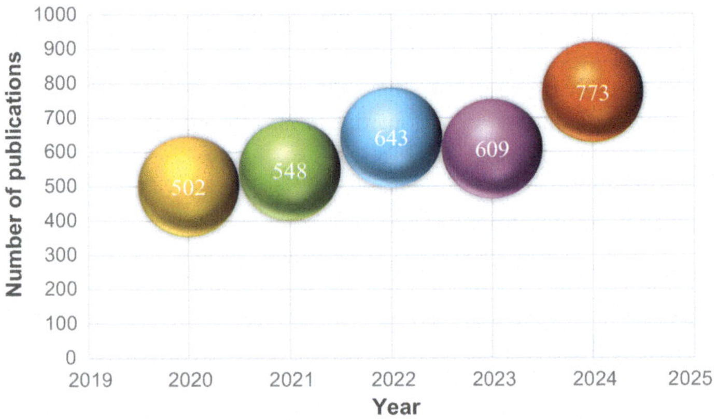

Fig. 3 Distribution of scientific papers by year. *Source* Own processing in Excel

attributed to the unexpected emergence of the pandemic, which has had an adverse effect on the global economy. Concerns about fraud prevention are also evident in the number of publications, with 643 in 2023 and 773 in 2024. Figure 3 shows the distribution of articles for each year.

Once we have obtained a sufficient number of publications on the research topic covered by this study, we will move on to the second stage: choosing the type of analysis and the programme with which to perform it.

3.2 Analysis Method

The bibliometric analysis was performed using the Bibliometrix and CiteSpace software. These two applications are among the most well-known for this type of analysis and are designed to explore literature and provide concrete information on a specific research topic (Wahib and Rohman 2024; Li et al. 2023; Nan et al. 2025).

4 Results and Discussion

To answer the first research question, we performed a quantitative analysis of data extracted from the Web of Science database. First, articles addressing fraud prevention during the analysed five-year period were identified, and their impact on the literature was determined by measuring the number of citations..

4.1 The Importance of Fraud Prevention

A descriptive analysis of the most frequently occurring keywords in the literature, as well as the number of publications each year, was conducted to find the clearest and most concise answer to the first question. Figure 4 shows the main keywords resulting from the bibliometric analysis performed in CiteSpace.

Figure 4 shows that the most common keywords in literature discussing fraud prevention are 'internal control', 'audit', 'corporate governance', 'fraud detection' and 'machine learning methods'. Based on these keywords, it can be seen that a key topic of debate in the specialised literature is who is responsible for fraud prevention. This responsibility primarily falls to corporate governance, internal control and internal audit. The emergence of the term 'machine learning' indicates that researchers are concerned about integrating artificial intelligence techniques into fraud prevention activities to maximise the effectiveness of mitigating fraud risk.

Additionally, it was deemed appropriate to present the most pertinent articles published during the analysed period that addressed issues related to fraud prevention within companies. It was noted that the selected articles addressed internal environmental responsibility in reducing fraudulent acts in financial reporting, as well as the development and application of deep learning-based techniques to minimise the risk of financial fraud. In the current context, the prevention of financial fraud remains a topic of the utmost importance. Researchers are currently considering topics closely related to who is responsible for preventing financial fraud and the effectiveness of introducing artificial intelligence as a method of reducing fraudulent acts (Table 1).

The 12 publications were hand-selected following an exploratory review of the specialized literature. All of these articles captured aspects related to financial fraud in the current business environment, with a particular emphasis on the prevention and detection of fraudulent acts.

4.2 Responsible for Fraud Prevention

Financial fraud is currently a serious and complex problem worldwide. The number of fraud cases is increasing every year. Although there has been much talk about

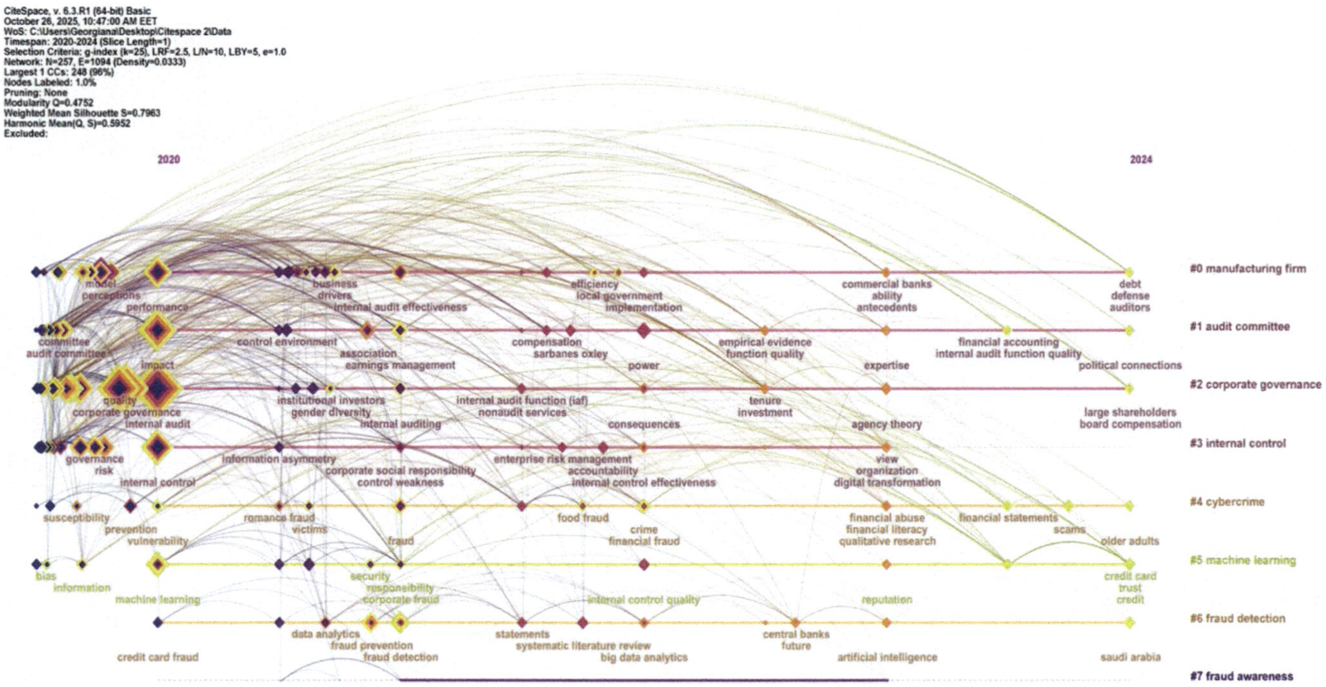

Fig. 4 Keywords used by authors in their research on the financial fraud prevention. *Source* Own processing in CiteSpace

Table 1 List of relevant articles on the topic of financial fraud prevention

No Crt	Scientific papers	Authors	Publishing year	Scientific journal	Research subject	Conclusions
1	The impact of audit committee information technology expertise on the reliability and timeliness of financial reporting	Ashraf, M., Michas, P. N., Russomanno, D.	2020	The Accounting Review	The influence of information technology within the audit committee on the reliability of financial reporting	The presence of an information technology expert on the audit committee has a positive influence on the quality of financial reporting
2	Fintech in financial reporting and audit for fraud prevention and safeguarding equity investments	Roszkowska, P.	2021	Journal of Accounting and Organizational Change	The importance of using artificial intelligence-based methods in reliable reporting of financial results	The integration of artificial intelligence into the process of preparing financial statements and in the auditor's work has a significant impact on reducing misstatements in financial reports
3	The influence of internal audit, risk management, whistleblowing system and big data analytics on the financial crime behavior prevention	Putra, I., Sulistiyo, U., Diah, E., Rahayu, S., Hidayat, S.	2022	Cogent Economics and Finance	Determining how fraud prevention mediates the effect of internal audits, risk management, whistle-blowing systems and big data analysis on preventing financial criminal behaviour	Within a company, fraud prevention mediates the effect of internal audits, risk management, whistle-blowing systems and big data analysis on the prevention of financial criminal behaviour
4	The effectiveness of internal audit for fraud prevention	Lonto, M. P., Sukoharsono, E. G., Prihatiningtias, Y. W.	2023	Australasian Accounting Business And Finance Journal	The impact of internal audit quality in fraud prevention	Auditor independence affects the quality of the audit with direct consequences on the prevention of financial fraud

(continued)

Table 1 (continued)

No Crt	Scientific papers	Authors	Publishing year	Scientific journal	Research subject	Conclusions
5	Preempting fraud: a financial distress prediction perspective on combating financial crime	Halteh, K., Tiwari, M.	2023	Journal of Money Laundering Control	Implications of financial difficulties in fraud prevention	There is a direct relationship between financial crime and financial difficulties. The more financial difficulties a company faces, the greater the fraud risk
6	Forensic accounting: a novel paradigm and relevant knowledge in fraud detection and prevention	Afriyie, S. O., Akomeah, M.O., Amoakohene, G., Ampimah, B. C., Ocloo, C. E., Kyei, M. O.	2023	International Journal Of Public Administration	The importance of forensic accounting in preventing financial fraud	The development of forensic accounting and its direct involvement in reducing fraudulent acts is an aspect that should be taken into account in the current context
7	Financial fraud detection and prevention: automated approach based on deep learning	Miao, Z. Y.	2024	Journal of Organizational and End User Computing	Using artificial intelligence techniques to prevent and detect financial fraud	The introduction of the Transformer-LOF-Random Forest model has had a significant impact on fraud prevention and detection
8	Identification and prevention of financial securities fraud based on deep learning	Guo, D. B.	2024	Journal of Computational Methods in Sciences and Engineering	Using deep learning methods to prevent fraud	Using and developing deep learning techniques can greatly improve the fraud prevention process
9	Fraud prevention in the indonesian banking sector using anti-fraud strategy	Shonhadji, N., Irwandi, S. A.	2024	Banks and Bank Systems	The importance of anti-fraud strategies in preventing fraud	The results showed that applying strategies and rigorously punishing fraud significantly reduces cases of fraud

(continued)

Table 1 (continued)

No Crt	Scientific papers	Authors	Publishing year	Scientific journal	Research subject	Conclusions
10	The effect of internal control mechanism towards fraud prevention in small and medium enterprises	Azizan, A. F., Ali, M. M.	2024	Indonesian Journal of Sustainability Accounting and Management	The impact of internal control systems on preventing financial fraud in small and medium-sized enterprises	A well-organized control system mitigates the occurrence of fraudulent acts within companies
11	Internal auditing's role in preventing and detecting fraud: An empirical analysis	Bonrath, A., Eulerich, M.	2024	International Journal of Auditing	The role of internal auditing in preventing illegal acts	The results confirm that internal audit involvement in preventing financial fraud is important and necessary for the company
12	Internal auditor competence and internal control: Improving internal audit quality to prevent fraudulent financial statements	Novatiani, R. A., Kusumah, R. W. R., Yadiati, W., Rachmat, R. A. H., Rachman, A. A.	2024	Cogent Business and Management	Investigating the extent to which the competence of internal auditors significantly impacts the prevention of fraudulent acts	The audit quality represented by the competence of the internal auditor has a positive effect in stopping the occurrence of financial fraud

Source Own processing

financial fraud over time, no solution has yet been found to prevent it from occurring. All these considerations lead us to a single question: who is responsible for preventing fraud? The answer to this question was obtained following an analysis in Bibliometrix, more specifically by linking articles according to key elements, as shown in Fig. 5.

Figure 5 shows that, within a company, those responsible for ensuring the accuracy of reported financial information, the normal conduct of business and the prevention of fraud are individuals who form part of the internal control system, the internal audit team and the corporate governance team. The internal control system may not always be entirely effective, and internal auditing may be influenced by certain factors, resulting in an inability to prevent fraudulent financial reporting. One factor that could affect the effectiveness of the three departments within the company is financial difficulty. A company facing financial difficulties is much more likely to commit financial fraud. Another factor influencing this is the quality of internal auditing, which can be affected by other factors. One such factor may be the competence of the auditor in analysing and assessing the risk of fraud.

4.3 Researchers Concerned with Fraud Prevention

As preventing financial fraud is a sensitive and important issue in business, it was deemed appropriate to analyse the connections between researchers who have written on this subject and highlight their collaborations.

Figure 6 shows the researchers who have published the most papers on topics related to financial fraud. Among the authors who have addressed the topic of financial fraud prevention is Annika Bonrath, who has published work on the role of internal auditing in fraud prevention. Bing Wang and Sri Mulyani have also shown a keen interest in the role of internal control in fraud prevention. Other researchers who have addressed the topic of fraud prevention include Salvatore Polizzi, Surya Abbas Dirvi, Mark Button, Agustia Dian, Rachel Barker, and so on.

While Fig. 6 highlights researchers and their countries of origin, it was also deemed appropriate to identify groups of countries with a history of collaboration between authors who have published on the topic of financial fraud. This is illustrated in Fig. 7.

Significant collaborations have taken place between researchers in Australia, China, the USA, Nigeria, Brazil and the United Kingdom. The most significant collaborations in the field of financial fraud research are those between the USA, Australia and China. The close relationship between the USA and China is due not only to their geographical proximity, but also to their economic power. In the context of a constantly evolving economic landscape, it is crucial to be mindful of potential risks that could impact ongoing operations. Financial fraud is one of the most important risks to analyse and evaluate due to the harmful consequences it can generate in the business environment. Accurately assessing this risk contributes to the economic and financial well-being of companies.

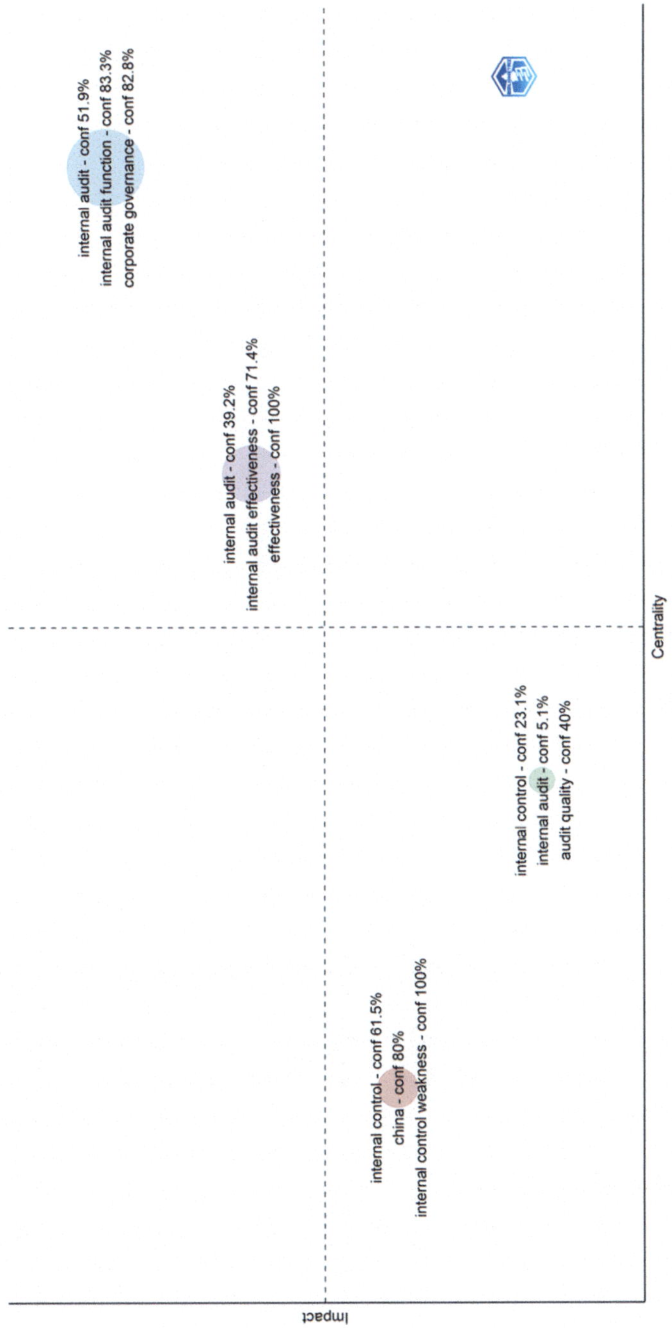

Fig. 5 Key aspects resulting from the coupling of documents. *Source* Own projection in Bibliometrix

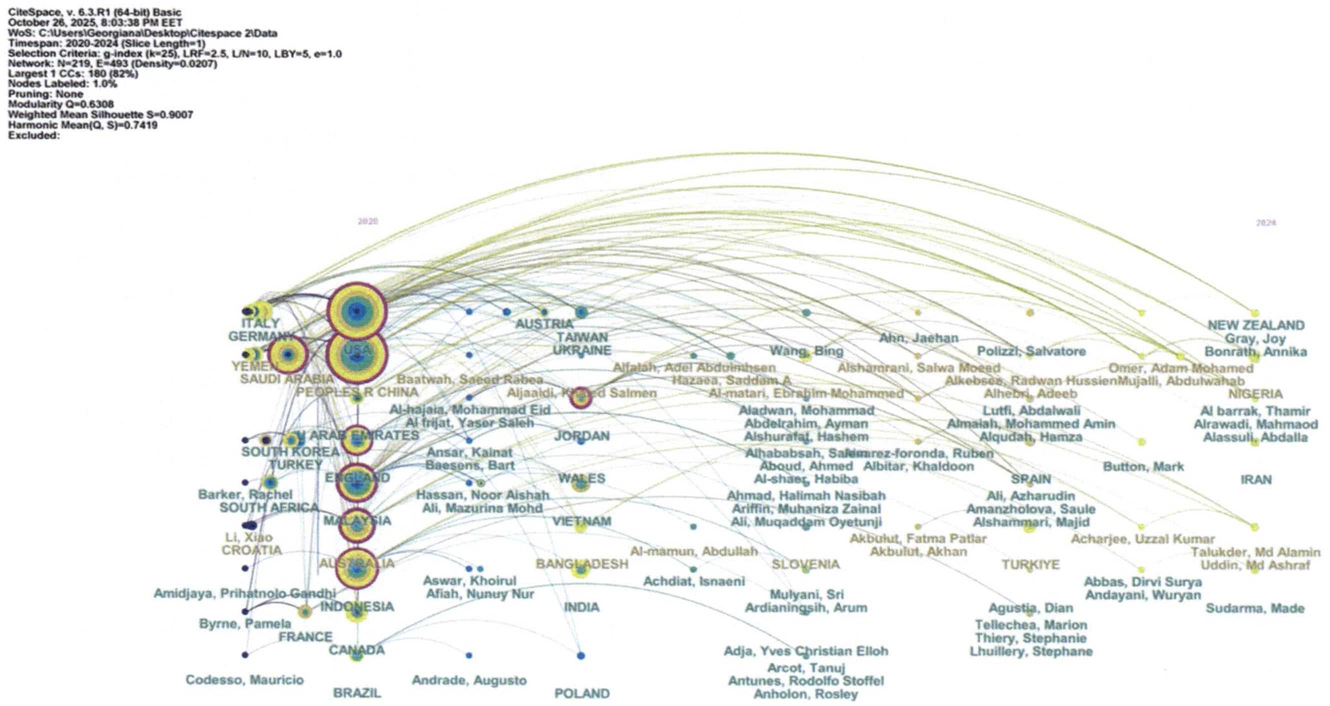

Fig. 6 The main authors who have published works on fraud prevention. *Source* Own procesings in CiteSpace

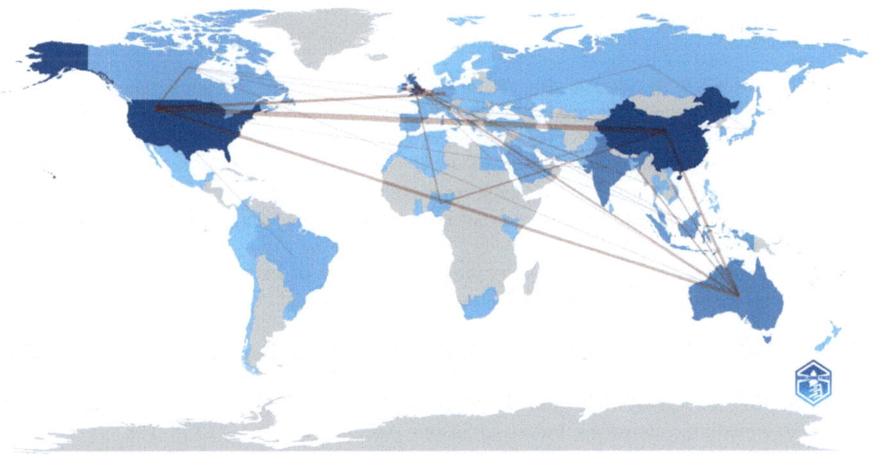

Fig. 7 Country Collaboration Map. *Source* Own processings in Bibliometrix

5 Conclusions

Financial fraud remains a particular concern for academia, regulatory bodies and other agencies responsible for tackling illegal activities. Most financial fraud is committed by private companies seeking financial gain.

Fraud prevention is a complex and rather difficult task, given the dynamics of the economic environment and external pressures affecting the internal environment of companies. Combating fraud requires constant and rigorous involvement on the part of internal control, internal auditors, management, and other external bodies. In order to prevent fraudulent acts, a series of strategies and rules are also necessary to support those responsible for preventing fraudulent acts.

This study employed bibliometric analysis to evaluate the impact of financial fraud prevention on specialised literature. The analysis covered the period from 2020 to 2024. The results obtained allowed us to conclude that financial fraud remains a pressing issue. All companies must take fraud prevention extremely seriously.

Future research should focus on practical strategies and methods for preventing financial fraud. This should include developing a set of rules for the company to follow, sanctions for not following these rules, and training for those responsible for internal control. Furthermore, future studies on the integration of artificial intelligence in financial fraud prevention should provide a clearer explanation of its real-time contribution to preventing fraudulent acts.

References

Achim MV, Borlea SN, Vaidean VL, Rus AI, Dobre F (2024) The impact of intelligence on economic and financial crime: a cross-country study. Singap Econ Rev 69(8):2522

Adejumo AP, Ogburie CP (2025) Forensic accounting in financial fraud detection: trends and challenges. Int J Sci Res Arch 14(3):1219–1232

Afriyie SO, Akomeah MO, Amoakohene G, Ampimah BC, Ocloo CE, Kyei MO (2023) Forensic accounting: a novel paradigm and relevant knowledge in fraud detection and prevention. Int J Public Adm 46(9):615–624

Alzeban A, Gwilliam D (2023) Examining the critical factors of internal audit effectiveness from the internal auditors' perspective: moderating role of extrinsic rewards. J Mod Account Audit 19(2):42–60

Awale AA, Abdullahi FA, Kulmie DA (2025) Understanding the realities of financial crime in public institutions: female public servants' insights. Int J Econ Financ Issues 15(1):319–329

Azizan AF, Ali MM (2024) The effect of internal control mechanism towards fraud prevention in small and medium enterprises. Indones J Sustain Account Manag 8(1):178–188

Bello OA, Folorunso A, Ejiofor OE, Budale FZ, Adebayo K, Babatunde OA (2023) Machine learning approaches for enhancing fraud prevention in financial transactions. Int J Manag Technol 10(1):85–109

Bello OA, Olufemi K (2024) Artificial intelligence in fraud prevention: exploring techniques and applications challenges and opportunities. Comput Sci IT Res J 5(6):1505–1520

Biyyapu NS, Chandolu SB, Gorintla S, Tirumalasetti NR, Chokka A, Praveen SP (2024) Advanced machine learning techniques for real-time fraud detection and prevention. J Theor Appl Inf Technol 102(20):7412–7422

Bonrath A, Eulerich M (2023) Internal auditing's role in preventing and detecting fraud: an empirical analysis. Int J Audit 28(4):615–631

Button M, Hock B, Shepherd D, Gilmour P (2024) What really works in preventing fraud against organisations and do decision-makers really need to know? Secur J 37:965–983

Chealsea A, Yuliastuty Asmara R (2025) The effect of competence, digital technology, and locus of control on fraud prevention. International Journal of Multidisciplinary Sciences and Arts 4(3):212

de Batz L, Kočenda E (2023) Financial crime and punishment: a meta-analysis. CESifo Working Paper, No. 10528, p. 1

Emran AKM, Rubel TH (2024) Big data analytics and AI-driven solutions for financial fraud detection: techniques. Appl Chall, AIM Int J 1(1):269–285

Eswar Prasad G, Hemanth Kumar G, Venkata Nagesh B, Manikanth S, Kiran P, Shravan Kumar R, Mohit Surender R (2023) Enhancing performance of financial fraud detection through machine learning model. J Contemp Educ Theory Artif Intell 1(1):1–7

Gotelaere S, Paoli L (2022) Prevention and control of financial fraud: a scoping review. Eur J Crim Policy Res 31:1–21

Gottschalk P (2022) Gender and crime: convenience for pink-collar offenders. Deviant Behav 43(2):213–227

Guo D (2024) Identification and prevention of financial securities fraud based on deep learning. J Comput Methods Sci Eng 24(4–5):2673–2688

Madolidi Handoyo BR, Bayunitri BI (2021) The influence of internal audit and internal control toward fraud prevention. Int J Financ Account Manag 3(1):45–64

Halteh K, Tiwari M (2024) Preempting fraud: a financial distress prediction perspective on combating financial crime. J Money Laund Control 26(6):1194–1202

Irianti LR, Nuswantara DA, Pujiono P (2025) The role of internal auditors in fraud prevention: a systematic literature review (SLR). J Bus Inf Syst 7(1):141–142

Islam T, Islam SAM, Sarkar A, Obaidur AJM, Khan R, Paul R, Bari MDS (2024) Artificial intelligence in fraud detection and financial risk mitigation: future directions and business applications. Int J Multidiscip Res 6(5):1–23

Ismail MM, Haq MA (2024) Enhancing enterprise financial fraud detection using machine learning. Eng Technol Appl Sci Res 14(4):14854–14861

Kamuangu P (2024) A review on financial fraud detection using AI and machine learning. J Econ Financ Account Stud 6(1):67–77

Lee C-W, Fu M-W, Wang C-C, Azis MI (2025) Evaluating machine learning algorithms for financial fraud detection: insights from Indonesia. Mathematics 13(4):1–35

Li C, Zong Z, Qie H, Fang Y, Liu Q (2023) CiteSpace and bibliometric analysis of published research on forest ecosystem services for the period 2018–2022. Land 12(845):1–16

Lin AK (2024) The AI revolution in financial services: emerging methods for fraud detection and prevention. Jurnal Galaksi (Global Knowledge, Artificial Intelligence and Information System) 1(1):43–51

Lonto MP, Sukoharsono EG, Baridwan Z, Prihatiningtias YW (2023) The effectiveness of internal audit for fraud prevention. Australas Account, Bus Financ J 17(3):171–190

Miao Z (2024) Financial fraud detection and prevention: automated approach based on deep learning. J Organ End User Comput 36(1):1–3

Muncahyani DA, Muhsyaf SA, Pituringsih E (2024) Determinants of fraud prevention with monitoring center for prevention (MCP) as moderation. Int J Multicult Multireligious Underst 11(2):380–396

Murtanto, Ferisanti, Banjarnahor E (2022) Determinants of fraud prevention in village fund management with organizational justice as moderator. Indones Manag Account Res 21(1):1–16

Mutua Musyoki K (2023) Internal control systems and their role in financial fraud prevention in Kenya. Afr J Commer Stud 3(3):173–180

Nan D, Zhao X, Chen C, Sun S, Lee KR, Kim JH (2025) Bibliometric analysis on ChatGPT research with CiteSpace. Information 16(38):1–13

Njoku DO, Iwuchukwu VC, Jibiri JE, Ikwuazom CT, Ofoegbu CI, Nwokoma FO (2024) Machine learning approach for fraud detection system in financial institution: a web base application. Int J Eng Res Dev 20(4):1–12

Novatiani RA, Kusumah RWR, Yadiati W, Rachmat RAH, Rachman AA (2024) Internal auditor competence and internal control: Improving internal audit quality to prevent fraudulent financial statements. Cogent Bus Manag 11(1):1–16

Nugroho DA, Sari R, Kuntadi C (2023) Factors affecting fraud prevention: organizational culture, human resource competence and the role of the internal auditor. Dinasti Int J Educ Manag Soc Sci 4(4):629

Premrl P, Dobovšek B, Slak B (2025) Complexities in defining and investigating financial crime. Secur J 38(55):1–31

Odufisan OI, Abhulimen OV, Ogunti EO (2025) Harnessing artificial intelligence and machine learning for fraud detection and prevention in Nigeria. J Econ Criminol 7:1–9

Oyedotun SA, Oise GP, Akilo BE, Nwabuokei OC, Ejenarhome PO, Fole M, Onwuzo CJ (2025) The role of internal audit in fraud detection and prevention: a multi-contextual review and research agenda. J Sci Res Rev 2(2):76–85

Putra I, Sulistiyo U, Diah E, Rahayu S, Hidayat S (2022) The influence of internal audit, risk management, whistleblowing system and big data analytics on the financial crime behavior prevention. Cogent Econ Financ 10(1):1–27

Roszkowska P (2021) Fintech in financial reporting and audit for fraud prevention and safeguarding equity investments. J Account Organ Chang 17(2):164–196

Shonhadji N, Irwandi SA (2024) Fraud prevention in the Indonesian banking sector using anti-fraud strategy. Banks Bank Syst 19(1):12–23

Sigetova K, Uzikova L, Dotsenko T, Boyko A (2022) Recent trends in the financial crime of the world. Financ Credit Act: Probl Theory Pract 5(46):259

Supriadi T, Tjakrawala K, Suryadnyana NA, Enyke Sjam JV, Marota R (2025) Fraud prevention in the public sector: the role of internal audit. Econ Stud J 34(3):170–183

Trabelsi MA (2024) The impact of artificial intelligence on economic development. J Electron Bus Digit Econ 3(2):142–155

Wahyuandari W (2025) The role of forensic auditing in detecting and preventing financial fraud in organizations. J Acad Sci 2(1):217

Wang Z, Shen Q, Bi S, Fu C (2024) AI empowers data mining models for financial fraud detection and prevention systems. Procedia Comput Sci 243:891–899

Wahib MFN, Rohman A (2024) A bibliometric analysis of the financial fraud detection literature-from 2004 to 2024. J Econ Financ Manag Stud 7(9):5855–5867

Wang B, Bian JJ, Xu YS, Liu D (2025) The role of internal control on financial fraud: evidence of pre-fraud and post-punishment from Chinese firms. Emerging markets finance and trade. Taylor Fr JS 61(5):1446–1459

Georgiana Burlacu is a third-year Ph.D. student in Accounting at the Doctoral School of Economics and Business Administration in Iaşi. Her interest in this field came after completing her bachelor's and master's studies, as well as after the practical experience that further amplified her desire for knowledge and contribution in the field of accounting.

Ioan-Bogdan Robu is a Ph.D. professor in the Department of Accounting, Economic Informatics, and Statistics and a Ph.D. supervisor in the Doctoral School of Economics and Business Administration at the Faculty of Economics and Business Administration at the "Alexandru Ioan Cuza" University of Iaşi. He has advanced training and has made numerous contributions in areas such as financial auditing, financial reporting, the quality of financial information, and financial statistics and econometrics.

Social, Ethical, and Regulatory Aspects of Financial Crime

The Asymmetric Impact of Different Types of Taxes on the Level of Corruption and Shadow Economy Among Developed and Developing Countries

Monica Violeta Achim, Viorela Ligia Văidean, Nawazish Mirza, and Neli Muntean

Abstract The purpose of our research is to estimate the effects of state revenues from various types of taxes upon the corruption and shadow economy phenomena for a generous sample of worldwide countries. We validate the quadratic approach for the impact of taxes upon financial and economic crime phenomena. Corporate and individual income taxes, as well as property and goods and services taxes hold a more pronounced impact on both corruption and shadow economy of developed countries, as compared to developing countries, the steepness of the (inversely) U-shaped curve being lighter for the latter. Social contributions and taxes on payroll and workforce slightly support the parametric approach. The inflection points stand as threshold values that draw important exclamation marks in terms of public policies, in order to use taxes as a means of decreasing financial and economic crime phenomena. Those thresholds express the resilience levels of those groups of countries, as maximum or minimum points of the specific taxes, beyond which the trend of financial and economic crime phenomena is reversed.

Keywords Taxes · Corruption · Shadow economy · Quadratic approach

JEL codes E62 · H26

M. V. Achim (✉) · V. L. Văidean
Faculty of Economics and Business Administration, Babeş-Bolyai University, Cluj-Napoca, Romania
e-mail: monica.achim@econ.ubbcluj.ro

V. L. Văidean
e-mail: viorela.vaidean@econ.ubbcluj.ro

N. Mirza
CERIIM, Excelia Business School, La Rochelle, France

N. Muntean
Faculty of Economic and Business Engineering, Technical University of Moldova, Chisinau, Republic of Moldova
e-mail: neli.muntean@adm.utm.md

M. V. Achim (ed.), *Financial Crime in the Digital Era*, Contributions to Finance and Accounting, https://doi.org/10.1007/978-3-032-20198-0_14

1 Introduction

Fiscal policy is frequently associated with corruption and shadow economy. People and firms bribe officials to achieve their personal objectives, which may include avoiding taxes and regulations or obtaining public contracts (Fjeldstad 2003; Amara and Khlif 2018; Sun 2021). However, the impact of different types of taxes is different among the incentives for corruption (Dreher and Schneider 2010; Torgler and Schneider 2009; McGee 2012; Achim et al. 2018). In addition, due to the specific patterns of countries, the impact of tax burden on the level corruption and shadow economy significantly differs among the developed and developing counties (Achim et al. 2023; Awasthi and Bayraktar 2015; Liu and Feng 2015). Tax laws imposed by the government play a significant role in both the corruption and shadow economy phenomena, in relation with economic growth. A wide range of studies have addressed the effect of tax burdens on corruption and shadow economy. The idea that the shadow economy is growing as fiscal pressure increases is supported by a main strand of papers (Torgler and Schneider 2009).

However, another set of studies (Friedman et al. 2000; Kawano and Slemrod 2016) refutes the existence of such a causal relationship. A relationship under a Laffer curve, however, is shown by a third category of studies (Busato and Chiarini 2013), which reflects how an increase in tax pressure determines the increase in tax revenues up to a maximum point, after which tax revenues start to drop (Wang et al. 2012; Achim et al. 2023). So, the literature suggests that certain fiscal policies may work in some countries, but not in others. This work intends to fill a gap in literature about the impact of taxes on the level of corruption and shadow economy, accounting both for the types of taxes and the degree of development of countries. So, we fundament the following working hypotheses:

(H1): Taxes impact corruption in an asymmetrical manner.
(H2): Taxes impact shadow economy in an asymmetrical manner.

For this purpose, we use a panel data analysis conducted for the 2005–2020 time period for 57 developed and 128 developing countries, respectively.

Our findings suggest that the impact of taxes on financial crime proxies is stronger in developed countries than in developing countries. Basically, income taxes and property and goods taxes impact corruption and shadow economy in a more abrupt manner, particularly in the case of the developed countries' subsample. The quadratic approach of data is supported, explicating the relationship with a gain of 1–4% in terms of Adjusted R^2, a net gain compared to the linear approach.

The remainder of this paper is structured as follows. Section 2 describes the employed methodology and the dataset. Section 3 presents and discusses the results. In the end, Sect. 4 briefly concludes.

2 Methodology and Data

The dependent variable (financial and economic crime—FinCrime) assesses two important dimensions of financial and economic crime phenomena: first as corruption, which is expressed with the subjectively assessed scores of the Corruption Perception Index CPI offered by Transparency International (2024) that reflects the cleanliness from corruption of a worldwide country, and second as a percentage of the shadow economy SE within the Gross Domestic Product (GDP), as provided by Schneider and Asllani (2022) on the other hand.

The independent variable (Taxes) is represented by various categories of taxes and social contributions as their percentage in the GDP, namely: a) Corporate Income Tax Revenue in Percent of GDP (CorpIncome); b) Individual Income Tax Revenue in percent of GDP (IndivIncome); c) Social Contributions in Percent of GDP (SocContrib); d) Taxes on Payroll and Workforce Revenue in Percent of GDP (PayrollWork); e) Property Tax Revenue in Percent of GDP (Property) and f) Goods and Services Tax Revenue in Percent of GDP (GoodsServices) as International Monetary Fund available data. These data are provided for 185 worldwide countries by the International Monetary Fund. The time period included in our analysis is 2005–2020 for which most data are available.

We intend to find whether there exist certain differences of the impact of taxes among worldwide countries, from the point of view of their development levels, classified according to the World Bank in 57 Developed countries (_HI) and 128 Developing countries (_LI) (Appendix). The employed methodology uses the Pooled OLS method for an unbalanced panel data set, the forward estimation approach, simple linear regression and multiple quadratic approach. The parametric equation approach is used for estimating Corruption and Shadow Economy as a function of various types of Taxes through a second degree polynomial as depicted in Eq. 1.

$$FinCrime_{it} = \beta_0 + \beta_1 Taxes_{it} + \beta_2 Taxes_{it}^2 + \varepsilon_{it} \quad (1)$$

where:

$FinCrime_{it}$—proxy for the financial and economic crime dimensions of country *i* in year *t* (subjectively assessed corruption CPI_{it} and shadow economy SE_{it});
β_1—linear effect parameter;
β_2—quadratic effect parameter;
$Taxes_{it}$ –proxy for various structures of taxes of country *i* in year *t*; it includes:
$CorpIncome_{it}$—Corporate Income Tax Revenue in Percent of GDP of country *i* in year *t*
$IndivIncome_{it}$—Individual Income Tax Revenue in percent of GDP of country *i* in year *t*
$SocContrib_{it}$—Social Contributions in Percent of GDP of country *i* in year *t*
$PayrollWork_{it}$ – Taxes on Payroll and Workforce Revenue in Percent of GDP of country *i* in year *t*
$Property_{it}$—Property Tax Revenue in Percent of GDP of country *i* in year *t*

GoodsServices$_{it}$—Goods and Services Tax Revenue in Percent of GDP in country i in year t;
ε_{it}—the residuals (the difference between the actual and predicted values of the dependent variables).

The inflection points of these curves have the coordinates given by Eqs. 2 and 3, allowing us to estimate the threshold values where the curvature of the function switches from a direct impact to an indirect one or vice versa.

$$Taxes_0 = -\frac{\beta_1}{2\beta_2} \tag{2}$$

$$FinCrime_0 = f(Taxes_0) = \frac{-\beta_1^2 + 4\beta_1\beta_2}{4\beta_2} \tag{3}$$

Figures 1 and 2 graphically represent the impact of various subcategories of taxes upon CPI and SE respectively, inspiring the asymmetric impact research hypotheses of ours.

3 Results and Discussions

Tables 1–3 estimate the CPI as a function of various types of Taxes through the parametric approach reflected by Eq. 1, for all sample (Table 1), developed countries' subsample (Table 2) and developing countries' subsample (Table 3).

With few exceptions (model [3] in Table 1, models [3] and [4] in Table 2), these estimations support the quadratic approach of corruption as a function of taxes for all the three samples. Just like Figure no 1 portrays, the impact of various types of taxes upon corruption is concave (β_1 positive and β_2 negative, when significant). Basically the higher the taxation levels are, be it on corporate or individual income, or property or goods and services), the higher the subjectively assessed corruption is, up to the threshold values, beyond which higher taxation levels would no longer increase corruption. The great majority of observations find themselves on the ascending part of this second degree polynomial function, with the exception of Goods and services tax revenues. The threshold levels indicate resilience levels of nations for those taxes. Beyond those bearable tax revenues as a GDP percentage, no matter how high tax revenues would be, corruption levels decrease below their maximum attained levels provided by Eq. 3. Corruption would be constrained by a higher understanding of the fact that collecting taxes performs well for nations, reflecting itself into improved public services and public security provided by countries.

Still, threshold levels differ as development levels of countries differ. The ones estimated by models (1) in Tables 1–3 place developing nations' curvature point of CPI as a function of CorpIncome (6.0932 in Table 3) just a little below the one of

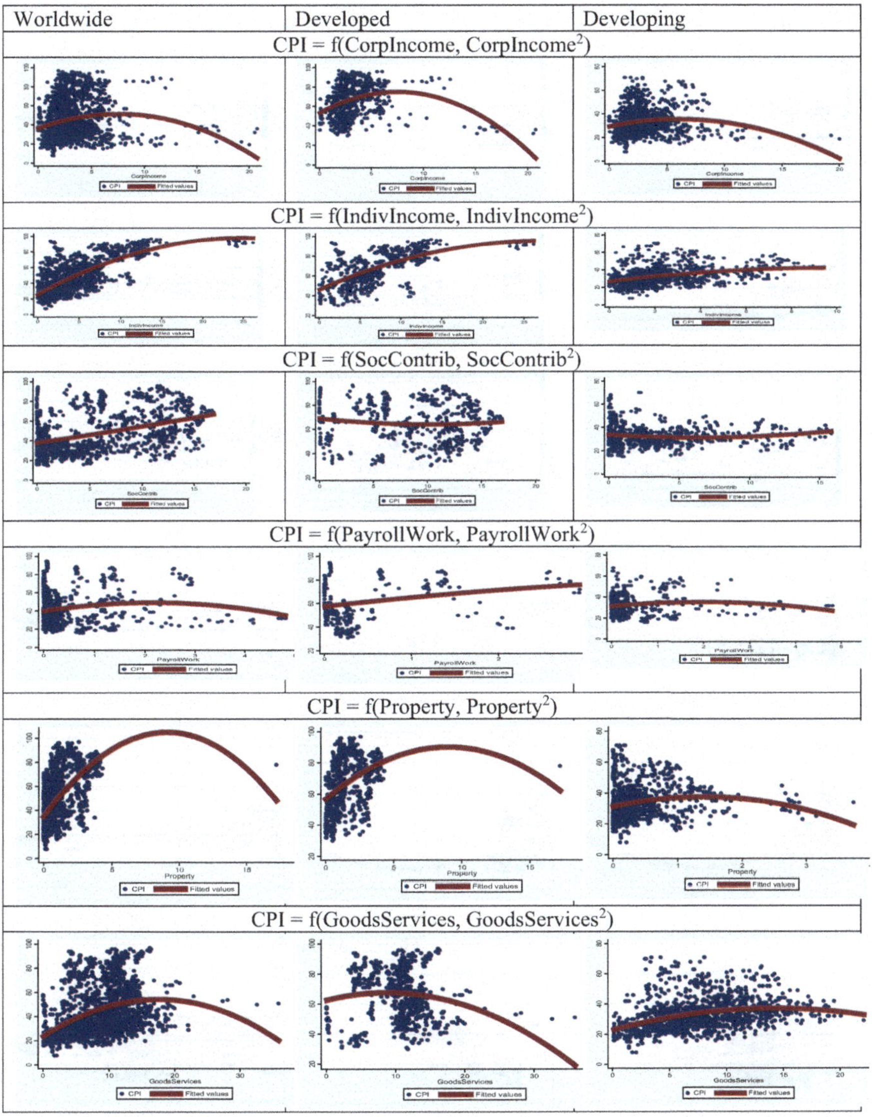

Fig. 1 Plot of taxes against CPI. *Source* Own processing

developed nations (7.5193 in Table 2). Models (2) prove individuals to be more sensitive in front of taxes than businesses are: the inflection points are 24.8438 in Table 1, for the entire sample, 27.2249 in Table 2 for the developed countries and 9.6635 in Table 3 for the developing countries, very close to the highest registered values in practice for IndivIncome. Still, the threshold is almost three times lower in developing countries compared to developed countries, the impact of individual income

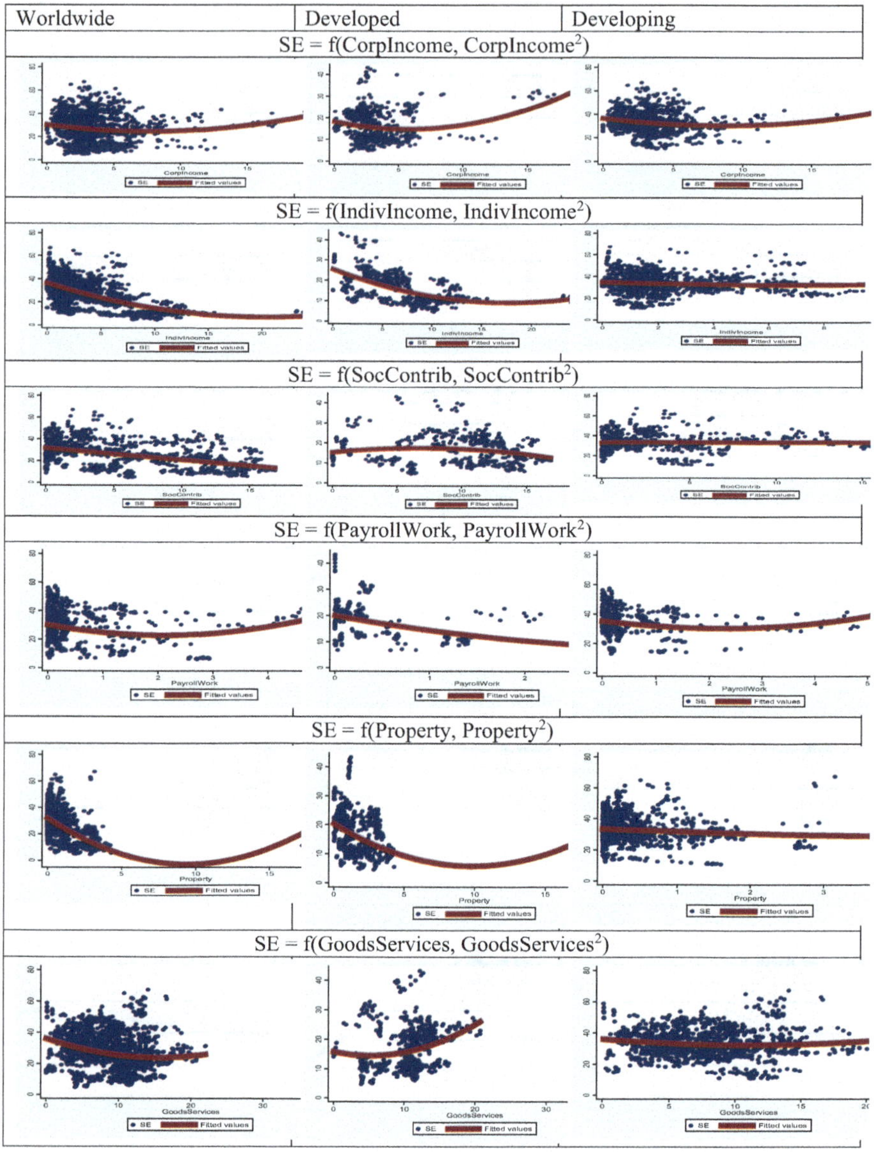

Fig. 2 Plot of taxes against SE. *Source* Own processing

taxes upon corruption being positive, with a lighter slope as taxation levels increase. A similar evolution is registered by CPI as a function of Property. Nonetheless, the evolution of CPI as a function of GoodsServices is almost flat, with lowers levels of perceived Corruption on the ordinate axis of developing countries, compared to developed ones. Summing up, from Table 1, as tax burden increase, states would

Table 1 Corruption (CPI_all), as a function of taxes (by structure), the full worldwide sample

	(1)		*(2)*		*(3)*		*(4)*	*(5)*			*(6)*	
	Simple regression OLS	Parametric regression OLS	Simple regression OLS	Parametric regression OLS	Simple regression OLS	Parametric regression OLS	Simple regression OLS	Parametric regression OLS	Simple regression OLS	Parametric regression OLS	Simple regression OLS	Parametric regression OLS
Constant	42.9276 ***	36.5736 ***	29.2454 ***	25.6589 ***	37.8622 ***	37.9687 ***	41.5881 ***	40.2711 ***	36.9701 ***	34.8587 ***	30.649 ***	23.6152 ***
CorpIncome	0.7239 ***	3.9848 ***										
CorpIncome^2		-0.2638 ***										
IndivIncome			4.0545 ***	5.8532 ***								
IndivIncome^2				-0.1178 ***								
SocContrib					1.7005 ***	1.6295 ***						
SocContrib^2						0.0051						
PayrollWork							2.652 ***	8.5444 ***				
PayrollWork^2								-1.9912 ***				
Property									11.1143 ***	15.4885 ***		
Property^2										-0.8544 ***		

(continued)

Table 1 (continued)

	(1)		*(2)*		*(3)*		*(4)*	*(5)*			*(6)*	
	Simple regression OLS	Parametric regression OLS	Simple regression OLS	Parametric regression OLS	Simple regression OLS	Parametric regression OLS	Simple regression OLS	Parametric regression OLS	Simple regression OLS	Parametric regression OLS	Simple regression OLS	Parametric regression OLS
GoodsServices											1.618 ***	3.5174 ***
$GoodsServices^2$												-0.1004 ***
Threshold ($Taxes_0$)	n/a	7.5526	n/a	24.8438	n/a	-	n/a	2.1455	n/a	9.0639	n/a	17.5169
R^2	0.0057	0.035	0.5261	0.5511	0.1645	0.1645	0.0112	0.0223	0.3009	0.3481	0.1152	0.1373
Adjusted R^2	0.0052	0.0341	0.5259	0.5506	0.1639	0.1633	0.01	0.0198	0.3006	0.3474	0.1148	0.1365
Observations	2033	2033	1980	1980	1445	1445	807	807	1893	1893	2121	2121

Notes *** designates the 1% significant coefficients, ** designates the 5% significant coefficients and * designates the 10% significant coefficients
Source Own processing

Table 2 Corruption (CPI_HI), as a function of taxes (by structure), the developed countries' subsample

	(1)		*(2)*		*(3)*		*(4)*		*(5)*		*(6)*	
	Simple regression OLS	Parametric regression OLS	Simple regression OLS	Parametric regression OLS	Simple regression OLS	Parametric regression OLS	Simple regression OLS	Parametric regression OLS	Simple regression OLS	Parametric regression OLS	Simple regression OLS	Parametric regression OLS
constant	65.3879 ***	53.2491 ***	50.5584 ***	46.1753 ***	67.7484 ***	69.3304 ***	58.0477 ***	57.7295 ***	59.6691 ***	56.8818 ***	69.8902 ***	62.6522 ***
CorpIncome	0.2209	5.8711 ***										
CorpIncome^2		-0.3904 ***										
IndivIncome			2.3498 ***	3.6427 ***								
IndivIncome^2				-0.0669 ***								
SocContrib					-0.2544 *	-0.9544 *						
SocContrib^2						0.0459						
PayrollWork							6.5982 ***	8.386 **				
PayrollWork^2								-0.7449				
Property									4.5455 ***	7.4436 ***		
Property^2										-0.4143 ***		
GoodsServices											-0.3347 **	1.1522 ***

(continued)

Table 2 (continued)

	(1)		*(2)*		*(3)*		*(4)*		*(5)*		*(6)*	
	Simple regression OLS	Parametric regression OLS	Simple regression OLS	Parametric regression OLS	Simple regression OLS	Parametric regression OLS	Simple regression OLS	Parametric regression OLS	Simple regression OLS	Parametric regression OLS	Simple regression OLS	Parametric regression OLS
$GoodsServices^2$												-0.0659 ***
Threshold ($Taxes_0$)	n/a	7.5193	n/a	27.2249	n/a	-	n/a	-	n/a	8.9833	n/a	8.742
R^2	0.001	0.1262	0.3804	0.4017	0.0055	0.0089	0.0768	0.0774	0.1162	0.1535	0.0068	0.0304
Adjusted R^2	0.0004	0.1238	0.3795	0.3999	0.0039	0.0057	0.0735	0.071	0.1149	0.1511	0.0054	0.0278
Observations	735	735	703	703	626	626	289	289	721	721	734	734

Notes *** designates the 1% significant coefficients, ** designates the 5% significant coefficients and * designates the 10% significant coefficients
Source Own processing

Table 3 Corruption (CPI_LI), as a function of taxes (by structure), the developing countries' subsample

	(1)		*(2)*		*(3)*		*(4)*		*(5)*		*(6)*	
	Simple regression OLS	Parametric regression OLS	Simple regression OLS	Parametric regression OLS	Simple regression OLS	Parametric regression OLS	Simple regression OLS	Parametric regression OLS	Simple regression OLS	Parametric regression OLS	Simple regression OLS	Parametric regression OLS
Constant	32.5305 ***	29.2867 ***	28.3092 ***	27.0019 ***	32.964 ***	33.7682 ***	32.2217 ***	31.3882 ***	32.5829 ***	31.2277 ***	26.8435 ***	22.8779 ***
CorpIncome	0.2613 *	2.0851 ***										
$CorpIncome^2$		-0.1711 ***										
IndivIncome			2.1048 ***	3.2972 ***								
$IndivIncome^2$				-0.1706 **								
SocContrib					-0.0211	-0.6921 **						
$SocContrib^2$						0.0571 ***						
PayrollWork							0.8405	4.3232 ***				
$PayrollWork^2$								-1.0779 ***				
Property									2.4146 ***	9.5601 ***		
$Property^2$										-3.4119 ***		

(continued)

Table 3 (continued)

	(1)		*(2)*		*(3)*		*(4)*		*(5)*		*(6)*	
	Simple regression OLS	Parametric regression OLS	Simple regression OLS	Parametric regression OLS	Simple regression OLS	Parametric regression OLS	Simple regression OLS	Parametric regression OLS	Simple regression OLS	Parametric regression OLS	Simple regression OLS	Parametric regression OLS
GoodsServices											0.8136 ***	2.0345 ***
GoodsServices^2												-0.0716 ***
Threshold (Taxes_0)	n/a	6.0932	n/a	9.6635	n/a	6.0604	n/a	2.0053	n/a	1.4009	n/a	14.2074
R^2	0.0024	0.034	0.1241	0.1287	0.0012	0.0086	0.0044	0.0193	0.0136	0.0389	0.0956	0.1156
Adjusted R^2	0.0017	0.0325	0.1234	0.1273	0.0001	0.0062	0.0025	0.0155	0.0128	0.0373	0.095	0.1143
Observations	1298	1298	1277	1277	819	819	518	518	1172	1172	1387	1387

Notes *** designates the 1% significant coefficients, ** designates the 5% significant coefficients and * designates the 10% significant coefficients
Source Own processing

collect less, due to enlarged corruption. Still, the steepness of the curves in Fig. 1 is milder for developing countries, as reflected by the estimations in Table 3 as well.

To continue with, Tables 4–6 estimate SE as a function of various types of tax burdens, both direct and indirect, through the parametric approach depicted in Eq. 1, for all sample (Table 4), developed countries' subsample (Table 5) and developing countries' subsample (Table 6).

With some exceptions (model [3] in Table 4, model [4] in Table 5 and models [2], [3] and [5] in Table 6), our estimations support the quadratic approach of SE as a function of taxes for all the three samples.

The graphical representations in Fig. 2 are convex. These U-shaped impacts of taxes on the SE point out the fact that as tax burdens increase, SE levels decrease, up to a certain level of threshold taxes beyond which the SE increases with taxes. Basically, worldwide shadow economy seems to be discouraged up to the threshold values of tax burdens in Table 4.

Keeping in mind that SE levels are higher on average in developing countries, as compared to developed countries (see the ordinate values in Fig. 2), it's interesting to notice that threshold tax burdens differ between sampled countries. The tax burden threshold in CorpIncome is 5.7464 for developed countries (model [1], Table 5) and 8.4834 for developing countries (model [1], Table 6), thus a higher endurance above which SE starts to increase with taxes in developing countries, compared to developed countries. This resilience is also validated by the threshold levels of GoodsServices tax burdens: 5.2426 in model (6), Table 5 and 11.23 in model (6), Table 6, so developing countries are more that two times more resilient than developed countries. Basically, resilience levels differ on types of taxes, and they vary with the development levels of countries supporting our working hypotheses *H1* and *H2*, robust to alternative measures of tax structures. Our models are robust to time fixed effects, the use of quantile regression analysis and the addition of unemployment rates and or population growth rates as control variables.

4 Conclusions

Our study is among the very few that validates the quadratic approach of taxes' impact upon financial crime phenomena. We believe fiscal policies of nations need to be adapted to the development levels of states, various tax burden resilience levels being innovatively validated through this study for several categories of taxes, up to which corruption and shadow economy are hampered. As such, for corporate income tax revenues above 7.55% in GDP (7.72% for shadow economy), these financial and economic crime phenomena start to develop, extra caution being needed on behalf of regulators. For property taxes, the resilience threshold is at 9.06% of GDP (9.46% for shadow economy), for the worldwide nations. Globally, these thresholds are higher than the mean values of these tax categories, thus taxation policies should consider these thresholds as red flags. The heterogeneity analysis of subsampled countries according to their development levels identifies peculiarities. Throughout

Table 4 Shadow Economy (SE_all), as a function of taxes (by structure), for the full worldwide sample

	(1)		*(2)*		*(3)*		*(4)*		*(5)*		*(6)*	
	Simple regression OLS	Parametric regression OLS	Simple regression OLS	Parametric regression OLS	Simple regression OLS	Parametric regression OLS	Simple regression OLS	Parametric regression OLS	Simple regression OLS	Parametric regression OLS	Simple regression OLS	Parametric regression OLS
constant	28.1645 ***	30.5809 ***	34.7026 ***	36.8797 ***	32.2377 ***	32.2816 ***	29.1738 ***	30.6265 ***	31.2405 ***	32.2245 ***	33.3575 ***	36.4563 ***
CorpIncome	-0.2748 **	-1.4825 ***										
CorpIncome^2		0.096 ***										
IndivIncome			-1.8005 ***	-2.8838 ***								
IndivIncome^2				0.0705 ***								
SocContrib					-1.0895 ***	-1.1186 ***						
SocContrib^2						0.0021						
PayrollWork							-1.2675 ***	-7.1432 ***				
PayrollWork^2								1.6858 ***				
Property									-5.3613 ***	-7.3711 ***		
Property^2										0.3894 ***		

(continued)

Table 4 (continued)

	(1)		*(2)*		*(3)*		*(4)*		*(5)*		*(6)*	
	Simple regression OLS	Parametric regression OLS	Simple regression OLS	Parametric regression OLS	Simple regression OLS	Parametric regression OLS	Simple regression OLS	Parametric regression OLS	Simple regression OLS	Parametric regression OLS	Simple regression OLS	Parametric regression OLS
GoodsServices											-0.6825 ***	-1.5715 ***
GoodsServices^2												0.0503 ***
Threshold (Taxes_0)	n/a	7.7213	n/a	20.4525	n/a	-	n/a	2.1186	n/a	9.4647	n/a	15.6213
R^2	0.0025	0.0145	0.326	0.3542	0.204	0.204	0.0091	0.0452	0.2358	0.2691	0.0550	0.0626
Adjusted R^2	0.0020	0.0135	0.3257	0.3535	0.2034	0.2028	0.0079	0.0428	0.2354	0.2683	0.0545	0.0616
Observations	1901	1901	1844	1844	1366	1366	798	798	1766	1766	1985	1985

Notes *** designates the 1% significant coefficients, ** designates the 5% significant coefficients and * designates the 10% significant coefficients
Source Own processing

Table 5 Shadow Economy (SE_HI), as a function of taxes (by structure), the developed countries' subsample

	(1)		*(2)*		*(3)*		*(4)*		*(5)*		*(6)*	
	Simple regression OLS	Parametric regression OLS	Simple regression OLS	Parametric regression OLS	Simple regression OLS	Parametric regression OLS	Simple regression OLS	Parametric regression OLS	Simple regression OLS	Parametric regression OLS	Simple regression OLS	Parametric regression OLS
constant	15.1201 ***	18.5199 ***	22.0533 ***	25.7224 ***	17.4431 ***	15.5057 ***	19.8908 ***	20.2286 ***	19.4986 ***	20.5611 ***	12.3943 ***	15.9774 ***
CorpIncome	0.3523 ***	-1.2171 ***										
$CorpIncome^2$		0.1059 ***										
IndivIncome			-0.8154 ***	-1.8335 ***								
$IndivIncome^2$				0.0511 ***								
SocContrib					-0.0983	0.6538 ***						
$SocContrib^2$						-0.0475 ***						
PayrollWork							-4.4896 ***	-6.4099 ***				
$PayrollWork^2$								0.8012				
Property									-1.8888 ***	-2.9551 ***		
$Property^2$										0.1495 ***		

(continued)

Table 5 (continued)

	(1)		*(2)*		*(3)*		*(4)*		*(5)*		*(6)*	
	Simple regression OLS	Parametric regression OLS	Simple regression OLS	Parametric regression OLS	Simple regression OLS	Parametric regression OLS	Simple regression OLS	Parametric regression OLS	Simple regression OLS	Parametric regression OLS	Simple regression OLS	Parametric regression OLS
GoodsServices											0.4021 ***	-0.4991 *
$GoodsServices^2$												0.0476 ***
Threshold ($Taxes_0$)	n/a	5.7464	n/a	17.9403	n/a	6.8821	n/a	-	n/a	9.8832	n/a	5.2426
R^2	0.014	0.0658	0.246	0.3131	0.0038	0.0212	0.1995	0.2038	0.1069	0.1334	0.0412	0.058
Adjusted R^2	0.0125	0.0631	0.2448	0.311	0.0021	0.0178	0.1966	0.198	0.1056	0.1308	0.0398	0.0552
Observations	687	687	655	655	581	581	276	276	679	679	691	691

Notes *** designates the 1% significant coefficients, ** designates the 5% significant coefficients and * designates the 10% significant coefficients
Source Own processing

Table 6 Shadow Economy (SE_LI), as a function of taxes (by structure), the developing countries' subsample

	(1)		*(2)*		*(3)*		*(4)*		*(5)*		*(6)*	
	Simple regression OLS	Parametric regression OLS	Simple regression OLS	Parametric regression OLS	Simple regression OLS	Parametric regression OLS	Simple regression OLS	Parametric regression OLS	Simple regression OLS	Parametric regression OLS	Simple regression OLS	Parametric regression OLS
constant	35.2034 ***	36.95 ***	34.5542 ***	34.9414 ***	33.5208 ***	33.4272 ***	34.5783 ***	35.6181 ***	33.6649 ***	33.7283 ***	34.6707 ***	36.35 ***
CorpIncome	-0.5371 ***	-1.4863 ***										
$CorpIncome^2$		0.0876 ***										
IndivIncome			-0.3561 **	-0.7141								
$IndivIncome^2$				0.0506								
SocContrib					0.0191	0.0991						
$SocContrib^2$						-0.0068						
PayrollWork							-0.6213	-4.5945 ***				
$PayrollWork^2$								1.0344 ***				
Property									-1.5389 ***	-1.8833		
$Property^2$										0.1622		
GoodsServices											-0.1576 **	-0.6604 ***

(continued)

Table 6 (continued)

	(1)		*(2)*		*(3)*		*(4)*		*(5)*		*(6)*	
	Simple regression OLS	Parametric regression OLS	Simple regression OLS	Parametric regression OLS	Simple regression OLS	Parametric regression OLS	Simple regression OLS	Parametric regression OLS	Simple regression OLS	Parametric regression OLS	Simple regression OLS	Parametric regression OLS
GoodsServices^2												0.0294 **
Threshold ($Taxes_0$)	n/a	8.4834	n/a	-	n/a	-	n/a	2.2208	n/a	-	n/a	11.23
R^2	0.0141	0.0254	0.0048	0.0053	0.0012	0.0024	0.0043	0.0307	0.0082	0.0083	0.0044	0.0086
Adjusted R^2	0.0133	0.0238	0039	0.0036	0.00001	0.0002	0.0024	0.0269	0.0073	0.0065	0.0036	0.0071
Observations	1214	1214	1189	1189	785	785	522	522	1087	1087	1294	1294

Notes *** designates the 1% significant coefficients, ** designates the 5% significant coefficients and * designates the 10% significant coefficients
Source Own processing

the covered time period Angola reduced its corporate income tax levels (their so called **"Imposto Industrial"**), and so have Kazakhstan, Norway and Papua New Guinea, further reducing their shadow economy levels. Still, the limitations of our study refer to more recent data constrains and the possibility to further develop this methodology. Supplementary research would be needed for the social contributions and payroll work taxes, further considering the opportunity to conduct mediation effect analysis as well.

References

Achim MV, Mirza N, Văidean VL (2023) The asymmetric impact of tax burden structures on the shadow economy: a panel analysis of old and new European Union countries. Appl Econ Lett 30(16):2179–2188. https://doi.org/10.1080/13504851.2022.2094876

Achim MV, Borlea NS, Anghelina A (2018) The impact of fiscal policies on corruption: a panel analysis. SAJEMS 21(1):1–9. https://doi.org/10.4102/sajems.v21i1.1970

Amara I, Khlif H (2018) Financial crime, corruption and tax evasion: a cross-country investigation. J Money Laund Control 21(4):545–554. https://doi.org/10.1108/JMLC-10-2017-0059

Awasthi R, Bayraktar N (2015) Can tax simplification help lower tax corruption? Eurasian Econ Rev 5:297–330. https://doi.org/10.1007/s40822-015-0014-9

Busato F, Chiarini B (2013) Steady state Laffer curve with the underground economy. Public Finance Rev 41(5):608–632. https://doi.org/10.1177/1091142113487006

Corruption Perception Index (2024) Corruption Perception Index statistics reports by Transparency International

Dreher A, Schneider F (2010) Corruption and the shadow economy. An empirical analysis. Public Choice 144(1):215–238. https://doi.org/10.1007/s11127-009-9513-0

Fjeldstad OH (2003) Fighting fiscal corruption: lessons from the Tanzania revenue authority. Public Adm Dev 23:165–175. https://doi.org/10.1002/pad.278

Friedman E, Johnson S, Kaufmann D, Zoido-Lobaton P (2000) Dodging the grabbing hand: the determinants of unofficial activities in 69 countries. J Public Econ 76:459–493. https://doi.org/10.1016/S0047-2727(99)00093-6

Kawano L, Slemrod J (2016) How do corporate tax bases change when corporate tax rates change? With implications for the tax rate elasticity of corporate tax revenues. Int Tax Public Financ 23(3):401–433. https://doi.org/10.1007/s10797-015-9375-y

Liu Y, Feng H (2015) Tax structure and corruption: cross-country evidence. Public Choice 162:57–78. https://doi.org/10.1007/s11127-014-0194-y

McGee RW (2012) The ethics of tax evasion: perspectives in theory and practice. Springer, North Miami, FL

Schneider FH, Asllani A (2022) Taxation of the informal economy in the EU. European Parliament

Sun Y (2021) Corporate tax avoidance and government corruption: evidence from Chinese firms. Econ Model 98:13–25. https://doi.org/10.1016/j.econmod.2021.02.008

Torgler B, Schneider F (2009) The impact of tax morale and institutional quality on the shadow economy. J Econ Psychol 30(3):228–245. https://doi.org/10.1016/j.joep.2008.08.004

Wang DH-M, Yu H-KT, Hu HC (2012) On the asymmetric relationship between the size of the underground economy and the change in effective tax rate in Taiwan. Econ Lett 117(1):340–343. https://doi.org/10.1016/j.econlet.2012.04.041

Monica Violeta Achim is a professor and doctoral supervisor in Finance at the Faculty of Economic Sciences and Business Administration, Babeş-Bolyai University, Cluj-Napoca. With over 27 years of experience in academia, she has published, as author and co-author, over 140 scientific articles and 27 books. The main research topics are financial analysis, business performance, finance, and economic and financial crime. In 2020, she obtained the Award for Excellence in Scientific Research, at Babeş-Bolyai University, Faculty of Economics and Business Administration, Cluj-Napoca, Romania, as a recognition of the results obtained in the research activity. She leads a main national project in the area of financial crime in the period 2020–2023. In the business environment, she works in liberal professions as an accountant expert, tax consultant, and judicial expert; from this perspective, being involved in solving many cases of economic and financial crime of the Palace of Justice, Cluj-Napoca.

Viorela Ligia Văidean obtained a Bachelor Degree in Finance and Banking from 'Babeş-Bolyai' University (BBU) Cluj-Napoca, Romania in 2006, further graduating a Master program in Corporate Finance and Insurances and another one in Project Management and Evaluation. She successfully followed a full time PhD program, obtaining the PhD title in the Finance field, in 2010. In 2015 she graduated a postdoctoral study program. She has worked as a Teaching Assistant and then a Lecturer, for the Finance Department within BBU Cluj-Napoca. She has also worked as an Expert for different EU financed projects and grants. She has published more than 40 research papers and attended several international conferences. She has been the author or coauthor of ten books and international book chapters. Her research interests cover the areas of Health Economics, Corporate Finance, Financial Management, Organized Crime and Fiscal Policies.

Dr. Nawazish Mirza obtained a Doctorate in Management Science, specialising in Finance, from the University of Paris Dauphine in 2010. He has more than 15 years of experience in consulting and teaching in Australia, Singapore, the United Arab Emirates and France. His areas of teaching and research focus on Financial Intermediation, Financial Valuation, Risk Management and Financial Statement Analysis. Dr Elahi regularly appears in renowned international media (CNBC, China Daily, Gulf News etc.) talking about international economic and financial issues. He is also the editor in chief of the *Journal of Risk Finance*, co-editor of *Economic Research*, associate editor of *Journal of Sustainable Finance and Investment*, and guest editor of *Energy Economics*, *Resources Policy*, and *Climate Change Economics*.

Neli Muntean holds a PhD in Economics and is an Associate Professor in the Department of Economics and Management, Faculty of Economic and Business Engineering, Technical University of Moldova, Chisinau, Republic of Moldova. She holds the quality of Doctoral Supervisor in the specialties of Accounting, Audit, Economic analysis and Finance. She has 23 years' experience in the academic field. She is author/co-author of more than 100 scientific works (monographs, books, scientific articles, conferences papers). Starting with June 2022 she became a titular member of the Regional Commission of Economic and Research Experts (CREES) of Francophone Universities Agency (AUF), Central and Eastern Europe Regional Directorate. During the period 2016–2025 she was director/member of more than 10 scientific/institutional projects. Now she is Member of the Commission of Experts in the field of Economic Sciences, Sociology, Media and Communication of the National Agency for Quality Assurance in Education and Research of Republic of Moldova. Since 2015s she is a Member of the Romanian Society of Economic and Financial Analysis, SRAEF.

Corporate Deception or the Illusion of Sustainability? A Critical Look at Greenwashing Practices

Ruben Pop and Monica Violeta Achim

Abstract Corporate controversies are publicly observable events that are expected to have negative implications for a company, as they jeopardize its reputation, undermine stakeholders' trust, and can seriously impact its environmental, social, and governance (ESG) sustainability.

Focusing on these negative, often unexpected news events plays a crucial role in analyzing the evolution of ESG scores. When public controversies arise—such as pollution scandals, human rights violations, or a lack of transparency in governance—ESG scores may be adjusted rapidly, reflecting a new, more realistic and critical understanding of the risks associated with the company.

The findings highlight that corporate controversies influence not only the assessment of reputation and long-term risks but also the investment decisions and social responsibility strategies adopted by market participants.

The analysis of controversies becomes a valuable tool for stakeholders to understand the dynamics of perception and to anticipate their impact on a company's value and sustainability.

Keywords Corporate controversies · Greenwashing · Non-financial reporting

1 Introducere

ESG (Environmental, Social, and Governance) controversies refer to incidents, activities, or practices of a company that have a negative impact or pose risks to the environment, society, or aspects of corporate governance (DasGupta 2022; Franco 2020; Passas et al. 2022).

R. Pop (✉) · M. V. Achim
Faculty of Economics and Business Administration, Babeş-Bolyai University, Cluj-Napoca, Romania
e-mail: ruben.pop@econ.ubbcluj.ro

M. V. Achim
e-mail: monica.achim@econ.ubbcluj.ro

M. V. Achim (ed.), *Financial Crime in the Digital Era*, Contributions to Finance and Accounting, https://doi.org/10.1007/978-3-032-20198-0_15

Aouadi and Marsat (2018) clarify that ESG controversies refer to corporate news related to ESG issues, including cases of questionable social conduct and product scandals, which attract substantial media coverage and, consequently, investor interest. Such news events can cast doubt on a firm's future prospects, pose a reputational risk, and influence the overall value of the firm.

In recent years, ESG controversies have received increasing attention due to companies' involvement in controversial activities. Companies are penalized by investors and regulators for their unethical practices (Carberry et al. 2018). Investors divest from companies' shares, and regulators impose fines and penalties (Karpoff et al. 2005).

ESG engagement can be shaped by informal institutions such as social norms, values, culture, and cognitive systems, in addition to formal institutional constraints. Among these, public perceptions serve as a dominant symbol of informal institutions to affect ESG adoptions. Public perceptions can be viewed from three aspects: knowledge, awareness, and sentiment. In the context of ESG development, the knowledge aspect reflects public understanding of the basic ideas and principles related to ESG. Public awareness focuses on attention and concerns about ESG issues, while sentiment reflects public feelings and attitudes toward ESG (Costa and Menichini 2013).

In the absence of mandatory disclosure, the media disseminates information about companies' ESG aspects, and the intensity and scope of media criticism can influence investors' assessment of ESG risks (Asante-Appiah 2020).

Although scientific literature on ESG has grown significantly over the past decade, there is still a notable gap in understanding and conceptualizing ESG controversies. Most studies focus on the positive impact of ESG performance on corporate reputation, market value, or access to finance, but insufficiently address the conflicting and ambiguous dimension of ESG practices. The lack of an integrative framework, the underanalysis of the pandemic's effect on the media coverage and credibility of ESG practices, and the insufficiency of comparative studies are the main gaps. The COVID-19 pandemic has brought intense media coverage of ESG controversies to the forefront, generating public pressure that has paradoxically led to an apparent improvement in non-financial reporting, often through greenwashing.

Based on the research objective and the contributions of this paper to the previous literature, the structure of the article is as follows: Sect. 1 provides a brief review of the previous studies to clarify the gaps in the literature, which the literature seeks to fill. Section 2 captures the research methodology used, Sect. 3 includes the results, Sect. 4 includes discussions and Sect. 5 includes conclusions, limitations of the research and the premises for future research.

2 Literature Review

The materiality of ESG controversies can affect firms' financial performance in several ways, such as violations of environmental policies leading to fines and penalties, damage to firms' reputations leading to stock price volatility, and increased cost of capital due to lower credit ratings (Agoraki et al. 2023; Jebe 2019).

Although significant clarifications have been made on how to mitigate the negative effects of ESG controversies, less is known about how to prevent ESG controversies from arising or what their potential might be. A recent study by Treepongkaruna et al. (2022), focusing on the effect of external governance instruments on ESG controversies, found that a decrease in the risk of shareholder litigation leads to a significant decrease in ESG controversies, as managers intentionally avoid risky and controversial activities.

Einwiller and Carroll (2020) concluded in their analysis of self-reported controversies that firms are expected to disclose those negative ESG issues that will inevitably become known, while concealing those that are less likely to become public. However, Schwoy et al. (2025) conclude that even within public controversies, there is prioritization around which deviations are disclosed and which are concealed, resulting in highly selective and minimal disclosure of ESG controversies. The fact that only truly controversial issues have been published in sustainability reports/sections further shows that companies are trying to keep their sustainability information as clean as possible from negative contributions and therefore continue to use their sustainability reports/sections primarily as marketing tools. The authors' main finding concerns the fact that companies adopt a certain disclosure strategy with regard to ESG controversies:

1. They disclose controversies involving anticipated litigation only in their annual reports, due to the legal obligation arising from financial reporting.
2. They disclose only controversies that have attracted significant media attention in reports/sections on sustainability.
3. All other controversies are not disclosed at all.

Corporate scandals can be defined as widely publicized incidents involving allegations of managerial misconduct or unethical behaviour by one or more members of the company (Dyck et al. 2010).

Corporate scandals can be grouped into four main categories: environmental disasters, human rights violations, product recalls, and corporate crimes. Environmental disasters are related to the company's environmental sustainability (E), human rights violations and product recalls to the company's social sustainability (S), and finally, corporate crimes are usually related to corporate governance (G) (Utz 2019).

Pop et al. (2025) highlight that before the COVID-19 pandemic, greenwashing focused mainly on communicating general concepts such as "eco-friendly," "biodegradable," or "sustainable," without providing concrete or standardized evidence. Companies targeted product attributes in particular (e.g., "green" packaging, "natural" ingredients), appealing to the emotions of environmentally conscious consumers. After the pandemic, however, greenwashing underwent a significant transition. The global context emphasized the importance of social responsibility and climate resilience. Nowadays, companies no longer promote individual products as "green," but position their entire business model as sustainable, using more complex terms such as "carbon neutrality," "net-zero emissions," "circular economy," and "diversity and inclusion" as part of their ESG reporting.

A company's risks reflect uncertainty about its future performance and should impact analysts' performance in terms of their reporting and forecasting about companies. Therefore, it is important to understand the impact that media reporting of ESG incidents has on risk. First, ESG scandals tarnish a firm's reputation and affect stakeholders' trust in the firm. Second, ESG incidents covered by the press could generate potential litigation costs, regulatory fines, and other costs, which are often uncertain in terms of the actual amount that will be incurred. Third, media coverage of ESG incidents could trigger strategic changes on the part of a firm, making its future prospects uncertain. Strategic changes by the firm, which are made in response to media exposure of ESG incidents rather than to increase its competitive advantage, could lead to uncertain performance by the firm. In addition, a company whose ESG incidents are reported by the media may conceal other negative news about the company to prevent damage to the company's reputation and mitigate the potential negative consequences of the reported ESG incidents. This inappropriate behaviour increases the opacity of information about the company. Thus, media coverage of ESG incidents could cause high commercial risk and high informational risk for companies (He and Li 2024).

Among the many components of reputation are aspects related to the perceptions of stakeholders, who form their opinions, feelings, and overall sentiments about companies as they interact with them or receive information (Gray and Balmer 1998). Based on this, Fombrun (2005) proposes that reputations are based on stakeholders' impressions of companies' actions and policies, mainly those related to meeting social and ethical criteria. Perceptions of trust, for example, indicate that stakeholders believe the organization will remain true to its goals, fulfilling what is expected of it.

Media coverage also plays a crucial role in influencing corporate ESG performance, serving as an external monitoring mechanism. For example, He et al. (2024) show that increased media attention correlates with improved ESG performance, as media coverage reduces information asymmetry and attracts the attention of analysts, increasing external oversight of firms. This effect is particularly pronounced for non-state-owned firms and those that voluntarily disclose ESG information.

Wong and Zhang (2022) show that negative ESG media coverage significantly affects firm valuation because investors consider corporate reputation to be a valuable intangible asset.

Firms can influence stakeholder perceptions and optimize their reputation through impression management behaviours. For example, public statements, CSR activities, and brand-building initiatives (Highhouse et al. 2009).

The use of impression management strategies, such as charitable donations, information concealment, and positive image promotion, can lead to significant divergences in stakeholders' perceptions of firms. Such disparities have the potential to lead to substantial losses for companies, including the loss of ESG investors and perceptions of hypocrisy among investors. Therefore, companies need to engage in CSR activities in a sustained, comprehensive, and consistent manner, focusing on institutional development and practicing genuine commitment to build a truly responsible image (He Chen and Zhu 2025).

The taxonomy considered by Ozsozgun Caliskan et al. (2021) divides communication tactics (impression management) into three different categories: assertive, performance-oriented, and defensive. Assertive tactics aim to create a positive image of the company's operations and enhance its reputation. Performance tactics inform stakeholders about the company's achievements in numerical or percentage terms and allow comparisons with previous years, highlighting the most positive data. Defensive tactics play a role when the company intends to repair its positive image as its reputation has diminished or to eliminate negative perceptions from stakeholders.

Broadly speaking, impression management strategies are classified into two forms: reactive and proactive impression management (Bolino et al. 2008; Elsbach et al. 1998; Short and Pfarrer 2023). Proactive impression management refers to companies' efforts to preventively mitigate negative evaluations (Bass et al. 2023; Bundy et al. 2017). However, beyond managing legitimacy crises, proactive impression management strategies are also used to shape stakeholder perceptions in routine disclosures, particularly in contexts such as ESG reports and annual reports, where regulatory flexibility gives managers significant discretion.

Similarly, the use of confusing narrative strategies in ESG reporting constitutes a form of proactive impression management (Leventis and Weetman 2004). Narrative strategy refers to the approach by which a company shapes public perception of its corporate image and reputation by constructing specific stories or narrative frameworks (Ogilvy et al. 2014).

Bass et al. (2023) classify the literature on proactive impression management into three main directions—voluntary disclosure, anticipatory impression management (AIM), and ceremonial behaviours.

Wu and Hui (2025) build on previous research on impression management strategies, such as "strategic noise" (Graffin et al. 2011; Jin et al. 2022) and "showing off" (Bass et al. 2023), identifying two potential forms of proactive impression management—clear ESG narratives and ambiguous ESG narratives—in the context of China's institutional environment, where firms face distinct legitimacy pressures.

Consequently, the research answers the following research questions:

RQ1. How have the themes and directions of research on ESG-related corporate controversies evolved between 2016 and 2025, and what are the emerging trends identified through bibliometric analysis?

RQ2. How are the strategies through which organizations attempt to mitigate or conceal ESG controversies reflected in comparison with theoretical trends in the literature?

3 Research Methodology

This research incorporates a bibliometric analysis in order to examine the evolution and manifestation of corporate controversies associated with ESG criteria. This mixed approach allows the correlation of trends identified in scientific literature with organizational realities observable in practice.

The bibliometric analysis was performed using the Bibliometrix (R) package, utilizing the Biblioshiny interface, to examine the structure, dynamics, and collaboration networks in the specialized literature published between 2016 and 2025. The dataset comprised 203 relevant documents extracted from the Web of Science database, which were evaluated according to indicators such as annual growth rate (63.61%), average number of citations per document (21.16), and proportion of international collaborations (32.02%). The key term used for the search was "ESG controversies." The bibliometric results showed a significant expansion of academic interest, the formation of thematic clusters focused on transparency, governance, and corporate reputation, as well as the strengthening of international collaboration networks.

The Bibliometrix package in R (Aria and Cuccurullo 2017) was used to analyse bibliometric data. This tool was used to perform performance analyses of ESG disclosure and greenwashing in scientific research and to select papers for content analysis. The performance analysis uses multiple publications and citations and allows for the analysis of scientific productivity, co-citations, the most influential papers, and research impact.

4 Results

The "Annual Scientific Production" graph shows a significant increase in academic interest in corporate controversies between 2016 and 2025, as shown in Fig. 1. In the early years analysed (2016–2018), scientific output was low. This indicates limited concern for an area considered marginal in business ethics and corporate governance. Topics such as social responsibility, transparency, and organizational ethics were discussed sporadically, without clear recognition of corporate controversy as a systemic phenomenon.

Between 2019 and 2020, there was a slight increase in the number of articles. This was probably driven by major corporate scandals and an emphasis on transparency and social responsibility. However, the instability of this period, amplified by the COVID-19 pandemic, led to a temporary stagnation in scientific output. After 2021, the trend became visibly upward. The steady increase in publications reflects the consolidation of the field and the diversification of theoretical and empirical approaches. At this stage, corporate controversies are analysed from the perspective of ESG criteria, ethical responsibility in supply chains, and phenomena such as greenwashing, organizational discrimination, or corporate reputation manipulation.

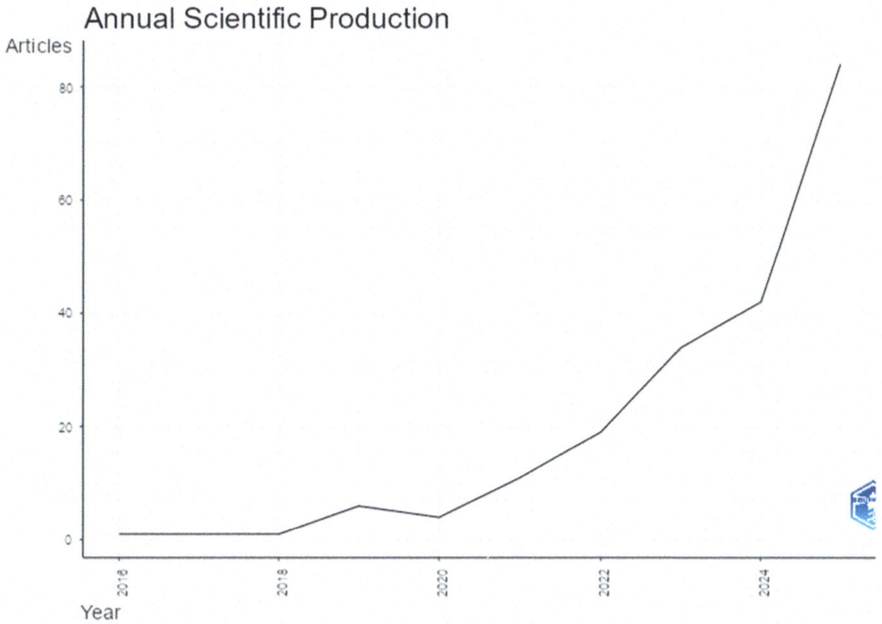

Fig. 1 Evolution of publications on ESG controversies. *Source* Authors' processing using Bibliometrix

The period 2024–2025 marks an explosion in scientific output, reaching record levels. This growth suggests that the field has become a topic of global relevance. It is stimulated by recent corporate crises, stricter international regulations on corporate responsibility, and ethical concerns generated by new technologies.

The evolution and frequency of key concepts in academic research on ESG topics between 2020 and 2025 are highlighted in Fig. 2. Each term represents a recurring theme in the literature. The size of the bubble shows how often each term is used in publications, suggesting the interest of the academic community.

In the early years (2020–2021), research focused on key concepts such as *corporate social responsibility*, *financial performance*, and *reporting*. At this stage, the emphasis was on the impact of non-financial reporting on company value and on clarifying the ESG framework. After 2022, terms such as *impact*, *company value*, *sustainability*, and *ESG* become increasingly frequent. This shows an expansion of the analysis from financial aspects to the assessment of the social and environmental effects of corporate activity. The increase in the frequency of the terms *corporate social responsibility* and *company performance* confirms the interest in the relationship between business ethics, economic performance, and organizational legitimacy, as shown in Fig. 3.

Between 2024 and 2025, the dominant term becomes *ESG controversies*, with the highest frequency and visibility. Attention shifts from the implementation of ESG principles to the critical analysis of the controversies, inconsistencies, and

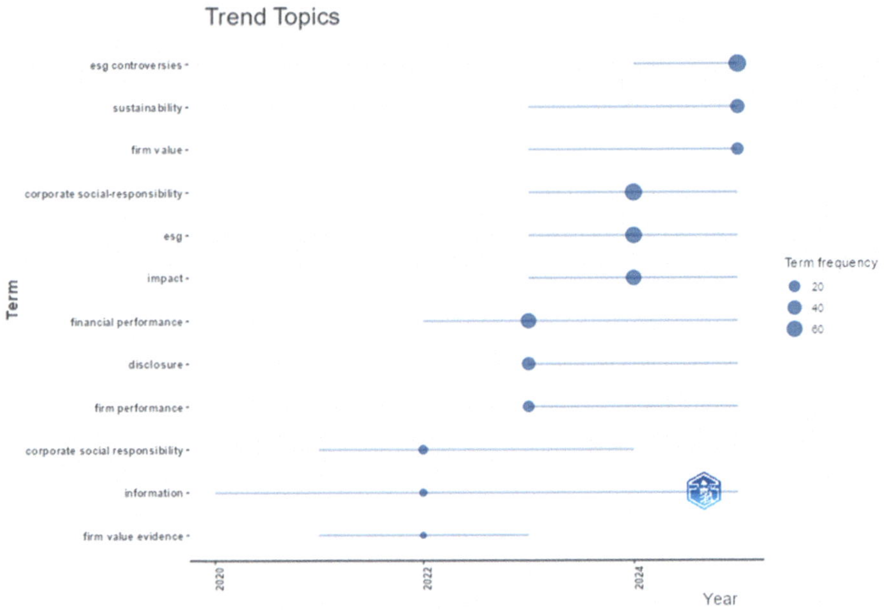

Fig. 2 Conceptual dynamics of research on ESG corporate controversies. *Source* Authors' processing using Bibliometrix

negative effects they generate. Topics such as greenwashing, selective reporting, the instrumentalization of social responsibility, and conflicts between financial and ethical performance become major topics of interest, according to Table 1.

The frequency analysis of relevant terms highlights the connection between corporate controversies and ESG dimensions, as shown in Fig. 4. Dominant terms such as *sustainability*, *CSR*, *greenwashing*, and *accountability* suggest the existence of a common thematic core that structures the academic discourse on corporate responsibility and legitimacy, as shown in Table 2.

The term *ESG controversies* appears most frequently (78 times). This confirms that recent studies have focused on tensions, inconsistencies, and limitations related to the application of ESG principles. The prevalence of this term indicates a shift in the literature from analysing the benefits of ESG to critically examining reputational risks, the lack of consistency between discourse and practice, and the impact of controversies on public trust and corporate performance. In second place is *corporate social responsibility* (71), which helps to understand the ethical and social dimensions of corporate controversies. The close relationship between CSR and ESG reflects the evolution of academic discourse, where traditional social responsibility is reinterpreted through the lens of sustainable governance and transparency.

The term *ESG* (64), often seen as an integrated governance structure, is central to this group of words. The high frequency of the terms *impact* (52), *financial performance* (49), and *performance* (45) shows researchers' concern with correlating ESG

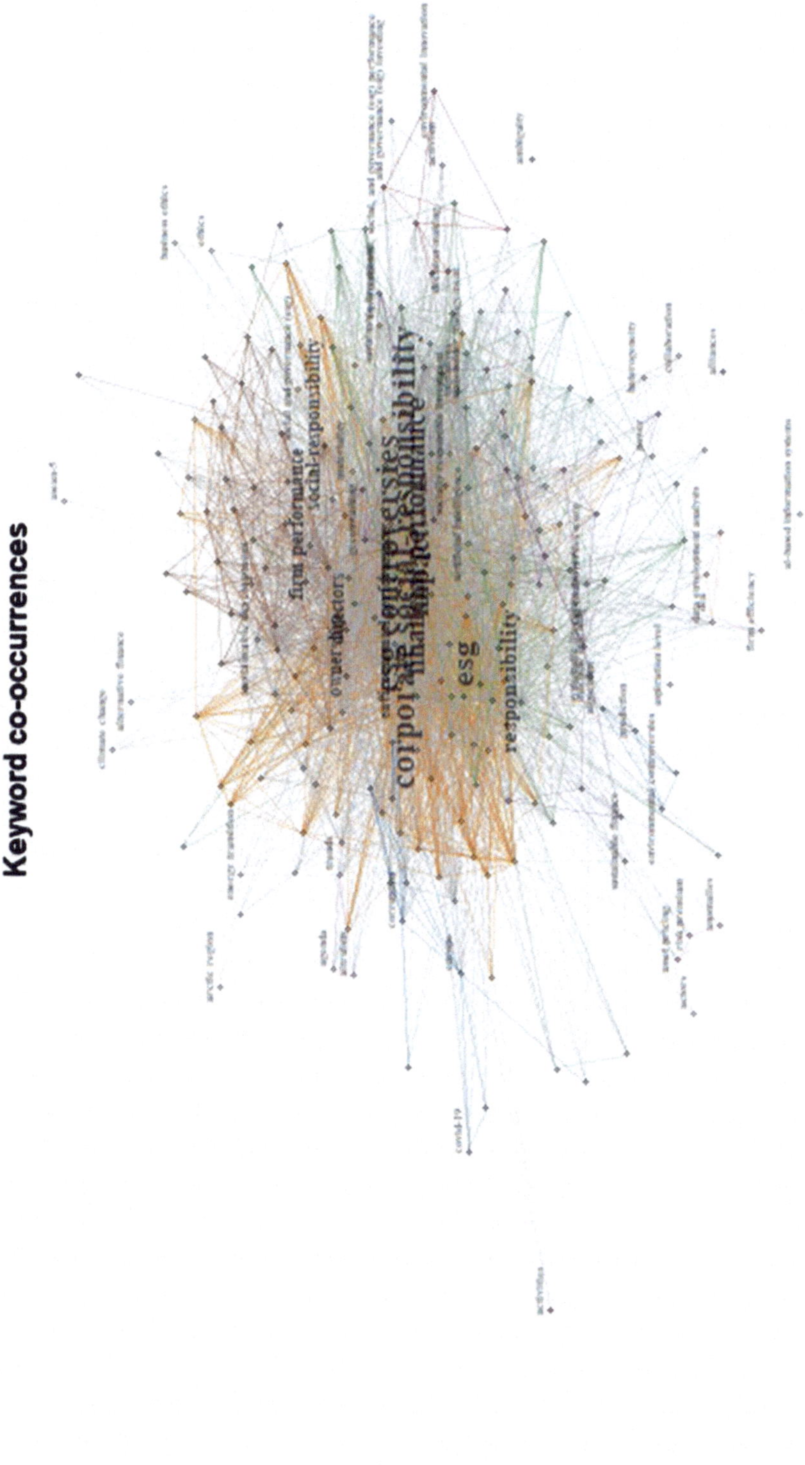

Fig. 3 Co-occurrence network of keywords in studies on ESG controversies. *Source* Authors' processing using Bibliometrix

Table 1 Dominant and emerging themes in the academic debate on ESG controversies

Term	Frequency	Year (Q1)	Year (Median)	Year (Q3)
Corporate social responsibility	10	2021	2022	2024
Information	6	2020	2022	2025
Firm value evidence	5	2021	2022	2023
Financial performance	49	2022	2023	2025
Disclosure	31	2023	2023	2025
Firm performance	19	2023	2023	2025
Corporate social-responsibility	71	2023	2024	2025
ESG	64	2023	2024	2025
Impact	52	2023	2024	2025
ESG controversies	77	2024	2025	2025
Sustainability	40	2023	2025	2025
Firm value	26	2023	2025	2025

Source Authors' processing using Bibliometrix

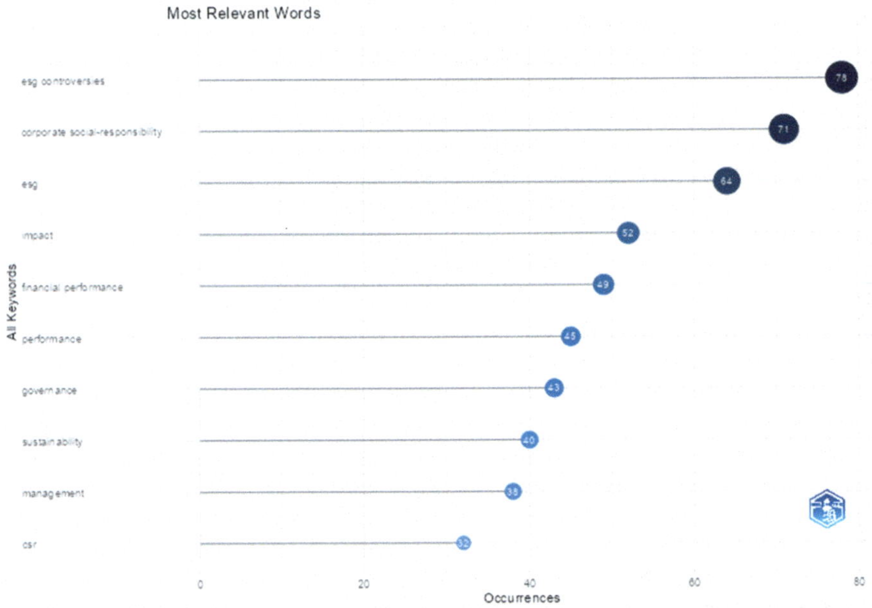

Fig. 4 Conceptual core of research on ESG corporate controversies. *Source* Authors' processing using Bibliometrix

Table 2 Most frequent terms in the literature on ESG corporate controversies

Words	Occurrences
ESG controversies	78
Corporate social-responsibility	71
ESG	64
Impact	52
Financial performance	49
Performance	45
Governance	43
Sustainability	40
Management	38
CSR	32
Disclosure	31
Corporate governance	28
Firm value	26
Responsibility	26
Risk	20
Firm performance	19

Source Authors' processing using Bibliometrix

controversies with companies' economic results, emphasizing the link between financial performance and ethical behaviour. Similarly, the terms *governance* (43), *sustainability* (40), and *management* (38) define the structural framework for controversies: governance establishes rules and responsibilities, sustainability provides moral purpose, and management defines how to implement and report.

Figure 5 shows a diverse geographical distribution, with a predominance in European and Asian countries. Italy leads the ranking with the most publications, followed by China, France, and India. Italy's position can be explained by the increased interest in corporate ethics and responsible governance, especially after recent financial scandals. Italy also has a high level of perceived corruption (according to Transparency International), which stimulates research on transparency, reporting, and social responsibility.

China ranks second, which reveals a paradox. Rapid economic growth and the internationalization of Chinese companies have led to an interest in ESG standards. However, corporate transparency regulations are still developing, and governance controversies remain frequent. Chinese literature often discusses the tension between economic performance and ethics.

France has advanced regulations on corporate responsibility (e.g., the "devoir de vigilance" law), stimulating academic literature on the subject. In India, although CSR legislation is strict (large companies must invest a percentage of their profits in social activities), controversies related to the application and transparency of these practices are frequent.

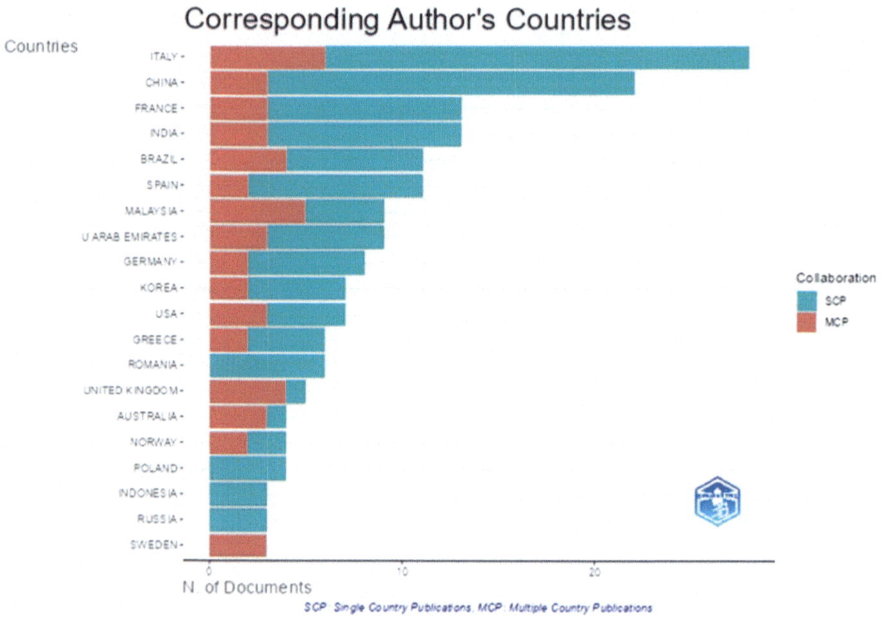

Fig. 5 Countries' contribution to scientific publications by type of collaboration. *Source* Authors' processing using Bibliometrix

Romania, Greece, the United Arab Emirates, and other emerging economies also have a moderate contribution. Here, high perceptions of corruption and unclear regulations on ESG reporting may stimulate research. The literature from these regions tends to examine institutional deficiencies and opportunistic corporate behaviour.

In contrast, countries with established governance systems (such as Germany, Norway, or the United Kingdom) publish fewer individual articles, preferring international collaborations. This may indicate a more mature theoretical approach, oriented towards a global analysis of the phenomenon. The geographical distribution of publications reflects not only scientific interest but also the socio-economic and institutional context of each country, as shown in Fig. 6.

The document coupling method uses common references between articles to identify thematic connections and form research clusters, as shown in Fig. 7.

The two axes of the graph define the role and relevance of these themes in the literature:

- The horizontal axis (Centrality) shows how connected a theme is to other topics. A high centrality means that the theme is pivotal in research, linking several fields.
- The vertical axis (Impact) indicates the level of academic influence, measured by the frequency of citations and the recognition of the theme in the scientific community.

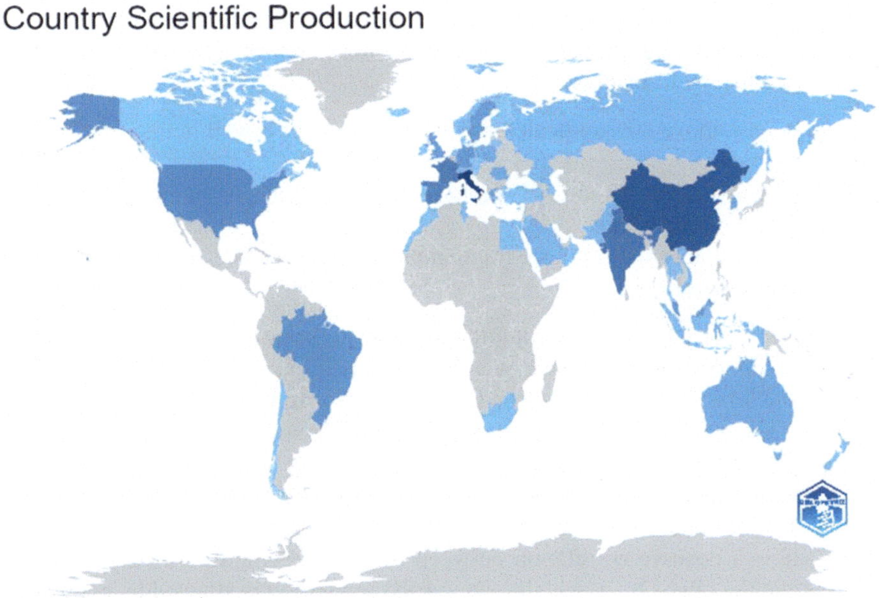

Fig. 6 Global distribution of scientific output on ESG controversies. *Source* Authors' processing using Bibliometrix

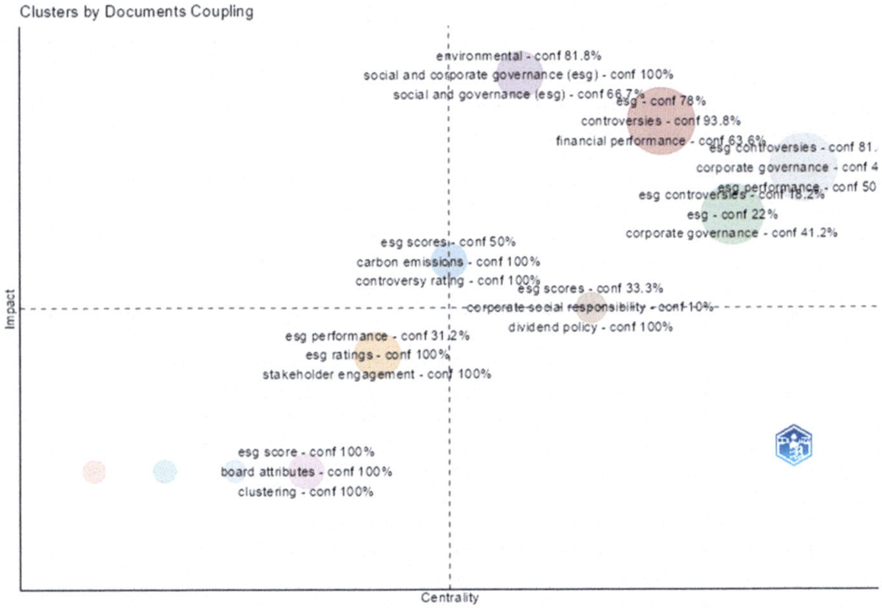

Fig. 7 Thematic structure of research on ESG controversies: cluster analysis through document coupling. *Source* Authors' processing using Bibliometrix

Each bubble has a consistency percentage (conf %), which reflects the thematic homogeneity of the cluster. It shows the proportion of papers that address the same theme in a convergent manner.

- Percentages above 80% indicate high consistency, i.e., a well-defined theoretical topic.
- Percentages between 40 and 70% indicate methodological or theoretical diversity, i.e., an area under debate.
- Percentages below 40% indicate fragmentation or emergence, i.e., a new field that is still being clarified.

The upper right quadrant—the dominant core of corporate controversy research—focuses on topics with high centrality and academic impact. The *ESG controversies* cluster (93.8%) is the most coherent and central, representing the main topic of current literature. The articles analyse the effects of controversies on company reputation, ESG scores, and investor perception.

Financial performance (63.8%) and *ESG performance* (50%) are at the intersection of ethics and economics. The average percentages suggest diversity: some studies show a positive correlation between transparency and performance, while others argue the opposite, especially when ESG reputation is affected by controversies. *Corporate governance* (41.2%) has lower coherence, suggesting a variety of interpretations regarding governance mechanisms.

The upper left quadrant—Theoretical and conceptual foundations of ESG—includes terms such as: Environmental—conf 81.8%; Social and corporate governance (ESG)—conf 100%; Social and governance (ESG)—conf 66.7%. These clusters have high levels of coherence (over 80%), showing that they are well defined theoretically. They form the conceptual basis for studies on controversies. *Environmental* (81.8%) reflects literature focused on the ecological impact of corporate activities. *Social and corporate governance* (ESG)—conf 100% shows total homogeneity: the articles discuss the ESG structure as an integrated system for assessing corporate responsibility.

The lower right quadrant—Operational and assessment themes—includes clusters with high centrality but moderate impact. *Corporate social responsibility*—conf 100%—shows that all papers treat CSR as a tool for assessing corporate responsibility. However, CSR is seen more as an operational variable. *Dividend policy*—conf 100%—has the same consistency, indicating a clear topic linking ethical controversies to financial decisions. *ESG scores*—conf 33.3%—has a low level of consistency, suggesting a lack of a unified methodology.

Lower left quadrant—Emerging and micro-analytical themes—Includes terms such as: *Board attributes*—conf 100%—analyses the role of boards of directors in preventing controversies. *Stakeholder engagement*—conf 100%—investigates stakeholder involvement in governance decisions. *Clustering*—conf 100%—refers to analytical methods for identifying controversial companies.

Figure 8 presents a thematic map based on bibliometric analysis of keyword frequency and co-occurrence, which positions research topics according to their degree of development (density) and central relevance (centrality) in the literature.

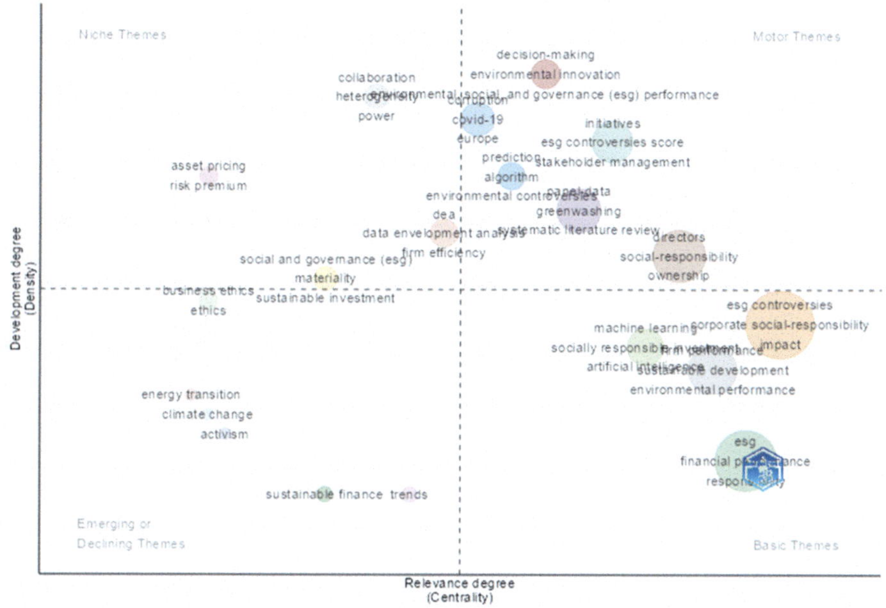

Fig. 8 Conceptual landscape of ESG controversy research: from emerging topics to dominant directions. *Source* Authors' processing using Bibliometrix

The upper right quadrant—Motor Themes (dynamic and consolidated themes) includes the most developed and influential topics at the center of current research. The main themes are: *ESG controversies*, *corporate social responsibility*, *environmental performance*, *impact*, and *financial performance*. These constitute the current core of research on corporate controversies and are recognized as interdisciplinary themes that integrate ethics, performance, and governance.

Lower right quadrant—Basic Themes contains essential topics widely used as a theoretical or empirical basis: *ESG*, *financial performance*, *responsibility*. These themes provide the conceptual framework for studies on corporate controversies and are used in almost all empirical analyses of the relationship between governance and performance.

Upper left quadrant—Niche Themes (specialized themes with limited relevance) highlights themes such as *asset pricing*, *risk premium*, *heterogeneity*, and *collaboration*. These are advanced and specialized areas focused on quantitative analysis or econometric models, with limited applicability in the context of ESG controversies.

Lower left quadrant—Emerging or Declining Themes includes topics such as *energy transition*, *climate change*, *activism*, and *sustainable finance*. These themes are gaining traction, reflecting recent concern about the link between climate crises, social activism, and corporate responsibility.

Figure 9 illustrates the evolution of the frequency of terms associated with controversies in publications indexed in Web of Science between 2015 and 2025. A steady

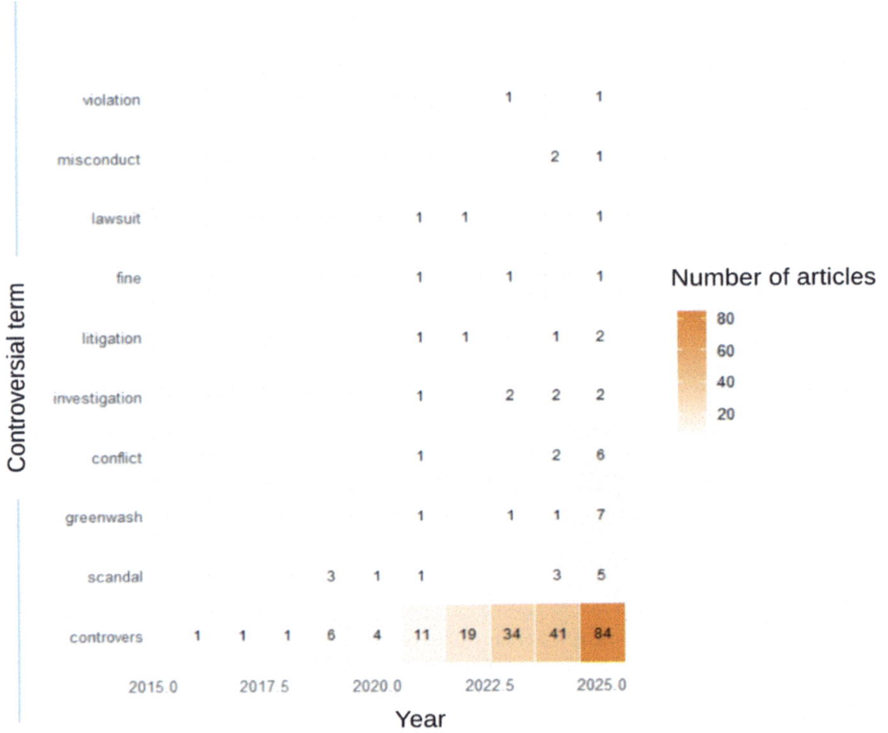

Fig. 9 Evolution of controversial terms in scientific literature (WoS) between 2015 and 2025. *Source* Authors' processing using R Studio

increase can be observed after 2020, when terms such as *controversy*, *scandal*, *greenwash*, and *conflict* become increasingly present in the literature.

While these terms appear sporadically between 2015 and 2019, after 2020 there is a noticeable diversification of the vocabulary associated with controversy. For example, the term *greenwash* reflects the increased interest in issues of sustainability and corporate responsibility, while *lawsuit*, *litigation*, and *misconduct* indicate an emphasis on the legal and ethical dimensions of academic discussions. The term *controversy* clearly dominates the period analysed, reaching 84 occurrences in 2025, which suggests an intensification of scientific concerns for sensitive, disputed, or ambiguous topics, often at the intersection of ethics, communication, and organizational practices.

Figure 10 shows the distribution of scientific articles mentioning controversies associated with the three ESG (Environment, Social, Governance) pillars for the top 20 countries, according to data from Web of Science. It can be seen that the "Governance" pillar clearly dominates in most countries, indicating that governance issues—corruption, transparency, managerial responsibility, and corporate ethics—are the most discussed in the literature. Italy (60 articles), China (40), India (31), the

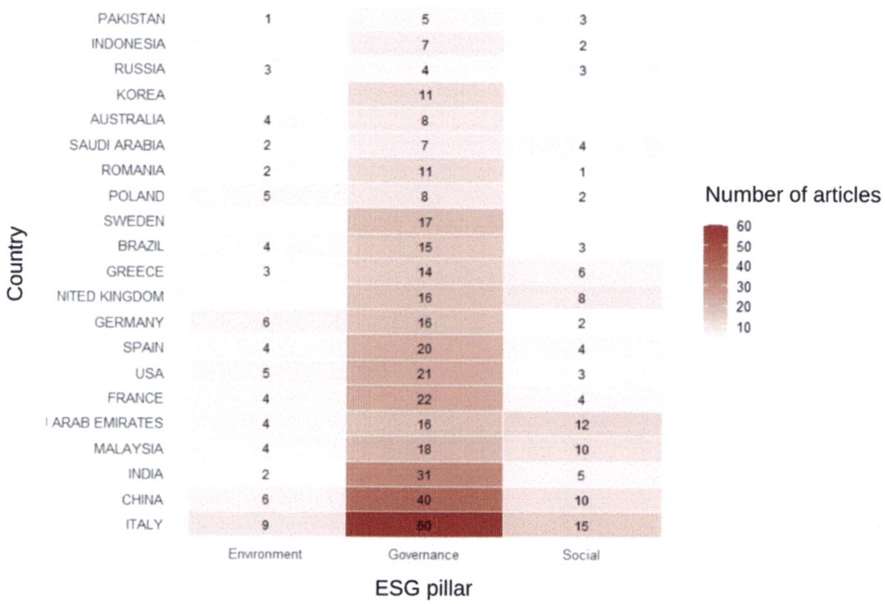

Fig. 10 Governance at the heart of ESG debates: a comparative analysis of global controversies. *Source* Authors' processing using R Studio

US (21), and France (22) have the highest values for this pillar, suggesting a global concern for corporate conduct and governance issues.

By comparison, the Environment and Social pillars are significantly less represented. Environmental controversies appear particularly in Italy, Poland, and China, probably associated with debates on sustainability and the ecological impact of companies. The Social pillar has the lowest frequency, reflecting limited coverage of issues related to equity, employee rights, and social impact. Overall, the figure shows that ESG controversies are predominantly addressed through the lens of governance, with national variations that may reflect differences in regulation, media visibility, and institutional maturity.

The evolution of controversial ESG (Environment, Social, Governance) subtopics in Web of Science, comparing the pre-pandemic (until 2019) and post-pandemic (2020–2025) periods, can be seen in Fig. 11. The results indicate a substantial increase in the volume of articles in the post-pandemic period, particularly on topics related to corporate governance. The terms *Corporate Ethics*, *Corruption*, *Disclosure*, and *Board Diversity* become more frequent after 2020, suggesting a reassessment of transparency, ethics, and organizational responsibility practices in the context of global crises.

Countries such as Italy, Sweden, China, Malaysia, and the United Arab Emirates are seeing significant activity, focused on sub-topics such as *Corruption*, *Corporate Ethics*, and *Disclosure*. In contrast, the pre-pandemic period is characterized by a

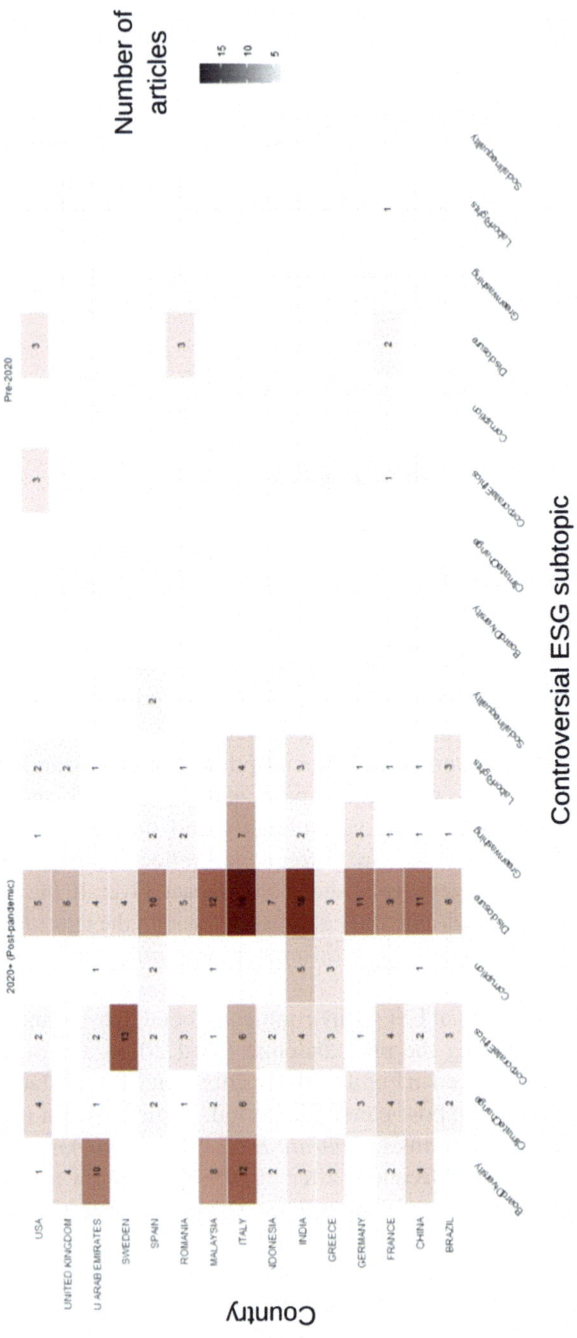

Fig. 11 Reconfiguration of ESG controversies post-pandemic: governance in the spotlight. *Source* Authors' processing using R Studio

small number of articles, focused mainly on *Greenwashing* and *Social Inequality*, indicating a more specific interest in environmental and social equity issues.

5 Discussions

The authors draw on what other researchers have previously demonstrated, namely that transparency is an essential factor for effective communication with stakeholders. In this context, Fig. 12 highlights how academic interest in ESG controversy subtopics evolved between 2015 and 2025, with the vertical line marking the beginning of the pandemic period (2020). There is a clear intensification of scientific interest after 2020, confirming that the pandemic was a major turning point in the debate on corporate responsibility, ethics, and transparency. Of all the sub-topics analysed, "*Disclosure*" (information transparency and ESG reporting) is rising the fastest, reaching a notable peak in 2025. This trend suggests increased pressure on companies for clarity, accountability, and ethical reporting in the context of new regulations and public interest in sustainability.

Sun et al. (2024) conclude that a higher ESG score is associated with:

1. a lower probability of ESG scandal;
2. higher losses in the event of a scandal. These findings convey two key messages, as follows:
    - ESG scores are informative because they can predict negative ESG events;
    - firms with high ESG ratings should maintain high standards to avoid scandals, as the losses incurred will otherwise be more significant compared to firms with low ESG ratings.

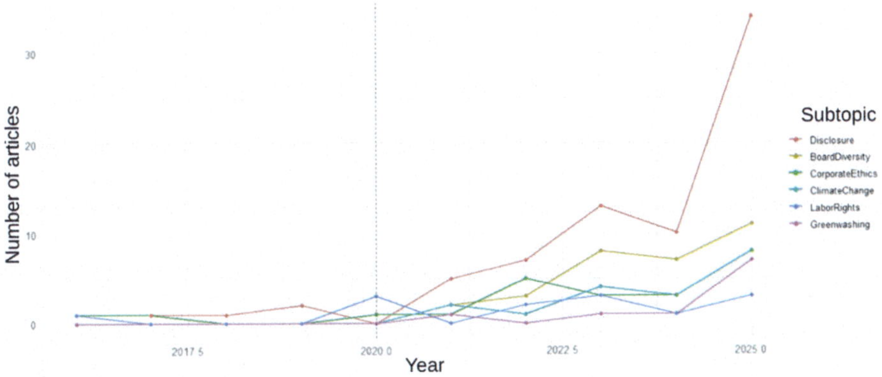

Fig. 12 The rise of post-pandemic ESG controversies: from corporate ethics to transparency. *Source* Authors' processing using R Studio

García Lara et al. (2025) highlight a comparison between substantive actions and symbolic actions. Substantive actions involve costly investments that change current practices and reduce the likelihood of another disaster occurring. Symbolic actions involve legitimizing actions to create a positive image and signal firms' social and environmental awareness through CSR, without changing their current practices. In both scenarios, CSR can help improve stakeholder relations and reduce the negative effects that firms suffer as a result of the disaster. Companies in affected industries improve their CSR performance in the post-disaster period. However, these CSR improvements are, on average, symbolic rather than substantial. That is, they are driven by an increase in strengths rather than a decrease in concerns and by CSR categories other than those related to the environment. When managers are forced to improve CSR performance over a short period of time, they implement symbolic practices that are not associated with real changes in corporate ethical or safety standards. This calls into question the effectiveness of external requirements for CSR practices, whether through regulation or social imposition.

The choice of ESG information disclosure strategy is equally strategic and plays a key role in either repairing or enhancing a company's reputation. In other words, strategically aligned (convergent) companies can use clear and positive information to convey to stakeholders that they are truly committed to good practices, thereby achieving optimal uniqueness in their ESG positioning. On the other hand, strategically divergent firms may adopt more ambiguous disclosure strategies to mitigate control and regulatory risks, thus avoiding the potential risk of "decoupling" in ESG practices (Bothello et al. 2023; Hawn and Ioannou 2016).

Thus, strategically convergent firms may adopt clear ESG disclosure strategies to enhance their reputation, such as demonstrating transparency, meeting external expectations, or differentiating themselves from competitors. In contrast, strategically distinctive firms may rely on ambiguous ESG disclosure strategies to navigate regulatory scrutiny and mitigate potential risks (Wu and Hui 2025).

6 Conclusions

The study of corporate controversies has evolved into a complex system of themes: from ethical and conceptual foundations (CSR, ESG) to relational analyses (governance, financial performance) and micro dimensions (board attributes, stakeholder engagement). High consistency percentages show conceptual consolidation, while average and low values signal areas of innovation. Corporate controversies are constantly changing, at the confluence of ethics, performance, and global governance.

The thematic map shows that *ESG controversies* are in the Motor Themes area, confirming their status as a central, mature, and high-impact theme in current literature. Concepts such as *corporate social responsibility*, *environmental performance*, and *financial performance*, which are the main pillars of research, gravitate around it. In contrast, themes in the lower area—such as *sustainable finance* and *climate change activism*—are expanding and suggest new directions for the development of studies on corporate controversies, as the academic debate extends to sustainability, green transition, and global ethics.

Nations with higher perceived corruption and incomplete regulations tend to have scientific output that is more focused on critical aspects of ESG controversies. In contrast, countries with clearer regulations focus on assessing and refining corporate responsibility.

The study highlights that the pandemic has acted as a catalyst for intensifying research on corporate governance and integrity, shifting the focus of ESG debates from social and environmental issues to transparency, ethics, and managerial responsibility.

Among the limitations of this study is that co-occurrence, coupling, or thematic mapping analyses provide a quantitative perspective but do not capture the qualitative content of controversies in depth (e.g., the nature of disputes, ethical positions, political or sectoral context). The results show how the themes are linked, but do not explain why controversies arise and how differences in approach manifest themselves between countries, industries, or periods. Another limitation is that ESG research is evolving rapidly, especially in the context of new regulations (e.g., CSRD, EU taxonomy) and the growth of non-financial reporting, and the resulting maps and clusters reflect the situation at a given moment but can quickly become outdated as new themes emerge (e.g., greenwashing, AI governance, impact investing).

References

Agoraki M-EK, Giaka M, Konstantios D, Patsika V (2023) Firms' sustainability, financial performance, and regulatory dynamics: evidence from European firms. J Int Money Finance 131:102785. https://doi.org/10.1016/j.jimonfin.2022.102785

Aouadi A, Marsat S (2018) Do ESG controversies matter for firm value? Evidence from international data. J Bus Ethics 151:1027–1047. https://doi.org/10.1007/s10551-016-3213-8

Aria M, Cuccurullo C (2017) Bibliometrix: an R-tool for comprehensive science mapping analysis. J Informetr 11(4):959–975. https://doi.org/10.1016/j.joi.2017.08.007

Asante-Appiah B (2020) Does the severity of a client's negative environmental, social and governance reputation affect audit effort and audit quality? J Account Public Policy 39(3):106713. https://doi.org/10.1016/j.jaccpubpol.2019.106713

Bass AE, Pfarrer MD, Milosevic I, Titus VK (2023) Better to be loved by some? Firm flaunting as an impression management strategy. Acad Manag Rev 48(2):292–312. https://doi.org/10.5465/amr.2020.0015

Bolino MC, Kacmar KM, Tumley WH, Gilstrap JB (2008) A multi-level review of impression management motives and behaviors. J Manag 34(6):1080–1109. https://doi.org/10.1177/0149206308324325

Bothello J, Ioannou I, Porumb VA, Zengin-Karaibrahimoglu Y (2023) CSR decoupling within business groups and the risk of perceived greenwashing. Strat Manag J 44(13):3217–3251. https://doi.org/10.1002/smj.3532

Bundy J, Pfarrer MD, Short CE, Coombs WT (2017) Crises and crisis management: Integration, interpretation, and research development. J Manag 43(6):1661–1692. https://doi.org/10.1177/0149206316680030

Carberry EJ, Engelen PJ, Van Essen M (2018) Which firms get punished for unethical behavior? Explaining variation in stock market reactions to corporate misconduct. Bus Ethics Q 28(2):119–151. https://doi.org/10.1017/beq.2017.46

Costa R, Menichini T (2013) A multidimensional approach for CSR assessment: the importance of the stakeholder perception. Expert Syst Appl 40. https://doi.org/10.1016/j.eswa.2012.07.028

DasGupta R (2022) Financial performance shortfall, ESG controversies, and ESG performance: evidence from firms around the world. Financ Res Lett 46:102487. https://doi.org/10.1016/j.frl.2021.102487

Dyck A, Morse A, Zingales L (2010) Who blows the whistle on corporate fraud. J Financ 65:2213–2252. https://doi.org/10.1111/j.1540-6261.2010.01614.x

Einwiller SA, Carroll CE (2020) Negative disclosures in corporate social responsibility reporting. Corp Commun: Int J 25(2):319–337. https://doi.org/10.1108/ccij-05-2019-0054

Elsbach KD, Sutton RI, Principe KE (1998) Averting expected challenges through anticipatory impression management: a study of hospital billing. Organ Sci 9(1):68–86. https://doi.org/10.1287/orsc.9.1.68

Fombrun CJ (2005) A world of reputation research, analysis and thinking—building corporate reputation through CSR initiatives: evolving standards. Corp Reput Rev 8:7–12. https://doi.org/10.1057/palgrave.crr.1540235

Franco CD (2020) ESG controversies and their impact on performance. The Journal of Investing 29(2):33–45. https://doi.org/10.3905/joi.2019.1.106

García Lara JM, García Osmaa B, Khalilovc A, Gazizova I (2025) Demand-driven corporate social responsibility: symbolic versus substantive change after environmental disasters. J Corp Finan 94:102816. https://doi.org/10.1016/j.jcorpfin.2025.102816

Graffin SD, Carpenter MA, Boivie S (2011) What's all that (strategic) noise? Anticipatory impression management in CEO succession. Strat Manag J 32(7):748–770. https://doi.org/10.1002/smj.906

Gray ER, Balmer JM (1998) Managing corporate image and corporate reputation. Long Range Plan 31(5):695–702. https://doi.org/10.1016/S0024-6301(98)00074-0

Hawn O, Ioannou I (2016) Mind the gap: the interplay between external and internal actions in the case of corporate social responsibility. Strat Manag J 37(13):2569–2588. https://www.jstor.org/stable/26155189

He F, Guo X, Yue P (2024) Media coverage and corporate ESG performance: evidence from China. Int Rev Financ Anal 91:103003. https://doi.org/10.1016/j.irfa.2023.103003

He G, Li AZ (2024) Does media coverage of firms' environment, social, and governance (ESG) incidents affect analyst coverage and forecasts? A risk perspective. Int Rev Financ Anal 94:103289. https://doi.org/10.1016/j.irfa.2024.103289

He R, Chen H, Zhu X (2025) Corporate hypocrisy and ESG rating divergence. Corp Soc Responsib Environ Manag 32(1):1122–1146. https://doi.org/10.1002/csr.3002

Highhouse S, Brooks ME, Gregarus G (2009) An organizational impression management perspective on the formation of corporate reputations. J Manag 35(6):1481–1493. https://doi.org/10.1177/0149206309348788

Jebe R (2019) The convergence of financial and ESG materiality: taking sustainability mainstream. Am Bus Law J 56(3):645–702. https://doi.org/10.1111/ablj.12148

Jin J, Li H, Hoskisson R (2022) The use of strategic noise in reactive impression management: How do market reactions matter? Acad Manag J 65(4):1303–1326. https://doi.org/10.5465/amj.2018.1054

Karpoff JM, Lott J, John R, Wehrly EW (2005) The reputational penalties for environmental violations: empirical evidence. J Law Econ 48(2):653–675. https://doi.org/10.1086/430806

Leventis S, Weetman P (2004) Impression management: Dual language reporting and voluntary disclosure. Accounting Forum 28(3):307–328. https://doi.org/10.1016/j.accfor.2004.07.004

Ogilvy J, Nonaka I, Konno N (2014) Toward narrative strategy. World Futures 70(1):5–18. https://doi.org/10.1080/02604027.2014.875718

Ozsozgun Caliskan A, Esen E, Barkemeyer R (2021) Impression management tactics in the CEO statements of Turkish sustainability reports. Bus Ethics, Environ Responsib 30(4):485–506. https://doi.org/10.1111/beer.12374

Passas I, Ragazou K, Zafeiriou E, Garefalakis A, Zopounidis C (2022) ESG controversies: a quantitative and qualitative analysis for the sociopolitical determinants in EU firms. Sustainability 14(19):12879. https://doi.org/10.3390/su141912879

Pop R, Achim MV, Bota-Avram C (2025) The shifting landscape of greenwashing—insights from a bibliometric analysis. Sustain Financ Rev. Ahead-of-print. https://doi.org/10.1108/SFR-05-2025-0005

Schwoy SM, Dutzi A, Messing J (2025) Silence is golden?—Analysing the transparency of ESG controversies in corporate reporting within the pharmaceutical and textile industry. Manag Decis 63(2):665–707. https://doi.org/10.1108/MD-10-2023-1988

Short CE, Pfarrer MD (2023) Managing asymmetric events with anticipatory and reactive strategies. J Manag. https://doi.org/10.1177/01492063231198174

Sun W, Luo Y, Yiu SM, Yu L, Ding W (2024) ESG scores, scandal probability, and event returns. Financial Innovation 10(1):121. https://doi.org/10.1186/s40854-024-00635-1

Treepongkaruna S, Kyaw K, Jiraporn P (2022) Shareholder litigation rights and ESG controversies: a quasi-natural experiment. Int Rev Financ Anal 84:102396. https://doi.org/10.1016/j.irfa.2022.102396

Utz S (2019) Corporate scandals and the reliability of ESG assessments: Evidence from an international sample. Rev Manag Sci 13:483–511. https://doi.org/10.1007/s11846-017-0256-x

Wong JB, Zhang Q (2022) Stock market reactions to adverse ESG disclosure via media channels. Br Account Rev 54(1):101045. https://doi.org/10.1016/j.bar.2021.101045

Wu X, Hui Q (2025) Exploring optimal distinctiveness through ESG impression management: implications for organizational reputation. Corp Reput Rev. https://doi.org/10.1057/s41299-025-00241-6

Ruben Pop is a PhD student in finance at the Faculty of Economics and Business Administration within Babeş-Bolyai University. He holds a bachelor's degree in business management, specializing in firm economics, and a master's degree in accounting, specializing in accounting expertise and audit. His greatest passion is mathematics.

Monica Violeta Achim is a professor and doctoral supervisor in Finance at the Faculty of Economic Sciences and Business Administration, Babeş-Bolyai University, Cluj-Napoca. With over 27 years of experience in academia, she has published, as author and co-author, over 140 scientific articles and 27 books. The main research topics are financial analysis, business performance, finance, and economic and financial crime. In 2020, she obtained the Award for Excellence in Scientific Research, at Babeş-Bolyai University, Faculty of Economics and Business Administration, Cluj-Napoca, Romania, as a recognition of the results obtained in the research activity. She leads a main national project in the area of financial crime in the period 2020–2023. In the business environment, she works in liberal professions as an accountant expert, tax consultant, and judicial expert; from this perspective, being involved in solving many cases of economic and financial crime of the Palace of Justice, Cluj-Napoca.

The Transparency Paradox of the Real Estate Markets: When Visibility Masks Vulnerability in the Digital Era

Elena Ionașcu

Abstract In the digital era, enhancing transparency has emerged as an important objective in combating financial crime, notably in high-value sectors such as real estate. The real estate sector is susceptible to illicit financial activities due to its capacity to cover the origin of criminal proceeds through high-value transactions, frequent cash use, and pricing manipulation, compounded by regulatory gaps and limited oversight that facilitate exploitation with minimal risk of detection. Paradoxically, efforts to increase transparency—particularly through digitalization—may also expose the real estate sector to new forms of risk, as greater information flows and automated systems can be exploited by sophisticated actors to legitimize fraudulent transactions under the guise of compliance. The purpose of this chapter is to document the contradictory relationship between market transparency and the incidence of financial fraud in the European Union real estate sector, facilitated by digital innovation, using a mixed research approach. Drawing on a comparative cross-country analysis, this chapter develops a conceptual framework for understanding the transparency paradox, highlighting how digital instruments can facilitate financial crimes in both low- and high-transparency real estate markets. The theoretical and empirical evidence suggests that a high degree of real estate market transparency is no guarantee against financial fraud; on contrary, when not embedded in enforceable and cross-linked institutional systems, transparency may become a tool to obscure illicit activities under a veneer of legitimacy. The chapter contributes to the broader understanding of how digitalization must be strategically governed to close the gap between transparency as policy and transparency as protection in the context of financial crime.

Keywords Real estate · Transparency paradox · Financial crime · Digital innovations · Vulnerabilities

---

E. Ionașcu (✉)
Department of Economic and Financial Analysis and Evaluation, Bucharest University of Economic Studies, Bucharest, Romania
e-mail: elena.ionascu@cig.ase.ro

M. V. Achim (ed.), *Financial Crime in the Digital Era*, Contributions to Finance and Accounting, https://doi.org/10.1007/978-3-032-20198-0_16

1 Introduction

Transparency has become a central topic in debates surrounding economic, social, political, and environmental issues, driven by events in recent decades that have underscored the growing need for transparency in economic activities. The global financial crisis of 2007–2008 exposed the significant risks associated with insufficient transparency in the use of complex financial instruments tied to real estate assets, as well as in the evaluation of the underlying risks (Gorton 2008). In the aftermath of the crisis, investors increasingly called for greater transparency in real estate markets, where it has since become a critical factor in supporting informed decision-making and aligning the actions of market participants. The emphasis on improving transparency in the real estate sector is also driven by its substantial contribution to economic growth and employment. In 2023, investment in real estate accounted for 65% of fixed capital formation in both the European Union (EU) and the United Kingdom (UK) (EPRA and INREV 2024). The industrial segment of commercial real estate alone generated €522.7 billion in gross value added (GVA), representing 2.9% of total economic output, and supported 4.4 million jobs, positioning it among the most economically significant sectors in the region (EPRA and INREV 2024).

At the same time, in addition to its major economic contribution, the real estate sector is frequently exploited as a channel for financial crime, including money laundering, corruption, and tax evasion (Europol 2024; FATF 2022b). Real estate is a common destination for the proceeds of illicit activity, due in part to the high value of assets, the potential for capital appreciation, and the ease with which ownership can be obscured (FATF 2007). Numerous investigative reports have linked luxury property markets in cities such as London, New York, and Miami to politically exposed persons and high-risk transactions (Bieler 2022). While precise estimates are difficult due to the clandestine nature of such activities, the UNODC (n.d.) suggests that between 2% and 5% of global GDP, roughly $800 billion to $2 trillion, is laundered globally each year, a significant share of which is believed to flow through real estate markets. This dual role of real estate as both an economic pillar and a channel of laundering illicit funds highlights the urgent need to critically examine how transparency mechanisms and regulatory frameworks can be designed to effectively address these vulnerabilities.

The literature evidence indicates that strong regulatory frameworks and beneficial ownership transparency significantly mitigate money laundering risks and promote investor confidence; however, enforcement inconsistencies and disclosure loopholes persist, even in the world's most advanced economies (Collin et al. 2023; Marinoni et al. 2025). The real estate sector in many countries continues to face high risks of money laundering and terrorist financing, often due to insufficient access to beneficial ownership data (FATF 2022b). Technological tools, such as blockchain, machine learning, and artificial intelligence (AI), show promise in improving transaction transparency and fraud detection, but face limited adoption and regulatory challenges (Giannoni and Medda 2023). At the same time, digital innovations that aim to improve transparency can also be misused to support illicit financial activities if they are not properly regulated and monitored. These contradictory findings describe a transparency paradox: while the completeness, accessibility, and openness of ownership and transaction data are essential elements of a transparent real estate market, they are not sufficient to prevent abuse. In many cases, financial crime, particularly money laundering, continues to occur through the use of opaque ownership structures and limited due diligence, even in markets where formal transparency standards appear to be met (Marinoni et al. 2025). The paradox lies in the fact that, despite the increasing availability of real estate data, key aspects of ownership and transaction processes often remain unclear or difficult to trace. Thus, the assumption that greater transparency inherently deters financial crime must be reconsidered. Without accountability and institutional coherence, transparency may not only fail to close existing gaps but it may also legitimise illicit flows under the appearance of compliance.

The purpose of this chapter is to document the paradox of real estate transparency in the digital era, focusing on how EU countries are operating to reduce financial crime. The study draws on recent regulatory development at EU level, combined with theoretical insights on the relationship between real estate transparency and financial crime. Special attention is given to instruments such as the Global Real Estate Transparency Index (GRETI) and the Opacity in Real Estate Ownership (OREO Index) to measure real estate transparency in selected EU countries. In addition, a selection of recent cases reported in the international press, suspected of involving financial crime through the real estate sector, was analysed to illustrate how the transparency paradox manifests in both highly and poorly transparent markets. By bringing together theoretical reflection and empirical observations, this chapter contributes to a more nuanced understanding of the role of transparency in mitigating, not just masking, financial crime risks in real estate markets.

The structure of the chapter is as follows: Sect. 2 presents the theoretical and regulatory background; Sect. 3 describes the research methodology approach; Sect. 4 illustrates empirically the real estate transparency paradox; and Sect. 5 outlines key conclusions and policy implications.

2 Theoretical and Regulatory Background

This section introduces the theoretical and regulatory foundations of the real estate market transparency paradox by outlining the key sources of property vulnerabilities to illicit financial practices, the main dimensions of transparency, the EU's AML/CFT framework, and the role of digitalisation in shaping transparency outcomes.

2.1 Structural Vulnerabilities of Real Estate Assets

The real estate sector, including both land and associated constructions, remains one of the preferred channels for criminals to launder illicit funds (OECD 2019). The intrinsic features of real estate, namely its tangibility, indivisibility, immobility, heterogeneity, and transactional complexity (Breuer and Nadler 2012), render the sector particularly susceptible to financial crime. These attributes create conditions that enable opacity, hinder market efficiency, and facilitate the concealment, movement, and legitimization of illicit funds, making real estate a structurally vulnerable asset class for criminal exploitation (Table 1).

The tangibility of real estate assets, defined by their physical form, intrinsic value, and income-generating potential, makes them particularly attractive for laundering illicit funds. Unlike financial instruments, property can be valued independently of its owner, based primarily on their intrinsic characteristics and market context, rather than the identity or creditworthiness of the owner (Breuer and Nadler 2012; Graaskamp 1992). The ability to disconnect ownership from asset value enables the use of complex financial arrangements that can obscure the origin of funds, reduce the transparency of transactions and facilitate the concealment of beneficial owners. The decoupling of ownership rights from the identity of the beneficial owner facilitates the use of offshore structures in the real estate sector, as it allows assets to be transferred and held through intermediary entities that obscure the true owner's identity. This disconnection creates a favourable environment for anonymity, tax evasion, and the integration of illicit funds into the legal economy (Johannesen et al. 2022).

Existing studies have highlighted the strategic use of tangible assets, particularly real estate, in financial crime schemes, as opposed to intangible assets and financial instruments, which appear less frequently in such operations (Dugato et al. 2015; Nazzari and Riccardi 2022). This observation is reinforced by recent data from Europol (2024), which reports that 41% of the 821 criminal networks operating across EU exploit the real estate sector as a primary channel for laundering illicit

Table 1 Special features of real estate and their implications for financial crime

Feature	Definition	Implications for financial crime
Tangibility	Physical nature of real estate as a tangible asset	Facilitates integration of illicit funds as stable physical assets; low scrutiny
Indivisibility	High capital required per unit; not easily divided	Allows use of layered financing and complex ownership structures to obscure origin of funds
Immobility	Fixed location; asset bound to a specific jurisdiction	Enables strategic investment in low-transparency jurisdictions; hampers cross-border investigations
Heterogeneity	Diverse property characteristics; market fragmentation and negotiation-based pricing	Permits price manipulation and valuation fraud due to market opacity and high transaction costs
Complexity	The involvement of multiple intermediaries	Exploitation through layering schemes involving multiple companies

Source Author's projection

profits. Other notable methods include the use of gold and luxury goods (27%), cash-intensive businesses (20%), and cryptocurrencies (10%) (Europol 2024), illustrating the diversification of laundering strategies across different asset classes. The attractiveness of tangible assets, such as real estate, luxury goods, and precious metals, for criminal networks seeking to integrate illicit funds into the legal economy lies in their physical presence, relative stability in value, and capacity to store wealth discreetly. These assets can often be transferred, inherited, or pledged as collateral with greater ease and without necessarily triggering immediate regulatory scrutiny, particularly in jurisdictions with weak oversight or opaque ownership structures. While tangible assets offer discretion and flexibility in concealing illicit wealth, intangible and digital financial assets are embedded in highly regulated environments, where transaction histories are traceable and enforcement mechanisms are stronger. This makes them a less favourable choice for criminal actors seeking anonymity and asset integration.

The indivisibility of real estate assets implies that they are typically acquired, transferred, and valued as whole units, rather than in divisible components, like financial instruments (Mooya 2016). This indivisible nature allows for the injection of large amounts of illicit funds into a single transaction, reducing the number of steps and lowering the risk of detection. At the same time, real estate is a long-term asset, subject to physical, functional, and economic depreciation, which introduces a degree of valuation uncertainty that can be strategically exploited. Criminal actors may take advantage of this by fabricating high-end renovations or inflated lease agreements to justify unexplained wealth or simulate legitimate income (Remeur 2019; Teichmann 2023). In opaque or weakly regulated markets, such practices frequently escape detection and contribute to the misuse of real estate as a vehicle for financial crime.

Real estate includes land and the buildings situated on it, along with all installations and facilities permanently attached, which defines its characteristic of immobility. The immobility of real estate assets makes location the primary driver of value, integrating both intrinsic attributes, such as structural features, and external attributes, including environmental quality and access to public amenities. Therefore, real estate values reflect not only the characteristics of the property itself but also the desirability of its surrounding area, which jointly shape market perceptions and final prices (Rosen 1974). This strong dependence on location, combined with the high value and relative opacity of real estate transactions, makes large cities with dynamic property markets particularly attractive for financial crime schemes (Johannesen et al. 2022; Teichmann 2023). Under such conditions, criminal actors may exploit genuine market appreciation to conceal the origins of illicit funds or to legitimize their wealth through investments in prestigious neighbourhoods, where high property values are common and regulatory oversight tends to be limited.

The numerous attributes that define real estate properties determine their inherent characteristic of heterogeneity, which consequently contributes to the high segmentation of real estate markets, with distinct sub-markets (residential, commercial, industrial) that operate independently, often at the local or regional level. The heterogeneous and decentralized nature of real estate markets significantly constraints their transparency. Unlike financial assets traded in regulated exchanges, real estate properties are unique, illiquid, and infrequently traded, with market information dispersed across multiple local actors. The lack of centralized data systems and standardized disclosure practices leads to significant information asymmetry between market participants. Consequently, price formation often depends on pairwise negotiations and subjective assessments rather than transparent market mechanisms (Quan and Quigley 1991). This structural opacity increases transaction costs and complicates the valuation process, while also creating conditions conducive to illicit financial flows. In such an environment, discrepancies between declared and actual values, the use of intermediaries, and the layering of ownership through complex legal entities can obscure the origin of funds and the identity of beneficial owners.

A related defining feature of real estate assets is their complexity, which derives from the extensive involvement of various entities throughout the lengthy development process and the long-life cycle of properties (Breuer and Nadler 2012). The prolonged development process and the participation of numerous actors (developers, contractors, financial institutions, notaries, appraisers, and public authorities) create a complex transactional network that can obscure financial flows and dilute accountability. This fragmentation makes it easier to layer transactions, disguise beneficial ownership, and introduce illicit funds under the guise of legitimate investments. The long holding periods and revaluation opportunities inherent to real estate assets make them particularly attractive for storing and legitimizing illicit wealth.

Collectively, these features of real estate assets establish a structural environment in which financial crime can thrive. This environment is characterized not by overt illegality, but by systemic opacity, information asymmetries, and regulatory fragmentation that weaken the effectiveness of market oversight and anti-money laundering frameworks.

2.2 Real Estate Transparency: Definitions and Dimensions

The concept of transparency has gained increasing prominence in academic, policy, and market discourse, particularly following systemic disruptions such as the global financial crisis of 2007–2008. The crisis exposed the profound vulnerabilities created by a lack of clarity and oversight in the management of complex financial instruments, many of which were underpinned by real estate assets (Gorton 2008). In response, transparency came to be seen not merely as a desirable feature of markets but as a structural necessity to ensure stability, accountability, and investor protection.

Transparency in real estate markets is commonly understood as the extent to which market participants have access to reliable, timely, and comprehensive information that supports informed decision-making and mitigates information asymmetry (Ionaşcu et al. 2019b). A transparent real estate market is one in which the mechanisms governing price formation, risk allocation, and contractual enforcement are clearly understood and predictably applied (Schulte et al. 2005). The functioning of transparent property markets is conditioned by multiple interrelated factors: the quality and accessibility of legal and cadastral data, the institutional environment (e.g., judicial efficiency, corruption control), the macroeconomic stability, the degree of technological innovation, and the broader social and environmental responsibilities embedded in property governance (Gholipour et al. 2023; Newell 2016). These dimensions collectively shape the ability of market participants to make informed decisions and assess both opportunities and vulnerabilities.

Due to its multidimensional nature, assessing the level of transparency in real estate markets is inherently complex. The Global Real Estate Transparency Index (GRETI), developed by Jones Lang LaSalle (JLL), remains the most comprehensive and widely recognised benchmark for measuring transparency in the real estate sector. It evaluates transparency across six thematic pillars: performance measurement, market fundamentals, governance of listed vehicles, regulatory and legal environment, transaction process, and sustainability (JLL 2024). According to GRETI, a highly transparent market is one in which real estate performance is measured using reliable and accessible indices; fundamental market data, such as rents, yields, and transactions, is available over time and across asset types; corporate and financial disclosure practices for listed vehicles meet high standards; land and property rights are clearly defined and publicly accessible; transaction processes are governed by fair, consistent, and enforceable rules; and sustainability metrics, such as energy performance and climate risk reporting, are integrated into the market infrastructure (JLL 2024).

Although transparency is widely regarded as a deterrent to financial fraud, its effectiveness largely depends on the extent to which it is embedded within enforceable, cross-linked institutional systems (Marinoni et al. 2025). The institutional environment is the main dimension of market transparency that determines the efficient functioning of real estate markets (Ionascu 2021). From this perspective, real estate transparency should be understood as comprising a formal layer, which refers to the existence of data, regulations, reporting standards, and a functional layer, reflecting the actual usability, clarity, and enforceability of that information.

Formal transparency is a necessary condition for the functioning of the real estate sector but it is not sufficient for ensuring effective enforcement, detecting illicit practices, or preventing the misuse of property for financial crime. A higher formal transparency, which provides the structural architecture for market oversight, through disclosure rules, registries, and reporting obligations, it does not automatically translate into functional transparency. In other words, merely recording of property data does not guarantee enhanced transparency if access to that data is restricted or if it is dispersed across multiple databases administered by different institutions that lack real-time interoperability (Graham et al. 2016). Although property data may be formally transparent—recorded, documented and ostensibly available—its functional transparency may be limited by procedures, restrictive formats, fragmented registers, or prohibitive fees (Marinoni et al. 2025). Such conditions restrict the ability of market participants, intermediaries, or authorities to verify transactions, trace ownership structures, or identify irregularities. Thus, formal transparency could create an illusory transparency of relevant information that is, in fact, inaccessible to the public. Similarly, the existence of formal property registers does not ensure clarity regarding the real beneficiary exercising control over a real estate asset. In many jurisdictions, property registries document only the immediate legal owner, leaving ultimate beneficial ownership undisclosed (FATF 2022b; Marinoni et al. 2025). This allows complex corporate structures, shell companies, and nominee arrangements to obscure the identity of the real controlling party. As a result, property registries fulfil their formal role as instruments of record-keeping, yet remain limited as tools for effective surveillance, ownership verification, or anti-money laundering risk assessment. This gap highlights a fundamental aspect of the transparency paradox: although transparency mechanisms may seem robust in terms of institutional design, they only provide partial visibility in practice, creating blind spots that illicit actors can exploit strategically.

Although most jurisdictions formally extend AML obligations to real estate intermediaries, the practical impact of these regulations is weakened by exemptions, inconsistent supervisory arrangements, and limited enforcement capacity. In several markets, important intermediaries like lawyers, notaries and real estate agents are either partly free from due diligence requirements or overseen by various bodies with limited resources or legal power (Marinoni et al. 2025). Consequently, AML rules create the appearance of robust governance, even though their implementation remains inconsistent or merely symbolic. This divergence between legal design and operational practice further exemplifies the transparency paradox, whereby states may have solid AML regulations that are nevertheless vulnerable to exploitation for financial crime purposes.

In response to these limitations, complementary instruments like the Open Real Estate Observatory (OREO) Index have emerged to assess vulnerabilities of real estate sector to financial crime, with a particular focus on ownership data and anti-money laundering measures (Marinoni et al. 2025). The OREO Index evaluates two critical dimensions: (1) the scope and accessibility of real estate ownership data, measured in terms of data completeness, public availability, and openness; and (2) the adequacy of anti-money laundering regulations applied to professionals in the real estate sector, assessed through criteria such as legal coverage, due diligence obligations, identification of beneficial owners, and the strength of supervisory and sanctioning mechanisms. Launched in 2025, the OREO Index remains a relevant and valuable instrument for assessing real estate vulnerabilities, despite its geographic limitation to only 24 jurisdictions, of which just four are EU member states, as it offers a focused lens on ownership opacity and anti-money laundering frameworks.

While transparency constitutes a foundational element of market integrity, it must be reinforced by robust anti-money laundering frameworks. The following section explores how such frameworks have been developed within the European Union to address structural weaknesses that transparency measures alone are insufficient to mitigate.

2.3 The Anti-Money Laundering and Counter-Terrorism Financing Framework in the EU

The European Union has been developing a comprehensive regulatory framework to prevent the misuse of the financial system, including the real estate sector, for money laundering and terrorism financing, in line with international anti-money laundering (AML) and counter-terrorism financing (CFT) standards set by the Financial Action Task Force (FATF). The EU regulatory regime comprises a series of AML Directives and regulations, first adopted in 1990 and subsequently revised regularly, to mitigate risks related to money laundering and terrorism financing among member states. These directives set out the minimum requirements for customer due diligence, including identifying and verifying clients' identities, monitoring transactions and reporting suspicious transactions. Of particular relevance to the real estate sector is the obligation to identify and verify the beneficial owner, which is the real person(s) who ultimately owns or controls a legal entity or arrangement, thus aiming to prevent the misuse of corporate structures to conceal illicit financial flows. In this context, a significant and ongoing vulnerability arises from the limited and often unreliable access to verified information about beneficial owners involved in real estate transactions. According to the FATF (2022a) many jurisdictions continue to face high risks of money laundering and terrorism financing in the real estate sector due to this lack of transparency. When beneficial ownership information is incomplete, inaccessible, or concealed through complex legal or cross-border structures, it greatly hinders the ability of authorities to detect, investigate, and prosecute illicit financial activities.

Based on the Anti-Money Laundering Directive (AMLD 6) (EU) 2024/1640, member states are required to ensure the interconnection and digital accessibility of land registry information, cadastral records, and beneficial ownership registers through the establishment of a single access point to real estate information. This mechanism aims to provide competent authorities with immediate and direct access, free of charge, to verified data necessary for identifying real estate assets, tracing beneficial ownership, and analysing related financial transactions. Such integration marks a significant institutional advance toward unified, machine-readable, and interoperable property information systems across the Union. Complementary policy instruments reinforce this direction: the Open Data Directive (EU) 2019/1024 sets out the principles for interoperability and re-use of public sector information, while the European Strategy for Data promote the creation of Common European Data Spaces (European Commission 2025). Although a dedicated data space for real estate has not yet been formally established, the progressive integration of property-related datasets under the AML framework could constitute the foundation for its future development. This would represent a natural extension of the EU's data governance architecture toward a more transparent, data-driven, and technology-enabled property information environment.

The progressive digitalisation of real estate-related information within the EU's AML/CFT context demonstrates the increasing reliance of regulatory systems on technology as a means of ensuring compliance, accountability, and traceability.

Although these developments establish the legislative foundations for a more transparent and data-driven property market, they are still in the early stages of implementation across member states and face institutional, technical, and governance challenges (Gołaczyński and Kaczorowska 2023; Oukes et al. 2024). The integration of property-related data through the single access point mechanism not only enhances the traceability of financial flows but also exposes new vulnerabilities linked to data accuracy, cybersecurity, and interoperability. Hence, the emerging model of data-driven governance reflects both the potential and the fragility of technology-based transparency.

2.4 Technology Adoption—An Instrument of Advancing Real Estate Transparency

The growing emphasis on transparency in real estate markets increasingly converges with the digital transformation of property systems across the European Union. Member states are expected to ensure the traceability of ownership and financial flows in property transactions through land registers, cadastral systems, and mechanisms for identifying beneficial ownership. However, significant disparities persist regarding the scope, accuracy, and digital accessibility of these registries, many of which still lack critical information such as transaction prices, funding sources, or entities involved in transactions (Transparency International 2025).

In this context, the digital transformation of the real estate sector, increasingly framed within the conceptual domain of property technology (PropTech) (Baum et al. 2020), emerges as both a regulatory necessity and a catalyst for structural change toward improving real estate market transparency (Ali et al. 2025; Gholipour et al. 2023). Digital land registries, open data portals, and automated AML verification systems are increasingly complemented by advanced technologies such as blockchain, artificial intelligence, internet of things, and machine learning, which enhance data integrity, enable real-time transaction monitoring, and support anomaly detection (Ali et al. 2025; Naz et al. 2022; Saari et al. 2022). Together, these innovations represent important advances toward integrated and accountable information systems for improving real estate transparency (Ionaşcu and Anghel 2020). Moreover, by minimising information asymmetries and reducing reliance on intermediaries, PropTech-driven innovation not only streamlines real estate operations but also strengthens trust and fairness within the market (Gabrielli et al. 2022; Gholipour et al. 2023; Ionaşcu and Anghel 2020).

The potential of technology to advance transparency is, however, undermined by emerging vulnerabilities associated with its implementation. The digitalisation of property information systems remains uneven across member states, often constrained by fragmented infrastructures, inconsistent data standards, and varying institutional capacities (Oukes et al. 2024). Such discrepancies may undermine interoperability and data reliability—the key mechanisms through which formal transparency (digital records) becomes functional transparency (usable, verifiable information)—thus limiting the effectiveness of transparency-oriented tools. In addition, the concentration of sensitive information within interconnected digital systems amplifies exposure to cybersecurity threats and risks of data misuse, while gaps in regulatory alignment may delay the full operationalisation of these technologies (Abualhamayl et al. 2024; Giannoni and Medda 2023). Therefore, increasing formal transparency by digitising property data could simultaneously weaken functional transparency because of cyber risks, data manipulation or system vulnerabilities.

In this context, the digitalization-driven enhancement in the real estate sector reveals a dual perspective. On the one hand, increased transparency through digitalisation can operate as a safeguard against financial crime by strengthening oversight and accountability mechanisms. On the other hand, reliance on digital infrastructures may amplify systemic risks, inadvertently introducing new cyber vulnerabilities that sophisticated actors can exploit. Under these conditions, the transparency paradox becomes evident, as digital information, although, is formally available, weaknesses in interoperability, regulatory alignment, and cyber resilience can generate new forms of functional opacity and, implicitly, blind spots that may be exploited for illicit purposes. Nevertheless, the existing body of research remains predominantly oriented toward the benefits of digital transparency, devoting comparatively limited attention to its associated digital risks and structural vulnerabilities (Ali et al. 2025).

Ensuring that technology enhances rather than compromises cybermarket integrity, therefore, depends not only on regulatory ambition but also on the maturity, resilience, and ethical governance of the systems through which transparency is operationalised.

3 Research Methodology

To document the relationship between market transparency and the incidence of financial fraud in the EU real estate sector, this study adopts a mixed-methods approach that integrates quantitative indicators of market transparency with qualitative case evidence of illicit practices.

The quantitative component relies on a descriptive analysis of the GRETI and OREO indices to assess the transparency of the real estate market across EU member states. GRETI provides a comparative evaluation of real estate transparency based on several dimensions, including regulatory quality, availability of market fundamentals and performance data, governance of listed real estate vehicles, the integrity of transaction processes and the degree to which sustainability considerations are integrated into market practices. GRETI is the most widely used international benchmark for assessing and comparing real estate transparency across countries. The index operationalises transparency as a composite numerical score on a five-point ordinal scale, where 1 denotes a highly transparent market and 5 indicates an opaque one.

Published biennially by JLL since 1999, GRETI has undergone periodic methodological refinements to incorporate emerging transparency dimensions and to align with the evolving informational requirements of cross-border investors and corporate occupiers (JLL 2024). The most recent edition of GRETI evaluates the transparency of 89 real estate markets worldwide, including 22 jurisdictions within the European Union (JLL 2024).

The OREO index measures the operational effectiveness of transparency infrastructure on a scale from 0 to 10, assessing the completeness, availability and openness of real estate data, as well as the robustness of AML frameworks. Although OREO currently covers only four EU real estate markets, its inclusion is justified by its unique analytical value. OREO is the only available instrument that assesses the operational dimension of transparency, which complements the structural transparency measured by GRETI. Even with limited geographical coverage, OREO provides essential insights into how transparency functions in practice and serves as a benchmark for understanding systemic vulnerabilities in advanced real estate markets. Methodologically, the combined use of GRETI and OREO enables differentiation among EU countries not only by the existence of formal transparency mechanisms but also by the degree to which these mechanisms are operational, effective, and enforceable.

Although transparency indices such as GRETI and OREO provide valuable aggregate benchmarks, they cannot fully capture the complexity of how real estate transparency operates or fails in specific market contexts. The absence of globally recognised and standardised frameworks for collecting data on financial crime results in fragmented, country-level reporting that relies on inconsistent definitions and scopes (Basel Institute on Governance 2024). This fragmentation not only obscures the true scale and typologies of illicit financial flows but also weakens the empirical foundations needed to evaluate the long-term impact of transparency on financial crime (Collin et al. 2023; Teichmann 2023). Against this background, the qualitative component consists of a set of purposefully selected case studies involving real estate—related financial crime in EU member states, based on the following criteria:

- *variation in transparency levels:* the cases were drawn from countries positioned at different GRETI transparency levels to observe potential differences in how illicit financial practices manifest across varying degrees of transparency;
- *relevance to real estate—based financial crime:* only cases involving money laundering, corruption, sanctions evasion, or manipulation of property values were included, ensuring a coherent empirical foundation for documenting the transparency paradox;
- *publicly documented evidence*: cases were sourced from national and international risk assessment reports and reputable investigative journalism, allowing for reliable and traceable empirical material.

By integrating quantitative transparency metrics with qualitative case evidence, this methodological approach presents how vulnerabilities, ranging from beneficial-ownership opacity to valuation manipulation, operate across different regulatory environments. In this way, the analysis offers a critical perspective on the transparency paradox by showing how illicit financial practices persist even in highly transparent real estate markets and revealing the structural and operational weaknesses embedded within their transparency frameworks.

4 Empirical Evidence of Real Estate Transparency Paradox

This section presents empirical insights into the transparency paradox by drawing on cross-country transparency indices and selected real estate-related financial crime cases to illustrate how vulnerabilities persist across both highly and less transparent EU markets.

4.1 Mapping Real Estate Transparency in EU Countries

The EU member states are collectively positioned among the most transparent real estate markets globally. The latest GRETI edition reports an average score of 2.27 for the 22 EU member states, placing the region within the "Transparent" tier, compared to a global average of 3.05, which corresponds to a "Semi-Transparent" profile (Fig. 1). Although several non-EU jurisdictions outperform the EU, most notably the United Kingdom, which ranks first globally with a score of 1.24, the Union follows a broadly aligned regulatory trajectory aimed at strengthening market visibility, disclosure requirements, and supervisory mechanisms. Even so, transparency outcomes differ markedly across jurisdictions, signalling persistent structural asymmetries within the Union. The standard deviation of 0.56 reflects a heterogeneous distribution of outcomes, ranging from highly transparent markets such as France (1.26) to considerably less transparent cases such as Malta (3.54). This dispersion suggests that a common EU legal framework does not automatically result in uniform transparency performance. Instead, national institutional capacity, data infrastructures and enforcement practices continue to shape country-specific results.

The 2024 GRETI results reveal a four-tier structure, ranging from highly transparent to low-transparent markets. The most advanced markets, such as France, the Netherlands, Ireland, Sweden, Germany and Belgium, combine mature governance frameworks with technology integration and climate reporting, resulting in high levels of reliability and accessibility of market information (JLL 2024). A second group, including Finland, Denmark, Spain, Italy, Poland, the Czech Republic, Luxembourg, Hungary, Portugal, Romania and Slovakia, also performs well, yet technology-enabled transparency instruments are unevenly implemented, limiting full interoperability and transaction traceability. A third cluster, comprising Greece, Bulgaria, Croatia and Slovenia, remains semi-transparent and continues to face structural vulnerabilities related to data accessibility, registry digitalization and supervisory capacity, which sustain persistent informational frictions. In the last cluster, Malta stands as the only low-transparent market in the EU, where limited access

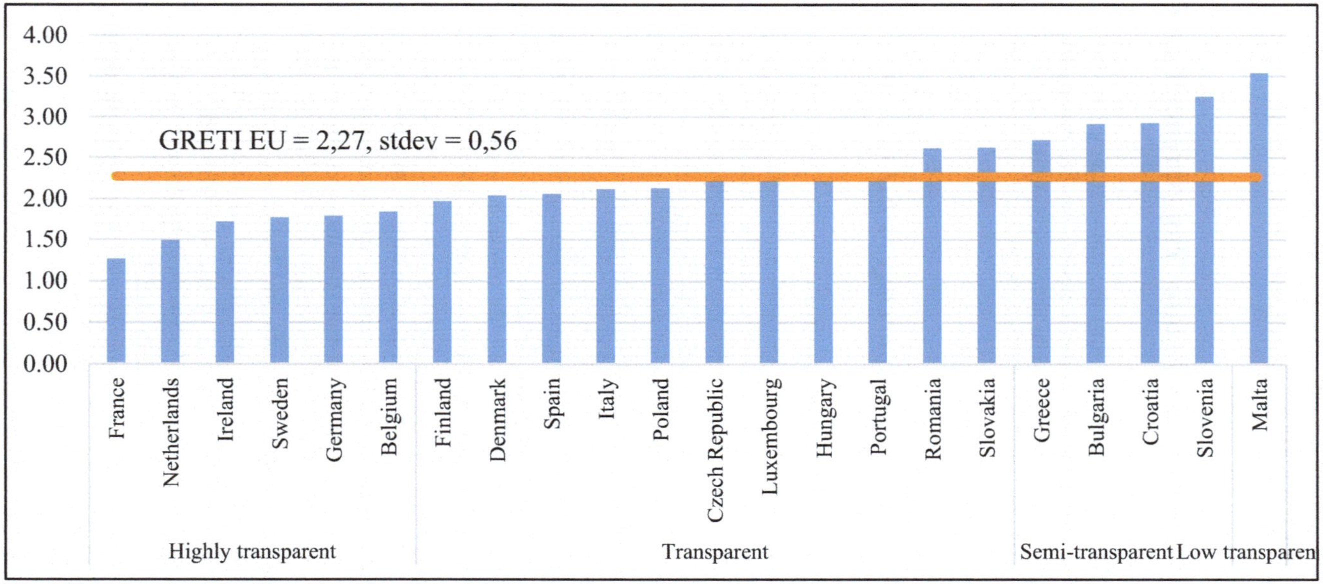

Fig. 1 Real estate transparency in 22 EU countries. *Source* Author's processing based on GRETI 2024 data, scored on 1 – to – 5 scale, where 1 denotes a highly transparent market and 5 an opaque one (JLL 2024)

to beneficial ownership information and weak enforcement of AML obligations contribute to increasing risks of financial crime in the real estate sector.

Sub-index variation further underscores the asymmetric nature of transparency performance. The strongest dimension at the EU level are the Transaction Process (1,42) and Regulatory and Legal framework (1.73), indicating both a relatively efficient procedural framework and a solid foundation of compliance structures. By contrast, weaker results are recorded for Market Fundamentals (2.52), Investment Performance (2.89) and Sustainability (2.93), where transparency is hindered by limited data harmonisation, inconsistent reporting practices and slower adoption of technology-enabled benchmarking and ESG monitoring tools (JLL 2024). These discrepancies could suggest that EU real estate transparency remains predominantly procedure and regulation-driven rather than data-driven, as institutional harmonisation has advanced faster than the modernisation of performance measurement tools, ESG reporting practices and PropTech-enabled data systems.

Although GRETI positions several EU markets among the most transparent globally, ownership transparency remains a more complex and uneven dimension. The OREO Index provides a complementary lens, revealing that even high-performing jurisdictions face persistent vulnerabilities in beneficial ownership disclosure and anti-money laundering enforcement (Marinoni et al. 2025). This asymmetry is further amplified by the limited country coverage of the OREO Index, which assesses only France, Germany, Spain, and Italy, thus restricting the extent to which ownership transparency and AML effectiveness can be evaluated across the Union as a whole (Table 2).

The comparison between GRETI and OREO reveals a structural transparency—enforcement gap within the EU. While GRETI captures formal and procedural transparency, OREO exposes a deeper layer of vulnerability: the traceability of real ownership and the effectiveness of AML controls, dimensions of functional transparency. The contrast between the two indicators of transparency reveals where formal transparency translates into functional transparency and where it does not.

Table 2 GRETI vs. OREO index in selected EU countries

EU countries	GRETI	Tier	OREO Index		
			Total score	**Real estate data**	**AML framework**
France	1.26	Highly transparent	7.16	7.63	6.69
Germany	1.79	Highly transparent	7.09	5.44	8.74
Spain	2.06	Transparent	5.91	3.88	7.94
Italy	2.12	Transparent	6.47	5.75	7.19

Source Author's processing based on GRETI 2024 data, scored on a 1 – to – 5 scale, where 1 denotes a highly transparent market and 5 an opaque one (JLL 2024), and OREO index 2024 data, presented on a 0 – to – 10 scale, where 0 reflects full opacity and 10 full ownership transparency (Marinoni et al. 2025)

Among the four countries assessed, France presents the most coherent profile, with high GRETI scores (1.26 out of 5, meaning highly transparent) mirrored by similarly strong OREO results (7.16 out of 10, meaning a low level of opacity). Both real estate data transparency and AML enforcement scores are comparatively high, suggesting that France's structural transparency aligns reasonably well with its operational transparency. Although France is widely regarded as a well-performing country in terms of overall real estate transparency, notable gaps persist in the practical applicability of its AML framework, particularly in relation to the verification of beneficial ownership and the detection of complex ownership structures (Marinoni et al. 2025). Germany illustrates a more complex configuration: although it ranks highly in GRETI (1.79 out of 5), reflecting strong market-level transparency, its OREO sub-score for real estate data (5.44) is considerably lower than its AML sub-score (8.74). This divergence shows that the functionality of transparency is constrained not by the strength of Germany's AML framework, but by gaps in the quality and interoperability of property-related data. In other words, even in a highly transparent market, missing or fragmented real estate information can restrict the effectiveness of enforcement and create blind spots for illicit financial activity.

Spain stands out as the most evident example of the transparency paradox. Categorised as a transparent market according to GRETI (2.06), Spain's average OREO score of 5.91, driven particularly by a very low real estate data sub-score of 3.88, reveals significant weaknesses in the completeness and openness of property-related information. The relatively strong AML sub-score (7.94) cannot compensate for the lack of reliable and interoperable data, producing a structural enforcement gap in which formal transparency coexists with pronounced functional opacity. Nevertheless, Spain has recently made notable progress in increasing real estate transparency, launching a centralised registry of beneficial ownership for real estate (JLL 2024). Italy ranks in the middle of the GRETI ranking (2.12), reflecting a transparent market environment but its OREO score of 6.47, although better than Spain's, highlights major shortcomings in real estate data availability and openness, as well as in due diligence requirements and beneficial ownership identification. Spain and Italy illustrate the same pattern, where compliance frameworks exist but fail to ensure systematic real-time traceability of beneficial ownership across transactions (Marinoni et al. 2025).

Taken together, these findings point to a transparency paradox, whereby strong regulatory frameworks do not guarantee full ownership clarity or effective oversight. High GRETI scores indicate that EU real estate markets have achieved robust structural transparency, yet OREO reveals persistent vulnerabilities in data interoperability, beneficial ownership verification, and AML enforcement. Even the highest-ranked EU markets, such as France and Germany, display critical weaknesses when ownership transparency is assessed, suggesting that procedural openness has not translated into full operational transparency. Transparency is most vulnerable at the enforcement interface, where digital infrastructure, data interoperability, and supervisory capacity shape the extent to which formal transparency becomes functional in practice.

4.2 Case Studies: Real Estate and Financial Crime

Table 3 summarises a set of illustrative case studies that document the transparency paradox in real estate markets. Analysing these cases provides insight into the mechanisms employed in financial crime and the real estate sector vulnerabilities exploited, both in countries with highly transparent property markets, such as France, Spain, and Italy, and in those with lower levels of transparency, including Bulgaria and Malta.

The comparative analysis of recent cases reveals several financial crime practices, adapted to different levels of real estate transparency and, implicitly, regulatory enforcement. In highly transparent markets, such as those in Germany, France and Spain, financial crime tends to be carried out using sophisticated ownership and financing structures. By contrast, in semi-transparent and low-transparency markets, like those in Bulgaria and Malta, criminal schemes exploit weak enforcement, administrative loopholes, and low-quality data integration.

Beyond differences in transparency, the cases analysed show that beneficial ownership opacity is the vulnerability most frequently exploited in illicit financial practices. In Germany, France, and Spain, countries characterised by high levels of real estate transparency, authorities have identified cases where offshore entities were used to purchase high-value properties with illicit money to conceal the identity of the real owner and avoid certain sanctions (FATF 2023). These examples underline the gap between formal transparency and functional transparency, illustrating how complex offshore structures and layered intermediaries can obscure beneficial ownership even in a highly transparent market. Despite robust disclosure frameworks and advanced property registries, functional transparency remains limited (Marinoni et al. 2025).

The Italian case, despite the country's relatively transparent real estate market, exposes the dual function of property as both a vehicle for concealing illicit wealth and a space of persistent opacity in tracing the origin of funds, revealing gaps between fiscal and anti-money laundering enforcement. In this example, the paradox emerges from the misalignment between fiscal and administrative transparency, on one hand, and the effectiveness of AML enforcement, on the other, revealing that transparent formal systems do not prevent the concealment of illicit capital when verification mechanisms are weak.

Germany's experience illustrates the paradox of strong institutional transparency coexisting with persistent opacity in practice. Although Germany is widely regarded as a highly transparent real estate market, the main money laundering and terrorist financing risks stem from its robust economy, cash-intensive sectors, and extensive international interconnectedness (FATF 2022a). Despite the presence of a comprehensive regulatory framework and a well-established transparency register, FATF (FATF 2022a, 2023) identified significant deficiencies in the supervision of non-financial intermediaries, inconsistent due diligence enforcement, and incomplete or outdated beneficial ownership information. The persistence of such gaps indicates that money laundering in Germany does not rely on the absence of information, but on the ability of illicit actors to navigate and manipulate the regulatory framework

Table 3 Selected cases of suspected financial crime across EU markets

Country	GRETI tier	Description	Mechanism	Vulnerability	Transparency paradox
France	Highly transparent	In 2024, French authorities seized €70 million in assets, including villas and luxury cars, tied to Russian businessmen using offshore entities in Cyprus and the British Virgin Islands (El Idrissi 2024)	Money laundering: use of offshore entities providing loans from tax-haven jurisdictions to finance property acquisitions and circumvent sanctions	Beneficial ownership opacity	High formal transparency (registries, disclosure rules) coexists with functional opacity due to complex offshore structures that bypass ownership verification
Spain	Transparent	In 2024, Spanish authorities investigated a high-value real estate laundering scheme involving the purchase of multiple luxury properties in Northeastern Spain. The assets, acquired through offshore companies and family intermediaries, were financed by funds linked to an international laundering network previously exposed in Europe. Transactions were structured as intra-family transfers and disguised loans to conceal beneficial ownership (Baquero 2025)	Money laundering: use of offshore shell companies and family intermediaries to acquire and conceal ownership of luxury properties and circumvent sanctions	Beneficial ownership opacity	Sophisticated opaque ownership structures exist in a formal transparent market

(continued)

Table 3 (continued)

Country	GRETI tier	Description	Mechanism	Vulnerability	Transparency paradox
Italy	Transparent	In 2024, the European Public Prosecutor's Office (EPPO) in Milan investigated an embezzlement and fraud scheme involving approximately €1 million in misused social funds. Two residential properties purchased with diverted public money were seized (EPPO 2024)	Conversion of embezzled public resources into residential properties to conceal illicit origin and preserve asset value	Origin of funds opacity	Fiscal/ administrative transparency does not prevent AML opacity
Bulgaria	Semi-transparent	In 2019, Bulgarian prosecutors launched investigations into the misuse of EU development funds for the construction of hundreds of private guest houses and into property acquisitions by officials at prices significantly below market value. The inquiry resulted in multiple resignations and financial sanctions imposed on beneficiaries (Saric 2019)	The misuse of EU public funds for private construction and the acquisition of luxury real estate by officials at prices significantly below market value	Manipulation of market values	Formal disclosure exists, but poor verification and inconsistent valuation practices produce systemic functional opacity
Malta	Low-transparency	Maltese authorities have uncovered a large-scale residency fraud scheme involving the fabrication of over 1,500 false lease agreements used to obtain residence permits. The scheme relied on intermediaries in the rental market who repeatedly registered dozens of individuals at identical addresses (Borg 2024)	Systematic falsification of rental contracts for foreign nationals, often associating several people at a single address, to legitimize addresses of residence in administrative systems and mask illicit cash flows with those derived from rents	Regulatory blind spots in verifying lease authenticity	Regulatory completeness is formal, but weak verification and fragmented data undermine functional transparency

Source Author's processing

itself. The evidence reinforces the observation that criminal actors tend to favour developed countries with mature real estate markets, as these environments offer both stability and the potential for high returns on property investments (Teichmann 2023).

The case of Bulgaria, whose real estate market is considered semi-transparent, provides an illustrative example of how property values can be deliberately manipulated by distorting the market. It reveals systemic weaknesses in property valuation, verification of income sources, and oversight of EU funds, demonstrating how real estate transactions can conceal political corruption and erode institutional transparency. The Bulgarian case exposes functional opacity despite formal reporting because of inconsistent valuation and weak institutional coordination.

The case of Malta, known as having the least transparent real estate market in the EU, represents a distinct manifestation of the transparency paradox, where the appearance of regulatory completeness conceals significant operational gaps. NCC (2023) acknowledges that Malta's real estate sector remains among the most prone to the risk of money laundering and terrorist financing. The Maltese case suggests vulnerabilities related to weak verification of rental contract authenticity, fragmented data reporting in state registers, and limited due diligence among real estate agents and other intermediaries involved. This case illustrates how low transparency and fragmented systems create blind spots behind the appearance of regulatory completeness. Even when regulatory frameworks appear comprehensive, weaknesses in enforcement and data coordination undermine functional transparency and allow illicit practices to remain undetected.

This evidence reveals the existence of institutional vulnerabilities in state systems that are exploited in the conduct of illicit financial activities, both in highly transparent markets and in those with low transparency. Taken together, these cases demonstrate how different facets of the transparency paradox materialise across diverse real estate markets. In highly transparent jurisdictions, such as France, Germany, Spain, and Italy, the paradox emerges through sophisticated forms of functional opacity that circumvent ownership verification and obscure the origin of funds despite robust formal frameworks. In semi-transparent and low-transparency environments, such as Bulgaria and Malta, inconsistencies in data quality, weak institutional coordination, and limited verification capacity translate formal disclosure requirements into incomplete or unreliable visibility. Across these contexts, the empirical evidence shows that vulnerabilities arise not from the absence of transparency mechanisms but from the persistent disconnect between their formal design and their functional performance. Thus, real estate transparency can only be effective when supported by coherent, interoperable, and enforceable governance systems. This idea reinforces the importance of institutional dimension as a fundamental pillar of formal and functional transparency (Ionaşcu et al. 2019a).

Real estate assets remain one of the primary channels for laundering proceeds derived from criminal activities. According to Europol (2024), around 41% of the criminal networks identified within the European Union use the real estate sector as a preferred vehicle for money laundering. From this perspective, transparency in real estate should be understood as a process of enforcement and verification, rather than a declarative principle. Policymakers and civil society actors must therefore move beyond the formal existence of transparency frameworks and focus on ensuring their operational effectiveness and institutional coherence.

5 Conclusions

The purpose of this chapter is to explore the relation between real estate transparency and financial crime in the digital era, with a particular focus on the EU context. The analysis revealed that while transparency and digitalisation are essential components of a resilient real estate market, they are not sufficient on their own to prevent financial crime. On the contrary, in the absence of robust enforcement regulation mechanisms, verified beneficial ownership data, and institutional interoperability, increased transparency may be exploited to simulate compliance and obscure illicit financial flows. In more advanced jurisdictions, with well-developed legal structures and reporting requirements, criminal actors often leverage legal complexity, professional intermediaries, and digital tools to conceal ownership or construct the appearance of legitimacy. In less transparent markets, the lack of access to ownership data and limited regulatory oversight create conditions in which financial crime can occur with minimal resistance. Collectively, this evidence sustains the need to shift from a predominantly formal (registries, disclosure requirements) to a functional (data usability, verification, interoperability, enforcement) understanding of real estate transparency. The paradox of transparency in real estate lies in the gap between formal transparency and functional transparency, which creates blind spots that could be exploited for illicit purposes. Across the analysed markets, vulnerabilities emerge not from the absence of transparency mechanisms, but from the misalignment between formal transparency and functional transparency.

Digital innovations are frequently perceived as tools for enhancing transparency, particularly in reducing anonymous ownership of real estate. However, the effectiveness of digital instruments depends heavily on how they are integrated into broader institutional and regulatory systems. Without proper governance, such technologies may have a limited impact or may even be exploited to simulate compliance rather than ensure genuine transparency.

The real estate vulnerabilities to financial crime practices require serious attention from policymakers. First, transparency reforms should move beyond input-based indicators and adopt an integrated approach that links land registries, corporate records, and beneficial ownership databases. Interoperable data systems, supported by common standards for property identifiers, beneficial ownership identification and transaction reporting, are essential for enabling meaningful oversight. Second, verification of beneficial ownership must be substantially strengthened by regular data audits, risk-based verification procedures, elimination of exemptions for high-risk intermediaries, and automated cross-checks between real estate, fiscal and corporate registers. This requirement aligns with the provisions of the EU AMLD, which mandate member states to establish centralised beneficial ownership registers accessible to competent authorities and, in some cases, civil society, but the implementation progress is uneven across jurisdictions. Third, AML obligations should also be extended to all professional intermediaries involved in real estate transactions, including lawyers, notaries, valuers, and developers, whose roles often provide critical gateways for money laundering. Fourth, digital tools such as automated red-flag detection, machine-learning models for anomaly detection and AI-assisted due diligence can enhance monitoring capacities, but only when embedded within well-resourced, independent and digital capable supervisory authorities. Finaly, transparency policy must prioritise building institutional capacity and encouraging cross-border cooperation, particularly for detecting complex layering schemes and offshore structures. In the absence of robust regulatory frameworks and effective mechanisms for verifying compliance, real estate transparency risks becoming a superficial measure—one that obscures rather than addresses the structural vulnerabilities, which enable financial crime within the sector.

Despite the breadth of the analysis, several limitations must be acknowledged. The empirical component relies on data from two transparency indices—GRETI and OREO—which, although conceptually complementary, differ in scope, methodology and country coverage. GRETI covers 22 EU member states, whereas the OREO index is currently available for only four EU countries. This asymmetry limits the extent to which conclusions about the alignment or divergence between market transparency, AML enforcement and ownership transparency can be generalised across the entire EU. Another limitation refers to the case studies analysed. While they are illustrative of structural vulnerabilities, the case studies reviewed do not constitute an exhaustive inventory of real estate-related financial crime within the Union. Their availability depends heavily on the degree of media scrutiny, judicial disclosure and institutional reporting in each country. This can result in certain forms of illicit activity being under-represented, particularly in jurisdictions with weaker investigative journalism or limited access to public records. The final limitation relates to the exploratory and descriptive nature of the research rather than an in-depth analysis mediated by statistical modelling, due to data limitations and inherent opacity of illicit financial flows.

These limitations also highlight important areas for future research. Geographical expansion of composite transparency measurement indices to allow for broader cross-country comparisons across all EU countries to facilitate empirical testing of the transparency paradox for the purpose of documenting future reforms. Future research could benefit from the construction of more comprehensive databases of financial crime cases linked to real estate, integrating data from judicial records, reports, property and beneficial ownership registries in order to better capture the breadth of illicit practices. A promising research direction lies in empirically evaluating digitalisation reforms, such as introducing interoperable registries, automated verification tools, and unique property identifiers, to measure their actual impact on transparency and enforcement capacity.

References

Abualhamayl A, Almalki M, Al-Doghman F, Alyoubi A, Hussain FK (2024) Blockchain for real estate provenance: an infrastructural step toward secure transactions in real estate E-Business. SOCA 18:333–347. https://doi.org/10.1007/s11761-024-00403-0

Ali W, Samarasinghe DAS, Feng Z, Wilkinson S, Rotimi JOB (2025) A systematic literature review on digital transformation in real estate: challenges and opportunities. Smart and Sustainable Built Environment. Ahead-of-print. https://doi.org/10.1108/SASBE-04-2024-0111

Baquero A (2025, July 12) Spanish police arrest son of Russian defense executive in money laundering probe. Organized Crime and Corruption Reporting Project (OCCRP). https://www.occrp.org/en/news/spanish-police-arrest-son-of-russian-defense-executive-in-money-laundering-probe?utm_source=chatgpt.com

Basel Institute on Governance (2024) Basel AML Index 2024: 13th Public Edition. Ranking money laundering risks around the world. https://index.baselgovernance.org/api/assets/0789b440-8537-45b4-8bfd-e44ac456c15d.pdf

Baum A, Saull A, Braesemann F (2020) Proptech 2020: the future of real estate. https://www.sbs.ox.ac.uk/research/oxford-future-real-estate

Bieler SA (2022) Peeking into the house of cards: money laundering, luxury real estate, and the necessity of data verification for the corporate transparency act's beneficial ownership registry. Fordham J Corp Financ Law 27(1):193–258. https://ir.lawnet.fordham.edu/jcfl/vol27/iss1/4

Borg J (2024, November 15) 'Fake mailbox' leads police to rental contract scam operated from barber shop. Times of Malta. https://timesofmalta.com/article/fake-mailbox-leads-police-rental-contract-scam-operated-barber-shop.1101085?utm_medium=Socialandutm_source=Facebookandfbclid=IwY2xjawNxRE9leHRuA2FlbQIxMQABHnrEgN6enVJKeZQ5vhPAzl554qADDsVrYuX4Ng-nE_VWOUALSl2nClIhsPJB_aem_Pn5mrdR53BzU2EApowDufQ#Echobox=1731679793

Breuer W, Nadler C (2012) Real estate and real estate finance as a research field—an international overview. J Bus Econ 82(1):5–52. https://doi.org/10.1007/978-3-8349-3864-0_2

Collin M, Hollenbach FM, Szakonyi D (2023) The end of Londongrad? The impact of beneficial ownership transparency on offshore investment in UK property (2023/11; WIDER Working Paper). https://www.wider.unu.edu/sites/default/files/Publications/Working-paper/PDF/wp2023-11-end-Londongrad-impact-beneficial-ownership-transparency-offshore-investment-UK-property.pdf

Dugato M, Favarin S, Giommoni L (2015) The risks and rewards of organized crime investments in real estate. Br J Criminol 55(5):944–965. https://doi.org/10.1093/BJC/AZV002

El Idrissi A (2024, October 14) Villas, luxury cars worth €70 million and belonging to Russian oligarchs seized in France. Le Monde. https://www.lemonde.fr/en/les-decodeurs/article/2024/10/14/villas-luxury-cars-worth-70-million-and-belonging-to-russian-oligarchs-seized-in-france_6729372_8.html?utm_source=chatgpt.com

EPPO (2024, October 30) Italy: Investigation into €1 million embezzlement fraud involving social funds—EPPO seizes two properties. European Public Prosecutor's Office. https://www.eppo.europa.eu/en/media/news/italy-investigation-eu1-million-embezzlement-fraud-involving-social-funds-eppo-seizes?utm_source=chatgpt.com

EPRA, INREV (2024) Real estate in the real economy: Supporting growth, jobs and sustainability. www.epra.com

European Commission (2025) A European strategy for data. Shaping Europe's Digital Future. https://digital-strategy.ec.europa.eu/en/policies/strategy-data

Europol (2024) Decoding the EU's most threatening criminal networks. https://doi.org/10.2813/811566

FATF (2007) Money laundering and terrorist financing through the real estate sector

FATF (2022a) Anti-money laundering and counter-terrorist financing measures—Germany, Fourth Round Mutual Evaluation Report. http://www.fatf-gafi.org/publications/mutualevaluations/documents/mer-germany-2022.html

FATF (2022b) Guidance for a risk-based approach to the real estate sector. www.fatf-gafi.org/publications/documents/Guidance-RBA-Real-Estate-Sector.html

FATF (2023) Anti-money laundering and counter-terrorist financing measures—Germany, 1st Enhanced Follow-up Report. www.fatf-gafi.org

Gabrielli L, Ruggeri AG, Scarpa M (2022) Detecting information transaprency in the Italian real estate market: a machine learning approach. Valori e Valutazione 31:33–47

Gholipour HF, Arjomandi A, Andargoli AE, Bennett R (2023) On real estate market transparency: the relationship with ICT trade and investment. Land Use Policy 133:106846. https://doi.org/10.1016/J.LANDUSEPOL.2023.106846

Giannoni C, Medda F (2023) Unlocking transparency: harnessing blockchain for anti-money laundering in alternative assets. The case of fine art and real estate. Sustainable and Impact Investments International Conference (SIIIC). https://ssrn.com/abstract=4662355

Gołaczyński J, Kaczorowska M (2023) Interconnecting Land Registers at the European Level: Technological Progress and Harmonization Aspects. Rev Eur Comp Law 55(4):29–68. https://doi.org/10.31743/RECL.16593

Gorton GB (2008) The panic of 2007 (14358; NBER Working Paper Series). http://www.nber.org/papers/w14358

Graaskamp JA (1992) Fundamentals of real estate development. J Prop Valuat Invest 10(3):619–639. https://doi.org/10.1108/14635789210031253

Graham FS, Gooden ST, Martin KJ (2016) Navigating the transparency-privacy paradox in public sector data sharing. Am Rev Public Adm 46(5):569–591. https://doi.org/10.1177/0275074014561116/FORMAT/EPUB

Ionascu E (2021) Asimetria informaţională şi transparenţa investiţională pe piaţa imobiliară. Editura Economică

Ionaşcu E, Anghel I (2020) Improvement of the real estate transparency through digitalisation. Proc Int Conf Bus Excel 14(1):371–384. https://doi.org/10.2478/PICBE-2020-0036

Ionaşcu E, Mironiuc M, Anghel I (2019a) Transparency of real estate markets: conceptual and empirical evidence. Audit Financiar 17(154):306–326. https://doi.org/10.20869/auditf/2019/154/013

Ionaşcu E, Taltavull de La Paz P, Mironiuc M (2019) The Relationship between housing prices and market transparency. In: Evidence from the metropolitan European markets. Housing, theory and society. https://doi.org/10.1080/14036096.2019.1672577

JLL (2024) Global real estate transparency Index, 2024: Tranparency in a time of transition

Johannesen N, Miethe J, Weishaar D (2022) Homes incorporated: Offshore ownership of real estate in the U.K. (10159; CESifo Working Paper). https://doi.org/10.2139/ssrn.4309211

Marinoni E, Rostomashvili E, Hornsby M (2025) Opacity in real estate ownership index. Assessing data transparency and anti-money laundering rules in global markets. www.transparency.org

Mooya MM (2016) Real estate valuation theory. A critical appraisal. Springer Nature. https://doi.org/10.1007/978-1-4615-0909-7

Naz F, Kumar A, Upadhyay A, Chokshi H, Trinkunas V, Magda R (2022) Property management enabled by artificial intelligence post Covid-19: an exploratory review and future propositions. Int J Strat Prop Manag 26(2):156–171. https://journals.vilniustech.lt/index.php/IJSPM/article/view/16923/11174

Nazzari M, Riccardi M (2022) Cleaning mafia cash: an empirical analysis of the money laundering behaviour of 2800 Italian criminals. The Third International Research Conference on Empirical Approaches to Anti-Money Laundering

NCC (2023) Money laundering, terrorist and proliferation financing and targeted financial sanctions: Malta's National Risk Assessment 2023

Newell G (2016) The changing real estate market transparency in the European real estate markets. J Prop Invest Financ 34(4):407–420. https://doi.org/10.1108/JPIF-07-2015-0053

OECD (2019) Money laundering and terrorist financing awareness handbook for tax examiners and tax auditors. OECD

Oukes P, Okembo C, Morales J, Lemmen C, Zevenbergen J, Kuria D (2024) Implementing data exchange and interoperability on LADM country profiles using the ISO framework for enterprise interoperability standard. Land Use Policy 146:107333. https://doi.org/10.1016/J.LANDUSEPOL.2024.107333

Quan DC, Quigley JM (1991) Price formation and the appraisal function in real estate markets. J R Estate Financ Econ 4(2):127–146. https://link.springer.com/content/pdf/10.1007%2FBF00173120.pdf

Remeur C (2019) Understanding money laundering through real estate transactions

Rosen S (1974) Hedonic prices and implicit markets: product differentiation in pure competition. J Polit Econ 82(1):34–55. https://pdfs.semanticscholar.org/c66b/420f81caa64ad7a8e1cce2fd6ea7218099ff.pdf

Saari A, Vimpari J, Junnila S (2022) Blockchain in real estate: recent developments and empirical applications. Land Use Policy 121:106334. https://doi.org/10.1016/J.LANDUSEPOL.2022.106334

Saric I (2019, May 15) Bulgarian Minister involved in property scandal quits. Organized Crime and Corruption Reporting Project (OCCRP). https://www.occrp.org/en/news/bulgarian-minister-involved-in-property-scandal-quits?utm_source=chatgpt.com

Schulte K, Rottke N, Pitschke C (2005) Transparency in the German real estate market. J Prop Invest Financ 23(1):90–108. https://doi.org/10.1108/14635780510575111

Teichmann FMJ (2023) Financial crimes in the real estate sector in Austria, Germany, Liechtenstein and Switzerland. J Money Laund Control 26(2):418–432. https://doi.org/10.1108/JMLC-05-2019-0044

Transparency International (2025) One click away? The barriers investigators face across the EU when tracing asset ownership. https://www.transparency.org/en/news/barriers-investigators-face-across-eu-tracing-asset-ownership?utm_source=chatgpt.com

UNODC (n.d.) Money laundering. United Nations Office on Drugs and Crime. Retrieved November 1, 2025, from https://www.unodc.org/unodc/en/money-laundering/overview.html

Elena Ionaşcu , BA (Bacau), MA (Iasi, Bucharest), PhD (Iasi), is an assistant professor at the Bucharest University of Economic Studies, where she teaches economic and financial analysis and business valuation. She is a certified real estate and business valuer, as well as a scientific researcher and lecturer in professional training programs for valuers organized by ANEVAR. Her research interests include: transparency of real estate markets, sustainable development of the real estate sector, digital innovation, and business valuation. She is the author and co-author of several articles and books published in prestigious peer-reviewed journals and academic publishing houses.

One More Time, the Dark Side of the Economy: Exploring the Shadow Economy in the European Union

Andreea-Roxana Danci, Ionuț-Adrian Lazar, and Gabriela-Mihaela Mureșan

Abstract This study examines the key drivers of the shadow economy in the European Union between 2003 and 2022, using panel data techniques that integrate socioeconomic, cultural, and institutional variables. Starting with the measure developed by Friedrich Schneider, the shadow economy refers to the dark side of the economy. Our findings confirm that cultural, institutional, and behavioral factors significantly influence the size of the shadow economy. Moreover, the study highlights the importance of interactions between institutional quality and fiscal pressure, suggesting that well-functioning governance systems can mitigate the unintended consequences of tax burdens. The results highlight the importance of complementing reforms with a focus on deeper institutional dynamics and cultural contexts to combat corruption. In addition to legal and fiscal reforms, European countries must make new efforts to promote behavioral change among citizens and foster civic engagement to combat all aspects of financial crime.

Keywords Shadow economy · Financial crime · Cultural · Institutional · Socioeconomic

JEL Classification E26 · E62 · O17

A.-R. Danci · I.-A. Lazar (✉) · G.-M. Mureșan
Faculty of Economics and Business Administration, Babeș-Bolyai University, Cluj-Napoca, Romania
e-mail: ionut.adrian.lazar@stud.ubbcluj.ro

A.-R. Danci
e-mail: andreea.roxana.danci@stud.ubbcluj.ro

G.-M. Mureșan
e-mail: gabriela.muresan@econ.ubbcluj.ro

M. V. Achim (ed.), *Financial Crime in the Digital Era*, Contributions to Finance and Accounting, https://doi.org/10.1007/978-3-032-20198-0_17

1 Introduction

The shadow economy, often referred to as the "dark side of the economy," remains a persistent structural issue for modern societies. It involves illegal market activities that are intentionally hidden from authorities to avoid taxes, social contributions, or regulations. More than just its definition, informality weakens tax revenue, distorts competition, erodes trust in institutions, and changes the implicit agreement between citizens and the government. Therefore, it is not merely a minor irregularity but a phenomenon driven by economic incentives, governance issues, and cultural factors.

Quantitatively, its size remains significant. Long-term estimates by Schneider and colleagues indicate that informal activity accounts for less than 10 percent of GDP in Nordic economies, but exceeds one-quarter in several Southern and Eastern European countries (Schneider 2015, 2022). This variation within a shared economic area highlights the paradox of European integration: unified supranational frameworks coexist with varying national abilities to control shadow activity.

The consequences go beyond financial losses. Governments see decreasing revenues, which limits their ability to fund public services, while legal businesses face unfair competition from untaxed rivals. Citizens facing widespread tax evasion may lose trust in the system, fueling a cycle of noncompliance. Therefore, the shadow economy is both a symptom of weak institutions and a contributor to governance problems.

Studies have approached this issue from three main perspectives. The economic approach emphasizes taxation, unemployment, and labor rigidities, drawing on early cost–benefit models of compliance (Allingham and Sandmo 1972). Empirical research indicates that high fiscal pressure and instability tend to increase informality, whereas growth and openness tend to decrease it (Neck et al. 2012; Khan et al. 2023). The institutional approach focuses on governance quality, regulatory efficiency, and the rule of law, with corruption and weak enforcement consistently linked to larger shadow economies (Buehn et al. 2018). Evidence from transition economies suggests that misalignments in institutions and norms undermine compliance (Gërxhani and Cichocki 2023). A third perspective considers cultural and behavioral factors, noting that compliance depends not only on deterrence but also on tax morale (Alm and Torgler 2011). Hofstede's cultural framework suggests that power distance and uncertainty avoidance are correlated with larger shadow economies, whereas individualism and long-term orientation tend to reduce them (Husted 1999; Buszko 2018; Saunoris 2024). However, religion has not consistently shown effects, implying that cultural influence mainly operates through trust and shared values (Shadabi 2013).

Despite these advances, much of the literature remains fragmented, treating each dimension separately. However, recent work highlights interaction effects: strong institutions can mitigate the negative impact of taxation (Schneider 2022), individualism enhances the effect of economic freedom in reducing informality (Saunoris 2024), while institutional-cultural misalignments may amplify shadow activity (Gërxhani and Cichocki 2023). They highlight the importance of integrated approaches that account for the interdependencies among economic, institutional, and cultural factors.

The EU offers an especially suitable setting for such analysis. Despite harmonized supranational frameworks, member states vary significantly in their levels of development, institutional strength, and cultural backgrounds. This diversity provides a natural laboratory for examining both direct effects and interactions in shaping shadow activity.

Against this background, the present study investigates the drivers of the shadow economy in EU countries from 2003 to 2022. Building on Schneider's estimates, we use panel econometric techniques to examine the impact of socioeconomic factors (taxation, unemployment, inflation), institutional indicators (governance quality, rule of law, regulatory efficiency), and cultural dimensions (individualism, power distance, uncertainty avoidance, among others). By analyzing both direct and moderating effects, the study provides a comprehensive understanding of informality. It offers policy insights into how fiscal reforms can be supported by institutional strengthening and cultural awareness.

2 Literature Review

The modern study of tax evasion and the shadow economy begins with the Allingham and Sandmo framework (1972), which views noncompliance as an expected utility maximization problem, balancing gains from evasion with the likelihood and severity of detection and punishment. Later research distinguished between tax avoidance and tax evasion, highlighting the impact of labor-market frictions. Complex tax systems, with many exemptions and deductions, can lead to tax avoidance, while oversimplified systems may paradoxically promote certain activities becoming informal (Neck et al. 2012).

Regarding its definition and measurement, the shadow economy is generally described as legally productive activities intentionally hidden from authorities to avoid taxes or regulations, excluding traditional criminal activities. Empirical research primarily relies on macro-indirect methods, particularly the MIMIC (Multiple Indicators Multiple Causes) approach, which is often calibrated using the currency demand method. Alternative proxies, like electricity consumption or survey-based data, are used to triangulate estimates. Although these methods offer relative size indicators as a percentage of GDP, they carry significant margins of error and should be interpreted with caution (Buehn and Schneider 2013; Schneider et al. 2015).

Regarding determinants, evidence from the 2000s highlighted the importance of unemployment, self-employment, and the tax burden, alongside regulation, bureaucracy, and tax morale. In a broad OECD panel (1999–2010), unemployment and self-employment were found to be the strongest drivers of shadow economy dynamics, followed by tax morale, GDP growth, and business freedom (Buehn and Schneider 2013). For Europe, estimates covering the period 2003–2014 confirmed a gradual decline in the shadow economy but persistent heterogeneity, with higher shares in Southern and Eastern Europe (Schneider et al. 2015).

Since the 2010s, two major strands of literature have broadened the field. First, scholars have incorporated cultural and institutional factors into their research. Cross-country analyses show that Hofstede's cultural dimensions (2011), such as uncertainty avoidance, individualism, and masculinity, along with governance quality (rule of law, control of corruption), influence levels of the informal sector, with evidence of spatial spillovers across neighboring countries (Achim 2016; Alarcón-García et al. 2020; Syed 2025). Second, there has been a shift toward ethics and trust. Compliance is increasingly seen not just as a deterrence issue but also as rooted in social norms and perceptions of fairness. The "enforcement-service-trust" model suggests that tax administrations can promote higher compliance through a combination of deterrence, facilitation, and building trust measures (Alm and Torgler 2011). In the same institutional-psychological context, corruption damages both well-being and trust, indirectly encouraging tolerance of informality (Tay et al. 2014).

Recent EU and OECD studies have documented how the global financial crisis (GFC) and COVID-19 pandemic reshaped informal activity. Following a pre-pandemic low in 2019, the shadow economy surged in 2020 to record-high levels, then experienced partial declines in 2021 and 2022 (Schneider 2022). A broader synthesis extending to 2022 confirms a long-term downward trend in the EU shadow economy, interrupted by temporary reversals during crises such as COVID-19 and the energy shock. The structural factors remain mostly stable, including tax burden, unemployment, self-employment, tax morale, and institutional quality. In contrast, effective policies focus on fiscal reform, digitalization, and stronger governance (Asllani and Schneider 2025).

For Eastern Europe and Romania, both macro- and micro-level studies agree that labor market dynamics (unemployment, part-time work, and self-employment) and institutional efficiency are the main factors explaining outcomes, rather than just tax levels. Policy options with higher success potential include strengthening administrative capacity, implementing measures to promote formal employment, and improving tax morale (Popescu et al. 2018).

2.1 *Bibliometric Analysis*

Given the limited research on the relationship between the shadow economy and cultural factors, we conducted a bibliometric analysis to examine the overlap between these two fields in the academic literature. Using the Web of Science Core Collection, we search for publications that contain the terms "shadow economy," "informal economy," or "underground economy," combined with "culture," "Hofstede," or "cultural values." The search yielded 235 relevant articles, and we used the VOSviewer to visualize the co-occurrence of author keywords and citations (Fig. 1).

The resulting network visualization reveals several distinct research clusters that collectively capture the main directions of the literature on this topic.

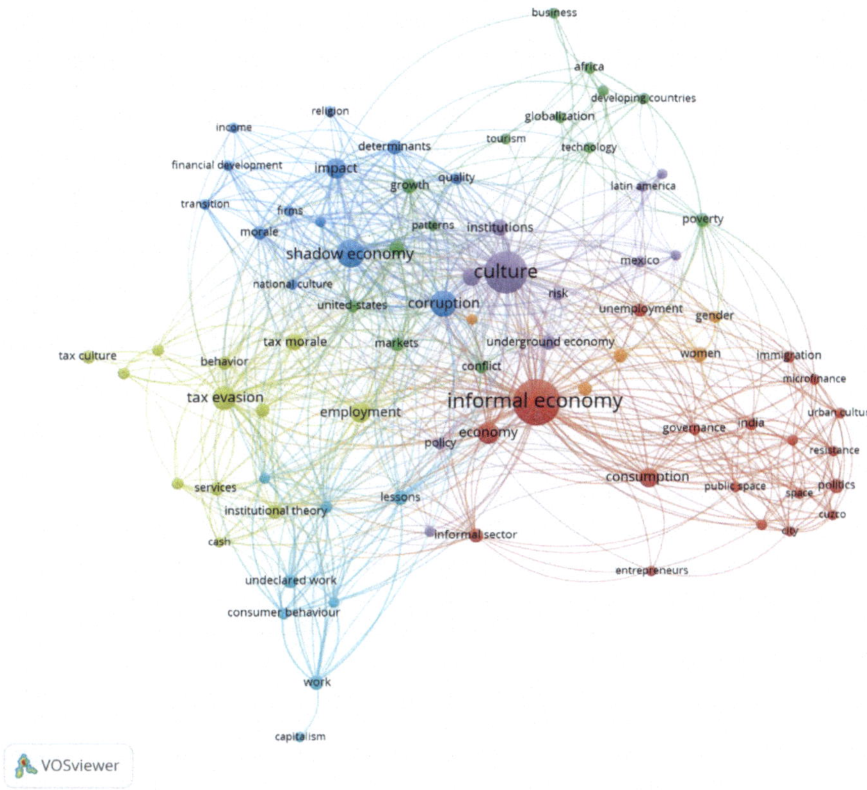

Fig. 1 Co-Occurrence analysis of key concepts. *Source* Created by the authors using Vosviewer

The bibliometric map shows that the most influential and frequently co-occurring keywords in the field are "shadow economy," "informal economy," and "culture." These three terms form the core of the literature and serve as central nodes within the network, linking various thematic areas across disciplines.

The keyword "shadow economy" is most closely associated with corruption, tax morale, national culture, institutions, and governance. These connections suggest that research on this term primarily focuses on the institutional and moral aspects of informality, highlighting how cultural and governance factors influence tax compliance and participation in the informal economy.

The "informal economy" cluster is more diverse and connected to employment, policy, consumption, governance, and urban development. This reflects a broader socioeconomic perspective, emphasizing labor markets, social protection, and policy responses to informality. Links between public space and urban culture also highlight a growing interest in how informal activities are perceived in spatial and community contexts.

The keyword "culture" serves as a bridge between the institutional and socioeconomic groups. It is most closely associated with corruption, governance, tax evasion, behavior, and morale, indicating that cultural factors are crucial mediators of informal conduct and the quality of governance. The frequent use of terms such as national culture, tax morale, and corruption underscores the role of Hofstede's cultural dimensions in explaining differences in shadow economic activity across countries.

Together, these patterns show that research on the shadow and informal economy is increasingly framed through a cultural-institutional lens, linking ethics, trust, and governance with economic behavior. The centrality of these three keywords demonstrates the convergence of economic, social, and moral perspectives in understanding the persistence and dynamics of informality, especially in European and comparative contexts.

The co-citation network (Fig. 2) reveals three major clusters that structure the academic field linking the shadow economy and culture.

The first cluster, led by Friedrich Schneider, reflects the quantitative and macroeconomic tradition. Authors in this group emphasize measuring the size and growth of the shadow economy using econometric estimation methods and cross-country comparisons. Works by Medina and Schneider (2018) form the empirical foundation for much of the field, providing standardized models and long-term data series that are used worldwide.

The second cluster, led by Benno Torgler, James Alm, and Erich Kirchler, focuses on the behavioral and cultural perspective. These authors highlight how social norms, perceived fairness, and cultural dimensions, often measured through Hofstede's indices, influence tax morale and compliance. Their research combines economics and psychology to enhance our understanding of why individuals choose to participate (or not) in the informal economy.

The third cluster, led by Colin C. Williams and including key institutional sources such as the OECD and European Commission, adopts a policy-oriented, and governance-focused approach. This body of work focuses on undeclared work and informal entrepreneurship in Europe, examining the relationship between informality and regulatory effectiveness, corruption control, and the institutional trust gap between citizens and the state.

This evolution demonstrates that the relationship between culture and the shadow economy is no longer viewed solely as an economic issue, but rather as a complex problem rooted in governance, ethics, and societal norms.

Recent studies, such as Danci et al. (2025) or Bota-Avram (2023), expand this discussion by connecting financial behavior under uncertainty to transparency and governance quality, highlighting the multidimensional nature of the shadow economy as an issue rooted in culture, ethics, and institutional trust.

Overall, the literature describes the shadow economy as a complex phenomenon that encompasses economic, institutional, and cultural factors that simultaneously respond to fiscal incentives, labor market rigidities, and broader governance quality, culture, and tax ethics. This theoretical view supports our research design, which examines the EU from 2003 to 2022 by incorporating cultural and institutional

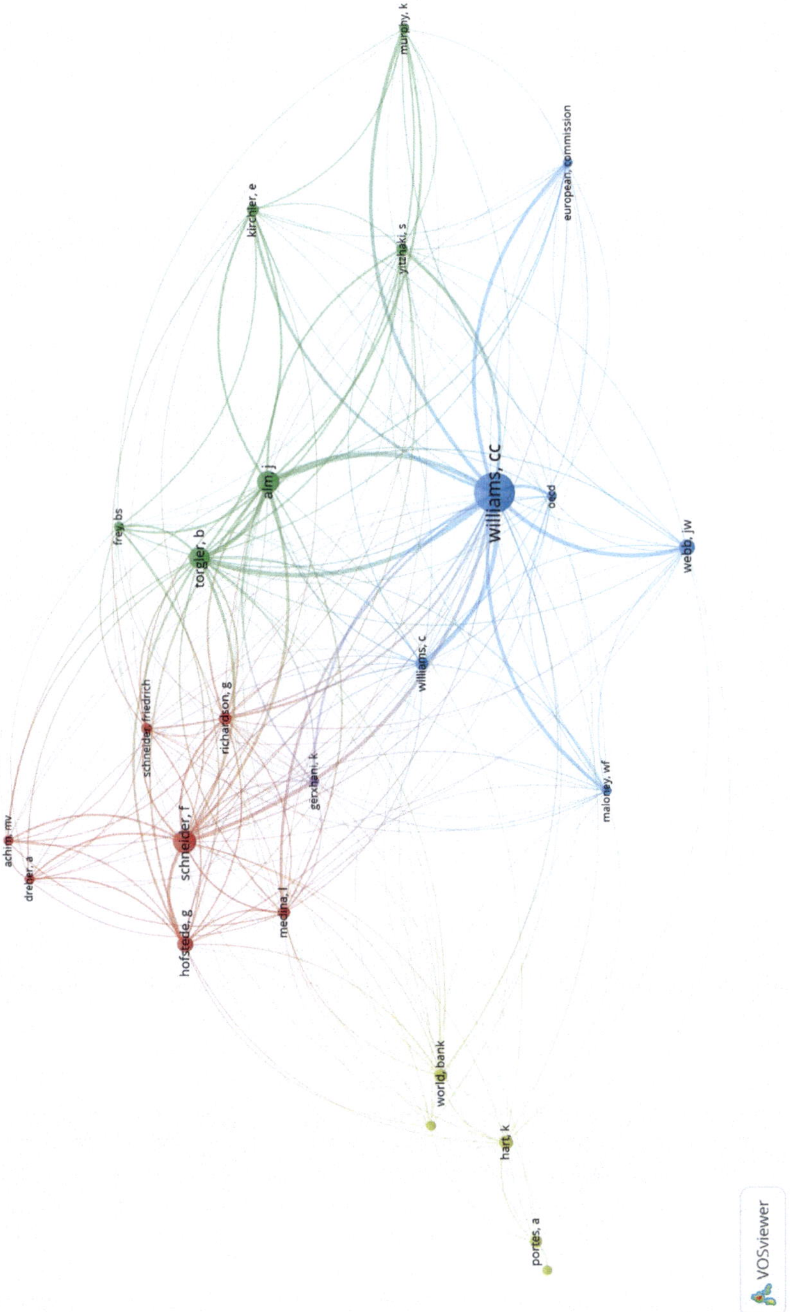

Fig. 2 Co-Citation network: key thematic clusters and influential authors. *Source* Created by the authors using Vosviewer

variables, using Schneider's estimates as the primary measure of the shadow economy.

2.2 Research Methodology

The empirical analysis relies on a balanced panel dataset covering 27 EU member states from 2003 to 2022 (20 years, 540 observations). The dependent variable is the shadow economy (SE), expressed as a percentage of GDP, estimated by Schneider and colleagues using the MIMIC model calibrated with the currency demand approach. This measure has been widely used in previous cross-country studies (Dell'Anno 2022; Buehn and Schneider 2013; Schneider et al. 2015; Asllani and Schneider 2025), ensuring comparability and consistency across time and countries.

Our set of explanatory variables is motivated by both economic theory and empirical evidence. We consider institutional quality, with control of corruption and rule of law as widely recognized determinants of informality, since poor governance erodes trust in state institutions and incentivizes hidden activity (Alarcón-García et al. 2020; Achim 2016). We also incorporate cultural dimensions based on Hofstede's framework (individualism, power distance, uncertainty avoidance, indulgence, and long-term orientation), which have been shown to influence tax morale and informal behavior (Syed 2025; Achim 2016). Additionally, macroeconomic and structural factors such as tax revenue (% of GDP), unemployment, self-employment (indirectly proxied through labor market variables), and income inequality (GINI) are considered classical predictors of the shadow economy, with unemployment repeatedly identified as a key driver (Buehn and Schneider 2013; Popescu et al. 2018). Finally, we include development and globalization controls, namely general government final consumption expenditure (GGFCE), foreign direct investment (FDI), education (as a proxy for human capital measured by government expenditure on this public sector), and political stability, as prior research emphasizes how economic openness and educational attainment can reduce informality (Goel and Nelson 2016; Schneider 2022; Asllani and Schneider 2025). Data for the explanatory variables are obtained from the World Development Indicators (World Bank) and Hofstede Insights, ensuring reliability and comparability across EU countries.

Measuring the shadow economy has always involved uncertainty, as hidden activities cannot be directly observed, and macro-indirect methods, such as MIMIC, depend on proxies and assumptions. Therefore, estimates show plausible ranges rather than precise values (Buehn and Schneider 2013; Schneider 2022). For consistency, this study uses the consolidated series from Schneider and colleagues, which has been widely validated in peer-reviewed research and is considered the standard for long-term cross-country analysis in the European Union (Schneider 2022; Asllani and Schneider 2025).

We estimate a panel least squares (PLS) model with period fixed effects, which accounts for time-specific shocks that are common to all countries, such as the global financial crisis and the COVID-19 pandemic. This method aligns with other cross-country studies of informality that use panel data techniques to control for unobserved heterogeneity and to capture both spatial and temporal variation (Dell'Anno 2022; Buehn and Schneider 2013; Alm and Torgler 2011; Alm and Embaye 2013). The general specification can be expressed as:

$$SE_{it} = \alpha + \beta_1 Inst_{it} + \beta_2 Cult_{it} + \beta_3 Econ_{it} + \mu_i + \lambda_t + \varepsilon_{it}$$

where:

SE_{it} is the size of the shadow economy in country i at time t;
$Inst_{it}$ denotes institutional indicators;
$Cult_{it}$ are cultural variables;
$Econ_{it}$ includes macroeconomic and structural controls;
μ_i and λ_t represent country and time effects, respectively.
The estimation was carried out in two stages:

1. A baseline specification that includes institutional and cultural variables, capturing the fundamental relationship between governance, culture, and informality.
2. A fully specified model that includes macroeconomic, fiscal, and structural controls, and tests the robustness of the main effects.

Such incremental modeling strategies are often employed to mitigate omitted variable bias and underscore the stability of key determinants (Torgler and Schneider 2009; Schneider et al. 2015; Popescu et al. 2018).

We include control of corruption and rule of law as governance indicators. Prior studies consistently show that weak institutions and high corruption are linked to larger shadow economies (Johnson et al. 1998; Dreher and Schneider 2010; Elgin and Öztunali 2012).

H1: Better institutional quality (higher control of corruption, stronger rule of law) is negatively linked to the size of the shadow economy.

Drawing on Hofstede's cultural framework, we include individualism, power distance, uncertainty avoidance, indulgence, and motivation. Cultural values shape tax morale, perceptions of fairness, and tolerance for informality (Torgler 2007; Alm and Torgler 2011; Achim et al. 2019).

H2a: Increased individualism reduces involvement in the shadow economy, as taxpayers prioritize personal responsibility and adherence to rules.
H2b: Greater power distance boosts the shadow economy, indicating acceptance of inequality and distrust in institutions.
H2c: Greater uncertainty avoidance increases informality, as strict regulations and risk aversion drive actors toward covert activities.
H2d: Greater indulgence is associated with lower informality, as societies with higher life satisfaction tend to trust institutions more.

We account for tax revenue (as a percentage of GDP), unemployment, GINI inequality, education, FDI inflows, and general government final consumption expenditure (GGFCE – a proxy for the size of the government in each country). Prior research has highlighted the tax burden (Johnson et al. 1998; Schneider and Enste 2000), unemployment as a driver of informal employment (Popescu et al. 2018; Vătavu et al. 2023), and inequality as a factor weakening tax morale (Williams 2014). Education and FDI are expected to reduce informality by enhancing human capital and market integration (Elgin and Öztunali 2012; Schneider 2022).

H3a: Higher tax revenue ratios are expected to reduce the shadow economy, reflecting improved fiscal capacity and stronger institutional enforcement.
H3b: Higher unemployment is positively linked to informality.
H3c: Higher income inequality promotes informality by reducing compliance and fairness perceptions.
H3d: Higher education levels and increased FDI inflows are expected to decrease the shadow economy.

Political variables and time-fixed effects account for EU-wide shocks such as the global financial crisis (2008–2009) and the COVID-19 pandemic (2020–2021), both of which temporarily increased informal activity (Medina and Schneider 2019; Schneider 2022).

H4: Political instability and economic crises are positively linked to the growth of the shadow economy.

By integrating institutional, cultural, and macroeconomic variables within a single panel framework, this study combines determinants that are often analyzed separately. This approach advances the debate on whether informality in the EU is mainly driven by economic incentives, institutional weaknesses, or cultural attitudes, while providing robustness through an expanded specification.

2.3 Descriptive Statistics

Before presenting the econometric estimates, it is essential to provide a descriptive overview of the dataset. This step not only illustrates the size and variation of the shadow economy across EU countries but also highlights the diversity of socioeconomic, institutional, and cultural factors involved. Descriptive statistics help us understand the central tendencies, distribution, and outliers, giving an initial perspective on the structural differences between member states. These differences are crucial for understanding why uniform fiscal or institutional reforms might produce different results across the Union. Additionally, presenting summary indicators promotes transparency about how key variables are distributed and provides a natural benchmark for interpreting the econometric results later on (Table 1).

The descriptive statistics confirm both the persistence and diversity of the shadow economy within the European Union. Across the 27 member states, the shadow

Table 1 Descriptive statistics of the variables (2003–2022)

Variable	Mean	Median	Min	Max	Standard Deviation
Shadow Economy	18.916	18.500	6.100	35.900	7.369
Control of Corruption	1.006	0.931	-0.411	2.459	0.797
Unemployment	8.276	7.255	2.015	27.686	4.163
Tax revenue	21.375	21.073	10.189	62.634	6.005
GGFCE	19.985	19.568	11.061	27.816	2.949
Individualism	66.734	67.000	42.000	100	14.126
Power Distance	51.400	50.000	11.000	100	20.457
Uncertainty Avoidance	70.593	74.000	23.000	100	21.595
Motivation towards Achievement and Success	45.978	43.000	5.000	100	24.138
Indulgence	43.409	44.000	13.000	78.000	19.338
FDI	11.617	3.371	-440.131	452.221	50.750
Political Stability	0.740	0.778	-0.475	1.687	0.383
GINI	31.343	31.400	23.200	41.300	3.795
Rule of Law	1.101	1.105	-0.210	2.125	0.614
Government expenditure on education	5.023	4.911	2.823	8.560	1.060

Source Personal proceedings

economy accounts for an average of approximately 19% of GDP, with a median of 18.5%. However, this figure varies substantially, ranging from 6.1% in Austria in 2019, one of the most formalized economies, to 35.9% in Bulgaria in 2003, where informality remains a structural challenge nowadays.

Labor market conditions display similar heterogeneity: the unemployment rate averages around 8.3%, but oscillates between 2% in the Czech Republic and nearly 28% in Greece during crisis periods. Fiscal indicators also differ markedly: tax revenues as a share of GDP range from 10% in Spain in 2009 to over 62% in Malta in 2007, while government expenditure on education ranges from 2% to 8% of GDP, reflecting distinct policy priorities across the Union.

Institutional indicators show relatively high average values, yet reveal wide disparities between member states. The Control of Corruption index spans from -0.41 in Romania to 2.46 in Sweden, highlighting the persistent North–South and East–West divide in governance quality.

Social and structural variables also exhibit diversity: the GINI index ranges from 23 to 41, with lower inequality in Slovakia and higher in Bulgaria. These descriptive patterns underscore the structural asymmetries within the European Union and the importance of jointly analyzing cultural, institutional, and economic factors in explaining the evolution of the shadow economy (Table 2).

Table 2 General presentation of the variables used in the model

Variable (abbreviation)	Way of measuring	Sign	Source
Shadow economy (SE) (Dependent variable)	% of GDP		Asllani, A., and Schneider, F. (2025), Table 2. Available at https://link.springer.com/article/doi.org/10.1007/s10797-024–09842-z/tables/2
Control of corruption (CC)	Governance indicator, -2.5 (weak) to +2.5 (strong)	–	World Bank Governance Indicators, The World Bank Available at https://www.worldbank.org/en/publication/worldwide-governance-indicators
Rule of law (RL)		–	
Individualism (IND)	Hofstede cultural dimension, 0–100 points	–	Hofstede Insights Available at https://www.theculturefactor.com/country-comparison-tool
Power distance (PD)	Hofstede cultural dimension, 0–100 points	+	
Uncertainty avoidance (UA)	Hofstede cultural dimension, 0–100 points	+	
Indulgence (INDUL)	Hofstede cultural dimension, 0–100 points	–	
Motivation (MOT)	Hofstede cultural dimension, 0–100 points	–	
Tax revenue (TAXREV)	% of GDP	–	World Development Indicators, The World Bank Available at http://data.worldbank.org/data-catalog/world-development-indicators
Unemployment (UNEMP)	% of labor force	+	
Income inequality (GINI)	Gini coefficient (0–100)	+	
General government final consumption expenditure (GGFCE)	% of GDP	–	
Foreign direct investment (FDI)	Net inflows (% of GDP)	–	
Education (EDU)	Government expenditure on education	–	
Political stability (POL)	Governance indicator, -2.5 to +2.5	–	

Source Personal proceedings

3 Results and Discussion

The results of the basic model align with recent literature, which shows that both institutions and culture play a significant role in determining the size of the underground economy. The robust adverse effect of corruption control confirms Mara's (2021) findings, which highlight that government integrity and respect for property rights reduce informality in EU countries, regardless of the welfare model. At the same time, the significant coefficients for individualism, power distance, and uncertainty avoidance support the evidence presented by Achim et al. (2019) and Alarcón-García et al. (2020), according to which culture strongly shapes tax compliance behaviors, with different results between collectivist and individualist societies or between countries with high versus low tolerance for uncertainty. Furthermore, the negative correlation between variables such as indulgence and motivation and the underground economy can be interpreted in light of the findings of Tay et al. (2014), which suggest that well-being and personal satisfaction increase institutional trust and reduce tolerance for corruption. The results for the cultural dimension power distance show a negative coefficient, contrary to initial expectations and some contributions from the specialized literature. In general, studies such as Tsakumis et al. (2007), Buszko (2018), and Achim et al. (2019) have reported a positive relationship between power distance and the underground economy, arguing that hierarchical and unequal societies perceive the tax system as less equitable and, therefore, are more prone to noncompliance. However, the fact that the coefficient is negative in our case suggests that in countries with a more hierarchical culture, compliance with the rules is stimulated by stronger authority or constraints, which could reduce the social propensity towards informal activities. To better understand this atypical relationship, we test the robustness of the estimates in subsequent analyses by including additional control variables, thereby clarifying whether the result reflects either a structural peculiarity of the sample or a more subtle causal relationship.

Overall, these results indicate that informality cannot be fully explained by cultural or institutional factors alone; an integrated approach is necessary. Studies by Buehn and Schneider (2013) and Popescu et al. (2018) demonstrate that unemployment, self-employment, and labor market conditions are among the most significant determinants. Mara (2021) further states that social protection policies and economic growth also influence the size of the underground economy. Therefore, including economic and structural variables in the model is a vital step toward accurately understanding the interaction among culture, institutions, and socioeconomic conditions in the European Union.

Although these initial results confirm the theoretical hypotheses and align with the literature, they only partially capture the complexity of the phenomenon. As Mara (2021) emphasizes, the size of the underground economy is influenced not only by institutional integrity and cultural values but also by structural economic factors, such as labor taxation, unemployment, and the level of development, which can amplify or reduce the effects of institutions and culture. Similarly, studies by Buehn and Schneider (2013) and Schneider et al. (2015) highlight that ignoring fiscal variables and labor market conditions can lead to incomplete or biased estimates. Therefore, to test the robustness of the identified relationships and gain a more comprehensive understanding of the factors driving the underground economy in the European Union, we expanded the model by including additional control variables that represent economic, fiscal, and social dimensions. This approach enables the investigation of interactions among culture, institutions, and the economic environment, providing a more comprehensive understanding of the causes and dynamics of informality (Table 3).

In the basic model, which includes only cultural variables and the institutional indicator for controlling corruption, the results primarily show a negative and significant effect of institutional quality on the size of the underground economy. A higher level of corruption control reduces informality, confirming consistent findings in the literature (Dreher and Schneider 2010; Medina and Schneider, 2018; Mara 2021), which suggest that good governance and administrative integrity are key factors in limiting the shadow economy.

From a cultural dimensions perspective, the obtained coefficients highlight several notable results. Individualism is negatively correlated with the size of the underground economy, which is in line with theoretical hypotheses and with the results reported by Achim et al. (2019), Saunoris (2024), Alm and Torgler (2011) or Buszko (2018), according to which more individualistic societies favor personal responsibility and fiscal compliance. In contrast, the estimates for power distance indicate a negative, significant coefficient, which contradicts expectations derived from studies such as Tsakumis et al. (2007), Buszko (2018), and Achim et al. (2019), which associate high power distance with higher levels of the underground economy. A possible explanation is that, in some EU member states, stronger hierarchies may induce compliance through social constraints or fear of authority, resulting in an effect opposite to that anticipated. Regarding uncertainty avoidance, the positive coefficient is consistent with the literature, which argues that societies with high uncertainty aversion tend to generate more informality due to institutional rigidities and risk aversion (Alm and Torgler 2011; Achim 2016). Similarly, the dimensions of motivation and indulgence are negatively associated with the underground economy,

Table 3 Panel least squares results 1—shadow economy in EU countries (2003–2022)

Variable	Coefficient	Std. Error	t-Statistic	Prob
C	39.25855	1.247958	31.45823	0.0000
CC	-6.082487	0.350920	-17.33297	0.0000
IND	-0.112670	0.014448	-7.789997	0.0000
PD	-0.031998	0.009717	-3.293060	0.0010
UA	0.027868	0.008668	3.411905	0.0007
MOT	-0.119359	0.006806	-19.61739	0.0000
INDUL	-0.034776	0.011055	-3.145740	0.0018

Notes The dependent variable is the Shadow Economy (% of GDP). Panel Least Squares estimates with period fixed effects, covering 27 EU countries from 2003 to 2022 (540 observations)

which supports the hypothesis that individual satisfaction and a positive orientation increase trust and reduce tolerance for corruption and evasion (Tay et al. 2014).

Overall, the simple model shows that both institutional and cultural factors consistently impact the size of the underground economy. However, some relationships, such as that between power distance and informality, differ from earlier results, highlighting the need to test robustness by adding more control variables (Table 4).

Expanding the model by including economic, fiscal, and institutional control variables produced more detailed results, facilitating comparisons with international and

Table 4 Panel least squares results 2—shadow economy in EU countries (2003–2022)

Variable	Model 1 (Cultural + Institutional)	Model 2 Full specification (no interactions)
CC	-6.082*** (-17.33)	-2.307*** (-4.42)
EDU		1.553*** (7.96)
FDI		0.012*** (4.70)
GGFCE		-0.22*** (-3.22)
GINI		-0.237*** (-5.02)
IND	-0.113*** (-7.79)	-0.121*** (-7.09)
INDUL	-0.035*** (-3.15)	-0.062*** (-5.51)
MOT	-0.119*** (-19.62)	-0.104*** (-18.40)
POL		-1.615*** (-3.58)
PD	-0.032*** (-3.29)	-0.067*** (-6.99)
RL		-6.425*** (-9.00)
TAXREV		0.020* (1.81)
UA	0.028*** (3.41)	0.043*** (6.12)
UNEMP		-0.096** (-2.68)

Notes The dependent variable is the Shadow Economy (% of GDP). Panel Least Squares estimates with period fixed effects, covering 27 EU countries from 2003 to 2022 (540 observations). Coefficients are reported with robust t-statistics in parentheses. ***, **, * indicate significance at the 1%, 5%, and 10% levels regional studies. First, institutional indicators remain strongly significant and negative: control of corruption, rule of law, and political stability reduce the size of the underground economy, corroborating the findings of Dreher and Schneider (2010), Medina and Schneider (2018), and Mara (2021), which suggest that good governance and political stability are critical to limiting informality.

Regarding taxation, the results differ from the traditional consensus. Classical literature suggests that a high tax burden encourages the development of the underground economy (Schneider and Enste 2000; Schneider 2022). However, our findings indicate a significant adverse effect: higher tax revenues are associated with increased informality. This difference can be attributed to the unique characteristics of the European Union, where high compliance and advanced tax collection systems mitigate the negative impacts of tax pressure.

The results on income inequality, measured by the GINI index, also contradict the literature. Studies, such as those by Williams (2014) and Dell'Anno (2016), show that inequality undermines fiscal morality and trust in institutions, thereby fueling the underground economy. In our model, however, the negative coefficient suggests that higher inequality is associated with a reduction in informality. This atypical relationship may reflect either methodological peculiarities or contextual factors, such as redistributive mechanisms or labor-market structures in some member states.

The effects on the labor market are also unconventional. While the literature (Popescu et al. 2018) highlights that high unemployment encourages the underground economy by pushing the workforce toward informal activities, our results show a negative coefficient, indicating that, during the period studied in the European Union, higher unemployment was linked to a decrease in informality. A possible explanation is the role of active employment policies and social protection systems, which may be more effective in European countries than in other regions.

The results regarding government size are consistent with those of Goel and Nelson (2016), who demonstrate that a larger public sector is associated with a smaller shadow economy, primarily because of its stronger enforcement capacity and institutional oversight. This alignment reinforces the view that an expansive government, when functioning effectively, can enhance compliance and limit informal activities by increasing administrative reach and monitoring efficiency. In contrast, education and foreign direct investment (FDI) show a positive and significant effect, contrary to initial expectations. Although the literature generally suggests that reducing informality can be achieved through more human capital and moral taxes (Elgin and Öztunali 2012), our findings indicate a more complex relationship, possibly affected by gaps between educational levels and labor market opportunities. Regarding FDI, however, the result aligns with previous research, which shows that, in specific contexts, foreign investment can boost the shadow economy through substitution effects and by exploiting areas with weaker regulation (Elgin and Öztunali 2012).

Overall, model 2 confirms the robustness of the institutional dimension but shows more ambiguous or even opposite relationships to those expected for certain economic and social variables. This suggests that the determinants of the underground economy in the European Union must be understood within the context of regional specificity and the complex interplay among institutions, culture, and economic factors. To better understand these relationships and test the sensitivity of the estimates, we re-estimated the complete model by adding interaction terms, which illustrate how institutions and economic conditions mutually reinforce each other in influencing informality (Table 5).

The introduction of interaction terms in the complete model enables a deeper understanding of the relationships between institutions, economic, and cultural factors. From an econometric perspective, these specifications capture how the effects of specific variables do not act in isolation but rather condition each other, as recent literature has highlighted (Torgler and Schneider 2009; Gërxhani and Cichocki 2023).

A key aspect is the change in the unemployment coefficient, shifting from a negative relationship in model 2 to a positive and significant one in model 3. This aligns the findings with the literature (Popescu et al. 2018), which suggests that high unemployment encourages the underground economy by putting pressure on the labor market. Additionally, the GINI × UNEMP interaction is negative and significant, indicating that inequality levels moderate the effect of unemployment on the underground economy. Specifically, in more unequal societies, the impact of unemployment on the underground economy is less pronounced, possibly because of redistributive policies or social safety nets. Notably, in this model, the simple GINI coefficient becomes insignificant, reinforcing the idea that the impact of inequality mainly occurs through its interaction with unemployment. This finding is consistent with recent empirical literature showing that the effect of inequality on informality often manifests primarily through interaction terms rather than in isolation. For instance, studies like Magwedere and Marozva (2025) illustrate that the relationship between GINI and informal activity becomes meaningful only when moderated by structural or institutional factors, a logic that supports our approach of considering this interaction.

For tax revenue, the coefficient remains positive and significant, and the stronger significance in the complete model indicates the robustness of the relationship. At the same time, the interaction between the RL × TAXREV is negative and significant, confirming the hypothesis put forward by Schneider (2022) and Asllani and Schneider (2025): the tax burden can stimulate the underground economy only when strong institutions are absent. In countries with a well-established rule of law, the effect of tax pressure is offset, thereby reducing the tendency to evade taxes and encouraging compliance. These results are in line with the findings of Achim et al. (2023), who document a non-linear relationship between tax burden and the shadow economy across EU member states. Their analysis shows that the effect of taxation depends on its structure and intensity: direct taxes display a U-shaped impact, while indirect taxes exhibit an inverted U-shaped pattern. Similarly, our results highlight that the influence of taxation on informality is not uniform but conditional on institutional quality, suggesting that efficient governance can mitigate the adverse effects of fiscal pressure.

The results regarding education remain surprising: the coefficient is positive and significant in both models 2 and 3, contrary to the consensus in the literature (Elgin and Öztunali, 2012), which suggests that education should reduce informality by enhancing human capital and moral taxes. However, the interaction term EDU × POL

Table 5 Panel least squares results 3—shadow economy in EU countries (2003–2022)

Variable	Model 1 (Cultural + Institutional)	Model 2 Full specification (no interactions)	Model 3 With interactions
CC	-6.082*** (-17.33)	-2.307*** (-4.42)	-2.730*** (-5.15)
EDU		1.553*** (7.96)	1.059*** (3.04)
EDU × POL			0.765*** (2.17)
FDI		0.012*** (4.70)	0.012*** (4.75)
GGFCE		-0.22*** (-3.22)	-0.270*** (-3.93)
GINI		-0.237*** (-5.02)	-0.045 (-0.55)
GINI × UNEMP			-0.024** (-2.62)
IND	-0.113*** (-7.79)	-0.121*** (-7.09)	-0.111*** (-6.48)
INDUL	-0.035*** (-3.15)	-0.062*** (-5.51)	-0.064*** (-5.51)
MOT	-0.119*** (-19.62)	-0.104*** (-18.40)	-0.106*** (-17.48)
POL		-1.615*** (-3.58)	-5.367*** (-3.12)
PD	-0.032*** (-3.29)	-0.067*** (-6.99)	-0.062*** (-5.93)
RL		-6.425*** (-9.00)	-3.02** (-1.99)
RL × TAXREV			-0.135** (-2.45)
TAXREV		0.020* (1.81)	0.233** (2.81)
UA	0.028*** (3.41)	0.043*** (6.12)	0.031*** (4.95)
UNEMP		-0.096** (-2.68)	0.697** (2.26)

Notes The dependent variable is the Shadow Economy (% of GDP). Panel Least Squares estimates with period fixed effects, covering 27 EU countries from 2003 to 2022 (540 observations). Coefficients are reported with robust t-statistics in parentheses. ***, **, * indicate significance at the 1%, 5%, and 10% levels is also positive and significant, indicating that, in the European context, higher education levels increase the underground economy's sensitivity to political instability. In other words, in unstable environments, individuals with higher levels of education may be more likely to seek opportunities outside the formal sector. A possible explanation for this finding is that the variable used measures government spending on education rather than the actual level of human capital. Consequently, the estimated effects may reflect additional fiscal pressure and budgetary constraints associated with an expanded public sector, rather than an immediate rise in tax compliance, leading to an apparently opposite relationship to that suggested by the literature based on human capital indicators. These results resonate with evidence from Bühn and Farzanegan (2013), which finds that higher educational levels can fuel shadow economy growth in environments with weak political institutions. This supports the idea that the interplay between education expenditure and institutional quality is critical. In stronger institutional settings, the compliance-enhancing effects of education may dominate, whereas in weaker ones, greater spending may exacerbate fiscal pressures and opportunistic informal behavior.

Overall, the entire model supports the idea that institutions (such as corruption control, rule of law, and political stability) are the main factors influencing the underground economy. It also shows that economic and social variables do not act independently but interact conditionally. This finding confirms recent approaches that argue policies to combat the underground economy should be carefully adjusted not only based on individual factors but also by understanding the interactions among institutions, the labor market, and social structures.

Our empirical analysis, which was developed through three successive specifications, confirms the complexity of the factors influencing the underground economy in the European Union.

The basic model, which focuses on cultural variables and the institutional indicator of corruption control, highlights the essential role of institutions and culture in shaping tax compliance. The findings show that individualism and anti-corruption efforts reduce the underground economy, while uncertainty avoidance increases it. Power distance has an opposite effect to traditional expectations, indicating specific contextual factors in European countries.

Including control variables in the model broadened the perspective, revealing significant economic and social effects and some findings that challenge existing literature. For example, unemployment and inequality initially showed signs that were the opposite of what theory predicts, while education spending was positively associated with the size of the underground economy. These inconsistencies highlighted the need for additional robustness checks and for analysis of interactions among factors.

The complete model, including interaction terms, clarified some of these inconsistencies and highlighted the conditional role of economic variables. As a result, unemployment once again became a positive and significant factor, confirming the literature's association between it and the growth of informality. Meanwhile, the effect of tax revenues was influenced by the rule of law: where institutions are strong, the tax burden does not lead to evasion but instead results in higher compliance. Moreover, the interaction between inequality and unemployment demonstrated that the negative impact of the labor market on compliance depends on the distribution of income and education spending. Although this finding is positive and unexpected, it reflects budgetary pressures rather than an adequate level of human capital, with an additional influence from increased sensitivity to political instability.

Overall, comparing the three models highlights the influence of institutional and cultural factors, as well as the conditional nature of economic and social determinants. The findings support existing research that emphasizes the interconnections among institutions, culture, and the economy, while also explaining some deviations from theoretical expectations through the roles of interactions and European-specific factors.

4 Conclusions, Limitations, and Future Research Directions

This study examined the determinants of the shadow economy in the European Union from 2003 to 2022, integrating institutional, cultural, and economic factors within a panel framework. Across all models, one key conclusion stands out: institutional quality is the most consistent and reliable factor influencing trends in the shadow economy. Stronger rule of law, better control of corruption, and political stability are consistently linked to lower levels of informality, aligning with previous findings by Dreher and Schneider (2010), Medina and Schneider (2018), and Mara (2021).

Cultural factors also play a significant role, although their effects differ across various dimensions. Individualism and indulgence tend to decrease informal activity, while uncertainty avoidance increases it. These findings align with studies by Alm and Torgler (2011), Achim et al. (2019), and Alarcón-García et al. (2020). However, the impact of power distance was negative, contrary to the expectations of Tsakumis et al. (2007) and Buszko (2018). This indicates that, in the European context, hierarchical structures may serve as mechanisms to promote compliance, reflecting particular institutional and cultural complementarities.

The inclusion of economic and social controls confirmed the importance of labor market conditions, fiscal variables, and inequality. It also produced results that, at first glance, seemed contradictory to much of the existing literature. Unemployment, inequality, and government spending on education exhibited unexpected trends when examined in isolation. However, once interaction terms were added, the results aligned more closely with theoretical expectations and previous research. For example, unemployment once again had a positive effect on the shadow economy, consistent with Buehn and Schneider (2013) and Popescu et al. (2018). The interaction between tax revenue and the rule of law showed that fiscal pressure increases informality only in contexts of weak institutions, as Schneider (2022) and Asllani and Schneider (2025) also indicated. Similarly, the interaction between inequality and unemployment suggested that the labor market effect depends on income distribution, highlighting the conditional nature of what drives the shadow economy. The consistently positive effect of education in this study can be explained by using government expenditure on education as a proxy, which reflects fiscal effort rather than actual human capital. This distinction is also discussed in related theoretical debates (Neck et al. 2012).

Taken together, these findings confirm that the shadow economy is a multifaceted phenomenon influenced not only by economic incentives but also by institutional capacity, cultural values, and their complex interactions. This supports the argument made by scholars such as Achim (2016), Alm and Torgler (2011), and Gërxhani and Cichocki (2023) that integrated approaches are essential for understanding and effectively addressing informality.

Like any empirical study, our analysis has limitations. First, measuring the shadow economy relies on the MIMIC method calibrated with the currency demand approach (Schneider and Enste 2000; Buehn and Schneider 2013), which involves significant uncertainty. Therefore, the results should be viewed as plausible ranges rather than exact estimates. Second, the proxies used for some variables, such as government expenditure on education or tax revenues as a percentage of GDP for tax burden, may reflect dimensions different from those intended, which could explain discrepancies with some findings in the literature. Third, although period fixed effects were included, unobserved country-level heterogeneity and potential endogeneity between the shadow economy and its determinants (e.g., institutions and taxation) remain concerns. Finally, the analysis does not account for spatial dependencies, although previous research (Alarcón-García et al. 2020) has demonstrated that the shadow economy shows regional clustering effects.

Future research should therefore aim to refine the measurement of key determinants by employing alternative indicators (e.g., years of schooling for education, tax wedges for fiscal pressure, or detailed measures of labor market dynamics such as self-employment and long-term unemployment). Addressing potential endogeneity with instrumental variable techniques or dynamic panel estimators, such as GMM, would also strengthen causal inference. Moreover, future work could explore additional interaction terms, non-linear relationships (e.g., inverted-U effects of FDI or taxation), and heterogeneity across welfare regimes within the EU. Finally, incorporating spatial econometric approaches would enable the capture of cross-border spillovers and regional interdependencies, while linking macro-level analysis with micro-level evidence on tax morale and trust (Alm and Torgler 2011; Tay et al. 2014).

In conclusion, our findings underscore that addressing the shadow economy in the European Union requires more than fiscal reforms alone. Efforts should be supported by strengthening institutions, increasing cultural awareness, and implementing policies tailored to the unique economic, institutional, and social dynamics of each member state.

Acknowledgements This work was supported by a "Contract for awarding special scholarships for a scientific activity to students based on research projects and the exploitation of their results", from Babes-Bolyai University, project number 35221/28.11.2025, period 2025–2026, manager of project Andreea-Roxana Danci. Also, Gabriela-Mihaela Mureşan acknowledges support from the Ministry of Research, Innovation and Digitization, CNCS-UEFISCDI, project number PN-IV-P2-2.1-TE-2023-1317, within PNCDI IV.

References

Achim MV (2016) Cultural dimension of corruption: a cross-country survey. Int Adv Econ Res 22(3):333–345

Achim MV, Borlea SN, Găban LV, Mihăilă AA (2019) The shadow economy and culture: evidence in European countries. East Eur Econ 57(5):352–374

Achim MV, Mirza N, Văidean VL (2023) The asymmetric impact of tax burden structures on the shadow economy: a panel analysis of old and new European Union countries. Appl Econ Lett 30(16):2179–2188

Alarcón-García G, Buendia Azorin JD, Sanchez De la Vega MDM (2020) Shadow economy and national culture: A spatial approach

Allingham MG, Sandmo A (1972) Income tax evasion: A theoretical analysis. J Public Econ 1(3–4):323–338

Alm J, Embaye A (2013) Using dynamic panel methods to estimate shadow economies around the world, 1984–2006. Public Finance Review 41(5):510–543

Alm J, Torgler B (2011) Do ethics matter? Tax compliance and morality. J Bus Ethics 101(4):635–651

Asllani A, Schneider F (2025) A review of the driving forces of the informal economy and policy measures for mitigation: an analysis of six EU countries. Int Tax Public Financ 32(1):310–344

Bota-Avram C (2023) Bibliometric analysis of sustainable business performance: where are we going? A science map of the field. Economic Research-Ekonomska Istraživanja 36(1):2137–2176

Bühn A, Farzanegan MR (2013) Impact of education on the shadow economy: institutions matter. Economics Bulletin 33(3):2052–2063

Buehn A, Schneider F (2013) Shadow Economies in highly developed OECD countries: What are the driving forces? (No. 2013-17)

Buehn A, Dell'Anno R, Schneider F (2018) Exploring the dark side of tax policy: an analysis of the interactions between fiscal illusion and the shadow economy. Empirical Economics 54(4):1609–1630

Buszko AT (2018) Cultural implications for the shadow economy. Engineering Economics 29(1):46–52

Danci AR, Lazar IA, Mureşan GM (2025) Financial analysis in the era of uncertainty: a comprehensive examination. Digital Finance 1–25

Dell'Anno R (2016) Analyzing the determinants of the shadow economy with a "separate approach". An application of the relationship between inequality and the shadow economy. World Dev 84:342–356

Dell'Anno R (2022) Theories and definitions of the informal economy: a survey. J Econ Surv 36(5):1610–1643

Dreher A, Schneider F (2010) Corruption and the shadow economy: an empirical analysis. Public Choice 144(1):215–238

Elgin C, Öztunali O (2012) Shadow economies around the world: model based estimates. Bogazici University, Department of Economics (No. 5). Working Papers.

Gërxhani K, Cichocki S (2023) Formal and informal institutions: understanding the shadow economy in transition countries. J Inst Econ 19(5):656–672

Goel RK, Nelson MA (2016) Shining a light on the shadows: Identifying robust determinants of the shadow economy. Econ Model 58:351–364

Hofstede G (2011) Dimensionalizing cultures: the Hofstede model in context. Online Read Psychol Cult 2(1):8

Husted BW (1999) Wealth, culture, and corruption. J Int Bus Stud 30(2):339–359

Johnson S, Kaufmann D, Zoido-Lobaton P (1998) Regulatory discretion and the unofficial economy. Am Econ Rev 88(2):387–392

Khan S, Abdul Hamid B, Rehman MZ (2023) Determinants of shadow economy in OIC and non-OIC countries: the role of financial development. Int J Emerg Mark 18(10):3373–3393

Magwedere MR, Marozva G (2025) Inequality and informal economy: the moderating role of financial technology. Econ-Innov Econ Res J 13(1):197–211

Mara ER (2021) Drivers of the shadow economy in European Union welfare states: a panel data analysis. Econ Anal Policy 72:309–325

Medina L, Schneider, MF (2018) Shadow economies around the world: what did we learn over the last 20 years? Int Monet Fund

Medina L, Schneider, MF (2019) Shedding light on the shadow economy: a global database and the interaction with the official one

Neck R, Wächter JU, Schneider F (2012) Tax avoidance versus tax evasion: on some determinants of the shadow economy. Int Tax Public Financ 19(1):104–117

Popescu GH, Davidescu AAM, Huidumac C (2018) Researching the leading causes of the Romanian shadow economy at the micro and macro levels: implications for sustainable development. Sustainability 10(10):3518

Saunoris JW (2024) Individualism, economic freedom, and the development of the shadow economy. Econ Syst 48(1):101168

Schneider F (2015) Size and development of the shadow economy of 31 European and 5 other OECD countries from 2003 to 2014: different developments? Journal of Self-Governance and Management Economics 3(4):7–29

Schneider F (2022) New COVID-related results for estimating the shadow economy in the global economy in 2021 and 2022. IEEP 19(2):299–313

Schneider F, Enste DH (2000) Shadow economies: Size, causes, and consequences. J Econ Lit 38(1):77–114

Schneider F, Raczkowski K, Mróz B (2015) Shadow economy and tax evasion in the EU. J Money Laund Control 18(1):34–51

Shadabi L (2013) The impact of religion on corruption. J Bus Inq 12(1):102–117

Syed AA (2025) Unveiling the nexus of shadow economy and economic growth through the lens of Hofstede's cultural dimensions: a case of emerging nations. Discov Sustain 6(1):1–24

Tay L, Herian MN, Diener E (2014) Detrimental effects of corruption and subjective well-being: Whether, how, and when. Soc Psychol Pers Sci 5(7):751–759

Torgler B (2007) Tax compliance and tax morale: a theoretical and empirical analysis. In Tax compliance and tax morale. Edward Elgar Publishing

Torgler B, Schneider F (2009) The impact of tax morale and institutional quality on the shadow economy. J Econ Psychol 30(2):228–245

Tsakumis GT, Curatola AP, Porcano TM (2007) The relation between national cultural dimensions and tax evasion. J Int Account Audit Tax 16(2):131–147

Vătavu S, Varadi AE, Manta EM, Ţăran AM, Lobonţ OR (2023) Causes and consequences of the shadow economy and its impact on economic development. Econ Comput Econ Cybern Stud Res 57(4).

Williams CC (2014) Confronting the shadow economy: evaluating tax compliance and behaviour policies. In: Confronting the shadow economy. Edward Elgar.

Andreea-Roxana Danci is a Master's student in Corporate Finance and Insurance at the Faculty of Economics and Business Administration, Babeş-Bolyai University, Cluj-Napoca. During his second year of study, she was awarded a one-year scientific scholarship, which significantly contributed to her academic and research development. She is a co-author of a recently published bibliometric analysis article and has additional papers currently under review. Her academic interests include Corporate Finance, Financial Ethics, Financial Crime, Manipulation of Financial Statements, Financial Analysis, and Bibliometric Studies. She serves as vice-president of an investment-focused academic club, actively contributing to financial research discussions and collaborative learning. Deeply involved in the research community, she regularly attends conferences, webinars, and workshops to develop both her academic profile and practical understanding of finance.

Ionuţ-Adrian Lazar is a Master's student in Corporate Finance and Insurance at the Faculty of Economics and Business Administration, Babeş-Bolyai University, Cluj-Napoca. During his first year of study, he was awarded a one-year scientific scholarship, which significantly contributed to his academic and research development. He is a co-author of a published bibliometric analysis article and has additional research currently under review. His academic focus covers Digital and Corporate Finance, Financial Analysis, Manipulation of Financial Statements, Behavioral Finance, Capital Markets, and Company Valuation, including risk and opportunity assessment following earnings releases and financial reporting. He is also interested in investments and currently serves as president of a university-level investment club. He actively participates in specialized academic events, such as conferences and workshops, to support his ongoing research and professional development.

Gabriela-Mihaela Mureşan holds a PhD in Finance and is currently an Associate Professor in the Department of Finance, Faculty of Economics and Business Administration, Babeş-Bolyai University, Cluj-Napoca. She has published academic papers and books and has participated in several international conferences. Her research interests include insurance, financial analysis, and economic psychology, with a particular focus on human behavior, manipulation, money addiction, happiness, ethics, corruption, fraud, corporate performance, bankruptcy, and creative accounting.

Variations in the Concept of Tax Evasion Between the Normative and Judicial Levels

Septimiu Ioan Puț

Abstract In a constantly changing world, in a system of positive law subject to systematic changes in tax legislation, where licit tax behaviors can be transformed overnight into illicit tax behavior, through the intervention of the legislator who seeks to include as many behaviors as possible within the scope of tax law in order to supplement budget revenues, the conceptual clarification of the possible legal classifications of certain types of atypical behaviors becomes crucial. This is due to the fact that, despite their use within a shared legal-fiscal register, tax fraud, tax evasion, abuse of rights in the field of taxation, and tax optimization cannot be equated. The substantiation of the regulation of illicit behaviors and the categorical classification of concepts is essential in circumstances where, in law, shades of gray can determine whether legal liability leans toward white (acquittal), or black (conviction). Our approach is syncretic, aiming at the practical application of the frameworks and classifications proposed at a theoretical level. We pursue a dual utility of the study, both from a theoretical perspective, where it may serve as a benchmark for the substantiation of new regulations in this field, and, above all, from a practical perspective, in order to distinguish *in concreto* between the different types of illicit behavior that have been artificially grouped under the same umbrella of "tax evasion".

Keywords Tax law · Tax fraud · Tax evasion · Legal liability

JEL Classification K34

1 Introduction

Between the inherent temptation of legal subjects to limit their tax exposure by means that push the boundaries of legality and the state's obsession with the multitude of evaders who plunder the state budget, a wide range of possibilities can be described that may arise in practice. In an ultra-normativized society, one would expect that the

S. I. Puț (✉)
Faculty of Law, Babeș-Bolyai University, Cluj-Napoca, Romania
e-mail: septimiu.put@law.ubbcluj.ro

M. V. Achim (ed.), *Financial Crime in the Digital Era*, Contributions to Finance and Accounting, https://doi.org/10.1007/978-3-032-20198-0_18

regulation of antisocial behaviors through dedicated legislation is to be carried out in a substantiated, appropriate, comprehensible, and predictable manner. However, in reality, the normative and subsequent administrative or judicial distinction between tax fraud and tax evasion, between tax evasion and abuse of rights in the field of taxation, or between abuse of rights in the field of taxation and tax optimization is not easy to achieve. This is particularly true where the regulation of these behaviors is imprecise or incomplete in terms of producing the effects intended by the legislator, who wishes to use the legal norms enacted to ensure the legal protection of the state budget, which, according to one opinion (Damarey 2006), is "in constant evolution."

Shortcomings and deficiencies in the regulation of tax evasion in Romania, the different perspectives of European and national tax law doctrine on the issue of tax evasion and the types of legal liability that may be engaged, which are unequivocally counterproductive both at the normative level and especially in judicial practice, have prompted us to formalize this study and strive to place the four types of tax behavior into well-defined legal categories: tax fraud, tax evasion, abuse of rights in the field of taxation, and tax optimization. The exact legal classification can constitute a legal model that can be adopted and, where appropriate, improved, so as to align with current trends in the regulation, prevention, and the adequate sanctioning of tax evasion. The paper comprises four main chapters presenting the state and popular perspectives on tax pressure, arguing for the need to reform the Romanian legal system and the reconceptualization of tax institutions, whilst presenting jurisprudential excerpts that illustrate the theoretical basis in the form of summarized case law.

2 The State Perspective and the Popular Perspective Regarding Fiscal Pressure

2.1 The Public Perspective

With a budget deficit of 5.39% of GDP in the first nine months of 2025, regulatory and administrative shortcomings, retrograde mentalities in a world of algorithms, and partially functional collection mechanisms, the Romanian state, through its competent fiscal institutions and bodies (the Parliament, the Government, ANAF[NAFA] with its four main pillars: the General Directorates of Public Finances, the Anti-Tax Fraud Directorates, the National Customs Authority, and the Directorate for Large Taxpayers) finds itself a difficult position.

During this year, multiple tax changes (set out in the two "fiscal packages") came into force, intended to bring about a fiscal-budgetary reform in Romania, providing the state budget with the resources necessary for social governance, with a third "tax package" to be approved by law and enter into force at the beginning of the next fiscal year.

One of the major objectives of the National Agency for Fiscal Administration's Strategy for 2023–2025 in the fight against tax evasion was to ensure a more effective identification of taxpayers with a high risk of tax evasion.

This general objective was to be achieved and materialized through secondary objectives such as: expanding the collection of data provided by third parties; establishing tax bases by estimation for lifestyle-based taxation; rational use of information received by notifications concerning acts of a tax evasion nature; increasing the proportion of documentation verifications; optimizing the quality of inspections/verifications in the high-risk segment; implementing a program of controls with an impact on the tax gap.

It is already certain that at the end of this period, the general objective and secondary objectives have not been achieved. Of course, at a declarative level, the strategic objectives of the tax authorities are diverse; however, the path toward their fulfillment is an arduous one. This is because, on the one hand, theory only partially overlaps with practice and, on the other hand, because in addition to the initial "assumed data," there is also "dynamic data," i.e., new elements or elements that, although known, were not known from the perspective of their effective weight. For example, the level of annual voluntary compliance can only be intuited at the time of developing the multiannual national strategy.

Through the fiscal measures adopted recently, the state has resorted to increases in tax rates and ceilings (increasing the standard VAT rate from 19% to 21% and the ceiling for social health contributions to a maximum of 72 minimum wages), the elimination of tax breaks (e.g. those concerning the IT industry), the introduction of new taxes (e.g. the additional tax for legal entities operating in the oil and gas sector—Article 46^2 of the Fiscal Code—Law No. 227/2015—published in the Romanian Official Gazette No. 688 of September 10, 2015), restrictions or additional conditions on the installment of tax obligations (e.g. regarding the requested guarantees), new rules for eliminating reduced rates or special tax regimes (e.g., waiving the reduced 5% and 9% VAT rates, and the introduction of a single reduced rate of 11% for VAT).

2.2 *Private Perspective*

In this context, characterized by excessive and abrupt fiscal interventions, the population perceives unfair exploitation by the state, which can be divided into two major components, depending on the legal subjects concerned: individuals (authorized or, without being authorized, openly fall within the scope of tax law due to the nature, complexity, or seriousness of their activities) and the entire spectrum of legal entities that fall within the scope of Romanian taxation: legal entities paying corporate income tax, entities paying microenterprise income tax, NGOs, and *societas europeas.*

From the perspective of individuals/natural persons, they suffer directly from changes in tax legislation both as taxpayers—legal entities that obtain at least one of the incomes covered by the provisions of the Tax Code (Art. 61), and as mere individuals—end consumers who bear the immediate consequences of the increase in indirect tax rates (VAT, excise duties, customs duties) and local tax rates subject to tax reforms. Certainly, in the context of illicit tax behavior, we are interested in the first perspective, the active one, in which not only is the temptation to evade tax pay, but the possible means that taxpayers could resort to are also extremely accessible.

From the perspective of legal entities, their activity has been completely disrupted by a series of fiscal measures aimed at increasing the level of taxation on their income and profits. Moreover, in the case of at least two important fiscal components, we are dealing with obvious overtaxation, which, in the constitutional-fiscal environment, is both unconstitutional and illegal. Thus, the newly introduced "additional" taxes: the tax on credit institutions—Romanian legal entities and branches in Romania of credit institutions—foreign legal entities—Art. 46^1 of the Fiscal Code and the tax on legal entities carrying out activities in the oil and natural gas sector—Art. 46^2 of the Tax Code oblige these companies to pay a new tax of 2% and 0.5%, respectively, in addition to the classic profit tax, only calculated in a different way.

Contextualized, this constant fiscal pressure predisposes legal entities to adopt fiscal behaviors that are at the upper limit of the law. An analysis of the behavioral determinants of economic-financial crime reveals that strictly economic explanations are insufficient to identify the causes of criminal phenomena, making it necessary to analyze the impact of culture, religion, fiscal morality, trust in the state, and happiness, which must be related to corruption or the underground economy in order to generate valid conclusions from a scientific point of view (Achim and Borlea 2019).

Naturally, at least two major open questions may arise. First: how will the two perspectives be synchronized, given that through the measures taken, the state is imposing additional fiscal pressure? Second: will voluntary compliance prove sufficiently defined and robust so as to eliminate the state coercive mechanisms that may be activated in the event of a violation of legal norms?

3 The Need for Regulatory Reform of the Romanian Legal System

It is well known in Romania that the reconceptualization of tax evasion is an immediate necessity. A number of indisputable arguments speak in favor of a new, modern law on tax evasion:

Firstly, Law No. 241/2005 on tax evasion (published in the Official Gazette No. 672 of July 27, 2005) is 20 years old. Despite the fact that regulatory changes have been made during this period, the structure and basis of the law have remained unchanged. Law No. 241/2005 was drafted at a time when Romania was not yet a member of the European Union (January 1, 2007), when the great financial crisis of 2007–2008 had not yet occurred, when social and economic dynamics were limited, when the challenges of intra-community operations did not exist, when a different Tax Code was in force, when profit shifting through and to off-shore companies was only occasional and isolated, when cryptocurrencies did not exist, and when criminal schemes were not very ingenious.

Secondly, because Law No. 241/2005 does not define what it incriminates. Paradoxically, by departing from technical standards in lawmaking and unlike the old regulation on tax evasion under Law No. 87/1994 (published in the Official Gazette No. 299 of October 24, 1994, which contained the following definition: evasion by any means, in whole or in part, from the payment of taxes, contributions, and other amounts owed to the state budget, local budgets, the state social security budget, and special extra-budgetary funds by taxpayers, natural or legal persons, Romanian or foreign) the normative act does not define the crime of tax evasion. We believe that this omission in defining the essential terms of the regulation is likely to affect the scope of the regulation. This is not the first omission of this type by the Romanian legislator. As we have pointed out on another occasion, tax authorities use customized formulas, such as "pipeline operations", "carousel operations", "bidet operations" or "ghost operations". The problem is that these words: "carousel", "bucket", "ghost", "pipeline", although used in conjunction or individually, are marked as such and recognized by state bodies: tax inspectors or criminal prosecution bodies, although they do not have a legal definition. (Puț 2018). Furthermore, in the same equivocal normative context, we sought to provide a composite sketch of the missing trader (ghost companies), which is an artificial construct used (also) for the purpose of tax evasion, by violating legal norms in various transactional circuits and are characterized by: not keeping accounting records or keeping them only formally/partially; not declaring purchases corresponding to deliveries; only performing a scriptic circuit of documents, not having the necessary resources to comply with the legal obligations highlighted in the documents; existing in a given market for a short period of time and, as a rule, without carrying out any activity at the registered office; generally, the actual administrator is different from the statutory administrator, who either has a precarious social or educational background or has an exotic citizenship; the money collected is withdrawn from accounts and divided among the persons involved in tax fraud (Costaș and Puț 2024).

Thirdly, because Law No. 241/2005 does not incriminate what it "defines." From a formal and terminological point of view, this normative act regulates tax evasion, although substantively it also addresses and regulates the most serious illegal behaviors in this area, namely criminal wrongdoings.

Thus, a conceptual distinction must be made between tax evasion and tax fraud. The correct approach would be to rigorously define the concepts, one of the possible options being the following: tax evasion would represent all acts of removing taxable income from the scope of tax law, without violating the legal provisions in force (corresponding to what in other legislations and in European approaches would mean tax avoidance), while tax fraud would represent acts and deeds of evading taxation by circumventing/eluding (violating) legal norms (corresponding to what in other legislations and in European approaches would mean tax evasion or tax fraud) (Minea et al. 2006).

Fourthly, the law must probe, respond to, and regulate current socio-legal situations and relationships. The partially retrograde nature of the law makes it inapplicable or ineffective. However, the current context and the multitude of economic challenges require uniform, up-to- date, modern, and predictable regulation. This can only be achieved through a new regulatory instrument, built from scratch, capable of differentiating between different forms of licit and illicit behaviors, between different levels of legal intensity.

Fifthly, given that the issue of tax fraud lies at the intersection of tax and criminal proceedings, it is noteworthy that in Romania it was not until 2022 that these proceedings were successfully correlated, in the sense that the commencement of criminal proceedings will lead to the interruption of tax proceedings. However, there are many other elements to be clarified: from the thesis, the generation and augmentation of damage in tax evasion cases (according to the regulations in force), to the actual synchronisation of court decisions handed down in the two procedures: criminal and tax.

Therefore, even if only for these reasons, the intervention of the legislator is imperative. But to do so, it will have to make a well-founded distinction between the different forms of illicit in this area of law.

The Romanian legislator will have to adequately define the relevant concepts, taking into account the fundamental objectives pursued. Thus, if it fails to strike an appropriate balance between the punitive, repressive, and sanctioning objective and the objective of redressing the damage, the normative act is compromised ab initio. This balance cannot be identified sequentially, solely through the regulatory mechanism, but is part of a macro-system that starts from mentalities, is culturally permeated, and is based on pre-existing legal values and reliable statistical data.

A comparative analysis (Drosu-Şaguna and Marin 2020) highlights interesting aspects related to the criminalization and punishment of tax evasion in certain EU member states. However, beyond the criminalization of illicit behavior, what stands out is that in all these tax law jurisdictions the emphasis is on recovering the damage, rather than on the severity of the penalties for tax fraud. Thus, in Belgium, income taxation reaches over 50% (including social contributions), compared to an average tax rate of 45% at EU level, and the risk of tax fraud seems, in theory, to be higher. With regard to income tax, fraud, which represents the taxpayer's direct intention to evade tax obligations, is punished in a simple form with a criminal fine or imprisonment, and in serious cases with imprisonment from 8 days to 5 years and/or a fine of between 250 and and 500.000 euro (which, according to the rules on additional increases in criminal fines, could reach up to €3 million). In France, where a progressive income tax of up to 45% is in place, tax evasion has non-criminal legal consequences, with tax fraud being punishable by either a fine of €500.000 and 5 years' imprisonment, or a fine of €2.000.000 and 7 years' imprisonment if committed by an organized group or in an aggravated form. In Austria, tax evasion (Abgabenhinterziehung) and negligent failure to provide information or fulfill reporting obligations, resulting in the understatement of the tax base, are punishable by up to double the unpaid tax and imprisonment for up to 2 years. In cases of tax fraud or if the taxpayer repeatedly violates their tax obligations, the penalties imposed are exponentially higher. Finally, in Hungary, the offense of tax fraud (where the fiscal authority has been misled regarding the payment of tax obligations or any other amounts payable or owed to the state budget, if relevant information regarding tax payment obligations has been concealed, or if declarations containing false/non-compliant information have been submitted, causing prejudice to the state budget) the guilty person is punished with imprisonment, and the actual classification of the act as a crime depends on the amount of damage caused to the state budget, on the basis of which the specific prison sentence is determined.

According to the provisions of Article 9(1) of Law No. 241/2005, which regulates the jurisdiction of tax evasion offences in Romania, the following acts committed for the purpose of evading tax obligations constitute tax evasion offences and are punishable by imprisonment of between 3 and 10 years and the deprivation of certain rights or a fine: (a). concealing taxable goods or sources of income; (b). the omission, in whole or in part, of recording commercial transactions or income in accounting records or other legal documents; (c). recording expenses in accounting records, electronic invoices, or other legal documents that are not based on actual transactions, or recording other fictitious transactions; (d). altering, destroying, or concealing accounting records, memories of electronic tax or fiscal cash registers, or other means of data storage, including electronic ones; (e). keeping double accounting records using documents or other means of data storage, including electronic ones; (f). evading financial, tax, or customs audits by failing to declare, making fictitious declarations, or making inaccurate declarations regarding the main or secondary premises of the persons being audited; (g). substitution, degradation or alienation by the debtor or by third parties of goods seized in accordance with the provisions of the Tax Procedure Code and the Criminal Procedure Code; (h). the taxpayer's use, in bad faith, of the national electronic invoicing system RO e-Factura, in order to create the appearance of legality of fictitious operations or to conceal the actual transaction circuit of goods/services; and (i). the use of electronic fiscal cash registers that are not connected to the national computer system for the supervision and monitoring of fiscal data, in accordance with the law, or the alteration of electronic fiscal cash registers for the non-transmission of fiscal data or the transmission of unreal fiscal data.

In summary, we may ask what other elements support the need for normative reform of this systemic component of Romanian positive law? Could it be the insufficient collection of damages in tax evasion cases? Or could it be the insufficient normative sharing and allocation of institutions?

4 Reconceptualization of Tax Institutions

As has been highlighted in doctrine, in order to emphasize the difference between the licit or illicit nature of the two categories of acts, namely tax evasion and tax fraud, the most appropriate seems to be a well-known English saying: "The difference between *tax avoidance* and *tax evasion* is the thickness of a prison wall" (Costaş and Tofan 2015).

However, the concept of tax evasion has multiple meanings: from legal conduct (in France, Belgium), an expression of abuse of rights (Switzerland) to tax fraud (in Italy and the *common law system*), and in national doctrine, the majority opinion is that tax evasion includes both licit methods of evading tax obligations (legal tax evasion) and illicit methods (illicit tax evasion) (Bugnar-Coldea 2021).

At the international level, through the mechanism and support of the OECD, an international economic forum at its base, the aim is, among other things, to limit the incidence of evasive behavior and to *avoid base erosion,* as well as the *shifting of profits* from one tax jurisdiction to another. As stated on the official website, although not all BEPS schemes are illegal *de plano,* for those that are illegal, additional efforts are needed to limit profit volatility. Base erosion and profit shifting (BEPS), where multinationals shift profits to low or no-tax locations where they have little or no economic activity or erode tax bases through deductible payments like interest or royalties, costs countries USD 100–240 billion in lost revenue annually. That is equivalent to 4%–10% of global corporate income tax revenue. Although some BEPS schemes are illegal, most are not. BEPS practices undermine the fairness and integrity of tax systems because businesses that operate across borders can use them to gain a competitive advantage over enterprises operating at a domestic level. In a broader context, when large corporations are seen to be avoiding income tax, it undermines voluntary compliance by all taxpayers (https://www.oecd.org/en/topics/base-erosion-and-profit-shifting-beps.html).

However, without questioning the legitimacy of these concerns, this is dependent on the relationship between law and globalization, which is constantly changing (Veitch et al. 2018).

Italian doctrine distinguishes between four types of behavior that lead to non-fulfillment of tax obligations, as follows:

(a) *Tax evasion (evasione fiscale)* proper. This type of behavior involves direct and open violation of tax rules, with the aim of concealing all or part of the taxable assets or taxable base from the tax authorities, thereby reducing or altering the level of tax obligations or generating undue tax credits.
(b) *Tax avoidance (elusiune fiscale).* Tax avoidance occurs mainly at the stage of determining taxes contributions and involves the existence of tax-related behaviors that do not violate legal rules but which, without being economically justified, are intended to circumvent the obligations or prohibitions of tax legislation and generate tax reductions or the reimbursement of undue amounts.
(c) *Abuse of rights in the field of taxation* (*abuso del diritto in ambito tributario*). Abuse of rights in the field of taxation is defined by Article 5 of Law No. 23/2014 as "*the distorted use of appropriate legal instruments to obtain a tax reduction, even if such conduct does not violate any specific legal provision.*"
(d) *Tax insolvency* (*insolvenza fiscale*). Finally, tax insolvency (sometimes referred to as "collection evasion") involves unlawful conduct by the taxpayer to evade enforcement for their own tax debts. This type of behavior can only occur if the

tax obligations are known to the tax authorities and is specific to the enforcement phase (Adolfini et al. 2015).

Portuguese tax doctrine highlights that the concept of tax evasion covers (all) types of offences (i.e. criminal offences proper, and administrative offences). In the middle of the scale, between crimes and licit behavior, we find a gray area, the size of which varies between legal systems, but which tends to be similar in OECD countries. This refers to behavior designated as tax evasion or abuse of rights in the field of taxation. This area includes legal acts or transactions that take legal forms not covered by the applicable rules or that circumvent certain rules for determining the tax base (Durado 2022).

Spanish doctrine distinguishes between *evasion fiscal licita (elusion)* and *evasion fiscal ilicita (fraude fiscal)*. Offenses regulated by Spanish law that fall under the category of *fraude fiscal* can cover a very broad spectrum, including, among others: violation of the obligation to declare taxable income or factual misrepresentation of payment obligations, with the resulting damage to tax collection, but also offenses related to reporting obligations, but without immediate economic damage, offenses relating to the obligation to declare taxable bases or tax results by entities subject to the income imputation regime, violations related to other purely formal or complementary obligations of taxpayers: (a) tax returns; (b) appointment of a representative; (c) obligation to declare tax residence; (d) accounting and registration obligations; (e) invoicing obligations (Perez Royo and Carrasco Gonzalez 2019).

As far as we are concerned in line with traditional Romanian doctrine, legal tax evasion refers to tax optimization procedures, tax-relevant behaviors that do not violate legal norms but which, without being economically justified, seek to reduce tax obligations, reimburse undue amounts, or circumvent prohibitions or obligations. Tax optimization, referred to in local doctrine as legal tax evasion, does not involve the specific aim of evading tax obligations, which distinguishes it from genuine tax evasion. We have shown on another occasion that illegal tax evasion is defined by the violation of tax laws with the aim of evading taxation. (Costaş and Puţ 2024) We subscribe to the thesis that tax evasion involves evading payment of amounts owed to the state, in violation of the law, without being limited to criminal conduct. Tax evasion occurs, for example, when taxpayers withhold and fail to pay in full the amounts representing taxes and contributions withheld at source, conduct that is punishable as an administrative offense under Article 336(1)(p) of the Tax Procedure Code (Bugnar-Coldea 2021), as is the case with generic conduct (without criminal connotations) involving the taxpayer/payer's failure to fulfill their legal obligations to declare taxable assets and income or, as the case may be, taxes, contributions, and other amounts, as well as any information related to taxes, contributions, taxable assets, and income, if the law provides for their declaration, as in Article 336(1)(b) of the Tax Procedure Code (Law No. 207/2015—published in the Official Gazette No. 688 of July 23, 2015).

The abuse of rights in the field of taxation essentially refers to the misuse of tax law provisions in order to obtain tax advantages that the taxpayer would not otherwise have been able to obtain. Because tax law is a matter of public policy and affects the essential interests of the state and the community (Dassesse and Minne 2001), it is likewise reactive whenever the fiscal normative commands are breached.

According to the provisions of Article 11(1) of the Tax Code: "When determining the amount of a tax or mandatory social contribution, the tax authorities may disregard a transaction that has no economic purpose, adjusting its tax effects, or may reclassify the form of a transaction/activity to reflect the economic content of the transaction/ activity. The tax authority is required to justify the tax assessment decision issued as a result of disregarding a transaction or, where applicable, as a result of reclassifying the form of a transaction, by indicating the relevant elements relating to the purpose and content of the transaction that is the subject of the non-consideration/reclassification, as well as all the evidence taken into account for this purpose."

Therefore, the tax authority has the *imperium* to assess *in concreto* whether a particular transaction invoked by the taxpayer for the exercise of subjective rights has an economic purpose and, should the conclusion be negative, to reclassify the form of a transaction/activity to reflect the economic content of that said transaction/ activity.

According to the provisions of paragraph 12) of Article 11 of the Tax Code, which filters and summarises the case law of the Court of Justice of the European Union on VAT abuse, two cumulative conditions must be met, combining the objective aspect (let. a) and the subjective aspect (let. b): "Where an abuse of rights is found to exist, the transactions involved in such abusive practices must be redefined so as to restore the situation that would have prevailed in the absence of the transactions constituting the abuse. The competent tax authorities have the right to cancel the VAT deducted in connection with each transaction whenever it is found that the right of deduction has been exercised abusively. In order to invoke abuse of rights, two conditions must be cumulatively met:

(a) the transactions in question, despite the formal application of the conditions laid down in the legal provisions, result in the granting of tax advantages that would be contrary to the purpose of those legal provisions;
(b) it must be objectively proven that the essential purpose of the transactions in question is to obtain a tax advantage.

From the perspective and in the specific context of VAT, the redefinition of transactions and the cancellation of the right to deduct VAT requires the corroboration of two components: objective and subjective. The objective aspect consists in the unjustified invocation of a right conferred by European Union law, which is only apparently invoked on valid grounds, but the purpose pursued by the European legislator in enacting that right is not respected, while the subjective aspect consists in proving the essential tax purpose of the transactions in question, which cannot seriously justify another commercial (lato sensu) non-tax purpose (Bufan 2016). Finally, in the natural-legal sense, tax optimization represents the taxpayer's inspired use of legal means that allow them to reduce their tax obligations. In turn, it also represents, stricto sensu "evasion", an avoidance of the burdensome tax obligation, only through the use of licit means.

As highlighted in doctrine, tax optimization involves identifying the means by which a taxpayer can benefit from tax breaks or other favorable provisions in the legislation for the economic activity they carry out. The purpose of tax optimization is to benefit from existing tax breaks and favorable provisions in legislation, which leads to a legal reduction in tax burdens. In other words, tax optimization could be considered a component of legal tax evasion, carried out with the aim of achieving maximum tax gains, and often involves relocation to different jurisdictions with low levels of income taxation. In a general classification, three major working techniques have been attributed to tax optimization:

- optimization through inaction—characterized by the ability of taxpayers to avoid paying taxes by refraining from entering into a legal act or performing a legal act that would generate a tax and, implicitly, the corresponding obligation to pay it by the taxpayer;
- optimization through choice—characterized by the taxpayer's ability to choose the most favorable tax solution, within the limits established by law;
- optimization through manipulation—characterized by the ability of taxpayers to exploit legislative loopholes for personal gain, taking advantage of either the lack of clarity of the tax rule or the lack of correlation between existing legal provisions at the national level (Costea 2019).

In summary, in an attempt to overlap the normative and applicative plans, it is necessary to associate each type of atypical tax behavior with a certain predictable type of legal liability, to the extent that it leads to a violation of legal provisions.

In general, as highlighted in legal theory, the issue of justifying punishment is the issue of substantiating the reasons that make the legal practice of imposing punishments fair and just. The question "why punish?" actually encompasses various additional aspects corresponding to the multiple aspects of criminal practice. Among these, the following should be mentioned in particular: determining the conduct that should be punished and, therefore, the behavior that should be prohibited; determining the persons to whom the sanctions apply; determining the procedures necessary for the application of sanctions; determining the nature and severity of the sanctions themselves. The question "why punish?" therefore encompasses six questions, which can be summarized as follows: "whether and how to prohibit, judge, and punish" (Jori and Pintore 1995).

In the specific context of criminal-tax law, tax fraud—as the most serious illegal act in this area—is subject to criminal liability, the most serious form of legal liability, with consequences that can reach up to 15 years in prison in our legal system if the damage exceeds €1.000.000.

From the perspective of tax evasion itself, without being limited to administrative liability, it concerns a level of legal intensity lower than the criminal level and should be placed in this position, and the register of liability should be, at least in principle, an administrative one.

With regard to abuse of rights in the field of taxation, tax liability will be attached to it, as the specific behaviors do not have criminal connotations. For example, tax liability may concern both the cancellation of the right to deduct certain expenses when calculating income or profit tax, and the cancellation of the VAT code or the right to deduct VAT, as well as the incurring of tax liability for the persons responsible for the insolvency of the legal entity.

Nevertheless, in order to construct an anti-abuse rule, the legislator has at its disposal only a provision that is as expressed in a manner as general as possible, capable of covering as wide a variety of situations as possible, since the multitude of types of abuse cannot be anticipated in each individual case. However, as practice has shown, such a "general" mechanism can be used without any limits or justification, even for situations that clearly do not fall within the scope of the case, leading to the abusive use of these general anti-abuse rules (Bufan 2016). Therefore, there are multiple situations in which the limits of "anti-abuse abuse" must be censored, and the last resort in this matter is exclusively represented by the courts.

Finally, we have previously highlighted that tax optimization involves tax planning, i.e., studying and choosing the most useful legal mechanisms to avoid taxpayers' tax exposure. In this environment, tax optimization is the only tax behavior that is immune to any type of accountability, obviously if the tax authority and the taxpayer are on the same wavelength, which in administrative practice happens extremely rarely.

In conclusion, from our point of view, it is useful to divide tax behaviors into the following categories: tax fraud, tax evasion, abuse of rights in the field of taxation, and tax optimization, and the new tax fraud law in Romania should exclusively substantiate and regulate the corresponding criminal elements.

Thus, is our reasoning and classification beyond any form of criticism? Certainly not, however it does establish, in a logically and legally coherent manner, the types of tax behavior that may be subject to sanctions!

Finally, the question remains as to the limits of the projection that these legal institutions would have in practice, and the various forms of legal interpretation that might be validated by the courts?!

5 Case Law Sequences Illustrating the Theoretical Basis

The purpose of theory is practice, the purpose of regulation is application. We theorize at the highest level of legal force—normative and we problematize at a lower level of legal force—doctrinal—in order to substantiate solutions in judicial practice. Thus, the theoretical distinctions articulated above are of particular significance in their application within jurisprudence. An examination of case law reveals extremely interesting legal situations that capture the idea that, in the legislative abyss, judicial practice tends to slip through the legal norms that regulate the matter:

5.1 First Case—Criminal Decision No. 193/2021 of the Cluj Court of Appeal (Unpublished)

In this case, it was held that the defendant G.B.A. had committed the crime of tax evasion provided for in Art. 9 para. (1) letter c and para. (3) of Law 241/2005—fictitious transactions, with damages of over EUR 1 million, in conjunction with embezzlement under Article 295 of the Criminal Code (Law No. 286/2009 published in the Official Gazette No. 510 of July 24, 2009) and with the application of Article 35(1) and Article 308 of the Criminal Code (corruption and service offences), and the defendant R.T. the offence of embezzlement in the same circumstances.

The defendant G.B.A. recorded in the accounts of two commercial companies fictitious supporting documents relating to purchases of goods and services that were not based on actual transactions. The acts were carried out in his capacity as partner and administrator in two companies, S.C. B SRL and S.C. SRL, through various economic transactions with nine other companies, causing a total loss of 3.443.095 lei. R.T. was also a partner in S.C. SRL.

The court rejected the claim of a de facto separation of the activities of the two companies, B. SRL and S.C. SRL, which would have invalidated the allegation of fraudulent collusion for the purpose of committing tax evasion, on the grounds that the witnesses' testimonies were insufficient to establish such a fact. The court found that another company, S.C. DVP SRL, with which the operations were carried out, was fictitiously taken over by two administrators who were not involved and that there were no employees or logistics to support the economic operations that took place between the three companies, the behavior being specific to "ghost companies." The defendant R.T. was convicted of embezzlement and sentenced to 3 years and 6 months in prison and an additional penalty of disqualification from exercising his rights, while the defendant G.B.A. was sentenced to 4 years and 6 months. Both defendants were ordered, on the basis of the civil action, to pay 7.587.235 lei in civil damages.

5.2 Second Case—Criminal Decision No. 1238/A/2019 of the Cluj Court of Appeal (Unpublished)

In a joint case concerning the unjustified refusal to present legal documents to the competent authorities for the purpose of preventing financial verifications, the same defendant, G.B.A., as administrator of I.S.S. SRL, recorded in the accounts eight tax invoices for purchases from DCP SRL, which did not reflect actual transactions, causing damage to the state budget of 3.286.831 lei. When summoned by the tax authorities, the defendant refused to provide them with the documents of I.S.S. SRL in order to prevent tax audits. In law, the offense is tax evasion under Article 9(1)(c) and (3) of Law 241/2005 and unjustified refusal to provide the competent authorities with legal documents in order to prevent financial audits (Article 4 of Law 241/

2005). (3) of Law 241/2005 and the unjustified refusal to submit legal documents to the competent authorities in order to prevent financial checks (Article 4 of Law 241/2005).

The defendant's claim that all the company's accounting documents had been sent to the company D.C. in the Seychelles was not considered credible. The photocopies of the two receipts from the Romanian Post Office submitted in defense do not prove the contents of the shipment and therefore cannot support the defendant's claim as credible. Regardless of the shipment, the court held that the defendant was obliged to fulfill this obligation. Furthermore, there is no logical reason why the defendant would have sent the accounting documents.

The eight invoices issued by the supplier D.C.P. SRL were not identified. The defendant claimed that the invoices could not be fictitious, as the goods purchased had been re-invoiced to third parties (without proving this claim). The tax returns do not include the date of any invoice, only the semester or month, so it was impossible to verify their accuracy.

The defendant was sentenced to five years in prison and the deprivation of certain rights.

5.3 *Third Case—Criminal Decision No. 1461/A/2020 of the Cluj Court of Appeal (Unpublished)*

The case stems from the alleged fictitious nature of the transactions recorded by SC S. SRL, consisting of the recording in the accounting records of 30 allegedly fictitious invoices issued by five companies to S. SRL as the beneficiary, with the effect of evading the company's income tax and VAT payments.

The criminal investigation authorities found that the transactions were fictitious because: the defendant was unable to provide relevant explanations regarding the identity of the persons who delivered the goods; there was an unpaid balance to SC T.I. SRL in the amount of 128.441 lei, for which this company did not register with the creditors' committee during the insolvency of SC S. SRL; inappropriate data in the "shipping data" section regarding transport; two witnesses stated that the two companies were not suppliers; the registered office of the suppliers coincides with an undeclared place of business of SC S. SRL; the goods were not received by a commission, but by the defendant; the administrators of the two companies are being prosecuted for tax evasion.

The court held that the mere fact that the two administrators were prosecuted did not constitute grounds for disregarding their statements. The payments were proven, having been made by bank transfer. Also, witnesses said that, because of the high flow of orders, they didn't see if there were any business relationships between the companies, and this can't prove that they didn't exist. The unpaid balance was supposed to be offset by labor. The problems with the invoices are irrelevant, because each company can create its own invoices, which do not have to comply with a fixed form.

The court noted that several witnesses attested to the commercial relations between the two companies. It has not been proven beyond reasonable doubt that the discrepancies in the tax records were intended to evade payment of obligations. The receipts were confirmed. Moreover, it is well known in the commercial field that it is possible and acceptable to pay a supplier from the administrator's personal account, who then withdraws the amount from his company's cash register into his account. There are more witnesses supporting innocence than guilt.

The final decision was to acquit (the act is not covered by criminal law), leaving the civil action brought by the tax authority unresolved.

5.4 Fourth Case—Criminal Judgment No. 47/2023 of the Sălaj Tribunal (Unpublished)

The defendant T.F.S. is accused of the crime of continuous tax evasion under Article 9(1)(b) and (2) of Law 241/2005. The indictment states that the defendant, as de facto administrator of P.R. SRL, together with C.A.F., failed to record in the company's accounting records tax invoices totaling 5.900.611 lei, representing deliveries of goods to P.P.H. SRL, I.D.B. SRL,

K.I.C.C. SRL T.G.P. SRL, with the aim of evading tax obligations and causing damage to the state budget in the total amount of 1.172.741 lei.

Following a tax inspection in August 2015, it was discovered that in 2013, P.R. SRL made intra-Community purchases of goods from Poland (powdered milk), which it did not declare to the competent tax authority.

As a result of the tax assessment, it was found that P.R. SRL made deliveries worth 2.038.96920 lei, of which 394.638 lei was VAT, but only one transaction worth 138.322 lei, of which 26.772 lei was VAT, was recorded in the company's accounts. The VAT payable and undeclared by P.R. SRL was set at 367.866 lei. The expert considers that the transactions have real economic substance, as the products delivered correspond to those purchased in Poland, but it is noted that the delivery transactions were not profitable, resulting in a net loss (excluding expenses) of 96.647 lei.

The court noted that, from the way in which the commercial operations were carried out and, in particular, from the fact that the sale price was below the purchase price, it is clear that there was an intention not to subsequently declare the deliveries and thus not to pay the VAT collected.

The failure to record in the accounts of P.R. SRL the commercial transactions carried out with P.P. SRL, namely the tax invoices issued to the company and the income obtained, does not meet the criteria for typicality, because the failure to record these transactions is natural and correct, being determined by the fact that the transactions did not actually take place. Because they did not take place, they cannot generate tax obligations. In fact, there were no documents to support this activity, only the evidence of the co-defendant C.A.F. The economic transfers between the two companies did not represent a real economic activity. Thus, from a criminal point of view, the defendant T.F.S. was acquitted due to the statute of limitations on criminal liability, and from a civil point of view, compensation for damages to the state budget in the total amount of 367.866 lei is required.

5.5 *Fifth Case—Criminal Decision No. 3/2025 of the Maramureș Tribunal (Unpublished)*

SC F. SRL's main activity is "driving schools" with the defendant S.A.R. as its administrator. The company pays tax on micro-enterprise income and salary income and has never been registered as a taxable person for VAT purposes. It is noted that the students paid the fee for the theoretical courses to the company, the courses being provided by the administrator. In contrast, the fees for the practical courses were paid directly to the driving instructors, who kept the fee, even though they were employed part-time or on the minimum wage, paid only the taxes related to their salary income and did not receive their actual salary. The contracts and other accounting records relating to the fees for the practical courses were recorded "only formally" in the relevant registers.

The students paid the fees for the practical courses directly to the instructors through an agreement they had with the administrator, as a result of the fact that they did not receive a salary and only paid their taxes and duties. The company should have registered for VAT purposes, exceeding the exemption threshold.

The court upheld the administrator's obligation "to take care of the accounting and recording in the accounts of all income obtained from the services provided, which the defendant knowingly failed to do."

The defendant was sentenced to three years' imprisonment, suspended, and an additional two years' disqualification from exercising certain rights. On the civil side, the tax authority's claim for payment of 200.999 lei (representing VAT and micro-enterprise income tax, plus interest and late payment penalties) was upheld.

5.6 *Sixth Case—Civil Judgment No. 1465/2023 of the Cluj Tribunal (Unpublished)*

Through Civil Judgment No. 1465/2023 of the Cluj Tribunal, in a case concerning the annulment of the tax assessment decision and the decision to settle the tax appeal, the court offered an unprecedented solution in that it dismissed the lawsuit as having been filed by a person without legal capacity.

The novelty of the solution lies in the fact that, in the course of the judicial proceedings seeking the annulment of the administrative acts, the company was compelled to initiate insolvency proceedings, given its state of insolvency. It is possible that the strategy was aimed at preventing possible sanctions resulting from the delay, such as, for example, the potential referral to the criminal authorities, the joint and several liability of the shareholders/directors, and the like.

In this regard, insolvency proceedings were initiated at the request of the debtor before the Cluj Specialized Court. The decision of the Cluj Specialized Tribunal was rendered without taking into account the ongoing tax dispute, which raises another issue regarding the synchronization of insolvency proceedings with tax proceedings, which currently does not exist in Romania. Admitting the request for closure of the insolvency proceedings, formulated by the judicial liquidator, the court ordered the closure of the debtor's bankruptcy proceedings and the removal of the debtor from the records of the Trade Registry Office attached to the Cluj Court.

Naturally, the legal question was: What will be the legal fate of the tax dispute seeking the annulment of the administrative tax acts in the context of the closure of the insolvency proceedings and the removal of the company from the register, given that the tax obligations have not been extinguished? Clearly, the lack of capacity to use legal personality automatically leads to the closure of the case, with the legal claim remaining unsupported.

The only issue remaining under discussion is that the main tax liabilities established by the tax decision in the amount of 185.375 lei, the ancillary tax liabilities representing interest and late payment penalties in the amount of 29.497 lei, and ancillary tax liabilities representing penalties for non-declaration in the amount of 117.912 lei.

6 Conclusions

At the level of positive tax law, we note that terminologically we do not meet the requirements of rigor, referring to tax evasion, but in reality criminalizing tax fraud. This calls for a reconceptualization of fiscal-criminal and legal-economic institutions, starting from a rigorous definition of tax fraud as the most serious form of fiscal-criminal behavior. Then, the legislator's objective should be recalibrated, from a tendency to maximize criminal penalties for these offenses (which reaches an unjustified maximum of 15 years in prison) to a constant tendency to obtain compensation for damages, including by "tempting" offenders with attractive reasons for non-punishment, in order to achieve this. Legal protection of the state budget remains a mere slogan if it is not accompanied by adequate regulation to balance the conflicting objectives: that of the state, which has suffered financial harm as a result of the offense, and that of the defendant, who is interested to avoid imprisonment or any legal consequences arising from the violation of the rules governing tax fraud.

This study aims to examine and articulate a legal foundation for the concept of tax evasion and its possible variations. We have signaled some points of concern, provided possible solutions, and outlined some directions, but future studies on the subjects may further refine and enhance the conclusions advanced by us, herein, conclusions which were intended, at this stage, to serve as a starting point for the legislative redimensioning of tax evasion, an area that should constitute a matter of pressing priority for the Romanian positive law legislator, respectively a legal benchmark for court solutions, until the entry into force of a new, modern normative act governing tax evasion.

References

Achim MV, Borlea SN (2019) Criminalitatea economico-financiară: corupţia, economia subterană şi spălarea banilor—cauze, efecte, soluţii—Abordări teoretice şi practice. Ed Economică, Bucureşti; pp 201–265

Adolfini M, Greco F, Mazzotta F, Tolla M, Thione M, Rapone F (2015) Istituzioni di Diritto tributario. Giuridica Editrice DIKE, Roma, p 517

Bufan, R. (2016). Tratat de drept fiscal. Volumul 1. Teoria generală a dreptului fiscal. Ed. Hamangiu, Bucureşti; p 384

Bugnar-Coldea O. (2021). Infracţiunile de evaziune prevăzute de art. 9 din Legea nr. 241/2005 pentru prevenirea şi combaterea evaziunii fiscale. Ed. Universul Juridic, Bucureşti; pp 28 and 35

Costaş CF, Puţ SI (2024) Drept fiscal şi financiar. Caiet de seminar. Ed. Hamangiu, Bucureşti; pp 89 and 99

Costaş CF, Tofan M (2015) Drept financiar. Ed. Universul Juridic, Bucureşti; p 484

Costea IM (2019) Evaziunea fiscală. Legea nr. 241/2005 comentată şi adnotată. Ed. Hamangiu, Bucureşti; p 21

Damarey S (2006) Finances publiques. Guliano Editeur, Paris; p 31

Dassesse M, Minne P (2001) Droit fiscal. Principes generaux et impots sur les revenus, 5eme edn. Bruylant Bruxelles, p 45

Durado AP (2022) Direito Fiscal, 7a Edisao. Almedina, p 309

Drosu-Şaguna D, Marin AA (2020) Evaziunea fiscală. Prevenire şi combatere. Ed. Universul Juridic, Bucureşti, pp 139–159

Jori M, Pintore A (1995) Manuale di Teoria Generale del Diritto, 2nd edizione. Giappichelli Editore, Torino, p 295

Minea MŞ, Costaş CF, Ionescu DM (2006) Legea evaziunii fiscale. Comentarii şi explicaţii. Ed. C.H. Beck, Bucureşti, p 15

Perez Royo F, Carrasco Gonzalez Fr. M (2019) Derecho Financiero y Tributario. Parte general, Thomas Reuters, Navarra, p 441

Puţ SI (2018) The use of legally undefined concepts in the practice of romanian tax authorities. In: Eufire. European Financial Regulation. Ed. Universităţii Alexandru Ioan Cuza, Iaşi, p 403

Veitch S, Christodoulidis E, Goldoni M (2018) Jurisprudence. Themes and Concepts, 3rd edn. Routledge, New York, p 100

https://www.oecd.org/en/topics/base-erosion-and-profit-shifting-beps.html

https://static.anaf.ro/static/10/Anaf/Informatii_R/Strategia_PIT_23112022.pdf

Septimiu Ioan Puţ is a a Senior Lecturer (PhD) and Vice-Dean at the Faculty of Law of Babeş-Bolyai University in Cluj-Napoca, where he teaches the following subjects: Theory of Law, Sports Law, Public Finance Law. He has published numerous books and dozens of scholarly articles in the fields of Tax and Financial Law, of Theory of Law, and Sports Law. He is a member of the

European Society for Comparative Legal History, a member of the International Fiscal Association—Romanian Branch, a member of the Romanian Association for the Study of Comparative Law, Private International Law, and International Trade Law, a member of the Society of Legal and Administrative Sciences, and a lawyer in the Cluj Bar Association.

Financial Crime in Stock Exchange: The Case on the Stock Exchanges of the Europen Union States

Yusuf Ekrem Akbaş, Mehmet Ali Polat, and Ahmet Şit

Abstract This study examines how financial crime dynamics shape equity market performance in the European Union. Using an unbalanced panel of 27 EU member states over 2013 to 2023, we estimate short run effects of seven offense categories on national stock indices via dynamic panel generalized method of moments with difference and system estimators. Diagnostic tests, including Wald, Sargan and Hansen, and Arellano and Bond AR(1) and AR(2), support instrument relevance and the absence of second order serial correlation. Results are consistent across estimators: corruption, migrant smuggling, and money laundering display positive short run associations with index levels, whereas fraud, theft, unlawful information technology access, and environmental crime are negatively associated. We argue that the positive coefficients for corruption and laundering related indicators reflect transitory liquidity and risk taking rather than sound fundamentals, which implies heightened long run fragility through institutional erosion and higher risk premia. By contrast, crimes that directly undermine property rights, contractual enforcement, cyber integrity, and environmental compliance depress valuations through profitability and investor confidence channels. Policy implications emphasize stronger deterrence and supervisory technology for market abuse and property crimes, risk based AML/CFT regimes with beneficial ownership transparency and cross border coordination, and the embedding of sustainability and cyber resilience into disclosure and enforcement frameworks. Limitations include measurement error in crime statistics, annual frequency that may mask higher frequency dynamics, and EU only coverage. Future research should examine sectoral and firm level heterogeneity, use higher frequency data to detect structural breaks, and apply designs that sharpen causal identification.

Y. E. Akbaş
Faculty of Economics and Administrative Sciences, Department of Economics, Adıyaman University, Altınşehir, Turkey

M. A. Polat (✉)
Faculty of Economics and Administrative Sciences, Department of Economics, Uludağ University, Bursa, Turkey

A. Şit (✉)
Faculty of Social and Human Sciences, Department of International Trade and Finance, Malatya Turgut Ozal University, Malatya, Turkey
e-mail: ahmet.sit@ozal.edu.tr

M. V. Achim (ed.), *Financial Crime in the Digital Era*, Contributions to Finance and Accounting, https://doi.org/10.1007/978-3-032-20198-0_19

Keywords Financial Crime · Stock Exchanges · European Union States · GMM

1 Introduction

Financial crime has become one of the most complex and multidimensional problems facing today's financial systems. The acceleration of digitalisation, the momentum gained by cross-border capital movements and the increasing integration of markets are increasing the scale and complexity of illegal activities such as fraud, corruption, theft, money laundering, cybercrime and economic activities that cause environmental damage. Such practices not only cause direct economic losses, but also erode investor confidence, undermine market stability and call into question the legitimacy of financial institutions and regulatory frameworks. Financial crime, which acts as an invisible tax on the functioning of the financial system, negatively affects firm performance at the micro level and the depth and integrity of capital markets at the macro level.

Corruption, theft, fraud and similar crimes weaken institutional structures, distort resource allocation and reduce social welfare. In addition, they trigger capital flight, distort income distribution and erode the credibility of legal regulations. For capital markets based on transparency, protection of property rights and reliable information flow, the increase in financial crime raises risk premiums, lowers asset valuations and limits financial deepening. In the long term, these dynamics mean low growth and high fragility as investors demand higher returns to compensate for increased oversight and enforcement risks.

Over the past thirty years, the relationship between financial crime and capital market performance has attracted increasing attention in the empirical literature. While early studies primarily examined the effects of corruption and governance quality on growth, investment, and institutional development, more recent studies have focused on the impact of specific types of crime on stock market indices, volatility, investor behaviour, and international capital flows. This literature demonstrates that the impact of financial crime varies depending on the strength of institutions, the rule of law, and the deterrent effect of sanctions. In countries with strong oversight and effective sanctions, financial crime is limited and swiftly punished, whereas in countries with weak institutional structures, it can become systemic and embedded in market operations.

Within this framework, the study examines the relationship between different types of financial and environmental crimes and stock market index performance in European Union countries. The empirical analysis is based on an unbalanced panel data set covering 27 EU member states, constructed using data from the period 2013–2023. The unbalanced panel structure stems from the fact that not all countries can provide data for all years due to missing observations in crime indicators for certain years in some countries. Therefore, Turkey and Cyprus were excluded from the analysis due to data gaps in various crime categories. Defining the sample in this way from the outset in a clear and consistent manner helps to ensure that the findings are interpreted correctly and that cross-country comparability is maintained.

In the study, each country's most actively traded national stock market index is used as an indicator of capital market performance. Seven categories of crime are analysed: corruption, fraud, theft, money laundering, migrant smuggling, illegal access to computer systems, and acts causing environmental pollution or degradation. These indicators cover a wide range, from traditional financial crimes to cybercrime and environmental violations, thus enabling the examination of whether the effects of different types of crime on stock markets are heterogeneous. This multidimensional approach makes it possible to assess whether certain types of crime may increase liquidity or speculative activity in the short term, while others directly undermine profitability, investor protection, and market integrity.

Methodologically, the study employs dynamic panel Generalised Method of Moments (GMM) approaches, specifically difference GMM and system GMM estimators, to analyse the relationship between financial crime indicators and stock market index performance. This choice is based on three fundamental reasons. First, since stock indices exhibit strong continuity over time, the inclusion of a lagged dependent variable in the model is inevitable, raising the issue of endogeneity in classical fixed or random effects models. Secondly, some crime indicators can be directly affected by the economic climate and market performance, increasing the risk of reverse causality and omitted variable bias. Thirdly, it is necessary to take into account structural differences between member countries that are constant over time but critical for analysis, such as legal traditions, supervisory capacity, and financial structure. Dynamic panel GMM estimators control both these endogeneity and reverse causality issues and country-specific fixed effects using instrumental variables, thereby enabling consistent and reliable estimates under relatively weak restrictions.

Empirical findings indicate that corruption, migrant smuggling and money laundering variables are positively correlated with the stock market index in the short term, while fraud, theft, illegal access to computer systems and environmental crimes exhibit negative correlations in the short term. At first glance, the positive coefficients of corruption and money laundering indicators suggest that illegal funds may inject liquidity into the market in the short term and increase speculative activity. However, from an institutional perspective, these effects are not permanent and, in the long term, weaken market credibility and the rule of law, thereby increasing capital costs, raising risk perception and deepening fragility. Conversely, crimes that undermine property rights, cyber infrastructure security, and environmental compliance negatively impact company valuations by reducing profitability and investor confidence.

This study contributes to various literatures by documenting the effects of different crime categories on capital markets in EU countries. Firstly, it positions financial crime and corporate quality among the determinants of stock market performance beyond macroeconomic fundamentals. Secondly, it contributes to discussions on the interaction between financial stability, governance and sustainability, and shows that environmental violations and cybercrime are increasingly priced in by investors. Finally, the study highlights the need to strengthen oversight and enforcement capacity in the fight against market abuses, fraud, and cybercrime; develop risk-based anti-money laundering and counter-terrorist financing regimes; and integrate transparency, sustainability, and cyber resilience into regulatory and supervisory frameworks. Thus, it is emphasised that combating financial crime is not only a legal or ethical imperative, but also a fundamental prerequisite for resilient, deep and inclusive capital markets in the European Union.

After literatüre review, the basic hypothesis of the study can be stated as follows:

H_0: Financial crimes occurring in stock markets have a negative impact on the stock markets of EU countries.

2 Literature Review

The relationship between financial crimes and capital market performance has gained increasing prominence in economic and financial literature over the past thirty years. Early studies in this field linked the relationship between corruption and corporate quality to macroeconomic growth (Mauro 1995), while subsequent research has focused on examining the direct effects of financial crimes on stock market indices, investor behaviour, and capital mobility. Acts such as corruption, fraud, money laundering, and cybercrime not only disrupt the redistribution of financial resources but also shape investors' risk perception and market confidence (Zhang 2012; Lakshmi et al. 2021). Therefore, analysing the effects of financial crimes is of paramount importance for understanding market stability.

In the literature, corruption has been described as the invisible tax on the financial system (Tanzi and Davoodi 1997). This metaphor emphasises that corruption not only reduces economic efficiency but also undermines investor confidence. The World Governance Indicators framework developed by Kaufmann et al. (2005) reveals that financial markets are deeper and more stable in countries with strong institutional quality. Conversely, high rates of financial crime in countries with weak institutional oversight accelerate capital outflows and increase stock market index volatility. More recent empirical evidence confirms and refines these insights. Using a panel of East Asia and Pacific countries, Phuong (2020) shows that higher levels of corruption significantly hinder stock market development, measured by market capitalisation and turnover, even after controlling for macroeconomic fundamentals. Similarly, Ahmed (2020) documents that corruption lowers equity market performance in a panel of emerging markets, while Islam et al. (2023) find both linear and non linear adverse effects of corruption and weak government integrity on sustainable stock market development in Pakistan. These studies underline that institutional quality and anti corruption enforcement are central determinants of market depth and resilience.

The impact of crimes such as fraud and theft on investor behaviour has been strongly documented in the literature. Hassan et al. (2024) show that an increase in financial fraud incidents leads to a permanent decline in investor confidence and causes long-term declines in stock indices. GMM analyses conducted by Dyck et al.

(2010) reveal that a one-unit increase in the fraud rate causes a loss of approximately 5–6 per cent in stock market indices. Similarly, theft and property violations steer investors towards less risky instruments, leading to an increase in demand for gold and bonds. New meta-analyses have also confirmed that the disclosure of financial crimes has a punitive effect on markets. De Batz and Kočenda (2023) show that financial crime disclosures generally lead to negative abnormal returns on stocks of between 0.5 and 1.4 per cent per day.

On the other hand, the effects of money laundering activities on the market present a dual picture in the literature. Schneider and Windischbauer (2008) and Ferwerda (2009) emphasise that money laundering can temporarily positively affect stock market performance by providing liquidity to capital markets in the short term, but weakens financial stability in the long term. This finding is consistent with the results obtained in GMM analyses: an increase in money laundering positively affects the stock market index in the short term but does not contribute to sustainable growth. Recent studies extend the focus from liquidity to systemic risk. Gerbrands (2022), using a large transactions level dataset, shows that criminal networks rapidly adapt to anti money laundering (AML) policies, which complicates detection and implies that observed financial flows only partially reflect underlying criminal activity. Eulaiwi et al. (2024) find that stronger money laundering governance reduces income shifting incentives among multinational firms in Australia, suggesting that robust AML frameworks can mitigate profit shifting and improve the informational quality of capital markets. At the policy level, recent network based analyses of the money laundering threat landscape highlight how complex cross border schemes propagate through the financial system and stress the need for coordinated supervision and data driven monitoring in the EU.

The positive outcome of the refugee smuggling variable in some countries is associated in the literature with demographic structure and the labour market. Particularly in European countries with low population growth rates, such migration flows can stimulate economic activity to a limited extent in the short term by increasing the labour supply (Schneider and Windischbauer 2008). However, the emergence and sustainability of this positive effect is considered to be highly sensitive to the institutional capacity of the country concerned, the migration policies implemented, and the success of social integration processes.

The positive correlation between corruption and stock market indices in some countries can be explained by the heterogeneity of institutional structures. Zhang (2012) argues that in certain markets, corruption serves an irregular but internal function, thereby facilitating short term investments. However, Lakshmi et al. (2021) note that this effect is not permanent, as increasing levels of corruption erode market confidence in the long term and raise capital costs. More recent work reinforces this heterogeneous view: some studies report that in weak governance environments, corruption may lubricate bureaucratic frictions and coincide with temporarily buoyant markets, whereas in countries with stronger institutions, corruption shocks are quickly penalised through higher risk premia and lower valuations. This view highlights the emphasis placed on the ethical foundations of the financial system: the sustainability of economic growth depends not only on production factors but also on social trust (Krueger et al. 2020).

In recent years, environmental crimes have also become part of financial analyses in the literature. Pastor et al. (2022) and Grossman and Krueger (1995) demonstrate that economic activities harmful to the environment influence investors' decisions based on sustainability criteria, and that the market values of companies associated with environmental pollution decline over time. Environmental crime's negative coefficient (Env) indicates that such activities impose social and economic costs and are viewed by investors as a risk factor, confirming the growing importance of ESG based financial approaches. Recent panel evidence from China shows that firms with better environmental performance earn significantly higher excess stock returns, consistent with the existence of "green returns" and growing investor demand for low carbon assets (Ma et al. 2024). Complementary work on US markets finds that ESG scores and, in particular, improvements in ESG performance (ESG momentum) are associated with changes in both returns and volatility, suggesting that investors increasingly price dynamic sustainability performance rather than static ratings alone (Escobar Saldívar et al. 2025).

Cybercrime and unlawful access to computer systems are directly related to the Unlawful variable used in this study. Akyildirim et al. (2024) show that, based on an international comprehensive data set, stock returns fell by approximately 0.24–0.25 per cent on the day following the announcement of cyber attacks, with this effect being stronger in the case of repeated or severe violations. Dewan and Muktadir Al Mukit (2025), in their study of 776 attack incidents in the US, reveal that market value losses are particularly pronounced in the finance, energy, and retail sectors. These findings demonstrate that cyber incidents directly damage both expected cash flows and investor confidence, supporting the notion that the negative coefficient obtained in this study is theoretically expected.

In general, the literature indicates that the impact of financial crimes on market performance requires the simultaneous assessment of both economic and institutional factors. Early studies on corruption and money laundering revealed that institutional quality is decisive in terms of growth and financial development (Mauro 1995; Tanzi and Davoodi 1997; Levi and Reuter 2006), recent studies have revealed the abnormal returns generated by financial crime disclosures, the sector-specific effects of cyber attacks, and the pricing of environmental risks. Empirical analyses show that although some types of financial crime can provide liquidity to markets in the short term, they create loss of confidence and financial fragility in the long term (Arellano and Bond 1991; Blundell and Bond 1998). It is also a widely confirmed finding in the literature that markets in countries with strong oversight and enforcement capacities react more quickly and more severely to financial crimes. Within this framework, the present study examines a broad set of financial and environmental crimes for the 27 European Union member states for the period 2013–2023, using a dynamic panel GMM approach to comparatively assess their short-term effects.

3 Data and Methodology

This section of the study provides theoretical information regarding the variables and methodology used. The aim of the study is to investigate the impact of unlawful and socially harmful situations in EU Member States on their stock markets. The variables used in the study are as follows (Table 1).

The most traded indices of countries are used as a proxy for effective financial development. The study aimed to investigate the 27 European Union member states and Turkey. However, because the data used for the independent variables did not pertain to Turkey and Southern Cyprus, these two countries were excluded from the analysis.

The method employed in this study was chosen by considering the characteristics of the panel dataset. The most common issues in panel data analyses are heteroskedasticity, autocorrelation, the endogeneity of explanatory variables, and the existence of unobserved country-specific effects. When the time dimension is relatively short and the cross-sectional dimension is large (N > T), conventional estimation methods such as Ordinary Least Squares (OLS), Fixed Effects (FE), or Random Effects (RE) often produce biased and inconsistent results. For these reasons, the Generalized Method of Moments (GMM), which is widely used in dynamic panel data analyses and provides more reliable estimates, has been preferred in this study. The model for the study is given below:

As seen in Fig. 1, all independent variables are expected to have an opposite effect on the dependent variable. Because financial crimes occurring in countries will increase the risk of the country in the eyes of investors and reduce its prestige. This situation will cause investors to flee. Because these outflows are partly from

Table 1 Variables used in the study

	Short name	Variables	Reference
Dependent Variable	SMI	Most Traded Stock Indices of Countries	Equityrt
Independent Variables	Corr	Corruption (Rate per 100,000 population)	The Official Website Of The United Nations
	Fraud	Fraud (Rate per 100,000 population)	
	Smugg	Smuggling of migrants (Rate per 100,000 population)	
	Theft	Theft (Rate per 100,000 population)	
	Money	Money laundering (Rate per 100,000 population)	
	Unlawful	Unlawful access to a computer System (Rate per 100,000 population)	
	Env	Acts that cause environmental pollution or degradation (Rate per 100,000 population)	

Source United Nations (2025)

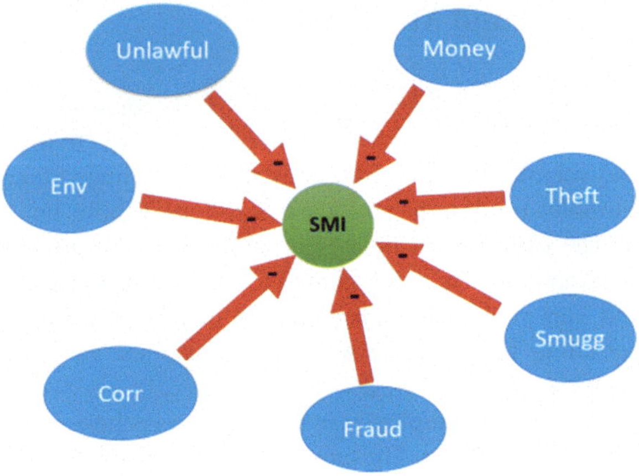

Fig. 1 The model of this paper. *Source* Prepared by Authors

exchanges in the form of hot money, they will have a negative impact on the stock market.

The general dynamic panel model can be expressed as follows:

$$y_{it} = \alpha y_{i,t-1} + \beta' X_{it} + \mu_i + \varepsilon_{it}, \quad i = 1..., N; t = 1, ...T$$

In this specification, y_{it} denotes the dependent variable (e.g., stock market index), $y_{i,t-1}$ is the lagged dependent variable, X_{it} is the vector of explanatory variables (e.g., fraud, corruption, money laundering, cybercrime), μiμirepresents unobserved country-specific effects, and ϵ_{it} is the idiosyncratic error term. The inclusion of the lagged dependent variable creates correlation with the error term, leading to inconsistency in OLS and FE estimators. The GMM approach overcomes this problem by eliminating fixed effects through differencing and addressing endogeneity by using appropriate instrumental variables.

The Difference GMM estimator proposed by Arellano and Bond (1991) removes fixed effects by taking the first difference of the model:

$$\Delta y_{it} = \alpha \Delta y_{i,t-1} + \beta' \Delta X_{it} + \Delta \varepsilon_{it}$$

In this transformation, the lagged dependent variable in differences is correlated with the error term. Therefore, lagged levels of the dependent variable (from two periods or more) are employed as valid instruments. However, Difference GMM may suffer from weak instruments. To overcome this limitation, Arellano and Bover (1995) and Blundell and Bond (1998) developed the System GMM estimator, which combines the differenced equation with the level equation to improve efficiency. In this framework, lagged differences are used as instruments for the level equation, while lagged levels are used as instruments for the differenced equation. This approach is particularly effective when the dependent variable exhibits strong persistence over time.

The final model estimated in this study is specified as follows:

$$SMI_{it} = \alpha_0 + \gamma SMI_{i,t-1} + \varphi_1 Fraud_{it} + \varphi_2 Embezzlement_{it} + \varphi_3 Corruption_{it} + \mu_i + \varepsilon_{it}$$

Here, SMI_{it} denotes the stock market index of country at time *t*, while the explanatory variables consist of indicators of financial and environmental crimes.

4 Results

This part contains information on analysis results and interpretations (Table 2).

The independent variables are measured in numbers per 100,000 people in each country. Furthermore, there are significant differences between the stock market indices of some countries. To better understand this difference, particularly based on the country's level of development, raw data were used without taking the logarithm of the stock market index (Table 3).

The correlation level between the variables is below 80%. There is an inverse relationship between the dependent variable, the most traded stock market indices of the countries, and financial crime transactions. The low correlation between the independent variables indicates that there is no multicollinearity problem among the independent variables (Table 4).

The System GMM method was also used to supplement the Difference GMM method used for variable analysis. The System GMM results are almost identical to the Difference GMM. These results indicate that the variables Corr, Fraud, Smugg, Theft, Money, and Unlawful have an impact on the countries' stock market indices.

While the variables Corr, Smugg, and Money have a positive effect on countries' stock market indices, the variables Fraud, Theft, Unlawful, and Env appear to have an inverse effect on countries' stock market indices. A 1-unit change in the Corr

Table 2 Statistical values related to variables

	Obs	Mean	Std. Dev	Min	Max
SMI	182	5103.83	9088.788	313	60,620
Corr	182	25.63794	40.63645	0.0384865	209.7364
Fraud	182	419.6345	534.2999	23.83229	2960.177
Smugg	182	5.393085	10.62961	0.0052281	101.3384
Theft	182	1105.275	824.4139	219.2159	3936.856
Money	182	11.61519	21.0134	0.1470877	142.6291
Unlawful	182	14.43115	28.36596	0.1044789	290.4385
Env	182	5.829426	16.92806	0.0050789	154.4664

Source Prepared by Authors

Table 3 Correlation table

	SMI	Corr	Fraud	Smugg	Theft	Money	Unlawful	Env
SMI	1.0000							
Corr	-0.0548	1.0000						
Fraud	-0.0220	-0.0211	1.0000					
Smugg	-0.0681	0.7653	0.1635	1.0000				
Theft	-0.0602	0.4137	0.2206	0.3876	1.0000			
Money	-0.0010	-0.0823	-0.0672	-0.1187	-0.0830	1.0000		
Unlawful	0.1302	0.3542	0.2407	0.4307	0.5398	0.0356	1.0000	
Env	0.0941	0.4071	0.2139	0.3358	0.5341	0.0882	0.4222	1.0000

Source: Prepared by Authors

Table 4 GMM results

	Difference GMM			System GMM		
	Coef	Std. Error	Prob	Coef	Std. Error	Prob
SMI (-1)	-0.334412	0.030245	0.0000	0.060925	0.025108	0.0168
Corr	91.00571	4.137826	0.0000 ***	97.23474	3.352611	0.0000 ***
Fraud	-6.506446	1.294891	0.0000 ***	-5.497883	1.394128	0.0001 ***
Smugg	209.7089	22.56778	0.0000 ***	59.79243	10.45075	0.0000 ***
Theft	-3.018280	0.527860	0.0000 ***	-1.978880	0.307627	0.0000 ***
Money	230.6641	17.65770	0.0000 ***	63.76422	24.87490	0.0116
Unlawful	-2.820022	2.920373	0.3362	0.629695	3.486851	0.8570
Env	-156.1089	14.94882	0.0000 ***	-71.30190	11.64569	0.0000 ***
Wald	2037.955 (0.0000)			3791.800 (0.0000)		
Sargan	0.726016			0.324241		
AR1/AR2	0.2211 / 0.2273			0.1628 / 0.1950		

Source Prepared by Authors

variable results in a 91-point increase according to the Difference GMM results and a 97.23-point increase according to the System GMM results. Corruption in countries appears to have a positive effect on stock market indices. This result is similar to Zhang (2012) and opposite to Lakshmi et al. (2021).

A 1-unit increase in the Fraud variable results in a 6,5 point decrease according to the Difference GMM results and a 5.49-point decrease according to the System GMM results. These results are similar to those of Hassan et al. (2024). In other words, an increase in fraud in countries reduces investor confidence in stock markets, negatively impacting the stock market index.

A 1-unit increase in the Smugg variable results in a 209.7-point increase according to the Difference GMM results, and a 59.79-point increase according to the System GMM results. In European Union countries with low young populations and low population growth rates, the labor force and employment rates also decline. In these countries, a portion of the workforce is provided by migrants. Therefore, increased migrant smuggling can contribute to national economies in terms of labor.

A 1-unit increase in the theft variable causes a decrease of 3.01 and 1.97 in the countries' stock market indices, respectively. Theft will reduce investor confidence in the country's stock markets. This decrease in investor confidence in the stock market will lead them to turn to lower-risk precious metals like gold and silver. A decrease in demand for the stock market will, in turn, lead to a decrease in the index's value.

A 1-unit increase in the Money variable results in increases of 230.66 and 63.76, respectively, according to the Difference GMM and System GMM results. This result is related to the shadow economy. While shadow economies are not a desired situation for countries, they are a systematic part of the economy in every country. When shadow money flows into the stock market, it can positively impact the stock market index by increasing demand for the stock market.

A 1-unit increase in the Env variable results in a 159.1-unit decrease according to the Difference GMM results and a 71.3-unit decrease according to the System GMM results. An increase in actions that cause environmental pollution or degradation will cause a decrease in the value of a country's stock market index. The increase in actions that are harmful to the environment will not only lead to social consequences but also to the heavy economic sanctions that will be imposed on actions that cause environmental pollution (Pastor et al. 2022; Krueger et al. 2020). It will impose additional costs on firms and reduce their profitability. Decreasing firm profits will have a cumulative negative impact on the index. This reduces the country's economic growth potential (Grossman and Krueger 1995).

5 Conclusion and Recommendations

This study investigates how indicators of financial crime shape equity market performance across 27 European Union member states over 2013–2023. Using dynamic panel GMM estimators (difference and system), we uncover consistent short-run patterns: corruption, migrant smuggling, and money laundering are positively associated with national stock indices, whereas fraud, theft, unlawful IT access, and environmental crimes are negatively associated. Diagnostic checks (Wald, Sargan/Hansen, and Arellano–Bond AR(1)/AR(2)) support the validity of the instruments and the absence of second-order serial correlation, lending credibility to these estimates.

It is seen that Corr, Fraud, Smugg, Theft, Money, Env variables have an effect on SMI. These effects are in the opposite direction for the Fradu, Theft, Env variants, as expected. However, contrary to expectations, this effect is isodirectional for the variables Corr, Smugg and Money. A 1 unit increase in the Corr, Smugg, Money variables will cause an increase of 91,005; 209,708; 230,664 units on the SMI variable, respectively, according to the Difference GMM results; and an increase of 97,234 and 59,792 units, respectively, according to the System GMM results. These results can be attributed to reasons such as the demand-driven rise of stock markets with unregistered money, and manipulative transactions artificially inflating country stock markets. In addition, a 1-unit increase in the Fraud, Theft and Env variables will cause a decrease of 6.506, 3.018 and 156.108 units on the SMI, respectively, according to the GMM results; and 5.497, 1.978 and 71.301 units, respectively, according to the System results. This situation can be explained by the decrease in confidence in the country's stock markets, the resulting flight from portfolio investments, the need to suppress the market, and the need to ensure stability by increasing the effectiveness of regulatory authorities.

The interpretation of the signs requires care. Short-run positive coefficients for corruption and money laundering likely reflect transitory liquidity injection and speculative activity rather than healthy fundamentals. Such dynamics can erode institutional trust, elevate risk premia, and heighten long-term fragility. By contrast, crimes that directly undermine property rights, contractual enforcement, cyber integrity, and environmental compliance—fraud, theft, unlawful access, and environmental offenses—depress valuations through profitability and investor-confidence channels.

The findings underscore that market resilience hinges not only on macroeconomic conditions but also on institutional quality, the rule of law, and ethical governance. Policy priorities therefore include strengthening deterrence and supervisory capacity (proactive surveillance, secure whistleblowing, real-time anomaly detection), tightening AML/CFT frameworks (risk-based KYC, beneficial-ownership transparency, cross-border supervisory coordination), and embedding sustainability and cyber-resilience (credible ESG disclosures, effective sanctions for environmental offenses, penetration testing and incident-response standards with mandatory breach reporting). These measures address both the sources of harmful short-run buoyancy and the mechanisms that directly damage market integrity.

Several limitations qualify our conclusions. Financial-crime statistics are prone to measurement error and under-detection of shadow activity; annual frequency can mask higher-frequency dynamics; and the EU-only sample constrains external validity. Future research should examine sectoral and firm-level heterogeneity, macroeconomic control variables should be added, exploit higher-frequency data to identify structural breaks associated with regulatory shocks, and employ designs that strengthen causal inference. Together, these extensions would clarify persistence, transmission channels, and welfare implications beyond the short run.

References

Ahmed W (2020) Corruption and equity market performance: international comparative evidence. Pac.-Basin Finan J 60:101282. https://doi.org/10.1016/j.pacfin.2020.101282

Arellano M, Bond S (1991) Some tests of specification for panel data: Monte Carlo evidence and an application to employment equations. Rev Econ Stud 58(2):277–297

Arellano M, Bover O (1995) Another look at the instrumental variable estimation of error-components models. J Econ 68(1):29–51

Blundell R, Bond S (1998) Initial conditions and moment restrictions in dynamic panel data models. J Econ 87(1):115–143

De Batz L, Kočenda E (2023) Financial crime and punishment: a meta-analysis. J Econ Surv (advance online publication). https://doi.org/10.1111/joes.12580

Dyck A, Morse A, Zingales L (2010) Who blows the whistle on corporate fraud? J Financ 65(6):2213–2253

Ferwerda J (2009) Corruption, trust and social capital: cultural drivers of institutional effectiveness and economic development (PhD thesis, University of Amsterdam)

Grossman GM, Krueger AB (1995) Economic growth and the environment. Q J Econ 110(2):353–377

Hassan M, Veena C, Singla A, Joshi A, ve Lourens M (2024) Fraud detection in Internet of Things based financial transactions using anomaly detection techniques. In: 2024 International conference on advances in computing, communications and applied informatics (ACCAI). IEEE, pp 1–6

Islam K, Bilal AR, Zaidi SAH, Sardar S, Kamboh MH (2023) Impact of government integrity and corruption on sustainable stock market development: linear and nonlinear evidence from Pakistan. Econ Change Restruct 56(4):2529–2556. https://doi.org/10.1007/s10644-023-09523-7

Kaufmann D, Kraay A, Mastruzzi M (2005) Governance matters IV: Governance indicators for 1996–2004 (Policy Research Working Paper No. 3630). Washington, DC: World Bank

Krueger P, Sautner Z, Starks LT (2020) The importance of climate risks for institutional investors. Rev Financ Stud 33(3):1067–1111

Lakshmi G, Saha S, Bhattarai K (2021) Does corruption matter for stock markets? The role of heterogeneous institutions. Econ Model 94:386–400

Levi M, Reuter P (2006) Money laundering. Crime Justice 34(1):289–375

Mauro P (1995) Corruption and growth. Q J Econ 110(3):681–712

Phuong NT (2020) Corruption and stock market development: evidence from East Asia and Pacific countries. J Asian Econ 69:101210. https://doi.org/10.1016/j.asieco.2020.101210

Pastor E, Sachs M, Selim S, Durrant JR, Bakulin AA, Walsh A (2022) Electronic defects in metal oxide photocatalysts. Nat Rev Mater 7(7):503–521

Schneider F, Windischbauer U (2008) Money laundering: some facts. Eur J Law Econ 26(3):387–404

Tanzi V, Davoodi HR (1997) Corruption, public investment, and growth (IMF Working Paper No. 97/139). International Monetary Fund

United Nations (2025) Corruption and economic crime. Retrieved on 23.09.2025 from https://dataunodc.un.org/dp-crime-corruption-offences

Zhang A (2012) An examination of the effects of corruption on financial market volatility. J Emerg Mark Financ 11(3):301–322

Yusuf Ekrem Akbaş is Prof. Dr. at Adıyaman University, Faculty of Economics and Administrative Sciences, Department of Economics. He graduated from the Department of Economics at Selçuk University, Faculty of Economics and Administrative Sciences in 2006. The same year, he started his master's degree in Economics at İnönü University, Institute of Social Sciences and completed this education in 2008. He completed his doctorate in Economics at İnönü University between 2008–2012. In 2009, he started working as a lecturer in the Foreign Trade Program at Kilis 7 December University Vocational School. He served there until January 2013. In January 2013, he started working as an Assistant Professor in the Department of Economics at Adıyaman University, Faculty of Economics and Administrative Sciences. Since 2019, he has been working as an Associate Professor at the same institution. In November 2021, he received his Professorship title at the same institution. He continues in the same position.

Mehmet Ali Polat is Assoc. Prof. Dr. at Uludağ University, Faculty of Economics and Administrative Sciences, Department of Economics, Dr. Polat graduated from the Department of Public Administration at Ankara University's Faculty of Political Sciences in 2003. He completed his master's degree at Gaziantep University in 2012 and his doctorate at Uludağ University in 2018. After 15 years of service at the Ministry of Environment and Urbanization and the Ministry of Transportation, he began working as an assistant professor at Malatya Turgut Ozal University. He received his associate professorship in economics in 2021 and has been working at Uludağ University since 2022. He has published numerous studies in economics in national and international journals.

Ahmet Şit is Assoc. Prof. Dr. at Malatya Turgut Ozal University, Faculty of Social and Human Sciences, Department of International Trade and Finance. He graduated from the Department of Business Administration at Inonu University's Faculty of Economics and Administrative Sciences in 2004. He completed his master's degree at Inonu University in 2012 and his doctorate in 2018. After working at a private bank and the Ministry of Finance, he began his teaching career at Kilis 7 Aralık University in 2011. He continued his career as an assistant professor at the same university in 2018. He started working with the same title at Malatya Turgut Ozal University, Faculty of Social and Human Sciences, Department of International Trade and Finance in 2021. 2022 yılında finans alanında doçent ünvanını alarak aynı bölümde doçent olarak görevine devam etmektedir. Dr. Şit has published numerous articles in the field of finance, particularly on financial analysis and corporate finance, in well-regarded national and international indices. He also has numerous projects and articles currently in preparation, including the completed European Union Horizon project.